NUCLEAR WEAPO
INTERNATION.

Nuclear Weapons Under International Law is a comprehensive treatment of nuclear weapons under key international law regimes. It critically reviews international law governing nuclear weapons with regard to the inter-state use of force, international humanitarian law, human rights law, disarmament law and environmental law, and discusses where relevant the International Court of Justice's 1996 Advisory Opinion. Unique in its approach, it draws upon contributions from expert legal scholars and international law practitioners who have worked with conventional and non-conventional arms control and disarmament issues. As a result, this book embraces academic consideration of legal questions within the context of broader political debates about the status of nuclear weapons under international law.

GRO NYSTUEN is a senior partner at the International Law and Policy Institute in Oslo where she works on public international law issues, including the ILPI Nuclear Weapons Project, humanitarian law, law of armed conflict and disarmament. She is also the Director of the ILPI Centre for International Humanitarian Law.

STUART CASEY-MASLEN is head of research at the Geneva Academy of International Humanitarian Law and Human Rights. He is an international human rights and humanitarian lawyer specialising in weapons law and the international law of law enforcement.

ANNIE GOLDEN BERSAGEL is a legal advisor at the International Law and Policy Institute, where she works on a broad range of international law issues, including human rights and corporate complicity, the laws of armed conflict, international economic transparency and treaty law.

NUCLEAR WEAPONS UNDER INTERNATIONAL LAW

Edited by

GRO NYSTUEN, STUART CASEY-MASLEN
AND ANNIE GOLDEN BERSAGEL

CAMBRIDGE
UNIVERSITY PRESS

CAMBRIDGE
UNIVERSITY PRESS

University Printing House, Cambridge CB2 8BS, United Kingdom

Cambridge University Press is part of the University of Cambridge.

It furthers the University's mission by disseminating knowledge in the pursuit of education, learning and research at the highest international levels of excellence.

www.cambridge.org
Information on this title: www.cambridge.org/9781316500699

© Cambridge University Press 2014

First published 2014
First paperback edition 2015

A catalogue record for this publication is available from the British Library

Library of Congress Cataloguing in Publication data
Nuclear weapons under international law / edited by Gro Nystuen, Stuart Casey-Maslen, Annie Golden Bersagel.
pages   cm
Includes bibliographical references and index.
ISBN 978-1-107-04274-2 (hardback)
1. Nuclear weapons (International law)   I. Nystuen, Gro, editor of compilation.
II. Casey-Maslen, Stuart, editor of compilation.   III. Bersagel, Annie
Golden, 1983–editor of compilation.
KZ5665.N83 2014
341.7′34–dc23
2014011305

ISBN 978-1-107-04274-2 Hardback
ISBN 978-1-316-50069-9 Paperback

CONTENTS

CONTRIBUTORS

ANNIE GOLDEN BERSAGEL is a legal advisor at the International Law and Policy Institute, where she works on a broad range of international law issues, including human rights and corporate complicity, the laws of armed conflict, international economic transparency and treaty law. She holds a JD (juris doctorate) degree from Stanford Law School, in addition to a Master of Philosophy degree in peace and conflict Studies from the University of Oslo and a Bachelor of Arts degree in economics and political science from Wake Forest University. She was a Fulbright scholar at the University of Oslo from 2006 to 2007. Golden Bersagel has published articles on business and human rights, Norway's legal relationship with the European Union and international sports arbitration.

STUART CASEY-MASLEN is head of research at the Geneva Academy of International Humanitarian Law and Human Rights. He is an international human rights and humanitarian lawyer specialising in weapons law and the international law of law enforcement. He has written a commentary on the 1997 Anti-Personnel Mine Ban Convention and co-edited with Gro Nystuen a commentary on the 2008 Convention on Cluster Munitions. He is the editor of *The War Report: 2012*, which classifies armed conflicts around the world, published in December 2013, and editor of *Weapons Under International Human Rights Law*, published by Cambridge University Press in January 2014.

LOUISE DOSWALD-BECK was appointed a professor of the Graduate Institute in 2003 and retired in 2012. She is a member of the Directorate of the Geneva Academy of International Humanitarian Law and Human Rights, created in September 2007. Professor Doswald-Beck was formerly the Director of the University Centre for International Humanitarian Law (CUDIH) from 2003 to 2007, and was Secretary General of the International Commission of Jurists (2001–2003). She was a legal adviser at the International Committee of the Red Cross (ICRC) from 1987 and became Head of the Legal Division in 1998. She began her career as a lecturer in law at Exeter University and then London University. During the 1990s Louise Doswald-Beck played an important role in the campaign to establish the International Criminal Court (ICC) and participated in the negotiations on the Rome Statute. In particular, she had a major role in negotiations that led to the establishment of the ICC's Elements of Crimes, Protocols II (amended) and IV of the Convention on Certain Conventional Weapons, the Anti-Personnel Mine Ban Convention, Protocol II of the Hague Convention on Cultural Property and the San Remo Manual on armed conflicts at sea. Professor Doswald-Beck has written extensively on subjects relating to the use of force, and humanitarian law and human rights law, including the ICRC's study on customary international humanitarian law (2005) for which she was awarded the Ciardi Prize at the time of the XVIIth Congress of the International Society for Military Law and the Law of War in 2006.

CHARLES GARRAWAY CBE served for thirty years as a legal officer in the United Kingdom Army Legal Services, initially as a criminal prosecutor but latterly as an adviser in the law of armed conflict and operational law. He represented the Ministry of Defence at numerous international conferences. He was also the senior Army lawyer deployed to the Gulf during the 1990/91 Gulf Conflict. On retirement, he spent three months in Baghdad working for the Foreign Office on transitional justice issues and six months as a Senior Research Fellow at the British Institute of International and Comparative Law before taking up the Stockton Chair in International Law at the United States Naval War College, Newport, Rhode Island in August 2004 for the year 2004/05. He was a Visiting Professor at King's College London from 2002 to 2008, teaching the Law of Armed Conflict, and an Associate Fellow at Chatham House from 2005 to 2012. He is currently a Fellow at the Human Rights Centre, University of Essex and was awarded an Honorary Doctorate by the University in 2012. In December 2006 he was elected to the International Humanitarian Fact Finding Commission under Article 90 of Additional Protocol I to the Geneva Conventions of 1949, of which he is now a Vice-President. He worked for the British Red Cross from 2007 to 2011 and now works as an independent consultant. He was appointed CBE in 2002. He has worked on a number of expert groups and is currently the General Editor of the United Kingdom Manual on the Law of Armed Conflict.

NOBUO HAYASHI is currently a researcher at PluriCourts, a project of the University of Oslo Law Faculty. He also maintains his affiliation as a Senior Advisor with the International Law and Policy Institute. His previous positions include Visiting Professor, International University of Japan; Researcher, Peace Research Institute Oslo; Legal Advisor, Norwegian Centre for Human Rights; and Legal Officer, Office of the Prosecutor, International Criminal Tribunal for the Former Yugoslavia. He specializes in the law of armed conflict, international criminal law, *jus ad bellum* and public international law.

CECILIE HELLESTVEIT has recently submitted her Ph.D. on Humanitarian Law and Non-international armed conflict at the Faculty of Law at the University of Oslo. She has previously worked at PRIO (Peace Research Institute, Oslo), and

NCHR (Norwegian Centre for Human Rights). For the past two years she has been a part of the Gulf Research Unit at the University of Oslo, with a particular focus on Saudi Arabia and Iraq. Hellestveit served as the Special Rapporteur on conduct of hostilities in military operations to the International Society for Military Law and the Laws of War 2008–2009. She has studied domestic Norwegian law (LLM), international law at Sorbonne Paris-X and Islamic law, and she holds the equivalent of an LLM in area and conflict studies and international relations with a particular emphasis on the Arab and Muslim world. Hellestveit has broad field experience, and she has also studied/worked in the USA (UN), France, Germany, Russia, Israel and several Arab countries. She is also attached to the ILPI Centre for International Humanitarian Law and the ILPI Centre for African Studies.

TORBJØRN GRAFF HUGO holds an M.Phil. in Peace and Conflict Studies and a BA in International Studies from the University of Oslo. He has worked on issues related to nuclear non-proliferation and disarmament for a number of years, and is currently attached to ILPI's Nuclear Weapons Project, which aims to shape and inform the debate on how to eliminate nuclear weapons by way of analysis, networking and outreach. Before joining ILPI Hugo worked in the Section for Disarmament and Non-proliferation in the Norwegian Ministry of Foreign Affairs in Oslo.

DANIEL H. JOYNER received a BA in Japanese from Brigham Young University, his JD from Duke Law School, an MA in political science from the University of Georgia and a Ph.D. in law from the University of Warwick School of Law in the United Kingdom. Prior to joining the University of Alabama Law faculty in 2007, Professor Joyner taught for four years on the faculty of the University of Warwick School of Law. During Michaelmas Term 2005 he was also a Senior Associate Member of St Antony's College, Oxford University. Professor Joyner teaches Public International Law, International Trade and Investment Law, The Law of War, WMD Law and Policy, and Contracts. Professor Joyner's research interests are focused on public international law, with particular interest in the area of nuclear weapons non-proliferation law and civilian nuclear energy law. His areas of expertise include nuclear non-proliferation treaties and international organisations, and sources of international trade, investment, safety, security, liability and export control law in the nuclear energy area. He has also written extensively on international use of force law, and on the UN Security Council.

ERIK V. KOPPE is an assistant professor of public international law at Leiden Law School and the Grotius Center for International Legal Studies. He is also Managing Editor of the Netherlands International Law Review. Koppe studied International and European Law as well as Dutch Law (Civil Law) at the University of Groningen and received his doctorate degree (*cum laude*) in 2006 at the same university for his research on *The Use of Nuclear Weapons and the Protection of the Environment During International Armed Conflict* (2008). Subsequently he worked as a researcher at the T.M.C. Asser Instituut in The Hague and as an associate at the Dispute Resolution Practice Group of Freshfields Bruckhaus Deringer LLP in Amsterdam.

MARTINA KUNZ is a Ph.D. candidate at the University of Cambridge, United Kingdom, and previously a teaching and research assistant at the Graduate Institute, Geneva. She studied international law at the Graduate Institute (LLM), Tsinghua University (China Scholarship Council Visiting Scholar) and the University of Geneva (LLB). She is fluent in German, English, Chinese, French and Spanish. Martina Kunz has worked on a number of international and comparative law research projects for universities, NGOs and international organisations, mainly in the fields of environmental law, economic law and public law at large.

DON MACKAY was New Zealand Ambassador for Disarmament and Permanent Representative to the United Nations and Specialised Agencies in Geneva from 2006 to 2009. Prior to that he served as New Zealand Permanent Representative to the United Nations in New York from 2001 to 2005. His positions within the New Zealand Ministry of Foreign Affairs and Trade have included Deputy Secretary responsible for legal and multilateral affairs, Legal Adviser and Director of the Legal Division, and Director of the Disarmament and International Security Division. Mr MacKay was Co-Agent and Counsel in the case of *New Zealand* v. *France* (*Nuclear Tests* case) before the International Court of Justice in 1995, and was Counsel in the *New Zealand* v. *France* Rainbow Warrior Arbitration in New York. He graduated from Victoria University of Wellington with first class honours in Law in 1970. He was a Visiting Fellow at the Research Centre for International Law at the University of Cambridge (United Kingdom) in 1996. He is currently an independent consultant in international law and international affairs.

DANIEL MEKONNEN obtained his primary legal education in Eritrea, where he served, among other things, as Judge of the Zoba Maekel Provincial Court in Asmara. His LLM in Human Rights and LLD in Public International Law are respectively from the University of Stellenbosch and the University of the Free State, both in South Africa. With a strong bias towards human rights, international humanitarian law and international criminal law, he also has a cumulative work experience in diverse areas ranging from development cooperation to corporate social responsibility, North–South relations, non-violent action, democratisation, peace and conflict studies and transitional justice. He has taught courses on human rights and international law at tertiary levels. He has thus far produced more than eighty academic publications and research outputs attached to his name, which include monographs, journal articles, chapters in edited volumes, conference papers, consultancies and expert legal advices. He is a frequent commentator in popular media and in online forums. Previously, Daniel was a research fellow at the School of Law at Queen's University Belfast, where he was involved in a research project dealing with the role of lawyers in conflict and transition. Daniel is associated with the ILPI Centre for African Studies.

JASMINE MOUSSA has a Ph.D. in Law from the University of Cambridge. Between 2008 and 2010 she was the desk officer in charge of Legal Affairs and Human Rights Affairs in the Cabinet of Egypt's Minister of Foreign Affairs, where she has also worked at the Legal Department and Multilateral Affairs Department. Other engagements include being a legal researcher at the Cabinet of the Secretary General of the League of Arab States and a legal consultant to several international non-governmental organisations and think tanks. She completed a BA in Political Science and MA in International Human Rights Law from the American University in Cairo, a Bachelor of Laws from Cairo University and a Master of Laws in Public International Law from the London School of Economics and Political Science before joining Magdalene College at the University of Cambridge as a Ph.D. candidate in Law. From 2012 to 2013 she was editor and editor-in-chief of the Cambridge Journal of International and Comparative Law.

GRO NYSTUEN is an international lawyer with a doctorate in public international law (dr. juris) from 2004. Nystuen worked in the Norwegian Ministry for Foreign Affairs from 1991 to 2005. From 2005 to 2013 she was Associate Professor of International Humanitarian Law/the Law on Armed Conflict at the University of Oslo and from 2008 also Associate Professor at the Defence Staff University College in Oslo. In addition to public international law and treaty law in general, she has worked in particular with international humanitarian law and the law of armed conflict, disarmament law and arms control law, arms export control law, constitutional law, peace agreements, international criminal law, penal law and procedural law, human rights law and corporate social responsibility. She has published extensively on the above issues. From 2004 to 2011, Nystuen also chaired the Council on Ethics of the Norwegian Government Pension Fund. Since 2009 she has been Senior Partner at ILPI and since June 2013 she has also been Director of the ILPI Centre for International Humanitarian Law.

SIMON O'CONNOR is a senior legal adviser at the Norwegian Red Cross. He is a Barrister and served in the British Army Legal Services from 2001 to 2006. He holds M.Phils. from the Universities of Tromsø and St Andrews in International Relations and lectures and publishes in international humanitarian law. In 2011 he was a Visiting Fellow at the Institute for Ethics Law and Armed Conflict at the University of Oxford where he remains a Research Associate.

MARCO ROSCINI is Reader in international law at the University of Westminster School of Law. He has a Ph.D. in international law from the

University of Rome 'La Sapienza'. Dr Roscini was previously a Research Fellow at the University of Verona School of Law and lectured on the international law of armed conflict at UCL, King's College London and Queen Mary University London. He also collaborated with the International Justice Project at the International Secretariat of Amnesty International, for which he prepared extensive commentaries on the implementation of the International Criminal Court's Statute in the Democratic Republic of the Congo and in Italy. Dr Roscini is the author of a monograph on nuclear weapon-free zones (2003) and the co-editor, with Daniel H. Joyner, of *Nonproliferation Law as a Special Regime* (Cambridge University Press, 2012). His book on cyber operations and the use of force in international law will be published in 2014.

JORGE VIÑUALES is the Harold Samuel Professor of Law and Environmental Policy at the University of Cambridge, United Kingdom, and a Visiting Professor of International Law at The Graduate Institute, during the academic year 2013–2014. Professor Viñuales has published widely in his speciality areas, most recently his books *Foreign Investment and the Environment in International Law* (Cambridge University Press, 2012), *Harnessing Foreign Investment to Promote Environmental Protection: Incentives and Safeguards* (Cambridge University Press, 2013, co-edited with P.-M. Dupuy) and *Diplomatic and Judicial Means of Dispute Settlement* (2012, co-edited with L. Boisson de Chazournes and M. G. Kohen). He has also wide experience as a practitioner. He has worked on many cases under ICSID, UNCITRAL, ICC or LCIA rules, including several high-profile inter-state, investor–state and commercial disputes, and he regularly advises companies, governments, international organisations or major NGOs on different matters of environmental law, investment law and public international law at large. Professor Viñuales was educated in France (Doctorat – Sciences Po, Paris), the United States (LLM – Harvard Law School), Switzerland (Licence and Diplôme d'études approfondies in international relations – HEI; liz jur – Universität Freiburg; Licence and Diplôme d'études approfondies in political science – Université de Genève) and Argentina (Abogado – UNICEN).

FOREWORD

We have recently commemorated the fiftieth anniversary of the assassin-ation of President John F. Kennedy on 22 November 1963. The regular ques-tion asked of my generation was: 'where were you when you heard the news?' Everybody could remember, just as, for a later generation, the news of '9/11' and the attacks on Washington and New York would provide similar memor-ies. And yet Kennedy's death overshadowed an equally momentous date, the night of 27/28 October 1962, when the world was on the brink of nuclear war in the Cuban Missile Crisis. As a schoolboy, I can remember going to bed that night wondering whether there would be a morning for me to wake up to. We lived that night in fear of nuclear annihilation.

Later, as a serving officer, I would be part of the forward UK division on the Inner German Border. Our task was to resist an invasion for as long as we could, though we knew in such an event our position was suicidal. Later at Supreme Headquarters Allied Powers Europe, I took part in exercises to resist such an invasion and such exercises almost inevitably ended in a nuclear exchange. On one such exercise, the first nuclear explosion in the UK missed its intended target, Greenham Common, and landed on a nearby village – where my family lived. It was a sobering moment.

Today the nuclear shadow cast during the Cold War has evaporated – but the danger has not gone away. The fear of nuclear proliferation remains and the new danger of nuclear technology falling into the hands of non-state actors is grounds enough for taking the issue seriously. As Gro Nystuen says in her conclusion, '[a] strongly polarised debate over nuclear weapons and their legality has taken place over the past decades' and almost twenty years have passed since the International Court of Justice gave its Advisory Opinion on the Legality of the Threat or Use of Nuclear Weapons. That Advisory Opinion did little to stem the debate, except that there emerged a new factor: 'both sides taking the Advisory Opinion as evidence that they were right.'

This book has sought to take a dispassionate view of the debate, taking into account the legal developments since 1996 in the various fields of inter-national law relevant to the use or threat of use of nuclear weapons. As should be expected, most if not all of the authors have strong views on the legality of nuclear weapons – which may or may not come across in their writings.

However, all have tried to view the issues dispassionately with the result that there are no firm conclusions on the legality or otherwise of nuclear weapons, contrary to what some would undoubtedly wish. Arguments are put forward and it is left to the reader to reach his or her own conclusions on the facts presented.

It is a relief to me – and to many – that the argument has now shifted from the political suspense of the Cold War into the more rarefied atmosphere of academia. However, we should not forget that this remains a real issue and a real threat. Regardless of the legal niceties, a nuclear conflict would be a catastrophe. There could be no winners. Any steps that can be taken to reduce such a risk are therefore to be welcomed. It is my hope that no child ever again has to go to sleep in the deep despair and fear of the unknown that I experienced on the night of 27/28 October 1962.

Charles Garraway

EDITORS' PREFACE

This book seeks to describe and assess the status of nuclear weapons under international law as it stands today, not as one might like to see it. Indeed, although many of the authors believe in the desirability of eliminating completely this category of non-conventional means of warfare, great care has been taken to focus on the identification of *lex lata* rules and to apply them dispassionately to nuclear weapons. Where authors believe the law is evolving in a particular field, such asserted *lex ferenda* is made explicit with contrary views duly reflected.

The book takes as its starting premise that the International Court of Justice (ICJ) did not, in its 1996 Advisory Opinion on the *Legality of the Threat or Use of Nuclear Weapons*, find that nuclear weapons were unlawful per se under any branch of international law. However, such is not the understanding of every international lawyer, for a number have argued fervently that the Court did rule nuclear weapons illegal (or at least that application of the rules deduced by the Court inevitably renders not only their use but also their stockpiling illegal). Certainly, where the ICJ did not address or apply a particular rule to nuclear weapons or, in the relevant author's view, did not assess its application correctly, the lacuna or error is acknowledged and discussed in this book. Further, where the state of the law in a particular field has evolved since the 1996 Advisory Opinion, this too is openly debated.

In identifying customary international law, authors have sought to discern a general practice of states (*usus*) accepted as law (*opinio juris*).[1] Where an issue under review calls for interpretation of a treaty provision, the approach taken is to employ the customary rules codified in the 1969 Vienna Convention on the Law of Treaties, especially its Articles 31 and 32. Thus, a treaty is interpreted in good faith in accordance with the ordinary meaning to be given to its terms in their context and in the light of the treaty's object and purpose. A special meaning is only given to a term if it is established that the negotiating parties

---

[1] Statute of the International Court of Justice, San Francisco, 26 June 1945, in force 24 October 1945, 3 Bevans 1179, Art. 38. For a more detailed description of customary international law, see I. Brownlie, *Principles of Public International Law*, 5th edn (Oxford University Press, 1998), pp. 4–11.

so intended.[2] Supplementary means of interpretation, particularly the *travaux préparatoires*, are used in order to confirm the meaning that is discerned, or to determine the meaning when the general rules of interpretation either leave it ambiguous or obscure, or lead to a manifestly absurd or unreasonable result.

As set out in more detail in the introduction to this book, we have sought to embrace all branches of international law deemed relevant to an assessment of the legality of nuclear weapons: the law on inter-state use of force (*jus ad bellum*); international humanitarian law;[3] international human rights law; international criminal law; disarmament law; and international environmental law. Although not the primary purpose of the book, we argue that this approach can be used to assess the legality of any weapon, whether conventional or non-conventional in nature.

We hope that readers will find this book engaging and thought-provoking, and that it will contribute to the various debates on nuclear weapons. Arguably, given the hugely destructive effects of all nuclear weapons, whatever their explosive yields, too few lawyers are currently involved in reflections and discussions in this area. If the book stimulates more to turn their minds to this critical humanitarian and security issue, then it can already be considered a success.

We would like to thank all the authors for their contributions. Two experts meetings were held during the course of the project to review the draft chapters, in December 2012 and June 2013. Special thanks are also owed to several hardworking interns at the International Law and Policy Institute for contributions to the editorial work: Marisol Nina Guttman, Lars Jørgen Røed and Kjølv Egeland. We are also very grateful to Charles Garraway for his careful review of the draft manuscript, which has further improved the text. Of course, any remaining errors of fact or law remain our responsibility.

---

[2] Vienna Convention on the Law of Treaties, Vienna, 23 May 1969, in force 27 January 1980, 1155 UNTS 331, Art. 31(1) and (4).

[3] By international humanitarian law is meant the entire international law of armed conflict, including Hague law governing the conduct of hostilities.

DISCLAIMER

This report is the work of the authors. The designation of armed non-state actors, states or territories does not imply any judgement by the International Law and Policy Institute or Cambridge University Press regarding the legal status of such actors, states or territories, or their authorities and institutions, or the delimitation of their boundaries, or the status of any states or territories that border them.

~

Introduction

GRO NYSTUEN AND STUART CASEY-MASLEN

Unlike biological and chemical weapons – the other 'weapons of mass destruction' (WMDs)[1] – nuclear weapons are not subject to a specific prohibition under international law. The 1968 Nuclear Non-Proliferation Treaty (NPT)[2] bans the possession and production of nuclear weapons by all non-nuclear weapon states that are party to the NPT, but it does not impose a prohibition on the use of nuclear weapons, and it is unspecific when it comes to disarmament obligations. In contrast, the other WMD treaties prohibit the possession, production and transfer of biological and chemical weapons, respectively,[3] and oblige states parties to destroy all stockpiles within specific timelines.[4] Given the assumed larger potential for harm and destruction that use of nuclear weapons could cause compared to other WMDs, this legal situation seems difficult to comprehend. In fact, despite the inherently dangerous nature of nuclear weapons, the fabric of the world's security politics as it has evolved since 1945 (including the significant link between nuclear weapons and the five permanent members of

---

[1] See the 1972 Convention on the Prohibition of the Development, Production and Stockpiling of Bacteriological (Biological) and Toxin Weapons and on Their Destruction (1972 Biological Weapons Convention), London, Moscow, and Washington DC, 10 April 1972, in force 26 March 1975, 1015 UNTS 163; and the 1992 Convention on the Prohibition of the Development, Production, Stockpiling and Use of Chemical Weapons and on their Destruction (1992 Chemical Weapons Convention), Geneva, 3 September 1992, in force 29 April 1993, 1974 UNTS 45.

[2] 1968 Treaty on the Non-Proliferation of Nuclear Weapons, London, Moscow, and Washington DC, 1 July 1968, in force 5 March 1970, 729 UNTS 161.

[3] It should be noted that the text of Article I of the 1972 Biological Weapons Convention itself does not explicitly prohibit use. The Convention's Review Conference has, however, specified that use of biological weapons 'is effectively a violation of Article I'. See, e.g. Final Document of the Fourth Review Conference, UN Doc. BWC/CONF/.IV/9 (25 November–6 December 1996). Moreover, the 1925 Geneva Gas Protocol already outlawed the use of bacteriological methods of warfare.

[4] In September 2013 Syria adhered to the 1992 Chemical Weapons Convention, but in an agreement forged between the Russian Federation and the United States was allowed only one year for the destruction of its huge chemical weapons stockpiles. See, e.g., 'Syria's chemical weapons stockpile', BBC, 20 September 2013, available at: www.bbc.co.uk/news/world-middle-east-22307705. Of UN member states, only Israel and Myanmar still have to ratify the Convention, while Angola, the Democratic People's Republic of Korea (DPR Korea), Egypt and South Sudan have neither signed nor acceded to it.

the Security Council) has made it very difficult to discuss nuclear weapons as weapons rather than as an overpowering political and security issue.

Many international legal rules do, however, apply to nuclear weapons, their unique political status notwithstanding. Some apply explicitly, such as the NPT and treaties on nuclear weapon-free zones. A number of other customary and conventional international legal rules apply generally or have an impact on use, possession, testing, transfer or production of nuclear weapons. These rules are the subject of this book. Before embarking on the legal discussions, however, it may prove useful to take a closer look at the more factual aspects of nuclear weapons. This introduction will proceed with an overview of the functioning and types of nuclear weapons, and a short history of use and testing of nuclear weapons and estimated stockpiles of nuclear weapons, before providing an overview of the layout of the book.

The functioning and types of nuclear weapons

A nuclear weapon[5] is an explosive device whose destructive force results from either nuclear fission chain reactions or combined nuclear fission and fusion reactions.[6] Nuclear weapons whose explosive force results exclusively from fission reactions are commonly referred to as atomic bombs,[7] while those that derive much or most of their energy in nuclear fusion reactions are termed thermonuclear weapons (or hydrogen bombs).[8]

---

[5] The precise date of origin of nuclear weapons is the subject of debate. Bernstein suggests that 3 March 1939, when two scientists first observed traces of 'prompt' neutrons (excess neutrons that are shed when uranium is fissioned), was the date when an atomic bomb first seemed a real possibility. J. Bernstein, *Nuclear Weapons: What You Need to Know* (Cambridge University Press, 2010), p. 74. Other key dates are 24 December 1938, when two scientists – one man, one woman – worked out how fission worked, reportedly while sitting on a tree trunk, and 2 December 1942, when a nuclear reactor being built by the Project was made to go critical for 28 minutes. *Ibid.*, pp. 112–14. See also B. Cameron Reed, *The Physics of the Manhattan Project* (Heidelberg/Dordrecht/London/New York: Springer, 2010).

[6] For details of the science behind and use of nuclear weapons, see, e.g., Bernstein, *Nuclear Weapons*; J. Cirincione, *Bomb Scare: The History and Future of Nuclear Weapons* (New York, Chichester, West Sussex: Columbia University Press, 2008).

[7] This is so even though the energy that is released in an atomic bomb comes from the nucleus of the atom, as it does in combined fission and fusion weapons.

[8] This is because these weapons rely on fusion reactions between isotopes of hydrogen. Research has been conducted into the possibility of developing pure fusion bombs: nuclear weapons consisting of fusion reactions without the need for a fission bomb to initiate them. Pure fusion weapons would create significantly less nuclear fallout than other thermonuclear weapons, because they would not disperse fission products. In 1998 the US Department of Energy divulged that it had, in the past, 'made a substantial investment' with a view to developing pure fusion weapons, but affirmed that the USA 'does not have and is not developing a pure fusion weapon', asserting that '[n]o credible design for a pure fusion weapon resulted' from that investment. US Department of Energy, 'Restricted data

In fission weapons, a mass of fissile material (enriched uranium or pluto-nium) is turned into a supercritical mass,[9] either by shooting one piece of sub-critical material into another (called the 'gun' method), or by using chemical explosives to compress a subcritical sphere of material into many times its ori-ginal density (the 'implosion' method).[10] Fission weapons produce explosive yields ranging from the equivalent of around one ton of TNT[11] to 500,000 tons (500 kilotons) of TNT. The detonation of any nuclear weapon is accompanied by a blast of radiation. Fission also produces radioactive debris, more com-monly known as fallout.

A thermonuclear weapon uses the heat generated by a fission bomb to com-press and ignite a nuclear fusion stage.[12] Thus, fission is still required to trigger the fusion reactions, and the fusion reactions can themselves trigger additional fission reactions. Thermonuclear weapons typically have a far higher explosive yield than do fission weapons, in the range of megatons rather than kilotons.[13] Fusion reactions do not create fission products, but because all thermonuclear weapons contain at least one fission stage, and many high-yield thermonuclear devices also have a final fission stage, thermonuclear weapons can generate at least as much nuclear fallout as fission-only weapons. A 'neutron' bomb, how-ever, is a thermonuclear weapon that yields a relatively small explosion but a large amount of neutron radiation.[14] A neutron bomb could be used to inflict

declassification decisions, 1946 to the present (RDD-8)', 1 January 2002, available at: www. fas.org/sgp/othergov/doe/decl/rdd-8.pdf.

[9] This is the amount of material needed to start a nuclear chain reaction.

[10] The implosion method is only possible if the fissile material is plutonium. The scientist Richard Tolman first suggested the method in the summer of 1942, but the idea was not followed through at the time. Bernstein, *Nuclear Weapons*, p. 122.

[11] 2,4,6-trinitrotoluene, whose explosive yield is the standard measure of strength of bombs and explosive devices.

[12] In nuclear fusion two or more atomic nuclei collide at very high speed and join to form a new type of atomic nucleus.

[13] 'Greenhouse George', fired by the USA in Nevada in May 1951, was the first fusion nuclear weapon to be detonated. Russia detonated a hydrogen bomb in 1952, the UK in 1955, China in 1967 and France in 1968. The largest nuclear explosion ever is believed to be Russian in origin – its explosive yield amounted to 50 megatons. The largest US nuclear detonation, which was equivalent to 15 megatons of TNT, occurred on Bikini Atoll in May 1954. The explosion was far larger than expected and the resulting radiation poisoned the crew of a Japanese fishing boat, leading to an international outcry. Bernstein, *Nuclear Weapons*, pp. 217, 222.

[14] BBC, 'Neutron bomb: Why "clean" is deadly', 15 July 1999, available at: http://news.bbc. co.uk/2/hi/science/nature/395689.stm. According to the BBC, research into the neutron bomb began seriously in the 1970s when military scientists in the USA sought to reduce the amount of blast produced by thermonuclear devices and increase the amount of gamma radiation emitted. Some of the lead work in the field is said to have been carried out in a French atmospheric detonation in 1967. The USA wanted to develop a nuclear weapon that would allow it to wipe out a Soviet army as it invaded Western Europe but leave towns and cities largely intact.

massive casualties while leaving infrastructure mostly intact and creating a minimal amount of fallout.

Surrounding a nuclear weapon with materials such as cobalt-60[15] or gold-98 would create a weapon known as a salted bomb. This device would produce exceptionally large quantities of radioactive contamination. A salted bomb should not be confused with a 'dirty bomb', an ordinary chemical explosive device containing radioactive material that is spread over the area when the device explodes. A salted bomb would contaminate a much larger area than a dirty bomb.

Antimatter has been considered as a trigger mechanism for nuclear weapons or even as a weapon in itself, at least in theory.[16] If electrons or protons collide with their antimatter counterparts, they annihilate each other. In so doing, they unleash more energy than any other known energy source, even thermonuclear weapons: the energy from colliding positrons and antielectrons is said to be 10 billion times that of high explosives. Unlike standard nuclear weapons, such 'positron' bombs could eject an extremely hazardous burst of gamma radiation that could kill massive numbers of people without ejecting radioactive fallout. There is, however, a huge obstacle to any positron bomb: the difficulty of producing antimatter in large enough quantities.[17]

Use and testing of nuclear weapons

In 1939 the Nobel Prize-winning scientist Niels Bohr[18] informed the United States that the Germans had split the atom. The fear that the Nazis could

---

[15] In 1957 in Australia, the UK tested 'Pixie', a small diameter implosion system with a plutonium core. The test later became notorious because of the experimental use of cobalt metal pellets as a test diagnostic for measuring yield. Discovery of (mildly) radioactive cobalt pellets around the test site later gave rise to rumours that the British had been developing a cobalt bomb radiological weapon. (A radiological weapon is any weapon designed to spread radioactive material with intent to kill.)

[16] See, e.g., K. Davidson, 'Air Force pursuing antimatter weapons', San Francisco Chronicle, 4 October 2004, available at: www.sfgate.com/science/article/Air-Force-pursuing-antimatter-weapons-Program-2689674.php. Another possibility is an antimatter-powered 'electromagnetic pulse' that could destroy power grids and communications networks.

[17] The first atoms of antihydrogen – the antimatter counterpart of the simplest atom, hydrogen – were created at the European Organization for Nuclear Research (CERN) in 1995. In 2011 the 'ALPHA' experiment at CERN reported succeeding in trapping antimatter atoms for more than 16 minutes, long enough to begin to study their properties in detail. CERN, 'CERN experiment traps antimatter atoms for 1000 seconds', Press release, 5 June 2011, http://press.web.cern.ch/press-releases/2011/06/cern-experiment-traps-antimatter-atoms-1000-seconds; see also G. B. Andresen et al., 'Confinement of antihydrogen for 1,000 seconds: The ALPHA Collaboration', Nature Physics 7 (2011), 558–64.

[18] From 1920 until his death in 1962, Bohr was head of the Institute for Theoretical Physics at Copenhagen University. Recognition of his work on the structure of atoms came with the award of the Nobel Prize for Physics in 1922. 'The Nobel Prize in Physics 1922: Niels Bohr; Niels Bohr – biographical', Nobelprize.org, undated but accessed on 12 October 2013 at: www.nobelprize.org/nobel_prizes/physics/laureates/1922/bohr-bio.html.

develop extremely powerful weapons prompted US President Theodore Roosevelt to establish the Manhattan Project[19] in 1941.[20] During the first week of April 1943, in Los Alamos, New Mexico, Robert Serber, assistant to the head of the Project's Los Alamos centre, J. Robert Oppenheimer, delivered a series of lectures summarising what was then known about the design of nuclear weapons. In his first lecture, Serber began: 'The object of the [Manhattan] project is to produce a practical military weapon in the form of a bomb in which the energy is released by a fast-neutron chain reaction in one or more of the materials known to show nuclear fission.'[21] The world's first detonation of a nuclear weapon, the result of their work, occurred just before 5.30 a.m. on 16 July 1945 at MacDonald's Ranch near Alamogordo in New Mexico.[22]

The first nuclear weapon attack occurred on 6 August 1945 over the city of Hiroshima in Japan.[23] According to one commentator, the use of the weapon was also simultaneously a test, as its design 'was considered to be so rudimentary'.[24] 'Little Boy', as the bomb was named, was famously dropped by parachute from the US Boeing B-29 Superfortress bomber aircraft Enola Gay, rendering an explosive yield of some 16 kilotons of TNT when it detonated. The bomb was dropped by parachute and exploded 580 metres (1,900 feet) above the ground.[25] No one knows exactly how many tens of thousands of people died.[26]

---

[19] The project was so named as the US Army Corps of Engineers made responsible for developing the atomic bomb was headquartered on Manhattan Island (at 270 Broadway). W. J. Broad, 'Why they called it the Manhattan Project', New York Times, 30 October 2007, available at: www.nytimes.com/2007/10/30/science/30manh.html?pagewanted=all&_r=0. The director of the Project, Leslie Groves, the engineer who designed the Pentagon, reportedly gave it the name. Bernstein, Nuclear Weapons, p. 114.

[20] PBS, 'People and discoveries: J. Robert Oppenheimer, 1904–1967', undated but accessed on 12 October 2013 at: www.pbs.org/wgbh/aso/databank/entries/baoppe.html.

[21] 'Manhattan Project history', The Manhattan Project Heritage Preservation Association, Inc., 3 August 2005, available at: www.mphpa.org/classic/HISTORY/H-06c10.htm.

[22] See, e.g., R. Serber, The Los Alamos Primer (Berkeley: University of California Press, 1992); J. Miller, Stockpile: The Story Behind 10,000 Strategic Nuclear Weapons (Annapolis: Naval Institute Press, 2010), p. 1.

[23] The initial recommendation by Manhattan Project staff – that of the ancient cultural city of Kyoto – was rejected by the US Secretary of State for War on the basis that it would complicate the post-war relationship with Japan. Miller, Stockpile, p. 9.

[24] Bernstein, Nuclear Weapons, p. 5.

[25] W. Wilson, Five Myths About Nuclear Weapons (Boston/New York: Houghton Mifflin Harcourt, 2013), p. 32. Ritchie asserts that the yield was closer to 14 kilotons. N. Ritchie, A Nuclear Weapons-Free World: Britain, Trident, and the Challenges Ahead (Basingstoke: Palgrave Macmillan, 2012), p. 11. Miller claims it was 15 kilotons. Miller, Stockpile, p. 195.

[26] The BBC includes on its website claims that between 60,000 and 80,000 people were killed instantly, with the final death toll estimated at 135,000 as a result of radiation poisoning. 'Fact file: Hiroshima and Nagasaki, 6 and 9 August 1945', BBC, updated in March 2012, available at: www.bbc.co.uk/history/ww2peopleswar/timeline/factfiles/nonflash/a6652262.shtml. As one authority notes: 'Chaotic conditions made accurate accounts most difficult. Some victims were vaporized instantly, many survivors were horribly disfigured, and death from radiation was uncertain – it might not claim its victims for days, weeks,

Three days later the United States detonated 'Fat Man', a plutonium bomb with a larger 20-kiloton yield (a 'clone' of the test device of July 1945), 610 metres (2,000 feet) above a suburb of Nagasaki,[27] killing some 74,000 people.[28] The height had been chosen to maximise the blast wave on the ground, while the fallout was distributed in areas far away from 'ground zero'.[29]

The explosion of a nuclear weapon creates phenomenal quantities of heat upon detonation – between 60 and 100 million degrees centigrade.[30] Anyone within a radius of one and a half miles from ground zero and who is unprotected will receive third-degree (full thickness) burns,[31] which will almost certainly be fatal.[32] At Hiroshima, collapsed buildings became tinder for the fires started largely by overturned cooking stoves and a firestorm started. At Nagasaki, fires broke out at many locations. Such fires are common to any high explosives. What is unique about nuclear weapons is the radiation, which occurs at different times. 'Prompt' radiation comes first, soon after the explosion, consisting of neutrons, gamma rays and electrons. Neutron radiation is an especially hazardous form of radiation to humans.[33] In the explosion of a nuclear weapon, the fireball rises, sucking the cooler air below as well as radioactive debris up from the ground. Water drops are extracted from the cooler air to form clouds.[34] Fallout begins one to two hours afterwards and lasts for a day or so.[35]

---

months, or even years.' 'Counting the dead', *AtomicBombMuseum.org*, available at: http://atomicbombmuseum.org/3_health.shtml.

[27] The original target was Kokura, but this was obscured by cloud so the bomb was dropped on nearby Nagasaki, an important port.

[28] The BBC reported claims that about 40,000 people were killed instantly and a third of the city was destroyed. The final death toll was calculated as at least 50,000. 'Fact File: Hiroshima and Nagasaki, 6 and 9 August 1945', BBC. The plutonium bomb used against Nagasaki was more powerful than the one used against Hiroshima, but its destructive range was limited by surrounding hills and mountains. Whatever the true figure, the massive loss of life in the bombing of a city was not the largest recorded in human history. A night attack on Tokyo on 9–10 March 1945 is believed to have killed up to 120,000 people or even more. Wilson, *Five Myths About Nuclear Weapons*, p. 32. Miller suggests the figure was closer to 100,000. Miller, *Stockpile*, p. 195.

[29] Bernstein, *Nuclear Weapons*, pp. 137–8.

[30] *Ibid.*, pp. 171–3. In comparison, the temperature of the surface of the sun is approximately 60,000 degrees centigrade.

[31] A burn that destroys both the epidermis and the dermis, often also involving the subcutaneous tissue. *Mosby's Medical Dictionary*, 8th edn (St Louis: Elsevier, 2009).

[32] Bernstein, *Nuclear Weapons*, p. 184.

[33] Neutron particles are released following nuclear fission of uranium or plutonium. In fact, it is neutrons that trigger the nuclear chain reaction to explode an atomic bomb. The human body contains a large amount of hydrogen, and when neutrons hit the nucleus of hydrogen, the proton causes ionisations in the body, leading to various types of damage. At equivalent absorbed doses, neutrons can cause more severe damage to the body than gamma rays. Radiation Effects Research Foundation, 'Basics about radiation', 2007, available at: www.rerf.jp/radefx/basickno_e/whatis.html.

[34] Bernstein, *Nuclear Weapons*, pp. 181–2.   [35] *Ibid.*, p. 184.

There were very high levels of short-term mortality in both Hiroshima and Nagasaki, with more than 90 per cent of those within 500 metres of ground zero in both cities dying. At 1.5 kilometres, more than two-thirds were casualties, and about one-third died. Of those at a distance of 2 kilometres, about half were casualties, 10 per cent of whom died. Casualties dropped to approximately 10 per cent at distances over 4 kilometres. Most of those close to ground zero who received high radiation dosages died immediately or during the first day. About one-third of all fatalities occurred by the fourth day; two-thirds by the tenth day; and 90 per cent by the end of three weeks. Four injury phases were discerned following the two attacks:

- During the first two weeks, injuries were mainly burns from rays and flames, and wounds (trauma) from blast and falling structures.
- In the third through eighth weeks, there were symptoms of damage by radioactive rays, for example, loss of hair, anaemia, loss of white cells, bleeding and diarrhoea. Approximately 10 per cent of cases in this group were fatal.
- In the third and fourth months, there was some improvement in burn, trauma, and even radiation injuries. But then came secondary injuries of disfiguration, severe scar formations (keloids), blood abnormalities, sterility (both sexes) and psychosomatic disorders.
- After more than half a century had passed, many after-effects remained: leukaemia; A-bomb cataracts; cancers of the thyroid, breast, lungs and salivary glands; birth defects, including mental retardation, and fears of birth defects in their children; and disfiguring keloid scars.[36]

Whether or not conventional wisdom is correct in holding that the United States' use of nuclear weapons against these two Japanese cities was the critical factor in prompting Japan's unconditional surrender a few days later is contested strongly by Ward Wilson. He argues that the declaration of war by Russia on Japan and Russia's invasion of Japanese territory was far more determinative in the Japanese Emperor's decision that Japan should surrender unconditionally.[37]

The second state after the United States to test a nuclear bomb successfully was Russia, which in 1949 detonated an atomic bomb, made with plutonium as its nuclear material.[38] In 1957 the United Nations established the International Atomic Energy Association (IAEA) as the world's 'Atoms for Peace' organisation within the UN family. The IAEA works with its member states and partners 'to promote safe, secure and peaceful nuclear technologies'.[39] According to the IAEA, its safeguards 'are generally acknowledged as the single credible

[36] 'Counting the dead', *AtomicBombMuseum.org*.
[37] See Wilson, *Five Myths About Nuclear Weapons*.   [38] Miller, *Stockpile*, p. 3.
[39] IAEA, 'About the IAEA: The "Atoms for Peace" Agency', undated but accessed on 12 October 2013 at: www.iaea.org/About/about-iaea.html.

means by which the international community can be assured that nuclear material and facilities are being used exclusively for peaceful purposes. This system functions not only as a confidence building measure, but also as an early warning mechanism.'[40]

In October 1962 the Cuban Missile Crisis brought the world to the brink of all-out nuclear war. Estimates suggested that had the United States struck first, it would still have suffered 100 million casualties, more than half of its 187 million population at the time.[41] The following month, the United States detonated a 10 megaton hydrogen bomb in space, 402 metres (250 miles) above the earth's surface.[42] As a result of Project Starfish, an electron belt was temporarily created that destroyed seven satellites, including the world's first communications satellite.[43] The following year, in August, the United States and the Soviet Union signed the Partial Test-Ban Treaty, prohibiting testing in the atmosphere. In 1966 a Comprehensive Test-Ban Treaty was adopted under United Nations auspices, but it has never entered into force, as it requires every single named state on a list annexed to the treaty to both sign and ratify it.[44]

In 1974 India tested its first nuclear weapon, while in 1998 Pakistan did the same.[45] In October 1986 Mordechai Vanunu, a former Israeli nuclear technician, publicly revealed in a British newspaper, the *Sunday Times*, that Israel had developed nuclear weapons. He was kidnapped in Rome by Israeli intelligence operatives and forcibly returned to Israel where he spent eighteen years in prison, more than half in solitary confinement.[46] The last above-ground test of a nuclear weapon is believed to have occurred in 1980, carried out by China.[47] In October 2006 the Democratic People's Republic of Korea conducted an underground test of a low-yield nuclear device, revealing it had joined the list of nuclear weapon states.[48]

Estimated stockpiles of nuclear weapons

No one knows (or agrees on) exactly how many nuclear weapons, or more pertinently how many nuclear warheads there are in the world.[49] Nine states

---

[40] IAEA, *IAEA Safeguards Agreements and Additional Protocols: Verifying Compliance with Nuclear Non-Proliferation Undertakings* (Vienna: IAEA, 2011), available at: www.iaea.org/Publications/Booklets/Safeguards3/safeguards0408.pdf, Foreword.

[41] Wilson, *Five Myths About Nuclear Weapons*, p. 73.

[42] Miller, *Stockpile*, p. 4.

[43] Bernstein, *Nuclear Weapons*, p. 178.

[44] As of 1 October 2013, China, DPR Korea, India and Pakistan had not signed the treaty, while Egypt, Iran, Israel and the United States had not ratified it.

[45] Bernstein, *Nuclear Weapons*, p. 5.

[46] M. Asser, 'Vanunu: Israel's nuclear telltale', BBC, 20 April 2004, available at: http://news.bbc.co.uk/2/hi/middle_east/3640613.stm.

[47] Bernstein, *Nuclear Weapons*, p. 4.   [48] Bernstein, *Nuclear Weapons*, p. 7.

[49] See Miller, *Stockpile*; S. N. Kile, 'World nuclear forces', *SIPRI Yearbook 2013* (Oxford University Press, 2013); Ritchie, *A Nuclear Weapons-Free World*, pp. 24–5; 'Get the facts',

Table I.1 *Global stockpiles of fissile material*

State	HEU, tonnes	Non-civilian Pu, tonnes	Civilian Pu, tonnes
Russia	695	128	50.1
USA	604	87	0
France	31	6	57.5
China	16	1.8	0.014
UK	21.2	3.5	91.2
Pakistan	3	0.15	0
India	0.8	5.2	0.24
Israel	0.3	0.84	0
DPR Korea	0	0.03	0
Others	15	0	61
TOTAL	1,390	234	260

are believed to have stockpiled a total of some 17,300 warheads.[50] The Russian Federation has the greatest number, believed to be around 8,500, closely followed by the United States (some 7,700). Far behind them are France (approximately 300), China (approximately 250), the United Kingdom (approximately 225), Pakistan (100–120), India (90–110), Israel (approximately 80) and the Democratic People's Republic of Korea (DPR Korea) (between 6 and 10). Of the total warheads in the world today, the Stockholm International Peace Research Institute (SIPRI) estimates that 4,400 are 'deployed' (i.e. potentially ready for use),[51] including 2,150 by the United States and approximately 1,800 by the Russian Federation.

Significant quantities of fissile material also exist that could be used in a nuclear weapon.[52] According to one estimate,[53] as of January 2013 the global stockpile of highly enriched uranium (HEU)[54] was approximately 1,390 tonnes (see Table I.1). The global stockpile of separated plutonium is about 490 tonnes,

Global Zero, available at: www.globalzero.org/get-the-facts/FAQs; 'Nuclear arsenals', International Campaign to Abolish Nuclear Weapons, available at: www.icanw.org/the-facts/nuclear-arsenals/#.UiROvhY7b_Q; 'China', Nuclear Threat Initiative, available at: www.nti.org/country-profiles/china/. The authors would like to thank Lars Jørgen Røed for his background research on stockpiled nuclear weapons and fissile material, accessed October 2013

[50] Wilson claims that the figure is more than 20,000. Wilson, *Five Myths About Nuclear Weapons*, p. 16.

[51] According to SIPRI, deployed means warheads placed on missiles or located on bases with operational force. Almost 2,000 are said to be kept in a state of high operational alert. Kile, 'World nuclear forces'.

[52] An isotope like uranium-235 is called fissile while an isotope like uranium-238 is called fissionable. Bernstein, *Nuclear Weapons*, p. 56.

[53] International Panel on Fissile Materials: Fissile material stocks, 31 July 2013, available at: http://fissilematerials.org. This subsection is based on the data contained therein.

[54] Enrichment is the process of separating, for example, uranium-235 from uranium-238.

of which about 260 tonnes is the material in civilian custody.[55] Production of military fissile materials is believed to continue in India, which is producing plutonium and HEU for naval propulsion; Pakistan, which produces plutonium and HEU for weapons; and Israel, which is believed to produce plutonium. DPR Korea has the capability to produce weapons-grade plutonium and HEU. France, India, Japan, Russia and the UK operate civilian reprocessing facilities that separate plutonium from spent fuel of power reactors. China is operating a pilot civilian reprocessing facility. A total of twelve states – Argentina, Brazil, France, Germany, India, Iran, Japan, the Netherlands, Pakistan, Russia, the UK and the United States – operate uranium enrichment facilities. DPR Korea is also believed to have an operational uranium enrichment plant.

The layout of the book

This book discusses nuclear weapons from the perspective of a number of international legal regimes. Starting with the law on the inter-state use of force (*jus ad bellum*), Part I begins by discussing the requirements of necessity and proportionality as well as the concept of threatening use of force. The separation between *jus ad bellum* and *jus in bello* and the rationale for maintaining this separation is also assessed.

Part II deals with the application of international humanitarian law (IHL) to nuclear weapons. The rules on conduct of hostilities including the rules of distinction and proportionality, as well as the prohibition on means of warfare of a nature to cause superfluous injury and unnecessary suffering are discussed with regard to nuclear weapons. The concept of whether threats of use of nuclear weapons might constitute a violation of IHL, and the use of nuclear weapons as a belligerent reprisal, are also discussed.

Part III, on nuclear weapons and international criminal law (ICL), discusses use of nuclear weapons as an act of genocide, a crime against humanity or a war crime. Another topic considered is the potential impact of the discrepancy between the 1998 Rome Statute of the International Criminal Court[56] and IHL when it comes to specific references to prohibited weapons.

Part IV, which deals with international environmental law, first discusses the requirements of IHL regarding protection of the environment. It goes on to discuss various international legal regimes pertaining to the environment and to the different aspects of nuclear weapons. Finally, it assesses the state

---

[55] Numbers for weapons plutonium for the UK and USA are based on official data. Most numbers for civilian plutonium are based on declarations submitted to the IAEA and reflect the status as of 31 December 2011. Other numbers are non-governmental estimates, often with large uncertainties. HEU amounts are 90 per cent enriched HEU equivalents (with the exception of the number for non-nuclear weapon states). The totals are rounded.

[56] Rome Statute of the International Criminal Court, Rome, 17 July 1998, entry into force 1 July 2002, 2187 UNTS 90.

of international law, including customary law, regarding the testing of nuclear weapons.

Part V addresses nuclear weapons disarmament and non-proliferation law. Several regional treaties establish nuclear weapon-free zones, which today encompass most states in Africa, Asia and Latin America. The legal and political impact of these treaties, as well as the proposed treaty on a WMD-free zone in the Middle East, is discussed here. Moreover, the NPT and its content, as well as the impact and meaning of its Article VI on general and complete disarmament of nuclear weapons, are considered. Lastly, the issue of armed non-state actors and nuclear terrorism is discussed.

The final section of the book, Part VI, considers the extent to which international human rights law is relevant to nuclear weapons. It discusses the applicability of human rights law in armed conflict, and the most relevant human rights at issue, such as the right to life and the right to health. The right to a remedy under human rights law for the harmful effects of any new use of nuclear weapons is also addressed here.

A conclusion on the status of nuclear weapons under international law completes the book.

PART I

Nuclear weapons and *jus ad bellum*

1

Using force by means of nuclear weapons and requirements of necessity and proportionality *ad bellum*

NOBUO HAYASHI

Introduction

This chapter examines necessity and proportionality *ad bellum* as applied to use of force involving nuclear weapons by states in self-defence against other states.

It is sometimes suggested that the very nature of these weapons renders their use neither necessary nor proportionate under any circumstances.[1] The situation under international law is, however, more equivocal. *Jus ad bellum* is weapon-neutral.[2] It authorises *some* force in self-defence under the right conditions. The lawfulness *ad bellum* of nuclear weapons depends on the specific circumstances of their use, and respect for both necessity and proportionality.[3] Frustrating as it may be, *jus ad bellum* is perhaps not the most suitable body of international law through which to restrict or ban nuclear weapons per se. This appears to remain the case, although various arguments have been advanced to the contrary.

Our discussion proceeds in the following order. Section A defines the scope of this inquiry. Section B considers necessity and proportionality *ad bellum* generally. In Section C, we examine issues surrounding their application to nuclear weapons used in self-defence.

A. Preliminary observations

Our focus is on use of force involving nuclear weapons by states in self-defence against other states. Accordingly, this chapter does not discuss *threats* of force.[4] Nor does it deal with force used in situations other than

---

[1] Written Statement of the Government of Mexico to the International Court of Justice (ICJ) in the *Legality of The Threat or Use of Nuclear Weapons Case*, 19 June 1995, pp. 10, 11; J. Burroughs, *The Illegality of Threat or Use of Nuclear Weapons: A Guide to the Historic Opinion of the International Court of Justice* (New Jersey: Transaction Publishers, 1998) pp. 39–40.

[2] International Court of Justice (ICJ), *Legality of the Threat or Use of Nuclear Weapons*, Advisory Opinion of 8 July 1996, *ICJ Reports* 1996 (hereafter, Nuclear Weapons Advisory Opinion), para. 41.

[3] Nuclear Weapons Advisory Opinion, paras. 42–3.

[4] See Chapter 2 for a discussion of nuclear weapons as a threat of force.

self-defence.[5] Defensive force that involves only conventional weapons is also excluded from this chapter.[6] Similarly, our investigation is limited to nuclear weapons used by one state against another state. We therefore defer to discussions elsewhere for issues such as whether *jus ad bellum* entitles a non-state entity to resort to force in self-defence,[7] and whether this body of law governs states using force in self-defence against non-state entities.[8]

Contemporary *jus ad bellum* restricts use of force in self-defence to situations where 'an armed attack occurs'.[9] It is not the purpose of this chapter to delve into questions of what it is and when it occurs. Suffice it to note here that the notion includes considerations of scale and effects,[10] rather than the specific type of weapons used. Thus, those situations of interest to this chapter include not only where the defending state uses nuclear weapons in response to a nuclear attack, but also where the attack involves exclusively conventional weapons. Regardless, when one state launches nuclear-armed intercontinental ballistic missiles against another, it scarcely matters to the latter state whether the launch itself constitutes an 'armed attack' within the meaning of Article 51 of the Charter of the United Nations 1945 (which it may not necessarily do prior to the actual explosion of the missiles), or whether it signifies the imminence of an attack (which, it is submitted here, it clearly does).[11]

---

[5] Regarding the application of necessity and proportionality *ad bellum* to such situations, see J. Gardam, *Necessity, Proportionality and the Use of Force by States* (Cambridge University Press, 2004), pp. 199–212.

[6] For the purpose of this chapter only, the expression 'conventional' is juxtaposed vis-à-vis 'nuclear'. Accordingly, chemical and bacteriological weapons fall under the former expression here.

[7] A. Randelzhofer, 'Article 2(4)' in B. Simma (ed.), *The Charter of the United Nations: A Commentary*, 2nd edn (Oxford University Press, 2002), pp. 128–9.

[8] ICJ, *Legal Consequences of the Construction of a Wall in the Occupied Palestinian Territory*, Advisory Opinion of 9 July 2004 (hereafter, Palestinian Wall Advisory Opinion), para. 139; ICJ, *Case Concerning Armed Activities on the Territory of the Congo (Democratic Republic of the Congo v. Uganda)*, Judgment of 19 December 2005 (hereafter, *Armed Activities* Judgment), paras. 146–7. Also, see Judge Kooijmans' Separate Opinion and Judge Buergenthal's Declaration in Palestinian Wall Advisory Opinion, paras. 35–9 (Kooijmans), para. 6 (Buergenthal); Judges Kooijmans and Simma's Dissenting Opinions in *Armed Activities* Judgment, paras. 4–15 (Simma), paras. 25–35 (Kooijmans); N. Lubell, *Extraterritorial Use of Force Against Non-State Actors* (Oxford University Press, 2010), pp. 30–6, 43–68.

[9] Charter of the United Nations, San Francisco, 26 June 1945, in force 24 October 1945, 1 UNTS XVI, Art. 51.

[10] ICJ, *Case Concerning Military and Paramilitary Activities in and against Nicaragua (Nicaragua v. United States of America)*, Judgment of 27 June 1986 (hereafter, *Nicaragua* Judgment), para. 195; ICJ, *Case Concerning Oil Platforms (Islamic Republic of Iran v. United States of America)*, Judgment of 6 November 2003, *ICJ Reports* 2003 (hereafter, *Oil Platforms* Judgment), para. 64; Eritrea–Ethiopia Claims Commission, *Partial Award* Jus Ad Bellum *Ethiopia's Claims 1–8*, 19 December 2005, paras. 11–12; D. Kretzmer, 'The inherent right to self-defence and proportionality in *jus ad bellum*', *European Journal of International Law* 24 (2013), 235–82 at 242–4.

[11] See discussions below regarding an attack's imminence as an element of necessity *ad bellum*.

B.   Necessity and proportionality *ad bellum*

The requirement to respect both necessity and proportionality *ad bellum* in any use of force in self-defence seems uncontroversial nowadays.[12] The International Court of Justice (ICJ)[13] and contemporary commentators[14] have repeatedly affirmed their applicability. The real difficulty concerns the numerous ambiguities and indeterminacies that imbue necessity and proportionality *ad bellum*. To begin with, distinguishing between them is not always straightforward. In Christine Gray's words:

> In theory it is possible to draw a distinction between necessity and proportionality, and the International Court of Justice typically applies the two requirements separately. Necessity is commonly interpreted as the requirement that no alternative response be possible. Proportionality relates to the size, duration and target of the response, but clearly these factors are also relevant to necessity. It is not clear how far the two concepts can operate separately. If a use of force is not necessary, it cannot be proportionate and, if it is not proportionate, it is difficult to see how it can be necessary. Commentators agree on a few, basic, uncontroversial principles: necessity and proportionality mean that self-defence must not be retaliatory or punitive; the aim should be to halt and repel an attack.[15]

As seen below, there is also disagreement about the content, timing and duration of the necessity and proportionality assessment. This mirrors larger differences regarding *jus ad bellum*'s temporal scope of application.[16]

1.   Necessity

Necessity *ad bellum*[17] concerns the circumstances in which the state exercising its right of self-defence may lawfully use force. Put simply, the circumstances must be such that they render recourse to force necessary. The standard formulation entails the requirement that there be no reasonable alternative to using

---

[12] For earlier views to the contrary, see J. L. Kuntz, 'Individual and collective self-defence in Article 51 of the Charter of the United Nations', *American Journal of International Law* 41 (1947), 872–9 at 876–7.

[13] *Nicaragua* Judgment, para. 176; *Oil Platforms* Judgment, paras. 43, 73, 74, 76; *Armed Activities* Judgment, para. 147; Nuclear Weapons Advisory Opinion, para. 41.

[14] C. Gray, *International Law and the Use of Force*, 3d edn (Oxford University Press, 2008), pp. 148–50; J. A. Green, *The International Court of Justice and Self-Defence in International Law* (Oxford: Hart Publishing, 2009), pp. 63–4.

[15] Gray, *International Law and the Use of Force*, p. 150. See also Green, *The International Court of Justice and Self-Defence*, p. 89.

[16] C. Greenwood, 'The relationship between *jus ad bellum* and *jus in bello*', Review of International Studies 9 (1983), 221–34.

[17] See generally, J. Gardam, 'Necessity and proportionality in *jus ad bellum* and *jus in bello*' in L. Boisson de Chazournes and P. Sands (eds.), *International Law, the International Court of Justice and Nuclear Weapons* (Cambridge University Press, 1999), pp. 278–9; Gardam,

force.[18] Beyond this, however, there is a conspicuous lack of guidance in case law[19] and only limited agreement among commentators.[20]

Force as a last resort

It seems generally agreed that necessity *ad bellum* requires the defending state to use force only as a last resort.[21] At least formally, it is always open to the defending state *not* to resist an armed attack with force (as Denmark chose to do during the Second World War). It would appear, however, that *jus ad bellum* does not demand that the defending state treat such a choice as among the relevant alternatives.[22] Nor does necessity appear to require exhaustion of all peaceful measures.[23] Only relevant alternatives that are reasonable need be shown to be unavailable. Admittedly, what is reasonable depends on the circumstances, and can only be assessed on a case-by-case basis. Commentators agree that an ongoing armed attack of a certain scale *ipso facto* satisfies the necessity requirement.[24] As one climbs down the scale, the proposition that a smaller-scale armed attack, or an isolated attack, also *ipso facto* satisfies necessity begins to look less certain.[25]

It is sometimes said that this line of reasoning conflates necessity with proportionality.[26] Whether such a criticism is apt is not entirely clear. Strictly speaking, holding that a given armed attack is *de minimis* amounts to asserting that the defending state is not entitled to use force in satisfaction of necessity. The issue is thus not (yet) how much force the defending state may lawfully use in accordance with proportionality.

Necessity, Proportionality and the Use of Force by States, pp. 148–55; Kretzmer, 'The inherent right to self-defence', 235.

[18] Gray, *International Law and the Use of Force*, p. 150.

[19] *Ibid.*, pp. 151–5; Green, *The International Court of Justice and Self-Defence*, pp. 105–7.

[20] See discussion below.

[21] J. Quigley, 'The Afghanistan war and self-defence', *Valparaiso University Law Review* 37 (2002–03), 541–62 at 546; R. Ago, *Addendum to the Eighth Report on State Responsibility*, UN doc. A/CN.4/318, Add 5–7, Y.B.I.L.C. I.1, 65–66 (1980); R. Jennings and A. Watts (eds.), *Oppenheim's International Law*, 9th edn (London: Longman, 1992), p. 422; Green, *The International Court of Justice and Self-Defence*, pp. 78–80.

[22] See discussion below regarding what the ICJ called an 'extreme circumstance of self-defence, in which the very survival of a State would be at stake' (Nuclear Weapons Advisory Opinion, para. 105(2)(E)).

[23] Green, *The International Court of Justice and Self-Defence*, pp. 84–5; Y. Dinstein, *War, Aggression and Self-Defence*, 5th edn (Cambridge University Press, 2011), p. 262.

[24] Green, *The International Court of Justice and Self-Defence*, p. 85; Gardam, 'Necessity and proportionality', p. 278; Dinstein, *War, Aggression and Self-Defence*, p. 262.

[25] O. Schachter, 'The right of states to use armed force', *Michigan Law Review* 82 (1984), 1620–46, at 1627, 1635; O. Schachter, 'The lawful resort to unilateral use of force', *Yale Law Journal* 10 (1985), 291–4, at 292; Ago, *Addendum to the Eighth Report*, 69; Gardam, 'Necessity and proportionality', p. 278; L. Moir, *Reappraising the Resort to Force* (Oxford: Hart Publishing, 2010), pp. 23–4; Dinstein, *War, Aggression and Self-Defence*, p. 262.

[26] Moir, *Reappraising the Resort to Force*, pp. 118–20.

Contemporaneous and bona fide belief of necessity?

The ICJ appears to have added, as a conclusive evidentiary ground for rejecting necessity claims, the absence of prior complaint specific to the mode and provenance of the (putative) armed attack, combined with prior non-identification of appropriate military targets. Thus, in the *Oil Platforms* case, the Court held:

> In the case both of the attack on the *Sea Isle City* and the mining of the USS Samuel B. Roberts, the Court is not satisfied that the attacks on the platform was necessary to respond to these incidents. In this connection, the Court notes that there is no evidence that the United States complained to Iran of the military activities of the platforms, in the same way as it complained repeatedly of minelaying and attacks on neutral shipping, which does not suggest that the targeting of the platforms was seen as a necessary act. The Court would also observe that in the case of the attack of 19 October 1987, the United States attacked the R-4 platforms as a 'target of opportunity', not one previously identified as an appropriate military target.[27]

Some critics[28] note with concern that the ICJ introduced the *jus in bello* principle of distinction into necessity *ad bellum*. Others[29] suggest that the Court simply reiterated its earlier view that the lawfulness of force involves compliance with both *jus ad bellum* and *jus in bello*.[30]

It is submitted here, however, that the Court apparently considered necessity *ad bellum* to require the contemporaneous and bona fide belief on the part of the state claiming self-defence that the necessity for its particular action existed. The *Oil Platforms* judgment appears to indicate, on its face at least, that necessity claims may fail on the absence alone of such belief. Note here that the Court took the absence of any prior complaint by the United States regarding the platforms' military activities to undermine the notion that 'the targeting of the platforms was seen as a necessary act'. The passive voice used here is curious. *Whose* view of targeting the R-4 platforms 'as a necessary act' is the absence of any US complaint meant to impugn? The only reasonable reading of the passage seems to be that, in the Court's view:

> there is no evidence that the United States complained to Iran of the military activities of the platforms ... which does not suggest that the targeting of the platforms was seen [by the United States] as a necessary act.[31]

In other words, the Court rejected the United States' necessity claims based on the absence of evidence that the claimant considered its own action to be

---

[27] *Oil Platforms* Judgment, para. 76.

[28] N. Ochoa-Ruiz and E. Salamanca-Aguado, 'Exploring the limits of international law relating to the use of force in self-defence', *European Journal of International Law* 16 (2005), 499–524 at 514.

[29] Moir, *Reappraising the Resort to Force*, pp. 124–5.

[30] Nuclear Weapons Advisory Opinion, para. 42.   [31] *Oil Platforms* Judgment, para. 76.

a necessary act. If this is indeed what the Court had in mind, it makes sense that it went on to mention the US designation of the platforms as opportunity targets rather than previously identified military targets.[32]

It is highly unlikely that, under modern *jus ad bellum*, the absence of contemporaneous and bona fide belief conclusively negates necessity claims. Nor, for that matter, does it appear that the existence of such belief conclusively establishes necessity.

Imminence of attack

For the purpose of this chapter, imminence means the temporal proximity between the offending state's future attack and the force to which the defending state resorts.[33] This notion is typically discussed in connection with anticipatory, that is non-imminent, self-defence.[34]

Some authority exists for the view that imminence is indeed an element of necessity *ad bellum*.[35] It has also been described as an element of proportionality *ad bellum*,[36] or as a temporal element of both necessity and proportionality.[37] This author agrees with those for whom imminence is best understood as an implicit aspect of necessity.[38] The imminence of an armed attack would be adequately captured by reference to the absence of reasonable alternatives to using force in response. The range of such alternatives, as well as the degree of

---

[32] To be sure, the Court did rule that '[t]he United States must show that its actions were necessary and proportionate to the armed attack made on it, and that the platforms were a legitimate military target open to attack in the exercise of self-defence' (*Oil Platforms* Judgment, para. 51). Nevertheless, the mere fact that the object of an attack is not previously identified as a legitimate military target does not per se preclude the possibility that it can constitute a military objective within the meaning of *jus in bello*.

[33] Green, *The International Court of Justice and Self-Defence*, p. 108. The ICJ itself has not pronounced on the matter. See *Nicaragua* Judgment, para. 194; *Armed Activities* Judgment, para. 143.

[34] I. Brownlie, *International Law and the Use of Force by States* (Oxford University Press, 1963), pp. 257–61; R. Higgins, *Problems and Process: International Law and How We Use It* (Oxford University Press, 1994), p. 242; T. Gazzini, *The Changing Rules on the Use of Force in International Law* (Manchester University Press, 2005), p. 143; Green, *The International Court of Justice and Self-Defence*, pp. 96–101; M. C. Alder, *The Inherent Right of Self-Defence in International Law* (Dordrecht: Springer, 2013), pp. 19, 119–20, 123, 173–4.

[35] Dinstein, *War, Aggression and Self-Defence*, pp. 230–1, 233–4, 267–8. But see, e.g., D. W. Bowett, *Self-Defence in International Law* (New York: Frederick A. Praeger, 1958), pp. 191–2; M. B. Occelli, 'Sinking the *Caroline*: why the Caroline doctrine's restrictions on self-defence should not be regarded as customary international law', *San Diego International Law Journal* 4 (2003), 467–90 at 483–8; Gardam, *Necessity, Proportionality and the Use of Force by States*, pp. 149–55.

[36] Brownlie, *International Law and the Use of Force by States*, p. 259; Gray, *International Law and the Use of Force*, p. 150.

[37] Green, *The International Court of Justice and Self-Defence*, pp. 96, 108.

[38] Gardam, 'Necessity and proportionality', p. 278; Gardam, *Necessity, Proportionality and the Use of Force by States*, pp. 149–53; Gazzini, *The Changing Rules on the Use of Force*, p. 144.

thoroughness with which the defending state would be expected to assess them, would in general increase or decrease with the amount of room for assessment that it had before deciding to resort to force. The more distant the attack is into the future, the less urgent it will be for the defending state to choose to use force in response, and the more carefully it will be expected to make that choice. Conversely, the more imminent the attack is, the more pressing it will be to respond quickly and decisively, and the less exhaustively the defending state will be required to explore alternatives.

Immediacy of force

Immediacy denotes the temporal proximity between the actual attack by one state that is either in progress or completed, and the force to which the defending state resorts in response.[39] All else being equal, immediacy is essentially what separates self-defence that is lawful under *jus ad bellum* from armed reprisals that are generally considered unlawful under *jus ad bellum*.[40]

Two unresolved questions may be mentioned. One involves potential changes in the character of the situation that initially established necessity *ad bellum*. Is necessity *ad bellum* strictly a matter of incidence,[41] or is it a matter of incidence and continuity?[42] The other question concerns whether use of force that lacks immediacy relative to one armed attack, such that it would constitute an instance of unlawful armed reprisals, might nevertheless retain its status as lawful self-defence on account of another, future armed attack that is sufficiently imminent.[43]

2. Proportionality

Proportionality *ad bellum*[44] demands some reasonable proportion between two variables. We know that one variable concerns the quantum of defensive

---

[39] Green, *The International Court of Justice and Self-Defence*, p. 108.

[40] Higgins, *Problems and Process*, p. 241; Gazzini, *The Changing Rules on the Use of Force*, pp. 164–9, 203–4; Gray, *International Law and the Use of Force*, pp. 151, 153, 155–6, 197–8, 203; Kretzmer, 'The inherent right to self-defence', 251–8.

[41] Gardam, 'Necessity and proportionality', p. 277; N. G. Printer, Jr, 'The use of force against non-state actors under international law: an analysis of the US Predator strike in Yemen', *UCLA Journal of International Law and Foreign Affairs* 8 (2003), 331–84 at 343; D. Rodin, *War and Self-Defence* (Oxford University Press, 2003), p. 112; Dinstein, *War, Aggression and Self-Defence*, p. 262.

[42] K. H. Kaikobad, 'Self-defence enforcement action and the Gulf Wars, 1980–88 and 1990–91', *British Yearbook of International Law* 63 (1992), 299–366 at 336ff.; Gardam, 'Necessity and proportionality', p. 277, n. 9; Gazzini, *The Changing Rules on the Use of Force*, pp. 143, 146–7.

[43] Gazzini, *The Changing Rules on the Use of Force*, p. 192; Green, *The International Court of Justice and Self-Defence*, pp. 101–4, 108.

[44] See generally, Gardam, 'Necessity and proportionality', pp. 279–81; Kretzmer, 'The inherent right to self-defence', 235.

force used. However, what the other variable entails, as well as the criteria, measurement and duration of comparison between the two variables, has not been given much clarification in ICJ jurisprudence[45] and continues to generate disagreement.[46]

Variables compared

To what does *jus ad bellum* require the quantum of defensive force used to be proportionate?[47] Several possibilities have been suggested. They range from the quantum of force used in the armed attack,[48] to the attack's successful repulsion,[49] to final and decisive victory (at least in cases of full-scale wars of self-defence).[50] Some commentators combine the defensive aim sought with the mode of the armed attack,[51] or a further benefit–harm comparison.[52]

Today the weight of authority appears to point to fulfilment of a state's strictly defensive purposes as the likeliest content of proportionality *ad bellum*'s second variable.[53] This is consistent with the notion that lawfulness *ad bellum* of force used in self-defence depends on its function rather than its form. In one sense, the assertion that the defensive force used should be compared to final and decisive victory is also a variation of the same theme. That such may indeed have been the second variable during the Second World War cannot be denied.[54] There is, however, no compelling evidence to suggest that it has

---

[45] Gray, *International Law and the Use of Force*, p. 151; Green, *The International Court of Justice and Self-Defence*, pp. 105–7.

[46] Brownlie, *International Law and the Use of Force by States*, p. 261; Gardam, 'Necessity and proportionality', p. 280.

[47] Gardam, 'Necessity and proportionality', p. 280; Green, *The International Court of Justice and Self-Defence*, p. 88.

[48] Brownlie, *International Law and the Use of Force by States*, p. 264; Schachter, 'The right of states to use armed force', 1637; K. W. Quigley, 'A framework for evaluating the legality of the United States intervention in Nicaragua', *New York University Journal of International Law and Policy* 17 (1984–5), 155–85, at 180 (cited in Dinstein, *War, Aggression and Self-Defence*, pp. 232–3).

[49] Dissenting Opinion of Judge Higgins, Nuclear Weapons Advisory Opinion, para. 5; C. Greenwood, '*Jus ad bellum* and *jus in bello* in the *Nuclear Weapons* Advisory Opinion' in L. Boisson de Chazournes and P. Sands (eds.), *International Law, the International Court of Justice and Nuclear Weapons* (Cambridge University Press, 1999), pp. 258–9; J. Gardam, 'Proportionality and force in international law', *American Journal of International Law* 87 (1993), 391–413 at 404; Gardam, *Necessity, Proportionality and the Use of Force by States*, pp. 156–9; Gazzini, *The Changing Rules on the Use of Force*, pp. 148, 197–8; Green, *The International Court of Justice and Self-Defence*, pp. 88–9, 92–3.

[50] Kuntz, 'Individual and collective self-defence', 876–7; Dinstein, *War, Aggression and Self-Defence*, pp. 264–7. But, see Green, *The International Court of Justice and Self-Defence*, p. 90.

[51] E. Cannizzaro, 'Contextualizing proportionality: *jus ad bellum* and *jus in bello* in the Lebanese war', *International Review of the Red Cross* 88 (2006), 779–92 at 783–4; Green, *The International Court of Justice and Self-Defence*, pp. 94–5.

[52] Kretzmer, 'The inherent right to self-defence', 235.   [53] But see *ibid.*, 260–2.

[54] Dinstein, *War, Aggression and Self-Defence*, pp. 265–7.

continued to be so to this day. In this author's view, neither the three authorities that Yoram Dinstein, a major proponent of the victory theory, invokes,[55] nor his own take on the situation stemming from the 1991 Gulf War to the 2003 Iraq War,[56] would be sufficient.

Nor does it appear realistic to expect that the defending state limit the quantum of its force in proportion to that used in the attack against it. In *Oil Platforms*, however, the ICJ apparently applied the force–counterforce test.[57] The Court held that, had the aforementioned attack on opportunity targets in October 1987 been necessary, then it 'might … have been considered proportionate'.[58] When making this ruling, the Court appears to have had the quantum of force used in the initial attack in mind. The same is arguably true regarding the April 1988 attacks on the Salman and Nasr complexes. According to the Court, whether taken on their own or as part of a larger operation, they were disproportionate '[a]s a response to the mining, by an unidentified agency, of a single United States warship, which was severely damaged but not sunk, and without loss of life'.[59]

Standard of comparison

It would appear that the standard of comparison between the two variables is not that of strict symmetry. This is so, whatever the second variable may be: that is the quantum of force involved in the armed attack,[60] the fulfilment of defensive purposes[61] or final and decisive victory.[62] However, the fact that, with the exception of force–counterforce proportionality, the two variables involved are dissimilar in character do not lend themselves to meaningful measurement.[63]

All things considered, what proportionality *ad bellum* requires appears to be twofold. First, the force used in self-defence should be assessed in light of the fulfilment of defensive purposes. Second, the quantum of the former should not be obviously excessive, rather than strictly proportionate, vis-à-vis the latter.

Temporal scope of assessment

As with necessity, two doctrinal positions regarding the temporal scope of proportionality assessment exist. According to the first position, proportionality should be assessed at one fixed moment while the defending state resorts to force.[64] For Dinstein, for instance, it should be assessed retrospectively when

---

[55] *Ibid.*, p. 266, nn.1541 (Schwebel), 1542 (Kuntz), 1543 (Zourek).

[56] *Ibid.*, pp. 266–7.   [57] See also *Nicaragua* Judgment, para. 176.

[58] *Oil Platforms* Judgment, para. 77.   [59] *Ibid.*

[60] Brownlie, *International Law and the Use of Force by States*, p. 264.

[61] Ago, *Addendum to the Eighth Report*, 69; Gazzini, *The Changing Rules on the Use of Force*, p. 148.

[62] Dinstein, *War, Aggression and Self-Defence*, pp. 262–3.

[63] Gardam, 'Necessity and proportionality', p. 280.

[64] Y. Ronen, 'Israel, Hizbollah and the second Lebanon war', *Yearbook of International Humanitarian Law* 9 (2006), 362–93 at 362; A. Zimmermann, 'The second Lebanon war: *jus*

on-the-spot reactions or defensive armed reprisals come to an end.[65] As regards a full-scale war, the relevant moment is not its termination but its inception.[66]

The other position holds that proportionality *ad bellum* is subject to constant assessment.[67] This, it is submitted here, is the correct view. Accepting the idea that the quantum of defensive force ought not to exceed the defensive purposes entails accepting potential changes in the latter while resorting to force. As seen below, the circumstances of self-defence may fluctuate between extreme and moderate, as well as between different degrees of extremeness. It would seem counterintuitive to tie the permissible quantum of force used by the defending state to the manner in which the circumstance of self-defence initially manifests itself, not least because it may progressively deteriorate from moderate to extreme.

C. Necessity and proportionality *ad bellum* applied to use of force by means of nuclear weapons

In its Nuclear Weapons Advisory Opinion, the ICJ held, unanimously, that '[a] threat or use of force by means of nuclear weapons … that fails to meet all the requirements of Article 51 [of the UN Charter] is unlawful'.[68] In doing so, however, the Court did little more than allude to necessity *ad bellum*.[69] Proportionality *ad bellum* attracted slightly greater attention:

> The proportionality principle may thus not in itself exclude the use of nuclear weapons in self-defence in all circumstances … Certain States have in their written and oral pleadings suggested that in the case of nuclear weapons, the condition of proportionality must be evaluated in the light of still further factors. They contend that the very nature of nuclear weapons, and the high probability of an escalation of nuclear exchanges, means that there is an extremely strong risk of devastation. The risk factor is said to negate the possibility of the condition of proportionality being complied with. The Court does not find it necessary to embark upon the quantification of such risks; nor does it need to enquire into the question whether tactical nuclear weapons exist which are sufficiently precise to limit those risks: it

---

ad bellum, jus in bello and the issue of proportionality', *Max Planck Yearbook of United Nations Law* 11 (2007), 99–141 at 99; Dinstein, *War, Aggression and Self-Defence*, p. 262.

[65] Dinstein, *War, Aggression and Self-Defence*, p. 262. One should approach Dinstein's reference to 'defensive armed reprisals' in light of his self-confessedly controversial opinion that they are, or should in any event be, a permissible form of self-defence. See *ibid.*, pp. 249–55.

[66] *Ibid.*, p. 263.

[67] Gardam, 'Proportionality and force in international law', 404; Gardam, 'Necessity and proportionality', pp. 280–1, esp. 280; Gardam, *Necessity, Proportionality and the Use of Force by States*, pp. 167–8; Gazzini, *The Changing Rules on the Use of Force*, p. 147.

[68] Nuclear Weapons Advisory Opinion, para. 105(2)(C).

[69] The opinion refers to it only once, and without elaboration. See *ibid.*, para. 41.

suffices for the Court to note that the very nature of all nuclear weapons and the profound risks associated therewith are further considerations to be borne in mind by States believing they can exercise a nuclear response in self-defence in accordance with the requirements of proportionality.[70]

The Advisory Opinion does not add much to the notion that necessity and proportionality *ad bellum* are weapon-neutral, and that the peculiarities of nuclear weapons are only incidentally relevant to them. Such peculiarities are, however, hard to ignore. Indeed, they affect commentators, courts and states alike, and shape their treatment of the law in a manner that is not always helpful.

1.   'Double' necessity for nuclear weapons?

Some suggest that the defending state may use its nuclear weapons only when its conventional weapons prove ineffective.[71] Could it be that using force involving nuclear weapons is subject to the requirement of necessity *ad bellum* twice? The first necessity requirement would be that, as a general rule, using force, whatever weapons it involves, comes only as a last resort in the sense described earlier. The second requirement would be that using nuclear weapons comes only as a last resort amongst all weapons.

Implicit in the double necessity argument is the (re)introduction of force–counterforce proportionality through the back door. Proponents of this view seem to assume that there is an inherent lack of symmetry between the defensive force involving nuclear weapons and the attack exclusively involving conventional weapons:

> In regard to the nature of the weapons used in self-defence, the quantum of force has to be strictly proportionate to the necessity of repelling the attack. Thus, if the attack was with conventional weapons, the right of self-defence would entitle the use of similar weapons to repel it. In the circumstances, the use of nuclear weapons would appear to exceed the right, since the quantum of force used would be out of proportion to the nature of attack necessary to repel.[72]

And yet there is no reason for the ineffectiveness of the defending state's conventional weapons to emanate exclusively from the attacking state using nuclear weapons. Whatever conventional weapons are at the disposal of the defending state may very well turn out to be ineffective in repelling a massive conventional invasion.

---

[70] *Ibid.*, paras. 42–3.

[71] N. Singh, 'The right of self-defence in relation to the use of nuclear weapons', *Indian Yearbook of International Affairs* 5 (1956), 32–4, cited in Gazzini, *The Changing Rules on the Use of Force*, p. 219, n.72.

[72] N. Singh and E. McWhinney, *Nuclear Weapons and Contemporary International Law* (Dordrecht: Kluwer, 1989), p. 100. See also N. Singh, *Nuclear Weapons and International*

Double necessity reveals the logical strain that one begins to feel where assertions specific to nuclear weapons are made in order to overcome perceived limitations of *jus ad bellum*'s weapon-neutrality.

2.   *Proportionality as teleological fitness*

As noted earlier, during the Second World War proportionality *ad bellum* may
have entailed comparing the defensive force to final and decisive victory. This
possibility remains, notwithstanding the law's arguable development thereafter
to the effect that the comparison should now be between the quantum of defensive force and the fulfilment of defensive purposes. It follows that proportionality *ad bellum* is essentially a matter of teleological fitness, as defined by the
relevant rules of *jus ad bellum* in force at the time.

Should this be so, however, we would be left with the dispiriting prospect
that the nuclear attacks on Hiroshima and Nagasaki were not disproportionate
ad bellum. Arguably, the United States did intend to hasten Japan's decision to
accept the Potsdam Declaration with nuclear attacks and, arguably, they did
have that effect.[73] If true, Hiroshima and Nagasaki would have been in keeping
with proportionality *ad bellum* then in force.[74]

3.   *'Extreme circumstance of self-defence'*

In its Nuclear Weapons Advisory Opinion, the ICJ found, by seven votes to
seven, with the president's casting vote, that:

> [I]n view of the current state of international law, and of the elements of fact
> at its disposal, the Court cannot conclude definitively whether the ... use of
> nuclear weapons would be lawful or unlawful in an extreme circumstance of
> self-defence, in which the very survival of a State would be at stake.[75]

Law (London: Stevens, 1959), pp. 132–3; Brownlie, *International Law and the Use of Force
by States*, pp. 262–4.; Burroughs, *The Illegality of Threat or Use of Nuclear Weapons*, p. 39;
Dinstein, *War, Aggression and Self-Defence*, p. 264.

[73] E. C. Stowell, 'The laws of war and the atomic bomb', *American Journal of International Law*
39 (1945), 784–88 at 786; R. J. Maddox, *Weapons for Victory: The Hiroshima Decision Fifty
Years Later* (Columbia: University of Missouri, 1995), p. 154; V. P. Nanda and D. Krieger,
Nuclear Weapons and the World Court (New York: Transnational Publishers, 1998), pp.
30–3, 35. But see W. Wilson, 'The myth of nuclear deterrence', *Nonproliferation Review* 15
(2008), 421–39 at 421–7; W. Wilson, *Five Myths About Nuclear Weapons* (Boston: Harcourt,
2013), pp. 21–52.

[74] That they might have been unlawful *in bello* is a separate proposition altogether. See
Tokyo District Court, *Ryuichi Shimoda v. The State*, 7 December 1963, *Japanese Annual of
International Law* 8 (1964), p. 212; R. A. Falk, 'The Shimoda case: a legal appraisal of the
atomic attacks upon Hiroshima and Nagasaki', *American Journal of International Law* 59
(1965), 759–93.

[75] Nuclear Weapons Advisory Opinion, para. 105(2)(E).

Although not entirely clear from the Opinion's structure,[76] this disclaimer seems to encompass questions of *jus ad bellum*.[77]

Relativity of extremeness

The very notion of extremeness reveals several layers of relativity. First, what exactly separates those circumstances of self-defence that are extreme from those that are not? It may lie with the survival of the state being or not being at stake, as the Court held. This merely displaces the problem from one location to another, however. Or, to two other locations, in this case: for the question now is what is meant by the 'state' (as opposed to, say, its constituent parts[78]), and what is meant by its 'very survival' (as opposed to, say, a temporary loss of some attributes of its statehood).

Second, even if we assume that the 'very survival of a state' has a settled core of meaning, the situation that puts it at stake and renders the circumstance of self-defence 'extreme' varies from one state to another. As early as 1961 Hart cited, among those qualities that distinguish international law from municipal law, the absence of what he termed 'approximate equality' in strength and vulnerability between states as opposed to individuals.[79] Similarly, Fawcett observed: '[a]rmed bands ... may constitute no threat at all to a powerful state but their operations may well amount to an "armed attack" upon a militarily weak or politically unstable state.'[80] The size of a state that finds itself in a situation of self-defence also affects how readily the situation reaches the requisite degree of extremeness.

Third, extremeness has an element of temporal relativity. The Court seems to have treated the relevant circumstance as if it were one initial moment, such as the onset of a massive invasion, when the right of self-defence would become

---

[76] Paras. 96–7 appear as part of the Court's consideration of *jus in bello*. Indeed, some judges who appended their separate and dissenting opinions did so on this basis. See Declaration of President Bedjaoui, Nuclear Weapons Advisory Opinion, para. 22; Declaration of Judge Vereshchetin, Nuclear Weapons Advisory Opinion, pp. 280–1.

[77] Declaration of Judge Herczegh, Nuclear Weapons Advisory Opinion, pp. 275–6; M. Kohen, 'The notion of "state survival" in international law' in L. Boisson de Chazournes and P. Sands (eds.), *International Law, the International Court of Justice and Nuclear Weapons* (Cambridge University Press, 1999), pp. 303–11; Gazzini, *The Changing Rules on the Use of Force*, p. 217; N. Stürchler, *The Threat of Force in International Law* (Cambridge University Press, 2007), pp. 87–9.

[78] Stürchler, *The Threat of Force in International Law*, p. 89, n. 110 (noting 'the disquieting question of what is meant by the survival of the "state", as opposed to, e.g., its government, people or territory. Smaller countries seem to be entitled to threaten and use nuclear force more quickly than the large ones. I owe this insight to James Crawford').

[79] H. L. A. Hart, *The Concept of Law*, 2nd edn (Oxford: Clarendon Press, 1994) p. 195.

[80] J. E. S. Fawcett, 'Intervention in international law: a study of some recent cases', *Recueil des Cours* 103 (1961), 343–423 at 363 (cited in M. J. Glennon, 'The fog of law: self-defense, inherence, and incoherence in Article 51 of the United Nations Charter', *Harvard Journal of Law and Public Policy* 25 (2001–02), 539–58 at 542, n. 12.).

operative. Surely, the initially 'moderate' circumstance of self-defence may progressively deteriorate to a point where it now becomes extreme, or vice versa. This would invariably affect the application of necessity and proportionality *ad bellum* to force used in self-defence.

Consequences of disclaimer

The Court's disclaimer gives rise to several plausible legal consequences. For example, it might be that it is merely mindful of the possibility where the extremeness of self-defence may, as a matter of fact, render even the extreme destructiveness of the force used involving nuclear weapons necessary and proportionate.[81] Upon reflection, however, this is unlikely to be the case. As noted earlier, the Court found that use of force involving nuclear weapons 'that fails to meet all the requirements of Article 51, is unlawful'.[82] These requirements already include necessity and proportionality *ad bellum*.[83] It cannot logically be that the Court is unable definitively to conclude whether their use 'would be lawful or unlawful', even where, *ex hypothesi*, the extremeness of self-defence is such as to render nuclear weapons necessary and proportionate.[84]

Alternatively, the Court's agnosticism may be seen to concern the possibility that use of force involving nuclear weapons in an extreme circumstance of self-defence *ipso facto* satisfies necessity and proportionality *ad bellum*.[85] Here, too, in the event that this possibility is affirmed, the lawfulness *ad bellum* of such force inescapably follows. This does not accord with the Court's conclusion that it is unable to resolve the matter.

The foregoing leaves the third plausible interpretation also the likeliest. Thus, the ruling might be taken to envisage situations where use of force involving nuclear weapons in extreme self-defence may be lawful *ad bellum* even when it lacks necessity and/or proportionality.[86] In other words, where the circumstance of self-defence is sufficiently extreme, this extremeness potentially 'rights' or 'repairs' even the lack of necessity and proportionality that would otherwise render the use of force involving nuclear weapons unlawful *ad bellum*.

Irrelevance of weapons

The fact that *jus ad bellum* is weapon-neutral means that there is no reason to confine the Court's agnosticism regarding extreme circumstances of self-defence to use of force involving nuclear weapons. On the contrary, it may

---

[81] Gazzini, *The Changing Rules on the Use of Force*, p. 218.

[82] Nuclear Weapons Advisory Opinion, para. 105(2)(C).

[83] *Ibid.*, para. 41.   [84] *Ibid.*, para. 105(2)(E).

[85] R. A. Falk, 'Nuclear weapons, international law and the World Court: a historic encounter', *American Journal of International Law* 91 (1997), 64–75 at 69; Gardam, 'Necessity and proportionality', p. 286; Kohen, 'The notion of "state survival"', pp. 304–5.

[86] Separate Opinion of Judge Guillaume, Nuclear Weapons Advisory Opinion, para. 8; Dissenting Opinion of Judge Fleischhauer, Nuclear Weapons Advisory Opinion, p. 307;

apply to any weapon type not otherwise prohibited under international law. Thus, but for the existence of total prohibitions elsewhere, chemical and bacteriological weapons might have been lawful as long as the particular circumstance of self-defence were so extreme as to put the defending state's very survival at stake.

4.   Assurances of non-use and no first use

Let us briefly consider assurances of non-use and no first use of nuclear weapons. They are problematic for *jus ad bellum* because of their non-binding character and weapon-specificity.

Non-use refers to promises given by nuclear weapon states vis-à-vis non-nuclear weapon states.[87] The latter are limited to those taking part in non-proliferation regimes or nuclear weapon-free zones and otherwise not involved in armed attacks in association with a nuclear weapon state against the promisor.[88] It appears that negative security assurances such as non-use of nuclear weapons do not amount to unilateral declarations.[89]

No first use is a variation of non-use. First use would involve a state using its nuclear weapons in self-defence in response to a conventional attack. It is immaterial whether the latter attack originates from a state with or without its own nuclear arsenal. Conversely, offering a promise of no first use would imply that the promisor refrains from using its nuclear weapons, even in self-defence, in the event of a conventional attack.[90] Such promises have been offered by the Soviet Union[91] (rescinded later by Russia[92]), China[93] (recently dropped from its annual White Paper on defence[94]) and Pakistan.[95] The North Atlantic Treaty Organization (NATO) and its member states have to date declined to offer such promises.[96] It stands to reason that a nuclear weapon state's inclination or disinclination to offer a promise of no first use would depend, in part, on its capacity

---

Stürchler, *The Threat of Force*, pp. 89–90. But see Kohen, 'The notion of "state survival"', pp. 308–10.

[87] Gazzini, *The Changing Rules on the Use of Force*, p. 214.

[88] *Ibid.*, pp. 213–4, 216.

[89] A. Rosas, 'Negative security assurances and non-use of nuclear weapons', *German Yearbook of International Law* 25 (1982), 199–218 at 204–10, 215–18; V. Rodriguez Cedeno, Eighth Report on Unilateral Acts of States, UN doc. A/CN.4/557, 26 May 2005, paras. 106–15; International Law Commission (ILC), Guiding Principles Applicable to Unilateral Declarations of States Capable of Creating Legal Obligations, with Commentaries Thereto (2006), p. 372 n. 940.

[90] Gazzini, *The Changing Rules on the Use of Force*, p. 214.   [91] *Ibid.*

[92] Burroughs, *The Illegality of Threat or Use of Nuclear Weapons*, p. 39.

[93] Gazzini, *The Changing Rules on the Use of Force*, p. 214.

[94] J. M. Acton, 'China and its nukes', *International Herald Tribune*, 20–21 April 2013. But, see 'China maintains no-first-use nuclear pledge', *Agence France Presse (AFP)*, 2 June 2013.

[95] Gazzini, *The Changing Rules on the Use of Force*, p. 215.   [96] *Ibid.*, pp. 214–15.

to repel an armed attack with its conventional weapons.[97] Notwithstanding earlier efforts to secure unlawfulness under *jus ad bellum*,[98] this body of law, as we know it today, does not appear to ban first use of nuclear weapons.

More importantly, one may ask whether it is fruitful to consider non-use and no first use of nuclear weapons under *jus ad bellum* in the first place. Chemical and bacteriological weapons have become the object of first-use prohibition (i.e. mandatory no first use), and then general prohibition (i.e. mandatory non-use). At no point, however, was *jus ad bellum* relevantly involved in this development. Tellingly, both promises of non-use and no first use of nuclear weapons were made at weapon-specific fora primarily concerned with non-proliferation and disarmament, respectively.

Conclusion

This chapter shows that the prospects of *jus ad bellum* comprehensively out-lawing use of nuclear weapons appear distinctly limited. This limitation emanates from the fact that *jus ad bellum* concerns itself with the function of force rather than its form, and that the possibility of nuclear weapons being used in compliance with necessity and proportionality cannot be ruled out in all conceivable circumstances. On the contrary, attempting to nail the square peg in the form of weapon-specific considerations into the round hole in the form of function-driven *jus ad bellum* only complicates the latter.

Perhaps the odds are better, if only marginally, with *jus in bello*, weapons regulations and disarmament. These are the paths that the other two weapons of mass destruction, that is chemical and bacteriological weapons, have taken with some success. Whether these avenues really are more suitable for nuclear weapons is a matter in which this author defers to those of other chapters in the book.

---

[97] *Ibid.*, p. 214.
[98] Falk, 'The Shimoda case', 782, 793; Rosas, 'Negative security assurances', 201–3; A. Carty, 'The significance of legal declarations on the non-use of force in international relations' in W. E. Butler (ed.), *The Non-Use of Force in International Law* (Dordrecht: Kluwer, 1989), pp. 61–6; M. Koskenniemi, 'The silence of law/the voice of justice' in L. Boisson de Chazournes and P. Sands (eds.), *International Law, the International Court of Justice and Nuclear Weapons* (Cambridge University Press, 1999), pp. 492–3.

2

Legality under *jus ad bellum* of the threat of use of nuclear weapons

NOBUO HAYASHI

Introduction

This chapter examines the current state of *jus ad bellum* regarding the threat of force by means of nuclear weapons. It does so in three steps. First, the chapter offers an overview of the normative background. Second, the chapter critically revisits the limited attention that the International Court of Justice (ICJ) paid to the subject in its 1996 Nuclear Weapons Advisory Opinion.[1] Third, the chapter endeavours to distinguish between questions of definition, effectiveness and lawfulness of nuclear threat.

This chapter concludes by identifying two major areas in need of further reflection. The first concerns the potentially dissimilar requirements of proportionality *ad bellum* governing threats of nuclear weapons as opposed to their use. The other area involves the legal consequences for non-nuclear weapon states where the nuclear force threatened on their behalf in collective self-defence by their nuclear-armed allies proves internationally wrongful.

A. Background to the Advisory Opinion

1. Threats of nuclear weapons and the legacies of the Cold War

As far as *jus ad bellum* is concerned, the post-Second World War period appears characterised by a curious duality. Despite Article 2(4) of the 1945 Charter of the United Nations (UN),[2] force has not only been used but also frequently threatened.[3] Indeed, one prominent commentator found the use of force so prevalent that he declared Article 2(4) dead.[4] And yet force involving nuclear weapons has first and foremost been a matter of threat. With the exception of

---

[1] International Court of Justice (ICJ), *Legality of The Threat or Use of Nuclear Weapons*, Advisory Opinion of 8 July 1996 (hereafter, Nuclear Weapons Advisory Opinion).

[2] 1945 Charter of the United Nations, San Francisco, 26 June 1945, in force 24 October 1945, 1 UNTS XVI.

[3] See, e.g., N. Stürchler, *The Threat of Force in International Law* (Cambridge University Press, 2007), pp. 291–310.

[4] See T. M. Franck, 'Who killed Article 2(4)? Or: changing norms governing the use of force by states', *American Journal of International Law* 64 (1970), 809–37.

Hiroshima and Nagasaki in 1945, no state has used nuclear weapons against another state. Meanwhile, thousands more nuclear weapons – whose yield is also thousands of times more powerful and destructive than the atomic weapons used in 1945 – have been tested, manufactured, deployed and placed on various levels of alert. It is often asserted that the 1945 nuclear attacks induced Japan to hasten its decision to surrender.[5] Even if true, deterrent threat is the only tangible value that states armed with nuclear weapons have asserted since the Second World War.

By the late 1980s discontent had been brewing among non-nuclear weapon states that their nuclear-armed counterparts were not delivering on their promise of achieving nuclear disarmament.[6] Nevertheless, despite the complete absence of actual use since 1945 and the pervasive threat of nuclear weapons, much of this debate has revolved mainly around use.[7] Both questions of force threatened in general, and those of force threatened by means of nuclear weapons in particular, are to this day often relegated to a position of secondary importance or overlooked altogether in the relevant literature[8] and judicial pronouncements.[9] The debate has also tended to focus on the weapons' status under *jus in bello* rather than under *jus ad bellum*.[10]

2. Advisory proceedings

On 15 December 1995 the UN General Assembly adopted a resolution requesting the ICJ to give an advisory opinion on the threat or use of nuclear weapons

---

[5] See, e.g., E. C. Stowell, 'The laws of war and the atomic bomb', *American Journal of International Law* 39 (1945), 784–88, at 786; R. J. Maddox, *Weapons for Victory: The Hiroshima Decision Fifty Years Later* (Columbia: University of Missouri, 1995), p. 154; V. P. Nanda and D. Krieger, *Nuclear Weapons and the World Court* (New York: Transnational Publishers, 1998), pp. 30–3, 35.

[6] See, e.g., Nanda and Krieger, *Nuclear Weapons and the World Court*, p. 152.

[7] See, e.g., *ibid.*

[8] See, e.g., O. Schachter, 'The right of states to use armed force', *Michigan Law Review* 82 (1984), 1620–46, at 1625; R. Sadurska, 'Threats of force', *American Journal of International Law* 82 (1988), 239–68, at 239–40, 248; A. Randelzhofer, 'Article 2(4)' in B. Simma (ed.), *The Charter of the United Nations: A Commentary*, 2nd edn (Oxford University Press, 2002), p. 124; M. Roscini, 'Threats of armed force and contemporary international law', *Netherlands International Law Review* 54 (2007), 229–77, at 231; M. C. Alder, *The Inherent Right of Self-Defence in International Law* (Dordrecht/New York: Springer, 2013), p. 78.

[9] See, e.g., Nuclear Weapons Advisory Opinion; Permanent Court of Arbitration (PCA), *Guyana* v. *Suriname*, ILM 47 (2008) (hereafter, *Guyana* v. *Suriname*). See also Stürchler, *The Threat of Force in International Law*, p. 84.

[10] See, e.g., Nanda and Krieger, *Nuclear Weapons and the World Court*, pp. 71–86; J. Burroughs, *The Illegality of Threat or Use of Nuclear Weapons: A Guide to the Historic Opinion of the International Court of Justice* (Piscataway: Transnational Publishers, 1998), p. 127.

under international law.[11] The part of the question that is of interest to this chapter reads as follows: 'Is the threat … of nuclear weapons in any circumstances permitted under international law?'[12]

Insofar as nuclear threats *ad bellum* were concerned, states found themselves divided roughly into three groups. The first were nuclear-armed states. Perhaps predictably, they invariably defended the lawfulness *ad bellum* of threatening force with nuclear weapons. The second group comprised states that were not nuclear-armed, yet had placed themselves under the nuclear 'umbrella' provided by their nuclear-armed allies. The third group, encompassing numerous states that were neither nuclear-armed nor covered by a nuclear umbrella, took a very different view indeed. Thus, for example, Indonesia asserted:

> [Since] the use of nuclear weapons is illegal in any circumstance, even by way of self-defence or reprisal, the threat to use nuclear weapons must also be illegal in any circumstance.[13]

Nuclear deterrence proved a particularly divisive issue. At one end of the spectrum were those states, such as Malaysia[14] and Nauru,[15] that strenuously pressed for the declaration of a total ban on nuclear weapons, including '[d]eterrence' and 'the deployment of nuclear arms to forestall an armed attack'.[16] At the opposite end stood those for whom discussions of threats would be best kept separate from questions of deterrence.[17] Examples include Australia[18] and Solomon Islands,[19] among others.

B. Advisory Opinion

The ICJ issued its Advisory Opinion on 8 July 1996. The Advisory Opinion is said to have offered several conclusions *ad bellum* on nuclear weapon threats.

---

[11] UN General Assembly Resolution 49/75K ('Request for an advisory opinion from the International Court of Justice on the legality of the threat or use of nuclear weapons'), adopted 15 December 1994 by 78 votes to 43 with 64 abstentions.

[12] *Ibid.*

[13] See Nuclear Weapons Advisory Opinion, Verbatim Record, 3 November 1995, para. 60 (internal citations omitted).

[14] See Nuclear Weapons Advisory Opinion, Verbatim Record, 7 November 1995, paras. 14–17.

[15] See Nuclear Weapons Advisory Opinion, Memorial of the Government of the Republic of Nauru, 15 June 1995, p. 29.

[16] Stürchler, *The Threat of Force in International Law*, p. 83.

[17] See *ibid.*, p. 82 ('it was not for the Court to comment on nuclear deterrence, let alone the deployment, manufacture or possession of nuclear weapons.'). See also *ibid.*, pp. 82–3.

[18] See Nuclear Weapons Advisory Opinion, Verbatim Record, 30 October 1995, paras. 2, 51–2.

[19] See Further Written Observations Submitted by the Government of Solomon Islands to the International Court of Justice, Nuclear Weapons Advisory Opinion, 20 September 1995, para. 5(b); Nuclear Weapons Advisory Opinion, Verbatim Record, 14 November 1995, p. 63.

First, a threat cannot be lawful unless carrying out the threat would also be lawful.[20] Second, the possession of nuclear weapons may amount to a threat in the sense of Article 2(4) of the UN Charter.[21] Third, the right of self-defence may justify possession of nuclear weapons.[22] Fourth, nuclear threats for purely self-defensive purposes and to secure the very survival of a state are potentially lawful.[23] Fifth, nuclear deterrence is arguably unlawful.[24] Sixth, the circumstance of extreme self-defence potentially rendering threatening use of nuclear weapons lawful does not encompass collective self-defence.[25]

As seen below, the Advisory Opinion's short passages on the subject raise more questions than they answer. This chapter looks at the Court's findings and the ambiguities it leaves unresolved. The latter include two matters of central concern here. The first is what nuclear threats really entail. One of the most remarkable aspects of the Advisory Opinion is that it does not define 'threatening force', let alone doing so by means of nuclear weapons. The other matter concerns the scope and content of *jus ad bellum* applicable to nuclear threats.

1.   *The Court's findings*

According to the Advisory Opinion, *jus ad bellum* is a body of rules that apply to the use or threat of force per se, rather than to the particular weapon involved.[26] It follows that the rules of *jus ad bellum* governing force threatened by means of nuclear weapons are identical to those governing force threatened generally. When considering the former's lawfulness or unlawfulness *ad bellum*, any peculiarities that nuclear weapons may have in comparison to other types of weapons are only incidentally relevant.

The Advisory Opinion's discussion of threatening use of nuclear weapons *ad bellum* is exceedingly brief. It dedicates just two full paragraphs specifically to the matter. For ease of reference, they are reproduced in full:

> In order to lessen or eliminate the risk of unlawful attack, States sometimes signal that they possess certain weapons to use in self-defence against any State violating their territorial integrity or political independence. Whether

---

[20] See Burroughs, *The Illegality of Threat or Use of Nuclear Weapons*, p. 41; Stürchler, *The Threat of Force in International Law*, pp. 83, 89; Roscini, 'Threats of armed force', 254–5.

[21] See Stürchler, *The Threat of Force in International Law*, p. 83.

[22] See *ibid.*

[23] See R. A. Falk, 'Nuclear weapons, international law and the World Court: a historic encounter', *American Journal of International Law* 91 (1997), 64–75, at 73; Stürchler, *The Threat of Force in International Law*, pp. 83, 89.

[24] See Burroughs, *The Illegality of Threat or Use of Nuclear Weapons*, p. 43; Nanda and Krieger, *Nuclear Weapons and the World Court*, pp. 164–5; Stürchler, *The Threat of Force in International Law*, p. 89.

[25] See, e.g., Burroughs, *The Illegality of Threat or Use of Nuclear Weapons*, p. 47.

[26] See Nuclear Weapons Advisory Opinion, para. 39.

a signalled intention to use force if certain events occur is or is not a 'threat' within Article 2, paragraph 4, of the Charter depends upon various factors. If the envisaged use of force is itself unlawful, the stated readiness to use it would be a threat prohibited under Article 2, paragraph 4. Thus it would be illegal for a State to threaten force to secure territory from another State, or to cause it to follow or not follow certain political or economic paths. The notion of 'threat' and 'use' of force under Article 2, paragraph 4, of the Charter stand together in the sense that if the use of force itself in a given case is illegal – for whatever reason – the threat to use such force will likewise be illegal. In short, if it is to be lawful, the declared readiness of a State to use force must be a use of force that is in conformity with the Charter. For the rest, no State – whether or not it defended the policy of deterrence – suggested to the Court that it would be lawful to threaten to use force if the use of force contemplated would be illegal.

Some States put forward the argument that possession of nuclear weapons is itself an unlawful threat to use force. Possession of nuclear weapons may indeed justify an inference of preparedness to use them. In order to be effective, the policy of deterrence, by which those States possessing or under the umbrella of nuclear weapons seek to discourage military aggression by demonstrating that it will serve no purpose, necessitates that the intention to use nuclear weapons be credible. Whether this is a 'threat' contrary to Article 2, paragraph 4, depends upon whether the particular use of force envisaged would be directed against the territorial integrity or political independence of a State, or against the Purposes of the United Nations or whether, in the event that it were intended as a means of defence, it would necessarily violate the principles of necessity and proportionality. In any of these circumstances the use of force, and threat to use it, would be unlawful under the law of the Charter.[27]

The Court found, unanimously, that '[a] threat ... of force by means of nuclear weapons that is contrary to Article 2, paragraph 4, of the United Nations Charter and that fails to meet all the requirements of Article 51, is unlawful'.[28] Accordingly, there are five specific circumstances where threatening force by means of nuclear weapons would be unlawful:

  i. where it is directed against the territorial integrity of a state;
 ii. where it is directed against the political independence of a state;
iii. where it is directed against the purposes of the UN;
 iv. where, in the event of self-defence, it would necessarily be lacking in necessity; and
  v. where, in the event of self-defence, it would necessarily be lacking in proportionality.

To this, one should add the Court's much-debated disclaimer that it 'cannot lose sight of the fundamental right of every State to survival, and thus its right

---

[27] *Ibid.*, paras. 47–8.   [28] *Ibid.*, para. 105(2)(C).

to resort to self-defence, in accordance with Article 51 of the Charter, when its survival is at stake'.[29] The Court proceeded to find, by seven votes to seven, with the president's casting vote, that:

> [I]n view of the current state of international law … the Court cannot conclude definitively whether the threat or use of nuclear weapons would be lawful or unlawful in an extreme circumstance of self-defence, in which the very survival of a State would be at stake.[30]

What does a 'state's survival' entail?[31] How exactly is a state's 'fundamental right' to survival to be understood?[32] When, and in what manner, does a circumstance of a state's self-defence become 'extreme'? The Advisory Opinion is silent on these questions, and its structure does not indicate clearly whether this disclaimer encompasses questions of *jus ad bellum*.[33] Some commentators appear to assume that it does.[34] If true, could this mean that the extremeness of self-defence might in some specific circumstances render even the extremeness of the force threatened by means of nuclear weapons necessary and proportionate?[35] Alternatively, could it mean that threatening nuclear weapons in an extreme circumstance of self-defence would *ipso facto* – that is necessarily and always – satisfy the necessity and proportionality requirements *ad bellum*?[36] Or could it perhaps mean that a nuclear threat in extreme self-defence might be

---

[29] *Ibid.*, para. 96.

[30] *Ibid.*, para. 105(2)(E). But see *ibid.*, para. 97, where no mention of 'threat of nuclear weapons' is made.

[31] See, e.g., Stürchler, *The Threat of Force in International Law*, p. 89, n. 110 ('This example raises the disquieting question of what is meant by the survival of the "state," as opposed to, e.g., its government, people or territory. Smaller countries seem to be entitled to threaten and use nuclear force more quickly than the large ones. I owe this insight to James Crawford').

[32] See, e.g., M. G. Kohen, 'The notion of "state survival" in international law' in L. Boisson de Chazournes and P. Sands (eds.), *International Law, the International Court of Justice and Nuclear Weapons* (Cambridge University Press, 1999), p. 293.

[33] Paras. 96 and 97 appear as part of the Court's consideration of *jus in bello*.

[34] See, e.g., Kohen, 'The notion of "state survival"', pp. 303–11; Stürchler, *The Threat of Force in International Law*, pp. 87–9.

[35] See Nuclear Weapons Advisory Opinion, para. 43 ('it suffices for the Court to note that the very nature of all nuclear weapons and the profound risks associated therewith are further considerations to be borne in mind by States believing they can exercise a nuclear response in self-defence in accordance with the requirements of proportionality').

[36] See, e.g., Falk, 'Nuclear weapons, international law and the World Court', 69 (discussing the impression conveyed through the Advisory Opinion that 'threats and uses of nuclear weapons are only legally available, if at all, under the pressure of necessity, that is, in the absence of alternatives when aggression threatens the survival of the state'); J. Gardam, 'Necessity and proportionality in *jus ad bellum* and *jus in bello*' in L. Boisson de Chazournes and P. Sands (eds.), *International Law, the International Court of Justice and Nuclear Weapons* (Cambridge University Press, 1999), p. 286 ('If a state is in extremis, necessity ipso facto is satisfied.'); Kohen, 'The notion of "state survival"', pp. 304–5 (discussing and rejecting the notion of 'qualified' self-defence).

lawful *ad bellum* even if it was in fact lacking in necessity and/or proportionality?[37] The Advisory Opinion does not discuss this matter further.

In addition to these general findings, the Advisory Opinion offers some observations regarding possible 'ingredients' of nuclear weapons threats. Thus, the Court held:

a. that possession of nuclear weapons may justify an inference of preparedness to use them;[38]

b. that the intention to use force by means of nuclear weapons needs to be credible if the policy of deterrence were to be effective;[39] and

c. that use of nuclear weapons may be said to be threatened within the meaning of Article 2(4) where, inter alia, the intention to use them if certain events occur is signalled.[40]

2. *Ambiguities*

Possession, preparedness and intention

The Advisory Opinion notes that '[p]ossession of nuclear weapons may indeed justify an inference of preparedness to use them'.[41] In his Dissenting Opinion, Judge Oda argued that the request for an Advisory Opinion should have looked more closely into states' possession of nuclear weapons, rather than their preparedness to use them:

> [T]he words 'the threat of nuclear weapons' are not clearly defined in the request and may not have been understood in an unequivocal manner by the Member States which supported the resolution. An important point seems to be overlooked in the request, namely a possibility that nuclear

---

[37] See, e.g., Nuclear Weapons Advisory Opinion, Separate Opinion of Judge Guillaume, para. 8 ('no system of law, whatever it may be, could deprive one of its subjects of the right to defend its own existence and safeguard its vital interests. Accordingly, international law cannot deprive a State of the right to resort to nuclear weapons if such action constitutes the ultimate means by which it can guarantee its survival'); Nuclear Weapons Advisory Opinion, Dissenting Opinion of Judge Fleischhauer (hereafter, Fleischhauer Dissenting Opinion), p. 307 ('the general principles of law recognised in all legal systems, contains a principle to the effect that no legal system is entitled to demand the self-abandonment, the suicide, of one of its subjects'). But see Kohen, 'The notion of "state survival"', pp. 308–10 (discussing and rejecting the possible existence of a new circumstance precluding wrongfulness comparable to *excuse absolutoire*); Stürchler, *The Threat of Force in International Law*, pp. 89–90 ('Securing "survival" may even justify threats (and uses) of nuclear force which under normal conditions would be prohibited under international law').

[38] Nuclear Weapons Advisory Opinion, para. 48.

[39] *Ibid.*   [40] *Ibid.*, para. 47.

[41] *Ibid.*, para. 48. The same can be said of possessing conventional weapons, for that matter. See M. Koskenniemi, 'The silence of law/the voice of justice' in L. Boisson de Chazournes and P. Sands (eds.), *International Law, the International Court of Justice and Nuclear Weapons* (Cambridge University Press, 1999), p. 490.

weapons may well be considered to constitute a 'threat' merely by being in a State's possession or being under construction by a State, considering that the phrase '*threat or* use of nuclear weapons' (emphasis added) was first used in the request while the phrase 'the use or *threat of use* of nuclear weapons' (emphasis added) had long been employed in the United Nations resolutions.[42]

Although Judge Oda points to this apparent ambiguity in the aforementioned passage of the Advisory Opinion, some commentators instead interpret the Advisory Opinion passage to mean that possession of nuclear weapons nearly always compels the inference of being prepared to use them.[43] This may be contrasted with Judge Weeramantry's emphatic insistence on distinguishing possession from deterrence (which, in his view, involves intent to use[44]):

> Deterrence is more than the mere accumulation of weapons in a storehouse. It means the possession of weapons in a state of readiness for actual use. This means the linkage of weapons ready for immediate take off, with a command and control system geared for immediate action. It means that weapons are attached to delivery vehicles. It means that personnel are ready night and day to render them operational at a moment's notice. There is clearly a vast difference between weapons stocked in a warehouse and weapons so readied for immediate action. Mere possession and deterrence are thus concepts which are clearly distinguishable from each other.[45]

Admittedly, Judge Weeramantry's observation concerns the process through which a fully nuclear-armed state brings its arsenal to a deployment stage.[46] Nonetheless, the mere fact that one is prepared to use nuclear weapons in its possession does not mean that the nuclear weapons in one's possession are ready for use generally, or, at any rate, ready for use in a particular manner as may be required by the circumstances. Take the Democratic People's Republic of Korea (DPR Korea), for example. It may be true that Pyongyang has successfully manufactured a limited number of rudimentary nuclear warheads. It seems likely, however, that the technological sophistication required for DPR Korea to put them to use reliably and according to its wishes may still be some years away.

This raises the matter as to what a state intends to do with the nuclear weapons at various stages of readiness in its possession. The Advisory Opinion

---

[42] Nuclear Weapons Advisory Opinion, Dissenting Opinion of Judge Oda, para. 4.

[43] See, e.g., Stürchler, *The Threat of Force in International Law*, pp. 84–5, pp. 255–6. It appears, however, that Stürchler himself sees some distinction. See *ibid.*, pp. 84–5, 263.

[44] Nuclear Weapons Advisory Opinion, Dissenting Opinion of Judge Weeramantry (hereafter, Weeramantry Dissenting Opinion), p. 540.

[45] *Ibid.*

[46] In this connection, see, e.g., Nanda and Krieger, *Nuclear Weapons and the World Court*, p. 13 (on 'de-alerting').

uses the expressions 'stated',[47] 'signalled'[48] and 'credible'[49] when describing the threatener's communications of its preparedness to use nuclear weapons to the threatenee. Nothing in the Advisory Opinion, however, connects stated or signalled intention to credible intention, or vice versa. Surely, not all instances of signalled intention to use nuclear weapons are per se credible. Here, too, DPR Korea arguably exemplifies a state whose intention to use nuclear weapons in its possession is loud and clear and yet, at least for the time being, lacks credibility. When considering the lawfulness *ad bellum* of a clearly signalled intention to use nuclear weapons, one has no reason to exclude instances where it is impossible to verify whether that intention is backed up by deployment-ready nuclear weapons. It would be odd to conclude that only verifiably credible threats are capable of being lawful or unlawful *ad bellum*.[50]

Conversely, not all credible intentions are, or need be, clearly signalled. Israel's doctrine of 'strategic ambiguity' is a case in point. It would be very strange if nuclear weapon threats within the meaning of Article 2(4) did not include instances involving credible yet unsignalled intentions to use them. Nevertheless, what the Advisory Opinion asks itself is whether 'a *signalled* intention to use force if certain events occur is or is not a "threat" within Article 2, paragraph 4, of the Charter'.[51]

As argued below, it is not an element of a threat that the intention be credible or signalled. While intention itself is indeed a prerequisite, what matters is its communication to, and apprehension as such by, the recipient.

Deterrence

According to the Court, credible intention is a *sine qua non* for effective deterrence,[52] whereas signalled intention would constitute a threat.[53] The Court's failure to connect the two kinds of intention mirrors its failure to distinguish between deterrence and threats.[54] To be sure, the Court observed:

> In order to be effective, the policy of deterrence, by which those States possessing or under the umbrella of nuclear weapons seek to discourage military

---

[47] Nuclear Weapons Advisory Opinion, para. 47.

[48] *Ibid.*   [49] *Ibid.*, para. 48.

[50] But see Weeramantry Dissenting Opinion, p. 540 ('Deterrence needs to carry the conviction to other parties that there is a real intention to use those weapons in the event of an attack by that other party. A game of bluff does not convey that intention, for it is difficult to persuade another of one's intention unless one really has that intention. Deterrence thus consists in a real intention to use such weapons. If deterrence is to operate, it leaves the world of make-believe and enters the field of seriously intended military threats'); Alder, *The Inherent Right of Self-Defence*, p. 75, n. 25 ('What was required was a credible threat to use force').

[51] Nuclear Weapons Advisory Opinion, para. 47 (emphasis added).

[52] See *ibid.*, para. 48.   [53] See *ibid.*, para. 47.

[54] See, e.g., Falk, 'Nuclear weapons, international law and the World Court', 73.

aggression by demonstrating that it will serve no purpose, necessitates that the intention to use nuclear weapons be credible. *Whether this is a 'threat'* contrary to Article 2, paragraph 4, depends upon whether the particular use of force envisaged would be directed against the territorial integrity or political independence of a State, or against the Purposes of the United Nations or whether, in the event that it were intended as a means of defence, it would necessarily violate the principles of necessity and proportionality.[55]

This passage is extremely ambiguous. Its first sentence specifies the intention's credibility as a prerequisite for effective deterrence. The expression 'this' in the next sentence is unhelpfully imprecise, however. Does 'this' refer to the policy of deterrence, intention *simpliciter* or credible intention? The Advisory Opinion does not assist its reader in this regard.[56] The question, therefore, is: do only effective deterrence policies constitute threats, or do all deterrence policies, effective or not, constitute threats?[57]

To make the matter worse, when the Court asked itself '[w]hether this is a "threat"',[58] the particular kind of threat it had in mind was that which is 'contrary to Article 2, paragraph 4'.[59] In other words, the Court was specifically and exclusively concerned with 'this' – whatever it refers to – being just that kind of threat that is unlawful *ad bellum*. The Court thereby excluded from its inquiry the question of whether conduct that is lawful *ad bellum* might nevertheless constitute a threat. As seen below, limiting the notion of 'threat' within the meaning of Article 2(4) to that which it prohibits is unilluminating. One should rather treat all relevant instances of threat as such, and then consider whether they would constitute that kind of threat that is forbidden or permitted according to Article 2(4).

The policy of nuclear deterrence became the subject of lively debate amongst its proponents and opponents alike as an *indicium* of *opinio juris*.[60] The Court itself declined to rule on the matter:

> The Court does not intend to pronounce here upon the practice known as the 'policy of deterrence'. It notes that it is a fact that a number of States adhered to that practice during the greater part of the Cold War and continue to adhere to it. Furthermore, the members of the international community are profoundly divided on the matter of whether non-recourse to nuclear weapons over the past 50 years constitutes the expression of an

---

[55] Nuclear Weapons Advisory Opinion, para. 48 (emphasis added).

[56] One commentator interprets the Opinion as suggesting that 'an expressed conditional intention of force may or may not amount to a threat of force of a nature capable of violating Article 2(4)'. See Alder, *The Inherent Right of Self-Defence*, p. 75.

[57] It will be suggested below that all deterrence policies, effective or otherwise, do indeed constitute threats.

[58] Nuclear Weapons Advisory Opinion, para. 48.   [59] *Ibid.*

[60] See *ibid.*, paras. 65–6.

opinio juris. Under these circumstances the Court does not consider itself able to find that there is such an *opinio juris*.[61]

In short, the Court treated the practice of deterrence as a potential indicator of *opinio juris* for the existence of a would-be customary rule regarding the *use* rather than the *threat* of force by means of nuclear weapons. The Court did, in fairness, query 'whether a prohibition of the *threat* or use of nuclear weapons as such flows from' customary law.[62] Nevertheless, the Court's findings on the matter refer only to the uncertainty of *opinio juris* regarding 'non-recourse to nuclear weapons',[63] and to whether the continuing tension hampered the emergence of customary law 'specifically prohibiting the use of nuclear weapons as such'.[64]

It may perhaps be intuitive to consider the policy of nuclear deterrence relative to the existence or otherwise of a customary prohibition against the use of nuclear weapons. After all, if one were to attempt to explain the non-use of nuclear weapons since 1945, nuclear deterrence is one prominent explanation (as the nuclear weapon states argued before the court[65]). Alternatively, the protracted non-use of nuclear weapons might be due to the nuclear weapon states' conviction that they were duty-bound not to use these weapons (as some of the non-nuclear weapon states argued).[66]

Of concern to this chapter, however, is an issue of a slightly different character. Whatever its evidentiary value as regards the existence of use-related *opinio juris*, would it not be possible, indeed preferable, to consider adherence to nuclear deterrence as an indication regarding the customary status *ad bellum* of nuclear deterrence as such? Further, would it not be possible that at least those states practising or purportedly benefiting from nuclear deterrence for the past half-century exhibit their *opinio juris* affirming its lawfulness *ad bellum*? It is apparent that the Court has entirely missed – or deliberately overlooked – this particular angle in its Advisory Opinion.[67]

The Court's failure to clarify the relationship between deterrence and threats appears to be partly responsible for the Advisory Opinion's deeply unsatisfactory treatment of the *ad bellum* principles of necessity and proportionality in relation to deterrent threats.[68] Where nuclear weapons are threatened

---

[61] *Ibid.*, para. 67.

[62] *Ibid.*, para. 64 (emphasis added); Stürchler, *The Threat of Force in International Law*, p. 85.

[63] Nuclear Weapons Advisory Opinion, para. 67.

[64] *Ibid.*, para. 73.   [65] See *ibid.*, para. 66.   [66] See *ibid.*, para. 65.

[67] Also see Falk, 'Nuclear weapons, international law and the World Court', 71 (regarding three dissenting opinions); *ibid.*, 70–1; H. Thirlway, 'The *Nuclear Weapons* Advisory Opinions: the declarations and separate and dissenting opinions' in L. Boisson de Chazournes and P. Sands (eds.), *International Law, the International Court of Justice and Nuclear Weapons* (Cambridge University Press, 1999), pp. 414–19; Stürchler, *The Threat of Force in International Law*, pp. 89, 105.

[68] It has been suggested that the court has treated these *ad bellum* principles only marginally in its jurisprudence. See, e.g., C. Gray, *International Law and the Use of Force*, 3rd edn

in self-defence to deter an attack, and if, as the Advisory Opinion states, the principle of necessity applies,[69] to what does the principle apply exactly? Does it apply to the *force* threatened, or to the *threat* of force? More specifically, according to the Advisory Opinion, does the law require:

i. that in order for a deterrent threat to be lawful as a measure of self-defence, the force threatened must be used only as a last resort?;[70] or
ii. that in order for a deterrent threat to be lawful as a measure of self-defence, the very act of threatening force must come as a last resort?

It is highly unlikely that the latter is the relevant question. One would otherwise be asking, counter-intuitively, whether the very act of threatening force might occur well before the fear of an armed attack emerged, or whether force should be threatened only once reasonable alternatives have been exhausted or become futile. Accordingly, the relevant question is likely to be the former one, that the force threatened must be used only as a last resort. Our focus would then be the threat's content. May the threatener use the force envisaged without first seeking to satisfy itself that no reasonable alternative exists, or can the threatener carry out the threat only in the event that it is satisfied that no reasonable alternative exists or needs to be explored? Threatening force that would be used in the absence of necessity would be unlawful. As a result, only that kind and degree of force whose use would be necessary may be lawfully threatened.

The 'Brownlie formula'

The Court proceeded on the assumption that the criteria for determining unlawfulness *ad bellum* of threatening force are the same as those for determining unlawfulness *ad bellum* of using force.[71] Sometimes called the 'Brownlie formula', this notion was phrased by Ian Brownlie in the following terms:

> A threat of force consists in an express or implied promise by a government
> of a resort to force conditional on non-acceptance of certain demands of

---

(Oxford University Press, 2008), p. 151; J. Green, *The International Court of Justice and Self-Defence in International Law* (Oxford: Hart Publishing, 2009), pp. 105–7. Nikolas Stürchler posits that deterrence entails no imminence requirement. See Stürchler, *The Threat of Force in International Law*, p. 85. His construal of 'imminence' is closely tied to that of the necessity principle. See *ibid.*, pp. 55–7, esp. p. 56. In Stürchler's view, therefore, deterrence does not entail an element of necessity and, because of this non-entailment, deterrence by means of nuclear weapons 'can be a *prima facie* infringement of the no-threat rule'. See *ibid.*, p. 85.

[69] See Nuclear Weapons Advisory Opinion, para. 48.

[70] In this and the following case, we are operating on the widely held assumption that the *ad bellum* principle of necessity requires the exhaustion or futility of alternatives not involving force. But see in this regard Chapter 1.

[71] Nuclear Weapons Advisory Opinion, para. 47. See also Weeramantry Dissenting Opinion, p. 541.

that government. If the promise is to resort to force in conditions for which no justification for the use of force exists, the threat itself is illegal.[72]

Unlike using force in actual fact, merely threatening to do so is a more subjective – or to be more precise, inter-subjective – phenomenon: in essence, a matter of perception and mutual position between the threatener and the threatenee. Threatening is said to be markedly less dramatic in terms of visibility and adverse consequences.[73] One might therefore be inclined, perhaps understandably, to subsume threatening force under using force and to treat the former essentially as a species of the latter.

During the Advisory Opinion proceedings, Indonesia, Malaysia and Nauru specifically referred to Brownlie's work.[74] The Advisory Opinion itself reveals little more than the Court's apparent acceptance of his formula.[75] This unexplained acceptance is also found in arbitral decisions.[76]

It appears that the formula has two versions. The first, broader version would involve the correspondence between the purpose for which force is threatened and the purpose for which it is used. Thus, according to this version, it would be unlawful *ad bellum* for a creditor state to threaten force in order to recover assets owed by a debtor state. It would be so because it is unlawful under modern *jus ad bellum* to use force for such a purpose. This version of the formula does not appear particularly controversial.[77]

The second version of the Brownlie formula is narrower in scope. Assume that force is threatened for an end for which it is lawful *ad bellum* to use force, for example self-defence. Assume further that the manner in which the force is threatened runs afoul of the conditions for the lawfulness *ad bellum* of its use, such that the actual use of the force threatened would be unlawful *ad bellum*. The threat of such force is then itself unlawful *ad bellum*, according to this version of the Brownlie formula.

---

[72] I. Brownlie, *International Law and the Use of Force by States* (Oxford University Press, 1963), p. 364. See also *ibid.*, p. 431 ('an illegal threat is a conditional promise to resort to force in circumstances in which the resort to force will be itself illegal').

[73] See, e.g., Sadurska, 'Threats of force', 257–8. But see, e.g., Roscini, 'Threats of armed force', 245–7.

[74] See Nuclear Weapons Advisory Opinion, Memorial of the Government of the Republic of Nauru, 15 June 1995, p. 11; Statement by the Government of Malaysia, 19 June 1995, p. 8; Nuclear Weapons Advisory Opinion, Verbatim Record, 3 November 1995, para. 60.

[75] This is also how Murray Colin Alder interprets the advisory opinion. See Alder, *The Inherent Right of Self-Defence*, pp. 75–6.

[76] See, e.g., *Guyana v. Suriname*, pp. 229–30 ('The ICJ has thrown some light on the circumstances, where a threat of force can be considered illegal', then citing Nuclear Weapons Advisory Opinion, para. 47).

[77] Brownlie, *International Law and the Use of Force by States*, pp. 112–13; A. Randelzhofer, 'Article 51' in B. Simma (ed.), *The Charter of the United Nations: A Commentary*, 2nd edn (Oxford University Press, 2002), p. 789; Alder, *The Inherent Right of Self-Defence*, p. 77.

The formula entails only the following consequence: where it is unlawful to use force, it is *ipso facto* unlawful to threaten to do so. The formula rejects the notion that it may be lawful to threaten force in circumstances where it would be unlawful to use it. Importantly, the formula does not concern itself with the circumstances under which one may lawfully threaten to use force. Nor is it concerned with the conditions that would render the threat of force unlawful that may exist in addition to, or independently of, those that would render the *use* of force unlawful.

And yet these limited consequences have not prevented the formula from being misconstrued. One misinterpretation invokes the formula *a contrario* for the proposition that '[n]ot only is every threat illegal where force is illegal, but, obviously, any justification put forward for the use of force will work equally well for the threat of such force'.[78] Where it is lawful *ad bellum* to use force, it is *ipso facto* lawful to threaten to do so. Plainly, the Brownlie formula does not warrant, let alone compel, such a corollary. The formula has likewise been treated as though it supported the view that '[f]or a threat of force to be unlawful, it has to relate to a projected use of force that is unlawful (*i.e.* in breach of the Charter)'.[79] This, of course, is a *non sequitur*. No proposition of the kind 'only where it is unlawful to use force is it unlawful to threaten to do so' logically emanates from the Brownlie formula.

Nor, strictly speaking, does the Brownlie formula address the possibility that it might be unlawful to threaten force even where it would be lawful to use it. Indeed, there may be additional condition(s) that threats of force must fulfil in order to be lawful *ad bellum*. Asserting that it is *never* lawful to threaten force by means of nuclear weapons exemplifies one variation of this theme.[80] Plausible though such a consequentialist proposition may be, it is not a matter upon which the Brownlie formula has any bearing.

Although the Brownlie formula finds widespread support,[81] is it legally correct? Is it possible that, even where the use of nuclear weapons would be unlawful, threatening to do so might not necessarily be unlawful? Critics of the

---

[78] Stürchler, *The Threat of Force in International Law*, p. 41.

[79] Y. Dinstein, *War, Aggression and Self-Defence*, 5th edn (Cambridge University Press, 2011), pp. 88, 89.

[80] It has been suggested, for example, that threats tend to invite counter-threats, thereby setting a dangerous spiral in motion and rapidly destabilising the existing international order. See, e.g., N. D. White and R. Cryer, 'Unilateral enforcement of Resolution 687: a threat too far?', *California Western International Law Journal* 29 (1999), 243–82, at 281; Stürchler, *The Threat of Force in International Law*, pp. 46, 48–51. See also Nuclear Weapons Advisory Opinion, para. 43.

[81] See, e.g., Nuclear Weapons Advisory Opinion, Verbatim Record, 6 November 1995, para. 32; Memorial of the Government of the Republic of Nauru, 15 June 1995, pp. 11, 23; Statement by the Government of Malaysia, 19 June 1995, p. 8; Written Statement by the Government of Mexico, 19 June 1995, para. 34; Verbatim Record, 10 November 1995, para. 15; Verbatim Record, 13 November 1995, p. 20; Verbatim Record, 15 November 1995, p. 79;

Brownlie formula have suggested that threatening force should be uncoupled from the use of force.[82] One reason for this suggestion is an essentially consequentialist claim that threatening sometimes helps to uphold international security. Thus, 'the preoccupation of international law with the political independence of states is not inspired by the concern of individualist liberalism with the freedom of political elites, but rather by the need for peace and order among nations'.[83] In his Dissenting Opinion, Judge Schwebel forcefully defended the effectiveness with which a thinly veiled threat of nuclear weapons in connection with Operation Desert Storm forestalled the use of chemical weapons by Saddam Hussein against coalition forces.[84] This claim is predicated on the viability of the deterrence model.[85]

Another reason proffered is more deontological in character. Threatening to do something is less grave than actually doing it, all else being equal.[86] 'All else being equal' needs careful consideration here. Lest any consequentialist elements creep into our strictly deontological investigation, we should concentrate on instances where threatening force, on the one hand, and using force, on the other, produces the same outcome. We should then compare threatening force that did or would succeed in forestalling the armed attack feared, with using the same force that did or would succeed in repelling it; or compare threatening force that did or would fail in its effort to forestall an armed attack feared, with using the same force that did or would fail in its effort to repel that attack. In this vein, one commentator noted:

> [T]he form of disapproval [by states] of the threatener's behavior indicates that, contrary to the appearances created by the language of Article 2(4), the threat of force is in actuality treated as a lesser international wrong, even if its consequences are comparable to the lasting effects of the use of force.[87]

To this, one may reply as follows. The apparently muted criticisms of force threatened as opposed to the often loud and public condemnations of force used do not, in fact, indicate that the two acts are held to dissimilar degrees of

---

Colombian member of the International Law Commission (ILC), Remarks by J. M. Yepes, *ILC Yearbook*, 2 vols. (New York: United Nations, 1951), Vol. I, p. 58; White and Cryer, 'Unilateral enforcement of Resolution 687', 254; Roscini, 'Threats of armed force', 245, 254–5.

[82] See, generally Sadurska, 'Threats of force'.

[83] *Ibid.*, 249. Here her arguments emanate primarily from the idea that '[t]he Charter prohibits the use of force in violation of the political independence and territorial integrity of a state *because* it may lead to international instability, breach of the peace and/or massive abuses of human rights. But if that is the rationale of Article 2(4), then there is no justification for the claim that the use of force and the threat of force should be treated equally.' *Ibid.*, 250 (emphasis in original).

[84] Nuclear Weapons Advisory Opinion, Dissenting Opinion of Judge Schwebel, pp. 323–9.

[85] See Stürchler, *The Threat of Force in International Law*, pp. 46, 47.

[86] See Sadurska, 'Threats of force', 258.   [87] *Ibid.*

wrongfulness. Rather, the discrepancy in international condemnation of threats versus use is the result of political and consequentialist considerations.[88] It cannot be denied that the latter considerations may colour the reaction of states to instances of threats of force. Even so, such considerations do not per se negate the possibility that threatening force is an act of a deontological status distinct in kind or degree from that of using force.

Threatening use of nuclear weapons within one's own territory

The Court declined to consider situations where states threaten to use nuclear weapons within their own territory.[89] It did so on the ground that no state addressing the Court raised this question during the Advisory Opinion proceedings.[90] The question may also have struck the Court as overly academic insofar as this scenario is exceedingly unlikely. After all, what state in its right mind would even consider threatening, let alone using, nuclear weapons on its own territory? Neither explanation for avoiding the question is entirely satisfactory, however. To begin with, by the Court's own admission, the question is in principle covered by the very (broad) terms of the General Assembly's request for an Advisory Opinion.[91] The mere fact that no state specifically discussed the matter hardly seems to warrant the conclusion that the Court is therefore 'not called upon' to deal with it.[92]

More importantly, the probability that a state would threaten to use nuclear weapons on its own territory may be greater than assumed at first blush. The relevant threatenee present on the threatener's territory need not comprise persons or entities of the threatener's own nationality. On the contrary, a state may very well threaten using nuclear weapons, including, in particular, low-yield nuclear warheads, against the armed forces of another state in the threatener's territory. For example, Kuwait in 1990 might have requested that nuclear-armed members of the coalition forces threaten to use tactical nuclear weapons against Iraqi military formations advancing through the desert of northern Kuwait.[93] Or, for that matter, a Kuwait armed with such weapons might have threatened to use them against columns of Iraq's armed forces.[94]

The application of *jus ad bellum* involving recourse to force between states does not appear to depend on whether the state acting in self-defence chooses to threaten or use force on its territory or on that of its adversary. The more relevant consideration would be whether the threatenee is also a state, that is an entity to which the relevant rules of *jus ad bellum* apply.

---

[88] Roscini, 'Threats of armed force', 245, 254–5.
[89] See Nuclear Weapons Advisory Opinion, para. 50.
[90] See *ibid.*   [91] See *ibid.*   [92] See *ibid.*
[93] See below for a further discussion of collective nuclear self-defence.
[94] During the advisory proceedings, several states did indeed raise similar possibilities. See Nuclear Weapons Advisory Opinion, para. 91. The Court declined to consider it, though on grounds of insufficient material rather than on the territorial status of the location concerned. See *ibid.*, para. 94.

Non-state entities

The foregoing discussion brings us to the question of non-state entities. Neither Article 2(4) nor Article 51 of the UN Charter, the two provisions on which the Advisory Opinion's discussion regarding the threat of nuclear weapons *ad bellum* rests, specifically deals with non-state entities. Article 2(4) makes it clear that states are both the duty-bearers and the beneficiaries of this provision.[95] The situation surrounding Article 51 is less clear. Whether an 'armed attack' within the meaning of that Article is capable of being launched by a non-state entity has become the subject of discussion in two post-1996 ICJ cases and, on both occasions, the Court studiously avoided the issue.[96]

Non-state entities do not appear to have much leeway under *jus ad bellum*. To be sure, they are sometimes alleged to have certain *ad bellum* prerogatives, such as national liberation movements pursuing armed struggles.[97] Even assuming that a national liberation movement resorting to arms is analogous to a state resorting to force in self-defence – a highly contentious idea at best – one cannot be certain that the same *ad bellum* rules apply to both, let alone whether the former can avail itself of the Court's 'extreme circumstance of self-defence' disclaimer.

A likelier situation is one in which a non-state entity finds itself on the receiving end of a nuclear weapon state's threat. There are several possibilities *ratione loci*, where a state might self-defensively threaten force involving nuclear weapons against non-state entities. Hypothetical scenarios might include:

a. within the threatener state's own territory (i.e. Russia against militants in remote Caucasus regions);
b. within the territory of another state (i.e. Israel against Hezbollah on Lebanese or Syrian territory); and
c. outside the territory of any state (i.e. Israel against Hezbollah on the high seas).

---

[95] Article 2(4) reads, in relevant parts (emphasis added): 'All *Members* [of the United Nations, i.e. states] shall refrain in their international relations from the threat or use of force against the territorial integrity or political independence of any *state*.'

[96] See ICJ, *Legal Consequences of the Construction of a Wall in the Occupied Palestinian Territory*, Advisory Opinion of 9 July 2004 (hereafter, Palestinian Wall Advisory Opinion), para. 139; ICJ, *Case Concerning Armed Activities on the Territory of the Congo (Democratic Republic of the Congo v. Uganda)*, Judgment of 19 December 2005 (hereafter, *Armed Activities* Judgment), paras. 146–7. See also Judge Kooijmans' Separate Opinion and Judge Buergenthal's Declaration in the Palestinian Wall Advisory Opinion, paras. 35–9 (Kooijmans); para. 6 (Buergenthal); Judges Kooijmans and Simma's Separate Opinions in *Armed Activities* Judgment, paras. 4–15 (Simma); paras. 25–35 (Kooijmans). See also, e.g., N. Lubell, *Extraterritorial Use of Force Against Non-State Actors* (Oxford University Press, 2010), pp. 30–6.

[97] For further discussion of this issue, see, e.g., Randelzhofer, 'Article 2(4)', pp. 128–9.

It would appear that the 'internal' recourse to nuclear weapons to which the Court declined to address itself[98] encompasses the first possibility. The second possibility would, in principle, render the threatener in breach of its obligation under Article 2(4) of the UN Charter vis-à-vis the other state on whose territory the non-state threatenee is based.[99] The third possibility remains unaddressed.

Collective self-defence

The Court appears to have limited its treatment of threateners to nuclear weapon states. This apparent limitation leaves at least three issues relating to collective nuclear self-defence unresolved. To begin, would a state be permitted to threaten to use nuclear weapons on behalf of its non-nuclear or lesser nuclear-armed ally in situations of extreme self-defence where the latter's, but not the former's, survival would be at stake? Some commentators took the Advisory Opinion's generally prohibitive language to mean that the 'extreme circumstance of self-defence' would be restricted to individual, rather than collective, self-defence.[100] For others, although the Advisory Opinion's restrictive undertone is undeniable, it makes no definitive finding as to whether 'extreme circumstance of self-defence' would include or exclude collective self-defence.[101]

---

[98] See Nuclear Weapons Advisory Opinion, para. 50.

[99] Such would not be the case, however, if one were to accept the notion that *jus ad bellum* entitles a state to threaten force in self-defence vis-à-vis acts emanating from a non-state entity operating in the territory of another state – directly and without consequence to the latter's otherwise protected territorial integrity and political independence – or vis-à-vis the state from whose territory the said act originates on account of attribution. See, e.g., Lubell, *Extraterritorial Use of Force*, pp. 36–42.

[100] See, e.g., Burroughs, *The Illegality of Threat or Use of Nuclear Weapons*, p. 47.

[101] See, e.g., Fleischhauer Dissenting Opinion, para. 6; Falk, 'Nuclear weapons, international law and the World Court', 68–9; Stürchler *The Threat of Force in International Law*, p. 89. The British position, though perhaps not entirely consistent, is that it is indeed covered. See, e.g., Burroughs, *The Illegality of Threat or Use of Nucelar Weapons*, p. 47, n. 138 ('The United Kingdom told the Court: "A decision to use nuclear weapons would only be taken in extreme cases and on the basis of the ultimate duty of a State to defend its people and their homeland." Nuclear Weapons Advisory Opinion, Verbatim Record, 15 November 1995, p. 39'). But see Transcript of United Kingdom House of Lords, 12 July 1996 (Lord Earl Howe) ('The opinion of the court has no implications at all for our defence policy. We see no reason to change the fundamental elements of UK and NATO defence policy. Like the court, we believe that the use of nuclear weapons would be considered only in self-defence in extreme circumstances. For the UK, self-defence must include collective self-defence. I believe that it is right for me to emphasise … that nuclear forces continue to have an essential role within our defence posture and that of NATO and that we shall retain them as long as they are necessary for our security'); T. Gazzini, *The Changing Rules on the Use of Force in International Law* (Manchester University Press, 2005), p. 215, n. 153 ('the British Government has categorically rejected that the conditions for individual self-defence may be different from those allowing collective self-defence. It stated: "We do not believe that the Court intended to make a distinction between individual and collective self-defence. If it had, that would been [*sic*] contrary to Article 51 of the UN Charter and we would not accept it"').

The second issue – assuming that collective self-defence is indeed encompassed by the notion of extreme self-defence – concerns how one should assess the necessity and proportionality requirements *ad bellum* for a nuclear-armed state's threats of force on behalf of its non-nuclear or lesser nuclear-armed ally. It is likely that, in order for a deterrent threat to be lawful as a measure of self-defence, the force threatened must be used only as a last resort. A nuclear-armed state may lawfully threaten force involving its nuclear weapons in collective self-defence on behalf of its non-nuclear or lesser nuclear-armed ally only in such a manner that the force threatened could lawfully be used where the latter had declared itself the victim of an armed attack and had requested assistance from the former.[102]

Questions of proportionality are likely to become very tricky. The survival of a smaller, typically non-nuclear or lesser nuclear-armed state is more likely to be at stake than that of a larger or nuclear-armed state.[103] Combine this consideration with the three possible ways of interpreting the Court's 'extreme circumstance of self-defence' agnosticism noted earlier:

a. The more vulnerable the non-nuclear weapon state, the more likely threats of nuclear weapons force made on the vulnerable state's behalf will be proportionate, whereas the same threats are likely to be disproportionate if issued by the nuclear-armed state on its own behalf;
b. The non-nuclear weapon state's vulnerability *ipso facto* renders the threatened force proportionate, whereas the same force threatened would not be proportionate if the nuclear-armed state issued the threat on its own behalf; or
c. A non-nuclear weapon state's vulnerability permits disproportionate nuclear force to be threatened on its behalf by its nuclear-armed ally, even where the same force threatened would be impermissibly disproportionate if the nuclear-armed state issued the threat on its own behalf.

The third issue related to collective self-defence involves attribution. This is an issue that would become one of far-reaching ramifications if it were held that certain or all instances of nuclear threat are unlawful *ad bellum*. Are non-nuclear states protected under the umbrella of their nuclear-armed allies to be considered threateners? In other words, can 'threatening to use force by means of nuclear weapons' include 'threatening to have such force used by one's ally'? Alternatively, how, if at all, would the (unlawful) force involving nuclear weapons threatened by a nuclear-armed state in collective self-defence be attributed to any of its non-nuclear allies? Might the latter assume some derivative responsibility through the provision of aid and assistance? Would it be responsible for failing to prevent

---

[102] See ICJ, *Military and Paramilitary Activities in and against Nicaragua (Nicaragua v. United States of America)*, Judgment of 27 June 1986, paras. 195, 199 (hereafter, *Nicaragua Judgment*).

[103] See also Stürchler, *The Threat of Force in International Law*, p. 89, n. 110.

the nuclear weapon state from (unlawfully) threatening force on its behalf? As seen below, the current law appears to be unclear on this particular matter.

C.   Incidence, effectiveness and legality

The Advisory Opinion does not define 'force threatened', let alone force threatened by means of nuclear weapons. It merely offers generic pronouncements that possessing such weapons may imply intending to use them and that signalling such an intention may amount to threatening. The Court discusses nuclear deterrence, but fails to treat it properly in connection with nuclear threat. The Advisory Opinion appears to accept the veracity of the Brownlie formula, yet offers no cogent reason for its acceptance. The Advisory Opinion effectively limits the possibility of lawful nuclear threats to extreme circumstances of self-defence, but leaves the status of collective self-defence unaddressed.

These ambiguities are not unique to the Advisory Opinion, however. There exists a pervasive conflation between (a) when force by means of nuclear weapons is or is not threatened; (b) when force thus threatened is effective or ineffective; and (c) when force thus threatened is lawful or unlawful.

One particular problem with the ambiguity surrounding the lawfulness of threats of force is the common doubtful perception that if something is a threat, it is already presumably unlawful.[104] Conversely, if something is lawful, then it is presumably not a threat. The idea of a warning in contradistinction to a threat exemplifies this perception. One occasionally comes across assertions that this or that instance was not a threat but a warning because it was not unlawful.[105] Tying the very notion of threat exclusively to unlawfulness *ad bellum* 'locks' the definition one step into the Brownlie formula. Thus, if using force in the manner envisaged is lawful, then threatening – nay, warning – to do so is lawful. Conversely, should it be unlawful to use force as envisaged, it would also be unlawful, and accordingly constitute a threat, to communicate one's intention to do so. As argued below, however, what would amount to a warning is merely a threat that is lawful.[106] Threatening is threatening, whether

---

[104] See, e.g., Roscini, 'Threats of armed force', 235.

[105] See, e.g., Dinstein, *War, Aggression and Self-Defence*, p. 88; Roscini, 'Threats of armed force', 236–7.

[106] For another questionable line of distinguishing threatening (hence unlawful) from warning (hence lawful), see, e.g., Roscini, 'Threats of armed force', 235 ('the realization of the threatened harm must depend on the threatenor's will, i.e. it can be caused or prevented by it. This is what distinguishes a threat from a (lawful) warning. For instance, state A has knowledge through its intelligence that state B is preparing an armed attack against state C and warns the latter about it. Such declaration would not amount to a threat by state A against state C, since the armed attack is being prepared by state B over which state A has no control'). With respect, State A's warning State C about State B's preparation of an armed attack against State C is surely not the relevant 'warning' in contradistinction to 'threat'. Of interest would rather be what to call State C's action *vis-à-vis* State B, once State C has been duly 'warned' by State A about State B's preparation of an armed attack against it. If,

the threatener is or is not duly authorised by law to do so in a given situation.[107] Similarly, a use of force remains a use of force, whether the state that uses it is or is not duly authorised to do so in a given situation. Treating force threatened as potentially lawful or unlawful accords with treating force used as potentially lawful and unlawful, which is the approach taken by most international lawyers active in *jus ad bellum*.

1.   Incidence or non-incidence of threat

Threat as communicated intention

This author proposes the following definition of threatening force: one entity threatens force against another entity where the former communicates its intention to use force, and its intention to do so is apprehended as such by the latter. This definition applies to cases where the force in question involves nuclear weapons. Thus defined, the notion contains two integral elements: the measure envisaged by the threatener, plus the communicated and apprehended intention. Often, though not always, there may be a third characteristic feature in the form of the behaviour demanded of the threatenee.

Measure envisaged by the threatener   For our purposes, the measure envisaged by the threatener consists of force involving nuclear weapons. There is no reason to assume that the kind and degree of nuclear force envisaged is, or need be, the kind and degree of nuclear force used, if at all, in the end. On the contrary, depending on the circumstances, it is possible that:

i.   the nuclear force envisaged is not used at all;[108]
ii.   it is used, but only of a lesser kind and/or degree than envisaged;[109]

---

for instance, State C communicated its intention to use force against State B unless State B desisted from carrying out the armed attack under preparation, then this communication would eminently be capable of constituting a 'threat' whose lawfulness or otherwise depends on its compliance with the applicable rules of *jus ad bellum*.

[107] Similarly, driving is driving, whether the vehicle is operated by a person with or without a valid licence to do so. It might be objected that the analogy is flawed, because threatening force by means of nuclear weapons lawfully under *jus ad bellum* concerns an exception from a general prohibition and hence must be construed narrowly, whereas driving a vehicle does not. To this, a two-fold rejoinder may be offered. First, driving lawfully also involves a narrow, licence-based exception from a general prohibition. Second, the narrow construal required of threatening force by means of nuclear weapons pertains to its lawfulness, not to its incidence, which is what is at stake here.

[108] Nor, for that matter, need it be the case that non-use of the force envisaged means the threat's success. Having threatened unsuccessfully, the threatener may very well decline or fail to act on it.

[109] It is indeed likely that a threat of force followed by its actual use, in whole or in part, signifies the threat's failure. Nevertheless, the threatener may threaten, successfully obtain its objective, and then still use force with a view to getting more out of the situation.

iii. it is used exactly as envisaged; or

iv. it is used, but of a greater kind and/or degree than envisaged.

These possibilities remain whatever other kinds and degrees of force may be envisaged and/or used alongside the nuclear force.

Communicated and apprehended intention　The aforementioned definition also entails one two-fold 'mental' element, so to speak. First, the entity intending to use force involving nuclear weapons communicates its intention. Second, the entity against whom the use of such force is intended apprehends this intention. Whereas the threatenee must receive and apprehend the threatener's communicated intention, the threatenee need not in fact feel threatened or intimidated by it.

There is, in principle, some degree of specificity regarding the threatenee's identity. Mutual nuclear deterrence of the classic Cold War-type typifies this construal. Another good recent example is India and Pakistan, where both are at once, and very clearly, each other's threatener and threatenee. In certain circumstances, however, the threatenee's identity need be neither so specific nor so singular. It may be said that Israel's strategic ambiguity, by its very design, has multiple unnamed threatenees in the Middle East, both near to and far from its borders.

In the context of collective self-defence, who exactly intends to use force by means of nuclear weapons and who communicates that intention? Where the arrangement envisages nuclear self-defence, those bearing nuclear arms intend to use force involving such weapons and communicate their intention to do so. Moreover, by offering an umbrella, they also communicate their intention to use nuclear weapons on behalf of non-nuclear or lesser nuclear-armed allies. Such would be the case, for example, for the United States within the context of the North Atlantic Treaty Organization (NATO) during the Cold War.

The situation concerning the beneficiaries of nuclear umbrellas is less straight-forward. By placing themselves thereunder, non-nuclear weapon states might be said to 'communicate' the intention of their nuclear-armed allies to use nuclear weapons on their behalf. Accordingly, while Norway with its NATO membership does not relevantly 'intend' to use force by means of its allies' nuclear weapons, it does 'communicate' the allies' intention to use such force on Norway's behalf. It follows that one and the same intention to use nuclear weapons may be communicated directly by the intender, that is the state that possesses these weapons, and indirectly by its non-nuclear ally on whose behalf the nuclear-armed state intends to use them.

The recipient of a communicated intention needs to apprehend that it is the intended target of the threatened use of nuclear weapons. Accordingly, there may be situations where the interaction between the parties fails to establish one or both of the elements in inter-subjective communication and apprehension.

Examples include: (1) an 'attempted' threat, where the would-be threatener's intention does not register with the would-be threatenee as such;[110] (2) a 'spurious' threat, where the would-be threatenee claims, in bad faith, to apprehend the would-be threatener's intention when the would-be threatener did not so intend; and (3) an 'inadvertent' threat, where the would-be threatenee genuinely feels it apprehends the would-be threatener's intention, although the would-be threatener actually did not intend to make the perceived threat.[111]

Behaviour demanded of the threatenee: 'compellence' v. deterrence   This author agrees that threats do not per se require demands of any specific behaviour from the threatenee.[112] Two kinds of force may be threatened: one meant to induce the threatenee into doing something ('compellence') and the other meant to deter the threatenee *from* doing something ('deterrence').[113] It has been suggested that 'compellence' tends to require the content of the behaviour demanded of the threatenee to be specific, whereas the same need not be true for deterrence.[114] If so, this could also explain the fact that not all communicated intentions to use nuclear force in self-defence specifically identify their recipients.

Means of communication

A state may communicate its intention to use nuclear weapons in various ways, including deliberate undertakings as well as physical actions.[115] The very fact of forming or joining a collective self-defence alliance may amount to communicating intention. Where such a pact is formally concluded between a nuclear weapon state and a non-nuclear weapon state in which the latter is placed under the former's nuclear umbrella, the former expresses its intention, publicly and unambiguously, to use its nuclear weapons either in its own self-defence, in defence of its non-nuclear ally or allies, or both, as the case may be. The non-nuclear weapon state arguably 'communicates' its nuclear-armed allies' intention to use nuclear weapons on the non-nuclear state's behalf. Certain types of

---

[110]   See, e.g., Sadurska, 'Threats of force', 244; Roscini, 'Threats of armed force', 237–8.

[111]   On the absence of relevant intention rendering the underlying act a non-threat, see, e.g., Roscini, 'Threats of armed force', 240.

[112]   See, e.g., White and Cryer, 'Unilateral enforcement of Resolution 687', 253–4; Stürchler, *The Threat of Force in International Law*, p. 273; Dinstein, *War, Aggression and Self-Defence*, p. 89; Roscini, 'Threats of armed force', 235. But see, e.g., Randelzhofer, 'Article 2(4)', p. 124.

[113]   See, e.g., Stürchler, *The Threat of Force in International Law*, p. 58; Roscini, 'Threats of armed force', 235.

[114]   See, e.g., Stürchler, *The Threat of Force in International Law*, p. 58.

[115]   See, e.g., Brownlie, *International Law and the Use of Force by States*, pp. 361–4; *ILC Yearbook*, 2 vols. (New York, United Nations: 1989–II, pt. 2), Vol. I, p. 68; Weeramantry Dissenting Opinion, p. 541; Roscini, 'Threats of armed force', 238–43, esp. 238; Alder, *The Inherent Right of Self-Defence*, p. 78.

calculated ambiguity may also count as a means of communication. Through its strategic ambiguity, Israel may be said to threaten force, as a deterrent and in self-defence, by means of nuclear weapons.

2. *Effectiveness or ineffectiveness of threat*

A threat is effective when it is taken seriously by the threatenee. Crucially, 'being taken seriously by the threatenee' may, but need not, mean 'being credible'. According to Stürchler:

> Overall, state practice since 1945 has converged into a single, overarching credibility test: *does a state credibly communicate its readiness to use force in a particular dispute?* A threat is credible when it appears rational to implement it, when there is a sufficiently serious commitment to run the risk of armed encounter. A calculated expectation is created that an unnamed challenge might incur the penalty of military force; no certainty is required as to whether force really will be used, or under what conditions it will be triggered or that there be an urgent and imminent danger of its deployment.[116]

It is suggested here that a threat would exist not only where the intention to use force is credible in the manner described above. Rather, it would also exist where it does not even appear entirely rational for the threatener to act on its communicated intention. Roscini speaks of a 'delirious dictator', for example.[117] Perhaps a more suitable point of reference might be the existence of some real risk. Such a risk may arise even where the threatener is known neither to possess nuclear weapons nor to have them placed in a state of readiness. In the Advisory Opinion, the Court found that 'possession of nuclear weapons may indeed justify an inference of preparedness to use them'.[118] It would also appear that the Court considered, albeit only implicitly, the notion of preparedness to be synonymous with that of intention. While such an interpretation seems by no means unreasonable, this author argues that it would be no less unreasonable to treat the communication of an 'empty' or 'exaggerated' intention, effectively in the form of nuclear bluffing, also as an instance of force threatened by means of nuclear weapons. Indeed, there is no epistemological reason to limit the notion of nuclear threats to situations where the threatener's communicated intention to use its nuclear weapons is accompanied by its actual ability to do so, this ability being somehow capable of verification – previously, contemporaneously or subsequently – by the threatenee or some third party. On the contrary, one would do well to regard instances of nuclear bluffing and posturing also as threats, particularly where the threatenee takes the bluffs and postures seriously.

---

[116] Stürchler, *The Threat of Force in International Law*, p. 259.
[117] Roscini, 'Threats of armed force', 235.
[118] Nuclear Weapons Advisory Opinion, para. 48.

Nor is it necessary that 'being taken seriously' means 'being successful in inducing the threatenee into behaving as demanded'. Clearly, where the threatenee apprehends the threatener's communicated intention as such, takes it seriously and chooses, however unwillingly, to behave as demanded by the threatener, the threat is effective. A threat would also be effective, however, where the threatenee chooses to resist the demand by seeking protection and taking measures with a view to neutralising the force threatened. It is effective in the sense that the threatenee 'gets the message' and decides to do something about it.[119]

In contrast, a threat is ineffective where the threatenee does not take the threatener's communicated intention to use nuclear weapons seriously. This would happen, for instance, where the threatenee calls the threatener's bluff, or takes a calculated risk, by ignoring the latter's communicated intention.

3. Lawfulness or unlawfulness of threats

All threats, effective or ineffective, are susceptible to being lawful or unlawful *ad bellum*. Force threatened that is neither against the territorial integrity or political independence of a state, nor contrary to the purposes of the UN, nor lacking in necessity or proportionality if it is a measure of self-defence, is lawful. That which fails to fulfil any one of the above requirements is unlawful. This now sets the stage for the examination of two major areas of ambiguity left unaddressed by the Advisory Opinion. The areas in question are, first, the veracity of the Brownlie formula as a matter of law, and second, the legal consequences of an unlawful nuclear threat in collective self-defence for non-nuclear beneficiaries.

The Brownlie formula redux

At stake here is the narrower version of the Brownlie formula noted above. In the interest of argumentative focus, let us agree that self-defence is an end towards which force may be used lawfully *ad bellum*, and that force's use would nevertheless be unlawful should it prove lacking in necessity and/or proportionality. Then the Brownlie formula will have been shown to be erroneous if there are possible criteria for the unlawfulness of threatening force that are distinct from the criteria for the unlawfulness of using it. In particular, the formula will have failed if it can be shown that unlawful use of force may nevertheless be lawfully threatened.

Could there be a more permissive or lenient set of criteria for determining the lawfulness or unlawfulness *ad bellum* of threatening force than those for its use?[120] Proportionality *ad bellum* does not necessarily connote parity between

---

[119] Such is arguably the case between DPR Korea, on the one hand, and the Republic of Korea, Japan and the United States, on the other.

[120] See, e.g., Sadurska, 'Threats of force', 240.

offensive and defence force used; rather, it is more often understood as parity between defensive force used and the repulsion of imminent or actual armed attack.[121] Proportionality *ad bellum* does not require parity between offensive force feared and defensive force threatened either. Surely, one reason for which the possession of armaments, however extensive, is not unlawful as such, is that a state cannot know in advance (a) the specific kind and degree of offensive force it may imminently or suddenly face in the future, or (b) the specific kind and degree of defensive force required at the relevant moment to repel such offensive force.[122] One would rather err on the side of over-preparation followed by underutilisation, rather than under-preparation followed by an inability to defend oneself.

Assuming this is so, proportionality *ad bellum* with respect to threatening force may be construed as entailing parity between two variables. The first variable is the kind and degree of force reasonably likely to be used in the armed attack threatened. The second variable is the kind and degree of force required in order to deter the threatener from launching that attack. There is a distinct possibility that the quantity and quality of force threatened differ in kind and degree from the force required for the victim to repel the attack. Thus construed, threat-related proportionality appears to comprise a reasonable prospect of successful deterrence combined with a similarly reasonable prospect of non-escalation. It is therefore conceivable that threatening force involving nuclear weapons that is proportionate in the sense just described may be lawful *ad bellum*, even though using the same force in the event of an actual armed attack may prove disproportionate vis-à-vis the need to repel that attack and, as a result, be unlawful *ad bellum*.

Collective self-defence and questions of attributing unlawful threats to non-nuclear weapon states under a nuclear umbrella

Where a particular instance of nuclear force threatened in collective self-defence constitutes a breach of *jus ad bellum*, would the non-nuclear weapon state on whose behalf it is threatened be internationally responsible for the breach?

Let us assume that State A, a nuclear-armed state, threatens force by means of its nuclear weapons in collective self-defence on behalf of State B, State A's much smaller, non-nuclear ally. Assume further that the kind and degree of nuclear force threatened by State A far exceed even the most extreme needs of deterrent self-defence that State B has, rendering this particular threat in

---

[121] See Chapter 1.

[122] It may be of interest to note that these criteria may very well underpin the reasons for which arms-building, even on a massive scale, is not per se unlawful. See *Nicaragua* Judgment, para. 209. But see Stürchler, *The Threat of Force in International Law*, p. 85 ('The idea that maintenance of arms may be a *prima facie* infringement of the no-threat rule, dead in the *Nicaragua* judgment, is alive and well here in regard to nuclear weapons').

breach of *jus ad bellum*. It seems fairly straightforward that this breach can be attributed to State A, and therefore constitutes an internationally wrongful act for which State A may be held internationally responsible.[123] Moreover, the act remains internationally wrongful so long as the force threatened continues to lack proportionality.[124]

A trickier question is whether and, if so, how, State B may also be held internationally responsible for this threat. Let us consider two distinct scenarios. In one, State B not only 'communicates' State A's intention to use nuclear weapons on its behalf, but also 'assists' State A by permitting the latter to deploy the said weapons on its territory. In this case, State B may arguably be held responsible for the internationally wrongful act committed by State A under Article 16 of the International Law Commission (ILC) Articles on State Responsibility.[125] In another scenario, State B 'communicates' State A's intention to use nuclear weapons, but does not permit its territory to be used to deploy such weapons. Can State B still be said to have 'assisted' or 'aided' State A in the commission of an internationally wrongful act within the meaning of Article 16? The answer is unclear. While there is no requirement that State B's conduct be essential to State A's,[126] one may doubt whether State B's act of 'communicating' State A's intention 'contributes significantly' to the unlawful threat coming into existence.[127]

There is another, more controversial interpretation of State B's legal situation vis-à-vis State A's unlawful nuclear threat. State B could be said to be bound by a separate obligation not to permit State A to threaten force in collective self-defence by means of nuclear weapons, even on State B's own behalf, if the force threatened is lacking in proportionality and therefore in breach of Article 2(4) of the UN Charter. If true, this would amount to requiring non-nuclear weapon states to refrain from forming collective nuclear self-defence alliances, or to withdraw from such alliances, should the nuclear force threatened therewith prove unlawful in the sense just described. If these states nevertheless choose to join or remain in such alliances, then this choice would constitute an internationally wrongful act for which they would be responsible.

Conclusion

Odd as it may sound, threats have never quite been at the forefront of our legal discourse when it comes to nuclear weapons. If it were found that such weapons may never, under any circumstances be used, then no need to consider

---

[123] See ILC, Draft Articles on Responsibility of States for Internationally Wrongful Acts, with commentaries, 2001, text adopted by the International Law Commission at its fifty-third session in 2001, and submitted to the General Assembly as part of the Commission's report covering the work of that session (A/56/10), p. 34, Art. 2.

[124] See *ibid.*, p. 59, Art. 14(2).   [125] See *ibid.*, pp. 65, Art. 16, and 66–7.

[126] See *ibid.*, p. 66.   [127] See *ibid.*

the lawfulness of their threat would arise. This certainly appears to have been the hope and expectation on the part of those who sought an ICJ Advisory Opinion. Understandable as such hopes and expectations are, the current state of *jus ad bellum* appears to fall well short of satisfying them. To begin with, *jus ad bellum* is not weapon-specific. It is therefore unsusceptible to pronouncements of the form: 'nuclear weapons may never be threatened or used even as an instrument of self-defence.' Since self-defence permits the use or threat of *some* force, it is, at least in principle, conceivable that use of nuclear force could be lawfully threatened in self-defence. To compound the difficulties, the very definition of threatening force by means of nuclear weapons is not easy to pin down. Complex notions such as deterrence, as well as collective and individual self-defence, overshadow much of the ambiguities highlighted in the preceding pages. Last but not least, the legality *ad bellum* of threatening nuclear weapons – its scope, relationship to using such weapons and the like – is exceedingly difficult to assess.

This chapter has endeavoured to bring some degree of clarity and food for thought to the table. First, threatening force by means of nuclear weapons equals a communicated intention to use them. This helps to explain collective and individual self-defence. Second, the Brownlie formula may not be correct as a matter of law. Even if proven correct, however, the criteria for determining the lawfulness and unlawfulness of nuclear threats require further investigations. Third, in cases where a nuclear threat proves unlawful *ad bellum*, the possible international legal responsibility of non-nuclear weapon states for a benefactor state's threat merits additional work and reflection.

Nuclear weapons and the separation of *jus ad bellum* and *jus in bello*

JASMINE MOUSSA

Introduction

The question of whether the legal categories of *jus ad bellum* and *jus in bello*[1] should remain conceptually distinct is one that has attracted much academic discussion among both moral and legal theorists. Originating in the debate on 'just war' theory, the principle of separation of *jus ad bellum* and *jus in bello* re-emerged as a contested topic as a result of the International Court of Justice (ICJ)'s 1996 Advisory Opinion on the *Legality of the Threat or Use of Nuclear Weapons*.[2] In its Opinion the Court stated that it could not rule out the lawfulness of the use of nuclear weapons 'in an extreme circumstance of self-defence, in which the very survival of a State would be at stake'.[3] The Court therefore appeared to leave open the vexing question of whether a state could lawfully justify its use of nuclear weapons – even when such use violated *jus in bello* – by reference to 'an extreme circumstance of self-defence'.

The proposition that *jus ad bellum* and *jus in bello* are, and should remain, conceptually distinct entails that international humanitarian law (IHL) binds all belligerents equally, regardless of the legality of their recourse to force. While mainstream publicists have defended the separation of *jus ad bellum* and *jus in bello* as 'fundamental',[4] the principle has also been challenged both on its

---

[1] The terms *jus in bello* and international humanitarian law (IHL) are used interchangeably throughout this chapter.

[2] ICJ, *Legality of the Threat or Use of Nuclear Weapons*, Advisory Opinion, of 8 July 1996, para. 78 (hereafter, Nuclear Weapons Advisory Opinion). Earlier considerations of the subject include C. Greenwood, 'The relationship between *ius ad bellum* and *ius in bello*', *Review of International Studies* 9 (1983), 221–34.

[3] Nuclear Weapons Advisory Opinion, dispositif E.

[4] See L. Blank, 'A new twist on an old story: lawfare and the mixing of proportionalities', *Case Western Reserve Journal of International Law* 43 (2010–11), 707–38; J. Weiler and A. Deshman, 'Far be it from thee to slay the righteous with the wicked: an historical and historiographical sketch of the bellicose debate concerning the distinction between *jus ad bellum* and *jus in bello*', *European Journal of International Law* 24(1) (2013), 25–61, at 26; M. Sassòli et al., *How does Law Protect in War?*, 3rd edn, 3 vols. (Geneva: International Committee of the Red Cross, 2011), Vol. I, p. 14; A. Bouvier, 'Assessing the relationship between jus in bello and jus ad bellum: an "orthodox" view', *Proceedings of the Annual Meeting of the American Society of International Law (ASIL)* 100 (2006), 109–12, at 110; L. Doswald-Beck,

own merits and on the grounds of state practice.[5] Indeed, doctrine has increasingly suggested the existence of a gap between theory and practice in this area. This is particularly so with respect to 'humanitarian intervention' and measures of armed force against non-state actors (under self-defence). The practice of the United Nations (UN) Security Council has also called into question the continued validity of the separation principle. Some scholars argue that emerging state practice is changing the law such that the separation principle is no longer valid. According to this view, in certain circumstances *jus in bello* has, and should be, subordinated to *ad bellum* considerations. Others claim that the gap indicates only a departure by states from respect for the letter of the law. They base their argument on the fact that ample evidence is found in international treaties and the jurisprudence of international courts (particularly international criminal courts and tribunals) for the complete separation of *jus ad bellum* and *jus in bello* in international law and for the equal application of *jus in bello* to all parties in a conflict.[6] This is the premise on which this chapter is based.

In particular, the implications of the separation principle are examined in the specific context of the use of nuclear weapons, an area where debate on the principle's validity has important practical consequences. The question addressed is whether use of nuclear weapons in a manner that violates *jus in bello* can ever be justified by reason that a state is using force in self-defence or is otherwise acting in compliance with the UN Charter (such as under the authority of the UN Security Council). This question, which has already arisen in one conflict in recent history, has important practical implications. Could it be argued that the use of the atomic bomb in Hiroshima and Nagasaki was legal *exclusively* by reference to the justness of the allied *casus belli*, namely self-defence against aggression by the Axis states (regardless of whether the attack complied with the applicable *jus in bello*)? The question is equally applicable

---

'International humanitarian law and the Advisory Opinion of the International Court of Justice on the Legality of the Threat or Use of Nuclear Weapons', *International Review of the Red Cross* 37(116) (1997), 35–55, at 53; T. Gill, 'The Nuclear Weapons Advisory Opinion of the International Court of Justice and the fundamental distinction between the *jus ad bellum* and the *jus in bello*', *Leiden Journal of International Law* 12 (1999) 613–24, at 614, 616; E. Koppe, 'Compensation for War Damages Under *jus ad bellum*' in *The 1998–2000 War Between Eritrea and Ethiopia: An International Legal Perspective*, de Guttry, Venturini, and Post (eds.) (2009), 418.

[5] M. Milanović, 'A non-response to Weiler and Deshman', *European Journal of International Law* 24(1) (2013), 63–6, at 65; Koppe, 419.

[6] See Protocol Additional to the Geneva Conventions of 12 August 1949, and relating to the Protection of Victims of International Armed Conflicts (Protocol I), Geneva, 8 June 1977, in force 7 December 1978, 1125 UNTS 3, Preamble (hereafter, Additional Protocol I); and The 1949 Geneva Conventions, Geneva, 12 August 1949, in force 21 October 1950, 75 UNTS 31, 75 UNTS 85, 75 UNTS 135, 75 UNTS 287, Common Articles 1 and 2. See Greenwood, 'The relationship between *jus ad bellum* and *jus in bello*', 225.

in the case of conventional warfare: for example, could purported violations of IHL by NATO forces in the 1999 Kosovo war[7] be justified on the grounds of 'humanitarian intervention', which is an *ad bellum* argument?[8]

Following this introduction, Section A of this chapter frames the contours of the discussion with preliminary observations regarding use of nuclear weapons in light of the separation principle. Section B puts this discussion into context by examining the implications and the legal and theoretical foundations of the separation principle. Section C analyses the contemporary challenges to the separation principle, beginning with a critique of the ICJ's Nuclear Weapons Advisory Opinion. The section then analyses the implications of the conflation of *ad bellum* proportionality with *in bello* proportionality in doctrine and state practice. It surveys contemporary doctrine, which has increasingly challenged the separation principle, particularly in light of the principle of concurrent application of *jus ad bellum* and *jus in bello*. It also examines recent state practice challenging the principle and the practice within the UN Security Council, where, arguably, the subordination of *in bello* considerations to *jus ad bellum* has been a feature of recently authorised interventions.

Section D highlights areas of law where the separation principle has been reaffirmed, asserting that the 'conflationist' trend amounts to misunderstanding and misapplication of the law. It also highlights the contribution of international criminal law and the law of state responsibility to reaffirmation of the separation principle. The chapter concludes that use of nuclear weapons in a manner that violates IHL is also a violation of international law no matter what its legality may be *ad bellum*.

A.   Use of nuclear weapons and the separation principle: preliminary observations

It has been argued that no use of nuclear weapons could possibly respect the core principles of IHL. According to this view, even the smallest nuclear weapons release huge amounts of heat, explosive energy and radioactivity, the effects of which cannot be contained in time and space (even in the case of an

---

[7] See Application filed by Banković *et al.* and rejected by the European Court of Human Rights on grounds of non-admissibility. *Banković and Others* v. *Belgium and Others*, Admissibility Decision (Grand Chamber) (App. No. 52207/99), 12 December 2001, 123 ILR 94. See also, Amnesty International, *Federal Republic of Yugoslavia (FRY)/NATO: 'Collateral Damage' or Unlawful Killings? Violations of the Laws of War by NATO during Operation Allied Force* (June 2000), available at: www.amnesty.org/en/library/info/EUR70/018/2000/en.

[8] The legality of 'humanitarian intervention' itself under *jus ad bellum* is highly questionable. For a brief discussion in relation to the proposed UK/US military intervention in Syria in 2013, see, e.g., Dapo Akande, 'The Legality of Military Action in Syria: Humanitarian Intervention and Responsibility to Protect', *EJIL Talk*, 28 August 2013, available at: www.ejiltalk.org/humanitarian-intervention-responsibility-to-protect-and-the-legality-of-military-action-in-syria/.

underground detonation). Radioactivity can travel to areas far from the detonation site (including to other states), contaminating the natural environment
and human populations for many years.[9] This view holds that such destructive
effects would be incapable of meeting the principle of distinction (although the
weapon's *accuracy of deployment* can meet the requisite standard). It is possible
that resulting civilian deaths would also be expected to be disproportionate
compared to the concrete and direct military advantage anticipated.

Proportionality, however, depends on the specific circumstances of the
attack. It is not impossible to envisage a situation in which a low-yield nuclear
weapon could be used in a manner that would effectively minimise civilian
casualties (for example, by using the weapon against a military vessel on the
high seas).[10] It has been contended that nuclear weapons are now being developed with yields as low as tens of tons, which could result in no radioactive
fissile material.[11] This was the view advanced by nuclear weapon states in their
submissions in the context of the Nuclear Weapons Advisory Opinion, in
which they argued that nuclear weapons were capable of being used in compliance with the principles and rules of IHL.[12] Conceivably, therefore, nuclear
weapons could be used in a manner that would respect both *jus ad bellum* and
jus in bello.

This chapter does not discuss further whether use of nuclear weapons can
meet the *in bello* requirements; this issue is addressed in Part II of this book.
What is of interest is the scenario that involves use of nuclear weapons in a
manner that clearly violates *jus in bello*. Could such use ever be justified by
reference to the legality of *jus ad bellum*? In other words, can the justness of
the *casus belli* somehow relax the IHL rules applicable in a particular conflict?
Could it confer legality on a use of nuclear weapons that would otherwise be
illegal by reference to *jus in bello*? This is the question that this chapter seeks to
answer.

B.   Rationale and implications of the separation between *jus ad bellum* and *jus in bello*

The separation principle has three important implications. First, it implies that
acts in conformity with *jus in bello* may nonetheless be prohibited under *jus
ad bellum*. Similarly, an attack that is inconsistent with *jus in bello* does not

---

[9] B. Bengs, 'Legal constraints on the use of a tactical nuclear weapon against the Natanz
nuclear facility in Iran', *George Washington International Law Review* 40 (2008), 323–400, at
366–7.

[10] Maj. R. P. Chatham, 'Tactical nuclear weapons: lawful use in the aftermath of the ICJ
Opinion', *The Reporter* 37(2) (2010), 41–6, at 42, 44–5.

[11] *Ibid.*, 46.

[12] Nuclear Weapons Advisory Opinion, Dissenting Opinion of Judge Schwebel.

(directly at least) affect the legality of the resort to force.[13] Second, the question of whether the resort to force was lawful under *jus ad bellum* is immaterial to whether and how *jus in bello* applies in a conflict. In other words, whether the conflict is one of legitimate self-defence or aggression, whether it constitutes armed intervention to rescue civilians, restore democratic government or illegally occupy another state's territory, whether it constitutes force authorised by the UN Security Council or is completely unilateral, indeed whether it is in flagrant violation of the UN Charter, has no bearing on the applicability of *jus in bello*. Third, and as a close corollary, *jus in bello* applies to all belligerents, irrespective of the cause of conflict. All parties are bound by the applicable limitations of IHL and can benefit from its protections. This principle, sometimes referred to as the 'equal application' of *jus in bello*, holds true for both international and non-international armed conflict. Its consequence in international armed conflict is that the act of bearing arms does not render a combatant a criminal, even if the initial use of force by the party on whose behalf s/he is fighting was itself unlawful.

Many scholars who challenge the separation principle premise their argument on rationalising the 'just war' model from a moral and philosophical standpoint, rather than a legal one. This position, also known as the 'conflationist' position, removes the application of IHL from the realm of law and exposes it to the subjective realm of morality. Instead of treating departures from the separation principle as violations of an established norm, the conflationist position is that such departures modify the substantive content of the norm.

One view that subordinates *jus in bello* to a 'just cause' is grounded in a form of consequentialist moral reasoning: the argument that the violation of IHL may be necessary to avert an even greater evil. According to this view, use of nuclear weapons in violation of IHL may be justified, at least in theory, if there is a circumstance so extreme such as to warrant their use, for example when the very survival of the state is threatened.[14] In this case, the violation of IHL can be tolerated to avoid an even greater evil (the destruction or extinction of the state). In contrast, proponents of categorical moral reasoning counter this utilitarian view. This opposing moral standpoint views any violation of IHL as categorically prohibited, regardless of the consequences (even if the violation is necessary to avoid a greater moral wrong). The debate is circular, and does not lend itself to a right or wrong answer. It is therefore imperative to base the case for the separation principle on practical and legal, rather than on moral grounds.

[13] See, e.g., J. Moussa 'Can *jus ad bellum* override *jus in bello*?', *International Review of the Red Cross* 90(872) (2008) 963–90, at 968; Greenwood, 'The relationship between *jus ad bellum* and *jus in bello*', 222; J. Gardam, 'Proportionality and force in international law', *American Journal of International Law* 87 (1993), 391–413, at 392.

[14] This view is reflected in the Separate Opinion of Judge Fleischhauer in the Advisory Opinion, para. 3. See also Chapters 1 and 2 in this volume.

Opponents of the separation principle base themselves on law and practice. First, they argue that the application of the legal maxim *ex injuria jus non oritor* necessitates that a state may not benefit from its own illegal conduct.[15] Second, they argue that the principle is not upheld in reality, and indeed cannot be realistically upheld.[16] Third, it is argued that doing away with the separation principle does not necessarily entail diminished respect for IHL.[17]

Proponents of the separation principle respond with the following. First, in practical terms it is nearly impossible to find a way of objectively identifying the aggressor in an armed conflict; thus, doing away with the separation principle would subject application of IHL to the vagaries of what is essentially a subjective determination. Furthermore, even if it were possible to institutionally determine the aggressor (for example through UN Security Council determination, which itself is not free from controversy), the ordinary soldier cannot be expected to be aware of this, at least not at the start of hostilities.[18] Second, the separation of *jus ad bellum* from *jus in bello* makes the conduct of warfare practically possible. Its absence would make a criminal out of every soldier fighting on the side of the undeterminable 'aggressor'.[19] Third, doing away with the separation principle would undermine respect for and application of IHL by absolving the party acting in conformity with *jus ad bellum* of its duty to respect IHL. Since, in practice, IHL often functions on the basis of reciprocity, the 'aggressor', who is not entitled to benefit from its protections, is unlikely to respect its limitations *vis-à-vis* the opponent.[20] Inevitably, this would result in poorer protection of civilians in armed conflict.[21]

---

[15] H. Lauterpacht, 'Rules of warfare in an unlawful war' in G. A. Lipsky (ed.), *Law and Politics in the World Community (Essays on Hans Kelsen's Pure Theory and Related Problems in International Law)* (Berkeley: University of California Press, 1953).

[16] I. Österdahl, 'Dangerous liaison? The disappearing dichotomy between *jus ad bellum* and *jus in bello*', *Nordic Journal of International Law* 78(4) (2009), 553–66, at 554.

[17] *Ibid.*, 557. Österdahl argues that the interplay between *jus ad bellum* and *jus in bello* might actually lead to increased respect for *jus in bello*, as *jus in bello* must be more scrupulously enforced in a 'just' war (such as a war of self-defense or humanitarian intervention).

[18] But, see A. Orakhelashvili, 'Overlap and convergence: the interaction between *jus ad bellum* and *jus in bello*', *Journal of Conflict and Security Law* 12(2) (2007), 157–96, at 170–2; and Weiler and Deshman, 'Far be it from thee to slay the righteous', 43, who state that 'for those separationists, whose argument is mostly rooted in the pragmatic difficulty of authoritatively, and ex ante, classifying which of the two parties is a just and an unjust warrior, the Security Council type authorized use of force poses a challenge: for it both clearly and authoritatively makes precisely that distinction'.

[19] But, see Orakhelashvili, 'Overlap and convergence', 179.

[20] See e.g. Österdahl, 'Dangerous liaison?', 556; Bouvier, 'Assessing the relationship between *jus in bello* and *jus ad bellum*', 112. But, see Orakhelashvili, 'Overlap and convergence', 178–9.

[21] Bouvier, 'Assessing the relationship between *jus in bello* and *jus ad bellum*', 112.

In the following two sections, this chapter will discuss the theoretical foundations and development of the separation principle, highlighting the legal basis for the complete distinction between *jus in bello* and *ad bellum*.

C.   Theoretical foundations of the separation between *jus ad bellum* and *jus in bello*

Jus ad bellum and *jus in bello* are theoretically distinct. They each have different historical origins as well as different aims and objectives.[22] The modern principles of *jus in bello* can be traced back to the nineteenth century,[23] particularly the establishment of the International Committee of the Red Cross (ICRC) in the aftermath of the 1859 Battle of Solferino, the promulgation of the 1863 Lieber Code,[24] and the conclusion of the 1864 Geneva Convention[25] and the 1868 St Petersburg Declaration.[26] Modern *jus ad bellum*, on the other hand, has its origins in the 1919 Covenant of the League of Nations and the 1928 Kellogg–Briand Pact, which renounced recourse to force between states.[27] Contemporary *jus ad bellum* is reflected in Articles 2(4) and 51 of the UN Charter and in customary international law.[28] Whereas *jus ad bellum* regulates when states can lawfully resort to force, *jus in bello* aims to place limitations on the conduct of warfare so as to make it more humane. Also, the consequences attaching to the violation of each of *jus in bello* and *jus ad bellum* differ.[29] The complete separation of the two branches of international law was also a product of the classical distinction between the law of peace and the law of war.[30]

---

[22] E. Cannizzaro, 'Contextualising proportionality: *jus ad bellum* and *jus in bello* in the Lebanese war', *International Review of the Red Cross* 88(864) (2006), 779–92, at 791. See also Gardam, 'Proportionality and force in international law', 391.

[23] See R. D. Sloane, 'The cost of conflation: preserving the dualism of *jus ad bellum* and *jus in bello* in the contemporary law of war', *Yale Journal of International Law* 34 (2009), 47–112, at 50, 63.

[24] Instructions for the Government of the Armies of the United States in the Field, General Orders No. 100, 'Lieber Code', published in D. Schindler and J. Toman (eds.), *The Laws of Armed Conflicts: A Collection of Conventions, Resolutions and Other Documents*, 3rd edn (Dordrecht: Martinus Nijhoff Publishers/Geneva: Henry Dunant Institute, 1988), pp. 3–23.

[25] Convention for the Amelioration of the Condition of the Wounded in Armies in the Field, Geneva, 22 August 1864, in force 22 June 1865, 129 CTS 361.

[26] Declaration Renouncing the Use in Time of War of Explosive Projectiles Under 400 Grammes Weight, Saint Petersburg, 11 December 1868, in force 11 December 1868, published in Schindler and Toman, *The Laws of Armed Conflicts*, p. 102.

[27] See M. N. Shaw, *International Law*, 4th edn (Cambridge University Press, 1997), pp. 807–8.

[28] Charter of the United Nations, San Francisco, 26 June 1945, in force 24 October 1945, 1 UNTS XVI. See Greenwood, 'The relationship between *jus ad bellum* and *jus in bello*', 222.

[29] Greenwood, 'The relationship between *jus ad bellum* and *jus in bello*', 227; Gardam, 'Proportionality and force in international law', 404–5.

[30] Greenwood, 'The relationship between *jus ad bellum* and *jus in bello*', 221.

The principle of separation of *jus ad bellum* and *jus in bello*, and its corollary the principle of 'equal application' of IHL, can thus be said to be the antithesis of 'just war' theory, under which war was considered 'just' if it was waged in response to illegal aggression. By relying on the validity of the *casus belli*, this doctrine did not place belligerents on an equal footing when it came to the application of IHL.[31] Many important scholarly works are concerned with a historiography of 'just war' theory and the separation principle.[32] There is only room in this contribution for a brief account of this development. 'Just war' theory can be traced back to both Roman law and the theological writings of Augustine and Aquinas. According to its original conception, a just cause justified any means of war, regardless of whether or not it respected standards of humanity.[33]

The separation principle began to take root with the emergence of the concept of the sovereign state after the Peace of Westphalia in 1648. The rise of the modern nation state and the doctrine of *raison d'état* meant that war was regarded as a neutral situation, no longer to be assessed by reference to the justness of its cause. War was to be regulated through application of *jus in bello*, which therefore applied equally to all belligerents.[34] The idea that *jus in bello* should apply equally to both just and unjust belligerents thus appeared in the writings of Vitoria, Suarez and Gentili, who recognised the difficulty of determining the aggressor in a world of multiple sovereigns. However, the separation principle only clearly began to take form in Grotius' *De jure belli ac pacis*. Grotius argued that humanitarian restraints should apply equally to all belligerents, basing his argument on a secular (natural law) rather than a theological perspective.[35]

Although Grotius is credited with developing the separation principle, it was Kant's writings that crystallised the principle in its current form in the late nineteenth century. Kant was the first theorist to clearly distinguish between 'the Right of going to War' and 'the Right during War'.[36]

The development of the separation principle was not, however, unchallenged. German doctrine, particularly during the First World War, challenged the notion that IHL was to be respected regardless of the cause of conflict or

---

[31] R. Kolb, 'Origin of the twin terms *jus ad bellum* and *jus in bello*', *International Review of the Red Cross* 37 (1997), 553–62, at 554–5; Gardam, 'Proportionality and force in international law', 397.

[32] R. Howse, 'Thucydides and just war: how to begin to read Walzer's *Just and Unjust Wars*' *European Journal of International Law*, 24(1) (2013), 17–24.

[33] Sloane, 'The cost of conflation', 57–8.

[34] Orakhelashvili, 'Overlap and convergence', 158; Blank, 'A new twist on an old story', 719; T. Meron, 'Shakespeare's Henry the Fifth and the law of war', *American Journal of International Law* 86(1) (1992), 1–45, at 12.

[35] Sloane, 'The cost of conflation', 59–61.

[36] I. Kant, *The Philosophy of Law. An Exposition on the Fundamental Principles of Jurisprudence as the Science of Right*, W. Hasle (transl.) (Edinburgh: Clark, 1887), para. 53.

the desired goal of military conduct. This notion took form in several related doctrines, including the maxim that *Not kennt kein Gebot* ('necessity knows no law')[37] and *Kriegsraison geht vor Kriegsmanier*, by virtue of which it was argued that obligations under the laws of armed conflict could be displaced 'by urgent and overwhelming necessity'.[38] These doctrines, which are based on the notion of a fundamental right of 'self-preservation', entailed that a belligerent was entitled to disregard IHL in cases where observing its rules would endanger its own armed forces. They were based on the practical consideration that commanders would inevitably act on the doctrine in spite of the existence of any rule to the contrary.[39] The *Kriegsraison* doctrine gave rise to the question of whether a distinction could be made between mere military necessity and another category of 'dire or genuine necessity'. This second category, based on the notion of 'overruling necessity' that arises out of 'an extreme emergency of a state as such',[40] has parallels with the notion of extreme circumstances of self-defence recognised by the ICJ in its Nuclear Weapons Advisory Opinion, discussed in detail below.

The development in international law of a prohibition of the use of force through the League of Nations Covenant, the 1928 Kellogg–Briand Pact and eventually the UN Charter led some scholars to question why an 'aggressor' should be allowed to benefit from the protections of *jus in bello*.[41] Although this modern version of 'just war' theory was tested and rejected before the International Military Tribunal at Nuremberg,[42] some scholars remained sympathetic to the idea that a belligerent acting in conformity with *jus ad bellum* should have an advantaged position when it came to the application of *jus in bello*. An early study by the Institut de Droit International concluded that there should not be complete equality between belligerents when there is a determination by the UN Security Council that one of the belligerents has resorted to force unlawfully.[43] In 1951 a Committee established by the American Society of International Law to examine whether the laws of war should apply to UN

---

[37] M. G. Kohen, 'The notion of state survival in international law' in L. Boisson de Chazournes and P. Sands (eds.), *International Law, the International Court of Justice and Nuclear Weapons* (Cambridge University Press, 1999), p. 311.

[38] N. C. H. Dunbar, 'Military necessity in war crimes trials', *British Yearbook of International Law* 29 (1952), 442–54, at 444–5.

[39] *Ibid.*, 446.

[40] P. Weidenbaum 'Necessity in international law', *Transactions of the Grotius Society* 24 (1938), 105–32, at 110, 112–13.

[41] See, e.g., Q. Wright, 'The outlawry of war and the law of war', *American Journal of International Law* 47(3) (1935), 365–76, at 370–1.

[42] G. Schwarzenberger, *International Law, as Applied by International Courts and Tribunals*, 3 vols. (London, Stevens & Sons, 1968), Vol. II: 'The Law of Armed Conflict', p. 104.

[43] Sloane, 'The cost of conflation', 70; Resolution, 'Equality of application of the rules of the law of war to parties to an armed conflict', *Annuaire de L'Institut de Droit International* 50(1) (Brussels Session, 1963).

enforcement action stated that the UN was not bound by IHL, but could volun-
tarily choose to respect some of its principles. The Committee added that the
UN would be justified in prohibiting 'the use of atomic bombs by a state while
reserving the right to use them itself'.[44] However, by and large the mainstream
view of lawyers rejected this contention.[45]

D.   The Nuclear Weapons Advisory Opinion and the notion of 'extreme circumstance of self-defence'

One of the most important challenges to the validity of the separation principle
is potentially the ICJ's 1996 Nuclear Weapons Advisory Opinion. Although the
Court's decision is vague, some commentators have interpreted it as stating
that nuclear weapons may be used in violation of IHL if *jus ad bellum* justi-
fies such use, as when the very survival of the state (whatever that means) is at
stake.[46]

In light of the very divergent interpretations of the Advisory Opinion, a
more detailed consideration of the decision is warranted. The Court clearly
stated that nothing in international law prohibited the threat or use of nuclear
weapons per se. Whether the use of nuclear weapons was legal therefore neces-
sitated an examination of each of *jus ad bellum* and *jus in bello*.[47] The Court
then stated that any threat or use of nuclear weapons in violation of the UN
Charter would be clearly illegal, and asserted that the exercise of the right to
self-defence was limited by the principles of necessity and proportionality. It
emphasised that proportionality under *jus ad bellum* did not rule out the use of
nuclear weapons a priori,[48] a clear recognition that proportionality analysis is
contextual. The Court also stated that 'a use of force that is proportionate under
the law of self-defence, must, in order to be lawful, also meet the requirements

[44] Report of the Committee on Study of Legal Problems of the UN, 'Should the laws of war
apply to United Nations enforcement action?' *Proceedings of the Annual Meeting of the
American Society of International Law (ASIL)* 46 (1952), 218. See Weiler and Deshman, 'Far
be it from thee to slay the righteous', 36.

[45] Some scholars exempted the law of occupation and *jus post bellum* from the operation of the
separation principle. Their view was that the validity of a *jus ad bellum* case could have implications for certain aspects of the law of occupation such as title to property, while generally
accepting that the rules relating to the actual conduct of hostilities were immune to such
an exception. According to the Harvard Research in International Law's Draft Convention
on Rights and Duties of States in Case of Aggression, 'an aggressor does not have any of the
rights which it would have if it were a belligerent'; however, this did not apply to 'a violation of the humanitarian rules concerning the conduct of hostilities'. Harvard Research in
International Law, 'Draft Convention on Rights and Duties of States in Case of Aggression',
American Journal of International Law Special Supplement 33 (1939), 827–30, at 828.

[46] See C. Greenwood '*Jus ad bellum* and *jus in bello* in the Nuclear Weapons Advisory Opinion'
in L. Boisson de Chazournes and P. Sands (eds.), *International Law, the ICJ and Nuclear
Weapons* (Cambridge University Press, 1999), p. 263.

[47] Nuclear Weapons Advisory Opinion, para. 36.   [48] *Ibid.*, para. 42.

of the law applicable in armed conflict which comprise in particular the principles and rules of humanitarian law'.[49] Some commentators have interpreted this statement to imply that a use of force in self-defence can only be considered proportionate if it respects IHL. However, this does not seem to reflect what the Court actually meant. It is more accurate to state that the Court found that a use of force in self-defence might only be considered lawful if it respects both *jus ad bellum* proportionality as well as IHL.

The Court then proceeded to examine the compliance of nuclear weapons with the principles of *jus in bello*. First, it affirmed that the principles of IHL applied to the use of nuclear weapons.[50] It then stated that whereas the use of nuclear weapons is 'scarcely reconcilable' with IHL, the Court was unable to ascertain that such use would necessarily violate IHL in every single circumstance. Again, this reflects the Court's recognition that compliance with IHL must be assessed in light of the particular context and circumstances of each individual case. This also signifies that the court accepted the view expressed by nuclear weapon states before the ICJ that nuclear weapons could be used in a variety of different circumstances with different effects, some of which could respect IHL.

The most controversial part of the decision is paragraph 2E of the *dispositif*. Here, the Court found that 'the threat or use of nuclear weapons would generally be contrary to the rules of international law applicable in armed conflict, and in particular the principles and rules of humanitarian law'. This finding was followed by the most divisive part of the Advisory Opinion, in which the Court held by a vote of seven in favour and seven against and with the casting vote of the President that:

> [it] cannot conclude definitively whether the threat or use of nuclear weapons would be lawful or unlawful in an extreme circumstance of self-defence, in which the very survival of a State would be at stake.[51]

Together, these two paragraphs could lead to the conclusion that in 'extreme circumstances of self-defence', the use of nuclear weapons may be justified even if such use violates *jus in bello*. Dispositif 2E could equally imply that recourse to nuclear weapons in compliance with *jus ad bellum* 'might *of itself* exceptionally make such a use compatible with humanitarian law'.[52] The Court did not adequately explain the legal reasoning behind its decision.

In the immediate aftermath of the Court's Advisory Opinion, a voluminous body of literature criticised this finding. Falk and Akande argued that it represented new doctrinal terrain[53] as 'there is no basis in international law for

---

[49] *Ibid.*, para. 42.   [50] *Ibid.*, para. 86.   [51] *Ibid.*, p. 266, Dispositif 2E.

[52] Nuclear Weapons Advisory Opinion, Dissenting Opinion of Judge Higgins, para. 25 (emphasis added).

[53] R. Falk, 'Nuclear weapons, international law and the World Court: a historic encounter', *American Journal of International Law* 91 (1997), 64–75.

introducing the notion of the survival of the state as a legitimate excuse for violating the law of armed conflict.[54] Such a proposition would allow states to justify any violation of IHL if they deemed their survival to be threatened. With no
international arbiter to determine the existence of such an 'extreme' circumstance,
allowing states to make a determination of 'extreme self-defence' would lead to
a situation of arbitrariness and unpredictability. The Court also failed to clarify
the scope of this 'new' category of self-defence or the definition of the 'survival
of a State'. According to one view, this concept could equally mean the political
survival of a state's ruling regime, the survival of a state's sovereignty and independence, or the physical survival of its population.[55] Another view was that an
extreme circumstance of self-defence threatening a state's survival was an exception that should be narrowly construed, but nonetheless might include annihilation of a state's inhabitants or absorption of the functions of statehood by another
state.[56] Weil claimed that the Court's pronouncement of a *non liquet* implies that
the use of nuclear weapons in violation of IHL is permitted, as per the *Lotus* principle, according to which anything not expressly prohibited by international law
is permitted.[57]

The extent of the controversy is reflected in the numerous separate and
Dissenting Opinions of the ICJ Judges.[58] It is possible to identify three main
positions in the Judges' opinions. Judges Fleischhauer and Vereshchetin supported the interpretation that recourse to nuclear weapons could be lawful even
if it violated IHL. According to Judge Fleischhauer, nuclear weapons could be
used in violation of IHL in extreme situations of self-defence threatening the
very existence of a state.[59] He criticised the Court's use of hesitating and vague
terms, and stated that prioritising IHL over the inherent right of self-defence
was an incorrect statement of the law. International law did not envision such
a denial of a state's legitimate right to self-defence, particularly if use of nuclear

---

[54] D. Akande, 'Nuclear weapons, unclear law? Deciphering the Nuclear Weapons Advisory
Opinion of the International Court', *British Yearbook of International Law* 68 (1997), 165–
217, at 209.

[55] M. Matheson, 'The opinions of the International Court of Justice on the threat or use of
nuclear weapons', *American Journal of International Law* 91 (1997), 417–35, at 430.

[56] See P. Weiss, 'The World Court tackles the fate of the Earth: an introduction to the ICJ
Advisory Opinion on the threat or use of nuclear weapons', *Transnational Law and
Contemporary Problems* 7 (1997), 313–32, at 325–6.

[57] P. Weil, '"The Court cannot conclude definitively …": non-liquet revisited', *Columbia
Journal of Transnational Law* 36 (1997), 109–19, at 112, 118.

[58] Every single judge found it necessary to explain their vote in an individual opinion.

[59] Nuclear Weapons Advisory Opinion, Separate Opinion of Judge Fleischhauer, para. 4. The
only other Judge in the Court who seems to share a similar opinion is Judge Vereshchetin,
who held that the Court was 'debarred' from finding a general rule of international humanitarian law that comprehensively proscribes recourse to nuclear weapons. See Nuclear
Weapons Advisory Opinion, Declaration of Judge Vereshchetin, p. 280.

weapons was the last means available to a victimised state.[60] He stated that 'no legal system is entitled to demand the self-abandonment, the suicide, of one its subjects'.[61] This finding goes beyond the claims of any of the nuclear weapon states that appeared before the Court, although it has subsequently been advanced by them to justify the possible use of nuclear weapons. For instance, in April 2002 British Defence Secretary Geoff Hoon defended the use of nuclear weapons in the following terms: 'the use of nuclear weapons is still a deterrent of last resort. However, for that to be a deterrent, a British Government must be able to express their view that, ultimately and in conditions of extreme self-defence, nuclear weapons would have to be used.'[62] Three years later, he used a similar argument to justify the Trident nuclear missile system, stating that: 'The justification of Trident is as an instrument of deterrence with the possibility of its use only in the "extreme circumstances of self-defence"'.[63]

Several critiques were directed at Judge Fleischhauer's Separate Opinion. Warner argued that the Judge's interpretation skewed the 'classical legal distinction between *jus ad bellum* and *jus in bello*' by linking application of *jus in bello* with the reasons for going to war.[64] He added that Fleischhauer's Hobbesian view relied on the outdated principle of '*raison d'État*' and obliterated 'the distinction between the limitations on self-defence and the limitations within humanitarian law'.[65]

Judges Shahabuddeen, Weeramantry, Koroma, Ranjeva, Ferrari Bravo and Herczegh held that the use of nuclear weapons was categorically unlawful. Judge Koroma criticised the Court's decision for creating a new standard – that of 'state survival' – that gave rise to a different level of self-defence: one in which a state would not be bound by IHL.[66] The right to self-defence thus became limitless, with huge implications for the rights of victims of armed conflict, as well as for the security of states.

---

[60] This is in sharp contrast to the view espoused by Higgins that 'in the present case, it is the physical survival of peoples that we must constantly have in view'. See Nuclear Weapons Advisory Opinion, Dissenting Opinion of Judge Higgins, para. 41.

[61] Nuclear Weapons Advisory Opinion, Separate Opinion of Judge Fleischhauer, para. 5.

[62] Mr Hoon, MP, Response in House of Commons Debate, 29 April 2002, *Hansard*, Column 666.

[63] Mr Hoon, MP, Response in House of Commons Debate, 24 April 2005, *Hansard*, Column 1210 W, reprinted at: www.publications.parliament.uk/pa/cm200607/cmselect/cmdfence/225/225we23.htm.

[64] D. Warner, 'The Nuclear Weapons Decision by the International Court of Justice: locating the *raison* behind *raison* d'état', *Millennium – Journal of International Studies* 27(2) (1998), 299–324, at 311.

[65] *Ibid*. He further contends that the 'right' to state survival is a right that 'has never been heard of before'.

[66] Nuclear Weapons Advisory Opinion, Dissenting Opinion of Judge Koroma, p. 571.

The third interpretation, which is reflected in the opinions of Judges Guillaume, Higgins and Schwebel, is that the Court envisioned a scenario in which nuclear weapons could be used within the limits of IHL.[67] According to Judge Schwebel:

> The use of nuclear weapons is ... exceptionally difficult to reconcile with the rules of international law applicable in armed conflict ... But that is by no means to say that the use of nuclear weapons, in any and all circumstances, would necessarily and invariably conflict with those rules of international law. On the contrary, as the *dispositif* in effect acknowledges, while they might 'generally' do so, in specific cases they might not.[68]

Judge Higgins embarked on the most serious attempt to reconcile the Court's decision with the separation principle, implicitly disagreeing with Judge Schwebel's interpretation. In her Dissenting Opinion, she critiqued the 'peculiar' wording of Dispositif 2E, particularly the use of the word 'generally' in the first sentence.[69] About this statement, she writes that because the Court was unable to conclude whether the threat or use of nuclear weapons would be lawful in extreme circumstances of self-defence, all situations in which the use of nuclear weapons complied with IHL were logically excluded. In such situations of compliance, the use of nuclear weapons would be in conformity with *both* Article 51 of the UN Charter *and* IHL; the Court could not possibly have meant that it was unable to decide whether such a use would be lawful (as clearly it would). By way of logic, the Court must therefore have been referring to those 'general' circumstances in which recourse to nuclear weapons contravened IHL and whether, in such cases, 'a use of force *in extremis* and in conformity with Article 51 of the Charter, might nonetheless be regarded as lawful'.[70] The Court was unable to 'definitively' answer that question, leaving open 'the possibility that a use of nuclear weapons contrary to humanitarian law might nonetheless be lawful'.[71]

According to Judge Higgins, the Court's controversial pronouncement of a *non liquet* opened the door to interpretations that subordinated *jus in bello* to *jus ad bellum*.[72] Her solution to avoiding this controversy was to try to reconcile

---

[67] See C. Greenwood 'The Advisory Opinion on nuclear weapons and the contribution of the International Court to international humanitarian law', *International Review of the Red Cross* 316 (1997), 65–75; Greenwood, '*Jus ad bellum* and *jus in bello* in the Nuclear Weapons Advisory Opinion', 264.

[68] Nuclear Weapons Advisory Opinion, Dissenting Opinion of Vice-President Schwebel, pp. 321–2.

[69] Nuclear Weapons Advisory Opinion, Dissenting Opinion of Judge Higgins, para. 25.

[70] *Ibid.*, para. 28.   [71] *Ibid.*, para. 29.

[72] Paragraph 90 set the stage for the controversy that resulted in the pronouncement of a *non liquet* in paragraph 105 2E of the *dispositif*. The Court's pronouncement of a *non liquet* is itself a matter of much controversy. Does it imply that the conduct in question is acceptable (as per the *Lotus* principle)? According to Judge Higgins, rather than pronouncing a

the use of nuclear weapons with IHL through the principles of necessity and proportionality. According to Judge Higgins, the large-scale humanitarian suffering associated with the use of nuclear weapons ('blast, radiation, shock, together with risk of escalation, risk of spread through space and time') could meet the test of proportionality when balanced against 'the most extreme circumstances' of 'defence against untold suffering or the obliteration of a state or peoples'.[73]

Judge Higgins proceeded to state that an attack by nuclear weapons could be considered 'proportionate' if the 'military advantage' anticipated is:

> one related to the very survival of a State or the avoidance of infliction (whether by nuclear or other weapons of mass destruction) of vast and severe suffering on its own population; and that no other method of eliminating this military target be available.[74]

This can be translated into a scenario where State A has attacked (or is about to attack) State B with a nuclear weapon that would obliterate State B or its people. According to Judge Higgins, State A would, in this case, be entitled to use a nuclear weapon against State B's nuclear weapon facilities (which are a legitimate military target), provided that no other method is available. The vast destruction caused to State A's territory and population as a result of the nuclear attack would be considered proportionate to the goal of repelling State A's nuclear attack. However, it could be argued that defence against the obliteration of a state is a *jus ad bellum* rather than a *jus in bello* consideration. Introducing language related to state survival, no matter how narrow this concept is interpreted, in the *jus in bello* proportionality equation still serves to blur the distinction between the two proportionality principles under *jus ad bellum* and *jus in bello*. This is a major contemporary challenge to the separation principle in doctrine and state practice.

E.   Other contemporary challenges to the separation principle

1.   *The rise of 'conflationism' in contemporary doctrine*

The initial reaction to the Nuclear Weapons Advisory Opinion was largely critical because of the perceived threat to the separation principle. Recently, however, some doctrine has been willing to abandon the separation principle in light of contemporary state practice. A number of recent scholarly works

---

non liquet, the Court should have embraced the difficult task of weighing the competing legal claims against each other. Nuclear Weapons Advisory Opinion, Dissenting Opinion of Judge Higgins, paras. 37–40. See also Falk, 'Nuclear weapons, international law and the World Court', 66.

[73] Nuclear Weapons Advisory Opinion, Dissenting Opinion of Judge Higgins, para. 18.

[74] *Ibid.*, para. 21.

explore the theoretical underpinnings of the separation principle, its historical development and modern applications.[75] Much of this literature challenges the continued validity of the principle. Weiler and Deshman refer to ongoing debates between proponents and opponents as the 'battle zone between Separationists and Conflationists'.[76] They note that 'it was primarily the work of publicists which "made" the distinction fundamental, and it is the work of publicists which is now destabilizing it'.[77] Positioning themselves as 'neutral' in the debate, Weiler and Deshman describe the historical development of the principle and its rise and fall in response to different political contexts. While their analysis is useful to understanding the reasons behind the popularity of the 'conflationist' position at different points in time, it does not discuss the merits of that position from a legal point of view.

Orakhelashvili is a strong proponent of what he calls the 'aggressor discrimination' thesis, a modern articulation of 'just war' theory. He states that 'the argument of the separation of the two bodies of law has no sound or consistent conceptual basis in doctrine ... In practice, states often act in disregard of the thesis that an aggressor and its victim shall be treated identically'.[78] He bases his assessment on an analysis of the principles of necessity and proportionality under *jus ad bellum* and military necessity and proportionality under *jus in bello*. He argues that 'military necessity under *jus in bello* is by no means a free-standing concept, but is linked to the very cause of the relevant conflict and thus, is an emanation of the causes of war under *jus ad bellum*'.[79]

Sloane hesitatingly endorses the separation principle, decrying its 'tacit and subtle erosion', while admitting exceptions to the principle.[80] He states that the principle, which he refers to as the 'dualistic axiom', is 'logically questionable, undertheorized, and at times disregarded or misapplied in practice – with troubling consequences for the policies that underwrite these components of the contemporary law of war'.[81] According to Sloane, the rise of the nation state and positivist international law reduced the principle to the realm of ethics rather than law. He argues that this principle emerged late in the development of the 'just war' theory and never enjoyed its current 'axiomatic character'. Throughout his article, however, Sloane's position oscillates. He asserts that,

---

[75] In April 2013 the *European Journal of International Law* published the results of its Symposium on 'Just and Unjust Warriors', convened to commemorate the 35th anniversary of Michael Walzer's *Just and Unjust Wars: A Moral Argument with Historical Illustrations*, 4th edn (New York: Basic Books, 2006), which included twenty-four important contributions by leading authorities in the field. In addition, two earlier articles by Orakhelashvili and Sloane discussed the erosion of the separation principle in light of modern state practice. See Sloane, 'The cost of conflation' and A. Orakhelashvili, 'The acts of the Security Council: meanings and standards of review', *Max Planck Yearbook of International Law* (2007), 143–95.

[76] Weiler and Deshman, 'Far be it from thee to slay the righteous', 27.
[77] *Ibid.*   [78] Orakhelashvili, 'Overlap and convergence', 196.
[79] *Ibid.*, 164.   [80] Sloane, 'The cost of conflation', 53.   [81] *Ibid.*, 50.

in spite of inconsistent state practice, the separation principle constitutes customary international law[82] and 'remains indispensable to IHL in practice'.[83]
Nonetheless, he advocates a more contextual appreciation of the so-called dualistic axiom, arguing that cases of asymmetrical warfare where 'one party is an
elusive non-state belligerent like al-Qaeda or a cognate "network of networks"'
should be treated differently.[84] In such cases, exceptions should be admitted to
the principle through the development of treaty law.[85]

Sloane depends in his analysis on the principle of 'concurrent' application
of *jus ad bellum* and *jus in bello*, which he finds logically inconsistent with the
notion of separation.[86] The principle of concurrent application is based on contemporary state practice; recent developments confirm that the two bodies of
law do, in fact, apply simultaneously. Each subsequent act involving the use of
force has to be justified by reference to the principles of both *jus ad bellum* and
of *jus in bello*. State practice has therefore departed from the classical model
where the *jus ad bellum* determination was made exclusively upon initial
recourse to force. Contemporary state practice indicates that this assessment
is made repeatedly at every subsequent use of force throughout the duration of
the armed conflict, in order to ensure conformity with the principles of necessity and proportionality. Simultaneously, *jus in bello* operates throughout the
armed conflict and necessitates an assessment of each attack in relation to the
jus in bello principles of distinction, military necessity and proportionality of
expected civilian harm to the direct military advantage anticipated.

Greenwood, who is a proponent of the separation principle, implies that *jus
in bello* claims can affect our assessment of the legality of an act in relation to *jus
ad bellum*. He states that 'it is difficult to see how any use of force which violates
the humanitarian rules of *jus in bello*, for example those rules prohibiting the
use of weapons likely to cause unnecessary suffering or rules governing the
humane treatment of prisoners of war, can be regarded as reasonable measures
of self-defence'.[87] In his analysis of the Nuclear Weapons Advisory Opinion,
Greenwood also states the following:

> The Court held that although neither article 2(4) nor article 51 refers to spe-
> cific weapons, the need to ensure that a use of force in self-defence was pro-
> portionate had implications for the degree of force and, consequently, for
> the weaponry which a state might lawfully use. The proportionality require-
> ment of self-defence thus had an effect upon the legality of the way in which
> a state conducted hostilities.[88]

---

[82] *Ibid.*, 67.   [83] *Ibid.*, 55.   [84] *Ibid.*, 105.
[85] *Ibid.*, 106.   [86] *Ibid.*, 67.
[87] Greenwood, 'The relationship between *jus ad bellum* and *jus in bello*', 227. See also
Greenwood '*Jus ad bellum* and *jus in bello* in the Nuclear Weapons Advisory Opinion',
p. 258.
[88] Greenwood '*Jus ad bellum* and *jus in bello* in the Nuclear Weapons Advisory Opinion', 258.

According to this view, applying the proportionality principle under *jus ad bellum* has implications for *jus in bello*, such as the choice of weaponry. However, the concurrent application of *jus ad bellum* and *jus in bello* should not necessarily mean that *jus ad bellum* and *jus in bello* considerations must inevitably influence each other. The fact that these two bodies of law apply simultaneously does not mean that they cannot apply separately. One commentator therefore describes the concept of 'concurrent' application as 'parallel' application of *jus ad bellum* and *jus in bello*.[89] The term 'parallel application' is better capable of capturing the notion that *jus ad bellum* and *jus in bello* are separate regimes that apply simultaneously. This should not imply that the two concepts are linked or interdependent.

Recent practice in the UN Security Council has arguably contributed to undermining the classical distinction between *jus ad bellum* and *jus in bello*. A large amount of scholarly literature has been devoted to examining the limits of Security Council action and the extent to which the Security Council is bound to respect IHL[90] in light of Article 103 of the UN Charter.[91]

Some commentators have also claimed that the Security Council is not only bound by the rules of IHL, but is also bound by the limits of *jus ad bellum* (necessity and proportionality). This argument – based on the premise that Security Council authorisation is 'akin to the overall *jus ad bellum* authorization pertaining to a mission' or to the question of why force is used – is controversial.[92] The limits of necessity and proportionality in exercising self-defence find no specific expression in the UN Charter and are derived from

[89] J. Lehmann, 'All necessary means to protect civilians: what the conflict in Libya says about the relationship between the *jus in bello* and the *jus ad bellum*', *Journal of Conflict and Security Law* 17 (2012), 117–46, at 129.

[90] This debate dates back to the immediate aftermath of the establishment of the UN. There is no need to revisit this debate within the context of this chapter; however, it shall be noted that there is at least a presumption that the Security Council must act in conformity with the rules of IHL. The controversy has been partially resolved by the UN Secretary-General's promulgation in 1999 of his Bulletin on the Observance by UN Forces of IHL, see e.g. Bulletin on the Observance by United Nations Forces of International Humanitarian Law, UN doc. ST/SGB/1999/13 (1999), reprinted in 13 ILM 1656 (1999). See D. Shraga, 'UN peacekeeping operations: applicability of international humanitarian law and responsibility for operations-related damage', *American Journal of International Law* 94 (2000), 406–12.

[91] See Orakhelashvili, 'The acts of the Security Council', 149; D. Schweigman, 'The authority of the Security Council under Chapter VII of the Charter. Legal limits and the role of the International Court of Justice', *Nordic Journal of International Law* 71 (2002), 443–7; K. Okimoto, *The Distinction and Relationship between Jus ad Bellum and Jus in Bello* (Portland, OR: Hart Publishing, 2011).

[92] R. McLaughlin, 'The legal regime applicable to use of lethal force when operating under a United Nations Security Council Chapter VII mandate authorising all necessary means', *Journal of Conflict and Security Law* 12 (2008), 389–417.

the customary international law notion of an 'inherent right to self-defence' in response to an armed attack. It is therefore not entirely clear that the limits of necessity and proportionality apply to Security Council-authorised action under Chapter VII of the UN Charter.[93] However, it is much less controversial to state that the Council is bound in its action by the limits of its own mandate as set out by member states in relevant resolutions.

A recent case that raises questions about the Security Council's compliance with the principle of separation between *jus ad bellum* and *jus in bello* is the military intervention in Libya in 2011. Operative paragraph 4 of Security Council Resolution 1973 (2011), which authorised the use of force in Libya, requires member states to:

> take all necessary measures ... to *protect civilians and civilian populated areas under threat of attack* in the Libyan Arab Jamahiriya, including Benghazi, while excluding a foreign occupation force of any form on any part of Libyan territory, and requests the Member States concerned to inform the Secretary-General immediately of the measures they take pursuant to the authorization conferred by this paragraph which shall be immediately reported to the Security Council [emphasis added].

Lehmann has argued that the implementation of Resolution 1973 has undermined the separation principle. He argues that because of the perceived justness of the use of force, the states acting under the authorisation of the Security Council overstepped the limits of the mandate. The mandate of Security Council action in Libya was to 'protect civilians and civilian populated areas under threat'. The use of force should therefore have been limited to the prevention of violations of IHL or the commission of international crimes *against civilians* strictly speaking.[94]

States acting under Security Council authorisation in Libya relied, in the view of some commentators, on an unduly wide interpretation of the term 'to protect civilians and civilian populated areas under threat of attack', arguably in order to fight the regime in support of the rebels, due to the perceived justness of the *casus belli*.[95]

F.   Reaffirming the validity of the separation principle

In spite of inconsistencies in recent state practice, there is ample evidence in both treaty law and customary international law for the existence of the separation principle and its corollary, the equal application of IHL to all parties to a conflict. The conflationist position therefore represents a misapplication of the

---

[93] Lehmann, 'All necessary means to protect civilians', 132.
[94] *Ibid.*, 125.   [95] *Ibid.*, 124.

relevant law, which is often the result of an incorrect merging of the proportionality principles under *jus ad bellum* and *jus in bello*.

1. Legal foundations of the separation principle

The UN Charter makes no direct reference to the relationship between *jus ad bellum* and *jus in bello*. Common Articles 1 and 2 of the 1949 Geneva Conventions, however, state that the Conventions apply 'in all circumstances', without distinction as to the cause of conflict.[96] According to the commentary on Article 1:

> no Power bound by the Convention can offer any valid pretext, legal or other, for not respecting the Convention in all its parts. The words 'in all circumstances' mean in short that the application of the Convention does not depend on the character of the conflict. Whether a war is 'just' or 'unjust', whether it is a war of aggression or of resistance to aggression, the protection and care due to the wounded and sick are in no way affected.[97]

The 1977 Additional Protocol I similarly endorses the principle that *jus ad bellum* and *jus in bello* are distinct and confirms that compliance with IHL does not have any bearing on the assessment of the legality of a conflict in terms of *jus ad bellum*. The Preamble provides that 'nothing in this Protocol or in the Geneva Conventions of 12 August 1949 can be construed as legitimizing or authorizing any act of aggression or any other use of force inconsistent with the Charter of the United Nations'.[98] It further stipulates that:

> the provisions of the Geneva Conventions of 12 August 1949 and of this Protocol must be fully applied in all circumstances to all persons who are protected by those instruments, without any adverse distinction based on the nature or origin of the armed conflict or on the causes espoused by or attributed to the Parties to the conflict.[99]

These two provisions reaffirm the principle that application of IHL will not legitimise unlawful use of force, and its corollary: that IHL applies equally to all belligerents, without consideration as to the cause or merits of the conflict.[100]

---

[96] Geneva Convention (I) for the Amelioration of the Condition of the Wounded and Sick in Armed Forces in the Field, Geneva, 12 August 1949, in force 21 October 1950, 75 UNTS 31.

[97] International Committee of the Red Cross, *Commentary on the Geneva Conventions of 12 August 1949*, 4 vols. (Geneva: International Committee of the Red Cross, 1952), Vol. I, p. 27. Nuclear Weapons Advisory Opinion, para. 78.

[98] Additional Protocol I, Preamble.

[99] *Ibid.*

[100] See Y. Sandoz, C. Swinarski, and B. Zimmermann (eds.), *Commentary on the Additional Protocols of 8 June 1977 to the Geneva Conventions of 12 August 1949* (Geneva: ICRC/ Martinus Nijhoff, 1987), pp. 29–30.

Proponents of the separation principle also refer to Articles 4[101] and 5(5)[102] of 1977 Additional Protocol I.

Opponents of the principle, on the other hand, refer to Article 1(4) of the Protocol. According to this provision, conflicts involving peoples 'fighting against colonial domination and alien occupation and against racist regimes in the exercise of their right of self-determination' are to be considered international armed conflicts, attracting the full application of the rules of IHL. This arguably undermines the separation principle by conferring belligerent privilege on some but not all non-state actors and thereby discriminating in the application of IHL.[103] This view, however, does not reflect an accurate interpretation of Article 1(4). The effect of this provision is simply to treat wars of national liberation as international armed conflicts; the parties to these conflicts (whether 'liberation' movements or 'colonial' regimes) remain equally bound by the Geneva Conventions and 1977 Additional Protocol I.[104] It does not affect the position of non-state actors in other types of conflict, whose rights and duties are governed by the rules applicable to non-international armed conflicts.

Article 44, which is concerned with combatants and prisoners of war, further reaffirms that all belligerents in an international armed conflict, including non-state actors, are to be treated equally. Article 44(2) is based on the premise that both regular and irregular armed forces must equally respect IHL. The fact that a combatant has violated the rules of IHL does not deprive them of prisoner of war (POW) status (whether they belong to regular or irregular armed forces). This constitutes a departure from the 1907 Hague Regulations and 1949 Geneva Convention III, under which this did not apply to members of irregular forces unless they could prove that they had respected IHL. Article 44 therefore extended the basis for POW status to a larger group of irregulars. Any combatant who violates IHL is to be prosecuted under the relevant provisions of 1977 Additional Protocol I without losing his/her POW status. Simultaneously, all combatants are required to comply with the rules of IHL in their entirety. No combatant can be prosecuted for the mere act of taking up arms against the enemy.[105]

---

[101] 'The application of the Conventions and of this Protocol, as well as the conclusion of the agreements provided for therein, shall not affect the legal status of the Parties to the conflict.' According to the commentary on Article 4, however, the reference to the 'legal status' of the parties to the conflict does not directly relate to *jus ad bellum* (whether they are acting in self-defence) but rather to questions such as whether a party qualifies as a state or a 'people' fighting against colonial occupation. Sandoz *et al.*, *Commentary on the Additional Protocols of 8 June 1977*, pp. 73–4.

[102] 'In accordance with article 4, the designation and acceptance of Protecting Powers for the purpose of applying the Conventions and this Protocol shall not affect the legal status of the Parties to the conflict.'

[103] See Sloane, 'The cost of conflation', 65.

[104] See also Greenwood, 'The relationship between *jus ad bellum* and *jus in bello*', 225.

[105] See Sandoz *et al.*, *Commentary on the Additional Protocols of 8 June 1977*, pp. 526–7.

In addition to this treaty-based evidence of the separation principle, customary international law also generally supports the separation of *jus ad bellum* and *in bello*. However, international custom is not entirely consistent in this area, which has contributed to the current state of confusion surrounding the status of the principle. According to some scholars, state practice indicates that the perceived legality of a state's recourse to force has a subtle impact on its assessment of the means legitimately available to achieve its goal.[106] In fact, no state will acknowledge that it has violated *jus in bello* because of what it perceives to be the justness of its cause.[107] This may indicate that, when disregarding the separation principle, states are aware that they are breaching a legal norm (the violation does not undermine the nature of the prohibition, but rather confirms it).

With the exception of the Nuclear Weapons Advisory Opinion, the ICJ's jurisprudence has clearly dealt with *jus ad bellum* and *jus in bello* as two separate legal regimes. The Court has had the opportunity to examine questions related to both bodies of law in a number of cases, including the *Corfu Channel* case, the *Nicaragua* case,[108] the Nuclear Weapons Advisory Opinion (discussed above), the *Oil Platforms* case, the *Congo/Uganda* case and the *Advisory Opinion on the Legality of the Wall*.[109]

In the *Oil Platforms* case and the Wall Advisory Opinion the Court focused on the legality of the initial recourse to force. The Court's finding implies that once the initial use of force was found to have been illegal, there was no need to examine issues of *ad bellum* proportionality throughout the rest of the conflict. This position has been criticised for purportedly marginalising proportionality analysis under *jus ad bellum*.[110]

2.   *Clarifying concepts: proportionality under* jus ad bellum *as distinct from proportionality under* jus in bello

In a comprehensive analysis of the different applications of proportionality under *jus ad bellum* and *jus in bello*, Gardam notes that in spite of concern about the limits of proportionality, legal commentators have not adequately addressed the relationship between its two aspects.[111] The difference between the two proportionality principles can briefly be described as follows: whereas

---

[106]   Gardam, 'Proportionality and force in international law', 393.

[107]   *Ibid.*, 66–7.

[108]   ICJ, *Military and Paramilitary activities in and against Nicaragua* (*Nicaragua* v. *United States of America*), Judgment of 27 June 1986, para. 194.

[109]   See Orakhelashvili, 'Overlap and convergence', 168.

[110]   Sloane, 'The cost of conflation', 86–7. Sloane argues that the Court's failure to examine *in bello* proportionality in the Wall Advisory Opinion denies the analytical independence of *jus ad bellum* and *jus in bello*.

[111]   Gardam, 'Proportionality and force in international law', 392.

under *jus ad bellum* proportionality limits the overall force that can be used to respond to an unlawful use of force, under *jus in bello* it seeks to weigh the anticipated military advantage of a particular attack against the expected civilian harm.[112] The proportionality equation in each of the two bodies of law is based on a different logic. According to Cannizzaro, whereas:

> the legal regulation of the use of force is based on a superior right of the attacked state in regard to the attacker, the legal regulation of the means and methods of warfare is dominated by the principle of the parity of the belligerents and by the concomitant principle of the respect owed by each of them to interests and values of a humanitarian nature.[113]

The difference in the normative values underlying *jus ad bellum* and *jus in bello*, with their associated different standards of legality, accounts for the different structure of the two proportionality principles. Although this distinction may be apparent in theory, in practice the two different proportionality principles are often merged.[114]

Proportionality under *jus ad bellum*

As noted above, necessity and proportionality under *jus ad bellum* derive from customary international law, namely from the notion of 'inherent right of self-defence' against an armed attack, preserved in Article 51 of the UN Charter.[115] Gardam asserts that the proportionality requirement under *jus ad bellum* has no humanitarian content. It relates exclusively to limitations on the damage that may be inflicted on the territory of a state and that of third states.[116] Under *jus ad bellum*, an attack is lawful if it is proportionate to overall goals such as subordinating the enemy or repelling an attack. No more force can be used than that strictly required to achieve that objective.[117] If applied as a principle of limitation, the practical end result of applying *jus ad bellum* proportionality will be to affect the degree of force used and hence the degree of suffering inflicted upon belligerents. It will therefore result in greater protection for the victims of armed conflict. However, this should be distinguished from the notion that proportionality under *jus ad bellum* is synonymous with, or has as its objective, humanitarian considerations.

---

[112] *Ibid.*, 391. See also Akande, 'Nuclear weapons, unclear law?', 191.

[113] Cannizzaro, 'Contextualising proportionality', 782.   [114] *Ibid.*, 781.

[115] ICJ, *Military and Paramilitary activities in and against Nicaragua* (*Nicaragua* v. *United States of America*), Judgment of 27 June 1986, paras. 94, 194; Nuclear Weapons Advisory Opinion, para. 41; J. Crawford, *Brownlie's Principles*, 8th edn (Oxford University Press, 2012), p. 748; C. Gray, *International Law and the Use of Force*, 3rd edn (Oxford University Press, 2008), pp. 171–3.

[116] J. Gardam, 'Necessity and proportionality in *jus ad bellum* and *jus in bello*' in L. Boisson de Chazournes and P. Sands (eds.), *International Law, the ICJ and Nuclear Weapons* (Cambridge University Press, 1999), p. 277.

[117] Akande, 'Nuclear weapons, unclear law?', 191.

As noted above, the requirement of proportionality in a *jus ad bellum* context limits the degree of force a state can lawfully use. Proportionality remains relevant throughout the whole of the conflict. Arguably, a state may not assess proportionality when determining the legality of its initial recourse to force only to dispense with it completely afterwards.[118]

One of the factors contributing to the complexity of proportionality analysis is that the question of 'proportionate to what' remains unresolved in international law doctrine. Since detailed analysis of this controversial issue is outside the scope of this chapter (see Chapter 1), it suffices to mention a few brief points. It is generally recognised that under *jus ad bellum* there are two types of proportionality analysis. In the first type of proportionality analysis (known as backward-looking proportionality) the proportionality of an attack is measured against the scale of the attack suffered. Proportionality therefore 'requires that the size, duration, and target of the response correspond to the attack' suffered.[119] It takes into consideration 'the scale of the action, the type of weaponry, and the magnitude of the damage'.[120] In the *Oil Platforms* case, the ICJ applied backward-looking proportionality to reach the conclusion that the US attacks against Iranian Oil Platforms did not amount to a proportionate use of force in self-defence.[121]

In the case of forward-looking proportionality, which measures the proportionality of the attack against the objective of the resort to force (the *casus belli*), proportionality analysis may depart from an 'exact correspondence' with the aggressive attack.[122] According to one view, the proportionality equation changes throughout the conflict, such that the initial use of force should be proportionate to the injury suffered, whereas subsequent uses of force throughout the conflict should be proportionate to the aims to be legitimately achieved.[123] Because of the indeterminacy of the principle of proportionality, it is a term that easily lends itself to confusion and abuse.[124]

Proportionality under *jus in bello*

The proportionality principle under *jus in bello* is based on a different structure and logic. It is based on the principle that attacks that may be expected to

[118] Gardam, 'Proportionality and force in international law', 404.

[119] Crawford, *Brownlie's Principles*, p. 749. See also Gray, *International Law and the Use of Force*, pp. 148–56.

[120] Cannizzaro, 'Contextualising proportionality', 783. See also Nuclear Weapons Advisory Opinion, Dissenting Opinion of Judge Higgins, para. 5.

[121] ICJ, *Oil Platforms (Islamic Republic of Iran v. United States of America)*, Judgment of 6 November 2003, pp. 198–9.

[122] Cannizzaro, 'Contextualising proportionality', 783–4.

[123] Sloane, 'The cost of conflation', 68; R. Higgins, *Problems and Process: International Law and How We Use It* (Oxford University Press, 1994), p. 231.

[124] However, it is possible that this infinite flexibility is both a strength and a weakness. See Gardam, 'Proportionality and force in international law', 412.

cause excessive harm to civilians are prohibited. According to Article 51(5)(b) of 1977 Additional Protocol I, and also reflected in Rule 14 of the ICRC study on Customary International Humanitarian Law:

> Launching an attack which may be expected to cause incidental loss of civilian life, injury to civilians, damage to civilian objects, or a combination thereof, which would be excessive in relation to the concrete and direct military advantage anticipated, is prohibited.[125]

Assessing proportionality under *jus in bello* entails balancing the harm expected to be caused by an attack – in terms of injury to civilians and/or damage to civilian objects – against the anticipated concrete and direct military advantage anticipated by the attack.[126] It is measured by reference to the aims of each military attack, rather than the ultimate goals of the broader military action.[127]

The proportionality analysis under *jus in bello* may render illegal an attack against an otherwise legitimate military target if the harm caused to civilians and their property is expected to be excessive in relation to the expected military advantage. Nonetheless, proportionality 'does not entirely preclude an attack simply because it would result in civilian casualties; it merely requires the anticipated military advantage to outweigh the anticipated civilian casualties'.[128] No consideration is given to the overall goal of the military action, even if it is self-defence against unlawful aggression that threatens to obliterate the state.

Although the proportionality equations under *jus ad bellum* and *jus in bello* are based on different rationales, in practice the two proportionality principles are sometimes merged. This is unfortunate. The 'concrete and direct military advantage', which constitutes the yardstick in the *jus in bello* proportionality equation, 'should never be confused with, or allowed to collapse back into, the ultimate *casus belli* of a party'.[129] The separation principle thus removes the assessment of *jus in bello* proportionality from the politicised objectives of *jus ad bellum* judgments. In other words, it attempts to 'halt the slippery slope from "concrete and direct military advantage" to "victory" '.[130]

---

[125] J.-M. Henckaerts and L. Doswald-Beck, *Customary International Humanitarian Law*, 3 vols. (Cambridge University Press, 2005), Vol. I, p. 46 (hereafter, Customary IHL Study).

[126] Akande, 'Nuclear weapons, unclear law?', 208.

[127] However, what constitutes an attack is disputed among states. In adhering to the Protocol, for instance, the United Kingdom stated, inter alia, that: '(i) Re: Article 51 and Article 57 In the view of the United Kingdom, the military advantage anticipated from an attack is intended to refer to the advantage anticipated from the attack considered as a whole and not only from isolated or particular parts of the attack.' United Kingdom, Declaration of 2 July 2002, Additional Protocol I, available at: www.icrc.org/ihl/NORM/0A9E03F0F2EE75 7CC1256402003FB6D2?OpenDocument. According to the ICRC Customary IHL Study, it may also include considerations related to the safety of the attacking forces. Customary IHL Study, p. 50.

[128] Bengs, 'Legal constraints on the use of a tactical nuclear weapon', 368.

[129] Sloane, 'The cost of conflation', 75.   [130] *Ibid.*, 76.

3. Contribution of international criminal law to the separation principle

The case law of the International Military Tribunal (IMT) confirms both the principle of separation of *jus ad bellum* and *jus in bello*, as well as the principle of 'equal application' of IHL.[131] This is established in the Court's decision in the Justice trial,[132] the Hostages trial,[133] the *High Command* case,[134] and *re Krupp*,[135] in spite of the prosecution's repeated attempts to argue that Germany, as an aggressor, was not entitled to benefit from the laws of war. A number of post-1945 domestic trials in the Netherlands, Germany and Denmark also confirmed this approach (*re Christiansen, re Rauter* and *re Gabre*).[136]

Recently, international criminal law has also confirmed the separation of *jus ad bellum* and *jus in bello*, particularly in areas where the criminal defence of 'self-defence' may be confused with a *jus ad bellum* argument of self-defence. The Rome Statute of the International Criminal Court clearly stipulates in Article 31(3)(c) that 'the fact that the person was involved in a defensive operation conducted by forces shall not in itself constitute a ground for excluding criminal responsibility'.[137]

The International Criminal Tribunal for the former Yugoslavia (ICTY) has affirmed the principles of 'separation' and 'equal application' in both the Appeal Chambers judgments in *Kordić and Čerkez*,[138] as well as in the final Report to

---

[131] Moussa 'Can *jus ad bellum* override *jus in bello*?', 981–5; Orakhelashvili, 'Overlap and convergence', 167.

[132] *United States of America* v. *Alstotter et al.*, Law Reports of Trials of War Criminals, Vol. VI, United Nations War Crimes Commission, London, 1947–49, p. 52.

[133] *United States of America* v. *William List et al.* (*Case No. 7*), Trials of War Criminals before the Nuremberg Military Tribunals, Vol. XI, 1950, p. 1247.

[134] *United States of America* v. *Wilhelm von Leeb et al.*, Law Reports of Trials of War Criminals, Vol. XII, Judgment of 27 October 1948, p. 124.

[135] *United States of America* v. *Krupp et al.* (*Case no. 10*), Trials of War Criminals before the Nuremberg Military Tribunals, Vol. IX, Judgment of 31 July 1948, pp. 1338–46.

[136] Orakhelashvili, 'Overlap and convergence', 169–70. Although there were a few exceptions to this approach, these were generally based on an erroneous confusion of the terms 'military necessity' and 'self-defence' rather than a denial or misapplication of the 'separation' principle. See *United States of America* v. *Weizsacker et al.* (The Ministries Trial), Trials of War Criminals before the Nuremberg Military Tribunals, Vol. XIV, Judgment of 11 April 1949. 'Military necessity' under *jus in bello* is not the same as 'necessity' under *jus ad bellum*. Under the latter, the principle of necessity means that 'the defending state must have no other option in the circumstances than to act in forceful self-defence'. In other words, it precludes any unnecessary use of force by requiring a justification for a state's initial resort to military force. Under IHL, on the other hand, military necessity is (according to some interpretations) intended to prevent needless death and destruction in an otherwise valid armed conflict.

[137] Rome Statute of the International Criminal Court, Rome 17 July 1998, in force 1 July 2002, 2187 UNTS 90, Art. 31(3)(c).

[138] ICTY, *Prosecutor* v. *Kordić and Čerkez*, Judgment (Trial Chamber) (Case No. IT-95-14/2-T), 26 February 2001, paras. 448–52; ICTY, *Prosecutor* v. *Kordić and Čerkez*, Judgment (Appeals Chamber) (Case No. IT-95-14/2-A), 17 December 2004, paras. 835–8.

the Prosecutor of the Committee Established to Review the NATO Bombing Campaign against the Federal Republic of Yugoslavia.[139] More recently, the Appeals Chamber of the Special Court for Sierra Leone overturned the Trial Court's decision to mitigate the sentences of Civil Defence Forces fighters because they were engaged in a 'legitimate war' to protect the government against the rebels.[140]

4. *State responsibility and the reaffirmation of the separation principle*

Further support for the separation of *jus ad bellum* and *in bello* can be found in the law of state responsibility. The 2001 Articles on the Responsibility of States for Internationally Wrongful Acts (2001 Articles on State Responsibility) indicate that international humanitarian law may not be subordinated to *jus ad bellum*. Although both necessity and self-defence are circumstances precluding wrongfulness under the 2001 Articles on State Responsibility, the Commentary clearly establishes that they may not be relied on to justify violations of IHL. According to Article 21, 'the wrongfulness of an act of state is precluded if the act constitutes a lawful measure of self-defence taken in conformity with the Charter of the United Nations'.[141] This might imply that a state acting in self-defence may not be held liable for violations of IHL. However, the accompanying Commentary by the International Law Commission clearly states that self-defence may not preclude the wrongfulness of violations of IHL and that a state acting in self-defence is 'totally restrained' by international obligations limiting conduct in armed conflict.[142] It further notes that self-defence must be exercised 'in conformity with the Charter of the United Nations'. Article 21 is intended to preclude the wrongfulness of the 'non-performance of certain obligations under Article 2(4)'. In other words, a state is justified in resorting to the threat or use of force (i.e. suspending Article 2(4) of the Charter) provided that it is itself responding to a breach of that provision.[143]

However, in the Nuclear Weapons Advisory Opinion, the ICJ referred to 'extreme circumstances' of self-defence. Is it possible that such a category exists, which falls under another provision of the 2001 Articles on State Responsibility? A likely candidate would be the principle of necessity (Article 25). Unlike self-defence, necessity 'does not presuppose a wrongful act on the

---

[139] 'Final report to the prosecutor' in A. Klip and G. Sluiter (eds.), *Annotated Leading Cases of International Criminal Tribunals* (Oxford: Intersentia, 2003), p. 21.

[140] *Prosecutor* v. *Fofana and Kondewa*, Judgment (Case No. SCSL-04-14-A), 28 May 2008. See also Blank, 'A new twist on an old story', 709.

[141] J. Crawford, *The International Law Commission's Articles on State Responsibility* (Cambridge University Press, 2002), p. 166.

[142] *Ibid.*, p. 167.   [143] *Ibid.*, p. 166.

part of the other State'.[144] According to Article 25, necessity may not be invoked unless the act in question:

(a) is the only way for the State to safeguard an essential interest against a grave and imminent peril; and
(b) does not seriously impair an essential interest of the State or States towards which the obligation exists, or of the international community as a whole.[145]

The negative wording of this Article highlights the exceptional nature of the plea. The ICJ has affirmed that this provision reflects customary international law.[146]

Necessity can also arise in a different context, namely as a pretext, in and of itself, for violating IHL. Defendants in war crimes trials attempt to rely on the pleas of necessity and military necessity to justify violations of IHL.[147] However, Article 25 of the 2001 Articles on State Responsibility does not cover the doctrine of military necessity. Rather, this doctrine is taken into account in the formulation of obligations under humanitarian law treaties, some of which 'expressly exclude reliance on military necessity'.[148] The concept of military necessity cannot justify violations of IHL, since the purpose of IHL is to balance the narrow interests of a belligerent with the higher interest of the dictates of humanity. States adopted IHL rules in complete awareness that they were restraining themselves from complete freedom of action in conducting warfare. According to Crawford, military necessity should be seen as a limitation on the conduct of belligerents, as it prevents them from engaging in any act that is not strictly necessary to achieving the military advantage anticipated. Its effect is one of 'non-necessity'; it is a circumstance that precludes the *lawfulness* of conduct normally allowed.[149] Attempts to widen the concept of military necessity or invoke a right of self-preservation to justify violations of IHL can therefore have no basis in the existing framework of the law of armed conflict.

---

[144] Kohen, 'The notion of state survival in international law', p. 307.
[145] International Law Commission (ILC), Draft Articles on Responsibility of States for Internationally Wrongful Acts, with commentaries, 2001, text adopted by the International Law Commission at its fifty-third session, in 2001, and submitted to the General Assembly as a part of the Commission's report covering the work of that session (A/56/10), Art. 25.
[146] ICJ, *Gabčíkovo-Nagymaros Project* (*Hungary/Slovakia*), Judgment of 25 September 1997, paras. 51–2.
[147] For a historical discussion of the distinction between military necessity, necessity as a criminal defence and necessity as a situation precluding the wrongfulness of a state, see Weidenbaum, 'Necessity in international law', 113.
[148] Crawford, *The International Law Commission's Articles on State Responsibility*, p. 185.
[149] International Law Commission (ILC), 'Commentary to Article 33 (Necessity) of 1996 Draft Articles on State Responsibility', in *ILC Annual Report* (1996), para. 27.

Conclusion

This chapter has examined the question of whether the legitimacy of an *ad bellum* cause may ever justify the use of nuclear weapons in violation of *jus in bello*. The question of whether the separation principle remains valid is central to this assessment. Although the debate on the validity of the separation principle is largely doctrinal, it also has important practical implications, particularly in relation to the use of nuclear weapons. This chapter argues that although state practice in some cases has disregarded the separation principle, this can be considered a departure from relevant treaty law and customary international law, as confirmed by international criminal courts and tribunals and the 2001 Articles on State Responsibility.

The 'conflationist' position, which seeks to subordinate *jus in bello* to *jus ad bellum*, is based on an incorrect understanding of the law. In practical (and legal) terms, IHL would disintegrate as a result of linking its application to the perceived lawfulness of the *ad bellum* use of force. Moreover, the 'conflationist' view appears to be linked in particular to an incorrect understanding of the two aspects of proportionality analysis under each of the two branches of international law. The application of the proportionality principle under *jus ad bellum* is intended to limit the degree of damage that can be inflicted on the enemy. Conflating the two proportionality principles in such a manner transforms it from a principle of limitation to one that can be invoked to justify a degree of injury and destruction that would otherwise be considered clearly excessive in the proportionality equation under *jus in bello*. Neither treaty law nor customary international law supports such a proposition, which is why justifying the use of nuclear weapons in a manner that violates IHL cannot be considered consistent with international law.

PART II

Nuclear weapons and international humanitarian law

4

The use of nuclear weapons under rules governing the conduct of hostilities

STUART CASEY-MASLEN

Introduction

This chapter focuses on the legality of the use of nuclear weapons under three core rules of international humanitarian law (IHL): distinction, proportionality and precautions in attacks. The International Court of Justice (ICJ)'s Nuclear Weapons Advisory Opinion, issued in 1996,[1] is naturally a primary frame of reference. Given, however, that the Court did not discuss either proportionality or precautions in attacks, and that its assessment of distinction was limited to international armed conflict, discussion in this chapter is not restricted to the Court's assessment of the application of IHL.

The chapter opens with a review of the fundamental principle whereby parties to an armed conflict do not have an 'unlimited right' to select and use means or methods of warfare. It then looks in turn at the IHL rules of distinction, proportionality and precautions in attack, considering their particular relevance for, and application to, the use of nuclear weapons.

A. Limitations on the choice of means and methods of warfare

Upon ratifying 1977 Additional Protocol I,[2] France and the United Kingdom each lodged reservations to the effect that they understood the new rules governing the conduct of hostilities introduced by the Protocol, and which do not form part of the corpus of customary international law today, not to apply to nuclear weapons.[3] For the purposes of this chapter, these reservations are not

---

[1] International Court of Justice (ICJ), *Legality of the Threat or Use of Nuclear Weapons*, Advisory Opinion of 8 July 1996 (hereafter, Nuclear Weapons Advisory Opinion).

[2] Protocol Additional to the Geneva Conventions of 12 August 1949, and relating to the Protection of Victims of International Armed Conflicts (Protocol I), Geneva, 8 June 1977, in force 7 December 1978 (hereafter, 1977 Additional Protocol I).

[3] UK, Reservation to 1977 Additional Protocol I, 28 January 1998, para. (a) ('It continues to be the understanding of the United Kingdom that the rules introduced by the Protocol apply exclusively to conventional weapons without prejudice to any other rules of international law applicable to other types of weapons. In particular, the rules so introduced do not have any effect on and do not regulate or prohibit the use of nuclear weapons'); France, Reservation to 1977 Additional Protocol I, 11 April 2001, para. 2.

relevant, as the principles discussed herein are rules of customary international humanitarian law binding upon all states and are therefore not among the 'new rules' of the Protocol to which France and the UK objected.

The principle whereby parties to an armed conflict are restricted by international law in the weapons they may use, as well as the way they may lawfully use them, is long-standing. Already in 1880 the Oxford Manual of the Laws of War on Land observed that the laws of war 'do not recognize in belligerents an unlimited liberty as to the means of injuring the enemy'.[4] This principle was reiterated in the Regulations annexed to 1907 Hague Convention IV (hereafter, the 1907 Hague Regulations) as follows: 'The right of belligerents to adopt means of injuring the enemy is not unlimited.'[5] In 1977 Additional Protocol I it was stipulated in Article 35 (Means and Methods of Warfare – Basic Rules) that:

> In any armed conflict, the right of the Parties to the conflict to choose methods or means of warfare is not unlimited.[6]

The substance of the principle is believed to be declaratory of customary international law.[7] Indeed, in its Nuclear Weapons Advisory Opinion, the ICJ

[4] Article 4, The Laws of War on Land, adopted by the Institute of International Law, Oxford, 9 September 1880. See, e.g., D. Schindler and J. Toman, *The Laws of Armed Conflicts* (Dordrecht: Martinus Nijhoff, 1988), p. 25.

[5] Article 22, Annex to Convention (IV) respecting the Laws and Customs of War on Land: Regulations Concerning the Laws and Customs of War on Land, The Hague, 18 October 1907, in force 26 January 1910, 187 CTS 227; 1 Bevans 631. The Nuremberg International Military Tribunal found in 1945 that the humanitarian rules included in the 1907 Hague Regulations 'were recognized by all civilized nations and were regarded as being declaratory of the laws and customs of war'. Trial of the Major War Criminals, 14 November 1945–1 October 1946, Nuremberg, 1947, Vol. I, p. 254, cited by the ICJ in its Nuclear Weapons Advisory Opinion, para. 80.

[6] 1977 Additional Protocol I, Art. 35(1).

[7] If not necessarily its exact formulation in 1977 Additional Protocol I (as opposed to the 1907 Hague Regulations). See, e.g., Maj. S. Condron (ed.), *Operational Law Handbook 2011* (Charlottesville: International and Operational Law Department, The Judge Advocate General's Legal Center and School, 2011), Chapter 2, p. 17 (hereafter, US Operational Law Handbook); UK Ministry of Defence, *The Manual of the Law of Armed Conflict* (Oxford University Press, 2004), paras. 2.1 and 6.1.1 (hereafter, UK Manual of the Law of Armed Conflict). According to the US Department of the Navy, 'it is a fundamental tenet of the law of armed conflict that the right of nations engaged in an armed conflict to choose methods or means of warfare is not unlimited.' US Department of the Navy, *The Commander's Handbook on the Law of Naval Operations*, NWP 1-14M, 2007, para. 9.1, available at: www.usnwc.edu/getattachment/a9b8e92d-2c8d-4779-9925-0defea93325c/1-14M_(Jul_2007)_ (NWP). The preamble to the 1980 Convention on Prohibitions or Restrictions on the Use of Certain Conventional Weapons which May Be Deemed to Be Excessively Injurious or to Have Indiscriminate Effects ('Convention on Certain Conventional Weapons'), Geneva, 10 October 1980, in force 2 December 1983, 1342 UNTS 137 (hereafter, the 1980 Convention on Certain Conventional Weapons) includes a preambular paragraph that provides that, in their agreement, states parties were '[b]asing themselves on the principle of international law that the right of the parties to an armed conflict to choose methods or means of warfare

reiterated that states 'do not have unlimited freedom of choice of means in the weapons they use'. Surprisingly, however, the Court applied the principle only to the rule whereby it is prohibited to cause unnecessary suffering to combatants.[8] With all due respect to the Court, there is no evidence to indicate that the principle is so limited.[9]

According to its commentary on 1977 Additional Protocol I, the International Committee of the Red Cross (ICRC) affirmed that the provision 'implies principally the obligation to respect the rules of international law applicable in case of armed conflict ... Military necessity cannot justify any derogation from rules which are drafted in a peremptory manner ... The Protocol does not impose a specific prohibition on any specific weapon.'[10] So while the provision does not prohibit any 'means of warfare' (i.e. any weapon) per se, it does insist that fundamental rules and prohibitions of IHL cannot be overridden by perceived military necessity. This is potentially relevant for the selection and use of nuclear weapons.[11]

There is, though, no requirement under IHL that each weapon be specifically 'authorised' for its use to be lawful; use will only be unlawful when, and to the extent that, it is prohibited by an applicable conventional or customary rule.[12]

---

is not unlimited'. This 'principle' was similarly formulated in the preamble of the Convention on the Prohibition of the Use, Stockpiling, Production and Transfer of Anti-Personnel Mines and on Their Destruction, Oslo, 18 September 1997, in force 1 March 1999, 2056 UNTS 211 (hereafter, the 1997 Anti-Personnel Mine Ban Convention). Although not expressly stipulated in these sources, the principle may also reasonably be considered applicable in armed conflicts of a non-international character (NIAC). Somewhat surprisingly, however, the study by the International Committee of the Red Cross (ICRC) of customary international humanitarian law – J.-M. Henckaerts and L. Doswald-Beck, *Customary International Humanitarian Law*, 3 vols. (Cambridge University Press, 2005) (hereafter, ICRC Study of Customary IHL) – did not reflect this principle directly in the 161 rules it deduced from state practice.

[8] Nuclear Weapons Advisory Opinion, para. 78.

[9] See generally Chapter 5 in this work, and also, e.g., Lt.-Col. M. N. Schmitt, 'The International Court of Justice and the use of nuclear weapons', *Naval War College Review* LI(2) (Spring 1998), 92–116, at 103.

[10] Y. Sandoz, C. Swinarski, and B. Zimmermann (eds.), *Commentary on the Additional Protocols of 8 June 1977 to the Geneva Conventions of 12 August 1949* (Geneva: ICRC/ Martinus Nijhoff, 1987), paras. 1404, 1405.

[11] See, e.g., C. Greenwood, '*Jus ad bellum* and *jus in bello* in the *Nuclear Weapons* Advisory Opinion' in L. Boisson de Chazournes and P. Sands (eds.), *International Law, the ICJ and Nuclear Weapons* (Cambridge University Press, 1999), pp. 263–4. Greenwood rejects an interpretation of the Court's dispositive whereby state survival would justify use of nuclear weapons in violation of IHL, arguing that the Court saw the extreme situation as a cumulative not alternative legal requirement, on the basis that it would have to satisfy necessity and proportionality requirements under *jus ad bellum*. *Ibid.*, p. 264.

[12] See, e.g., Schmitt, 'The International Court of Justice and the use of nuclear weapons', 100; Greenwood, '*Jus ad bellum* and *jus in bello* in the *Nuclear Weapons* Advisory Opinion', p. 251. As Dinstein observes, unlike biological and chemical weapons, nuclear weapons are

As the ICRC commentary on 1977 Additional Protocol I states, 'prohibitions are those of customary law, or are contained in other international agreements'.[13]

In its Written Statement to the ICJ for its Nuclear Weapons Advisory Opinion, the UK stated that:

> While that principle is undoubtedly well established as part of custom-ary international law, however, it cannot stand alone as a prohibition of a particular category of weapons. In any event, there is no incompatibility between the two propositions (i) that States do not have an unlimited choice of the methods and means of warfare and (ii) that States may use nuclear weapons where this is consistent with their right of self-defence. There is no suggestion that self-defence is 'unlimited'. On the contrary, self-defence is always limited to the necessities of the case.[14]

The UK's mixing of *jus ad bellum* and *jus in bello* is unfortunate.[15] The issue is not whether nuclear weapons may or may not be used in self-defence per se, but whether their use would be legal or illegal under the law applicable in armed conflict. A state's inherent right to self-defence cannot override IHL rules. Indeed, although the Russian Federation did not discuss in detail the application of customary international humanitarian law to nuclear weapons, in its Written Statement to the ICJ it noted that use must occur 'within the framework of limitations imposed by humanitarian law with respect to means and methods of conducting military activities', and affirmed that the relevant limitations were 'under customary rather than treaty law'.[16] The Netherlands' Written Statement to the ICJ, which concluded that the use of nuclear weapons was lawful in certain circumstances, similarly affirmed the application of 'gen-eral principles' of IHL to nuclear weapons, including 'the principle laid down in Article 22 of the 1907 Hague Regulations that the right of a belligerent to adopt means of injuring the enemy is not unlimited'.[17]

---

not subject to any treaty ban on their use. Y. Dinstein, *The Conduct of Hostilities under the Law of International Armed Conflict*, 2nd edn (Cambridge University Press, 2010), p. 83. Any prohibition must therefore be sought in applicable customary law. See also Nuclear Weapons Advisory Opinion, para. 105.

[13] Sandoz *et al.*, *Commentary on the Additional Protocols of 8 June 1997*, para. 1408.

[14] Written Statement of the UK, Nuclear Weapons Advisory Opinion, June 1995, p. 47.

[15] See, further, Chapter 3 of the present book.

[16] Written Statement of the Russian Federation, Nuclear Weapons Advisory Opinion, Moscow, 16 June 1995, p. 18.

[17] 'The applicability of general principles of international humanitarian law in armed con-flict – among which must also be counted the principle laid down in Article 22 of the 1907 Hague Regulations that the right of a belligerent to adopt means of injuring the enemy is not unlimited – to the use of nuclear weapons was also confirmed as long ago as 1965 in Resolution XXVIII of the 20th International Conference of the Red Cross (Vienna) which was passed unanimously. Consensus on this point was also reached at the diplomatic con-ference on Additional Protocol I to the 1949 Geneva Conventions.' Written Statement of the Netherlands, Nuclear Weapons Advisory Opinion, 16 June 1995, p. 13.

In 2010, at the Review Conference of the Nuclear Non-Proliferation Treaty, states parties reaffirmed in the Final Document 'the need for all States at all times to comply with applicable international law, including international humanitarian law'.[18]

B. The rule of distinction

It is a fundamental rule of IHL that parties to a conflict must direct attacks only against lawful military objectives (whether military personnel or objects of concrete military value).[19] Its formulation as a 'basic rule' affording 'general protection' to the civilian population against the effects of hostilities in international armed conflict is set out as follows in 1977 Additional Protocol I:

> In order to ensure respect for and protection of the civilian population and civilian objects, the Parties to the conflict shall at all times distinguish between the civilian population and combatants and between civilian objects and military objectives and accordingly shall direct their operations only against military objectives.[20]

The rule of distinction – sometimes referred to as a principle either of distinction or of discrimination[21] – is declaratory of customary international law,[22]

---

[18] 2010 Review Conference of the Parties to the Treaty on the Non-Proliferation of Nuclear Weapons, Final Document, Vol. I, UN doc. NPT/CONF.2010/50 (Vol. I), New York, p. 19, available at: www.un.org/ga/search/view_doc.asp?symbol=NPT/CONF.2010/50%20(VOL.I).

[19] Military objectives – in so far as objects are concerned – are defined in 1977 Additional Protocol I as being 'limited to those objects which by their nature, location, purpose or use make an effective contribution to military action and whose total or partial destruction, capture or neutralization, in the circumstances ruling at the time, offers a definite military advantage.' 1977 Additional Protocol I, Art. 52(2).

[20] 1977 Additional Protocol I, Art. 48.

[21] The United States treats the terms as synonyms: see US Operational Law Handbook, Chapter 2, p. 11; US Department of the Air Force, *The Military Commander and the Law*, Updated August 2012, pp. 667–8, available at: www.afjag.af.mil/shared/media/document/AFD-120828-043.pdf; Joint Chiefs of Staff, *Joint Targeting*, Joint Publication 3–60, 13 April 2007, Appendix E, para. E2, available at: www.aclu.org/files/dronefoia/dod/drone_dod_jp3_60.pdf. In its 2006 doctrine on targeting, the US Department of the Air Force states that the principle of distinction (discrimination) 'requires parties to direct operations only against combatants and military objectives. It prohibits "indiscriminate attacks"'. US Department of the Air Force, *Targeting, Air Force Doctrine Document 2-1.9*, 8 June 2006, p. 90, available at: www.globalsecurity.org/military/library/policy/usaf/afdd/2-1-9/afdd2-1-9.pdf. Stefan Oeter refers to 'the principle of distinction between combatants and civilians and the corresponding prohibition of indiscriminate warfare'. S. Oeter, 'Methods and means of combat' in D. Fleck (ed.), *The Handbook of International Humanitarian Law*, 2nd edn (Oxford University Press, 2008), p. 163, and see also p. 168.

[22] See, inter alia, US Operational Law Handbook, Chapter 2, p. 11; UK Manual of the Law of Armed Conflict, paras. 2.5, 2.5.1; Sweden, *International Humanitarian Law in Armed Conflict* (Stockholm: Swedish Ministry of Defence, 1991), para. 29; preambles to both the

and is applicable in armed conflicts of a non-international character (NIACs)[23] as well as in international armed conflicts (IACs).[24] There is also a strong case to be made that the rule of distinction, the most fundamental of all IHL rules, is a peremptory norm[25] of international law.[26]

1. *Indiscriminate weapons*

Given the rule of distinction that governs all 'attacks' in an armed conflict (i.e. all military operations whether offensive or defensive in nature),[27] it is both

1980 Convention on Certain Conventional Weapons and the 1997 Anti-Personnel Mine Ban Convention. See also Dinstein, *The Conduct of Hostilities under the Law of International Armed Conflict*, p. 89; L. C. Green, *The Contemporary Law of Armed Conflict*, 3rd edn (Melland Schill Studies in International Law, Manchester University Press, 2008), p. 149; Schmitt, 'The International Court of Justice and the use of nuclear weapons'; and G. D. Solis, *The Law of Armed Conflict: International Humanitarian Law in War* (New York: Cambridge University Press, 2010), Section 7.1, pp. 251ff. According to Solis, distinction 'is the most significant concept a combatant must observe'. *Ibid.*, p. 251. As Michael Schmitt noted with respect to the Nuclear Weapons Advisory Opinion: 'That the principles of distinction and unnecessary suffering had become customary law was not controverted in any of the states' submissions.' Schmitt, 'The International Court of Justice and the use of nuclear weapons', p. 104.

23 See, inter alia, Article 13 of Protocol Additional to the Geneva Conventions of 12 August 1949, and relating to the Protection of Victims of Non-International Armed Conflicts (Protocol II), Geneva, 8 June 1977, in force 7 December 1978 (hereafter, 1977 Additional Protocol II).

24 According to the ICRC Study of Customary IHL, Rule 1 provides that: 'The parties to the conflict must at all times distinguish between civilians and combatants. Attacks may only be directed against combatants. Attacks must not be directed against civilians.' Available at: www.icrc.org/customary-ihl/eng/docs/v1_rul_rule1. The ICRC asserts that state practice establishes this rule as a norm of customary international law applicable in both IACs and NIACs. This is not controversial.

25 The existence of norms of *jus cogens* – peremptory norms under international law from which no derogation is possible – was first reflected in the 1969 Vienna Convention on the Law of Treaties. According to Article 53 (Treaties conflicting with a peremptory norm of general international law ('jus cogens')): 'A treaty is void if, at the time of its conclusion, it conflicts with a peremptory norm of general international law. For the purposes of the present Convention, a peremptory norm of general international law is a norm accepted and recognized by the international community of states as a whole as a norm from which no derogation is permitted and which can be modified only by a subsequent norm of general international law having the same character.' Vienna Convention on the Law of Treaties, Vienna, 23 May 1969, in force 27 January 1980, 1155 UNTS 331; (1969) 8 ILM 679; UKTS (1980) 58.

26 As discussed below, the ICJ stated in its Nuclear Weapons Advisory Opinion that this and other fundamental IHL rules were 'intransgressible'. According to the International Law Commission (ILC): 'In the light of the description by ICJ of the basic rules of international humanitarian law applicable in armed conflict as "intransgressible" in character, it would also seem justified to treat these as peremptory.' ILC, *Draft Articles on Responsibility of States for Internationally Wrongful Acts, with commentaries, 2001* (United Nations, 2008), Commentary on Article 40, p. 113, para. 5.

27 See Article 49(1), 1977 Additional Protocol I ('Definition of attacks and scope of application'), whereby: '"Attacks" means acts of violence against the adversary, whether in offence or in defence.'

logical and necessary for the respect of IHL that any weapon that is 'incapable of distinguishing between civilian and military targets'[28] is unlawful. The ICJ described this as a 'cardinal' principle[29] and affirms that it is among the 'fundamental rules' that must be 'observed by all States whether or not they have ratified the conventions that contain them, because they constitute *intransgressible* principles of international customary law'.[30] The Court's *dispositif*,[31] in which it appears to open the door for *ad bellum* considerations to prevail over IHL rules, might explain the choice of terminology here, as the precise meaning of the term 'intransgressible'[32] is uncertain. Notwithstanding the Advisory Opinion, the prohibition on indiscriminate weapons is arguably a norm of *jus cogens*, either directly, or indirectly by virtue of the rule requiring discrimination in attacks.[33]

Writing a year after the ICJ's Nuclear Weapons Advisory Opinion, Doswald-Beck referred to the identification by the Court of a prohibition on indiscriminate weapons as customary law in the following terms:

> The significance of this statement cannot be overestimated. First, it is important that the prohibition of indiscriminate weapons has been confirmed as

---

[28] Nuclear Weapons Advisory Opinion, para. 78. The Court's exact formulation is rather unfortunate, given that it implies there are civilian 'targets'. A better formulation might have been 'incapable of distinguishing between civilians and civilian objects and military objectives'.

[29] The US Operational Law Handbook describes it rather quaintly as a 'grandfather' principle. US Operational Law Handbook, Chapter 2, p. 11.

[30] Nuclear Weapons Advisory Opinion, para. 79 (emphasis added).

[31] *Ibid.*, para. 105(E).

[32] Notwithstanding the ILC's interpretation of the term, as set out in note 26, above, the precise meaning of the word 'intransgressible' remains unclear, in particular whether it is to be considered as a synonym for a norm of *jus cogens*. Condorelli notes that the term 'intransgressible' is close to a peremptory norm, but claims that it should not be assimilated to it given that the Court specifically stated that it did not need to assess whether fundamental norms of IHL were to be considered *jus cogens*. L. Condorelli, 'Le droit international humanitaire ou de l'exploration par la cour d'une *terra* à peu près *incognita* pour elle' in L. Boisson de Chazournes and P. Sands (eds.), *International Law, the International Court of Justice and Nuclear Weapons* (Cambridge University Press, 1999), p. 234. See also, generally, J. Werksman and R. Khalastchi, 'Nuclear weapons and jus cogens: peremptory norms and justice pre-empted?' in L. Boisson de Chazournes and P. Sands (eds.), *International Law, the International Court of Justice and Nuclear Weapons* (Cambridge University Press, 1999), esp. pp. 183ff.

[33] According to Judge Weeramantry: 'The rules of the humanitarian law of war have clearly acquired the status of *jus cogens*, for they are fundamental rules of a humanitarian character, from which no derogation is possible without negating the basic considerations of humanity which they are intended to protect … The question under consideration is not whether there is a prohibition in peremptory terms of nuclear weapons specifically so mentioned, but whether there are basic principles of a *jus cogens* nature which are violated by nuclear weapons. If there are such principles which are of a *jus cogens* nature, then it would follow that the weapon itself would be prohibited under the *jus cogens* concept.' Nuclear Weapons Advisory Opinion, Separate Opinion of Judge Weeramantry, Section 10, p. 274. In his

customary, for the only treaty formulation of the prohibition of indiscriminate attacks is to be found in Additional Protocol I, which has not yet been ratified by all States, and only in that treaty is there a general statement as to which types of weapons would fall foul of this rule. Secondly, following the Court's logic, the prohibition against deliberately attacking civilians found in Additional Protocol II automatically means that indiscriminate weapons must not be used in non-international armed conflicts to which that Protocol applies. Thirdly, it means that any weapon can be tested against these criteria and if it falls foul of them, its use would be prohibited without there being a need for any special treaty or even State practice prohibiting the use of that particular weapon.[34]

The ICRC study of customary international humanitarian law, published in 2005, similarly concluded that: 'The use of weapons which are by nature indiscriminate is prohibited.'[35] The ICRC affirms that state practice has established the rule as a norm of customary international law applicable in both international and non-international armed conflicts.[36] The United States, in its Written Statement to the ICJ, did not seek to argue that the rule against inherently indiscriminate weapons did not apply to nuclear weapons.[37]

Separate Opinion (at para. 21), ICJ President Bedjaoui stated that: 'I have no doubt that most of the principles and rules of humanitarian law and, in any event, the two principles, one of which prohibits the use of weapons with indiscriminate effects and the other the use of arms causing unnecessary suffering, form part of jus cogens. The Court raised this question in the present Opinion; but it nevertheless stated that it did not have to make a finding on the point since the question of the nature of the humanitarian law applicable to nuclear weapons did not fall within the framework of the request addressed to it by the General Assembly of the United Nations. Nonetheless, the Court expressly stated the view that these fundamental rules constitute "intransgressible principles of international customary law"'.

[34] L. Doswald-Beck, 'International humanitarian law and the Advisory Opinion of the International Court of Justice on the legality of the threat or use of nuclear weapons', *International Review of the Red Cross* 316 (1997), 35–55, available at: www.icrc.org/eng/resources/documents/misc/57jnfm.htm.

[35] ICRC Study of Customary IHL, Rule 71, available at: www.icrc.org/customary-ihl/eng/docs/v1_rul_rule71.

[36] *Ibid.* The evidence is primarily that: 'No official contrary practice was found with respect to either international or non-international armed conflicts. No state has indicated that it may use indiscriminate weapons in any type of armed conflict.' As noted above, however, Doswald-Beck also argued that, 'following the Court's logic, the prohibition against deliberately attacking civilians found in Additional Protocol II automatically means that indiscriminate weapons must not be used in non-international armed conflicts to which that Protocol applies.' Doswald-Beck, 'International humanitarian law and the Nuclear Weapons Advisory Opinion.' Boothby states that: '[t]o the extent that the rule against indiscriminate weapons applies to international armed conflict, the conclusion that it will also apply to non-international armed conflict seems uncontroversial.' W. H. Boothby, *Weapons and the Law of Armed Conflict* (Oxford University Press, 2009), p. 82.

[37] See also Nuclear Weapons Advisory Opinion, Dissenting Opinion of Judge Rosalyn Higgins, para. 24. Judge Higgins asserts that the rule covers only weapons that are 'incapable of being targeted at a military objective'.

Instead, it pleaded that nuclear weapons can be directed at a military object-ive and can be used in a discriminate manner and are therefore not inherently indiscriminate.[38]

The *UK Manual on the Law of Armed Conflict* sets out the applicable rule as follows:

> It is prohibited to employ weapons which cannot be directed at a specific military objective or the effects of which cannot be limited as required by Additional Protocol I and consequently are of a nature to strike military objectives and civilians or civilian objects without distinction.[39]

This UK formulation of the rule has two alternative tests to it: first, is any given weapon *inherently incapable* of being targeted against a specific military objective; and second, can the effects of any given weapon be limited to a military objective or will they, *inevitably*, constitute an indiscriminate attack, inter alia, because they have uncontrolled effects?[40] Under the rule as expressed by the UK, any weapon that possesses either of these two intrinsic characteristics will be adjudged inher-ently indiscriminate and therefore its use will be unlawful in all circumstances.

While it is uncontested that a prohibition on inherently indiscriminate weap-ons is, at least today,[41] a customary rule of IHL, its overall scope and its appli-cation to specific weapons remain controversial. The issues will be addressed in turn.

2.   What is an inherently indiscriminate weapon?

A weapon that cannot be targeted

It is generally admitted that any weapon whose guidance system is so rudi-mentary or unreliable that there is no way of knowing where it will land – for

---

[38] Written Statement of the United States to the ICJ, Nuclear Weapons Advisory Opinion, 20 June 1995. In his most recent treatise, Boothby argues that 'the elements of article 51(4) [of 1977 Additional Protocol I] that prohibit weapons that are indiscriminate by nature, do not apply to nuclear weapons'. The point is in fact moot, given the customary nature of the prohibition. Indeed, as he goes on to acknowledge, 'The customary law position in respect of nuclear weapons will of course depend on the practice of States, and the official statements by States to which reference has been made in this section will constitute State practice in this regard ... There is no rule of law that prohibits the use of nuclear weapons. However, customary law principles, in particular the principles of distinction, proportion-ality, and of superfluous injury and unnecessary suffering would constrain any such use.' W. H. Boothby, *The Law of Targeting* (Oxford University Press, 2012), pp. 79 and 296; and see also pp. 292–3.

[39] UK Manual of the Law of Armed Conflict, para. 6.4. The UK adhered 1977 Additional Protocol I in January 1998. The United States has signed but not ratified the Protocol.

[40] 1977 Additional Protocol I, Art. 51(5)(b).

[41] See, e.g., Boothby's claim that, as of 1974 when the first two Additional Protocols to the four 1949 Geneva Conventions were being negotiated, 'no rule prohibiting indiscriminate weapons existed'. Boothby, *Weapons and the Law of Armed Conflict*, p. 75.

example a 'long-range'[42] rocket or missile – is inherently indiscriminate and therefore unlawful. Examples of weapons said to fall foul of this test are, among others, V1 or V2 rockets[43] or Scud missiles.[44, 45]

Of course, weapons may be used indiscriminately without being inherently indiscriminate, especially when they are aimed at targets from a distance that represents the high end of their effective operational range. Further, certain weapons are more prone to indiscriminate use than others; this helps to explain why treaties have been adopted to outlaw anti-personnel mines[46] and cluster munitions.[47] Indeed, in its judgment in the *Martić case* before the International Criminal Tribunal for the former Yugoslavia (ICTY), which concerned the firing of cluster munitions against Zagreb in May 1995, the ICTY's Trial Chamber noted:

> that the weapon was fired from the extreme of its range. Moreover, the Trial Chamber notes the characteristics of the weapon, it being a non-guided high dispersion weapon. The Trial Chamber therefore concludes that the M-87 Orkan, by virtue of its characteristics and the firing range in this specific instance, was incapable of hitting specific targets. For these reasons, the Trial Chamber also finds that the M-87 Orkan is an indiscriminate weapon,

---

[42] According to the ICRC Commentary on the 1977 Additional Protocols: 'As regards the weapons, those relevant here are primarily long-range missiles which cannot be aimed exactly at the objective. The V2 rockets used at the end of the Second World War are an example of this.' Sandoz *et al.*, *Commentary on the Additional Protocols of 8 June 1977*, para. 1958.

[43] Sandoz *et al.*, *Commentary on the Additional Protocols of 8 June 1977*, para. 1958; see also Boothby, *Weapons and the Law of Armed Conflict*, p. 80; and M. N. Schmitt, 'Future war and the principle of discrimination', *Israeli Yearbook of Human Rights* 28 (1999), 51–90, at 55.

[44] During the Cold War, NATO used the term 'Scud' to refer to a specific missile, the R-11, a Soviet theatre-range weapon intended to strike targets in Western Europe. Scuds were manufactured from 1959 to 1984. Because their gyros and electronics date back to the 1950s, the missiles are notoriously inaccurate. The original Scud missiles had a circular error probable (CEP) of about 3,300 feet, meaning that half the missiles aimed at a target would land more than two-thirds of a mile away. B. Berkowitz, 'What's a scud?', *Air & Space Magazine* (May 2003), available at: www.airspacemag.com/history-of-flight/whats-a-scud-4510864/?no-ist.

[45] The ICRC cites in evidence to support the assertion (though without necessarily endorsing the conclusion) the military manual of Canada and statements by Israel, the United Kingdom and the United States, as well as reported practice of Israel. ICRC Study of Customary IHL, Rule 71, n. 42, available at: www.icrc.org/customary-ihl/eng/docs/v1_rul_rule71. Solis argues that the V-1 flying bomb and V-2 rockets and Scud missiles are 'by their nature indiscriminate'. Solis, *The Law of Armed Conflict*, Section 14.7, p. 537. The United Kingdom affirms that the V-1 flying bomb and the Scud rocket 'are examples of weapons likely to be caught by this provision'. UK Manual on the Law of Armed Conflict, p. 104, para. 6.4.1.

[46] 1997 Anti-Personnel Mine Ban Convention.

[47] Convention on Cluster Munitions, Dublin, 30 May 2008, in force 1 August 2010, 48 ILM 354.

the use of which in densely populated civilian areas, such as Zagreb, will result in the infliction of severe casualties.[48]

Prima facie, the statement of the Trial Chamber appears to affirm that the Orkan is an inherently indiscriminate weapon, partly 'by virtue of its characteristics'.[49] But the Court went on to add that the firing range 'in this specific instance' and its use in 'densely populated civilian areas' would lead to many casualties.[50] It was thus not entirely clear what made it an indiscriminate weapon in this case.[51] Would a different (i.e. shorter) firing range and a dissimilar environment for its use potentially have led to a different outcome? Accordingly, the Trial Chamber's reasoning indicates that it did not necessarily deem the Orkan to be an inherently unlawful weapon. This would require a determination that no reasonable scenario of the use of a given weapon would comply with the rule on discrimination. The Appeal Chamber did not clarify this issue any further, stating only: 'The Trial Chamber concluded that the M-87 Orkan *was used* as an indiscriminate weapon.'[52]

In November 2012 the ICTY's decision on appeal in the case of *Prosecutor* v. *Ante Gotovina and Mladen Markač* was potentially controversial for a number of reasons, not least in that it seemed to offer a narrow notion of what would

[48] ICTY, *Prosecutor* v. *Milan Martić*, Judgment (Trial Chamber) (Case No. IT-95-11), 12 June 2007, para. 463, available at: www.icty.org/x/cases/martic/tjug/en/070612.pdf.

[49] *Ibid.*, para. 463.   [50] *Ibid.*

[51] As the Trial Chamber explained: 'The M-87 Orkan is a non-guided projectile, the primary military use of which is to target soldiers and armoured vehicles. Each rocket may contain either a cluster warhead with 288 so-called bomblets or 24 anti-tank shells … Each bomblet contains 420 pellets of 3mm in diameter. The bomblets are ejected from the rocket at a height of 800–1,000m above the targeted area and explode upon impact, releasing the pellets. The maximum firing range of the M-87 Orkan is 50 kilometres. The dispersion error of the rocket at 800–1,000m in the air increases with the firing range. Fired from the maximum range, this error is about 1,000m in any direction. The area of dispersion of the bomblets on the ground is about two hectares. Each pellet has a lethal range of ten metres.' *Ibid.*, para. 462 (internal citations omitted).

[52] ICTY, *Prosecutor* v. *Milan Martić*, Judgment (Appeals Chamber) (Case No. IT-95-11-A), 8 October 2008, para. 247 (emphasis added), available at: www.icty.org/x/cases/martic/acjug/en/mar-aj081008e.pdf. A similar 'mistake' appears to have been made by the Trial Chamber in the *Perišić* case (involving the same use of cluster munitions against Zagreb that had been the subject of the case against Martić). The Trial Chamber stated that: 'The Trial Chamber finds that due to its characteristics, especially its high dispersion pattern, the Orkan rocket system is an indiscriminate weapon. It follows that its use in a densely populated civilian area cannot but result in the infliction of severe civilian casualties.' ICTY, *Prosecutor* v. *Momčilo Perišić*, Judgment (Trial Chamber) (Case No. IT-04-81-T), 6 September 2011, para. 590, available at: www.icty.org/x/cases/perisic/tjug/en/110906_judgement.pdf. The issue of whether cluster munitions were an indiscriminate weapon was never addressed by the Appeal Chamber in Perišić's appeal against conviction for crimes against humanity and war crimes as he was acquitted on unrelated grounds at the end of February 2013. ICTY, *Prosecutor* v. *Momčilo Perišić*, Judgment (Appeals Chamber) (Case No. IT-04-81-A), 28 February 2013, available at: www.icty.org/x/cases/perisic/acjug/en/130228_judgement.pdf.

constitute 'indiscriminate' use of a weapon in a populated area. The original trial judgment had concluded that Croatian army artillery attacks on Benkovac, Gračac, Knin and Obrovac (the 'Four Towns'), were unlawful, in part on the basis that many shells fell more than 200 metres away from any lawful military objective. Gotovina's lawyers argued that during the Appeal Hearing, the Prosecution raised 'certain new, and therefore inadmissible, arguments', including that 'the use of certain artillery weapons was "inherently indiscriminate" in an urban environment'.[53] The Prosecution also asserted, however, that the broad spread of artillery impacts all over Knin demonstrates that the attack on that town was indiscriminate. It further contended that some shells impacted 700–800 metres from identified legitimate targets in the Four Towns, suggesting that this would be an unreasonable margin of error.[54]

In allowing the appeal by a majority decision, the Appeals Chamber unanimously agreed that the Trial Chamber had not sufficiently explained the basis on which it arrived at a 200-metre margin of error as a reasonable measure of an indiscriminate attack.[55] More controversially, the judgment also asserted that the fact that a relatively large number of shells fell more than 200 metres from fixed artillery targets could be consistent with a much broader range of error.[56] In a strongly worded Dissenting Opinion, Judge Fausto Pocar referred to 'the sheer volume of errors and misconstructions in the Majority's reasoning' and asserted that the Appeal Judgment had misrepresented the Trial Chamber's analysis. His opinion merits citation in detail, as follows:

> By not articulating the correct legal standard, the Majority falls short of correcting any legal errors in the Trial Judgement and clarifying the law the Trial Chamber should have applied when assessing the legality of an attack directed on civilians and civilian objects. It also fails to consider whether the artillery attacks on the Four Towns were lawful or not when the evidence is assessed in light of the principles of international humanitarian law ('IHL'). First, the Majority fails to give any indication as to what the correct legal standard was. Does the Majority consider that the correct legal standard was a 400-metre standard? A 100-metre standard? A 0-metre standard? The Appeal Judgement provides no answer to this question. Second, the Majority also fails to clarify on which basis the correct legal standard should have been established. Does the Majority consider that a legal standard can be established on a margin of error of artillery weapons? Does the Majority consider that a trial chamber is entitled in law to establish a presumption of legality to assess the evidence of the shelling attacks and the artillery impacts in order to establish the lawfulness of the attack? Is a trial chamber not limited in its analysis to the strict application of IHL

---

[53] ICTY, *Prosecutor v. Ante Gotovina and Mladen Markač*, Judgment (Appeals Chamber) (Case No. IT-06-90-A), 16 November 2012, para. 16. The Court declined to consider this reasoning.

[54] *Ibid.*, para. 41.   [55] *Ibid.*, para. 58.   [56] *Ibid.*, para. 65.

principles? Here again, the Appeal Judgement is mute on these issues. Third, if the Majority considers that applying a presumption of legality to analyse the evidence of the shelling attacks and the artillery impacts in order to establish its lawfulness is incorrect, it further fails to articulate which legal principles the Trial Chamber should have applied. Does the Majority consider that the Trial Chamber should have applied the principles of customary IHL in its analysis? If so, which exact IHL principles should the Trial Chamber have applied in assessing whether the artillery attack was lawful? Does the Majority consider that the minimum applicable legal standard was to analyse whether the shelling was aimed at targeting military objectives offering a definite military advantage, whether it was done in respect of the principle of proportionality and after all precautionary measures had been taken? Silence.[57]

As Pocar observes, we are potentially left with serious doubt as to what, in practice, would constitute an indiscriminate attack – and therefore what would constitute an inherently indiscriminate weapon. Of course, it is very difficult to say what is indiscriminate out of context. The figure fixed upon by the Trial Chamber was unreasonable as a general standard for artillery fire as it took no account of circumstances. However, the standard it proposed might have been reasonable *in those circumstances*.[58]

A weapon with indiscriminate effects

Notwithstanding the practical implications of the Gotovina judgment on appeal, whereas a means of warfare that cannot effectively be targeted at a lawful military objective clearly constitutes an inherently indiscriminate weapon,[59] the extent to which other IHL prohibitions on indiscriminate attacks[60] form part of the test is more controversial. One such prohibition is given expression in Article 51(4)(c) of 1977 Additional Protocol I:

> Indiscriminate attacks are prohibited. Indiscriminate attacks are: … (c) those which employ a method or means of combat the effects of which cannot be limited as required by this Protocol; and consequently … are of a nature to strike military objectives and civilians or civilian objects without distinction.

---

[57] *Ibid.*, Dissenting Opinion of Judge Fausto Pocar, §13.

[58] The author is indebted to Charles Garraway for this observation.

[59] According to 1977 Additional Protocol I, Article 51(4)(b), indiscriminate attacks include 'those which employ a method or means of combat which cannot be directed at a specific military objective'.

[60] As Dinstein notes: 'Indiscriminate attacks differ from direct attacks against civilians in that "the attacker is not actually *trying* to harm the civilian population": the injury/damage to civilians is merely a matter of "no concern to the attacker". From the standpoint of LOAIC [Law of International Armed Conflict], an indiscriminate attack is not better than a premeditated attack against civilians (or civilian objects): either course of action is equally irreconcilable with the cardinal principle of distinction.' Dinstein, *The Conduct of Hostilities*

According to paragraph 5 of the same provision:

> Among others, the following types of attacks are to be considered as indiscriminate:
> (a) an attack by bombardment by any methods or means which treats as a single military objective a number of clearly separated and distinct military objectives located in a city, town, village or other area containing a similar concentration of civilians or civilian objects; and
> (b) an attack which may be expected to cause incidental loss of civilian life, injury to civilians, damage to civilian objects, or a combination thereof, which would be excessive in relation to the concrete and direct military advantage anticipated.

There are three separate but related issues to consider. The first relates to 'uncontrolled effects' (i.e. a means of combat the effects of which cannot be limited as required by the Protocol or other IHL applicable rules). The second concerns a bombardment by any methods or means which treat as a single military objective several 'clearly separated and distinct military objectives' located in a populated area. The third prohibits an attack that causes excessive deaths or injuries of civilians, or damage to civilian objects, or a combination thereof, when balanced with the expected concrete and direct military advantage of an attack. The remainder of this section considers the first and second questions. The third issue, the rule of proportionality in attacks, is addressed in Section C below.

Are the effects of the weapon 'uncontrolled'?   The US Air Force's 1976 Manual on International Law defines indiscriminate weapons as those 'incapable of being controlled, through design or function', such that they 'cannot, with any degree of certainty, be directed at military objectives'.[61] In its commentary of the relevant provision contained in Article 51(4)(c) of 1977 Additional Protocol I, the ICRC referred to the *travaux préparatoires*, citing the report on discussions in the relevant negotiating committee that dealt with the issue of indiscriminate effects. It noted that:

> Many but not all of those who commented [in the Committee] were of the view that the definition was not intended to mean that there are means or methods of combat whose use would involve an indiscriminate attack in all circumstances. Rather it was intended to take account of the fact that means or methods of combat which can be used perfectly legitimately in

---

under the Law of International Armed Conflict, p. 127 (citing H. M. Hanke, 'The 1923 Hague Rules of Air Warfare', *International Review of the Red Cross* 33(12) (1996), 12–44, at 26 (original emphasis)).

[61] US Department of the Air Force, 'International law – the conduct of armed conflict and air operations', Air Force Pamphlet 110–31 (19 November 1976), para. 6–3. See also US Department of the Air Force, *The Military Commander and the Law*, updated August 2012, p. 669, available at: www.afjag.af.mil/shared/media/document/AFD-120828-043.pdf.

some situations could, in other circumstances, have effects that would be contrary to some limitations contained in the Protocol, in which event their use in those circumstances would involve an indiscriminate attack.[62]

It continued, however, with its view that:

there are some means of warfare of which the effects cannot be limited in any circumstances. It is different with regard to other means, such as fire or water which, depending on the circumstances of their use, can have either a restricted effect or, on the contrary, be completely out of the control of those using them, causing significant losses among the civilian population and extensive damage to civilian objects. The nature of the means used is not the only criterion: the power of the weapons used can have the same consequences. For example, if a 10 ton bomb is used to destroy a single building, it is inevitable that the effects will be very extensive and will annihilate or damage neighbouring buildings, while a less powerful missile would suffice to destroy the building. There are also methods which by their very nature have an indiscriminate character, such as poisoning wells.[63]

The ICRC Commentary goes on to note that 'several delegations' considered it necessary to confirm, in their explanations for their vote, their view that the provision contained in Article 51(4)(c) does not mean that there are means of combat the use of which would constitute an indiscriminate attack in all circumstances.[64] According to the ICRC, though, while it is true that in most cases the indiscriminate character of an attack depends not on the nature of the weapons concerned but on the way in which they are used:

there are some weapons which by their very nature have an indiscriminate effect. The example of bacteriological means of warfare is an obvious illustration of this point. There are also other weapons which have similar indiscriminate effects, such as poisoning sources of drinking water. Of course, bacteriological means of warfare have been prohibited since 1925, and the use of poison was prohibited in 1899 by the Hague Regulations.[65]

Dinstein similarly implies that weapons with 'uncontrolled effects', which 'by their very nature or design cannot possibly maintain the distinction in any set of circumstances', fall within the test of inherently indiscriminate weapons.[66] The US Air Force's 1976 Manual on International Law cites biological weapons as a 'universally agreed illustration of ... an indiscriminate weapon', noting that

---

[62] Sandoz *et al.*, *Commentary on the Additional Protocols of 8 June 1977*, para. 1962 (citing the Geneva Diplomatic Conference on the Reaffirmation and Development of International Humanitarian Law, Ordinary Records XV, p. 274, para. 55, Doc. CDDH/215/Rev.1, Annex).

[63] *Ibid.*, para. 1963.   [64] *Ibid.*, para. 1964.

[65] *Ibid.*, para. 1965. Presumably, the commentary means to refer to poisoning sources of drinking water as a method of warfare rather than a means of warfare.

[66] Dinstein, *The Conduct of Hostilities under the Law of International Armed Conflict*, p. 62.

the uncontrollable effects from such weapons 'may include injury to the civilian population of other states as well as injury to an enemy's civilian population'.[67] The Naval/Marine Commander's Handbook states that such weapons are 'inherently indiscriminate and uncontrollable'.[68] Citing a 1999 article by Schmitt, Dinstein likewise refers to biological weapons with respect to which 'the crux of the matter is that, when unchecked by an antidote, they can spread contagious disease far and wide without being capable of sanitizing civilians (or even neutrals)'.[69] These uncontrolled effects concern both spatial and time issues.

The extent to which the effects of nuclear weapons are uncontrolled depends on a variety of factors, such as the size and type of nuclear weapon used; whether the weapon is ground- or underwater-burst, or detonated in the air or at high altitude;[70] terrain; and climate. However, the effects can still be highly unpredictable even when such factors are known.[71]

There is a particular problem resulting from radioactive fallout. Indeed, 'the most fundamental difference between nuclear and conventional weapons is that the former release radioactive rays at the time of explosion'.[72] Nuclear fallout refers to the particles of matter in the air made radioactive from a nuclear explosion.[73] Some of these particles fall in the immediate area and some get blown many thousands of miles by upper winds. When they eventually fall to the earth, this is called fallout. The effects of radiation on the body are said to be prodromal, hematologic, gastrointestinal, pulmonary, cutaneous and neurovascular.[74]

---

[67] C. J. Moxley, Jr, '2002 Nuclear Posture Review: Strategic and Legal Ramifications', 16 April 2002, p. 30, available at: www.nuclearweaponslaw.com/2002_NPR_Moxley.pdf (hereafter, 2002 Nuclear Posture Review) (citing US Department of the Air Force, 'International law – the conduct of armed conflict and air operations', para. 6–3).

[68] *Ibid.* (citing US Department of the Navy Annotated Supplement to the Commander's Handbook on the Law of Naval Operations 10–21, Naval Warfare Publication 9, 1987 with Revision A (5 October 1989)).

[69] *Ibid.*, pp. 62–3 (citing Schmitt, 'Future war and the principle of discrimination', 55). See also Boothby, *Weapons and the Law of Armed Conflict*, p. 84.

[70] A nuclear weapon detonated in the air, called an air burst, produces less fallout than a comparable explosion near the ground.

[71] For an example of how inaccurate forecasts of the area affected by a nuclear weapon strike can be, see, e.g. Col. J. R. Mercier, 'Nuclear Weapons Effects', US Armed Forces Radiobiology Research Institute, July 2008, p. 31, available at: www.usuhs.mil/afrri/outreach/pdf/sci-update-Mercier-July08.pdf.

[72] Statement of the Mayor of Nagasaki to the International Court of Justice, Nuclear Weapons Advisory Opinion, 7 November 1995, p. 36, available at: www.icj-cij.org/docket/files/95/5935.pdf.

[73] Fallout is a complex mixture of more than 200 different isotopes of 36 elements. Two ounces of fission products are said to be formed for each kiloton (kT) of yield. See, e.g., Fun Fong *et al.*, 'In-Depth Medical Management for Nuclear/Radiological/Conventional Terrorism Agents', PowerPoint Presentation, undated, available at: www.powershow.com/view/17e3-NTY4Y/Medical_Effects_of_Nuclear_Weapons_powerpoint_ppt_presentation.

[74] *Ibid.*

According to the Mayor of Nagasaki:

> All people exposed to large doses of radiation generated during the one-minute period after the Nagasaki atomic bomb explosion died within two weeks. Induced radiation due to the absorption of neutrons by substances on the ground, as well as plutonium particles, products of nuclear fission and other radioactive fallout scattered by the wind, caused widespread, long-term radio-contamination. Therefore, not only directly exposed people, but also those who came into the hypocenter area after the bombing and those exposed to fallout carried by the wind suffered radiation-induced injuries ... A high incidence of disease was observed among the survivors exposed to large doses of radiation. Particularly noteworthy is the high frequency of diseases such as leukaemia and malignant tumours appearing after long periods of latency. It has been reported that leukaemia appears two or three years after an atomic bombing and that the incidence declines after reaching a peak six or seven years after the bombing. Cancer meanwhile is said to appear after a latency of more than 10 years and then to increase in frequency over time.[75]

The details of the actual fallout pattern from a nuclear weapon blast depend on wind speed and direction as well as on the terrain.[76] The fallout will typically contain about 60 per cent of the total radioactivity.[77] For instance, from the 15-megaton thermonuclear device tested at Bikini Atoll on 1 March 1954, the fallout caused substantial contamination across more than 7,000 square miles. The contaminated region was roughly cigar-shaped and extended more than 20 miles upwind but over 350 miles downwind. Fallout can also enter into the stratosphere where radioactive particles can remain for between one to three years before returning to the surface of the planet.[78]

Does the use of the weapon constitute area bombing? A second element in indiscriminate attacks is 'area' or 'saturation' bombing.[79] Repeating the provision set out in 1977 Additional Protocol I,[80] the ICRC expresses the prohibition on such attacks as a customary rule as follows:

> Attacks by bombardment by any method or means which treats as a single military objective a number of clearly separated and distinct military

---

[75] Statement of the Mayor of Nagasaki to the ICJ, p. 36.
[76] Atomic Archive, 'Effects of Nuclear Weapons: The Fallout Pattern', undated, available at: www.atomicarchive.com/Effects/effects19.shtml.
[77] *Ibid.*   [78] *Ibid.*
[79] In the *Shimoda* case, a Japanese court concluded in 1963 that the bombings of Hiroshima and Nagasaki were unlawful, in part on the basis that they were 'undefended cities'. Of note, it concluded that at the relevant time, 'the indiscriminate bombing of a defended city or defended area [was] ... permissible'. With regard to undefended cities, however, 'the aerial bombardment of military objectives only, is permitted'. District Court of Tokyo, *Ryuichi Shimoda et al.* v. *State*, Judgment (Merits), 7 December 1963.
[80] 1977 Additional Protocol I, Art. 51(5)(a).

objectives located in a city, town, village or other area containing a similar concentration of civilians or civilian objects are prohibited.[81]

Thus, military targets dispersed around populated areas have to be attacked separately.[82] It implies that the use of a weapon that cannot be limited to an attack on a single military objective in a populated area would be unlawful. Yet, as Doswald-Beck has observed, this would be difficult to use as a test for the legality of a weapon, for the words of this provision 'presuppose the intention to attack several distinct military objectives in a populated area, treating them as if they were one objective. One cannot assume this when deciding on the nature of any particular weapon, for one of the planned uses of the weapon may well be to attack one military objective far from a civilian centre.'[83]

With respect to nuclear weapons, the extent of damage would depend on the power of the device. According to one estimate, even a 'low-yield' 1-kiloton[84] 'earth-penetrating "mininuke"' used in an urban environment would spread a lethal dose of radioactive fallout over several square kilometres, resulting in tens of thousands of civilian fatalities.[85] In addressing the US Senate in 2003, Senator Feinstein stated that: 'According to models done by the Natural Resources Defense Council, detonating a similar weapon on the surface of a city would kill a quarter of a million people and injure hundreds of thousands more ... So there really is no such thing as a "usable nuclear weapon".'[86] In case of a 1-megaton (Mt) explosion,[87] 10 seconds after

---

[81] ICRC Study of Customary IHL, Rule 13, available at: www.icrc.org/customary-ihl/eng/docs/v1_rul_rule13.

[82] UK Manual of the Law of Armed Conflict, para. 5.23.2.

[83] Doswald-Beck, 'International humanitarian law and the Advisory Opinion'.

[84] As Solomon Islands observed in its written statement to the ICJ, in the case of 1 to 75 kilotons (1 kiloton = 1,000 tonnes of dynamite) for atomic bombs, 'the minimum level of one kilotonne corresponds to the minimum critical mass of fissile material necessary to unleash a nuclear reaction (the bombardment of uranium-235 atoms or plutonium-239 atoms by neutrons – when bursting (fission) these atoms free other neutrons and a great amount of energy). It is now possible to go below the level of 1 kilotonne through the use of certain "compression" techniques of fissile material, and it has been suggested that nuclear weapons with a power equivalent to 10 or 100 tonnes of TNT might be constructed.' Written Statement of Solomon Islands, Nuclear Weapons Advisory Opinion, 19 June 1995, p. 44, para. 3.44.

[85] R. W. Nelson, 'Low-yield earth-penetrating nuclear weapons', *Science and Global Security* 10 (2002), 1–20, available at: http://scienceandglobalsecurity.org/archive/sgs10nelson.pdf.

[86] See, e.g., R. M. Jones, 'Senators debate low-yield nuclear weapons initiative', *FYI: The AIP Bulletin of Science Policy News* 77 (19 June 2003), available at: www.aip.org/fyi/2003/077.html.

[87] Solomon Islands referred to devices of 'between several kilotonnes and several megatonnes (1 megatonne = 1,000 kilotonnes) for hydrogen bombs (thermonuclear weapons) which comprise two bombs: a thermonuclear bomb with virtually unlimited power and an atomic explosive which allows the necessary temperature of several million degrees to be reached to unleash a nuclear reaction where isotopes of heavy hydrogen (tritium and deutenum) unite (fusion) to create a helium core, thereby unleashing a vast quantity of energy; the atomic explosive which triggers the fusion is approximately 1 kilotonne, the amount of

detonation the diameter of the fireball will be 5,700 feet, while the distance of the shock front will be 3 miles.[88]

Concluding remarks

There is strong, though not overwhelming, evidence that the inherently indiscriminate test of the legality of a weapon under IHL encompasses both weapons that cannot be targeted and those that have indiscriminate effects. The ICJ itself used the words 'weapons that are incapable of distinguishing between civilian and military targets',[89] rather than a narrower formulation such as 'weapons that cannot be targeted at a military objective'.

State practice is obviously relevant to the analysis. The United States' Written Statement to the ICJ in 1995 in connection with the Nuclear Weapons Advisory Opinion declared that: 'Since nuclear weapons can be directed at a military objective, they can be used in a discriminate manner and are not inherently indiscriminate.'[90] This appears to limit the term inherently indiscriminate to weapons that cannot be directed at a military objective. Yet the United States also referred in the same paragraph to 'the ability of modern delivery systems to target specific military objectives with nuclear weapons, and the ability of modern weapon designers to tailor the effects of a nuclear weapon to deal with various types of military objectives'.[91] The latter reference to the ability to 'tailor the *effects* of a nuclear weapon to deal with various types of military objectives' is more akin to the issue of indiscriminate effects.

A similar position was taken by the UK in its Written Statement to the Court. The UK argued that: 'Modern nuclear weapons are capable of far more precise targeting and can therefore be directed against specific military objectives without the indiscriminate effect on the civilian population which the older literature assumed to be inevitable.'[92] Again, however, the reference to

fissile material necessary for a nuclear reaction; these materials are generally then encased in a mass of uranium-238 which is more stable than uranium-235, but which as a result of the fusion and the intense bombardment of neutrons itself enters the reaction (fission). The whole process thereby comprises one of fission–fusion–fission. The maximum power of such a weapon is limited only by limitations relating to packaging and transportation, and certain attempts have been made to create larger weapons, although it seems that at present the majority of nuclear weapons arsenals comprise bombs of between 55 [kilotonnes] and 1 megatonne (some 38 to 76 times more powerful than the bomb used at Hiroshima).' Written Statement of the Government of Solomon Islands, Nuclear Weapons Advisory Opinion, 19 June 1995, p. 44, §3.44.

[88] A. Glaser, 'Effects of Nuclear Weapons', PowerPoint Presentation, Princeton University, 12 February 2007, available at: www.princeton.edu/~aglaser/lecture2007_weaponeffects.pdf.

[89] Nuclear Weapons Advisory Opinion, para. 78.

[90] Written Statement of the United States, Nuclear Weapons Advisory Opinion, 20 June 1995, p. 23.

[91] *Ibid.*

[92] Written Statement of the UK, Nuclear Weapons Advisory Opinion, June 1995, p. 52, para. 3.68.

the *indiscriminate effect* on the civilian population appears to support the argument that such effects are covered by the test in addition to the ability to strike a lawful military objective with any degree of accuracy.

In contrast, France and Russia, in their Written Statement, did not engage in any assessment of what constituted an inherently indiscriminate weapon. Russia cited Blix in support of its argument – unpersuasive in the view of the present author – that it was only the indiscriminate use of a weapon, and not the nature of the weapon itself, that was unlawful:

> As Hans Blix said, 'it is certainly correct to say that the legality of the use of most weapons depends upon the manner in which they are employed. A rifle may be lawfully aimed at the enemy or it may be employed indiscriminately against civilians and soldiers alike. Bombs may be aimed at specific military targets or thrown at random. The indiscriminate use of the weapon will be prohibited, not the weapon as such.' We should add that it is a duly qualified use rather than the use of weapons as such at large that will be regarded as illegal.[93]

Opinions among the ICJ judges in the Nuclear Weapons Advisory Opinion differed as to the nature of the inherently indiscriminate test of the legality of a weapon under IHL. Judge Higgins in her Dissenting Opinion asserted that 'it may be concluded that a weapon will be unlawful per se if it is incapable of being targeted at a military objective only, even if collateral harm occurs'.[94] She thus appeared to exclude the possibility that uncontrolled (or disproportionate) effects could form part of the test of an inherently indiscriminate weapon. In contrast, the ICJ President Mohammed Bedjaoui, in his Separate Opinion, declared that:

> I have no doubt that most of the principles and rules of humanitarian law and, in any event, the two principles, one of which prohibits the use of weapons *with indiscriminate effects* and the other the use of arms causing unnecessary suffering, form part of jus cogens.[95]

3.   Are nuclear weapons inherently indiscriminate?

Notwithstanding a conclusion that the prohibition on inherently indiscriminate weapons does apply to nuclear weapons, applying the legal test to them

---

[93] Written Statement of the Russian Federation, Nuclear Weapons Advisory Opinion, 16 June 1995, p. 18 (citing Hans Blix, 'Means and methods of combat' in Institut Henry-Dunant, UNESCO, *International Dimensions of Humanitarian Law* (Paris/Dordrecht: UNESCO/ Martinus Nijhoff, 1988), pp. 144–5).

[94] Dissenting Opinion of Judge Rosalyn Higgins, Nuclear Weapons Advisory Opinion, para. 24. Solis claims that the term 'collateral damage' was first coined during the 1991 Gulf War. Solis, *The Law of Armed Conflict*, Section 7.4, p. 275.

[95] Separate Opinion of ICJ President Mohammed Bedjaoui, Nuclear Weapons Advisory Opinion, para. 21 (emphasis added).

is practically challenging. Thus, for example, as ICJ Vice-President Schwebel wrote in his Dissenting Opinion: 'While it is not difficult to conclude that the principles of international humanitarian law – ... discrimination between military and civilian targets – govern the use of nuclear weapons, it does not follow that the application of those principles ... is easy.'[96] Nonetheless, the following section attempts such application, looking first at the accuracy of targeting, then at one of the two main elements of indiscriminate attacks: uncontrolled effects.[97]

Can nuclear weapons be targeted at a lawful military objective?

As already cited, in its submission to the ICJ in connection with the Nuclear Weapons Advisory Opinion, the United States argued that nuclear weapons 'can be directed at a military objective, they can be used in a discriminate manner and are not inherently indiscriminate.'[98] Similarly, the UK affirmed that '[m]odern nuclear weapons are capable of far more precise targeting and can therefore be directed against specific military objectives.'[99] It further affirmed that all weapons, 'nuclear weapons included', can be used 'against centres of civilian population or in an indiscriminate way'. Subject to their lawful use in reprisal, 'such use would be illegal'.[100] 'What is not true is that nuclear weapons cannot be used in any other way.'[101] The UK asserted that the use of nuclear weapons against specific military objectives 'would undoubtedly not be contrary' to the rule requiring parties to an armed conflict to discriminate between civilians and civilian objects on the one hand, and combatants and military objectives on the other, and to direct their attacks only against the latter.[102]

Such claims are (relatively) uncontroversial. There is little credible evidence that delivery mechanisms for nuclear weapons are not – let alone cannot be – accurate;[103] what is far more open to contrary interpretation is whether the weapons are indiscriminate in their effects.

Several individual judges, in either separate or dissenting opinions, made their own conclusions regarding whether nuclear weapons were inherently indiscriminate. Judge Schwebel, for example, speculated on different types of uses and which of these might be lawful or not. After discussing the legality

---

[96] Separate Opinion of Judge Stephen M. Schwebel, Nuclear Weapons Advisory Opinion, p. 98, available at: www.icj-cij.org/docket/files/95/7515.pdf.

[97] As noted above, the issue of proportionality is addressed separately in Section C below.

[98] Written Statement of the United States, Nuclear Weapons Advisory Opinion, 20 June 1995, p. 23.

[99] Written Statement of the UK, Nuclear Weapons Advisory Opinion, June 1995, p. 52, para. 3.68.

[100] *Ibid.*, pp. 53, 52, paras. 3.69, 3.67.   [101] *Ibid.*, p. 52, para. 3.69.   [102] *Ibid.*

[103] Even Solomon Islands, which adjudged that nuclear weapons were unlawful, referred to the 'surgical precision of a nuclear attack' while dismissing such attacks as 'entirely theoretical'. Written Statement of Solomon Islands, Nuclear Weapons Advisory Opinion, 19 June 1995, p. 51, para. 3.57.

of a massive attack against an enemy's cities, he refers to the regularly projected scenario of use of tactical nuclear weapons against submarines that are
themselves equipped with nuclear weapons: 'discrete military or naval targets
so situated that substantial civilian casualties would not ensue'.[104] He cites the
example of the use of a nuclear 'depth-charge' to destroy a submarine about to
fire nuclear missiles, or which has already fired one or more of its nuclear missiles, and concludes that this 'might well be lawful':

> By the circumstance of its use, the nuclear depth-charge would not give rise
> to immediate civilian casualties ... The submarine's destruction by a nuclear
> weapon would produce radiation in the sea, but far less than the radiation
> that firing of its missiles would produce on and over land.[105]

He went on to cite what he referred to as an 'intermediate' case, namely the
use of nuclear weapons to destroy an enemy army situated in a desert. He concluded that '[i]n certain circumstances, such a use of nuclear weapons might
meet the tests of discrimination and proportionality; in others not.'[106] Although
this conclusion does not constitute a particularly helpful analysis, it is clear
that, in Schwebel's view, nuclear weapons are not by nature indiscriminate.[107]

Are the effects of nuclear weapons capable of being controlled?

The destructive power of the nuclear weapon will have a significant impact on
whether its effects can be controlled as required by customary law. It is hard to
see how the effects of anything other than a low-yield nuclear weapon[108] could
be said to be controllable. Indeed, the Nuclear Weapons Advisory Opinion
contained the following affirmation whereby the ICJ:

> also notes that nuclear weapons are explosive devices whose energy results
> from the fusion or fission of the atom. By its very nature, that process, in
> nuclear weapons as they exist today, releases not only immense quantities of
> heat and energy, but also powerful and prolonged radiation. According to

---

[104] Separate Opinion of Judge Schwebel, Nuclear Weapons Advisory Opinion, p. 98.

[105] *Ibid.*, pp. 98–9. See also, e.g., M. Koskenniemi, 'The silence of law/the voice of justice' in
L. Boisson de Chazournes and P. Sands (eds.), *International Law, the International Court of
Justice and Nuclear Weapons* (Cambridge University Press, 1999), p. 493.

[106] Separate Opinion of Judge Schwebel, Nuclear Weapons Advisory Opinion, p. 99.

[107] In contrast, India, itself now a nuclear weapon power, stated in 1995 that 'it is easy to come
to the conclusion that the use of nuclear weapons in an armed conflict is unlawful being
contrary to the conventional as well as customary international law because such use
cannot distinguish between combatants and non-combatants'. Written Statement of the
Government of India to the ICJ, Nuclear Weapons Advisory Opinion, 20 June 1995, p. 4,
available at: www.icj-cij.org/docket/files/95/8688.pdf.

[108] There is no agreed definition of what constitutes 'low-yield'. Burroughs *et al.*, refer to a definition from the Joint Chiefs of Staff manual, *Doctrine for Joint Nuclear Operations*, wherein
it is stated: '**nuclear yields**. The energy released in the detonation of a nuclear weapon,
measured in terms of the kilotons or megatons of trinitrotoluene required to produce the
same energy release.' Yields are categorized as:

the material before the Court, the first two causes of damage are vastly more powerful than the damage caused by other weapons, while the phenomenon of radiation is said to be peculiar to nuclear weapons. These characteristics render the nuclear weapon potentially catastrophic. *The destructive power of nuclear weapons cannot be contained in either space or time.* They have the potential to destroy all civilization and the entire ecosystem of the planet.[109]

Dinstein refers to possible use of a 'clean' nuclear weapon, without specifying what such a device would be. One possibility could be so-called 'neutron' bombs. Solomon Islands described these in the following terms:

> bombs from 1 to several kilotonnes: these are actually thermonuclear bombs of limited power which are not surrounded by a belt of uranium-238; the effect of the shockwaves is less significant than other nuclear weapons. Although neutron bombs have less of an effect on solid objects (buildings, vehicles) they produce proportionately more radiation and hence create greater damage to victims and the environment in relation to their actual size.[110]

As the BBC has reported, whereas a standard thermonuclear device would destroy buildings in a vast shockwave of heat and pressure, a neutron bomb would detonate above a battlefield with, 'theoretically', little risk of destroying the surrounding area. The blast would be confined to a radius of no more than a couple of hundred metres but a massive wave of radiation would knock out tank crews, infantry and other personnel. Even if the buildings did remain, survivors would soon find their bodies filled with elements such as strontium,

- very low – less than 1 kiloton.
- low – 1 kiloton to 10 kilotons.
- medium – over 10 kilotons to 50 kilotons.
- high – over 50 kilotons to 500 kilotons.
- very high – over 500 kilotons.

Joint Chiefs of Staff, *Doctrine for Joint Theater Nuclear Operations*, Joint Publication 3–12.1, 9 February 1996, GL-2, available at: www.fas.org/nuke/guide/usa/doctrine/dod/jp3_12_1.pdf. See C. J. Moxley Jr, J. Burroughs and J. Granoff, 'Nuclear weapons and compliance with international humanitarian law and the Nuclear Non-Proliferation Treaty', *Fordham International Law Journal* 34 (2011), 595–696, available at: http://ir.lawnet.fordham.edu/ilj/vol34/iss4/1.

[109] Nuclear Weapons Advisory Opinion, para. 35 (emphasis added). See also, in a similar vein, E. David, 'The Status of Nuclear Weapons in the Light of the Court's Opinion of 8 July 1996' in L. Boisson de Chazournes and P. Sands (eds.), *International Law, the International Court of Justice and Nuclear Weapons* (Cambridge University Press, 1999), p. 212.

[110] Written Statement of Solomon Islands, Nuclear Weapons Advisory Opinion, 19 June 1995, p. 45, para. 3.44, citing *L'Encyclopaedia Universalis*, Vth, 'Nucléaire (armement)'; Etude d'ensemble des armes nucléaires; Rapport du Secrétaire général, doc. ONU A/35/392, 12 septembre 1980 … Appendix 1, p. 180, §23; Etude d'ensemble des armes nucléaires, Rapport du Secrétaire général, doc. ONU A/45/373, 18 septembre 1990. See also A. Resibois and A. Joffroy, Armes nucléaires: les médecins désarmés (Brussels: Association Médicale pour la Prévention de la Guerre Nucléaire, 1981), pp. 12–13; H. Firket. 'Effets biologiques et médicaux des explosions nucléaires' in *Vivre ensemble ou mourir: le dilemme nucléaire* (Brussels: Association Médicale pour la Prévention de la Guerre Nucléaire, 1986), pp. 17–18.

ensuring that they eventually die of radiation poisoning.[111] According to one anti-nuclear campaigner, 'The neutron bomb became a way of legitimising nuclear weapons. The radiation would clear up after a strike and it was regarded as the magic wand of nuclear weapons – you could wave it and all the people would be gone.'[112]

C. A 'disproportionate' weapon?

Even where a lawful military objective is targeted by a party to an armed conflict, that attack may still be unlawful where it causes incidental civilian deaths or injuries, destruction of, or damage to, civilian objects, or a combination of both, which are 'excessive' compared to the expected military advantage. Thus, as Dinstein rightly notes, proportionality has 'nothing to do with injury to combatants or damage to military objectives'.[113] It is also irrelevant *for the purposes of IHL* that a use of nuclear weapons by one party to a conflict may rapidly lead to an escalating use of such weapons.[114] This is a critical political and moral consideration, undoubtedly, as well as an element in determining proportionality within the realm of *jus ad bellum*, but not a legal one relevant for *jus in bello*.

In 1977 Additional Protocol I the rule of proportionality *in bello* is seen as a form of indiscriminate attack.[115] Thus, according to Article 51(5) of the Protocol: 'Among others, the following types of attacks are to be considered as indiscriminate: ... (b) an attack which may be expected to cause incidental loss of civilian life, injury to civilians, damage to civilian objects, or a combination thereof, which would be excessive in relation to the concrete and direct military advantage anticipated.' This provision is said by the UK to be the codification

---

[111] BBC, 'Neutron bomb: why "clean" is deadly', 15 July 1999, available at: http://news.bbc.co.uk/2/hi/science/nature/395689.stm.

[112] *Ibid.* According to reported remarks by Christopher Paine of the US Natural Resources Defense Council, 'The quest for fourth-generation nuclear weapons – based on new physical principles and new ways to compress fusion fuel – goes back to the early years of the nuclear labs ... It's been a Holy Grail of the [nuclear weapons] labs, to find a clean, low-yield, very compact nuclear explosive device.' The frustration is almost equally old: 'They've had classified projects since the '50s ... and have never gotten there.' 'Opening Pandora's Nuclear War Chest' (University of Wisconsin, 2002), available at: http://whyfiles.org/167new_nukes/3.html.

[113] Dinstein, *The Conduct of Hostilities under the Law of International Armed Conflict*, p. 129.

[114] Nuclear Weapons Advisory Opinion, para. 43; and see, e.g., David, 'The Status of Nuclear Weapons', p. 219.

[115] This chapter treats the rule separately as a distinct rule, as does the ICRC in its 2005 assessment of the state of customary international humanitarian law. See ICRC Study of Customary IHL, Rules 11, 12, and 14. See also Solis, who claims proportionality is one of the four core principles of the law of armed conflict, the other three being distinction, military necessity and unnecessary suffering. Solis, *The Law of Armed Conflict*, Section 7.0, p. 250.

'for the first time as a treaty rule' of an already 'longstanding principle'.[116] In her Dissenting Opinion to the Nuclear Weapons Advisory Opinion, Judge Higgins observed that the 'principle' of proportionality, 'even if finding no specific mention, is reflected in many provisions' of 1977 Additional Protocol 1. 'Thus even a legitimate target may not be attacked if the collateral civilian casualties would be disproportionate to the specific military gain from the attack.'[117]

Mirroring the language used in the Protocol, the ICRC has expressed this customary rule as follows:

> Launching an attack which may be expected to cause incidental loss of civilian life, injury to civilians, damage to civilian objects, or a combination thereof, which would be excessive in relation to the concrete and direct military advantage anticipated, is prohibited.[118]

It affirms that state practice establishes this rule as a norm of customary international law applicable in both international and non-international armed conflicts.[119]

1. What is 'excessive'?

The question of what constitutes 'excessive' is, predictably, a thorny one – 'not an exact science' in the words of Dinstein.[120] As the ICRC observes: 'Of course, the disproportion between losses and damages caused and the military advantages anticipated raises a delicate problem; in some situations there will be no room for doubt, while in other situations there may be reason for hesitation. In such situations the interests of the civilian population should prevail.'[121] Dinstein claims that the damage is excessive when 'the disproportion is not in doubt'. He notes that in the 1998 Rome Statute of the International Criminal Court, the adverb 'clearly' is added to qualify

---

[116] UK Manual of the Law of Armed Conflict, §5.33.2.

[117] Dissenting Opinion of Judge Rosalyn Higgins, Nuclear Weapons Advisory Opinion, §20.

[118] ICRC Study of Customary IHL, Rule 14, available at: www.icrc.org/customary-ihl/eng/docs/v1_rul_rule14. Dinstein notes that the 'exact formulation of the principle of proportionality in the Protocol has been criticized by some commentators, but nobody seriously denies the validity of the principle of proportionality as such.' Dinstein, *The Conduct of Hostilities under the Law of International Armed Conflict*, p. 130, referring particularly to W. Hays Parks, 'Air war and the law of war', *Air Force Law Review* 32 (1990), 1–225, at 171–4.

[119] See *ibid*. The rule of proportionality in attacks does not appear in either of the primary texts governing NIACs: Common Article 3 to the 1949 Geneva Conventions or 1977 Additional Protocol II.

[120] Dinstein, *The Conduct of Hostilities under the Law of International Armed Conflict*, p. 132. See also UK Manual of the Law of Armed Conflict, para. 2.7.1; and, for useful case examples, Solis, *The Law of Armed Conflict*, Section 7.4, pp. 272–85.

[121] Sandoz *et al.*, *Commentary on the Additional Protocols of 8 June 1997*, para. 1979.

the word excessive.[122] He cautions, however, that the view that the notion would only apply 'when the disproportion is unbearably large' goes 'too far'.[123]

The ICRC Commentary, referring to the claim occasionally made 'whereby even if they are very high, civilian losses and damage may be justified if the military advantage at stake is of great importance', affirms that such a claim is 'contrary to the fundamental rules of the Protocol' and that 'in particular' it conflicts with Article 48 ('Basic rule') and with paragraphs 1 and 2 of Article 51. In its view: 'The Protocol does not provide any justification for attacks which cause extensive civilian losses and damages. Incidental losses and damages should never be extensive.'[124] Dinstein, however, rejects this as a 'misreading of the text'.[125] He claims that extensive civilian casualties need not be excessive in light of the concrete and direct military advantage expected from an attack.[126]

Whatever the precise nature of the balancing of expected military advantage and civilian harm, Boothby argues that the proportionality rule has 'no direct applicability to the legitimacy of a weapon'.[127] This is not wholly persuasive given the UK's own view of the state of the law,[128] but even were it accepted that disproportionate effects were covered by the prohibition on inherently indiscriminate weapons, according to Doswald-Beck:

> Although not impossible, it is very difficult to use proportionality to test whether a weapon is indiscriminate in nature. To do so, one would have to decide in advance if any use of the weapon in question would inevitably lead to civilian casualties or civilian damage which would be excessive in relation to any military objective that could be attacked using that weapon.[129]

---

[122] Thus, according to Article 8(2)(b)(iv) of the 1998 Rome Statute of the International Criminal Court, a serious violation of the laws and customs applicable in international armed conflict includes: 'Intentionally launching an attack in the knowledge that such attack will cause incidental loss of life or injury to civilians or damage to civilian objects or widespread, long-term and severe damage to the natural environment which would be clearly excessive in relation to the concrete and direct overall military advantage anticipated.' Rome Statute of the International Criminal Court, Rome 17 July 1998, in force 1 July 2002, 2187 UNTS 90.

[123] Dinstein, *The Conduct of Hostilities under the Law of International Armed Conflict*, p. 131, citing A. Randelzhofer, 'Civilian objects', *Encyclopaedia of Public International Law* (Amsterdam: Elsevier Science Publications, 1992), p. 606.

[124] Sandoz et al., *Commentary on the Additional Protocols of 8 June 1997*, para. 1980.

[125] Dinstein, *The Conduct of Hostilities under the Law of International Armed Conflict*, p. 131.

[126] *Ibid.*

[127] Boothby, *Weapons and the Law of Armed Conflict*, p. 79.

[128] See *UK Manual on the Law of Armed Conflict*, para. 6.4.

[129] Doswald-Beck, 'International humanitarian law and the Advisory Opinion'.

2. Are nuclear weapons inherently 'disproportionate' in the harm they cause to civilians?

Surprisingly, the ICJ did not discuss the rule of proportionality in attacks in its Advisory Opinion, especially given that several states, including nuclear weapon states, did raise the issue. The UK, for example, specifically discussed the application of the rule to nuclear weapons in its Written Statement to the ICJ. It did not assert that the rule is inapplicable, only that its application to nuclear weapons is not such as to render the weapons inherently unlawful:

> The reality … is that nuclear weapons might be used in a wide variety of circumstances with very different results in terms of likely civilian casualties. … It is by no means the case that every use of nuclear weapons against a military objective would inevitably cause very great collateral civilian casualties.[130]

Similarly, in its Written Statement to the ICJ, the United States referred to the argument that the use of nuclear weapons would be unlawful 'because it would cause collateral injury or damage to civilians or civilian objects that would be excessive in relation to the military advantage anticipated from the attacks'.[131] It affirmed that a determination as to whether an attack with nuclear weapons would be disproportionate would depend 'entirely' on the circumstances, 'including the nature of the enemy threat, the importance of destroying the objective, the character, size and likely effects of the device, and the magnitude of the risk to civilians'. It ended with the simple assertion that nuclear weapons 'are not inherently disproportionate'.[132] This is, however, as Schmitt rightly opines, merely a 'conclusory' argument.[133] Indeed, he refers to the Court's statement that those opposing the illegality of use of nuclear weapons were unable to give precise examples of where such use would meet all of the requirements of IHL.[134]

The UK also discussed the application of the rule of proportionality to nuclear weapons. As the UK recognised, it has often been assumed, both that any use of nuclear weapons would cause extensive civilian losses, and that such

---

[130] Written Statement of the United Kingdom to the ICJ, Nuclear Weapons Advisory Opinion, June 1995, p. 53, para. 3.70.

[131] Written Statement of the United States to the ICJ, Nuclear Weapons Advisory Opinion, 20 June 1995, p. 23.

[132] *Ibid.*

[133] Schmitt, 'The International Court of Justice and the use of nuclear weapons', 105.

[134] *Ibid.*, referring to the Nuclear Weapons Advisory Opinion, para. 94: 'The Court would observe that none of the States advocating the legality of the use of nuclear weapons under certain circumstances, including the "clean" use of smaller, low yield, tactical nuclear weapons, has indicated what, supposing such limited use were feasible, would be the precise circumstances justifying such use.' As Schmitt observes in a footnote, the United Kingdom came closest to formulating such examples.

losses would necessarily be excessive in relation to any military advantage that might result.[135] It cited the Written Statement of Solomon Islands to the ICJ whereby that state had argued that 'the use of nuclear weapon [*sic*] with enhanced power' increases its effects 'and adds indiscriminate effects which cannot be limited to any permitted military objectives'.[136] The UK affirmed, however, that such:

> assumptions tend to be based on assessments of the likely effects of a nuclear attack on or near a city. The reality, however, is that nuclear weapons might be used in a wide variety of circumstances with very different results in terms of likely civilian casualties. In some cases, such as the use of a low-yield nuclear weapon against warships on the High Seas or troops in sparsely populated areas, it is possible to envisage a nuclear attack which caused comparatively few civilian casualties. It is by no means the case that every use of nuclear weapons against a military objective would inevitably cause very great collateral civilian casualties.[137]

Neither France nor the Russian Federation engaged in any discussion of proportionality in their written statements.

In his Dissenting Opinion, Judge Schwebel claimed that the use of tactical nuclear weapons against submarines that were themselves equipped with nuclear weapons:

> would easily meet the test of proportionality; the damage that the submarine's missiles could inflict on the population and territory of the target state would infinitely outweigh that entailed in the destruction of the submarine and its crew. The submarine's destruction by a nuclear weapon would produce radiation in the sea, but far less than the radiation that firing of its missiles would produce on and over land.[138]

With the greatest respect to the former president of the ICJ, however, this appears to be something of a mischaracterisation of the proportionality rule. As the citation of Dinstein on the applicable rule, noted above, helped to clarify, proportionality is a balance between 'collateral damage' (i.e. civilian death and injuries and damage to civilian objects) which might be expected on the one hand, and expected military advantage resulting from striking lawful military objectives on the other. Instead, Schwebel apparently sees the balancing to be conducted between the attacker destroying a lawful military objective (the submarine as well its crew), and the potential damage to civilians that would

---

[135] Written Statement of the UK, Nuclear Weapons Advisory Opinion, June 1995, p. 53, para. 3.70.

[136] Written Statement of Solomon Islands, Nuclear Weapons Advisory Opinion, 19 June 1995, p. 48, para. 3.50.

[137] Written Statement of the UK, Nuclear Weapons Advisory Opinion, June 1995, p. 53, para. 3.70.

[138] *Ibid.*, pp. 98–9.

result from a presumably unlawful and speculative strike on the attacker's own civilian population.

His conclusion, however, seems robust. In the case he describes, the use of the low-yield nuclear weapon would seemingly inflict few or even no civilian casualties, and cause no damage to civilian objects (except and insofar as the high seas around a submarine equipped with nuclear weapons can be deemed a civilian object or IHL protecting the environment would form part of the proportionality equation).[139] They might, though, have a very significant expected military advantage.

More problematic is the UK's other example of possible lawful use, namely of a low-yield nuclear weapon against 'troops in sparsely populated areas'. Presumably 'sparsely populated' excludes entirely a city or town and would encompass a desert or other extremely remote rural area 'in conditions of no wind'.[140] It might even cover the use of such a weapon by the Democratic People's Republic of Korea (DPR Korea) in repelling a combined attack against it by South Korean and US troops across the demilitarised zone that lies between DPR Korea and the Republic of Korea.[141]

A more widespread use of nuclear weapons would be significantly harder to justify than a pinpoint strike against a lawful military objective. In practice, multiple use of nuclear weapons would likely have to be justified under

---

[139] It is unclear to what extent Schwebel was considering radiation as purely potential harm to a civilian object (i.e. the sea) and to what extent he was incorporating environmental concerns into a proportionality equation. According to Article 8(2)(b)(iv) of the 1998 Rome Statute of the International Criminal Court, in an international armed conflict the Court potentially has jurisdiction over the war crime of 'Intentionally launching an attack in the knowledge that such attack will cause incidental loss of life or injury to civilians or damage to civilian objects or widespread, long-term and severe damage to the natural environment which would be clearly excessive in relation to the concrete and direct overall military advantage anticipated.' This could be read as distinguishing *physical* damage to civilian objects with longer-term damage to the natural environment, which presumably would not be merely physical in nature. There is also no notion of cumulative harm ('a combination thereof'), as set out in Article 57(2)(a)(iii) of 1977 Additional Protocol I. See generally Chapter 10 of this work.

[140] See, e.g., Boothby, *Weapons and the Law of Armed Conflict*, p. 216.

[141] The DPR Korean statement in 1995 that it was clearly 'against the threat or use of nuclear weapons' (Letter dated 18 May 1995 from the Permanent Representative of the Democratic People's Republic of Korea to the UN) must be seen in the light of its subsequent acquisition of such weapons and its withdrawal in 2003 from the Nuclear Non-Proliferation Treaty. Moreover, in early March 2013 DPR Korea threatened a pre-emptive strike against the 'headquarters of the aggressors'. T. Branigan and E. MacAskill, 'UN backs expansion of North Korea sanctions after nuclear threat', *Guardian*, 7 March 2013, available at: www.guardian.co.uk/world/2013/mar/07/north-korea-threat-un-sanctions. Later the same month, DPR Korea said that it would attack US military bases in Japan in retaliation for the use of B-52 bombers in joint exercises with South Korea. See, e.g., M. Stone, 'North Korea issues fresh threat to America', *Sky News*, 21 March 2013, available at: http://news.sky.com/story/1067695/north-korea-issues-fresh-threat-to-america.

international law – if such justification is even possible – by reference to the law governing belligerent reprisals.[142]

The UK has stated that the legality of the use of nuclear weapons 'fall[s] to be dealt with by reference to the same general principles as apply to other weapons'.[143] In applying these principles (some prefer the term rules), the ICJ's assertion that the use of nuclear weapons would 'generally be contrary to the rules of international law applicable in armed conflict, and in particular the principles and rules of humanitarian law' appears correct, at a minimum in the case of the application of the rules of distinction and proportionality.

D.   Precautions in attacks

Nonetheless, if it is accepted that there are exceptional, extreme circumstances in which the use of nuclear weapons might conceivably satisfy the rules of distinction and proportionality, parties to an armed conflict are still required to take precautions in attacks in accordance with customary law. The notion of taking 'precautions' in attacks was first codified in Article 57 of 1977 Additional Protocol I. Paragraph 1 of the provision states as follows:

> In the conduct of military operations, constant care shall be taken to spare the civilian population, civilians and civilian objects.

It is then stipulated that those who plan or decide upon an attack are required to do 'everything feasible' to verify that the objectives to be attacked are neither civilians nor civilian objects and are not subject to special protection but are lawful military objectives and that it is not otherwise prohibited by the Protocol to attack them.[144] In the choice of means and methods of attack, 'all feasible precautions' must be taken 'with a view to avoiding, and in any event to minimizing, incidental loss of civilian life, injury to civilians and damage to civilian objects'.[145] Parties to an international armed conflict must 'refrain from deciding to launch any attack which may be expected to cause incidental loss of civilian life, injury to civilians, damage to civilian objects, or a combination thereof, which would be excessive in relation to the concrete and direct military advantage anticipated'.[146]

---

[142] See, in this regard, Chapter 7 of this work.

[143] UK Manual of the Law of Armed Conflict, p. 117, para. 6.17.

[144] 1977 Additional Protocol I, Art. 57(2)(a)(i).

[145] 1977 Additional Protocol I, Art. 57(2)(a)(ii).

[146] 1977 Additional Protocol I, Art. 57(2)(a)(iii). Similarly, according to paragraph (b), an attack shall be cancelled or suspended if it becomes apparent that the objective is not a military one or is subject to special protection or that the attack may be expected to cause incidental loss of civilian life, injury to civilians, damage to civilian objects, or a combination thereof, which would be excessive in relation to the concrete and direct military advantage anticipated.

According to sub-paragraph (c), effective advance warning 'shall be given' of attacks that may affect the civilian population, 'unless circumstances do not permit'. Further, when a choice is possible between several military objectives for obtaining a similar military advantage, the objective to be selected shall be that where the attack may be expected to cause the least danger to civilian lives and to civilian objects.[147] Article 57 concludes with the statement that no provision contained within the Article 'may be construed as authorizing any attacks against the civilian population, civilians or civilian objects'.[148]

The ICRC Commentary on the provision notes that it was 'a subject that required lengthy discussions and difficult negotiations in the Diplomatic Conference, and the text which was finally agreed upon is the fruit of laborious compromise between the various points of view'.[149] Nonetheless, the notion of an obligation to take precautions in attacks is both important and generally accepted.[150] It is therefore rather surprising that the ICJ did not even refer to the issue in its Nuclear Weapons Advisory Opinion.

The ICRC has subsequently expressed the concept as a customary rule applicable in NIACs as well as IACs in the following terms:

> In the conduct of military operations, constant care must be taken to spare the civilian population, civilians and civilian objects. All feasible precautions must be taken to avoid, and in any event to minimize, incidental loss of civilian life, injury to civilians and damage to civilian objects.[151]

The twin requirements of taking constant care to spare civilians as well as taking all feasible precautions to, at least, minimise civilian harm, are considered in turn.

1. Taking constant care to spare civilians

In the conduct of military operations,[152] constant care must be taken to spare the civilian population, civilians and civilian objects. This obligation of due diligence is, as the ICRC has noted, a corollary of the basic rule set out

---

[147] 1977 Additional Protocol I, Art. 57(3).   [148] 1977 Additional Protocol I, Art. 57(5).

[149] Sandoz *et al.*, *Commentary on the Additional Protocols of 8 June 1977*, para. 2184.

[150] In its study of customary IHL, the ICRC notes that when it appealed to the parties to the conflict in the Middle East in October 1973, the so-called Yom Kippur War, to respect the obligation to take precautions in attack, 'the States concerned (Egypt, Iraq, Israel, and Syria) replied favourably'. See ICRC Study of Customary IHL, Rule 15, available at: www.icrc.org/customary-ihl/eng/docs/v1_rul_rule15.

[151] ICRC Study of Customary IHL, Rule 15. Boothby affirms that there 'can be little doubt' that the requirement in Article 57(1) of 1977 Additional Protocol I 'is a customary principle'. Boothby, *The Law of Targeting*, p. 72.

[152] The United Kingdom notes that this term has a 'wider connotation than "attacks" and would include the movement or deployment of armed forces'. The ICRC commentary on the provision similarly specifies that the term should be understood to mean 'any

in Article 48 whereby parties to an armed conflict must always 'distinguish' between the civilian population and combatants, as well as between civilian objects and military objectives.[153] In its 2005 study of customary IHL, the ICRC even argued that the principle of distinction 'inherently requires respect for this rule'. According to the UK, 'the commander will have to bear in mind the effect on the civilian population of what he is planning to do and take steps to reduce that impact as much as possible'.[154]

2. Feasible precautions

The term 'feasible' with respect to precautions is not defined in 1977 Additional Protocol I, but the following definition is offered by Amended Protocol II to the 1980 Convention on Certain Conventional Weapons (CCW):

> Feasible precautions are those precautions which are practicable or practically possible taking into account all circumstances ruling at the time, including humanitarian and military considerations.[155]

Those feasible precautions most relevant to a proposed use of nuclear weapons are set out in Article 57, paragraph 2(a)(ii) of 1977 Additional Protocol I. This provision stipulates that those who plan or decide upon an attack shall take all feasible precautions in the choice of means and methods of attack with a view to avoiding, and in any event to minimising, incidental loss of civilian life, injury to civilians and damage to civilian objects. As the UK has observed, this is an obligation to select the weapons and tactics 'which will cause the least incidental damage commensurate with military success'.[156] While Dinstein may well be correct in asserting that the current state of the law is not yet such as to oblige parties to a conflict to use precision-guided munitions in urban settings, any

---

movements, manoeuvres and other activities whatsoever carried out by the armed forces with a view to combat'. Sandoz *et al.*, *Commentary on the Additional Protocols of 8 June 1997*, para. 2191.

[153] *Ibid.*

[154] UK Manual of the Law of Armed Conflict, para. 5.31.1.

[155] Article 3(10), Protocol on Prohibitions or Restrictions on the Use of Mines, Booby-Traps and Other Devices as Amended on 3 May 1996 (Amended Protocol II). Dinstein cites the Eritrea–Ethiopia Claims Commission, which noted that feasible precautions are 'not precautions that are practically impossible'. Dinstein, *The Conduct of Hostilities under the Law of International Armed Conflict*, p. 139, citing Eritrea–Ethiopia Claims Commission, Partial Award, Central Front, Ethiopia's Claim 2 (2004), 43 ILM 1275 (2004), p. 1295. See also Green, *The Contemporary Law of Armed Conflict*, p. 181.

[156] UK Manual of the Law of Armed Conflict, pp. 82–3, para. 5.32.4. But see an official amendment to the Manual in July 2011, in which the wording of the obligation was somewhat softened. See UK, 'Joint Services Publication 383 – The Manual of the Law of Armed Conflict, Amendment 4 (July 2011)', para. 31, available at: www.gov.uk/government/uploads/system/uploads/attachment_data/file/27870/20110725JSP383Amendment4Jul11.pdf.

attack using a weapon that is expected to cause excessive civilian harm would be unlawful.[157] According to the ICRC:

> As regards weapons, their precision and range should be taken into account; such precautions coincide with the concerns of military commanders wishing to economise on ammunition and to avoid hitting points of no military interest. When a well-placed 500 kg projectile is sufficient to render a military objective useless, there is no reason to use a 10 ton bomb or a series of projectiles aimed without sufficient precision.[158]

This requirement for precautions in attacks can be most appropriately seen as taking the rule of proportionality one step further. The ICRC rightly opines that '[i]n itself this rule does not imply any prohibition of specific weapons'.[159] But even should a proposed use of nuclear weapons satisfy both the rule of distinction and the rule of proportionality, a further assessment must be made as to whether alternative, less destructive weapons might adequately fulfil the military task.[160] Given the 'unique' characteristics of nuclear weapons, in many instances this threshold would not be met. In one example, as discussed briefly above, Judge Schwebel refers to the use of nuclear weapons against a submarine equipped with nuclear weapons. He asserts that:

> Nor is it as certain that the use of a conventional depth-charge would discharge the mission successfully; the far greater force of a nuclear weapon could ensure destruction of the submarine whereas a conventional depth-charge might not.[161]

This is a specific and exceptional example. It assumes that the location of the submarine is known precisely (no small assumption in the case of nuclear-powered and nuclear weapon-equipped submarines); that nuclear weapons can be deployed in a timely fashion (having first secured the necessary authority high up the chain of command) and with sufficient accuracy; and that the necessary proportionality calculations have been made, including the determination that alternative, less harmful weapons would not be sufficient to achieve the military task.

Finally, in accordance with Article 57, paragraph 2(c), 'effective advance warning shall be given of attacks which may affect the civilian population, unless circumstances do not permit.' Green notes that before the use of the

---

[157] Dinstein suggests only that such an attack must 'be recoiled from'. Dinstein, *The Conduct of Hostilities under the Law of International Armed Conflict*, pp. 142–3. See also Solis, *The Law of Armed Conflict*, Section 7.4, pp. 274–5.

[158] Sandoz *et al.*, *Commentary on the Additional Protocols of 8 June 1977*, para. 2200.

[159] *Ibid.*, para. 2201.

[160] The UK states that in considering the means of methods of attack to be used, a commander should have regard to factors including 'what weapons are available, their range, accuracy, and radius of effect'. UK Manual of the Law of Armed Conflict, p. 83, para. 5.32.5.

[161] Separate Opinion of Judge Schwebel, Nuclear Weapons Advisory Opinion, p. 99.

atomic bomb against Hiroshima in 1945, the Japanese authorities were warned that named cities were likely to be heavily bombarded and that civilians should be evacuated.[162]

Conclusion

Absent 'new rules' laid down by 1977 Additional Protocol I that have not become customary international law,[163] it does not appear to be seriously contested that international humanitarian law applies to nuclear weapons. The ICJ stated in its Nuclear Weapons Advisory Opinion that:

> In the view of the vast majority of States as well as writers there can be no doubt as to the applicability of humanitarian law to nuclear weapons ... The Court shares that view ... [I]t cannot be concluded ... that the established principles and rules of humanitarian law applicable in armed conflict did not apply to nuclear weapons. Such a conclusion would be incompatible with the intrinsically humanitarian character of the legal principles in question which permeates the entire law of armed conflict and applies to all forms of warfare and to all kinds of weapons, those of the past, those of the present and those of the future.[164]

Thus, the rule that there is no unlimited right to select and use means of warfare, the rules of distinction and proportionality, and the obligation to take all feasible precautions in attack, all form part of the corpus of customary international law, and, as such, are all applicable to nuclear weapons.[165] Greenwood claimed that the question posed by the UN General Assembly to the ICJ placed the Court:

> in an exceptionally difficult position, because it could not possibly consider all the combinations of circumstances in which nuclear weapons might be used or their use threatened. Yet unless one takes the position that the use of nuclear weapons is always lawful (which is obvious

---

[162] Green, *The Contemporary Law of Armed Conflict*, p. 182.

[163] See, e.g., Boothby, *Weapons and the Law of Armed Conflict*, pp. 216–20.

[164] Nuclear Weapons Advisory Opinion, paras. 85–6.

[165] According to the ICRC, 'The principles and rules of international humanitarian law, and in particular the principles of distinction and proportionality and the prohibition on causing superfluous injury or unnecessary suffering, apply to the use of nuclear weapons. The ICRC finds it difficult to envisage how the use of nuclear weapons could be compatible with the principles and rules of international humanitarian law.' See F. Bugnion, 'The International Committee of the Red Cross and nuclear weapons: from Hiroshima to the dawn of the 21st century', *International Review of the Red Cross* 87(859) (2005), 511–24, at 522. See also, e.g., R. A. Falk, 'Nuclear weapons, international law and the World Court: a historic encounter', *American Journal of International Law* 91 (1997), 64–75, at 65; and Boothby, *Weapons and the Law of Armed Conflict*, p. 216. Boothby does not specifically cite the requirement to take precautions – indeed he cites a 1985 article by Kalshoven in support of his assertion that the 'sophisticated rules' governing precautions in attack are not

nonsense), falls outside the law (which no state suggested) or is always unlawful (a view which has had some supporters but which the majority of the Court quite rightly rejected), then the answer to the General Assembly's question would have to depend upon a careful examination of those circumstances.[166]

Of course, if the question had been straightforward, it is unlikely that recourse to the Court would have been necessary. As is well known, the ICJ concluded that any use of nuclear weapons would 'generally be contrary to the rules of international law applicable in armed conflict, and in particular the principles and rules of humanitarian law'.[167] For any given use of nuclear weapons to satisfy these requirements, the circumstances of such use would have to be truly exceptional. But such circumstances, however exceptional they may be, do exist, notably with respect to low-yield nuclear weapons, and it therefore remains unpersuasive to argue that all nuclear weapons are either inherently indiscriminate or inherently disproportionate. As Schmitt has argued:

> Of course, it is no longer the case that use of nuclear weapons would necessarily result in the horrendous human suffering and physical damage caused by the US attacks in 1945. On the contrary, use of small-yield tactical

applicable to nuclear weapons – but their relevance and application is nonetheless asserted here as being integral to ensuring respect for the rules of distinction and proportionality. See Boothby, *Weapons and the Law of Armed Conflict*, p. 219, citing F. Kalshoven, 'Arms, armaments and international law', *Hague Receuil des Cours*, 191 (1985), 183–342. Alone, Boothby even appears to suggest that the principle of discrimination as set out in Article 51 of 1977 Additional Protocol I is also not applicable. He further claims, however, that the reference to the rule of discrimination 'should not, however, be taken to imply any suggestion that nuclear weapons are inherently indiscriminate'. Boothby, *Weapons and the Law of Armed Conflict*, p. 219.

[166] Greenwood, '*Jus ad bellum* and *jus in bello* in the *Nuclear Weapons* Advisory Opinion', p. 249. For example, in its oral statement to the ICJ with respect to the Nuclear Weapons Advisory Opinion, Australia claimed that 'nuclear weapons are by their nature illegal under customary international law, by virtue of fundamental general principles of humanity'. Remarks to the ICJ by the Honourable Gareth Evans, QC, Senator, Minister for Foreign Affairs of Australia, Counsel, The Hague, 30 October 1995.

[167] Nuclear Weapons Advisory Opinion, para. 78. In her Dissenting Judgment, Judge Higgins affirmed that 'in the present stage of weapon development, there may be very limited prospects of a State being able to comply with the requirements of humanitarian law. But that is different from finding the use of nuclear weapons "generally unlawful"'. Dissenting Opinion of Judge Rosalyn Higgins, Nuclear Weapons Advisory Opinion, para. 26. With all due deference, Judge Higgins' affirmation merely seems to confirm, not contradict, an ordinary reading of the Court's Opinion here. Asserting that use of nuclear weapons would be generally unlawful does not mean that such use would always be unlawful; indeed, it accepts that there 'may be very limited prospects of a State being able to comply with the requirements of humanitarian law'.

nuclear weapons in particular circumstances might result in minimal civilian losses.[168]

Based on the Court's reasoning in its 1996 Advisory Opinion, the ICRC stated in 2005 that it found it 'difficult to envisage how a use of nuclear weapons could be compatible with the rules of international humanitarian law'.[169] In 2011 the Council of Delegates of the International Red Cross and Red Crescent Movement adopted a resolution entitled 'Working Towards the Elimination of Nuclear Weapons', which found it:

> difficult to envisage how any use of nuclear weapons could be compatible with the rules of international humanitarian law, in particular the rules of distinction, precaution and proportionality.[170]

The present author concurs. Only low-yield tactical nuclear weapons could realistically be used in accordance with the rules of distinction and proportionality and then only in very specific and highly improbable scenarios in an international armed conflict between nuclear powers.[171]

Moreover, if it is already hard – though not impossible – to envisage lawful use of nuclear weapons in armed conflicts between states, a lawful use in an NIAC is even harder to conceive of.[172] In addition to violating rules of discrimination and proportionality, such use could arguably also violate

---

[168] M. N. Schmitt, 'Book Review: Nuclear Weapons and the World Court', 1998, pp. 1–2, available at: www.usafa.edu/df/dfl/documents/JLS Volume 9/schmitt.pdf. See also, inter alia, Dinstein, *The Conduct of Hostilities under the Law of International Armed Conflict*, p. 86.

[169] 'ICRC statement to the United Nations General Assembly on the Advisory Opinion of the International Court of Justice on the legality of the threat or use of nuclear weapons', *International Review of the Red Cross* 316 (January–February 1997), pp. 118–9. See also C. Greenwood, 'The Advisory Opinion on nuclear weapons and the contribution of the International Court to international humanitarian law', *International Review of the Red Cross* 316 (28 February 1997), 65–75, available at: www.icrc.org/eng/resources/documents/misc/57jnfp.htm.

[170] ICRC, Resolution 1 of the 2011 Council of Delegates, adopted on 26 November 2011, para. 2.

[171] In 2001 the Bush Administration cited, inter alia, 'immediate contingencies' that could lead to US use of nuclear weapons: 'an Iraqi attack on Israel or its neighbors, a North Korean attack on South Korea, or a military confrontation over the status of Taiwan'. United States, 'Nuclear Posture Review Report', Reconstructed report, Submitted to Congress on 31 December 2001, 8 January 2002, p. 16. While DPR Korea and China are nuclear weapon powers, Iraq was not.

[172] In its Advisory Opinion, the ICJ noted that: 'The terms of the question put to the Court by the General Assembly in resolution 49175 K could in principle also cover a threat or use of nuclear weapons by a State within its own boundaries. However, this particular aspect has not been dealt with by any of the States which addressed the Court orally or in writing in these proceedings. The Court finds that it is not called upon to deal with an internal use of nuclear weapons.' Nuclear Weapons Advisory Opinion, para. 50.

the prohibition on acts of terror set out in Article 13(2) of 1977 Additional Protocol II.[173] According to the ICRC, state practice establishes this rule as a norm of customary international law applicable in both international and non-international armed conflicts.[174]

---

[173] 'Acts or threats of violence the primary purpose of which is to spread terror among the civilian population are prohibited.' Protocol Additional to the Geneva Conventions of 12 August 1949, and relating to the Protection of Victims of Non-International Armed Conflicts (Protocol II), Geneva, 8 June 1977, in force 7 December 1978, 1125 UNTS 609.

[174] ICRC Study of Customary IHL, Rule 2, available at: www.icrc.org/customary-ihl/eng/docs/v1_rul_rule2.

5

Nuclear weapons and the unnecessary suffering rule

SIMON O'CONNOR

Introduction

Of the rules of international humanitarian law (IHL) considered in the *Legality of the Threat or Use of Nuclear Weapons* Advisory Opinion, the International Court of Justice (ICJ) determined two to be both 'cardinal' and 'intransgressible'.[1] The first was the rule of distinction while the second was the prohibition on means and methods of warfare of a nature to cause unnecessary suffering (hereafter, the unnecessary suffering rule).[2] But notwithstanding the claimed cardinality of the unnecessary suffering rule and its recognition as a norm of customary international law,[3] its exact content is far from clear. As has been observed:

> [t]he concept of superfluous injury or unnecessary suffering, its objective effect on the victim (severity of the injury, intensity of suffering), and its relation to military necessity (rendering the enemy *hors de combat*) are not interpreted in a consistent and generally accepted manner. This concept continues to be the basis on which judgment is formed, but debates have shown its relative and imprecise character.[4]

Moreover, many of the arguments concerning the legality of any use of nuclear weapons – understandably – centre on the issue of indiscriminate use. This reflects a number of factors, especially the demonstrable consequences for

The views expressed in this chapter reflect the author's opinions and do not necessarily reflect those of the Norwegian Red Cross.

[1] ICJ, *Legality of the Threat or Use of Nuclear Weapons*, Advisory Opinion, 8 July 1996, paras. 78–9 (hereafter, Nuclear Weapons Advisory Opinion).

[2] *Ibid.*, and see Protocol Additional to the Geneva Conventions of 12 August 1949, and relating to the Protection of Victims of International Armed Conflicts (Protocol I), Geneva, 8 June 1977, in force 7 December 1978, 1125 UNTS 3, Art. 35(2) (hereafter, 1977 Additional Protocol I).

[3] See J.-M. Henckaerts and L. Doswald-Beck, *Customary International Humanitarian Law*, 3 vols. (Cambridge University Press, 2005), Vol. I, p. 237 (hereafter, Customary IHL Study).

[4] Y. Sandoz, C. Swinarski and B. Zimmerman (eds.), *Commentary on the Additional Protocols of 8 June 1977 to the Geneva Conventions of 12 August 1949* (Geneva: ICRC/Martinus Nijhoff, 1987), pp. 409–10.

civilian populations of use of atomic weapons in Hiroshima and then in Nagasaki in 1945.[5] Thus, while significant attention is paid to whether any nuclear weapon use would, or could, comply with the rules of distinction and proportionality in attacks, there has been insufficient discussion of its legality under the unnecessary suffering rule.[6] This chapter seeks to help fill that lacuna.

Section A of this chapter summarises the development over time of the unnecessary suffering rule.[7] Section B discusses how the ICJ addressed the rule in its Advisory Opinion and the (limited) extent to which it applied the rule to nuclear weapons. It also looks more particularly at assessments by the Court's judges in their respective separate or dissenting opinions. Section C discusses key factors to be considered when interpreting the rule, including humanitarian concerns and military utility. The predictable long- and medium-term effects of nuclear weapon use are also discussed, as these must inform deliberations regarding compliance with the rule. The conclusion argues that it is almost impossible to conceive of circumstances when engendering the horrific short-, medium- and long-term injuries and suffering among those engaged in combat that are the foreseeable result of nuclear weapon use could truly be deemed necessary.

A.   A brief history of the unnecessary suffering rule

1.   Classicists, Lieber, St Petersburg and The Hague

The notion that international law limits the manner in which parties to an armed conflict conduct hostilities and that certain weapons, given the harm they inflict, ought never to be used, dates back centuries. Two classicists of international law, Grotius and Vattel, both address weapons with particular reference to poison. While one could certainly identify differences between the two authors' views, for present purposes it may be noted that both Vattel (who cites Grotius as a source) and Grotius himself indicate that poisoned weapons

---

[5] For a detailed account of those effects see, e.g., S. Iijima, S. Imahori and K. Gushima, *Hiroshima and Nagasaki: The Physical, Medical and Social Effects of the Atomic Bombings*, Committee for the Compilation of Materials on the Damage Caused by the Atomic Bombs in Hiroshima and Nagasaki, E. Ishikawa and D. L. Swain (trans.) (London: Hutchison, 1981).

[6] This is not to suggest that the general rule has not been subject to much consideration. For an indicative list of writers who have addressed the topic, see, e.g., M. Sassòli, A. A. Bouvier and A. Quintin (eds.), *How Does Law Protect in War*, 3rd edn (Geneva: ICRC, 2011), p. 284. The most recent comprehensive review of the rule is perhaps T. Boutruche, 'L'Interdiction des Maux Superflus: Contribution à l'Étude des Principes et Règles Relatifs aux Moyens et Méthodes de Guerre en Droit International Humanitaire', Ph.D. Thesis (Geneva, 2008).

[7] For a comprehensive history of the rule see, e.g., H. Meyrowitz, 'The principle of superfluous injury or unnecessary suffering: from the Declaration of St. Petersburg of 1868 to Additional Protocol 1 of 1977', *International Review of the Red Cross*, 34 (1994), 98–122.

should never be used.[8] In the words of Vattel, the use of poisoned weapons 'is prohibited by the law of nature, which does not allow us to multiply the evils of war beyond all bounds'.[9]

In its modern iteration, the unnecessary suffering rule can be traced back to the late nineteenth century. The *Instructions for the Government of Armies of the United States in the Field*, promulgated as General Order No. 100 and more popularly known as the Lieber Code[10] after its author Francis Lieber, includes three provisions addressing military necessity. Two of the Lieber Code's Articles in particular illustrate the essence of the unnecessary suffering rule. Article 14 provides that '[m]ilitary necessity, as understood by modern civilized nations, consists in the necessity of those measures which are indispensable for securing the ends of the war, and which are lawful according to the modern law and usages of war'. Then, although Article 15 acknowledges that such military necessity 'admits of all direct destruction of life or limb of armed enemies, and of other persons whose destruction is incidentally unavoidable in the armed contests of the war', Article 16 qualifies this permissiveness by clarifying that it 'does not admit of cruelty – that is, the infliction of suffering for the sake of suffering'. Although much more could be said about the context and how permissible harm was viewed in the mid to late nineteenth century, these remarks mark the beginning of modern considerations of the unnecessary suffering rule.

If the Lieber Code laid the foundations for the construction of this modern rule, then the 1868 St Petersburg Declaration,[11] negotiated by military representatives from seventeen states, could be said to have ushered it in to the corpus of international weapons law. A short instrument directed at prohibiting a particular type of weaponry (materially limited to the use of explosive projectiles under 400 grams that are either explosive or charged with fulminating or inflammable substances), the Declaration articulates the arguments on which the prohibition is based in the following sequential terms, determining:

> That the only legitimate object which states should endeavour to accomplish during war is to weaken the military forces of the enemy;

[8] H. Grotius, *The Rights of War and Peace, Book III*, R. Tuck (ed.) (Indianapolis: Liberty Fund, 2005), pp. 1290–2; E. de Vattel, *The Law of Nations or the Principles of Natural Law*, J. B. Scott (ed.) (Washington: Carnegie Institute of Washington), 1916, p. 289.

[9] E. de Vattel, *The Law of Nations*, B. Kapossy and R. Whatmore (eds.) (Indianapolis: Liberty Fund, 2008), §156, p. 562.

[10] *Instructions for the Government of the Armies of the United States in the Field*, General Order No. 100, 24 April 1863.

[11] Declaration Renouncing the Use, in Time of War, of Explosive Projectiles Under 400 Grammes Weight, St Petersburg, 11 December 1868, in force 11 December 1868, reproduced in A. Roberts and R. Guelff, *Documents on the Laws of War*, 3rd edn (Oxford University Press, 2001), pp. 54–5.

That for this purpose it is sufficient to disable the greatest possible number of men;

That this object would be exceeded by the employment of arms which uselessly aggravate the sufferings of disabled men, or render their death inevitable; [and]

That the employment of such arms would, therefore, be contrary to the laws of humanity.

The Declaration, when referring to the use of weapons that 'uselessly aggravate the sufferings' of the wounded ('disabled men'), seems to articulate the standard in light of (or, one might say, in proportion to) the legitimate purpose of rendering *hors de combat* the greatest number of men, so as to 'weaken' the forces of the enemy. According to that view, the phrase that follows would demand emphasis on the incompatibility of such use with the 'laws of humanity'.[12] But another reading might well be that the proscription in those laws (which are arguably ill-defined, if indeed they are defined at all) refers only to use that causes clearly gratuitous, 'aggravated' suffering – an absolute standard.

The 'sentiments which found expression in the Declaration' are specifically cited as inspiration for two further weapon-specific instruments: the 1899 Hague Declaration prohibiting the use of asphyxiating gases and the 1899 Hague Declaration prohibiting the use of expanding bullets.[13] In terms of lineage, the rhetorical question Vattel posed in 1758 that once an adversary is disabled, 'is there any need that he should inevitably die of his wounds?', resonates in the sentiments informing these two 1899 instruments. Interestingly, among comments by participants in The Hague peace conferences between May and July 1899, phrases such as 'needless cruelty', 'needlessly cruel' or 'uselessly cruel' appear to be the most recurrent.[14] In addition to the three declarations prohibiting particular weapons, Article 23 of the 1899 Hague Regulations[15] generally prohibited employment of arms, projectiles or material of a nature to cause superfluous injury. Adopted at the subsequent Hague Peace Conference in 1907, the 1907 Hague Regulations[16] reiterated Article 23 of their 1899 predecessor, albeit in a slightly amended, perhaps even erroneous formulation. The

---

[12] For detailed analysis of challenges in discerning the principle of humanity, see, e.g., K. Mujezinović Larsen, C. Guldahl Cooper and G. Nystuen (eds.), *Searching for a 'Principle of Humanity' in International Humanitarian Law* (Cambridge University Press, 2012).

[13] Declaration (IV,2) concerning Asphyxiating Gases, The Hague, 29 July 1899, in force 4 September 1900, first preambular paragraph. Declaration (IV,3) concerning Expanding Bullets, The Hague, 29 July 1899, in force 4 September 1900, first preambular paragraph.

[14] *The Proceedings of the Hague Peace Conferences: The Conference of 1899*, J. B. Scott (trans.) (New York: Oxford University Press, 1920), pp. 80–1, 83, 272, and 278.

[15] Regulations annexed to the Convention with Respect to the Laws and Customs of War on Land, The Hague, 29 July 1899, in force 4 September 1900 (1899 Hague Regulations).

[16] Regulations annexed to the Convention With Respect to the Laws and Customs of War on Land, The Hague, 18 October 1907, in force 26 January 1910 (1907 Hague Regulations).

1868 St Petersburg Declaration used the word 'suffering', which appeared in the 1907 Hague Regulations despite the difficulty in defining this term. The original French words '*maux superflus*', used in both the 1899 and 1907 text, have a wider meaning than the English translation used in 1907: 'calculated to cause unnecessary suffering'. French is the authentic text and this broader scope is reflected in the language of Article 35(2) of 1977 Additional Protocol I, which refers to: 'of a nature to cause superfluous injury or unnecessary suffering'.

2. 1977 Additional Protocol I

The decade preceding the adoption in 1977 of the first two additional protocols to the 1949 Geneva Conventions saw significant efforts to formulate general and specific rules governing use of weapons during armed conflict.[17] At the Second Session of the Conference of Government Experts on the Reaffirmation and Development of International Law Applicable in Armed Conflict in 1972, the International Committee of the Red Cross (ICRC) introduced its initial version of the first draft Additional Protocol. Article 30 of the draft, under the general heading of 'Combatants' and a specific provision headed 'Means of Combat', comprised three paragraphs. They read as follows:

1. Combatants' choice of means of combat is not unlimited.
2. It is forbidden to use weapons, projectiles or substances calculated to cause unnecessary suffering, or particularly cruel methods and means.
3. In cases for which no provision is made in the present Protocol, the principle of humanity and the dictates of public conscience shall continue to safeguard populations and combatants pending adoption of fuller regulations.[18]

Twenty-two states proposed amendments: some proposed more than one amendment while certain proposals were made in conjunction with other states.[19] In February 1975 Jean de Preux, a member of the ICRC delegation to the 1974–77 Diplomatic Conference on the Reaffirmation and Development of International Humanitarian Law Applicable in Armed Conflicts, introduced

---

[17] A number of chronologies detail the fora in which such efforts were undertaken. See, e.g., M. Lumsden, 'The prohibition of inhumane and indiscriminate weapons' in *SIPRI Yearbook 1973* (SIPRI/Oxford University Press, 1973), pp. 153–6; F. Kalshoven, *Constraints on the Waging of War* (Geneva: ICRC, 1991), pp. 19–23; see also A. Cassese, 'Weapons causing unnecessary suffering: are they prohibited?', *Riviste di diritto internazionale* 12 (1975), 12–42, reprinted in A. Cassese, *The Human Dimension of International Law: Selected Papers* (Oxford University Press, 2008).

[18] Conference of Government Experts on the Reaffirmation and Development of International Humanitarian Law Applicable in Armed Conflicts, Second Session, Report of the Work of the Conference (Geneva: ICRC, 1972), Vol. 2, p. 5. An identical provision was proposed as Article 18 of the Draft Additional Protocol to Common Article 3 to the four 1949 Geneva Conventions. *Ibid.*, p. 18.

[19] *Ibid.*, pp. 51–7, 59, 61 and 63.

Article 33 of the Draft Protocols at the twenty-sixth meeting of the Diplomatic Conference.[20] The Article had two paragraphs, which under the title 'Prohibition of unnecessary injury' read:

1. The right of Parties to the conflict and of members of their armed forces to adopt methods and means of combat is not unlimited.
2. It is forbidden to employ weapons, projectiles, substances, methods and means which uselessly aggravate the sufferings of disabled adversaries or render their death inevitable in all circumstances.

Citing both the 1907 Hague Regulations (Article 23) and the 1868 St Petersburg Declaration as the basis for paragraph 2 of draft Article 33, de Preux indicated that the purpose of the paragraph was 'in substance, to prohibit unnecessary injury, a concept which was well known but difficult to define'. In the text as ultimately adopted, however, Article 35(2) of 1977 Additional Protocol I prohibits parties to a conflict 'to employ weapons, projectiles and material and methods of warfare *of a nature to cause* superfluous injury or unnecessary suffering' (author's emphasis). This gives specificity to the general rule in paragraph 1 of Article 35: that the parties' choice of 'means and methods of warfare' is not unlimited.

3. The unnecessary suffering rule in other humanitarian law instruments

The large number of permanently and severely injured soldiers as a result of poisoned gas after the First World War was a main rationale for the adoption of the 1925 Gas Protocol.[21] Decades later, this protocol was supplemented by the 1972 Biological Weapons Convention,[22] and reinforced by the Chemical Weapons Convention in 1992.[23] Arguably, these instruments had the rule prohibiting unnecessary suffering at their core, even if the weapons banned under these regimes also necessarily in most cases violate the rule on distinction, if used.

---

[20] Official Records of the Diplomatic Conference on the Reaffirmation and Development of International Humanitarian Law Applicable in Armed Conflicts, Vol. 14, CDDH/III/SR.26, p. 233. De Preux subsequently authored the ICRC's commentary on Article 35 of 1977 Additional Protocol I.

[21] Protocol for the Prohibition of the Use in War of Asphyxiating, Poisonous or Other Gases, and of Bacteriological Methods of Warfare ('Geneva Protocol'), Geneva, 17 June 1925, in force 8 February 1928, 94 LNTS 65.

[22] Convention on the Prohibition of the Development, Production and Stockpiling of Bacteriological (Biological) and Toxin Weapons and on Their Destruction ('Biological Weapons Convention'), London, Moscow and Washington, DC, 10 April 1972, in force 26 March 1975, 1015 UNTS 163.

[23] Convention on the Prohibition of the Development, Production, Stockpiling and Use of Chemical Weapons and on Their Destruction ('Chemical Weapons Convention'), Paris and New York, 13 January 1993, in force 29 April 1997, 1974 UNTS 45.

A further line can be drawn from the discussions on 1977 Additional Protocol I in the early 1970s that resulted in the 1980 Convention on Certain Conventional Weapons (CCW).[24] Resolution 22 of the 1974–77 Diplomatic Conference,[25] recalling in essence efforts from the previous negotiations on the matter and the desirability of taking steps to prohibit certain weapons, sketched out what would ultimately be contained in the protocols annexed to the CCW. The premise for those protocols, which today total five in number, is found in the full title of the CCW: Convention on Prohibitions or Restrictions on the Use of Certain Conventional Weapons which May Be Deemed to Be Excessively Injurious or to Have Indiscriminate Effects. The third preambular paragraph of the Convention thus emphasises that the states parties are:

> *Basing themselves* on the principle of international law that the right of the parties to an armed conflict to choose methods or means of warfare is not unlimited, and on the principle that prohibits the employment in armed conflicts of weapons, projectiles, material and methods of warfare of a nature to cause superfluous injury or unnecessary suffering [original emphasis].

Protocols I, II and IV under the CCW, addressing non-detectable fragments, incendiary weapons and blinding laser weapons respectively, all address weapons that may be 'deemed to be excessively injurious'. Protocol II[26] is mainly aimed at weapons that may be deemed to have 'indiscriminate effects', namely booby traps, anti-vehicle mines and anti-personnel landmines,[27] but its Article 3(3) reads: 'It is prohibited in all circumstances to use any mine, booby-trap or other device which is designed or of a nature to cause superfluous injury or unnecessary suffering.' As such, the unnecessary suffering rule can thus be seen as a main rationale behind four of the five CCW protocols.

The ICRC, in its 2005 Study of Customary International Humanitarian Law, gives a long list of weapons that 'have been cited in practice as having caused unnecessary suffering if used in certain or all contexts',[28] including nuclear weapons. The ICRC makes it clear, however, that '[t]here is insufficient

---

[24] Convention on Prohibitions or Restrictions on the Use of Certain Conventional Weapons Which May Be Deemed to Be Excessively Injurious or To Have Indiscriminate Effects, Geneva, 10 October 1980, in force 2 December 1983, as amended on 21 December 2001, 19 ILM 1823 (1980).

[25] Official Records of the Diplomatic Conference on the Reaffirmation and Development of International Humanitarian Law Applicable in Armed Conflicts, Vol. 1., pp. 215–16.

[26] An amended Protocol was adopted by states parties to the CCW in 1996.

[27] Protocol II is largely superseded by the 1997 Convention on the Prohibition of the Use, Stockpiling, Production and Transfer of Anti-Personnel Mines and on their Destruction, Oslo, 18 September 1997, in force 1 March 1999, 2056 UNTS 211, 36 ILM 1507, save for its provisions on anti-vehicle mines.

[28] See: www.icrc.org/customary-ihl/eng/docs/v1_rul_rule70. Lances or spears with a barbed head; serrated-edged bayonets; expanding bullets; explosive bullets; poison and poisoned weapons, including projectiles smeared with substances that inflame wounds; biological and chemical weapons; weapons that primarily injure by fragments not detectable by

consensus concerning all of these examples to conclude that, under customary international law, they all violate the rule prohibiting unnecessary suffering'. [29]

4.   Deliberate infliction of unnecessary suffering as a war crime

The unnecessary suffering rule has also found its way into international criminal law. Article 3 of the Statute of the International Criminal Tribunal for the former Yugoslavia (ICTY) included in its list of violations of the laws and customs of war the employment of weapons 'calculated to cause unnecessary suffering' as a crime within its jurisdiction. No prosecution of this particular crime appears to have taken place before the ICTY, however. As a result, the Tribunal has not had the occasion to discuss its detailed elements. The first part of Article 8(b)(xx) of the Rome Statute of the International Criminal Court (ICC Statute)[30] reiterates the prohibition in Article 35(2) of 1977 Additional Protocol I, although it includes in the same provision a prohibition on inherently indiscriminate means and methods of warfare. For the Court to exercise jurisdiction over the crime, however, a statutory amendment is required to add, in an annex to the ICC Statute, a weapon that is of a nature to cause superfluous injury or unnecessary suffering or which is inherently indiscriminate. Any such weapon must already have been the subject of a comprehensive (treaty) prohibition. The elements of the crime (both the *actus reus* and the *mens rea*) must await such statutory addition.

The likelihood of nuclear weapons being included in such an annex any time soon is low, to say the least.[31] The issue of nuclear weapons was problematic in the 1998 negotiations that led to the adoption of the ICC Statute[32] and a proposal by Mexico at the First Review Conference in Kampala in 2010 to criminalise use of nuclear weapons was not adopted.[33]

X-ray, including projectiles filled with broken glass; certain booby traps; anti-personnel landmines; torpedoes without self-destruction mechanisms; incendiary weapons; blinding laser weapons; and nuclear weapons.

[29] Customary IHL Study, p. 244.

[30] Rome Statute of the International Criminal Court, Rome, 17 July 1998, in force 1 July 2002, 2187 UNTS 90.

[31] See Chapter 9.

[32] See D. McGoldrick, P. Rowe and E. Donnelly, *The Permanent International Criminal Court: Legal and Policy Issues* (Oxford: Hart, 2004), p. 225; R. S. Lee (ed.), *The International Criminal Court: The Making of the Rome Statute* (The Hague: Kluwer Law International, 1999), pp. 114–16.

[33] See 'Report of the Working Group on Amendments', Doc. ICC-ASP/10/32, pp. 13–16, for details of the proposal, and p. 3 for a report on consideration of the proposal. In its position paper, Mexico references the unnecessary suffering rule, though does so in a perhaps inconsistent manner. It cites the rule under a heading asserting the incompatibility of nuclear weapon use with the rules on distinction and proportionality and then refers to 'unnecessary injuries and harm to civilians', making no mention of combatant harm.

B.   The Nuclear Weapons Advisory Opinion and the views of individual judges on the unnecessary suffering rule

As noted in the introduction to this chapter, in its Nuclear Weapons Advisory Opinion the ICJ identified the unnecessary suffering rule as one of the two cardinal principles of IHL. In paragraph 78, the Court declared that:

> In conformity with the aforementioned principles, humanitarian law, at a very early stage, prohibited certain types of weapons either because of their indiscriminate effect on combatants and civilians or because of the unnecessary suffering caused to combatants, that is to say, a harm greater than that unavoidable to achieve legitimate military objectives.

Thus, the only description the Court gave of the unnecessary suffering rule was that such suffering constituted 'harm greater than that unavoidable to achieve legitimate military objectives'.[34] Beyond those remarks, however, the Court had little to say about how the rule should be understood or applied to nuclear weapons. It might be interesting, therefore, to consider the judges' individual opinions for further elucidation of the views they each held.

Of the fourteen ICJ judges, five made no mention of the rule in their declarations or appended opinions.[35] Among the other nine, Judges Guillaume and Fleischhauer and Vice-President Schwebel mention it on only one page of their opinions. Judge Herczegh makes one general comment on principles, including the unnecessary suffering rule, and President Bedjaoui addresses it twice. Judge Shahabuddeen addresses the issue in more detail, as do Judges Koroma and Higgins, although Judge Weeramantry allocated more space to its consideration than did any other of the Court's judges.

President Bedjaoui makes two references to the unnecessary suffering rule. In his view, with the caveat that scientific advances might allow for what he terms 'clean' nuclear weapons, there is an expectation that such weapons would both be inherently indiscriminate and would cause unnecessary suffering.[36] While the Court in its Advisory Opinion did not make a firm determination on this point, the ICJ President found that the unnecessary suffering rule (along with the rule of distinction) was a norm of *jus cogens*. Having reached this conclusion, he opined that nuclear weapons and IHL appeared to be mutually incompatible. President Bedjaoui concluded his remarks with the assertion that even in a situation of self-defence a state could not 'exonerate itself from compliance with the "intransgressible" norms' of IHL and stated that the survival of a state would not trump such rules.[37]

---

[34] Nuclear Weapons Advisory Opinion, para. 78.

[35] Thus, Judges Shi, Vereshchetin, Ferrari Bravo, Ranjeva and Oda saw no need to elaborate on how the Court had or ought to view the rule, or rather preferred to focus their comments elsewhere.

[36] Nuclear Weapons Advisory Opinion, Declaration of President Bedjaoui, p. 272.

[37] *Ibid.*, p. 273.

Without using the term directly, Judge Herczegh remarks that '[t]he fundamental principles of international law, rightly emphasized in the reasons of the Advisory Opinion, categorically and unequivocally prohibit the use of weapons of mass destruction, including nuclear weapons'.[38] Judge Guillaume, in his Separate Opinion, observes that, following the Court's dictum of unnecessary suffering as 'harm greater than that unavoidable to achieve legitimate military objectives', nuclear weapons 'could not be regarded as illegal' solely by virtue of the suffering that they are likely to cause. Such suffering must be compared with the 'military advantage anticipated' or with 'military objectives pursued'.[39]

In his Separate Opinion, Judge Fleischhauer, after listing the rules governing distinction, unnecessary suffering and neutrality, considers that 'the nuclear weapon is, in many ways, the negation of the humanitarian considerations underlying the law applicable in armed conflict and of the principle of neutrality. The nuclear weapon cannot distinguish between civilian and military targets. It causes immeasurable suffering. The radiation released by it is unable to respect the territorial integrity of a neutral state'.[40]

In his Dissenting Opinion, Judge Shahabuddeen is the first to deal in significant detail with the unnecessary suffering rule.[41] He offers a slight variation on the test the Court offered in its Advisory Opinion, namely that 'suffering is superfluous or unnecessary if it is materially in excess of the degree of suffering which is justified by the military advantage sought to be achieved'. While acknowledging the primacy of states in determining this balance, he still considers the Court bound to identify what states ought to assess as permissible. The guidance states ought to heed in making any legal determination is, for Judge Shahabuddeen, the public conscience. Although he subsequently deals with the Martens Clause,[42] the essence of his finding is that the Court could hold that nuclear weapons violate the principle (which he deems applicable to civilians as well as to combatants). He affirms that on the evidence the Court had considered, 'it could reasonably find that the public conscience considers that the use of nuclear weapons causes suffering which is unacceptable whatever might be the military advantage derivable from such use'.[43]

Judge Koroma in his Dissenting Opinion cites extensively the physical effects resulting from use of nuclear weapons, referring to the testimony provided to the Court by the Mayor of Hiroshima and the Government of Japan,[44] and, in

---

[38] Nuclear Weapons Advisory Opinion, Declaration of Judge Herczegh, p. 275.
[39] Nuclear Weapons Advisory Opinion, Separate Opinion of Judge Guillaume, p. 289.
[40] Nuclear Weapons Advisory Opinion, Separate Opinion of Judge Fleischhauer, p. 306.
[41] Nuclear Weapons Advisory Opinion, Dissenting Opinion of Judge Shahabuddeen, pp. 402–5.
[42] Ibid., p. 405ff.
[43] Ibid., p. 403. It should perhaps be noted that he considers only one type of weapon by analogy, namely poison gas, as being impermissible regardless of the military advantage gained.
[44] Nuclear Weapons Advisory Opinion, Dissenting Opinion of Judge Koroma, pp. 566–9.

the context of physical effects attributable to testing, from the delegation of the Marshall Islands.[45] He asserts subsequently that in light of those effects, the Court had concluded, inter alia, 'that such [nuclear] weapons cause unnecessary suffering and superfluous injury to combatants and non-combatants alike'.[46] While he clearly considers that the Court erred in not concluding definitively a prohibition on use in any circumstances,[47] in the context of reprisals he refers to the 'likelihood' of violating the rule, with the tone of his opinion clearly reflecting a belief that no circumstances would permit use that would not violate the rule. Although critics of his remarks might suggest he does not recognise the balance others purport is to be struck, he does not necessarily dispute it. It is probably incorrect to say he ignores the context; rather, he appears to conceive of no advantage that would outweigh the suffering caused.

In her Dissenting Opinion, Judge Higgins clearly avows that what is unnecessary is not identical to what might be deemed horrendous suffering. She makes this explicit, perhaps more clearly so than others, in her remark that: 'The principle does not stipulate that a legitimate target is not to be attacked if it would cause great suffering.'[48] Her next, and concluding paragraph on this topic begins with 'the crucial question: *what* military necessity is so great that the sort of suffering that would be inflicted on military personnel by the use of nuclear weapons would ever be justified'.[49] She indicates that this is dependent upon 'knowing the dimensions of the suffering of which we speak and the circumstances which occasion it'. Regarding the purported limited effects of tactical use as uncertain, she ends with the observation that:

> If the suffering is of the sort traditionally associated with the use of nuclear weapons – blast, radiation, shock, together with the risk of escalation, risk of spread through space and time – then only the most extreme circumstances (defence against untold suffering or the obliteration of a State or peoples) could conceivably 'balance' the equation between necessity and humanity.[50]

It is evident that Judge Higgins believed that great harm can only be occasioned to achieve great gains and that adding in the subsequent effects in time and space to those affecting individuals suggest that it is only such cumulative effects that would weigh against the gravest of circumstances, not the harm occasioned to combatants (howsoever grave that might be).

---

[45] *Ibid.*, pp. 569–70.   [46] *Ibid.*, p. 570.

[47] *Ibid.*, p. 571. When commenting on paragraph 2E of the dispositive, Judge Koroma remarks that: 'In my considered opinion, the unlawfulness of the use of nuclear weapons is not predicated on the circumstances in which the use takes place, but rather on the unique and established characteristics of those weapons which under any circumstances would violate international law by their use.'

[48] Nuclear Weapons Advisory Opinion, Dissenting Opinion of Judge Higgins, p. 587.

[49] *Ibid.* (emphasis added).   [50] *Ibid.*

Judge Weeramantry offers by far the most detailed remarks on both the effects of nuclear weapons and the unnecessary suffering rule, in what is the longest of all of the dissenting opinions. However, his conclusions as to the unnecessary suffering rule may be quickly summarised. Over twenty pages he describes the effects of nuclear weapons use, covering physical, environmental and societal consequences (indeed he lists in total twenty-two effects of nuclear weapons distinct from conventional arms that, he suggests, are not even exhaustive).[51] Based on these effects, he considers them 'more than sufficient to establish that the nuclear weapon causes unnecessary suffering going far beyond the purposes of war'.[52] And in what he terms a short examination of the principles of IHL that 'could be violated in self-defence', he begins:

> 1. *Unnecessary Suffering*. The harrowing suffering caused by nuclear weapons, as outlined earlier in this opinion, is not confined to the aggressive use of such weapons. The lingering sufferings caused by radiation do not lose their intensity merely because the weapon is used in self-defence.[53]

Although some might consider this an unusual elocution, he does seem to indicate that not even acts in self-defence could outweigh the prohibition of any nuclear weapon use. This sentiment would confirm the principle that *jus in bello* must apply independent of the *jus ad bellum* circumstances, and is not particular to the use or indeed long-term effects of nuclear weapons.

In their written statements, comments or observations to the Court prior to oral hearings, a marked difference may be noted among states in the views expressed. States such as the United States,[54] the United Kingdom[55] and the Netherlands[56] each make variations on the argument that a balancing between harm and necessity or advantage is required under the unnecessary suffering rule and that any *in abstracto* consideration cannot determine the likelihood of such unnecessary suffering occurring.

A number of other states do not address the point directly in written submissions (one example is New Zealand, which cites the rule but then offers no conclusion as to its precise application to nuclear weapons).[57] Other states do, however, and do so in clear opposition to the views just expressed. Thus,

---

[51] Nuclear Weapons Advisory Opinion, Dissenting Opinion of judge Weeramantry, pp. 471–2.

[52] *Ibid.*, p. 498. [53] *Ibid.*, p. 514.

[54] Written Statement of the USA, Nuclear Weapons Advisory Opinion, 20 June 1995, pp. 28–9.

[55] Written Statement of the UK, Nuclear Weapons Advisory Opinion, 16 June 1995, pp. 51–2.

[56] Written Statement of the Netherlands, Nuclear Weapons Advisory Opinion, 16 June 1995, pp. 7–8.

[57] Written Statement of New Zealand, Nuclear Weapons Advisory Opinion, 20 June 1995, pp. 22 and 23.

among others, Egypt,[58] Mexico[59] and Nauru[60] each consider any use of nuclear weapons as violating the unnecessary suffering rule, although they do not consider it in extensive detail. The one state that does, Solomon Islands, has a somewhat more extensive consideration in its submissions to the World Health Organization (WHO) proceedings[61] than to the General Assembly question that was the basis of the Advisory Opinion.[62]

Summing up, the ICJ did not discuss or analyse in any detail the question of the extent to which the rule against using means of warfare that causes unnecessary suffering or superfluous injury applies to nuclear weapons. While individual judges do so to a certain extent in their separate or dissenting opinions, divergences remain. The following section attempts to discuss in some more detail how the unnecessary suffering rule is interpreted in practice.

C.   Interpreting the unnecessary suffering rule

The very term 'unnecessary' implies a balancing act. An ICRC Conference of Experts held at Lucerne in 1975 noted that the unnecessary suffering rule 'involved some sort of equation between, on the one hand, the degree of injury or suffering inflicted (the humanitarian aspect) and, on the other, the degree of necessity underlying the choice of a particular weapon (the military aspect)'.[63] Such a balancing act is not easy to apply in practice, however. As Greenwood has pointed out, the balancing act is 'easier to state in the abstract than it is to apply, since it is not comparing like with like and there is considerable uncertainty regarding the factors to be placed on each side of the scales'.[64]

The elements to be considered when carrying out the balancing act should comprise not only the humanitarian aspect and the military aspect, but also whether the unnecessary suffering rule contains an obligation to consider alternative weapons.

---

[58] Written Statement of Egypt, Nuclear Weapons Advisory Opinion, 1 February 1995, p. 25, with a footnote referring to UN General Assembly Resolution 1653 (XVI) of 24 November 1961.

[59] Written Statement of Mexico, Nuclear Weapons Advisory Opinion, 19 June 1995, p. 13 (although potentially it is less categorical if one believes that the term 'excessive' as used here is equally concerned with civilian injury).

[60] Written Statement of Nauru, Nuclear Weapons Advisory Opinion, 15 June 1995, pp. 10, 17, and 22.

[61] Letter dated 19 June 1995 from the Honorary Counsel of Solomon Islands in London, Together with Written Comments of the Government of Solomon Islands, Response to the World Health Organization's Request for an Advisory Opinion, 19 June 1995.

[62] Letter dated 19 June 1995, from the Permanent Representative of Solomon Islands to the United Nations, Together with Written Statement of the Government of Solomon Islands, Nuclear Weapons Advisory Opinion, 19 June 1995.

[63] ICRC, Conference of Government Experts on the Use of Certain Conventional Weapons, Lucerne 1974 (Geneva: ICRC, 1975), para. 24.

[64] C. Greenwood, 'The law of weaponry at the start of the new millennium' in M. Schmitt and L. C. Green (eds.), The Law of Armed Conflict: Into the Next Millennium, International Law Studies, Vol. VII (Newport: US Naval War College, 1998), pp. 185–232, at p. 194.

Starting with the humanitarian aspect, there is no general or detailed agreement on the degree of suffering or injury that would constitute a violation of the rule. In 1997 the ICRC published a report on its SIrUS Project,[65] the result of detailed analysis of data from ICRC field hospitals relating to more than 26,000 patients. It sets out four tables concerning the grade of injury suffered as a result of use of conventional weapons (denoted by the length of skin wound and presence or absence of a cavity): hospital mortality; the regions of the body injured and details of period of hospital stay; surgical interventions, units of blood transfusion and the proportion transfused; and number of lower limbs amputated, all cross-referenced to the type or cause of injury (fragment, bullet, burn or mine) of those who survive to be discharged. The SIrUS Project proposed:

> that what constitute 'superfluous injury and unnecessary suffering' be determined by design-dependant foreseeable effects of weapons when they are used against human beings and cause
> - specific disease, specific abnormal physiological state, specific abnormal psychological state, specific and permanent disability or specific disfigurement (*Criterion 1*); or
> - field mortality of more than 25% or a hospital mortality of more than 5% (*Criterion 2*); or
> - Grade 3 wounds as measured by the Red Cross wound classification (*Criterion 3*); or
> - effects for which there is no well recognized and proven treatment (*Criterion 4*).[66]

Although the study concerned the effects of conventional weapons, the report does note that 'one cannot consider the effects of weapons in general without referring to nuclear weapons. Here criteria 1, 2 and 4 would apply (burns and radiation sickness). The nuclear debate, which is discussed extensively in other fora, is not taken further in this document.'[67]

It is fair to say that the SIrUS project has not been without its critics,[68] and indeed, while states have recognised the evident need to identify harm, the proposals of the SIrUS project have not been generally accepted.[69] In part, the lack of acceptance is consonant with the views of many commentators on

---

[65] R. Coupland (ed.), *The SIrUS Project: Towards a Determination of which Weapons Cause 'Superfluous Injury or Unnecessary Suffering'* (Geneva: ICRC, 1997). Additionally, Coupland authored a piece in 1999 with the then Head of the ICRC Legal Division's Arms Unit summarising the project and offering further proposals. See R. M. Coupland and P. Herby, 'Review of the legality of weapons: a new approach: the SIrUS project', *International Review of the Red Cross* 81(835) (1999), 583–92.

[66] *Ibid.*, p. 23.   [67] *Ibid.*, p. 26.

[68] Maj. D. M. Verchio, 'Just say no! The SIrUS project: well intentioned, but unnecessary and superfluous', *Air Force Law Review* 51 (2001), 183–227.

[69] I. Daoust, 'ICRC Expert Meeting on Legal Review of Weapons and the SIrUS project, Jongny sur Vevey, 29–31 January 2001', *International Review of the Red Cross* 83(842) (2001), 539–42.

the application of the unnecessary suffering rule. Schmitt, for example, remarks that: 'Necessity also appears as a limiting factor in the second cardinal principle, unnecessary suffering, which implicitly recognizes the lawful nature of weapons that cause militarily necessary suffering.'[70] Greenwood notes that, while the 'identification of these criteria and the medical study on which they are based is of considerable value in helping to show how the balancing act required by the unnecessary suffering principle can be made more precise and less anecdotal than at present', it is not sufficient that a weapon meets one of these criteria to 'brand it unlawful without consideration of the military advantages which that weapon may offer'.[71]

Thus, the humanitarian aspect cannot be treated separately from the military aspect. Sassòli *et al.* remark that:

> In practice, the application of this basic rule is always a compromise between military necessity and humanity, as the principle of 'superfluous injury or unnecessary suffering' has been interpreted as referring to harm that would not be justified by military utility, either because of the lack of even the slightest utility or because the utility is considerably outweighed by the suffering caused.[72]

The Manual on International Law Applicable to Air and Missile Warfare asserts that weapons must comply with the prohibition of unnecessary suffering and superfluous injury.[73] In its commentary, the Program on Humanitarian Policy and Conflict Research at Harvard University states: 'The prohibition of weapons calculated, or of a nature to cause, superfluous injury or unnecessary suffering acknowledges that necessary suffering to combatants is lawful, and may include severe injury or death. The prohibition is violated when the weapon in question will, when employed for its intended purpose and with reasonable foresight, cause injuries that serve no military purpose.' Solis notes that 'great suffering is not the measurement by which a weapon is banned; the question is whether the suffering caused is substantially disproportionate to the military advantage gained'.[74]

Boothby, in one of the most recent monographs on weapons and IHL, cites the original version of the US Department of Defense weapons review directive – an authority that is, in his opinion, the most 'clear and accurate formulation

[70] M. N. Schmitt, 'Military necessity and humanity in international humanitarian law: preserving the delicate balance', *Virginia Journal of International Law* 50(4) (2010), 795–839, at 803.

[71] Greenwood, 'The law of weaponry at the start of the new millennium', p. 197.

[72] Sassòli *et al.*, *How Does Law Protect in War*, p. 284.

[73] Humanitarian Policy and Conflict Research (HPCR) Manual on International Law Applicable to Air and Missile Warfare, Bern, 15 May 2009 (Cambridge, MA: Harvard, 2009), Section C(5)(b).

[74] *Ibid.*, p. 272.

of the superfluous injury and unnecessary suffering test currently available'.[75] This document, which was drafted by Cummings, Solf and Almond, reads:

> The prohibition of unnecessary suffering constitutes acknowledgement that necessary suffering to combatants is lawful in armed conflict, and may include severe injury or loss of life justified by military necessity ... A weapon or munition would be deemed to cause unnecessary suffering only if it inevitably or in its normal use has a particular effect, and the injury caused thereby is considered by governments as disproportionate to the military necessity for that effect, that is, the military advantage to be gained from use.[76]

It seems that the practical application of the balancing act between humanitarian and military considerations remains difficult to pin down in concrete terms, even if most writers seem to agree that a balancing act must be undertaken. A more practical discussion in this context is, therefore, whether the unnecessary suffering rule includes an obligation to consider alternative weapons.

The term *unnecessary* suffering implies that some amount of suffering is *necessary*. Another word for necessary is unavoidable. Dinstein opines that:

> In essence the injunction against 'superfluous injury or unnecessary suffering' hangs on a distinction between injury/suffering that is avoidable and unavoidable. This requires comparison between the weapon in question and other options. Two issues arise in particular: (a) whether an alternative weapon would cause or inflict less injury or suffering; and (b) whether the effects produced by the alternative are sufficiently effective in neutralizing enemy personnel.[77]

When looking at the military objective to be achieved, one must therefore assume that there is an obligation to assess whether this military objective can be achieved with a weapon that causes less suffering. As Greenwood points out, the unnecessary suffering principle in essence involves 'a comparison between different weapons in determining whether the injuries and suffering caused by a particular weapon are necessary'.[78]

---

[75] W. H. Boothby, *Weapons and the Law of Armed Conflict* (Oxford University Press, 2009), p. 63 n. 28.

[76] International and Operational Law Department, *Law of Armed Conflict Deskbook* (Charlottesville: United States Army Judge Advocate General's Legal Center and School of the United States Army, 2012), p. 151. See also, UK Ministry of Defence, *Manual of The Law of Armed Conflict* (Oxford University Press, 2004), Ss. 6.1.4 and 6.2. Note that in an official amendment to the Manual in July 2011, the 'Cummings formula' was clearly reflected. See UK, 'Joint Services Publication 383 – The Manual of the Law of Armed Conflict, Amendment 4 (July 2011)', para. 43, available at: www.gov.uk/government/uploads/system/uploads/attachment_data/file/27870/20110725JSP383Amendment4Jul11.pdf.

[77] Y. Dinstein, *The Conduct of Hostilities under the Law of International Armed Conflict* (Cambridge University Press, 2004), p. 60.

[78] Greenwood, 'The law of weaponry at the start of the new millennium', p. 197.

In addition, the Humanitarian Policy and Conflict Research (HPCR) Commentary to the Manual on International Law Applicable to Air and Missile Warfare notes that assessments on alternative means must be understood as part of the unnecessary suffering rule:[79] 'a weapon's effects must be considered in light of other weapons currently in use that can achieve an equivalent military purpose. Reduced to basics, two questions permeate the assessment: (i) is a less injurious alternative weapon available?; and (ii) is the alternative sufficiently effective in achieving the intended military purpose?'[80]

The US Department of Defense weapons review directive similarly states that the balancing between humanitarian aspects and military aspects cannot be carried out in isolation:[81] 'A weapon's or munition's effects must be weighed in light of comparable, lawful weapons or munitions in use on the modern battlefield.'[82]

Applied to nuclear weapons, the obligation to consider, and choose, alternative means of warfare if the foreseen suffering is disproportionate to its military effectiveness, arguably renders the actual option to use nuclear weapons very slim. Clarity in understanding the scope of effects is of course a prerequisite for the obligations under IHL that would be incumbent on those contemplating the use of nuclear weapons. When considering the rule on unnecessary suffering, even if a proportionality assessment balancing the suffering against military necessity must be made, it is important to assess the effects. Also, when considering the implicit obligation to consider using alternative means of warfare, it is worth noting the stark differences in effects said to result from use of nuclear weapons compared to those that result from conventional munitions. For instance, Appendix F to *The Nuclear Matters Handbook*[83] begins with the following overview: 'A nuclear weapon produces effects that are overwhelmingly more significant than those produced by a conventional explosive, even if the nuclear yield is low.' It then lists the following differences, in that a nuclear detonation:

> produces energy which, weight for weight, is millions of times more powerful than that produced by a conventional explosive; instantaneously

---

[79] HPCR Commentary to the Manual on International Law Applicable to Air and Missile Warfare, Commentary to Rule 6, p. 64.

[80] The Manual at footnote 142 offers the alternative view expressed by the ICRC representative involved in the Manual's elaboration whereby, for the ICRC, the questions to be posed are: (1) What is the design-dependant nature of the foreseeable injury? (2) Is this more than is necessary to render a combatant *hors de combat*?

[81] The text is equally cited approvingly by W. Hays Parks in 'Means and methods of warfare', Symposium issue in honour of Edward R. Cummings, *George Washington International Law Review* 38 (2006), 511–39, at 511 n. 25.

[82] Maj. Marie Anderson and Ms. Emily Zukauskas (eds.), *Operational Law Handbook 2008*, International and Operational Law Department, The Judge Advocate General's Legal Center and School, Charlottesville, Virginia, p. 14.

[83] Office of the Assistant US Secretary of Defense for Nuclear, Chemical, and Biological Defense Programs, *The Nuclear Matters Handbook*, available at: www.acq.osd.mil/ncbdp/nm/nm_book_5_11/index.htm.

produces a very large and very hot nuclear fireball ... transmits a large percentage of energy in the form of heat and light within a few seconds that can produce burns and ignite fires at great distances; emits within the first minute, highly penetrating nuclear radiation that can be harmful to life ... creates, if it occurs in the lower atmosphere, an air blast wave that can cause casualties and damage at significant distances ... emits residual nuclear radiation over an extended period of time.[84]

Of course, each of these descriptions is rudimentary in form. Nevertheless, it is worth noting that, in terms of comparable harm, effects from ordinary use of a nuclear weapon differ to a very great degree from those from conventional explosives, even in terms of like-for-like tonnage. Documented effects of the limited use of nuclear weapons and their subsequent testing, together with projected effects, can be found in a number of sources.

Arguably, use of any nuclear weapon will produce three main effects on individuals: thermal injury, blast injury and radiation injury.[85] Each effect is the consequence of the threefold simultaneous effects of a fireball, air blast and the radiation released upon detonation of a nuclear device. These events and effects are said to act directly, simultaneously and in a complex fashion on the human body.[86] That complexity does not, however, detract from the obligation to determine predictable effects concomitant with the use of any given weapon. Those effects help to determine whether less injurious alternatives are available than the use of a nuclear weapon.

In addition, for a variety of reasons, our ability to predict injuries and suffering subsequent to use is now better than at any point in the past. Arguably, the ability to make more accurate predictions heightens the IHL obligations to assess limitations on means or methods to be used to achieve any sought military advantage and precautions to be taken in attack. Both obligations by their nature are ones in which the assessment must be prior to the purported use.

Immediate effects on thermal and blast injuries can be predicted with a high degree of confidence. Beyond factors of topography and meteorological conditions, the likelihood of injuries and their severity and the probability of fatalities can be considered for all intents and purposes inevitable in relation to close proximity to the detonation site, dependant of course on the yield of any given weapon. Epidemiological studies have been routinely undertaken on the survivors of the atomic bombs dropped on Hiroshima and Nagasaki since 1945. Since 1950 the Atomic Bomb Casualty Commission and its successor the Radiation Effects Research Foundation (RERF) have conducted mortality studies on atomic bomb survivors and residents of those cities not

---

[84] *Ibid.*, pp. 211–12.
[85] E. Ishikawa and D. L. Swain, *Hiroshima and Nagasaki: The Physical, Medical and Social Effects of the Atomic Bombings* (New York: Basic Books, 1979), p. 105.
[86] *Ibid.*

present at the time of the bombings[87] and studies of the incidence of cancer in atomic bomb survivors.[88] These studies offer significant scientific analysis over the long term, and describe continuing effects of atomic bombing. The mortality study noted that 'the most important finding regarding the late effects of A-bomb radiation exposure on mortality is an increased risk of cancer mortality throughout life'.[89] Equally a study on the incidence of hematopoietic malignancies found evidence of persistent risks for a particular leukaemia – acute myeloid leukaemia – thirty to fifty years after exposure: in effect a lifetime of excess or heightened risk.[90]

This temporal aspect of nuclear weapons use is important when considering whether suffering caused by a weapon is necessary or unnecessary. It also applies to the proportionality rule on excessive harm to civilians found in 1977 Additional Protocol I. To isolate the unnecessary suffering rule from the distinction and proportionality rules and give it an independent meaning, it is necessary to imagine a scenario where no civilians would be affected by a given use of nuclear weapons. One often cited example is bombing of a military installation in a desert area, far away from population centres. Such an attack would arguably not (necessarily)[91] constitute a violation of the rule on distinction. Nevertheless, would it still be a violation of the rule against unnecessary suffering, inasmuch as the surviving military personnel might be affected by disease weeks and even years later?

The balancing act requires that the suffering is weighed against military necessity. The question that must be raised in this connection is to what extent the effects of the weapon must be considered necessary from a military point of view, and not just the immediate effects but also the medium- and long-term effects. In other words, is it a requirement that all, or at least most, of the effects of the attack serve a military purpose? And is it possible to measure which effects serve the military purpose and which effects do not? It clearly gives the user of nuclear weapons no military advantage that people exposed to nuclear weapons use develop cancer or other diseases long after the attack. Because of the nature of nuclear weapons in their extreme medium- and long-term effects on human life (and on the environment), this seems to be a justified question.

---

[87] The most recent mortality study by the RERF is K. Ozasa et al., 'Studies of the mortality of atomic bomb survivors, Report 14, 1950–2003: an overview of cancer and noncancer diseases', Radiation Research 177 (2012), 229–43.

[88] For the latest study on haematological malignances, see W. L. Wsu et al., 'The incidence of leukemia, lymphona and multiple myeloma among atomic bomb survivors: 1951–2001', Radiation Research 179 (2013), 361–82.

[89] Ozasa et al., 'Studies of the mortality of atomic bomb survivors', 229.

[90] Wsu et al., 'The incidence of leukemia, lymphona and multiple myeloma among atomic bomb survivors', 378 and 380.

[91] Radioactive fallout could of course be a consequence of such an attack.

Conclusion

The horrific blast and burn injuries nuclear weapons would inflict on hundreds of thousands of people across a huge area in the instant following a nuclear detonation are dramatically enhanced by the lethal doses of radiation that would kill in the ensuing days and weeks. It is thus the rule on distinction and not the rule on unnecessary suffering that has taken up most of the debate on nuclear weapons use and IHL. The aim of this chapter has been to illustrate how the unnecessary suffering rule relates to the use of nuclear weapons. The weapons of concern at the beginning of the twentieth century when the rule was first articulated were typically those one combatant would use against another. Despite the likelihood of instantaneous mass casualties from any nuclear weapon use, however, the focus on the weapon's effects on the individual is nonetheless integral to the assessment of their legality.

The long-term impact of nuclear weapons also means a significantly increased risk of cancer mortality throughout the life of the survivors. How the temporal aspect of the rule on unnecessary suffering, namely the fact that injury or suffering does not manifest itself immediately, is to be understood, requires further analysis. That said, given the characteristics that would ordinarily manifest themselves from exposure to radiation, it is fair to contend that this issue must be taken into account in applying the unnecessary suffering rule. The comparable short- and long-term effects between conventional and nuclear weapons must be considered proper variables for this equation.

The unnecessary suffering rule does not operate as an absolute standard. It is a comparative rule. However, in light of the demonstrable consequences of nuclear weapons use discussed in this chapter and the obligation under IHL to use less injurious weapons where alternatives exist, it is almost impossible to conceive of circumstances when engendering such injuries and suffering, even among those engaged in combat, could be deemed truly necessary.

6

Threats of use of nuclear weapons and international humanitarian law

GRO NYSTUEN

Introduction

This chapter focuses on the extent to which threats of use of nuclear weapons can violate international humanitarian law (IHL). The reason for debating this question, which seems rather limited in scope and impact, is that it appears to play a role in the general confusion that was generated by the International Court of Justice (ICJ)'s Nuclear Weapons Advisory Opinion as regards the separation between *jus in bello* and *jus ad bellum*. The Court stated that the threat of use of nuclear weapons would be a violation of not only *jus ad bellum* as reflected in the UN Charter, but also of IHL:

> The *threat or use* of nuclear weapons would generally be contrary to the rules of international law applicable in armed conflict, *and in particular the principles and rules of humanitarian law.*[1]

The Court did not, however, substantiate this finding with legal reasoning. The purpose of this chapter is to discuss the validity of this statement, not merely for the sake of clarifying the content of IHL, but more importantly to reinforce the legal foundation for upholding the distinction between *jus ad bellum* and *jus in bello*.

The chapter proceeds as follows. Section A describes the context surrounding the ICJ Advisory Opinion, including the Court's vague and arguably often non-existent distinction between *jus ad bellum* and *jus in bello*. Section B examines the written statements that states submitted to the Court, to ascertain the legal basis for the claim that the 'threat ... of nuclear weapons' violates IHL. Only a few states made an attempt to provide a legal rationale for this assertion. For their part, states opposed to the notion that nuclear weapons are illegal per se generally focused their attention on threats *ad bellum*, not *in bello*. Section C analyses the discussion of threats in the Advisory Opinion. Lastly, Section D attempts some of the legal analysis the ICJ avoided, regarding whether IHL

---

[1] International Court of Justice (ICJ), *Legality of the Threat or Use of Nuclear Weapons*, Advisory Opinion of 8 July 1996, para. 105(2)E (hereafter, Nuclear Weapons Advisory Opinion) (emphasis added).

forbids the threat of nuclear weapons. This chapter concludes that threats are generally not prohibited under IHL, and that the ICJ's claim to the contrary merely underlined the Court's blurring of the boundaries between *jus ad bellum* and *jus in bello*.

A. Background

The question put to the ICJ by the General Assembly was formulated as follows: 'Is the threat or use of nuclear weapons in any circumstance permitted under international law?'[2] The Court itself described its task as 'clear' in that it was to 'determine the legality or illegality of the threat or use of nuclear weapons'.[3] The ICJ, in applying Article 38 of its Statute with regard to the relevant legal sources to be relied on, stated that the 'most relevant applicable law … is that relating to the use of force enshrined in the United Nations Charter and the law applicable in armed conflict which regulates the conduct of hostilities'.[4]

It is thus clear that the Court recognised, as a point of departure, the two distinct and separate legal regimes of *jus ad bellum* (*when* is it lawful to resort to the use or threat of armed force against another state) and *jus in bello* (*what means and methods* can lawfully be used in war – regardless of the war's justification). It is equally clear, however, that these two legal regimes are not sufficiently separated throughout the Advisory Opinion.

Chapter 3 of this book specifically discusses the potentially unfortunate implication of the (in)famous paragraph 2E of the dispositive of the Advisory Opinion, which could be read to indicate that *jus ad bellum* considerations can override *jus in bello* obligations.[5] The second half of paragraph 2E fails to clarify

---

[2] Nuclear Weapons Advisory Opinion, para. 1 (referring to UN General Assembly Resolution 49/75 K, adopted on 15 December 1994).

[3] Nuclear Weapons Advisory Opinion, para. 20.

[4] Nuclear Weapons Advisory Opinion, para. 34.

[5] See also T. Gill, 'The nuclear weapons advisory opinion of the International Court of Justice and the fundamental distinction between the *jus ad bellum* and the *jus in bello*', *Leiden Journal of International Law* 12(3) (1999) 613–24; J. Moussa, 'Can "*jus ad bellum*" override "*jus in bello*"? Reaffirming the separation of the two bodies of law', *International Review of the Red Cross* 872 (2008), 341–68; R. Sloane, 'The cost of conflation: preserving the dualism of *jus ad bellum* and *jus in bello* in the contemporary law of war', *Yale Journal of International Law* 34 (2009), 47–112, at 90 ('In its advisory opinion in *Nuclear Weapons*, the consequences of the ICJ's myopic focus on regulating the contingencies for resort to self-defence in the first instance rather than on the more difficult issues of *ad bellum* and *in bello* law led to a holding that most regard as, at best, confused.') But see C. Greenwood, '*Jus ad bellum* and *jus in bello* in the *Nuclear Weapons* advisory opinion' in L. Boisson de Chazournes and P. Sands (eds.), *International Law, the International Court of Justice and Nuclear Weapons* (Cambridge University Press, 1999), p. 264 (stating that the Court's opinion recognises that the rules of *jus ad bellum* and *jus in bello* are 'cumulative, not alternative', and that 'there is, therefore, no need to read the second part of that [the dispositive] paragraph as setting up the *jus ad bellum* in opposition to the *jus in bello*').

that the obligations under IHL cannot be set aside if the security of a state is at stake. Instead, the Court states that it cannot 'conclude definitively whether the threat or use of nuclear weapons would be lawful or unlawful in an extreme circumstance of self-defence, in which the very survival of the State would be at stake'. Even though the Court thus declared a *non liquet* as it refrained from giving a definite answer regarding the question of legality,[6] the implication of the statement is that use of nuclear weapons contrary to IHL might still be lawful in extreme circumstances of self-defence.

As discussed in Chapter 3, such an inference is hardly consistent with international treaty law or customary law. It is precisely in an extreme situation of self-defence (or aggression, for that matter) that the rules of IHL are meant to apply, in order to protect those not taking part in hostilities and regulate the actual conduct of hostilities. Probably because the Court issued a 'disclaimer' in declaring the question *non liquet*, the Advisory Opinion made no attempt to justify this inference with legal reasoning.

The suggestion that considerations *jus ad bellum* can potentially override obligations *jus in bello* remains controversial, and many lawyers have discussed this issue at length over the nearly two decades that have passed since the Advisory Opinion was issued.[7] The distinction between *jus ad bellum* and *jus in bello* appears blurred throughout the Advisory Opinion, because the two bodies of law are often mentioned together, and because the wording 'threat or use of force' of the main *ad bellum* international law instrument, the 1945 Charter of the United Nations (UN), is frequently used as a qualifier for the applicability of IHL.

Even though the term 'threat or use of force' applies *ad bellum*, the phrase is used throughout the Advisory Opinion as if it were also part of IHL. The Court even states explicitly that if the use of nuclear weapons would be prohibited *in bello*, then the threat of use of nuclear weapons would also be prohibited under the same rules.[8]

As has been pointed out in Chapter 3, respect for and application of IHL and thus the means of protecting those affected by armed conflict would disintegrate if *jus ad bellum* considerations were used to determine whether such protection should apply. As eloquently put by Greenwood:

> To allow the necessities of self defence to override the principles of humanitarian law would put at risk all the progress in that law which has been made over the last hundred years or so and raise the spectre of a return to theories of 'just war'.[9]

[6] See for example Nuclear Weapons Advisory Opinion, Dissenting Opinion of Judge Higgins, 8 July 1996, para. 2.

[7] See, e.g., the sources quoted in note 5, above.

[8] Nuclear Weapons Advisory Opinion, para. 78.

[9] C. Greenwood, 'The Advisory Opinion on nuclear weapons and the contribution of the International Court to international humanitarian law', *International Red Cross Review*, 316 (1997), 65–75.

Addressing the fact that the ICJ, in its 1996 Advisory Opinion, seemed to mix the concepts of *ad bellum* and *in bello* also with regard to the manner in which it deals with threats will hopefully contribute to inform the discussion on the more fundamental issue of the relationship between *jus ad bellum* and *jus in bello*.

1. *The question put to the ICJ by the General Assembly*

As noted above, the ICJ was asked whether the threat or use of nuclear weapons was 'in any circumstance permitted under international law'.[10] Although not limited to certain regimes of international law, this question was nevertheless framed on the basis of the very core *ad bellum* legal provision, Article 2(4) of the UN Charter. The background for why the question was formulated in this way will not be discussed here.[11] Suffice to say that it was deemed important to include considerations both *ad bellum* and *in bello*. Many civil society organisations had argued that possession of nuclear weapons, and the policy of deterrence, constituted threats of use and wanted the Court to confirm this view. It was thus no coincidence that the question was framed around the UN Charter's prohibition on the threat or use of force, despite the lack of an apparent link between rules *ad bellum* and specific weapons. The prohibition on the use or threat of use of force applies to all uses of force against another state.[12] Article 2(4) regulates the circumstances under which it is legal to use force, not the means or methods of conducting hostilities.

The question posed to the Court thus confuses the issue profoundly. If dissected, the question could look like this:

- Is the *threat* of use of nuclear weapons in any circumstance permitted *ad bellum*?
- Is the *use* of nuclear weapons in any circumstance permitted *ad bellum*?
- Is the *threat* of use of nuclear weapons in any circumstance permitted *in bello*?
- Is the *use* of nuclear weapons in any circumstance permitted *in bello*?

Three of these questions are discussed elsewhere in this book.[13] Here, the third question, namely whether the threat of use of nuclear weapons is permitted or prohibited *jus in bello*, will be subject to closer scrutiny.

[10] Nuclear Weapons Advisory Opinion, para. 1 (referring to UN General Assembly Resolution 49/75 K, adopted on 15 December 1994).

[11] But see, e.g., M. Koskenniemi, 'Faith, identity, and the killing of the innocent: international lawyers and nuclear weapons', *Leiden Journal of International Law* 10(137) (1997), 137–62, and Nuclear Weapons Advisory Opinion, Dissenting Opinion of Judge Oda, paras. 4–5.

[12] According to Simma, 'State practice reveals a relatively high degree of tolerance towards mere threats of force, one decisive reason for which seems to be that some of the most obvious threats of force are legitimized by the right of self defence embodied in Article 51 of the Charter.' B. Simma (ed.), *The Charter of the United Nations – A Commentary*, 2nd edn (Oxford University Press, 2002), p. 124.

[13] See Chapters 2, 1, and 4 of this book, respectively.

B.   Discussion of threats *in bello* in written statements by governments

The issue of threats *in bello* was not subject to extensive discussion in the written statements submitted by governments to the ICJ in connection with the
Advisory Opinion. In general, the statements refer to 'use' or 'threat of use'
almost interchangeably.[14] In fact, only Malaysia, Nauru, New Zealand and
Solomon Islands provided any rationale for the claim that threats in particular
violate IHL.[15] For its part, the United Kingdom stated briefly that threats of use
are a matter solely of *jus ad bellum*, not *jus in bello*.[16]

In the Written Statements by Nauru and Malaysia, a case was made for the
assumption that 'threats of use' in fact equals 'use'. Nauru wrote: 'Thus, the concepts of "threats" and "use" in Article 2(4) merge into each other in most circumstances: The threat of use is a kind of use.'[17]

Malaysia made the same point.[18] These are clearly comments that relate to *jus
ad bellum*, pertaining to the scope of the term 'use', or the relationship between
'use' and 'threat' in Article 2(4) of the UN Charter.

New Zealand appeared to mix the concepts of 'threats' and 'use' throughout
its Written Statement, much in the same vein as the Court consequently did. In
its section on 'Application of international humanitarian law to nuclear weapons', New Zealand stated: 'In general, international humanitarian law bears
on the threat or use of nuclear weapons in general as it does of other weapons.'[19] No legal reasoning is offered for this assertion. A few paragraphs later,
the New Zealand Written Statement nevertheless stated: 'The general application of international humanitarian law to the *use* of nuclear weapons has also
been acknowledged by nuclear weapons States.'[20] New Zealand thus indicated
that threats of use of weapons in general (not only threats of use of nuclear
weapons) could be in violation of IHL, but on the same page of their Statement
asserted that the nuclear weapon states agreed that IHL governs *use*.

New Zealand did refer to Article 51(2) of 1977 Additional Protocol I to the
Geneva Conventions, which states that 'Acts or *threats* of violence, the primary
purpose of which is to spread terror amongst the population, are prohibited'
(emphasis added). There was no further discussion of how this provision

---

[14] See, e.g., Written Statement of New Zealand, Nuclear Weapons Advisory Opinion, 20 June
      1995, p. 15, paras. 63–6.
[15] Written Statement of Nauru, Nuclear Weapons Advisory Opinion, pp. 22–3, 31–6; Written
      Statement of New Zealand, p. 15; Written Statement of Malaysia, 19 June 1995, pp. 2–3,
      14–6, 20; Written Statement of Solomon Islands, 19 June 1995, pp. 25–6.
[16] Written Statement of the UK, Nuclear Weapons Advisory Opinion, 16 June 1995, p. 72,
      para. 3.117.
[17] Written Statement of Nauru, Nuclear Weapons Advisory Opinion, at p. 31.
[18] Written Statement of Malaysia, Nuclear Weapons Advisory Opinion, at pp. 14–16.
[19] Written Statement of New Zealand, Nuclear Weapons Advisory Opinion, at p. 15, para. 63.
[20] *Ibid.*, para. 66 (emphasis added).

related to the threats of use of nuclear weapons. This is, however, one of the few legal bases suggested for the assertion that threats are prohibited *in bello*, and will be discussed below.

In its final comments, New Zealand noted that several other categories of weapons were subject to comprehensive prohibitions, including 'biological weapons, chemical weapons, exploding bullets, certain booby traps and weapons based on non-detectable fragments'.[21] It went on to state that: 'Treaties in the arms control and disarmament field circumscribe the threat or use in various respects.'[22] This is incorrect. None of the disarmament instruments mentioned in the quote above circumscribes any kind of threat: they prohibit use, along with development, production, transfer and stockpiling.[23]

Interestingly, both Malaysia and NewZealand discussed the Genocide Convention in relation to threats of use of nuclear weapons. Malaysia stated:

> [T]he Convention on the Prevention and Punishment of the Crime of Genocide renders punishable not only genocide, but also conspiracy to commit genocide, direct and public incitement to commit genocide, attempt to commit genocide, and complicity in genocide, *all of which might be perceived as the threat of genocide by the human targets of nuclear weapons.*[24]

This rather sweeping interpretation of the term 'threat' was not discussed further.

---

[21] *Ibid.*, p. 23, para. 100. Of course, as noted in the Introduction to this book, the 1972 Biological Weapons Convention does not explicitly prohibit the use of biological weapons. The Convention's Review Conference has, however, specified that use of biological weapons 'is effectively a violation of Article I'. See, e.g. Final Document of the Fourth Review Conference, UN Doc. BWC/CONF/.IV/9 (25 November – 6 December 1996). Moreover, the 1925 Geneva Gas Protocol already outlawed the use of bacteriological methods of warfare.

[22] *Ibid.*

[23] See, e.g., Article 1 of the 1992 Chemical Weapons Convention, which prohibits: '(a) To develop, produce, otherwise acquire, stockpile or retain chemical weapons, or transfer, directly or indirectly, chemical weapons to anyone; (b) To use chemical weapons; (c) To engage in any military preparations to use chemical weapons; (d) To assist, encourage or induce, in any way, anyone to engage in any activity prohibited to a State Party under this Convention.' Convention on the Prohibition of the Development, Production, Stockpiling and Use of Chemical Weapons and on their Destruction, Geneva, 3 September 1992, in force 29 April 1993, 32 ILM 800. See also, corresponding articles in similar conventions including the Conventions prohibiting anti-personnel mines and cluster munitions. Convention on the Prohibition of the Use, Stockpiling, Production and Transfer of Anti-Personnel Mines and their Destruction, Oslo, 18 September 1997, in force 1 March 1999, 2056 UNTS 211, 36 ILM 1507; Convention on Cluster Munitions, Dublin, 30 May 2008, in force 1 August 2010, 48 ILM 354.

[24] Written Statement of Malaysia, Nuclear Weapons Advisory Opinion, at p. 20 (emphasis added).

The Written Statement by New Zealand noted the requirement of *intent* to destroy national, ethnic or religious groups in the Genocide Convention, but then it went on to say:

> Nevertheless, it has been argued that owing to their uniquely devastating effect the threat or use of nuclear weapons is likely to breach this convention, especially given the likelihood of escalation. Adherents of this view tend to claim that once the nuclear threshold is crossed escalation is extremely likely if not unavoidable, and that such escalation will lead to the inevitable annihilation of populations.[25]

This could be taken to mean that there can be devastating effects of threats alone. Such effects of mere threats, however, are unlikely. The better interpretation is probably that a threat is likely to lead to escalation, and eventually annihilation of populations, so that the threat itself must be banned under the Convention.

Solomon Islands was the other government (together with New Zealand) that took an explicit position on the matter of threats *in bello*, and moreover offered a legal argument in support of this view:

> The threat of their [nuclear weapons] use must be considered as totally incompatible with the solemn obligation undertaken by States under common Article 1 of the four Geneva Conventions of 1949 and Article 1(1) of the 1st 1977 Additional Protocol 'to respect and ensure respect' of the four Conventions and the Protocol. Given the inevitability of the lethal effects of nuclear weapons, threatening their use must surely also violate the rights of potential victims as set forth in Article 40 of the 1st Additional Protocol, which provides that
>   'It is prohibited to order that there shall be no survivors, to threaten an adversary therewith or to conduct hostilities on that basis.'[26]

The Written Statement by Solomon Islands concluded:

> In summary, the threat of the use of nuclear weapons is clearly unlawful when it is accompanied by a threat prohibited by international law or when it appears in relation to the use of force or intervention also prohibited by international law. Even if the threat to use nuclear weapons might be used for apparently lawful purposes, such threat is unlawful by operation of general rules of international law and specific rules requiring respect for humanitarian and environmental objectives.[27]

The legal justification by Solomon Islands for considering threats of use of nuclear weapons as a violation of IHL was thus based on 'operation of general

---

[25] Written Statement of New Zealand, Nuclear Weapons Advisory Opinion, p. 20, paras. 84–5.
[26] Written Statement of Solomon Islands, Nuclear Weapons Advisory Opinion, pp. 25–6, para. 3.10.
[27] *Ibid.*, p. 26, para. 3.11.

rules of international law', as well as Article 1 Common to the 1949 Geneva Conventions, Article 1 of 1977 Additional Protocol I and finally Article 40 of the Protocol. Together with Article 51(2) of 1977 Additional Protocol I, these legal bases will be discussed as possible bases for the prohibition of threats of nuclear weapon use under IHL.

C.   Discussions of threats in the Advisory Opinion

As mentioned above, the Court started its substantive discussion in the Advisory Opinion with the following description of its task – '[T]o determine the legality or illegality of the threat or use of nuclear weapons'[28] – thus more or less replicating the very dense question from the UN General Assembly.

1.   *Threats* ad bellum

Having discussed briefly the possible implications of human rights law and environmental law, the Court moved on to *ad bellum* as it discussed 'the legality or illegality of recourse to nuclear weapons in light of the provisions of the Charter relating to the threat or use of force'.[29] Here, the Court noted that the provisions of the Charter 'do not refer to specific weapons. They apply to any use of force, regardless of the weapons employed.'[30]

When the Court embarked on the discussion of the relationship between 'threats' and 'use' of force *ad bellum*, it specifically pointed to the wording of the Charter, in paragraph 47:

> The notions of 'threat' and 'use' of force under Article 2, paragraph 4, of the Charter stand together in the sense that if the use of force itself in a given case is illegal – for whatever reason – the threat to use such force will likewise be illegal.[31]

The Court went on to state that no state – whether a supporter of nuclear deterrence or not – had 'suggested to the Court that it would be lawful to threaten to use force if the use of force contemplated would be illegal'.[32] This approach is consistent with the so-called 'Brownlie Formula' often cited in discussions about the use of force: '[if] the promise is to resort to force in conditions in which no justification for the use of force exists, the threat is itself illegal.'[33]

Notwithstanding this assumption and further deliberations and discussions among scholars regarding the concept of threats of use of force,[34] these are limited to the use of force *ad bellum*, not *in bello*.

---

[28] Nuclear Weapons Advisory Opinion, para. 20.
[29] *Ibid.*, para. 37.   [30] *Ibid.*, para. 38.   [31] *Ibid.*, para. 47.   [32] *Ibid.*
[33] I. Brownlie, *International Law and the Use of Force by States* (Oxford: Clarendon Press, 1963), p. 364. See generally Chapter 2 of the present book.
[34] See for example R. Sadurska, 'Threats of force', *American Journal of International Law* 82(2) (1988), 239–68; J. Green and F. Grimal, 'The threat of force as an action in self-defense under

The discussion in paragraph 47 of the Advisory Opinion, combined with the wording of paragraph 51, makes it clear that the Court discussed only *jus ad bellum* issues in paragraph 47: 'Having dealt with the Charter provisions relating to the threat or use of force, the Court *will now turn* to the law applicable *in situations of armed conflict*' (emphasis added). The Court thus made an attempt to keep these two legal regimes separate in its deliberations.

The Court's conclusion on threats under *jus ad bellum* is hardly controversial: Article 2(4) of the UN Charter, which explicitly states that both threats of use of force and use of force are illegal, save in the very limited exceptions specified in the Charter, is unambiguous in its wording, although it is not necessarily clear what would constitute a threat in practice. Article 2(4), moreover, is considered to constitute a norm of *jus cogens*.[35] Thus, the Court's finding that threats to use nuclear weapons violate *jus ad bellum* was unsurprising.

2.   *Threats* in bello

Turning to the discussion of *jus in bello*, the Court stated that it would address the question of whether there might be specific rules of international law regulating what the Court calls 'recourse' to nuclear weapons.[36] The Court offered no indication that the term 'recourse' was meant to indicate anything other than a synonym for 'use'. The Court proceeded by stating that it would 'examine the question put to it in the light of the law applicable in armed conflict proper, i.e. the principles and rules of international humanitarian law applicable in armed conflict'.[37]

Hence, the Court signalled a clear shift from the previous discussion of the law applicable to the justification for use of force (*jus ad bellum*), to an analysis of the law applicable when the armed conflict is a fact, or *jus in bello*. In its analysis of whether existing treaty law pertaining to other weapons, such as poisonous weapons or gas and weapons of mass destruction, can be used analogously with regard to nuclear weapons, the Court limited its discussions to use and did not bring up the question of threats.[38] The reason for not discussing threats here would seem to be that none of the relevant treaty provisions the Court discusses in this section of the Advisory Opinion regulate threats. For example, upon signing the 1925 Geneva Gas Protocol, states parties made clear

international law', *Vanderbilt Journal of Transnational Law* 44(285) (2011), 285–329; and N. Stürchler, *The Threat of Force in International Law* (Cambridge University Press, 2007).
[35] See the International Law Commission's commentary on Draft Article 50 (the Final Article 53 on peremptory norms) where it stated that the prohibition of the use of force 'in itself constitutes a conspicuous example of a rule in international law having the character of *jus cogens*'. *Yearbook of the International Law Commission 1966, 18th Session*, 2 vols. (New York: United Nations, 1967), Vol. II, p. 23.
[36] Nuclear Weapons Advisory Opinion, para. 51.
[37] *Ibid.*   [38] *Ibid.*, paras. 53–7.

that they understood the Treaty to prohibit only 'first-use', with the assumption that a state that violated the Treaty risked facing a reprisal from the injured state.[39] Thus, if one equates possession of the prohibited weapon with threats, these treaties in fact implicitly embraced such threats. Also, when the Court ventured to look at various other treaties relevant to nuclear weapons, such as treaties on nuclear weapon-free zones, its discussions were limited to use or deployment,[40] probably for the same reason: these instruments do not regulate threats.

In its discussion of IHL, the Court began by affirming that 'the right of belligerents to adopt means of injuring the enemy is not unlimited',[41] thereafter referring to the St Petersburg Declaration and its prohibition against the use of 'weapons which uselessly aggravate the suffering of disabled men or make their death inevitable'.[42] The Court then outlined a synopsis of IHL and its core rules and principles, emphasising that 'States do not have unlimited freedom of choice of means in the weapons they *use*'.[43]

After summing up the core content of IHL and the underlying rationale for these rules, the Court stated: 'If an envisaged use of weapons would not meet the requirements of humanitarian law, a threat to engage in such use would also be contrary to that law.'[44] Thus, the Court gave an explicit statement of law, expressing the view that threats of using weapons in violation of IHL must be equally illegal as the actual use. The Court did not, however, explain why it would reach such a conclusion. One might speculate whether the Court simply reiterated this passage from the *ad bellum* discussion without considering the implications.

The remainder of the IHL discussion, pertaining to the development of customary law, revolved around use,[45] with the exception of paragraph 83, in which the Court approvingly quotes the New Zealand Written Statement's assertion that: 'In general, international humanitarian law bears on the threat or use of nuclear weapons, as it does of other weapons.' New Zealand did not, however, provide a rationale for this claim with respect to *threats* of use of nuclear weapons or any other weapons, and as pointed out, the Court failed to supply one as well.

After asserting that IHL applies to both threats and use, the Court shifted the argument's premises by noting that all states that filed Written Statements with the Court acknowledged that international humanitarian law applies to use.[46] The Court failed to note that the states quoted in this regard also only

---

[39] See, e.g. W. Boothby, *Poison, Poisoned Weapons, Asphyxiating Gases, Biological and Chemical Weapons* (Cambridge University Press, 2011), p. 7 (noting 'the 1925 [Geneva Gas] Protocol was for many years regarded as "a ban on first use" of the relevant weapons').

[40] Nuclear Weapons Advisory Opinion, paras. 58–9.

[41] *Ibid.*, para. 77.   [42] *Ibid.*   [43] *Ibid.*, para. 78 (emphasis added).

[44] Nuclear Weapons Advisory Opinion, para. 78.

[45] *Ibid.*, paras. 79–83.   [46] *Ibid.*, para. 87.

mentioned use, and not threats.[47] In keeping up this approach, paragraph 86 of the Advisory Opinion tracks closely the structure of New Zealand's arguments in paragraphs 63 to 66 of that state's Written Statement.[48]

In its final discussion weighing the different arguments against each other, the Court concluded in paragraph 97:

> Accordingly, in view of the present state of international law viewed as a whole, as examined above by the Court, and of the elements of fact at its disposal, the Court is led to observe that it cannot reach a definitive conclusion as to the legality or illegality of the *use* of nuclear weapons by a State in an extreme circumstance of self-defence, in which its very survival would be at stake [emphasis added].

In the Advisory Opinion's *dispositif*, the court slightly rephrased this paragraph in litra D and E:

> A *threat or use* of force by means of nuclear weapons should also be compatible with the requirements of the international law applicable in armed conflict, *particularly those of the principles and rules of international humanitarian law* … It follows from the above-mentioned requirements that the *threat or use* of nuclear weapons would generally be contrary to the rules of international law applicable in armed conflict, *and in particular the principles and rules of humanitarian law* [emphasis added].

The lack of consistency with regard to the terms 'threat or use' or only 'use' throughout the Advisory Opinion begs the question of whether the Court simply has not been aware of the implications of mixing these two concepts. Variations in the text between references to 'use' or 'threat or use' appear largely random. The sentence in paragraph 78, however, which states explicitly that if an act is illegal under IHL, then a threat to carry out such an act must also be illegal under IHL, makes it clear that the Court did mean to express that threats of use of force are generally prohibited under this particular legal regime, but without explaining why.

None of the separate or dissenting opinions by the ICJ judges dealt to any large degree with the question of whether the Court intentionally asserted that threats of use of nuclear weapons are prohibited *in bello*. Judge Oda did, however, comment on the lack of clarity regarding the concept of a 'threat' and linked this omission to the ambiguity of the question posed to the Court:

> I would like further to point out that the words 'the threat of nuclear weapons' are not clearly defined in the request and may not have been understood in an unequivocal manner by the Member States which supported the resolution. An important point seems to be overlooked in the request, namely a possibility that nuclear weapons may well be considered to constitute a

---

[47] *Ibid.*, paras. 86–92.
[48] Written Statement of New Zealand, Nuclear Weapons Advisory Opinion, p. 15.

'threat' merely by being in a State's possession or being under production by a State, considering that the phrase *'threat or* use of nuclear weapons' (emphasis added) was first used in the request while the phrase 'the use *or threat of use* of nuclear weapons' (emphasis added) had long been employed in the United Nations resolutions. In my view it was quite possible, at the time of the request, for some Member States of the United Nations to consider that the actual 'possession' or 'production' of nuclear weapons constituted a 'threat'. In other words, the request might have been prepared by some States who strongly upheld the straightforward notion of the illegality of nuclear weapons as a whole.[49]

Judge Oda did not go into the difference between *jus ad bellum* and *jus in bello* with regard to threats, but rather focused on the alleged political motivations possibly underlying efforts to generate the question the General Assembly posed to the ICJ.

Judge Weeramantry specifically stated that threats would be in violation of *jus in bello*: 'I have voted against this clause as I am of the view that the threat or use of nuclear weapons would not be lawful in any circumstances whatsoever, as it offends the fundamental principles of the jus in bello.'[50] As was the case with the Advisory Opinion itself, no legal reasoning was offered to substantiate this understanding.

D.   Are threats illegal under international law in general?

As indicated above, the Court wrote in paragraph 78: 'If an envisaged use of weapons would not meet the requirements of humanitarian law, a threat to engage in such use would also be contrary to that law.'[51] This conclusion could be based on a general assumption that international law typically prohibits threatening to violate one's international legal obligations. This assumption appears, for example, to be made in the International Committee of the Red Cross (ICRC) study of customary international humanitarian law, in relation to the discussion of Rule 46 on ordering or threatening that no quarter will be given. The commentary to this rule states, without citation: 'The prohibition on threatening to carry out a prohibited act is generally recognized in international law.'[52]

It is not easy to find substantive legal bases for this rather sweeping assumption.[53] The Articles on State Responsibility do not refer to threats of violating

---

[49] Nuclear Weapons Advisory Opinion, Dissenting Opinion of Judge Oda, para. 4.

[50] Nuclear Weapons Advisory Opinion, Dissenting Opinion of Judge Weeramantry, p. 513.

[51] Nuclear Weapons Advisory Opinion, para. 78.

[52] J.-M. Henckaerts and L. Doswald-Beck, *Customary International Humanitarian Law*, 3 vols. (Cambridge University Press, 2005), Vol. I, p. 162.

[53] In a separate article, Doswald-Beck questioned whether the ICJ intended to declare that 'a threat to violate any rule of humanitarian law is also unlawful in itself', noting that 'the effect

international law, save in the case where a state coerces (possibly through threats) another state to commit a violation of international law.[54] Normally, threatening non-compliance with international law obligations would not constitute a violation in itself. On the contrary, threatening non-compliance is often what is needed to incite the other party to comply. Threatening countermeasures or other forms of reprisals in order to incite another party to an international agreement to fulfil its obligations is normally not considered unlawful.[55]

1.   *Threats in international humanitarian law*

Introduction/overview

As mentioned, the ICJ stated that if the use of nuclear weapons were illegal under IHL, then threats of use of nuclear weapons would likewise be prohibited under IHL.[56] Several international lawyers have repeated this point of view. For example, the authors Moxley, Burroughs and Granoff claim:

> There is a robust body of conventional and customary international law governing the use *and threat of use* of nuclear weapons ... This is the body of international humanitarian law, known variously as IHL, the law of armed conflict, and *jus in bello*, terms that are generally synonymous.[57]

In this article, the authors produce a 'Summary of the Main Rules of International Humanitarian Law Applicable to Nuclear Weapons', in which they go through the rule of distinction, the rule of proportionality, the rule of necessity, the 'corollary rule' of controllability and the law on reprisals (as well as the state's right of self-defence, which is not part of IHL), without explaining how any of these rules regulate threats.[58] In the section of the article that deals with 'Threats and Deterrence', the authors conclude that use of nuclear weapons would be

---

is far-reaching and it would also be superfluous to add threats to any treaty text (unless the commission itself would not be unlawful – not a likely eventuality)'. L. Doswald-Beck, 'International humanitarian law and the Advisory Opinion of the International Court of Justice on the legality of the threat or use of nuclear weapons', *International Review of the Red Cross* 37(316) (1997), 35–55.

[54] International Law Commission (ILC), Draft articles on Responsibility of States for Internationally Wrongful Acts, with commentaries, 2001, Text adopted by the International Law Commission at its fifty-third session, in 2001, and submitted to the General Assembly as a part of the Commission's report covering the work of that session (A/56/10), Art. 18.

[55] See Chapter 7 in this book on 'The use of nuclear weapons as a reprisal under international humanitarian law'.

[56] Nuclear Weapons Advisory Opinion, para. 78.

[57] C. L. Moxley, Jr, J. Burroughs and J. Granoff, 'Nuclear weapons and compliance with international humanitarian law and the Nuclear Non-Proliferation Treaty', *Fordham International Law Journal* 34 (2011), 595–696, at 606 (emphasis added).

[58] *Ibid.*, pp. 612–13.

unlawful under IHL, and therefore, because of the statement made by the ICJ to this effect, threats to use them would be unlawful as a result of the use being unlawful.[59] Hence, these authors do not produce any independent legal argumentation for why threats of the use of a weapon should be generally banned under IHL. They simply repeat the assertion made by the ICJ[60] – an assertion that, as noted above, lacks legal reasoning.[61]

Aside from the general statements referring to threats and IHL offered by the ICJ and other legal writers, some of the discussants have offered specific legal bases for the assertion that threats violate IHL, Solomon Islands and New Zealand being among these. The claims put forward in this regard are that threats of use of nuclear weapons would be prohibited under (1) Article 1 Common to the Geneva Conventions as well as Article 1(1) in 1977 Additional Protocol I; (2) Article 40 of 1977 Additional Protocol I; and (3) Article 51 (2) of 1977 Additional Protocol I. These three possible bases for the proposition that IHL prohibits threats to use nuclear weapons will be discussed in the following section.

2. Threats of use of nuclear weapons and the duty to 'respect and ensure respect for' IHL

As noted above, Solomon Islands argued that the threat of use of nuclear weapons could be a violation of Article 1 Common to the Geneva Conventions as well as Article 1(1) in 1977 Additional Protocol I.[62] In its Written Statement to the ICJ, Solomon Islands stated that the threat of use of nuclear weapons:

> must be considered as totally incompatible with the solemn obligation undertaken by States under common Article 1 of the four Geneva Conventions of 1949 and Article 1(1) of the 1st 1977 Additional Protocol 'to respect and ensure respect' of the four Conventions and the Protocol.[63]

The text of the relevant provisions is as follows: 'The High Contracting Parties undertake to respect and ensure respect for this Convention/Protocol in all circumstances.'

The point of departure for Solomon Islands, in its letter to the ICJ, was that 'any use of nuclear weapons would *prima facie* violate international humanitarian

---

[59] *Ibid.*, p. 675.   [60] See, e.g. *ibid.*, p. 638.

[61] See also, Nuclear Weapons Advisory Opinion, Dissenting Opinion of Judge Higgins, p. 584, para. 9 (stating: 'At no point in its Opinion does the Court engage in the task that is surely at the heart of the question asked: the systematic application of the relevant law to the use or threat of nuclear weapons. It reaches its conclusions without the benefit of detailed analysis. An essential step in the judicial process – that of legal reasoning – has been omitted').

[62] Written Statement of Solomon Islands, Nuclear Weapons Advisory Opinion, at pp. 25–6.

[63] *Ibid.*, pp. 25–6, para 3.10.

law'.[64] Thus, the logic is that threatening to violate IHL cannot be consistent with the obligation to respect and ensure respect for this body of law.

First of all, any use of nuclear or other weapons would not be regulated by any of the four Geneva Conventions, so the following discussion will be limited to Article 1 of 1977 Additional Protocol 1. Second, the interpretation seems to rest on the assumption that any use of nuclear weapons would *always* be inconsistent with IHL. Is it, in other words, prohibited under Article 1 to *threaten* to violate IHL?

Notwithstanding the issue of whether nuclear weapons could be used without violating IHL, it is not easy to find support, either in the Commentaries to 1977 Additional Protocol I or in legal literature, for the assumption that threats of IHL violations are generally prohibited under Article 1. In a 2012 article in the *European Journal of International Law*, Carlo Focarelli argues that 'common Article 1 is no more than a reminder of all obligations (negative and positive) to "respect" the Geneva Conventions'.[65] In other words, this provision does not impose obligations on states beyond the specific obligations laid down in the Conventions and Protocols themselves. Article 1 moreover refers to an obligation to 'ensure respect' for the provisions in the Conventions/Protocols. The Commentary on Article 1 addresses the provision's specific formulation:

> The use of the words 'and to ensure respect' was, however, deliberate: they were intended to emphasize and strengthen the responsibility of the Contracting Parties. It would not, for example, be enough for a State to give orders or directives to a few civilian or military authorities, leaving it to them to arrange as they pleased for the details of their execution.[66]

Solomon Islands did not offer any reasoning for how Article 1 could be understood to ban threatening the prohibited acts. It thus seems that this argument pertaining to threats and Article 1 did not add anything more to the discourse than the ICJ's general statement on threats *in bello*.[67] If threats of use of nuclear weapons were in fact prohibited under IHL, then clearly it would be incompatible with the general obligations in Article 1(1) of 1977 Additional Protocol I to carry out such threats. Solomon Islands did not discuss in its statement the underlying question of whether such threats are in fact outlawed by IHL.

---

[64] *Ibid.*
[65] C. Focarelli, 'Common Article 1 of the Geneva Conventions: A soap bubble?', *European Journal of International Law* 21(1) (2010), 125–71, at 171.
[66] International Committee of the Red Cross, *Commentary on the Geneva Conventions of 12 August 1949*, 4 vols. (Geneva: International Committee of the Red Cross, 1952), Vol. I, p. 404.
[67] Nuclear Weapons Advisory Opinion, para. 78.

3.   Orders or threats that no quarter will be given

Threats are mentioned specifically in two provisions in 1977 Additional Protocol I: Articles 40 and 51(2). Similarly, threats are mentioned in 1977 Additional Protocol II, in Articles 4 and 13(2).[68]

As noted above, Solomon Islands was one of the few governments that attempted to justify the assumption that threats *in bello* violate IHL using legal argumentation. One of Solomon Islands' arguments was linked to Article 40 of 1977 Additional Protocol I and the prohibition on threatening that there would be no survivors. In its Written Statement, Solomon Islands stated: 'Given the inevitability of the lethal effects of nuclear weapons, threatening their use must surely also violate the rights of potential victims as set forth in Article 40 of the 1st Additional Protocol'.[69]

Before determining whether the prohibition against orders or threats that no quarter will be given constitutes a prohibition on threats of nuclear weapons, a threshold question must be answered: to what extent does the rule embodied in Article 40 apply to the nuclear weapon states? The United States has signed, but not ratified 1977 Additional Protocol I.[70] The United States,[71] United Kingdom[72] and France[73] also maintain that the Protocol, or at least the new rules introduced by the Protocol, does not apply to nuclear weapons, while Russia and China did not make any reservations or declarations to this effect.

Nevertheless, if a treaty provision reflects an element of customary international law, it applies to all states that are not persistent objectors, regardless of

---

[68] It seems clear that the ICJ did choose to limit itself to the question of states using or threatening to use nuclear weapons, and thus did not specifically refer to the provisions in 1977 Additional Protocol II (applicable to non-international armed conflicts). That said, there is a real concern today about nuclear weapons ending up in the hands of non-state armed groups. This issue will, however, not be discussed in this chapter.

[69] Written Statement of Solomon Islands, Nuclear Weapons Advisory Opinion, pp. 25–6, para. 3.10.

[70] Signatories to Protocol Additional to the Geneva Conventions of 12 August 1949, and relating to the Protection of Victims of International Armed Conflicts (Protocol I), 8 June 1977, available at: www.icrc.org/ihl.nsf/WebSign?ReadForm&id=470&ps=S.

[71] 'It is, however, clear from the negotiating and ratification record of Protocol 1 that the new rules contained in the Protocol were not intended to apply to nuclear weapons.' Written Statement of the United States, Nuclear Weapons Advisory Opinion, 20 June 1995, p. 25.

[72] 'It continues to be the understanding of the United Kingdom that the rules introduced by the Protocol apply exclusively to conventional weapons without prejudice to any other rules of international law applicable to other types of weapons. In particular, the rules so introduced do not have any effect on and do not regulate or prohibit the use of nuclear weapons.' Reservation/Declaration text of the United Kingdom, Protocol Additional to the Geneva Conventions of 12 August 1949, and relating to the Protection of Victims of International Armed Conflicts (Protocol I), 8 June 1977.

[73] Reservation/Declaration text of France, Protocol Additional to the Geneva Conventions of 12 August 1949, and relating to the Protection of Victims of International Armed Conflicts (Protocol I), 8 June 1977.

whether a state has ratified the relevant treaty. This would seem to be the case for Article 40 of the Protocol. The United States, the United Kingdom and France are all parties to the Hague Regulations of 1907, on which inter alia Article 40 is based, and which were concluded well before the advent of nuclear weapons.[74] Article 23 of the Hague Regulations of 1907 provides: 'In addition to the pro-hibitions provided by special Conventions, it is especially forbidden … (d) To declare that no quarter will be given.' In addition, the ICRC study of customary international humanitarian law notes that this rule is also found in the US, UK, and French military manuals.[75] Thus, the rule found in Article 40 would seem to apply to these three states also with respect to nuclear weapons. Article 40 states that: 'It is prohibited to order that there shall be no survivors, to threaten an adversary therewith or to conduct hostilities on this basis.'

This rule is related to the prohibition against killing prisoners of war or soldiers *hors de combat*, but its core function is essentially that it ensures that adversaries should not be killed *unnecessarily* – there must be a possibility of surrendering or taking prisoners of war at the end of hostilities. Soldiers *hors de combat* must be treated according to the rules of IHL.

In addition to the prohibition against ordering that there will be no sur-vivors and to conducting hostilities on that basis, there is also a prohibition against making threats that there will be no survivors. It is easy to imagine the escalation of intensity of hostilities if an adversary fears that surrender or capitulation equals certain death. Soldiers in the hands of the adversary or in the process of surrendering are already entitled to protection under several provisions of IHL, including under the rules of Article 41 of 1977 Additional Protocol I. Hence, other provisions of IHL cover the last part of Article 40. It is clear that hostilities must not be conducted on the basis that there shall be no survivors.

The specific prohibition against making threats to conduct hostilities on this basis is, according to the ICRC study of customary international humanitar-ian law, outlawed in numerous military manuals.[76] The assertion in the ICRC customary IHL study is that threatening an adversary that there will be no survivors, regardless of whether it is in an international armed conflict (IAC) or a non-international armed conflict (NIAC), is prohibited under custom-ary international law.[77] The Rome Statute's provisions on war crimes in an IAC

---

[74] State Parties, Convention (IV) respecting the Laws and Customs of War on Land and its annex: Regulations concerning the Laws and Customs of War on Land. The Hague, 18 October 1907, available at: www.icrc.org/ihl.nsf/WebSign?ReadForm&id=195&ps=P.

[75] Henckaerts and Doswald-Beck, *Customary International Humanitarian Law*, pp. 918 and 920.

[76] See Rule 46, *ibid.*, pp. 161–3.

[77] *Ibid.*, p. 161. But see the Rome Statute of the International Criminal Court, Rome, 17 July 1998, in force 1 July 2002, 2187 UNTS 90, Art. 8(2)(b)xii, where this rule is linked only to international armed conflicts.

explicitly prohibit only declaring (not threatening) that there will be no survivors (see Article 8(2)(b)(xii)). In the Elements of Crimes, however, this omission appears to be remedied; in the elements to Article 8(2)(b)(xii) – War crime of denying quarter – threat is incorporated in the following way: '1. The perpetrator declared or ordered that there shall be no survivors. 2. Such declaration or order was given *in order to threaten* an adversary or to conduct hostilities on the basis that there shall be no survivors' (emphasis added).

The question in this context, however, is whether the threat to use nuclear weapons would constitute a violation of Article 40 of 1977 Additional Protocol I per se. In other words, could it be argued that *any* use of nuclear weapons would *always* and *inevitably* lead to a situation where there would be no survivors?

Despite limited experience with the use of nuclear weapons in hostilities,[78] there seem to exist ways of using these weapons that would not necessarily have such an effect. Even in Hiroshima and Nagasaki there were many survivors. Depending on the size of the nuclear warhead and the location attacked, it would not be an inevitable result that all adversaries would be killed.

In the ICRC Commentary to Article 40, it is noted that the provision:

> does not imply that the Parties to the conflict abandon the use of a particular weapon, but that they forgo using it in such a way that it would amount to a refusal to give quarter … As regards nuclear weapons, whether tactical or strategic, these form the object of a controversy which is examined elsewhere. However, it would be wrong to infer from this controversy that the constraints imposed by Article 40 in favour of enemy combatants concerning the use of conventional weapons are only of marginal importance on the argument that, if a nuclear weapon were used, the situation of these combatants would in any event be much worse. The rule is the rule and nuclear weapons raise questions which should be examined in their own right in the context of the recognized rules.[79]

In other words, there is not much support here for the assumption that threats of use of nuclear weapons per se would violate Article 40 of 1977 Additional Protocol I.

It seems very doubtful that the prohibition against threatening that there will be no survivors can be taken to imply bans on specific weapons. Also, other provisions more specifically aimed at means of warfare, such as Article 51(4) of the Protocol, which prohibits indiscriminate attacks, have not been interpreted to constitute prohibitions of specific weapons. During the processes to ban anti-personnel landmines as well as cluster munitions, it was argued that use of these weapons normally constituted violations of Article 51(4)(b), which

---

[78] Hiroshima and Nagasaki, August 1945.
[79] Y. Sandoz, C. Swinarski and B. Zimmermann (eds.), *Commentary on the Additional Protocols of 8 June 1977 to the Geneva Conventions of 12 August 1949* (Geneva: ICRC/ Martinus Nijhoff, 1987), p. 477 (hereafter, *Commentary on the Additional Protocols*).

prohibits the use of means of warfare that 'cannot be directed at a specific military objective'.[80] The same is true for the arguments with regard to banning biological weapons and chemical weapons. In all of these cases (with the possible exception of biological weapons) it could be argued that it would be conceivable to deploy them without violating the rule on distinction. The argument was, therefore, that since it was highly probable that these weapons, if available, would inevitably be used in ways that did not uphold the rule on distinction, the weapons ought to be outlawed.

It seems difficult to sustain the point of view that if Article 51(4)(b) did not constitute a de facto prohibition against the use of, for example, biological or chemical weapons, it nevertheless would constitute a ban on nuclear weapons.

4.   Threats of terror against the civilian population

New Zealand, in its Written Statement submitted to the ICJ before the issuance of the Advisory Opinion, argued that threats to use nuclear weapons would be prohibited under Article 51(2) of 1977 Additional Protocol I. The ICJ did not pick up this explicit legal argument. This provision is, however, the only provision besides Article 40 that deals with threats in the Protocol, and the ICRC study of customary IHL states that the rule embodied in Article 51(2) reflects customary law.[81]

Article 51(2) states: 'The civilian population as such, as well as individual civilians, shall not be the object of attack. Acts or threats of violence the primary purpose of which is to spread terror among the civilian population are prohibited.'

According to the ICRC commentary on this provision, the second sentence of Article 51(2) applies to acts or threats of terror that go beyond ordinary acts of war. Notwithstanding that ordinary acts of war in most circumstances are terrifying to those who might be at the receiving end or in the vicinity of such acts, the prohibition against acts or threats against civilians requires the primary purpose of spreading terror:

---

[80] See, e.g. T. Boutruche *et al.*, 'The title and preamble of the convention' in G. Nystuen and S. Casey-Maslen (eds.), *The Convention on Cluster Munitions: A Commentary* (Oxford University Press, 2010), p. 93, para. 0.190 (stating 'The potential for cluster munitions to have extensive indiscriminate effects served as the main incentive to campaign for an international ban'); S. Maslen, *Commentaries on Arms Control Treaties: Volume I: The Convention on the Prohibition of the Use, Stockpiling, Production, and Transfer of Anti-Personnel Mines and on their Destruction* (Oxford University Press, 2004), p. 68, para. 0.139; J. Borrie, *Unacceptable Harm: A History of How the Treaty to Ban Cluster Munitions Was Won* (Geneva: United Nations Institute for Disarmament Research, 2009), p. 25.

[81] Henckaerts and Doswald-Beck, *Customary International Humanitarian Law*, pp. 72–3. The USA also cited approvingly 1977 Additional Protocol I, Article 51(2) in its Written Statement to the ICJ in the *Nuclear Weapons* case. Written Statement of the USA, Nuclear Weapons Advisory Opinion, p. 26, n. 73.

[T]he prohibition covers acts intended to spread terror; there is no doubt that acts of violence related to a state of war almost always give rise to some degree of terror among the population and sometimes also among the armed forces. It also happens that attacks on armed forces are purposely conducted brutally in order to intimidate the enemy soldiers and persuade them to surrender. This is not the sort of terror envisaged here. This provision is intended to prohibit acts of violence the primary purpose of which is to spread terror among the civilian population *without offering substantial military advantage*. It is interesting to note that threats of such acts are also prohibited. This calls to mind some of the proclamations made in the past threatening the annihilation of civilian populations.[82]

The UK military manual supports this interpretation; it asserts that this rule would apply, for instance to:

car bombs installed in busy shopping streets, even if no civilians are killed or injured by them, their object being to create panic among the civilian population … It does not apply to terror caused as a by-product of attacks on military objectives or as a result of genuine warnings of impending attacks on such objectives.[83]

Likewise, the Eritrea–Ethiopia Claims Commission discussed precisely this issue of whether warnings of imminent attack constitute a violation of Article 51(2) of 1977 Additional Protocol I. Both Ethiopia and Eritrea claimed the other side violated Article 51(2) by terrorising civilians with the threat of imminent invasion, leading to internal displacement of both states' populations. Eritrea charged that Ethiopia issued explicit warnings to Eritrean citizens to flee their homes. The Claims Commission found no violation of Article 51(2) for either side, writing in its assessment of Eritrea's claims:

The Commission referred to this matter in its Partial Award in Ethiopia's Central Front Claim, in terms that are equally valid for the present claim.

'The flight of civilians from the perceived danger of hostilities is a common, and often tragic, occurrence in warfare, but it does not, as such, give rise to liability under international humanitarian law. While Protocol I prohibits "acts or threats of violence the primary purpose of which is to spread terror among the civilian population", it implicitly recognizes that civilians may, nevertheless, be terrorized because of the hostilities. Moreover, Ethiopia does not allege or prove that Eritrea deliberately tried to cause the civilian inhabitants of the wereda to flee by terrorizing them, let alone that spreading terror was the primary purpose of its acts during its invasion and occupation.'[84]

---

[82] *Commentary on the Additional Protocols*, p. 618, para. 1940 (emphasis added).
[83] UK Ministry of Defence, *The Manual of the Law of Armed Conflict* (Oxford University Press, 2004), p. 67, para. 5.21.1.
[84] Eritrea–Ethiopia Claims Commission, *Partial Award, Western Front, Aerial Bombardment and Related Claims: Eritrea's Claims 1, 3, 5, 9–13, 14, 21, 25 and 26, between the Federal*

It cannot be excluded that a threat to use nuclear weapons could be made in violation of Article 51(2). It would depend on the circumstances and on the intent behind the threat. This is not, however, the same as saying that *all* cases of threats to use nuclear weapons would violate this provision. The criterion of the primary purpose of the threat must be fulfilled. Article 51(2) cannot therefore reasonably constitute a general ban on a specific weapon.

5. Can threats equal possession under IHL?

There is a distinction between the two different types of threats that states referred to in their written opinions. The first, that possession of nuclear weapons equals a threat of use that violates international humanitarian law, can be dismissed relatively summarily. *Jus in bello*, as a rule, applies only within the context of an armed conflict.[85] Thus, the policy of nuclear deterrence in peacetime remains outside the scope of IHL. During an armed conflict, the legality under IHL of possessing nuclear weapons must be judged by the same standards as for any other type of weapon.

Although IHL regulates the use of weapons, there is no general legal basis for prohibiting the possession of weapons whose use would violate IHL. For example, although biological weapons are often named as the textbook example of inherently indiscriminate weapons, their possession would not violate IHL. This is not to say that possession of biological weapons would be legal. Clearly, no state party to the 1972 Biological Weapons Convention could possess such weapons without violating the terms of this Treaty. However, it is not IHL, but rather the Biological Weapons Convention that prohibits the possession of biological weapons. The same is true for chemical weapons, anti-personnel landmines and cluster munitions. The same argument would apply to nuclear weapons. As a result, there is no basis under IHL for prohibiting the possession of nuclear weapons. The remainder of this discussion will analyse whether an explicit threat to use nuclear weapons would violate IHL.

6. Threats in light of the purpose(s) of international humanitarian law

The discussion so far has concentrated on the actual claims made by different actors and commentators in relation to the ICJ Advisory Opinion. If one were to take a step back and look at the ICJ conclusion on this point, one might ask: why would threats of violations of IHL constitute actual violations of IHL? To

---

Democratic Republic of Ethiopia and the State of Eritrea (19 December 2005), p. 40, para. 135.

[85] Certain provisions of the Geneva Conventions and 1977 Additional Protocol I also apply outside of armed conflict, for example rules on placement of military buildings, protection of emblems and dissemination.

answer this, one must look at the purpose of IHL as a legal regime. It is a very specific legal regime, for most purposes only applicable in armed conflict, and regulating acts that under normal circumstances are considered appalling and unlawful.

The rules of IHL aim to, inter alia, separate combatants from civilians and thus make it possible to protect those who should not be adversely affected by acts of hostilities, and to protect combatants from unnecessary suffering. As Robert Kolb illustrates, the motivating forces underlying IHL have evolved considerably over the past century and a half – from an emphasis on creating international model military rules for domestic enforcement to the regime's emphasis since the 1990s on the plight of individual victims of armed conflicts.[86] Hence, there is strictly speaking no explicit and general prohibition on threats to violate IHL.[87] Throughout IHL's history, the consequences of the conduct of hostilities have been the concern of IHL, not threats. It is not unusual to threaten the adversary in a situation of armed conflict.[88] Sometimes, such threats may even prevent an attack or diminish the humanitarian impact of an attack.[89]

Another could be that as 1977 Additional Protocol I (and II) specifically mentions threats in two provisions, this could be indicative of an assumption that as far as the other provisions of 1977 Additional Protocol I are concerned, they do not cover threats.[90] In the instances where threats have been outlawed for very specific reasons, as shown above, this has been made explicit in the provisions in the relevant IHL instruments. One should, however, be careful in drawing strong conclusions solely based on *au contraire* interpretations.

[86] R. Kolb, 'The main epochs of modern international humanitarian law since 1864 and their related dominant legal constructions' in K. Mujezinovic, C. Cooper Guldal and G. Nystuen (eds.), *Searching for a 'Principle of Humanity' in International Humanitarian Law* (Cambridge University Press, 2012), pp. 23–71.

[87] 'But a threat to use nuclear (or other) weapons in a defensive response to aggression does not endanger the interests protected by international humanitarian law.' Also: 'as a general principle, international humanitarian law is concerned with consequences of the conduct of hostilities and is not offended by mere threats.' R. F. Turner, 'Nuclear weapons and the World Court: the ICJ's Advisory Opinion and its significance for US Strategic Doctrine', *International Legal Studies Series US Naval War College* 72 (1998), 309–64, at 350.

[88] See, e.g.,Doswald-Beck, 'International humanitarian law and the Advisory Opinion of the International Court of Justice', 4 (noting that if the 'policy of deterrence' constitutes a threat to violate IHL, then, if anything, 'State practice since 1945' demonstrates widespread acceptance of threats to violate IHL).

[89] 'If a particular use of nuclear weapons is thought to be unlawful because of disproportionate civilian casualties, why should a mere threat of such use be regarded as unlawful, when such a threat would cause no such casualties but might deter or halt an unlawful attack?' M. J. Matheson, 'The opinions of the International Court of Justice on the threat or use of nuclear weapons', *American Journal of International Law* 91(3) (1997), 417–35, at 432.

[90] See, e.g., Doswald-Beck, 'International humanitarian law and the Advisory Opinion of the International Court of Justice', 4.

Conclusion

The main ambition of this chapter has been to demonstrate that the statement in the ICJ Advisory Opinion contained inter alia in paragraph 78, that 'If an envisaged use of weapons would not meet the requirements of humanitarian law, a threat to engage in such use would also be contrary to that law', seems to be largely without legal support, at least from a *lex lata* point of view. It is futile to speculate as to the reasons for this; however, it is clear that this was a particularly difficult case for the Court, for a number of reasons.

Although this chapter addresses a rather narrow element of the legal debate pertaining to the lawfulness of nuclear weapons, the debate is nonetheless worth highlighting as an illustration of the tendency towards conflation of *jus ad bellum* and *jus in bello* evident in the Nuclear Weapons Advisory Opinion. It appears that the threat of use of force, prohibited under the UN Charter, has been subject to 'mission creep' and has landed in the *jus in bello* debate without sufficient legal justification. And if *jus ad bellum* and *jus in bello* cannot be kept as separate regimes, then *jus in bello* cannot survive. This is what is at stake here.

7

The use of nuclear weapons as a reprisal under international humanitarian law

STUART CASEY-MASLEN

It cannot be denied that reprisals against civilians are inherently a barbarous means of seeking compliance with international law. The most blatant reason for the universal revulsion that usually accompanies reprisals is that they may not only be arbitrary but are also not directed specifically at the individual authors of the initial violation … These retaliatory measures are aimed instead at other more vulnerable individuals or groups. They are individuals or groups who may not even have any degree of solidarity with the presumed authors of the initial violation; they may share with them only the links of nationality and allegiance to the same rulers.

Trial Chamber of the International Criminal Tribunal for
the former Yugoslavia[1]

Given the highly successful nuclear deterrence strategy of the United States and the refined state of modern weapons delivery systems, the threat of reprisals has probably done more for humanity in the past three decades than the sum total of the damage occasioned by the execution of reprisals throughout recorded history.

Maj. M. C. C. Bristol III, United States Air Force[2]

Introduction

There are few issues in international humanitarian law (IHL) that are more contentious than 'belligerent' reprisals[3] and even fewer that are of such obvious relevance to nuclear weapons. Accordingly, this chapter looks at the extent to

---

[1] International Criminal Tribunal for the former Yugoslavia (ICTY), *Prosecutor* v. *Zoran Kupreškić* et al., Judgment (Trial Chamber) (Case No. IT-95-16-T), 14 January 2000, para. 528 (hereafter, *Kupreškić* Trial Judgment).

[2] Maj. M. C. C. Bristol III, USAF, 'Laws of war and belligerent reprisals against enemy civilian populations', *Air Force Law Review* 21 (1979), 397–431, at 420, 422.

[3] Reference is occasionally made in the literature to 'pacific' reprisals. See, e.g., D. Alland, 'The definition of countermeasures' in J. Crawford, A. Pellet and S. Olleson (eds.), *The Law of International Responsibility* (Oxford University Press, 2010), p. 1131. Hereafter, when the

which use of nuclear weapons that would otherwise be unlawful under IHL could be justified under *jus in bello* rules governing reprisals. A 'trend'[4] towards a comprehensive prohibition on reprisals, notably against civilians in enemy territory during the conduct of hostilities,[5] has not yet crystallised into a norm of customary law. In the words of the United States Air Force:

> Under law of armed conflict treaties signed following World War II, the international community has sought to significantly limit the circumstances in which reprisals can be used. Notwithstanding these limitations, there is no customary international law prohibition on reprisals per se, and recent State practice indicates that States have yet to give up the possibility of exercising a right of reprisal in response to serious violations of the law of armed conflict to prevent further violations.[6]

The Nuclear Weapons Advisory Opinion, issued by the International Court of Justice (ICJ) in 1996,[7] included reference to reprisals in only two paragraphs and without addressing their legality in any detail.[8] The first instance concerned the prohibition under 1977 Additional Protocol I on reprisals against the natural environment,[9] while the second referred to reprisals more broadly. Given the alleged centrality of reprisals to the foreseen use of nuclear weapons, it is surprising that the Court did not accord the issue greater attention.

This chapter opens with a definition of the notion of a reprisal (distinguishing it from other similar notions) and then assesses the conditions for the exercise of a lawful reprisal under *jus in bello*. It subsequently applies the principle of lawful reprisals to a series of hypothetical uses of nuclear weapons in an international armed conflict. As will be seen, the specific use of nuclear weapons as a means of reprisal poses particular challenges to the applicable law. The

---

term 'reprisal' is referred to in this chapter, it refers to 'belligerent' reprisals in a situation of armed conflict. It does not cover armed reprisals *ad bellum*.

[4] J.-M. Henckaerts and L. Doswald-Beck, *Customary International Humanitarian Law*, 3 vols. (Cambridge University Press, 2005), Vol. I, pp. 520, 523.

[5] Already in 1970, prior to the adoption of 1977 Additional Protocol I, United Nations General Assembly Resolution 2675 (XXV) affirmed the principle that 'civilian populations, or individual members thereof, should not be the object of reprisals' as a basic principle for the protection of civilian populations in armed conflict. The Resolution was adopted by 109 votes to 0 with 8 abstentions, but because it was not adopted by a roll-call vote, it is not certain which states voted in favour and which abstained. See Henckaerts and Doswald-Beck, *Customary International Humanitarian Law*, p. 520.

[6] US Air Force, *Air Force Operations and The Law, A Guide for Air, Space, and Cyber Forces* (Washington DC: The Judge Advocate General School, 2009), p. 44.

[7] International Court of Justice (ICJ), *Legality of the Threat or Use of Nuclear Weapons*, Advisory Opinion of 8 July 1996 (hereafter, Nuclear Weapons Advisory Opinion).

[8] Nuclear Weapons Advisory Opinion, paras. 31, 46.

[9] Protocol Additional to the Geneva Conventions of 12 August 1949, and relating to the Protection of Victims of International Armed Conflicts (Protocol I), Geneva, 8 June 1977, in force 7 December 1977, 1125 UNTS 3, Art. 55(2) (hereafter, 1977 Additional Protocol I).

chapter then turns to the (disputed) legality of reprisals under the rules applicable to armed conflicts of a non-international character. The conclusion seeks to summarise the law governing the use of nuclear weapons as a reprisal.

A. The definition of a reprisal under IHL

The term reprisal describes an act that would normally be unlawful under IHL, but which is not prohibited insofar as it seeks, within tightly defined circumstances and criteria, to bring another party to the conflict back into compliance with *jus in bello*. As a working definition, Kalshoven suggested that they are acts 'in breach of a rule of the law of armed conflict directed by one belligerent party against the other with a view to inducing the latter party to stop violating that or another rule of [IHL]'.[10] As the term is not formally defined, nor its parameters prescribed, in any IHL treaty,[11] the precise conditions for its exercise are ultimately unsettled, although it is possible to trace many such conditions with a high degree of confidence.

In seeking to do so, a reprisal must, at the outset, be compared and contrasted with four other concepts with which it is sometimes confused. First, it is clearly not a synonym for *tu quoque*,[12] the (non-)defence to a criminal charge,[13]

---

[10] F. Kalshoven, 'Belligerent reprisals revisited', *Netherlands Yearbook of International Law* 21 (1990), 43–80, at 44. In *USA* v. *Ohlendorf et al.*, a US military court at Nuremberg defined reprisals in the following terms: 'Reprisals in war are the commission of acts which, although illegal in themselves, may, under the specific circumstances of the given case, become justified because the guilty adversary has himself behaved illegally, and the action is taken in the last resort, in order to prevent the adversary from behaving illegally in the future.' Military Tribunal II, *USA* v. *Otto Ohlendorf et al.* ('The *Einsatzgruppen* Case'), Case No. 9, Opinion and Judgment of 8–9 April 1948, printed in *Trials of War Criminals Before The Nuernberg Military Tribunals under Control Council Law No. 10*, Vol. IV (US Government Printing Office, 1950), p. 493.

[11] 'Neither the 1949 Geneva Conventions nor the 1977 Additional Protocols provide a definition of "reprisal". They are also silent on the requirements for legitimate reprisals in cases where they are not explicitly prohibited.' Henckaerts and Doswald-Beck, *Customary International Humanitarian Law*, pp. 513–18.

[12] As Yee explains: 'Simply put, tu quoque is the Latin rendition of "you too", with the argument built-in, though often unstated: "Since you have committed the same crime, why are you prosecuting me?" Cast in more affirmative terms, the argument is that if one side in a conflict has committed certain crimes, it has no authority to prosecute or punish nationals of the other side for the same or closely similar crimes.' S. Yee, 'The tu quoque argument as a defence to international crimes, prosecution or punishment', *Chinese Journal of International Law* 3 (2004), 87–133, at 87.

[13] As the ICTY noted in the *Kupreškić* case, the US Military Tribunal in the so-called High Command trial 'categorically stated that under general principles of law, an accused does not exculpate himself from a crime by showing that another has committed a similar crime, either before or after the commission of the crime by the accused'. *Kupreškić* Trial Judgment, para. 516 (citing US Military Tribunal, *US* v. *Wilhelm von Leeb et al.* ('The *High Command* Case'), Case No. 12, Judgment of 27 October 1948, printed in *Law Reports of the Trials of*

especially in an international criminal law tribunal.[14] *Tu quoque* differs materially from a reprisal on the basis of the intent of the act. The sole legitimate purpose of a reprisal is to bring a party to conflict that is acting unlawfully back into compliance with *jus in bello*, whereas, fundamentally, *tu quoque* asserts an implied justification to violate the law generally. Or, in the vernacular, 'what's sauce for the goose is sauce for the gander'.

Second, an act of reprisal should not be assimilated to an act of *collective punishment*.[15] Again, it is the intent of the act that distinguishes the two concepts. As the name clearly indicates, a collective punishment is intentionally punitive or retributive; accordingly, its aim is not to restore compliance with the law, as is the case with a reprisal. Of course, determining on the facts – and notwithstanding any public rhetoric to the contrary – whether any given act is a lawful reprisal or merely a collective punishment may be challenging.

Third, a reprisal differs materially from an act of *retorsion* in that the act that constitutes a reprisal would otherwise be unlawful, whereas acts of retorsion are not per se illegal (though they may well be 'unfriendly' in the words of the International Law Commission (ILC)).[16] Examples of such acts are 'the

---

War Criminals, Vol. XII: The German High Command Trial (London: United Nations War Crimes Commission, 1949), p. 64.

[14] *Tu quoque* was attempted as a defence by German Admiral Karl Doenitz during the International Military Tribunal at Nuremberg that followed the end of the Second World War. Doenitz argued that he should be acquitted of war crimes charges brought against him on the basis that other leaders and nations had also committed the same crimes. He was nonetheless ultimately convicted of the offence of waging unrestricted submarine warfare in the Atlantic even though US Admiral Chester Nimitz had admitted that the United States had done the same thing in the Pacific. Doenitz was, however, not given a prison sentence for the offence, suggesting that *tu quoque* may at least serve as a mitigating factor in sentencing. For a discussion of the case, see e.g. N. A. Heise, 'Deciding not to decide: Nuremberg and the ambiguous history of the tu quoque defense', *The Concord Review*, 2009, available at: http://ssrn.com/abstract=1354048.

[15] Collective punishments are always unlawful. Rule 103 of the ICRC Customary IHL Study states simply that collective punishments 'are prohibited', with state practice establishing the rule as a norm of customary international law applicable in both international and non-international armed conflicts. Henckaerts and Doswald-Beck, *Customary International Humanitarian Law*, pp. 374–5.

[16] According to the International Law Commission (ILC), acts of retorsion are '"unfriendly" conduct which is not inconsistent with any international obligation of the state engaging in it even though it may be a response to an internationally wrongful act'. ILC, Draft Articles on Responsibility of States for Internationally Wrongful Acts, with commentaries, 2001, Text adopted by the International Law Commission at its fifty-third session, in 2001, and submitted to the General Assembly as a part of the Commission's report covering the work of that session (A/56/10), p. 128 (hereafter, ILC Articles on State Responsibility). See also Alland, 'The definition of countermeasures', pp. 1131–2; M. Kamto, 'The time factor in the application of countermeasures' in J. Crawford, A. Pellet, S. Olleson and K. Pellet (eds.), *The Law of International Responsibility* (Oxford University Press, 2010), pp. 1186–7.

prohibition of or limitations upon normal diplomatic relations or other contacts, embargoes of various kinds or withdrawal of voluntary aid programmes'.[17]

More akin to reprisals are *countermeasures*, which are 'measures that would otherwise be contrary to the international obligations of an injured state vis-à-vis the responsible state, if they were not taken by the former in response to an internationally wrongful act by the latter in order to procure cessation and reparation'.[18] Countermeasures are sometimes distinguished from reprisals on the basis that they also apply in peacetime, although it is quite possible to see belligerent reprisals as a specific form of countermeasure.[19] According to the ILC's discussion of countermeasures, '[q]uestions concerning the use of force in international relations and of the legality of belligerent reprisals are governed by the relevant primary rules'.[20]

B.   The requirements for a lawful reprisal

It is possible to identify at least six core requirements for a lawful reprisal.[21] It should, though, be acknowledged that the exact conditions are not finally

[17] ILC Articles on State Responsibility, p. 128. Kamto cites economic sanctions 'insofar as they do not involve the suspension of performance of any obligation owed to the target State'. Kamto, 'The time factor in the application of countermeasures', p. 1186.

[18] ILC Articles on State Responsibility, p. 128.

[19] See, e.g., Kamto, 'The time factor in the application of countermeasures', pp. 1188–9.

[20] ILC Articles on State Responsibility, p. 128. With respect to the treaty law principle of *pacta sunt servanda*, Article 60(5) of the 1969 Vienna Convention on the Law of Treaties states that the principle of reciprocity does not apply 'to provisions relating to the protection of the human person contained in treaties of a humanitarian character, in particular to provisions prohibiting any form of reprisals against persons protected by such treaties'. See Vienna Convention on the Law of Treaties, Vienna, 23 May 1969, in force 27 January 1980, 1155 UNTS 331; 8 ILM 679, Art. 60(5).

[21] In 1976 the Department of the US Air Force set out the following eight characteristics that an act must have in order to be considered a reprisal:

(1) It must respond to grave and manifestly unlawful acts, committed by an adversary government, its military commanders, or combatants for whom the adversary is responsible.

(2) It must be for the purpose of compelling the adversary to observe the law of armed conflict … to induce him to refrain from further violations …

(3) There must be reasonable notice that reprisals will be taken.

(4) Other reasonable means to secure compliance must be attempted. The victim of a violation in order to justify taking a reprisal must first exhaust other reasonable means of securing compliance.

(5) A reprisal must be directed against the personnel or property of an adversary.

(6) A reprisal must be proportional to the original violation. Although a reprisal need not conform in kind to the same type of acts complained of … it may not significantly exceed the adversary's violation either in violence or effect.

(7) It must be … announced as a reprisal and publicized so that the adversary is aware of its obligation to abide by the law.

(8) It must be authorized by national authorities at the highest political level and entails full state responsibility.

settled in the literature and leave some room for disagreement. In most cases, however, such disagreement is peripheral, relating more to the precise scope of a condition than its existence.

1.   As a response to a prior unlawful act

The first requirement for a lawful reprisal is that the act allegedly undertaken in reprisal must be in response to a *prior* unlawful act or acts by the target state (and not one of its allies). Thus, if the prior act or acts are not clearly unlawful, there is no possibility of recourse to an act of reprisal. Of critical importance for nuclear weapons, 'pre-emptive' reprisals do not exist as a matter of IHL.

2.   In response to serious violations of IHL

The second requirement for a lawful reprisal is that the unlawful act or acts by the target state that justify the need for a reprisal must be serious in nature. According to the United Kingdom, for example, in order to qualify as a legitimate reprisal, an act must be 'in response to serious and manifestly unlawful acts, committed by an adverse government, its military commanders or combatants for whom the adversary is responsible'.[22] The notion of seriousness clearly brings with it the risk of subjectivity, but implies that either violations of *jus in bello* are widespread or that there have been isolated but exceptionally grave violations of that law.

3.   As a necessary measure

The third requirement is that recourse to a reprisal must be necessary. Accordingly, other measures must be attempted first (the so-called principle of subsidiarity), unless they are clearly doomed to be ineffective.[23] Such measures should include a warning to the offending state to cease its unlawful behaviour. The measures could clearly include acts that are lawful under IHL (and so not falling within the scope of a reprisal). Furthermore, the offending state must be explicitly warned of the consequences should it not return to compliance

---

Department of the US Air Force, *International Law – The Conduct of Armed Conflict and Air Operations*, AFP 110–31, 19 November 1976, para. 10–7c.

[22]   UK Ministry of Defence, *The Manual on the Law of Armed Conflict* (Oxford University Press, 2004), para. 16.17.

[23]   According to the US Army Manual on the Law of Land Warfare, 'Other means of securing compliance with the law of war should normally be exhausted before resort is had to reprisals. This course should be pursued unless the safety of the troops requires immediate drastic action and the persons who actually committed the offenses cannot be secured. Even when appeal to the enemy for redress has failed, it may be a matter of policy to consider, before resorting to reprisals, whether the opposing forces are not more likely to be influenced by a steady adherence to the law of war on the part of their adversary.' US Department of the Army, *The Law of Land Warfare*, Department of the Army Field Manual, FM 27–10, 1956 as amended on 15 July 1976 (hereafter, US Army Manual on the Law of Land Warfare), para. 497(c).

with *jus in bello* and, presumably, given adequate time to do so.[24] This appears to allow for the legality of a *threat* of lawful reprisals as a preventive measure.[25] Indeed, in his Dissenting Judgment in the Nuclear Weapons Advisory Opinion, Judge Schwebel refers to statements by then US Secretary of State James Baker III in the run-up to the 1990 Gulf War against Iraq and concludes that:

> [T]here is on record remarkable evidence indicating that an aggressor was or may have been deterred from using outlawed weapons of mass destruction against forces and countries arrayed against its aggression at the call of the United Nations by what the aggressor perceived to be a threat to use nuclear weapons against it should it first use weapons of mass destruction against the forces of the coalition. Can it seriously be maintained that Mr Baker's calculated threat was unlawful?
>
> [Thus] in some circumstances, the threat of the use of nuclear weapons – as long as they remain weapons unproscribed by international law – may be both lawful and rational.[26]

Finally, to ensure that the necessity requirement is satisfied, there is broad (though not universal) agreement[27] that reprisals must be authorised at the most senior level within a party to armed conflict.[28]

4.   With the intent to restore compliance with IHL

The fourth requirement, as noted above in the discussion of the definition of a reprisal, refers to the intent of a reprisal.[29] The relevant acts claimed to be of

---

[24] In the *Martić* case, Martić conceded in his appeal against conviction that there was no evidence that the Republic of Serbian Krajina (RSK) had formally warned Croatia before shelling Zagreb in May 1995, but asserted that there had been repeated warnings that Zagreb would be shelled in the case of 'aggression' against the RSK. The Appeals Chamber rejected his argument. ICTY, *Prosecutor* v. *Milan Martić*, Judgment (Appeals Chamber) (Case No. IT-95-11-A), 8 October 2008, paras. 238, 266. The Appeals Chamber also endorsed the finding of the Trial Chamber that the shelling 'was not a measure of last resort, because peace negotiations were conducted during Operation Flash until 3 May 1995'. *Ibid.*, para. 263.

[25] Indeed, as Michael Walzer has argued, 'We threaten evil in order not to do it, and the doing of it would be so terrible that the threat seems in comparison to be morally defensible.' M. Walzer, *Just and Unjust Wars: A Moral Argument with Historical Illustrations*, 4th edn (New York: Basic Books, 2006), p. 274.

[26] Dissenting Judgment of Judge Stephen Schwebel, Nuclear Weapons Advisory Opinion, pp. 327, 328.

[27] According to the US Army Manual on the Law of Land Warfare, para. 497(d): 'The highest accessible military authority should be consulted unless immediate action is demanded, in which event a subordinate commander may order appropriate reprisals upon his own initiative.'

[28] Whether this authorisation must be given by civilian or military authorities is not settled. The ICTY in the *Kupreškić* case implied that either was possible. *Kupreškić* Trial Judgment, para. 535. See also S. Darcy, 'The evolution of the law of belligerent reprisals', *Military Law Review* 175 (2003), 184–251, at 192–3.

[29] Intent is inferred both from pertinent acts by members of the armed forces and from relevant declarations or statements by state officials.

reprisal must be conducted with a view to bringing the target state back into compliance with *jus in bello* and should be announced as such. Unlawful acts carried out as mere retaliation or punishment therefore remain unlawful.[30] In this regard, Sivakumaran refers to the *Martić* Trial Chamber judgment, which asserted that the aim of ensuring a return to respect for the law must be the *sole* purpose of the acts taken.[31] As he notes, however, this:

> overstates the point. While reprisals must be undertaken to enforce compliance with the law on the part of the opposing party, they may be taken also for other reasons, for example to satisfy public pressure, or a particular domestic constituency. Likewise, the form that the reprisal takes may be motivated by military concerns. These other reasons do not render unlawful the use of belligerent reprisals. The relevant test should be whether the employment of belligerent reprisals was for the *primary* purpose of seeking compliance with the law by the opposing party.[32]

5.   A proportionate response

The fifth requirement for a lawful reprisal is that the act or acts of reprisal must be proportionate to the original breach.[33] At the same time, it is generally agreed that the acts may be of such nature and extent to be sufficient (but no more) to effect a return to compliance by the offending state. Greenwood, for example, argues that reprisals 'should exceed neither what is proportionate to the prior violation nor what is necessary if they are to achieve their aim of restoring respect for the law'.[34] Accordingly, as with the notion of proportionality in self-defence under *jus ad bellum*,[35] punitive or retributive force is unlawful and any

---

[30] According to the US Army Manual on the Law of Land Warfare, para. 497(d): 'Reprisals are never adopted merely for revenge, but only as an unavoidable last resort to induce the enemy to desist from unlawful practices.'

[31] ICTY, *Prosecutor* v. *Milan Martić*, Judgment (Trial Chamber) (Case No. IT-95-11-T), 12 June 2007, para. 465.

[32] S. Sivakumaran, *The Law of Non-International Armed Conflict* (Oxford University Press, 2012), p. 455 (original emphasis).

[33] In dodging the question of the legality of belligerent reprisals using nuclear weapons, the ICJ stated the following on the issue of proportionality: 'Certain States asserted that the use of nuclear weapons in the conduct of reprisals would be lawful. The Court does not have to examine, in this context, the question of armed reprisals in time of peace, which are considered to be unlawful. Nor does it have to pronounce on the question of belligerent reprisals save to observe that in any case any right of recourse to such reprisals would, like self-defence, be governed inter alia by the principle of proportionality.' Nuclear Weapons Advisory Opinion, para. 46.

[34] C. Greenwood, 'The twilight of the law of belligerent reprisals?', *Netherlands Yearbook of International Law* 20 (1989), 35–69, at 44.

[35] In the words of Elizabeth Wilmshurst, with respect to a state's right of self-defence, 'The proportionality requirement has been said to mean in addition that the physical and economic consequences of the force used must not be excessive in relation to the harm

such action would not constitute a lawful reprisal. Respecting proportionality does not, however, demand that an act of reprisal use the same prohibited weapon or commit the same violation against a similar group of people. As the US Army Manual on the Law of Land Warfare states, 'The acts resorted to by way of reprisal need not conform to those complained of by the injured party, but should not be excessive or exceed the degree of violence committed by the enemy.'[36]

Finally, the requirement of proportionality also demands that acts of reprisal cease as soon as compliance has been restored.[37] To allow otherwise could potentially lead to the original target state's having recourse to acts of 'counter-reprisal' and a spiral of abuse could ensue.

6.   Not against prohibited targets

Certain persons or objects may not be targeted with reprisals. A treaty rule prohibiting reprisals against prisoners of war was first introduced in the 1929 Geneva Convention on the Treatment of Prisoners of War.[38] Each of the four 1949 Geneva Conventions[39] included provisions prohibiting reprisals against

expected from the attack. But because the right of self-defence does not allow the use of force to "punish" an aggressor, proportionality should not be thought to refer to parity between a response and the harm already suffered from an attack, as this could either turn the concept of self-defence into a justification for retributive force, or limit the use of force to less than what is necessary to repel the attack.' E. Wilmshurst, 'Principles of international law on the use of force by states in self-defence', Chatham House Working Paper, London, October 2005 (footnote omitted), available at: www.chathamhouse.org/publications/papers/view/108106.

[36] US Army Manual on the Law of Land Warfare, para. 497(e). See further the arbitral award regarding the *Naulilaa* incident (*Responsabilité de l'Allemagne à raison des dommages causés dans les colonies portugaises du sud de l'Afrique (sentence sur le principe de la responsabilité (Portugal* c. *Allemagne)*, Arbitral Award of 31 July 1928, printed in *RIAA* 2 (2006), 1026–8). See also, e.g., L. C. Green, *The Contemporary Law of Armed Conflict*, 3rd edn (Manchester University Press, 2008), p. 148.

[37] *Kupreškić* Trial Judgment, para. 535.

[38] According to Article 2: 'Prisoners of war ... shall at all times be humanely treated and protected, particularly against acts of violence, from insults and from public curiosity. Measures of reprisal against them are forbidden.' Convention relative to the Treatment of Prisoners of War, Geneva, 27 July 1929, in force 19 June 1931, Art. 2.

[39] Geneva Convention for the Amelioration of the Condition of the Wounded and Sick in Armed Forces in the Field, Geneva, 12 August 1949, in force 21 October 1950, 75 UNTS 31, Art. 46 (hereafter, 1949 Geneva Convention I); Geneva Convention for the Amelioration of the Condition of Wounded, Sick and Shipwrecked Members of Armed Forces at Sea, Geneva, 12 August 1949, in force 21 October 1950, 75 UNTS 85, Art. 47 (hereafter, 1949 Geneva Convention II); Geneva Convention relative to the Treatment of Prisoners of War, Geneva, 12 August 1949, in force 21 October 1950, 75 UNTS 135, Art. 13(3); and Geneva Convention relative to the Protection of Civilian Persons in Time of War, Geneva, 12 August 1949, in force 21 October 1950, 75 UNTS 287, Art. 33(3), respectively.

protected persons and these prohibitions today constitute customary law.[40] It is therefore unlawful in any circumstances to conduct reprisals against persons in the power of a party to an international armed conflict, including the wounded, sick and shipwrecked; medical and religious personnel; captured combatants; civilians in occupied territory; and other categories of civilians in the power of an adverse party to the conflict, notably civilian internees.

It is also unlawful to conduct reprisals against medical buildings, vessels and equipment protected by 1949 Geneva Conventions I and II.[41] It is further unlawful to conduct reprisals against cultural property protected under the 1954 Hague Convention for the Protection of Cultural Property.[42] These rules are similarly reflective of customary law.[43] The International Committee of the Red Cross (ICRC) notes:

> According to the Report on the Practice of the Islamic Republic of Iran, during the Iran–Iraq War, the Islamic Republic of Iran offered a special protection to four Iraqi holy cities. Each time the Islamic Republic of Iran resorted to reprisals against Iraqi cities, it issued a statement asking Iraqi people to leave the cities to be attacked and go to the protected holy cities. According to the report, it committed itself not to attack these historic sites.[44]

The extent to which other treaty rules prohibiting reprisals constitute customary law is, though, far more controversial. In particular, this concerns the prohibition on reprisals against civilians and civilian objects in enemy territory during the conduct of hostilities. Thus, 1977 Additional Protocol I stipulates that:

> Attacks against the civilian population or civilians by way of reprisals are prohibited;[45]

---

[40] According to the ICRC Customary IHL Study, 'belligerent reprisals against persons protected by the Geneva Conventions are prohibited … State practice establishes this rule as a norm of customary international law applicable in international armed conflicts.' Henckaerts and Doswald-Beck, *Customary International Humanitarian Law*, p. 519. According to the US Army Manual on the Law of Land Warfare, para. 497(c), for example, 'Reprisals against the persons or property of prisoners of war, including the wounded and sick, and protected civilians are forbidden … Collective penalties and punishment of prisoners of war and protected civilians are likewise prohibited … However, reprisals may still be visited on enemy troops who have not yet fallen into the hands of the forces making the reprisals.'

[41] 1949 Geneva Convention I, Art. 46; and 1949 Geneva Convention II, Art. 47, respectively.

[42] Convention for the Protection of Cultural Property in the Event of Armed Conflict, The Hague, 14 May 1954, in force 7 August 1956, 249 UNTS 240, Art. 4(4) (hereafter, 1954 Hague Convention on Cultural Property).

[43] According to the ICRC Customary IHL Study, 'Reprisals against objects protected under the Geneva Conventions and Hague Convention for the Protection of Cultural Property are prohibited.' Rule 147, Henckaerts and Doswald-Beck, *Customary International Humanitarian Law*, p. 523.

[44] ICRC, 'Islamic Republic of Iran: practice relating to Rule 147. Reprisals against protected objects', www.icrc.org/customary-ihl/eng/docs/v2_cou_ir_rule147.

[45] 1977 Additional Protocol I, Art. 51(6).

and that:

> Civilian objects shall not be the object of attack or of reprisals.[46]

Furthermore, according to 1996 Amended Protocol II[47] to the Convention on Certain Conventional Weapons,[48] 'It is prohibited in all circumstances to direct weapons to which this Article applies, either in offence, defence or by way of reprisals, against the civilian population as such or against individual civilians or civilian objects.'[49]

In its commentary on Article 51(6) of 1977 Additional Protocol I, the ICRC stated that:

> This provision is very important. In fact, the belligerents in the Second World War recognized in their public declarations that attacks may be directed only at military objectives, but on the pretext that their own population had been hit by attacks carried out by the adversary, they went so far, by way of reprisals, as to wage war almost indiscriminately, and this resulted in countless civilian victims ...
>
> The prohibition contained in this article is not subject to any conditions and it therefore has a peremptory character; in particular it leaves out the possibility of derogating from this rule by invoking military necessity. As in the 1949 Conventions, this provision confirms the right of an individual not to be punished for acts which he has not himself committed.
>
> This prohibition of attacks by way of reprisals and other prohibitions of the same type contained in the Protocol and in the Conventions have considerably reduced the scope for reprisals in time of war. At most, such meas-

---

[46] *Ibid.*, Art. 52(1). Also worthy of mention are the prohibitions on reprisals set out in Art. 54(4) (protection of objects indispensable to the survival of the civilian population – examples given of such objects include foodstuffs, agricultural areas for the production of foodstuffs, crops, livestock, drinking water installations and supplies, and irrigation works), Art. 55(2) (protection of the natural environment) and Art. 56(4) (protection of works and installations containing dangerous forces).

[47] Protocol on Prohibitions or Restrictions on the Use of Mines, Booby-Traps and Other Devices, Geneva, 10 October 1980, in force 2 December 1983, 1342 UNTS 168, 19 ILM 1529; as amended on 3 May 1996 (Protocol II to the 1980 Convention as amended on 3 May 1996), Geneva, 3 May 1996, in force 3 December 1998, 35 ILM 1206 (hereafter, 1996 Amended Protocol II).

[48] Convention on Prohibitions or Restrictions on the Use of Certain Conventional Weapons Which May be Deemed to be Excessively Injurious or to Have Indiscriminate Effects, Geneva, 10 October 1980, in force 2 December 1983, 1342 UNTS 137; as amended, Geneva, 21 December 2001, in force 18 May 2004.

[49] 1996 Amended Protocol II, Art. 3(7). The language reflects that introduced in the original protocol. See Protocol on Prohibitions or Restrictions on the Use of Mines, Booby-Traps and Other Devices (1980 Protocol II), Geneva, 10 October 1980, in force 2 December 1983, 1342 UNTS 168, 19 ILM 1529, Art. 2(3).

ures could now be envisaged in the choice of weapons and in methods of combat used against military objectives.[50]

Certain states, notably (but not only) the United States, protested strongly during the negotiation of 1977 Additional Protocol I that the comprehensive prohibition on reprisals against civilians and civilian objects installed by the Protocol went too far. One US Air Force major, for instance, argued:

> It is unfortunate that Protocol I opted for outright prohibition in lieu of a rational compromise limiting reprisals against enemy civilian populations to responses in kind, i.e., in response to prior unlawful enemy attacks against the repriser's own civilian population ... The rationale underlying the absolute prohibitions of reprisals contained in the four Geneva Conventions of 1949 simply does not apply to enemy civilian populations in enemy territory. To artificially clothe them with immunity from reciprocation-in-kind is to offend the principle of military necessity and ignore the lessons of history.[51]

The United States has made clear its view of the prohibitions on reprisals in 1977 Additional Protocol I[52] and its signature of the Protocol was subject to an understanding that 'the rules established by this Protocol were not intended to have any effect on and do not regulate or prohibit the use of nuclear weapons'.[53]

In ratifying the Protocol in 1998, the United Kingdom attached the following 'understanding':

> Re: ARTICLES 51–55: The obligations of Articles 51 and 55 are accepted on the basis that any adverse party against which the United Kingdom might be engaged will itself scrupulously observe those obligations. If an adverse party makes serious and deliberate attacks, in violation of Article 51 or Article 52 against the civilian population or civilians or against civilian objects, or, in violation of Articles 53, 54 and 55, on objects or items protected by those Articles, the United Kingdom will regard itself as entitled to take measures otherwise prohibited by the Articles in question to the extent

---

[50] Y. Sandoz, C. Swinarski, and B. Zimmermann (eds.), *Commentary on the Additional Protocols of 8 June 1977 to the Geneva Conventions of 12 August 1949* (Geneva: ICRC/ Martinus Nijhoff, 1987), paras. 1982, 1984, 1985.

[51] Bristol, 'Laws of war and belligerent reprisals', 426–7.

[52] 'The Joint Chiefs of Staff, after a careful and extensive study, concluded that Protocol I is unacceptable from the point of view of military operations. The reasons ... include the fact ... that it eliminates significant remedies in cases where an enemy violates the Protocol. The total elimination of the right of reprisal, for example, would hamper the ability of the United States to respond to an enemy's intentional disregard of the limitations established in the Geneva Conventions of 1949 or Protocol I, for the purpose of deterring such disregard.' A. D. Sofaer, 'The rationale for the United States decision', *American Journal of International Law* 82 (1988), 784–7, at 785.

[53] Reproduced in A. Roberts and R. Guelff, *Documents on the Law of War*, 3rd edn (Oxford University Press, 2001), p. 512.

that it considers such measures necessary for the sole purpose of compelling the adverse party to cease committing violations under those Articles,
but only after formal warning to the adverse party requiring cessation of
the violations has been disregarded and then only after a decision taken at
the highest level of government. Any measures thus taken by the United
Kingdom will not be disproportionate to the violations giving rise thereto
and will not involve any action prohibited by the Geneva Conventions of
1949 nor will such measures be continued after the violations have ceased.
The United Kingdom will notify the Protecting Powers of any such formal
warning given to an adverse party, and if that warning has been disregarded,
of any measures taken as a result.[54]

A similar 'reservation' was made by France upon its adherence to the Protocol
in 2001.[55] The ICRC Customary IHL Study concluded:

> Because of existing contrary practice, albeit limited, it is difficult to con-
> clude that there has yet crystallized a customary rule specifically prohibiting
> reprisals against civilians during the conduct of hostilities. Nevertheless, it
> is also difficult to assert that a right to resort to such reprisals continues to
> exist based on the practice of only a limited number of States, some of which
> is also ambiguous. Hence, there appears, at a minimum, to exist a trend in
> favour of prohibiting such reprisals.[56]

For example, the ICRC Customary IHL Study observed in 2005 that:

> In the course of the many armed conflicts that have marked the past two
> decades, belligerent reprisals have not been resorted to as a measure of
> enforcing international humanitarian law, the main exception being the
> Iran–Iraq War, where such measures were severely criticized by the UN
> Security Council and UN Secretary-General.[57]

However, the question of when a customary rule ends or is displaced by a different customary rule is a vexed one. One of the few public international lawyers to have written on the issue is Ian Brownlie. In the sixth edition of his
Principles of Public International Law, he argues that:

---

[54] *Ibid.*, p. 511.
[55] France stated that it would apply Article 51(8) 'to the extent that its interpretation does
not pose an obstacle to the adoption, in conformity with international law, of measures
which it considers indispensable for the protection of its civilian population from serious,
clear and deliberate violations of the Geneva Conventions and this Protocol by the enemy'.
Declaration of 11 April 2001 upon ratification, available in French original at: www.icrc.
org/applic/ihl/ihl.nsf/Notification.xsp?action=openDocument&documentId=D80410
36B40EBC44C1256A34004897B2 (author's translation). The erstwhile USSR (with the
Russian Federation as successor state) did not make any reservation when adhering to the
Protocol in 1989.
[56] Henckaerts and Doswald-Beck, *Customary International Humanitarian Law*, p. 523.
[57] *Ibid.*, p. 513.

Presumably, if a substantial number of states assert a new rule, the momentum of increased defection, complemented by acquiescence, may result in a new rule ... If the process is slow and neither the new rule nor the old have a majority of adherents then the consequence is a network of special relations based opposability, acquiescence, and historic rule.[58]

With all due respect to the late Professor Brownlie, in the instance of belligerent reprisals using nuclear weapons, it cannot really be a mere numbers game. Perhaps, as Louise Doswald-Beck has suggested, in the case of belligerent reprisals against civilian populations in the opposing party's own territory there is, today, simply no customary *lex lata* rule at all?[59]

C.   The use of nuclear weapons as a lawful reprisal in an international armed conflict

Let us now apply the requirements for a lawful reprisal to theoretical uses of nuclear weapons. The first general condition is that the alleged act of reprisal must be in response to a *prior* unlawful act or acts by the target state (and not one of its allies). To reiterate the accepted position, an unlawful act *ad bellum* does not give rise to the possibility of recourse to a reprisal *in bello*.[60] Should the Democratic People's Republic of Korea (DPR Korea) ever carry out its threat to attack the US military or naval base on the island of Guam or US military bases in Japan,[61] this could constitute an attack on a legitimate military objective in conformity with IHL.[62] Accordingly, a lawful attack *in bello* would not entitle the United States to target cities in DPR Korea, so any US attack in response – and one should not doubt that such an attack would be mounted – would have to conform strictly to IHL. To the extent nuclear weapons are not prohibited

---

[58] Ian Brownlie, *Principles of Public International Law*, 6th edn (Oxford University Press, 2003), pp. 11–12.

[59] Remarks to experts meeting, Oslo, 17 June 2013, author's notes.

[60] As Sassòli has stated: 'As for obligations of international humanitarian law not covered by those prohibitions of reprisals, they may not be affected by countermeasures contrary to obligations for the protection of fundamental rights ... [T]hey may likewise not be affected by countermeasures against violations of rules of international law other than those of international humanitarian law. When the original violation is one of "jus ad bellum" this limitation is a necessary consequence of the fundamental distinction and separation between jus ad bellum and jus in bello.' M. Sassòli, 'State responsibility for violations of international humanitarian law', *International Review of the Red Cross* 84 (2002), 401–34, at 425 (footnotes omitted).

[61] See, e.g., C. Sang-Hun and S. Erlanger, 'North Korea threatens US military bases in Pacific', *New York Times*, 21 March 2013.

[62] Unless, of course, the nuclear weapon used could be considered a means of warfare of a nature to cause superfluous injury or unnecessary suffering or the attack was indiscriminate, for example by violating the rule of proportionality in attacks. The United States would be highly unlikely to frame the issue in these terms for obvious reasons.

by IHL, any response would therefore have to respect the rules of distinction, proportionality and precautions in attacks.

The second requirement for a lawful reprisal is that the unlawful act or acts by the target state that justify the need for a reprisal must be serious in nature. As discussed below with regard to proportionality, an unlawful act or acts that could possibly give risk to a lawful reprisal involving the use of nuclear weapons would need to be of the utmost gravity, presumably involving massive loss of civilian life.

The third requirement is that recourse to a reprisal must be necessary. This demands that other measures (political, diplomatic, economic) first be exhausted and the enemy given due warning of the consequences of any repeat action before recourse to a reprisal. Let us say, for the sake of legal argument, that Pakistan attacked an Indian city with a nuclear weapon. How realistic is it to expect that India should make diplomatic remonstrations to Pakistan before conducting a similar act in reprisal? To delay might invite further attacks. In reality, the response – insofar as the origin of the attack was clearly traceable and attributable to its correct author – would likely be almost instantaneous. Thus, as Kalshoven states, 'the possibility cannot be excluded of situations where the fruitlessness of any other remedy but reprisals is apparent from the outset. In such exceptional circumstances … recourse to reprisals can be regarded as an ultimate remedy and, hence, as meeting the requirement of subsidiarity.'[63] Or, as Hampson observes, if the victim state 'is seeking to deter the offending State from repeating its offence, it is hardly likely to be prepared to give it the time to strike again. Practical considerations limit the scope of this requirement.'[64]

The fourth requirement is that the intent of a reprisal must be to bring the offending state back into compliance with IHL. In the case of a 'limited' nuclear strike, it is at least conceivable that a tit-for-tat exchange between two nuclear powers, such as that envisaged between India and Pakistan, could be brought to a close after each party had obliterated 'only' one city on the other's territory. *Quid* a major exchange between nuclear powers, for instance the Russian Federation and the United States? Writing in 1979, a US major affirmed that:

> Especially in a general war involving the major powers, modern weaponry's potential for destruction of enemy population centers tends to subsume the issue of reprisals into the larger issue of self-defense. There are only two practical responses to a first use, for example, of nuclear weapons against population centers: 'short of surrender … the victim could have retaliation in kind as the only remedy'.[65]

---

[63] F. Kalshoven, *Belligerent Reprisals* (Leiden: A. W. Sijthof, 1971), p. 340.

[64] F. J. Hampson, 'Belligerent reprisals and the 1977 Protocols to the Geneva Conventions of 1949', *International and Comparative Law Quarterly* 37 (1988), 818–43, at 823.

[65] Bristol, 'Laws of war and belligerent reprisals', 408–9 (citing N. Singh, *Nuclear Weapons and International Law* (New York: Frederick A. Praeger, 1959), p. 222).

The words he chooses are apposite. The 'remedy' is 'retaliation' and the response is 'self-defence', not a reprisal. Were either the Russian Federation or the United States ever to launch a major strike against the other, owing to the inevitability of the response such a first strike attack would presumably be all-out, with a view to total destruction, or as near to it as could be achieved. The intent of the huge nuclear response that would likely ensue could hardly be claimed to be pursuant to any intent to restore compliance with the law; it would be simple, uncloaked retaliation – collective punishment for as massive a violation of IHL as it is possible to contemplate. Such a nuclear response could thus not be considered a reprisal and, as unfair as it might seem, equally wrong in the eyes of the law.[66]

Furthermore, even if this issue of intent were not fatal to the legitimacy of the response as an act of reprisal, at what moment could the strike lawfully be envisaged? The first requirement of any reprisal is that there has been a *prior* violation of IHL.[67] This appears to mean that the nuclear missiles must already have struck home soil, not just have been fired and be threatening. How can the responding state be certain that the weapons will actually detonate? The fundamental prohibition on pre-emptive reprisals demands that the state sit tight and wait for the missiles to hit. Here again, the likelihood that such a delay would be countenanced is as close to nil as one can imagine.

The fifth requirement for a lawful reprisal is that while the act or acts of reprisal may well need to be sufficient to effect a return to compliance by the offending state, they must also be proportionate to the original breach. Even though it is not possible to be unequivocal in strictly legal terms, it is hard to see how any use of a nuclear weapon in reprisal could be justified other than in response to one or more attacks using a weapon of mass destruction (i.e. biological, chemical or nuclear in nature) against a population centre *and* that caused huge numbers of casualties. It is highly unlikely that other violations of IHL, such as even very widespread murder or inhumane treatment of prisoners of war, could justify recourse to such retaliation.[68]

Horrific as it may be to contemplate, the proportionality equation in the tit-for-tat limited exchange between India and Pakistan cited above does not tax the callous legal mind too much; but what of a major nuclear exchange?

---

[66] I would thus dispute the assertion by Singh and McWhinney that 'the only *permissible* use of thermo-nuclear weapons would appear to be retaliation in kind alone'. N. Singh and E. McWhinney, *Nuclear Weapons and Contemporary International Law* (Dordrecht: Martinus Nijhoff, 1989), p. 174 (emphasis added).

[67] Thus, for example, an Israeli nuclear strike against an Iranian nuclear power station that was suspected to be in the process of producing a nuclear weapon could not be justified as a reprisal under IHL.

[68] As Singh and McWhinney opine, the use of nuclear weapons 'as a reprisal for any normal violation of the laws of war would clearly be excessive'. Singh and McWhinney, *Nuclear Weapons and Contemporary International Law*, p. 172.

Proportionality is then, in the circumstances of our discussion, almost obscene. How many hundreds of millions may you kill[69] – *do you need to kill?* – to cause the offending state once more to respect *jus in bello* (if, indeed, such is even possible)?

D. The use of nuclear weapons as a lawful reprisal in an armed conflict of a non-international character

Whether it is possible under any circumstances to have recourse to reprisals in an armed conflict of a non-international character (NIAC) remains contested.[70] Certainly, there is no express, generalised treaty prohibition of reprisals in an NIAC,[71] although attempts have been made to read one in to Common Article 3 to the 1949 Geneva Conventions and 1977 Additional Protocol II.[72] At the same time, there are good legal and policy reasons for excluding reprisals in an NIAC (inter alia, based on *jus cogens* human rights obligations) and it is unlikely that many states would agree to grant an organised armed group a right to conduct reprisals for its own unlawful behaviour.

It has been argued that given the nature of reprisals – that is, it is authorising a normally unlawful act – such authority should be explicit.[73] Indeed, in

[69] In the *Kappler* case (hereafter, *Ardeatine Cave* case), the Security Service headed by Lt.-Col. Kappler executed ten Italian prisoners for every German policeman killed in a particular bombing. In all, the Security Service retaliated for the bombing by executing 335 prisoners in the Ardeatine caves; 320 for the 32 policemen killed in the bomb attack, 10 for another German killed subsequently, and 5 others murdered 'due to a culpable mistake'. Darcy, 'The evolution of the law of belligerent reprisals', 195 (citing *In re Kappler*, Military Tribunal of Rome (20 July 1948), in H. Lauterpacht (ed.), *Annotated Digest and Reports of Public International Law Cases*, 16 vols. (London: Butterworth and Company, 1948), Vol. XV, p. 471). The Court concluded that the executions were disproportionate 'not only as regards numbers, but also for the reason that those shot in the Ardeatine caves included five generals, eleven senior officers … twenty-one subalterns and six non-commissioned officers'.

[70] In 1948 the Italian Military Tribunal held in the *Ardeatine Cave* case that 'the right to take reprisals arises only in consequence of an illegal act which can be attributed, directly or indirectly, to a State'. See, e.g., Darcy, 'The evolution of the law of belligerent reprisals', 190. If correct, this would imply that the use of a nuclear weapon by an armed non-state actor on the territory of a state could not give rise to a lawful reprisal by the victim state.

[71] See, e.g., S. Borelli and S. Olleson, 'Obligations relating to human rights and humanitarian law' in J. Crawford, A. Pellet, S. Olleson and K. Pellet (eds.), *The Law of International Responsibility* (Oxford University Press, 2010), pp. 1190–1. The two treaty prohibitions on reprisals in NIACs that do exist are found in 1954 Hague Convention on Cultural Property and 1996 Amended Protocol II.

[72] Protocol Additional to the Geneva Conventions of 12 August 1949, and relating to the Protection of Victims of Non-International Armed Conflicts (Protocol II), Geneva, 8 June 1977, in force 7 December 1978.

[73] This is the position of Professor Louise Doswald-Beck, for instance. Remarks to experts meeting, Oslo, 17 June 2013, author's notes. In the ICRC Customary Law Study that she oversaw, only a very few examples of state practice in favour of allowing (or not prohibiting)

2000 the International Criminal Tribunal for the former Yugoslavia (ICTY) concluded, controversially, in the *Kupreškić* case that:

> the reprisal killing of innocent persons, more or less chosen at random, without any requirement of guilt or any form of trial, can safely be characterized as a blatant infringement of the most fundamental principles of human rights. It is difficult to deny that a slow but profound transformation of humanitarian law under the pervasive influence of human rights has occurred. As a result belligerent reprisals against civilians and fundamental rights of human beings are absolutely inconsistent legal concepts ...
>
> Due to the pressure exerted by the requirements of humanity and the dictates of public conscience, a customary rule of international law has emerged on the matter under discussion.[74]

Others agree. Moir, among others, stated simply in 2002 that there is no place for reprisals in an NIAC.[75] In 2005 the ICRC Customary IHL Study concluded unequivocally that parties to NIACs 'do not have the right to resort to belligerent reprisals.'[76] That, one might say, would seem to be that.

Sivakumaran expounds a more nuanced position in his 2012 work, *The Law of Non-International Armed Conflict*. Noting that the United Kingdom has specifically contested the findings in the *Kupreškić* case as to the existence of a customary law prohibition, he argues that the view that belligerent reprisals are prohibited in NIACs as a matter of customary IHL 'may be overstating the existing position.'[77] As he notes, the *Martić* case, which concerned what could realistically be qualified as an NIAC between Croatia and the self-styled Republic of Serbian Krajina, did not, at least at trial or on appeal against conviction,[78] consider reprisals per se unlawful, adjudging instead that the claims that Martić made for his attacks against Zagreb amounting to a reprisal were

---

limited reprisals in an NIAC were identified, including Cameroon, Finland, Germany and Yugoslavia. See ICRC, Practice Relating to Rule 148. Reprisals in Non-International Armed Conflicts, available at: www.icrc.org/customary-ihl/eng/docs/v2_rul_rule148.

[74] *Kupreškić* Trial Judgment, paras. 529, 531.

[75] L. Moir, *The Law of Internal Armed Conflict* (Cambridge University Press, 2002), p. 240.

[76] Rule 148, Henckaerts and Doswald-Beck, *Customary International Humanitarian Law*, p. 526. Further, '[o]ther countermeasures against persons who do not or who have ceased to take a direct part in hostilities are prohibited.' *Ibid.*

[77] Sivakumaran, *The Law of Non-International Armed Conflict*, p. 452. Writing in 2003, i.e. prior to the publication of the ICRC Customary IHL Study, Darcy argued that: 'However undesirable reprisals may be from a humanitarian perspective, a strictly legal interpretation of the foregoing instruments would show that their use during a non-international armed conflict is not completely proscribed.' Darcy, 'The evolution of the law of belligerent reprisals', 219.

[78] However, in the pre-trial Rule 61 procedure (a process whereby the indictment against an accused not yet in custody is submitted to the Trial Chamber to determine whether 'there are reasonable grounds for believing that the accused has committed all or any of the crimes charged'), the Trial Chamber ruled that reprisals in an NIAC were outlawed under customary law. ICTY, *Prosecutor v. Milan Martić*, Decision (Case No. IT-95-11-R61), 8 March

not sustained on the facts.[79] And while policy reasons may be cited for endorsing a prohibition on any reprisals in NIACs,[80] it is perhaps premature to assert that a total prohibition reflects extant customary law.

Conclusion

As McDougal and Feliciano acknowledged in 1961:

> Obviously the doctrine of reprisals, like all authoritative policies, is vulnerable to perversion and abuse. By itself, however, this vulnerability cannot be decisive of the utility or desirability of the reprisals doctrine. In the context of continuing hostilities, and until a comprehensive, centralized, and effective sanctions process is achieved in the world arena, belligerents have to police one another and enforce the laws of war against each other.[81]

The ICTY Trial Chamber has declared that the development of international criminal law and tribunals to enforce it represents such an effective sanctions process:

> while reprisals could have had a modicum of justification in the past, when they constituted practically the only effective means of compelling the enemy to abandon unlawful acts of warfare and to comply in future with international law, at present they can no longer be justified in this manner. A means of inducing compliance with international law is at present more widely available and, more importantly, is beginning to prove fairly efficacious: the prosecution and punishment of war crimes and crimes against humanity by national or international courts. This means serves the purpose of bringing to justice those who are responsible for any such crime, as well as, albeit to a limited extent, the purpose of deterring at least the most blatant violations of international humanitarian law.[82]

While high-minded, this argument is not persuasive. As Sivakumaran observes, 'criminal prosecution tends to be retrospective in nature rather than ending violations existing at the time resort is had to belligerent

---

1996, paras. 13–7. See, e.g., Darcy, 'The evolution of the law of belligerent reprisals', 231–3; Borelli and Olleson, 'Obligations relating to human rights and humanitarian law', p. 1193. Following criticism of this assertion – by Christopher Greenwood and Frits Kalshoven in particular – the Trial Chamber conveniently forgot about its decision a decade earlier when subsequently rendering its judgment in the *Martić* case in 2007.

[79] Sivakumaran, *The Law of Non-International Armed Conflict*, p. 455.

[80] Sivakumaran himself notes that a prohibition on reprisals in NIACs is 'desirable' and asserts that 'foolish would be the state that undertakes belligerent reprisals against its own population in a non-international armed conflict'. *Ibid.*, pp. 452–3.

[81] M. McDougal and F. Feliciano, *Law and Minimum World Public Order: The Legal Regulation of International Coercion* (New Haven: Yale University Press, 1961), pp. 681–2.

[82] *Kupreškić* Trial Judgment, para. 530.

reprisals'.[83] Notwithstanding the important work of the Fact-Finding Missions and Commissions of Inquiry initiated, particularly, by the UN Human Rights Council, we are a long way from a situation where enforcement of IHL can be said to be taking place with any regularity and consistency.

In conclusion, it is argued that customary law has not yet outlawed belligerent reprisals against civilians in enemy territory, nor has it unequivocally outlawed reprisals in a non-international armed conflict. It is still the case that custom 'grants a state party to an armed conflict a qualified privilege to commit an otherwise unlawful act against its enemy if done according to certain recognized procedural requirements and substantive limitations and for the specific purpose of deterring repetition of prior unlawful acts committed by the same enemy'.[84] This is not to deny that resort to belligerent reprisals does indeed remain 'an unfortunate means by which to enforce the law'.[85] With specific regard to nuclear weapons, however, it is extremely hard to envisage any circumstances in which their use against civilians could meet the necessary criteria to constitute a lawful reprisal.

---

[83] Sivakumaran, *The Law of Non-International Armed Conflict*, p. 456.
[84] Bristol, 'Laws of war and belligerent reprisals', 397.
[85] Sivakumaran, *The Law of Non-International Armed Conflict*, p. 457.

PART III

International criminal law

8

Use of nuclear weapons as genocide, a crime against humanity or a war crime

STUART CASEY-MASLEN

Introduction

This chapter discusses the use of nuclear weapons as an international crime, focusing on genocide, war crimes and crimes against humanity, including three modes of liability for such crimes (joint criminal enterprise, joint criminal responsibility (according to control theory) and aiding and abetting an international crime). The Nuclear Weapons Advisory Opinion issued by the International Court of Justice (ICJ) in 1996[1] did not discuss any of these crimes in detail.[2]

The chapter begins by summarising international criminal law (ICL) and its relevance for the use of nuclear weapons. It then looks in turn at the extent to which use of nuclear weapons could be considered an act of genocide, a war crime or a crime against humanity, potentially engaging individual criminal responsibility under ICL not only for the adjudged principal of any violation, but also for a participant of a joint criminal enterprise, an individual sharing joint criminal responsibility or an individual as an aider or abettor.

ICL is, as Cassese observed, 'a body of international rules designed both to proscribe certain categories of conduct (war crimes, crimes against humanity, genocide, torture, aggression, international terrorism) and to make those persons who engage in such conduct criminally liable.'[3] As such, ICL either

---

[1] ICJ, *Legality of the Threat or Use of Nuclear Weapons*, Advisory Opinion of 8 July 1996 (hereafter, the Nuclear Weapons Advisory Opinion).

[2] As discussed below, the Court specifically addressed the issue of genocide in one paragraph of its Advisory Opinion, but did not refer at any stage to the possibility that a use of nuclear weapons might amount either to a war crime per se (although they obviously assessed the likelihood of a use of nuclear weapons violating international humanitarian law) or a crime against humanity.

[3] A. Cassese, *International Criminal Law*, 3rd edn (Oxford University Press, 2013), p. 3. Cryer states that the 'better view' is that individual acts of torture or terrorism that do not fall within the definitions of war crimes, crimes against humanity, genocide and aggression are not directly criminalised by international law. R. Cryer, 'International criminal law' in D. Moeckli, S. Shah and S. Sivakumaran (eds.), *International Human Rights Law* (Oxford University Press, 2010), p. 541.

authorises states, or imposes upon them the obligation, to prosecute and punish offenders.[4] In so doing, ICL draws on customary and conventional international humanitarian law and international human rights law, as well as on domestic criminal legislation and jurisprudence, making it a 'hybrid' branch of law.[5]

In accordance with practice across domestic legal systems, for a person to be held guilty of an international crime, there must be a culpable act, known as *actus reus*, allied to a 'frame of mind' for that conduct to be adjudged blameworthy, referred to as *mens rea*.[6] The different forms of frame of mind (e.g. *dolus directus*, *dolus eventualis*, recklessness,[7] *dolus specialis* or culpable negligence) are discussed as relevant below. For certain international crimes, an additional contextual element may be required. For instance, for a crime to be judged a crime against humanity, the *actus reus* and *mens rea* must occur as part of a widespread or systematic attack on the civilian population, whether in time of armed conflict or in peacetime, and for an individual to be held responsible under international criminal law, he or she must be aware of that broader context.[8]

---

[4] *Ibid.* Thus ICL should be clearly distinguished from state responsibility, to which certain conduct prohibited under ICL may also give rise.

[5] *Ibid.*, pp. 6–7. Consonant with the sources of international law set out in the Statute of the International Court of Justice, ICL tribunals and courts may apply, as a primary source of law, 'the general principles of law recognized by civilized nations' (Article 38(1)(c) – presumably general principles both of international law and, as relevant, of national law), and, as a subsidiary source of law, 'judicial decisions … of the various nations' (Article 38(1)(d)).

[6] Moeckli *et al.*, *International Human Rights Law*, p. 53 and generally Chapter 3: and see, e.g., D. Ormerod, *Smith and Hogan's Criminal Law*, 13th edn (Oxford University Press, 2011), Chapters 4 and 5. Schabas notes that the phrase *mens rea* originates in the Latin phrase *actus non facit reum nisi mens sit rea*. W. A. Schabas, *An Introduction to the International Criminal Court*, 4th edn (Cambridge University Press, 2012), p. 235 (hereafter, Schabas, *Introduction to the ICC*).

[7] Some authors consider *dolus eventualis* and recklessness as synonyms, but the better view is that there is a distinction between them. As Gaeta states, 'the difference between the two forms of mens rea can be identified in the fact that the perpetrator in the former case acts with a degree of intent, ie awareness that the forbidden results will likely occur in the ordinary course of events.' P. Gaeta, 'Serious violations of the law on the conduct of hostilities: a neglected class of war crimes?' in F. Pocar (ed.), *War Crimes and the Conduct of Hostilities: Challenges to Adjudication and Investigation* (London: Elgar, 2013), n. 54. She cites in this regard the decision of the International Criminal Court (ICC) in the *Lubanga* case: ICC, *Prosecutor v. Thomas Lubanga Dyilo*, Judgment (Trial Chamber I) (Case No. ICC-01/04–01/06), 14 March 2012, paras. 1011–2. But, see also Cassese, *International Criminal Law* (3rd edn), p. 41.

[8] Cassese, *International Criminal Law* (3rd edn), pp. 99–100.

A.   Use of nuclear weapons as an act of genocide

Genocide, the so-called 'crime of crimes',[9] was first coined as a term by Raphael Lemkin in his 1944 book *Axis Rule in Occupied Europe*.[10] Lemkin wrote that:

> Generally speaking, genocide does not necessarily mean the immediate destruction of a nation, except when accomplished by mass killings of all members of a nation. It is intended rather to signify a coordinated plan of different actions aiming at the destruction of essential foundations of the life of national groups, with the aim of annihilating the groups themselves. Genocide is directed against the national group as an entity, and the actions involved are directed against individuals, not in their individual capacity, but as members of the national group.[11]

In 1946 genocide was proclaimed as a crime under international law by United Nations General Assembly Resolution 96(I).[12] It was formally prohibited by multilateral treaty in the form of the 1948 Genocide Convention.[13] Its prohibition, which was recognised as a general principle of law in 1951,[14] has attained the status of a norm of *jus cogens*: 'assuredly the case with regard to the prohibition of genocide', in the words of the ICJ.[15] Acts of genocide may be committed in time of 'peace' as well as in a situation of armed conflict.[16]

---

[9] See, e.g., W. A. Schabas, 'National courts finally begin to prosecute genocide, the "crime of crimes"', *Journal of International Criminal Justice* 1(1) (2003), 39–63.

[10] United States Holocaust Memorial Museum, 'Coining a word and championing a cause: the story of Raphael Lemkin', *Holocaust Encyclopedia*, available at: www.ushmm.org/wlc/en/article.php?ModuleId=10007050 (last updated 11 May 2012).

[11] *Ibid.*

[12] The Resolution stated that genocide 'is a denial of the right of existence of entire human groups, as homicide is the denial of the right to life of individual human beings'. See R. Cryer, H. Friman, D. Robinson and E. Wilmshurst, *An Introduction to International Criminal Law and Procedure*, 2nd edn (Cambridge University Press, 2010), p. 203.

[13] Convention on the Prevention and Punishment of the Crime of Genocide, Paris, 9 December 1948, in force 12 January 1951, 78 UNTS 277. For a history of the drafting of the 1948 Genocide Convention, see, e.g., Y. Shany, 'The road to the Genocide Convention and beyond', Chapter 1 in Paola Gaeta (ed.), *The UN Genocide Convention, A Commentary* (Oxford University Press, 2009) (hereafter, Gaeta, *Commentary on the 1948 Genocide Convention*).

[14] ICJ, *Reservations to the Convention on the Prevention and Punishment of the Crime of Genocide*, Advisory Opinion of 28 May 1951, p. 12. Cryer *et al.* suggest that the ICJ had declared that the prohibition was of a customary nature, when in truth the Court referred to 'principles which are recognized by civilized nations as binding on states, even without any conventional obligation'. Cryer *et al.*, *An Introduction to International Criminal Law*, p. 205.

[15] ICJ, *Case Concerning Armed Activities on the Territory of the Congo* (New Application: 2002) (*Democratic Republic of the Congo* v. *Rwanda*), Jurisdiction of the Court and Admissibility of the Application, Judgment of 3 February 2006, para. 64; see Cryer *et al.*, *An Introduction to International Criminal Law*, p. 204.

[16] *Ibid.*, p. 206.

In its Nuclear Weapons Advisory Opinion, the ICJ noted that some states had contended that the prohibition on genocide, contained in the 1948 Genocide Convention, is 'a relevant rule of customary international law which the Court must apply'.[17] The Court cited the definition of the crime, as set out in Article 2 of the Convention, which is considered to have attained customary law status:[18]

> any of the following acts committed with intent to destroy, in whole or in part, a national, ethnical, racial or religious group, as such:
> (a) Killing members of the group;
> (b) Causing serious bodily or mental harm to members of the group;
> (c) Deliberately inflicting on the group conditions of life calculated to bring about its physical destruction in whole or in part;
> (d) Imposing measures intended to prevent births within the group;
> (e) Forcibly transferring children of the group to another group.

With respect to the *actus reus* of the crime of genocide, while the central and obvious consequences of use of a nuclear weapon would be swift and widespread death and widespread injury (i.e. the acts set out in points (a) and (b) above), the radioactive fallout provoked by a nuclear strike could also potentially be considered to invoke issues under point (c). In this regard, the Elements of Crimes of the Rome Statute of the International Criminal Court (ICC) interpret the term 'conditions of life' to include (but not necessarily to be restricted to) 'deliberate deprivation of resources indispensable for survival, such as food or medical services'.[19] The ICC Elements of Crimes for each point (a) to (c) states that the conduct must have taken place 'in the context of a manifest pattern of similar conduct directed against that group or was conduct that could itself effect such destruction'. The second part of this requirement covers situations where a nuclear or biological weapon is used without the necessary pattern of similar conduct.[20]

Thus, *dolus specialis* (special intent) is explicitly required for the crime of genocide under international law: 'intent to destroy, in whole or in part,[21] a

---

[17] Nuclear Weapons Advisory Opinion, para. 26.

[18] See, e.g., A. Cassese, *International Criminal Law*, 2nd edn (Oxford University Press, 2008), p. 57.

[19] 'Article 6(c): Genocide by deliberately inflicting conditions of life calculated to bring about physical destruction', note 4, in Official Records of the Assembly of States Parties to the Rome Statute of the International Criminal Court, *Elements of Crimes*, First session, New York (3–10 September 2002).

[20] Cryer *et al.*, *An Introduction to International Criminal Law*, p. 218.

[21] Case law within the ICTR as well as the ICJ evidences that the intent must be to target a 'substantial' part of the particular group. 'That is demanded by the very nature of the crime of genocide: since the object and purpose of the Convention as a whole is to prevent the intentional destruction of groups, the part targeted must be significant enough to have an impact on the group as a whole. That requirement of substantiality is supported by consistent rulings of the ICTY and the … ICTR … and by the Commentary of the ILC to its

national, ethnical, racial or religious group, as such'.[22] Indeed, in the Nuclear Weapons Advisory Opinion the ICJ correctly pointed out that the prohibition of genocide 'would be pertinent' in such cases where recourse to nuclear weapons entailed the requisite 'element of intent, towards a group as such. In the view of the Court, it would only be possible to arrive at such a conclusion after having taken due account of the circumstances specific to each case'.[23] This is persuasive. Thus, while claims before the Court and cited in its Advisory Opinion that 'the number of deaths occasioned by the use of nuclear weapons would be enormous' and that 'the victims could, in certain cases, include persons of a particular national, ethnic, racial or religious group'[24] are factually accurate, they are inadequate to constitute the crime of genocide. As Cassese observes, it is not sufficient for an alleged perpetrator of genocide to intend to kill, it 'also must be proved that he did … this with the (further and dominant) intention of destroying a group'.[25]

Similarly, assertions to the ICJ 'that the intention to destroy such groups could be inferred from the fact that the user of the nuclear weapon would have omitted to take account of the well-known effects of the use of such weapons' fail to meet the requisite *mens rea*.[26] It must be demonstrated that use of a

Articles in the draft Code of Crimes against the Peace and Security of Mankind.' ICJ, *Case Concerning Application of the Convention on the Prevention and Punishment of the Crime of Genocide* (*Bosnia and Herzegovina* v. *Serbia and Montenegro*), Judgment of 26 February 2007, para. 198.

[22] In the words of the Trial Chamber of the International Criminal Tribunal for Rwanda (ICTR): 'Special intent is a well-known criminal law concept in the Roman-continental legal systems. It is required as a constituent element of certain offences and demands that the perpetrator have the clear intent to cause the offence charged. According to this meaning, special intent is the key element of an intentional offence, which offence is characterized by a psychological relationship between the physical result and the mental state of the perpetrator.' ICTR, *Prosecutor* v. *Jean-Paul Akayesu*, Judgment (Trial Chamber) (Case No. ICTR-96-4-T), 2 September 1998, para. 518.

[23] Nuclear Weapons Advisory Opinion, para. 26.   [24] *Ibid.*

[25] Cassese, *International Criminal Law* (2nd edn), p. 65. Thus, for example, in July 2010 the ICC issued an international arrest warrant for the President of Sudan, Omar Al Bashir, for genocide. ICC, *Prosecutor* v. *Omar Hassan Ahmad Al Bashir* ('*Omar Al Bashir*'), Second Arrest Warrant (Pre-Trial Chamber I) (Case No. ICC-02/05-01/09), 12 July 2010. The warrant included the following reference to the requisite intent: '*Considering* that, on the basis of the standard of proof as identified by the Appeals Chamber, there are reasonable grounds to believe that Omar Al Bashir acted with *dolus specialis*/specific intent to destroy in part the Fur, Masalit and Zaghawa ethnic groups'. *Ibid.*, p. 8 (original emphasis).

[26] Nuclear Weapons Advisory Opinion, para. 26. Though note, for example, the broad definition incorporated into domestic legislation in Canada: '"genocide" means an act or omission committed with intent to destroy, in whole or in part, an *identifiable group of persons*, as such, that, at the time and in the place of its commission, constitutes genocide according to customary international law or conventional international law or by virtue of its being criminal according to the general principles of law recognized by the community of nations, whether or not it constitutes a contravention of the law in force at the time and in

nuclear weapon sought to target a defined 'national, ethnical, racial or religious group, as such'.[27] As the International Criminal Tribunal for Rwanda (ICTR) has opined:

> In concrete terms, for any of the acts charged to constitute genocide, the said acts must have been committed against one or more persons because such person or persons were members of a specific group, and specifically, because of their membership in this group. Thus, the victim is singled out not by reason of his individual identity, but rather on account of his being a member of a national, ethnical, racial or religious group. The victim of the act is, therefore, a member of a given group selected as such, which, ultimately, means the victim of the crime of genocide is the group itself and not the individual alone. The perpetration of the act charged, therefore, extends beyond its actual commission, for example, the murder of a particular person, to encompass the realization of the ulterior purpose to destroy, in whole or in part, the group of which the person is only a member.[28]

Furthermore, as Martin states, 'establishing the *dolus specialis* of an alleged perpetrator can only take place in conjunction with or subsequent to identifying the group at which the conduct is aimed'.[29] Unfortunately, the 1948 Genocide Convention offers little help in such identification. The *travaux préparatoires* evidence little discussion of the four categories, especially with respect to a national, racial or religious group, and what does exist offers little guidance. Martin notes, for instance, that 'the notion of a national group was alternatively described as "a group enjoying civic rights in a given State" or as a national minority'.[30] She further notes that summary records 'do not reveal a clear delineation of the concept of ethnic group, which was referred to as a "sub-group of a national group" but also as a synonym for "racial group" and for "linguistic group"'.[31]

The two ad hoc international criminal tribunals have had occasion to address the notion of the four protected groups. On 2 September 1998 the ICTR handed down the first guilty verdict by an international criminal court for the crime of genocide in the case of *Prosecutor* v. *Jean-Paul Akayesu*:[32]

---

the place of its commission.' Crimes Against Humanity and War Crimes Act, Codification (Current to 4 March 2013), S.C. 2000, c. 24, S. 4(3) (emphasis added).

[27] Thus, as Cryer *et al.* have observed: 'Most of the crimes committed by the Pol Pot regime in Cambodia in 1975–78, for example, are atrocities which do not easily fit within the narrow definition [of genocide], however dreadful the suffering they caused.' Cryer *et al.*, *An Introduction to International Criminal Law*, p. 203.

[28] ICTR, *Prosecutor* v. *Georges Anderson Nderubumwe Rutaganda*, Judgment (Trial Chamber) (Case No. ICTR-96-3-T), 6 December 1999, para. 59.

[29] F. Martin, 'The notion of "protected group" in the Genocide Convention and its application', Chapter 5 in Gaeta, *Commentary on the 1948 Genocide Convention*, pp. 112–13.

[30] *Ibid.*, p. 115.   [31] *Ibid.*, pp. 114–15.

[32] Martin, 'The notion of "protected group" in the Genocide Convention', p. 118.

On reading through the travaux préparatoires of the Genocide Convention … it appears that the crime of genocide was allegedly perceived as targeting only 'stable' groups, constituted in a permanent fashion and membership of which is determined by birth, with the exclusion of the more 'mobile' groups which one joins through individual voluntary commitment, such as political and economic groups. Therefore, a common criterion in the four types of groups protected by the Genocide Convention is that membership in such groups would seem to be normally not challengeable by its members, who belong to it automatically, by birth, in a continuous and often irremediable manner …

Based on the Nottebohm decision[33] … by the International Court of Justice, the Chamber holds that a national group is defined as a collection of people who are perceived to share a legal bond based on common citizenship, coupled with reciprocity of rights and duties …

An ethnic group is generally defined as a group whose members share a common language or culture …

The conventional definition of racial group is based on the hereditary physical traits often identified with a geographical region, irrespective of linguistic, cultural, national or religious factors …

The religious group is one whose members share the same religion, denomination or mode of worship.[34]

While the Trial Chamber's criteria of 'stable' and 'permanent' have certainly been criticised, especially controversial has been its opinion whereby an intent to destroy, in whole or in part, *any* stable and permanent group could meet the threshold to be considered genocide.[35] The Trial Chamber argued (unpersuasively, in this author's view) that 'the intention of the drafters of the Genocide Convention. … according to the travaux préparatoires, was patently to ensure the protection of any stable and permanent group'.[36] Moreover, as Martin notes, in most subsequent judgments Trial Chambers have followed a more contextual path with regard to the definition of national, ethnical, racial and religious groups:

The Chamber notes that the concepts of national, ethnical, racial and religious groups have been researched extensively and that, at present, there are no generally and internationally accepted precise definitions thereof. Each of these concepts must be assessed in the light of a particular political, social and cultural context.[37]

---

[33] ICJ, *Nottebohm (Liechtenstein v. Guatemala)*, Judgment of 18 November 1953.

[34] ICTR, *Prosecutor v. Jean-Paul Akayesu*, Judgment (Trial Chamber) (Case No. ICTR-96-4-T), 2 September 1998, paras. 511–15.

[35] See, e.g., W. A. Schabas, *Genocide in International Law* (Cambridge University Press, 2000), pp. 132–3; Martin, 'The notion of "protected group" in the Genocide Convention', pp. 119-20 and citations at n. 37.

[36] ICTR, *Prosecutor v. Akayesu*, Judgment (Trial Chamber), para. 516.

[37] ICTR, *Prosecutor v. Rutaganda*, Judgment (Trial Chamber), para. 55; see Martin, 'The notion of "protected group" in the Genocide Convention', p. 120 and citations at n. 40.

The International Criminal Tribunal for the former Yugoslavia (ICTY) has taken a slightly different approach. In *Prosecutor* v. *Krstić*, which concerned the mass executions at Srebrenica, the Trial Chamber argued that the four categories were actually more akin to a single category, namely that of a national minority:

> The preparatory work of the Convention shows that setting out such a list was designed more to describe a single phenomenon, roughly corresponding to what was recognised, before the second world war, as 'national minorities', rather than to refer to several distinct prototypes of human groups. To attempt to differentiate each of the named groups on the basis of scientifically objective criteria would thus be inconsistent with the object and purpose of the Convention.[38]

Despite strong criticism from certain quarters, this 'ensemble construction' has been endorsed in subsequent trial judgments.[39]

The question of whether a 'lone individual' could perpetrate genocide is controversial, but is of potential pertinence to a use of a nuclear weapon. As Cryer *et al.* point out, in the *Jelisić* case the ICTY Trial Chamber stated that killings committed by a single perpetrator were sufficient 'to establish the material element of the crime of genocide' and that it was 'a priori possible to conceive that the accused harboured the plan to exterminate an entire group without this intent having been supported by any other organisation in which other individuals participated'. The Chamber 'did not discount the possibility of a lone individual seeking to destroy a group as such'.[40] Given the uniquely powerful nature of a nuclear weapon, it could be asserted that, given the necessary *actus reus* and *mens rea* as set out above, an individual who made a 'dirty bomb' or a rogue submarine commander or pilot who launched a nuclear weapon could be solely responsible for an act of genocide.

In sum, notwithstanding an overall lack of clarity as to the definition of the four groups set out in Article 2 of the 1948 Genocide Convention, it appears to be the case that absent the intent to destroy in whole or in part at least one such group, a use of nuclear weapons will not constitute genocide under international criminal law. Targeting enemy combatants during combat or members of armed groups participating directly in hostilities will not meet the

---

[38] ICTY, *Prosecutor* v. *Radislav Krstić*, Judgment (Trial Chamber) (Case No. IT-98-33-T), 2 August 2001, para. 556. At para. 571 the Trial Chamber cited with apparent approval the ICJ's dicta pertaining to genocide as a result of the use of nuclear weapons.

[39] See, e.g., C. Kress, 'The crime of genocide under international law', *International Criminal Law Review* 6 (2006), 461–502, at 475–6, cited by Martin, 'The notion of "protected group" in the Genocide Convention', p. 122 and citations at nn. 48, 49, 51 and 52. Cryer holds the view that this 'national minorities' approach is preferable. Cryer, 'International criminal law', p. 545.

[40] ICTY, *Prosecutor* v. *Jelisić*, Judgment (Trial Chamber) (Case No. IT-95-10-T), 14 December 1999, para. 100; see Cryer *et al.*, *An Introduction to International Criminal Law*, p. 207.

requisite criteria. In seeking to discern the requisite intent, the relevant court will look primarily at the factual circumstances, for as a Judge Advocate stated in a Canadian military court in the 1946 case against Johann Neitz:

> Intention is not capable of positive proof, and, accordingly, it is inferred from the overt acts. Evidence of concrete acts is frequently much better evidence than the evidence of an individual for, after all, an individual honestly knows what he is thinking.[41]

This inferred intent from factual circumstances is an approach that has been adopted by the ICTY and ICTR.[42]

The *Krstić* case is also relevant for an understanding of the interaction between the *actus reus* and *mens rea*, in particular that given the requisite intent, a localised attack (such as an individual use of a nuclear weapon) could be sufficient. Thus, the Trial Chamber stated that:

> Several other sources confirm that the intent to eradicate a group within a limited geographical area such as the region of a country or even a municipality may be characterised as genocide. The United Nations General Assembly characterised as an act of genocide the murder of approximately 800 Palestinians ... detained at Sabra and Shatila, most of whom were women, children and elderly ... The Jelisić Judgement held that genocide could target a limited geographic zone ... Two Judgements recently rendered by German courts took the view that genocide could be perpetrated within a limited geographical area. The Federal Constitutional Court of Germany, in the Nikola Jorgić case, upheld the Judgement of the Düsseldorf Supreme Court ... interpreting the intent to destroy the group 'in part' as including the intention to destroy a group within a limited geographical area ... In a Judgement against Novislav Djajić on 23 May 1997, the Bavarian Appeals Chamber similarly found that acts of genocide were committed in June 1992 though confined within the administrative district of Foča.[43]

B. Use of nuclear weapons as a crime against humanity

As Cryer *et al.* have observed, '[m]any acts which do not constitute genocide will constitute crimes against humanity.'[44] The notion of crimes against humanity was first cited in 1915 in a protest from the British, French and Russian governments following mass killings of Armenians in the Ottoman Empire by Turkish forces. The Russian Foreign Minister's original proposed text had referred to 'crimes against Christianity and civilisation'.[45] The proposal for an

---

[41] Cited in Cassese, *International Criminal Law* (2nd edn), p. 75.

[42] See, e.g., *ibid.*, pp. 141–4.

[43] ICTY, *Prosecutor v. Radislav Krstić*, Judgment (Trial Chamber) (Case No. IT-98-33-T), 2 August 2001, para. 589.

[44] Cryer *et al.*, *An Introduction to International Criminal Law*, p. 203.

[45] See, e.g., Cassese, *International Criminal Law* (2nd edn), pp. 101–2.

international criminal tribunal after the 1914–18 War included the recommendation that it cover 'offences against the laws of humanity'. Following a suggestion by Hersch Lauterpacht, the Charter of the International Military Tribunal (IMT) included a provision authorising the IMT to prosecute persons guilty of crimes against humanity.[46]

In a 1991 resolution, the UN General Assembly 'reaffirmed' in a preambular paragraph that 'the use of nuclear weapons ... would be a crime against humanity'.[47] The Assembly has regularly reaffirmed this unequivocal claim, most recently in December 2012.[48] As with genocide, however, a given use of a nuclear weapon may constitute a crime against humanity, but will not necessarily do so. The ICJ, in its Nuclear Weapons Advisory Opinion, did not address the issue of nuclear weapon use as a possible crime against humanity.

Cassese affirms that under international law 'the category of crimes against humanity is sweeping but sufficiently well defined'.[49] He describes four elements that characterise a crime against humanity under contemporary international law, three of which are not contentious and a fourth that is disputable. First, they are particularly odious offences in that they constitute a serious attack on human dignity or a grave humiliation or degradation of one or more persons. Second, and critically, they are not isolated or sporadic events but are part of a widespread or systematic practice of atrocities.[50] Third, they are prohibited and may be punished regardless of whether they are perpetrated in time of war or peace.[51] Fourth, while the victims may be civilians, Cassese argues (controversially) that under customary international law they may also be enemy combatants.[52]

In August 2012 the report of the independent international commission of inquiry on the Syrian Arab Republic concluded that the Syrian regime and the

---

[46] *Ibid.*, pp. 102–4.

[47] UN General Assembly Resolution 46/37D, adopted on 6 December 1991 by 122 votes to 16 with 22 abstentions, eighth preambular paragraph.

[48] UN General Assembly Resolution 67/64 ('Convention on the Prohibition of the Use of Nuclear Weapons'), adopted on 3 December 2012 by 129 votes to 49 with 10 abstentions, sixth preambular paragraph.

[49] Cassese, *International Criminal Law* (2nd edn), p. 98.

[50] *Ibid.*

[51] An earlier need for a link between crimes against humanity and war was 'gradually dropped' after 1945. *Ibid.*, p. 108. The ICTY Statute limited crimes against humanity to relevant acts committed in armed conflict, although the ICTR Statute was adopted without such a requirement (Article 3). Cryer *et al.*, *An Introduction to International Criminal Law*, pp. 234–5.

[52] Cassese, *International Criminal Law* (2nd edn), pp. 99 and 112–3. His argument that since crimes against humanity may be committed in times of peace, 'it no longer makes sense to require that such crimes be perpetrated against civilians alone' is not yet persuasive as *lex lata*, although the suggestion, based on ICTY jurisprudence, that former combatants who are *hors de combat* be protected (see further note 56 below) can be more readily accepted. Nonetheless, in the revision of his 2008 work, which was completed after his death by a

Shabbiha government militia had committed the crimes against humanity of murder and of torture.[53] It set out the Commission's view of the applicable law as follows:

> Crimes against humanity are those crimes which 'shock the conscience of humanity'. Under the Rome Statute, crimes against humanity occur where certain acts are undertaken as part of a widespread or systematic attack against a civilian population where the perpetrator has knowledge of the attack.[54] The elements of crimes against humanity are well established in international criminal law:
>
> 1. There must be one or more attacks;
> 2. The acts of the perpetrator must be part of the attack(s);
> 3. The attack(s) must be directed against any civilian population;
> 4. The attack(s) must be widespread or systematic;
> 5. The perpetrator must know that his or her acts constitute part of a pattern of widespread or systematic crimes directed against a civilian population and know that his or her acts fit into such a pattern.[55]

Aside from noting the limitation to attacks against a civilian population,[56] particular consideration needs to be given to the need for the attack to be either 'widespread' or 'systematic'.[57] With respect to the term 'widespread', the

number of leading international criminal lawyers, the thrust of Cassese's argument is not only sustained but also actively promoted. See Cassese, *International Criminal Law* (3rd edn), pp. 101–5.

[53] 'Third report of the independent international commission of inquiry on the Syrian Arab Republic', Human Rights Council, UN doc. A/HRC/21/50, 16 August 2012, pp. 1–2 (hereafter, Third report of the commission of inquiry on Syria).

[54] Such acts are the following: murder, extermination, enslavement, forcible transfer of population, imprisonment, torture, rape, sexual slavery, enforced prostitution, forced pregnancy, enforced sterilization, sexual violence, persecution, enforced disappearance, apartheid, and other inhumane acts. Rome Statute of the International Criminal Court, Rome, 17 July 1998, in force 1 July 2002, 2187 UNTS 90, Art. 7(1)(a–k) (hereafter, Rome Statute).

[55] Third report of the commission of inquiry on Syria, p. 48, para. 16.

[56] Earlier jurisprudence in the ad hoc international criminal tribunals suggests that civilians no longer participating in hostilities could be the victims of crimes against humanity as could, in certain circumstances, combatants placed *hors de combat*. See, e.g., ICTY, *Prosecutor* v. *Blaškić*, Judgment (Trial Chamber) (Case No. IT-95-14-T), 3 March 2000, paras. 208–14. As Cryer *et al.* observe, however, the Appeals Chamber judgment in the *Martić* case affirmed that 'civilian' does not include persons *hors de combat* and that therefore such persons would not be the victims of crimes against humanity unless the broader attack was directed at civilians defined narrowly. 'The unfortunate effect of this interpretation is that large-scale extermination or torture directed against prisoners of war would not constitute crimes against humanity.' Cryer *et al.*, *An Introduction to International Criminal Law*, p. 242 (citing ICTY, *Prosecutor* v. *Martić*, Judgment (Trial Chamber) (Case No. IT-95-11-A), 8 October 2008, paras. 295–314).

[57] 'It is important to note that crimes against humanity need not be both widespread and systematic. The test is disjunctive, and therefore reaching either element suffices.' Third report of the commission of inquiry on Syria, p. 49, para. 18.

Commission cited the ICC Pre-Trial Chamber decision to authorise an investigation into the violence in Kenya following disputed elections in 2010.[58] It
noted that the term widespread 'has long been defined as encompassing "the
large scale nature of the attack, which should be massive, frequent, carried out
collectively with considerable seriousness and directed against a multiplicity
of victims". As such, the element of "widespread" refers both to the large-scale
nature of the attack and the number of resultant victims.'[59] With obvious relevance to an isolated use of a nuclear weapon against a civilian population centre, it further asserted, based on the *Tadić* case judgment, that: 'Accordingly, a
widespread attack may be the "cumulative effect of a series of inhumane acts or
the singular effect of an inhumane act of extraordinary magnitude".'[60]

The notion of systematic, in contrast, entails the:

> 'organised nature of the acts of violence and the improbability of their ran-
> dom occurrence' ... An attack's systematic nature can 'often be expressed
> through patterns of crimes, in the sense of non-accidental repetition of
> similar criminal conduct on a regular basis'. The Chamber notes that the
> 'systematic' element has been defined by the ICTR as (i) being thoroughly
> organised, (ii) following a regular pattern, (iii) on the basis of a common
> policy, and (iv) involving substantial public or private resources ... whilst
> the ICTY has determined that the element requires (i) a political object-
> ive or plan, (ii) large-scale or continuous commission of crimes which are
> linked, (iii) use of significant public or private resources, and (iv) the impli-
> cation of high-level political and/or military authorities.[61]

In terms of the relevant criminal conduct, particularly relevant for any use of
nuclear weapons are obviously murder and extermination. With respect to
murder, jurisprudence in the ad hoc international criminal tribunals suggests
that *dolus eventualis*/recklessness is sufficient to constitute the *mens rea* of the
offence. Extermination is said in the 1998 Rome Statute of the ICC to go beyond
mass or large-scale killing to mean also 'the intentional infliction of conditions
of life, inter alia the deprivation of access to food and medicine, calculated to

---

[58] ICC Pre-Trial Chamber, 'Situation in the Republic of Kenya, Decision Pursuant to Article
15 of the Rome Statute on the Authorization of an Investigation into the Situation in the
Republic of Kenya', Doc. ICC-01/09-19, 31 March 2010.

[59] Third report of the commission of inquiry on Syria, p. 49, para. 17.

[60] *Ibid.* (citing ICTY, *Prosecutor* v. *Dusko Tadić (a.k.a 'DULE')*, Judgment (Trial Chamber)
(Case No. IT-94-1), 7 May 1997, para. 648). See also, e.g., ICTY, *Prosecutor* v. *Kordić*,
Judgment (Trial Chamber) (Case No. IT-95-14/2-T), 26 February 2001, para. 179 (citing
Prosecutor v. *Blaškić*, Judgment (Trial Chamber) (Case No. IT-95-14-T), 3 March 2000,
para. 206). See further International Law Commission (ILC), *Draft Code of Crimes against
the Peace and Security of Mankind with Commentaries: 1996* (New York: United Nations,
2005), p. 47.

[61] Third report of the commission of inquiry on Syria, para. 18 (citing ICC Pre-Trial Chamber,
'Situation in the Republic of Kenya, Decision Pursuant to Article 15 of the Rome Statute on
the Authorization of an Investigation into the Situation in the Republic of Kenya', Doc. ICC-
01/09-19, 31 March 2010, para. 96).

bring about the destruction of part of a population'.[62] Cassese prefers the definition offered by the ICTY in *Prosecutor* v. *Krstić*, whereby:

> for the crime of extermination to be established, in addition to the general requirements for a crime against humanity, there must be evidence that a particular population was targeted and that its members were killed or otherwise subjected to conditions of life calculated to bring about the destruction of a numerically significant part of the population.[63]

This could potentially encompass use by a terrorist organisation or armed non-state actor of a 'dirty bomb' provided that the other conditions for a crime against humanity were met.[64]

These conditions include the requisite *mens rea* to commit a crime against humanity, above and beyond the *mens rea* to commit one or more of the constituent crimes. As cited above, the Syria Commission rightly affirms that the perpetrator must know that his or her acts constitute part of a pattern of widespread or systematic crimes directed against a civilian population *and* that his or her acts fit into such a pattern. It does not, though, appear necessary that (s)he know all the details of that pattern.[65]

C.   Use of nuclear weapons as a war crime

A number of possible uses of a nuclear weapon would constitute a war crime, generally defined as a *serious* violation of international humanitarian law (IHL).[66] This may result first and foremost from the characteristics of the weapon itself, particularly whether it is deemed to be inherently indiscriminate (see Chapter 4) or to be of a nature to cause superfluous injury or unnecessary suffering (see Chapter 5). If such is not the case, then a particular use of a nuclear weapon may still be a war crime, notably when the weapon is directed against the civilian population, thereby violating the rule of distinction, or when it is used indiscriminately. Fundamental prerequisites for any war crime are also, of course, that (a) there must be an armed conflict in progress (whether international or non-international in character), and (b) the relevant conduct (here, the use of a nuclear weapon) must have a sufficient nexus to an armed conflict to fall within its ambit.

---

[62] Rome Statute, Art. 7(2)(b).

[63] ICTY, *Prosecutor* v. *Radislav Krstić*, Judgment (Trial Chamber) (Case No. IT-98-33-T), 2 August 2001, para. 503.

[64] Cassese, *International Criminal Law* (2nd edn), p. 110.   [65] *Ibid.*, pp. 115–16.

[66] See, e.g., International Committee of the Red Cross (ICRC), 'What are "serious violations of international humanitarian law"? Explanatory Note', July 2012, available at: www.icrc.org/eng/assets/files/2012/att-what-are-serious-violations-of-ihl-icrc.pdf. The ICRC's explanatory note listed as war crimes specified grave breaches of the 1949 Geneva Conventions and 1977 Additional Protocol I, war crimes under Article 8 of the 1998 Rome Statute of the ICC, and other war crimes in customary IHL. See further Cassese's *International Criminal Law* (2nd edn), pp. 81 and 84–6. Thus, as Cassese notes, not all violations of IHL amount to war crimes, although they may give rise to state responsibility.

A generally accepted definition of armed conflict is set out in a seminal decision on a defence appeal on jurisdiction by the ICTY in the *Tadić* case:

> an armed conflict exists whenever there is a resort to armed force between
> States or protracted armed violence between governmental author-
> ities and organized armed groups or between such groups within a State.
> International humanitarian law applies from the initiation of such armed
> conflicts and extends beyond the cessation of hostilities until a general con-
> clusion of peace is reached; or, in the case of internal conflicts, a peaceful
> settlement is achieved. Until that moment, international humanitarian law
> continues to apply in the whole territory of the warring States or, in the
> case of internal conflicts, the whole territory under the control of a party,
> whether or not actual combat takes place there.[67]

This chapter will not discuss this definition in depth. What is most relevant for
our purposes is the apparent requirement for an international armed conflict
(IAC) that there be 'resort to armed force *between* States'. I would argue that a
state that uses overwhelming force against another state through the employment of nuclear weapons is still constrained by *jus in bello*, and may thus commit a war crime, even if that latter state is unable or unwilling to respond.[68]

Since the ICTY's decision in *Tadić* and the adoption of the 1998 Rome Statute
of the ICC, it appears relatively undisputed that war crimes may be committed
in a non-international armed conflict (NIAC). However, use by a governmental regime of a nuclear weapon within national territory against its own population might not fall within an NIAC, for example where armed opposition
to the regime was not sufficiently organised to constitute a party to a conflict.
Such use may still, of course, amount to an act of genocide or a crime against
humanity.

1.   Use of a nuclear weapon as a prohibited means of warfare

The use of a prohibited weapon in an armed conflict has been said by Cassese
to be per se an international crime.[69] As he noted, this particular crime is
unusual for ICL as it does not have a 'domestic' criminal law underpinning.

---

[67] ICTY, *Prosecutor* v. *Dusko Tadić (a.k.a 'DULE')*, Decision on the Defence Motion for
Interlocutory Appeal on Jurisdiction (Case No. IT-94-1), 2 October 1995, §70, available at:
www.icty.org/x/cases/tadic/acdec/en/51002.htm.

[68] Cryer *et al.*, for example, argue that aerial bombing by one state against another would constitute an armed conflict. Cryer *et al.*, *An Introduction to International Criminal Law*, p. 279.
Furthermore, in accordance with Common Article 2 to the four 1949 Geneva Conventions,
this is also the case where one army occupies another state, even where no shot is fired in
defence. One should perhaps, therefore, not read the *Tadić* dicta as defining the criteria that
would constitute an IAC as necessarily excluding other scenarios.

[69] Cassese, *International Criminal Law* (2nd edn), p. 54.

It is also a crime of 'conduct' rather than one of 'result', in that no damage need be caused to an enemy. The constituent elements are thus that a weapon proscribed by a rule of international law has been used, combined with intent to use the weapon.[70] Cassese also claims, however, that the use of a weapon that is inherently indiscriminate or of a nature to cause superfluous injury or unnecessary suffering in an IAC only 'arguably ... constitutes a war crime under customary international law, at least in those instances where the weapon at issue or the way it is used indisputably infringes those two principles or one of them'.[71]

Indeed, as Gaeta notes, Article 85 of 1977 Additional Protocol I[72] does not include, as a grave breach, the violation of Article 35(2) on using 'weapons, projectiles and material and methods of warfare of a nature to cause superfluous injury or unnecessary suffering'.[73] Furthermore, even if the general prohibition has attained the status of an international crime, where a particular nuclear (or indeed any) weapon is subsequently adjudged to be either inherently indiscriminate or of a nature to cause superfluous injury or unnecessary suffering, the alleged criminal user(s) must either have known, or be reasonably expected to have known, that such was indeed the case.[74] This is potentially a tricky threshold. Indeed, as Cassese rightly asserts, rules on means of warfare are 'even more difficult to apply than the legal standards on the conduct of hostilities' (which, he states, are 'purposely loose').[75]

2. Use of a nuclear weapon as a prohibited method of warfare

As Chapter 4 describes, direct attacks on civilians and indiscriminate attacks are prohibited under IHL, whether committed in an IAC or an NIAC. In addition to state responsibility, they constitute a war crime entailing individual criminal responsibility under ICL. These are crimes of result, which, in our concern, encompass three main scenarios: (1) a direct attack on the civilian population using a nuclear weapon; (2) where a nuclear weapon has been used

---

[70] *Ibid.*, pp. 54–5.   [71] *Ibid.*, p. 95.

[72] Protocol Additional to the Geneva Conventions of 12 August 1949, and relating to the Protection of Victims of International Armed Conflicts (Protocol I), Geneva, 8 June 1977, in force 7 December 1978, 1125 UNTS 3 (herafter, 1977 Aditional Protocol I).

[73] Gaeta, 'Serious violations of the law on the conduct of hostilities', p. 5.

[74] See, e.g., with respect to the particular *mens rea* requirement with regard to the use of expanding bullets under Article 8 of the 1998 Rome Statute (as amended), A. Alamuddin and P. Webb, 'Expanding jurisdiction over war crimes under Article 8 of the ICC Statute', *Journal of International Criminal Justice* 8 (2010), 1219–43, at 1233.

[75] Cassese, *International Criminal Law* (2nd edn), pp. 91, 90. At certain points in his analysis, however, he seems to have confused means and methods of warfare. His assertion, for example, that employing anti-personnel mines indiscriminately is a prohibited *means* of warfare (p. 91) is not persuasive.

without concern as to whether it is targeted against a lawful military objective or not; and (3) where a lawful military objective has indeed been targeted by a nuclear weapon, but where excessive harm is caused to the civilian population or civilian objects or a combination of both.

In general, targeting civilian areas, such as a city, with a nuclear weapon would clearly be unlawful and there would be little difficulty in proving the requisite *mens rea*. More difficult to assess might be where a use of nuclear weapons is claimed to have been used as a reprisal (see Chapter 6), but any realistic prospect of an attack being deemed lawful under IHL would likely demand a prior use of a nuclear weapon by another state in an IAC to be deemed proportionate and therefore potentially lawful.[76]

A limited and proportionate attack using nuclear weapons could be somewhat more easily envisaged, at least (and hopefully only) in legal theory. For example, an attack on an enemy military base using a tactical nuclear weapon would still reasonably be expected to cause civilian deaths and injuries (e.g. to civilian suppliers, cleaners, cooks, visitors and the like), but might not fall foul of the prohibition on attacks that could reasonably be expected to be disproportionate. Moreover, in accordance with the prohibition of a disproportionate attack as a grave breach of 1977 Additional Protocol I,[77] there must be *knowledge*[78] that the attack 'will cause excessive loss of life, injury to civilians or damage to civilian objects'[79] when compared with 'the concrete and direct military advantage anticipated'.[80]

The scope of individual criminal responsibility was further narrowed in the 1998 Rome Statute of the ICC, which included within the jurisdiction of the Court, within an IAC only, the offence of 'Intentionally launching an attack in the knowledge that such attack will cause incidental loss of life or injury to civilians or damage to civilian objects or widespread, long-term and severe damage to the natural environment which would be *clearly excessive* in relation to the concrete and direct overall military advantage anticipated'.[81] Although there is no international treaty formulation of the proportionality rule as a war

---

[76] It is argued by some that no use of nuclear weapons in the form of a lawful reprisal in an NIAC is possible under the law as it stands (though see Chapter 7 for a discussion of this issue).

[77] The duty in Article 57 of the Protocol is thus wider than the international criminal law prohibition: to 'refrain from deciding to launch any attack *which may be expected to cause* incidental loss of civilian life, injury to civilians, damage to civilian objects, or a combination thereof, which would be excessive in relation to the concrete and direct military advantage anticipated' (emphasis added).

[78] Cassese asserts that recklessness is sufficient to constitute knowledge, but this is not wholly persuasive. Cassese, *International Criminal Law* (2nd edn), p. 64.

[79] 1977 Additional Protocol I, Art. 85(3)(b).

[80] 1977 Additional Protocol I, Art. 57(2)(iii).

[81] Rome Statute, Art. 8(2)(b)(iv) (emphasis added).

crime in an NIAC,[82] it is generally uncontested that the rule on proportionality in attacks exists under customary IHL.[83]

Finally, it is also at least arguable that the use of a nuclear weapon could be considered an act of violence 'the primary purpose of which is to spread terror among the civilian population'.[84] According to the International Committee of the Red Cross (ICRC) study of customary IHL, state practice establishes this rule as a norm of customary international law applicable in both IACs and NIACs.[85] Article 4(d) of the 1994 ICTR Statute provides that the Tribunal has jurisdiction over violations of 1977 Additional Protocol II, including acts of terrorism. In his report on the establishment of a Special Court for Sierra Leone, the UN Secretary-General noted that violations of Article 4 of 1977 Additional Protocol II have long been considered violations of customary international law.[86] In the *Galić* case, which concerned an alleged 'campaign of sniping and shelling against the civilian population of Sarajevo with the intent to spread terror among that population' upheld by the Accused, the ICTY concluded that there was, already in 1992, individual criminal responsibility for a person committing a serious violation of the rule prohibiting terror, at least 'where the serious violation took the form of serious injury or death caused to civilians'.[87] It stated that the elements constituting that criminal responsibility included the following:

1. Acts of violence directed against the civilian population or individual civilians not taking direct part in hostilities causing death or serious injury to body or health within the civilian population.

---

[82] Article 3(8)(c) of 1996 Amended Protocol II to the Convention on Certain Conventional Weapons prohibits any placement of mines, booby traps and other devices 'which may be expected to cause incidental loss of civilian life, injury to civilians, damage to civilian objects, or a combination thereof, which would be excessive in relation to the concrete and direct military advantage anticipated'. Protocol on Prohibitions or Restrictions on the Use of Mines, Booby-Traps and Other Devices, Geneva, 10 October 1980, in force 2 December 1983, 1342 UNTS 168, 19 ILM 1529; as amended on 3 May 1996 (Protocol II to the 1980 Convention as amended on 3 May 1996), Geneva, 3 May 1996, in force 3 December 1998, 35 ILM 1206.

[83] See, e.g., ICRC, 'Rule 14. Proportionality in Attack', available at: www.icrc.org/customary-ihl/eng/docs/v1_cha_chapter4_rule14.

[84] Article 51(2) of 1977 Additional Protocol I prohibits 'acts or threats of violence the primary purpose of which is to spread terror among the civilian population' as does Article 13(2), 1977 Additional Protocol II, while Article 4, 1977 Additional Protocol II prohibits 'acts of terrorism'. See also R. Cryer, 'Prosecutor v Galić and the war crime of terror bombing', *IDF Law Review* 2 (2005–06), 73–102.

[85] ICRC, 'Rule 2. Violence Aimed at Spreading Terror among the Civilian Population', available at: www.icrc.org/customary-ihl/eng/docs/v1_rul_rule2.

[86] UN Secretary-General, Report on the establishment of a Special Court for Sierra Leone, UN doc. S/2000/915, 4 October 2000, para. 545.

[87] ICTY, *Prosecutor v. Stanislav Galić*, Judgment (Trial Chamber) (Case No. IT-98-29-T), 5 December 2003, para. 127.

2. The offender wilfully made the civilian population or individual civilians not taking direct part in hostilities the object of those acts of violence.

3. The above offence was committed with the primary purpose of spreading terror among the civilian population.[88]

D. Modes of liability

As under national criminal law, also in ICL individual criminal responsibility arises 'not only when a person materially commits a crime but also when he or she engages in other forms or modalities of criminal conduct'.[89] The ICTY, in the so-called *Lašva Valley* case, has affirmed that two types of liability for criminal participation 'appear to have crystallised in international law – co-perpetrators who participate in a joint criminal enterprise, on the one hand, and aiders and abettors, on the other'.[90] The ICC, on the other hand, has embraced 'control' theory instead of joint criminal enterprise (JCE). These modes of liability are each addressed below.

1.   Joint criminal enterprise

As in most legal systems, every participant in a common criminal plan is equally responsible when he or she participates in the criminal acts and intends to engage in the common criminal plan. They are all to be treated as principals in the crime although, naturally, varying degrees of culpability can be taken into account in sentencing following conviction.[91] As the ICTY Appeals Chamber stated in its judgment in the *Tadić* case:

---

[88] *Ibid.*, para. 133. It was not, however, deemed necessary that terror was the result of those actions. With respect to intent, the Tribunal stated that: '"Primary purpose" signifies the mens rea of the crime of terror. It is to be understood as excluding dolus eventualis or recklessness from the intentional state specific to terror. Thus the Prosecution is required to prove not only that the Accused accepted the likelihood that terror would result from the illegal acts – or, in other words, that he was aware of the possibility that terror would result – but that that was the result which he specifically intended. The crime of terror is a specific-intent crime.' *Ibid.*, para. 136. See further Chapter 6 in this volume.

[89] Cassese, *International Criminal Law* (2nd edn), p. 187. In the words of US prosecutor Telford Taylor at the Nuremburg trials: '[not under any] known system of criminal law is guilt for murder confined to the man who pulls the trigger or buries the corpse … [N]ot only are principals guilty but also accessories, those who take a consenting part in the commission of crime or are connected with plans or enterprises involved in its commission, those who order or abet crime, and those who belong to an organization or group engaged in the commission of crime. These provisions embody no harsh or novel principles of criminal responsibility.' Cited in *ibid.*, p. 190.

[90] ICTY, *Prosecutor v. Furundžija ('Lašva Valley')*, Judgment (Trial Chamber) (Case No. IT-95-17/1), 10 December 1998, para. 216.

[91] Cassese, *International Criminal Law* (2nd edn), p. 190.

the doctrine of acting in pursuance of a common purpose is rooted in the national law of many States. Some countries act upon the principle that where multiple persons participate in a common purpose or common design, all are responsible for the ensuing criminal conduct, whatever their degree or form of participation, provided all had the intent to perpetrate the crime envisaged in the common purpose. If one of the participants commits a crime not envisaged in the common purpose or common design, he alone will incur criminal responsibility for such a crime.[92]

As with national law,[93] the situation under ICL with respect to criminal liability in a joint criminal enterprise is complex and continues to evolve.

The concept of JCE – closely associated with the late Antonio Cassese[94] – is a mode of criminal liability that encompasses all the participants in a common criminal plan. It holds all such individuals criminally responsible for all criminal acts foreseen by the plan (whether or not they materially participated in the commission of these acts) as well as, in certain circumstances, criminal acts that fall outside the plan but that might foreseeably result from that plan.[95] Three categories of criminal liability exist under JCE, as set out in the *Tadić* Appeals Chamber decision: (1) for a common intentional purpose; (2) for participation in a common criminal plan within an institutional framework; and (3) incidental liability based on foresight and voluntary assumption of risk.[96] All three types share a common *actus reus*, namely that there is (1) a plurality of persons; (2) the existence of a common plan, design or purpose that amounts to or involves the commission of a crime provided for in the Statute; and (3) participation of the accused in the common design involving the perpetration of one of the crimes provided for in the Statute.[97]

With respect to the first category (for a common intentional purpose), common intent is clearly critical. Cassese argues that in addition to *dolus directus*, *dolus eventualis* (awareness of the likely consequences of one's acts) may be sufficient.[98] As he notes, all actors are guilty, even though in some instances the requisite *mens rea* (for example, intent to murder) is not accompanied by the corresponding *actus reus* (for example, firing a gun).[99] If sufficient intent is not established, a defendant cannot be held responsible under this category of

[92] ICTY, *Prosecutor v. Tadić*, Judgment (Appeals Chamber) (Case No. IT-94-1-A), 15 July 1999, para. 224.

[93] For the situation under English law with regard to 'joint enterprise liability', see, e.g., Ormerod, *Smith and Hogan's Criminal Law*, Section 8.5, pp. 213–30.

[94] See, e.g., J. D. Ohlin, 'Lubanga Decision Roundtable: Lubanga and the Control Theory', Blog post on *Opinio Juris*, 15 March 2012, available at: http://opiniojuris.org/2012/03/15/lubanga-and-the-control-theory-2/.

[95] Cassese, *International Criminal Law* (2nd edn), p. 191.

[96] ICTY, *Prosecutor v. Tadić*, Judgment (Appeals Chamber) (Case No. IT-94-1-A), 15 July 1999, para. 220 (hereafter, *Tadić* Appeal Judgment). See Cassese, *International Criminal Law* (2nd edn), p. 191; Cryer *et al.*, *An Introduction to International Criminal Law*, p. 369.

[97] *Tadić* Appeal Judgment, para. 227.   [98] *Ibid.*, p. 191.   [99] *Ibid.*, p. 192.

JCE (although another category or mode of criminal liability may still exist). In *Prosecutor* v. *Krstić*, the Trial Chamber held the defendant responsible for genocide under the basis of the first category of JCE, even though he had initially only shared intent to forcibly expel Bosnian Muslims from Srebrenica.[100] On appeal against conviction, however, the Appeals Chamber adjudged that Krstić had not shared the genocidal intent (although they found that he had aided and abetted the crime of genocide):

> all that the evidence can establish is that Krstić was aware of the intent to commit genocide on the part of some members of the VRS [Bosnian Serb army] Main Staff, and with that knowledge, he did nothing to prevent the use of Drina Corps personnel and resources to facilitate those killings. This knowledge on his part alone cannot support an inference of genocidal intent.
>
> Genocide is one of the worst crimes known to humankind, and its gravity is reflected in the stringent requirement of specific intent. Convictions for genocide can be entered only where that intent has been unequivocally established. There was a demonstrable failure by the Trial Chamber to supply adequate proof that Radislav Krstić possessed the genocidal intent. Krstić, therefore, is not guilty of genocide as a principal perpetrator.[101]

This implies that the provision of material support to the use of a nuclear weapon, but without having the intent to destroy in whole or in part one of the groups defined under the Genocide Convention, would mean that an individual would likely not be found guilty under the mode of liability of joint criminal enterprise. Indeed, in the *Gotovina and Markač* case[102] the ICTY Trial Chamber cited with approval the *Tadić* definition of the first category of liability:

> all co-defendants, acting pursuant to a common design, possess the same criminal intention; for instance, the formulation of a plan among the co-perpetrators to kill, where, in effecting this common design (and even if each co-perpetrator carries out a different role within it), they … all possess the intent to kill.
>
> The objective and subjective prerequisites for imputing criminal responsibility to a participant who did not, or cannot be proven to have effected the killing are as follows:
>
> (i) the accused must voluntarily participate in one aspect of the common design (for instance, by inflicting non-fatal violence upon the victim, or by providing material assistance to or facilitating the activities of his co-perpetrators); and

---

[100] ICTY, *Prosecutor* v. *Krstić*, Judgment (Trial Chamber) (Case No. IT-98-33-T), 2 August 2001.

[101] ICTY, *Prosecutor* v. *Krstić*, Judgment (Appeals Chamber) (Case No. IT-98-33-A), 19 April 2004, para. 134.

[102] ICTY, *Prosecutor* v. *Ante Gotovina and Mladen Markač*, Judgment (Trial Chamber) (Case No. IT-06-90-T), 15 April 2011.

(ii) the accused, even if not personally effecting the killing, must nevertheless intend this result.[103]

The ICTY Trial Chamber found that Gotovina shared the objective of and significantly contributed to a JCE, whose common purpose was to permanently remove the Serb civilian population from the Krajina region, by ordering unlawful attacks against civilians and civilian objects in Knin, Benkovac and Obrovac and by failing to make a serious effort to prevent or investigate crimes committed against Serb civilians in the Split Military District. The Trial Chamber found Gotovina guilty, under the first form of JCE, of persecution (deportation, forcible transfer, unlawful attacks against civilians and civilian objects, and discriminatory and restrictive measures) and deportation as crimes against humanity. It also found him guilty, under the third form of JCE, of murder and inhumane acts as crimes against humanity, and of plunder of public and private property, wanton destruction, murder and cruel treatment as violations of the laws or customs of war, either 'on their own or as underlying acts of persecution'. Gotovina was sentenced to a single term of imprisonment of twenty-four years.

On appeal, however, albeit without questioning the legal basis of JCE, the Appeals Chamber by majority decision acquitted Gotovina[104] in what one commentator has described as 'the most radical reversal in the ICTY's history'.[105] The Appeals Chamber focused on the decision by the Trial Chamber to consider artillery strikes falling 200 metres or more away from a military objective as potentially indiscriminate, with every Appeals Chamber judge agreeing that there was insufficient basis for this determination. As Decoeur notes, the Majority of the Appeals Chamber drew the conclusion that the Trial Chamber had erred in finding that the artillery attacks were unlawful. As a result, it also concluded that absent unlawful attacks on the Serb civilian population, there was no evidence of a JCE.[106] However, according to the Appeal Chamber's own judgment:

> Where the Appeals Chamber finds an error of law in the trial judgement arising from the application of an incorrect legal standard, the Appeals Chamber will articulate the correct legal standard and review the relevant factual findings of the trial chamber accordingly. In so doing, the Appeals Chamber not

---

[103] *Ibid.*, para. 1950.

[104] ICTY, *Prosecutor* v. *Ante Gotovina and Mladen Markač*, Judgment (Appeals Chamber) (Case No. IT-06-90-A), 16 November 2012.

[105] H. Decoeur, 'The ICTY Appeals Judgement in Prosecutor v Gotovina and Markač: Scratching below the Surface', Blog post, *Cambridge Journal of International and Comparative Law Blog*, 19 November 2012, available at: http://cjicl.org.uk/2012/11/19/the-icty-appeals-judgement-in-prosecutor-v-gotovina-and-markac-scratching-below-the-surface-2/.

[106] *Ibid.*

only corrects the legal error, but, when necessary, also applies the correct legal standard to the evidence contained in the trial record and determines whether it is itself convinced beyond reasonable doubt as to the factual finding challenged by the appellant before that finding is confirmed on appeal.[107]

This it did not do.[108]

2.   Joint criminal responsibility and 'control' theory

The ICC has not, to date at least, explicitly adopted JCE as a mode of liability, preferring instead Claus Roxin's Control Theory of Perpetration.[109] The theory, which dates back to the 1960s, requires a finding that the defendant performed an essential contribution to a crime. As Ohlin has noted, this 'is, necessarily, a counterfactual question, and the theory also gives too little guidance about how different the counterfactual crime must be before we declare it to be a different crime altogether, and therefore whether the defendant's contribution was essential or not'.[110] The relevant mode of liability is set out in Article 25(3)(a) of the Rome Statute:

> In accordance with this Statute, a person shall be criminally responsible and liable for punishment for a crime within the jurisdiction of the Court if that person:
> (a) Commits such a crime, whether as an individual, jointly with another or through another person, regardless of whether that other person is criminally responsible.

In its March 2012 judgment in the *Lubanga* case, the ICC Trial Chamber held that to be liable as a co-perpetrator the accused must, at a minimum, associate with a group whose purpose entails 'a sufficient risk that, if events follow the ordinary course, a crime will be committed'.[111] As Davids observes, this is somewhat akin to the – criticised[112] – third form of liability for JCE (incidental liability based on foresight and voluntary assumption of risk) and is potentially

---

[107]   ICTY, *Prosecutor v. Gotovina and Markač*, Judgment (Appeals Chamber) (Case No. IT-06-90-A), 16 November 2012, para. 12.

[108]   See, further, in this regard, Chapter 4.

[109]   As Davids notes, 'There is a simple reason for this. The Rome Statute of the ICC was adopted in 1998 and the Tadić appeals judgment was issued in 1999.' J. W. Davids, 'Some initial thoughts on the judgment in Prosecutor v. Lubanga', Blog post on *The {New} International Law*, 15 March 2012, available at: http://thenewinternationallaw.wordpress.com/tag/joint-criminal-enterprise/#_ftn4. See generally also Schabas, *Introduction to the ICC*, pp. 226–8.

[110]   Ohlin, 'Lubanga Decision Roundtable'.

[111]   ICC, *Situation in the Democratic Republic of the Congo in the Case of the Prosecutor v. Thomas Lubanga Dyilo*, Judgment pursuant to Article 74 of the Statute (Trial Chamber) (Case No. ICC-01/04-01/06), 14 March 2012 (hereafter, *Lubanga* case), para. 984.

[112]   See, e.g., Cryer *et al.*, *An Introduction to International Criminal Law and Procedure*, p. 373.

very wide in scope.[113] The Trial Chamber further stated that 'the prosecution does not need to demonstrate that the contribution of the accused, taken alone, caused the crime; rather, the responsibility of the co-perpetrators for the crimes resulting from the execution of the common plan arises from mutual attribution, based on the joint agreement or common plan'.[114]

Thus, in terms of the *actus reus* under Article 25(3)(a) of the Rome Statute, the majority of the Chamber concluded that 'the commission of a crime jointly with another person involves two objective requirements: (i) the existence of an agreement or common plan between two or more persons that, if implemented, will result in the commission of a crime; and (ii) that the accused provided an essential contribution to the common plan that resulted in the commission of the relevant crime'. It asserted that these two requirements 'must be assessed on the basis of all the evidence related to the alleged crime'.[115] With respect to the requisite *mens rea*, the majority decided that the standard was 'awareness that a consequence will occur in the ordinary course of events', meaning that 'the participants anticipate, based on their knowledge of how events ordinarily develop, that the consequence will occur in the future ... A low risk will not be sufficient.'[116] As Lieflländer suggests, however, 'Taken to the extreme, the combination of not requiring an inherently criminal purpose and having a rather unclear conception of the required risk might result in the adoption of a very broad doctrine of co-perpetration.'[117]

3.   Aiding and abetting an international crime

According to Article 25(3)(c) of the 1998 Rome Statute of the ICC, the Court has jurisdiction over anyone who, with respect to a crime within the jurisdiction of the Court, 'for the purpose of facilitating the commission of such a crime, aids, abets or otherwise assists in its commission or its attempted commission, including providing the means for its commission'. Thus, as under national criminal law, a person may be convicted of aiding or abetting an international crime where he or she assists a principal in the commission of a crime, but without sharing his/her criminal intent to commit that crime.[118] Indeed,

---

[113] Davids, 'Some initial thoughts on the judgment in Prosecutor v. Lubanga'. As he points out, 'Both doctrines assign criminal liability based on the foreseeable criminal actions of others in connection to the implementation of a common plan. The new formulation departs from the "customary" definition of the UN tribunals in one very important way: it does not require that the overall plan be criminal in essence. The result is criminal responsibility as a direct perpetrator for those who willingly contribute to a common plan in an essential way even when that the plan itself is not criminal' (footnotes omitted).

[114] *Lubanga* case, para. 994.   [115] *Ibid.*, para. 1006.   [116] *Ibid.*, para. 1012.

[117] T. R. Lieflländer, 'The Lubanga judgment of the ICC: more than just the first step?' *Cambridge Journal of International and Comparative Law* 1(1) (2012), 191–212, at 208.

[118] Compare and contrast aiding and abetting with the 'outside contribution' foreseen by Article 25(3)(d) of the 1998 Rome Statute of the ICC: 'In accordance with this Statute, a

as implied by the Appeal Chamber's decision in the *Krstić* case, the key difference between JCE and aiding and abetting an international crime is found in the *mens rea*.[119] In the so-called *Lašva Valley* case, the ICTY Trial Chamber stated that:

> With regard to mens rea, the Trial Chamber must determine whether it is necessary for the accomplice to share the mens rea of the principal or whether mere knowledge that his actions assist the perpetrator in the commission of the crime is sufficient to constitute mens rea in aiding and abetting the crime. The case law indicates that the latter will suffice.[120]

In general, 'the acts of a participant in a joint criminal enterprise are more serious than those of an aider and abettor to the principal offender since a participant in a joint criminal enterprise shares the intent of the principal offender whereas an aider and abettor need only be aware of that intent'.[121] In the *Ngirabatware* case, the ICTR Trial Chamber observed that the *actus reus* of aiding and abetting is constituted by:

> acts or omissions specifically aimed at assisting, encouraging or lending moral support to the perpetration of a certain specific crime, and which have a substantial effect on the perpetration of the crime. Whether a particular contribution qualifies as substantial is a fact-based inquiry, and need not serve as condition precedent for the commission of the crime. The contribution may occur before, during or after the principal crime has been perpetrated, and the location where the actus reus takes place may be removed from the location of the principal crime.[122]

Furthermore:

> The actus reus of aiding and abetting may also be constituted through tacit approval and encouragement of a crime, which substantially contributes to the perpetration of the crime. The authority of the accused, combined with his presence at or very near the crime scene, especially if considered

---

person shall be criminally responsible and liable for punishment for a crime within the jurisdiction of the Court if that person: ... (d) In any other way contributes to the commission or attempted commission of such a crime by a group of persons acting with a common purpose. Such contribution shall be intentional and shall either: ... (i) Be made with the aim of furthering the criminal activity or criminal purpose of the group, where such activity or purpose involves the commission of a crime within the jurisdiction of the Court; or ... (ii) Be made in the knowledge of the intention of the group to commit the crime.'

[119] Cassese, *International Criminal Law* (2nd edn), p. 211.

[120] ICTY, *Prosecutor v. Furundžija ('Lašva Valley')*, Judgment (Trial Chamber), para. 236.

[121] ICTY, *Prosecutor v. Krnojelac*, Judgment (Appeals Chamber) (Case No. IT-97-25-A), 17 September 2003, para. 75.

[122] ICTR, *Prosecutor v. Ngirabatware*, Judgment (Trial Chamber) (Case No. Case No. ICTR-99-54-T), 20 December 2012 (*Ngirabatware* case), para. 1294.

together with the prior conduct of the accused, may amount to an official sanction of the crime and thus substantially contribute to it.[123]

The Trial Chamber felt the need to clarify that this form of aiding and abetting 'is not, strictly speaking, criminal responsibility for omission'.[124]

In February 2013, however, the ICTY Appeals Chamber issued its judgment in the *Perišić* case, deciding to acquit (by four votes to one) the erstwhile Chief of Staff of the Yugoslav army for aiding and abetting war crimes and crimes against humanity.[125] In assessing Perišić's liability as an aider and abettor, the Trial Chamber had stated that 'specific direction'[126] was not a requisite element of the *actus reus* of aiding and abetting.[127] Before the Appeals Chamber, the Prosecution maintained that case law in other jurisdictions does not require specific direction in cases where an aider and abettor's conduct is remote from relevant crimes. The Appeals Chamber, however, 'reaffirmed' (despite acknowledged inconsistencies in its own prior jurisprudence) 'that no conviction for aiding and abetting may be entered if the element of specific direction is not established beyond reasonable doubt, either explicitly or implicitly'.[128] It stated further that where:

> an accused aider and abettor is remote from relevant crimes, evidence proving other elements of aiding and abetting may not be sufficient to prove specific direction. In such circumstances, the Appeals Chamber, Judge Liu dissenting, holds that explicit consideration of specific direction is required.[129]

While finding some 'intuitive appeal in this reasoning', and asserting that the Appeals Chamber 'is surely correct that there should be a difference between contributions to the war effort as such and to the commission of specific crimes', Milanović justly points out that Perišić:

> had every reason to know that the aid that he was providing to the Bosnian Serbs would be used in the commission of war crimes and crimes against

---

[123] *Ibid.*, para. 1295.   [124] *Ibid.*

[125] Murder, inhumane acts (injuring and wounding civilians, inflicting serious injuries, wounding, and forcible transfer) and persecutions on political, racial, or religious grounds as crimes against humanity; and murder and attacks on civilians as violations of the laws or customs of war.

[126] The notion was first cited in the *Tadić* Appeal Chamber judgment in 1999: 'The aider and abettor carries out acts *specifically directed* to assist, encourage or lend moral support to the perpetration of a certain specific crime (murder, extermination, rape, torture, wanton destruction of civilian property, etc.), and this support has a substantial effect upon the perpetration of the crime.' *Tadić* Appeal Judgment, para. 229 (emphasis added).

[127] ICTY, *Prosecutor* v. *Perišić*, Judgment (Trial Chamber) (Case No. IT-04-81-T), 6 September 2011, para. 126.

[128] ICTY, *Prosecutor* v. *Perišić*, Judgment (Appeals Chamber) (Case No. IT-04-81-A), 28 February 2013, para. 36.

[129] *Ibid.*, para. 39.

humanity. The commission of such crimes was perhaps not an intrinsic feature of their war effort, yet these crimes were not being committed by some random bad apples, but as part of a deliberate, systematic policy of ethnic cleansing. In such circumstances it is profoundly unsatisfactory to say that Perišić was not guilty at all under any pertinent theory of criminal liability – without the aid that he was providing, the Bosnian Serbs would never have been able to commit crimes on such a scale.[130]

The implications of the *Perišić* judgment for the supply of nuclear weapons and weapons technology 'remotely' are potentially significant and troubling, although the requirement for specific direction has since been dismissed in jurisprudence in the Special Court for Sierra Leone[131] and by the Appeals Chamber of the ICTY in the January 2014 judgment in the *Šainović and ors* case.[132] The precise *mens rea* element still remains to be settled, however.

With respect to *mens rea*, to be guilty of aiding and abetting, it has generally been held not to be necessary that the accessory knows exactly what crime will be committed, let alone be aware of the specific criminal intent of the perpetrator. The aider and abettor must be aware of either a criminal intent on the part of the perpetrator or at least the risk that the perpetrator will engage in criminal conduct.[133] As the Trial Chamber of the Special Court for Sierra Leone (SCSL) in *Brima and others* observed:

> The mens rea required for aiding and abetting is that the accused knew that his acts would assist the commission of the crime by the perpetrator or that he was aware of the substantial likelihood that his acts would assist the commission of a crime by the perpetrator. However, it is not necessary that the aider and abettor had knowledge of the precise crime that was intended and which was actually committed, as long as he was aware that one of a number of crimes would probably be committed, including the one actually committed.[134]

The SCSL Appeals Chamber endorsed the Trial Chamber's analysis. It referred to the Appeals Chamber of the ICTY in both *Blaškić* and *Simić*, which held that 'liability for aiding and abetting requires proof that the accused knew that one of a number of crimes would probably be committed, that one of those crimes

---

[130] M. Milanović, 'The Limits of Aiding and Abetting Liability: The ICTY Appeals Chamber Acquits Momcilo Perisic', Blog post on EJIL: *Talk*, 11 March 2013, available at: www.ejiltalk. org/the-limits-of-aiding-and-abetting-liability-the-icty-appeals-chamber-acquits-momcilo-perisic/.

[131] SCSL, *Prosecutor v. Charles Ghankay Taylor*, Judgment (Appeals Chamber) (Case No. SCSL-03-01-A), 26 September 2013, §6905.

[132] ICTY, *Prosecutor v. Nikola Šainović and ors*, Judgment (Appeals Chamber) (Case No. IT-05-87-A), 23 January 2014, paras. 1617–50.

[133] Cassese, *International Criminal Law* (2nd edn), pp. 215–16.

[134] SCSL, *Prosecutor v. Alex Tamba Brima et al.*, Judgment (Trial Chamber) (Case No. SCSL-04-16-T), 20 June 2007, para. 776.

was in fact committed, and that the accused was aware that his conduct assisted the commission of that crime'.[135] The SCSL Appeals Chamber endorsed that principle.[136]

In the *Ngirabatware* case, however, the ICTR Trial Chamber stated that 'The mens rea for aiding and abetting is knowledge that the acts performed by the aider and abettor assist the commission of the *specific* crime of the principal perpetrator. Specific intent crimes, such as genocide, do not require that the aider and abettor share the mens rea of the principal perpetrator; it suffices to prove that *he knew of the principal perpetrator's specific intent*.'[137] This is a significantly higher threshold, implying that, for example, an individual who supplied weapons-grade plutonium would not be guilty of aiding or abetting genocide unless (s)he was told that the device would be used 'to get' a certain group. This decision is consistent with the decisions of Dutch courts in the *van Anraat* case.

Frans van Anraat had initially been charged with complicity in genocide as well as in war crimes. On 23 December 2005, however, the District Court of The Hague acquitted him of the charge of complicity in genocide on the basis that he was not aware of Sadaam Hussein's genocidal intent. It stated that:

> The court considers that the requirement of knowledge of the accomplice in relation to the main offense of genocide is an essential component of liability under international criminal law on this subject and that Dutch law, which seems to result in a larger liability, cannot be applied in this respect ... This is different with respect to complicity in war crimes, which do not require a special intent of the perpetrator.[138]

The Hague Court of Appeal upheld his conviction for war crimes, concluding that it was foreseeable that the provision of Thiodiglycol (TDG) to Iraq would be used for the production of mustard gas.[139] Indeed, in the words of the Court:

> that TDG, in the quantities as supplied by the defendant – more than eleven hundred (1,100) tons altogether – could only serve for the production of

---

[135] SCSL, *Prosecutor* v. *Alex Tamba Brima et al.*, Judgment (Appeals Chamber) (Case No. SCSL-04-16-A), 22 February 2008, para. 243.

[136] *Ibid.* As Cassese notes, this corresponds to fundamental principles of [national] criminal law: if I give a gun to a criminal, I may reasonably expect that he will use it to commit criminal acts using that gun, and I will therefore be liable for aiding or abetting whatever crime he reasonably foreseeably commits. Cassese, *International Criminal Law* (2nd edn), p. 216.

[137] *Ngirabatware* case, para. 1296 (emphasis added).

[138] District Court of The Hague, *Prosecutor* v. *Frans van Anraat*, Judgment of 23 December 2005, paras. 6.5.1–6.5.2 (unofficial translation), available at: www.asser.nl/upload/documents/DomCLIC/Docs/NLP/Netherlands/vanAnraat_Judgment_23-12-2005_En.pdf.

[139] Van Anraat was charged with aiding and abetting violations of the laws and customs of war committed by named individuals including Saddam Hussein and Ali Hassan al-Majid

mustard gas and not – as continuously argued by the defendant and his defence – for use in the textile industry, has been stated by expert witness [A], among others, during the court session of 4 April 2007. [A] confirmed his earlier statement of 30 May 2007 before the examining magistrate in which he said that it is totally unthinkable that during the 1980s TDG was used in Iraq as textile 'additive' and that in Iraq not one factory had been found that was equipped for the production of textile paint or printing ink.[140]

The risk of such gas being used for violation of international law was also held to be reasonably foreseeable: 'the defendant was very aware of the fact that – "in the ordinary cause of events" – the gas was going to be used. In this respect the Court assumes that the defendant, notwithstanding his statements concerning his relevant knowledge, was aware of the – also then known – unscrupulous character of the then Iraqi regime.'[141]

Thus, providing weapons-grade nuclear material or essential nuclear weapons technology may constitute aiding or abetting an international crime where the provider knows that his action will assist the commission of a crime. But whether, in the case of nuclear weapons, that crime involves a war crime, a crime against humanity or genocide will likely depend on the extent of his/her knowledge of the principal's intentions.

Conclusion

Clearly, the use of nuclear weapons as well as the supply of nuclear materials could, under certain circumstances and according to varying liability modes, constitute genocide, crimes against humanity and/or war crimes. But the implications of the *Perišić* judgment for the supply of nuclear weapons and weapons technology 'remotely' are potentially significant and troubling. It remains to be seen whether the *Perišić* judgment is an exception or the start of a new trend limiting responsibility for aiding and abetting international crimes.

---

al-Tikriti, as regards gas attacks on the Kurdish population of northern Iraq in Halabja and elsewhere; and aiding and abetting violations of the laws and customs of war committed by named individuals including Saddam Hussein and Ali Hassan al-Majid al-Tikriti, as regards gas attacks on the territory of Iran. See European Court of Human Rights, *Frans Cornelis Adrianus van Anraat v. The Netherlands*, Decision on Admissibility (App. No. 65389/09), 6 July 2010, para. 8.

[140] Court of Appeal in The Hague, *State v. Frans van Anraat*, Judgment (Case No. 22-000509-06), 9 May 2007, para. 11.10, available at: www.haguejusticeportal.net/index.php?id=7548.

[141] *Ibid.*, para. 11.16.

9

Use of nuclear weapons as an international crime and the Rome Statute of the International Criminal Court

ANNIE GOLDEN BERSAGEL

Introduction

At the November 2009 Assembly of States Parties to the Rome Statute of the International Criminal Court (the Rome Statute),[1] the Government of Mexico submitted a proposal to ban the use or threat of use of nuclear weapons as a war crime under Article 8 of the Rome Statute. Although the proposal was unsuccessful, it highlights a recurring debate over the status of nuclear weapons under international humanitarian law (IHL) – a debate left largely unresolved by the International Court of Justice (ICJ)'s 1996 Advisory Opinion on the *Legality of the Threat or Use of Nuclear Weapons*.[2]

At the Rome Statute's founding, the debate over whether to explicitly classify the use of nuclear weapons as a war crime proved one of the most contentious issues of the negotiations. In order to achieve compromise, the drafters not only eliminated any explicit mention of nuclear weapons, but also limited the Court's jurisdiction over weapons 'of a nature to cause superfluous injury or unnecessary suffering or which are inherently indiscriminate' to weapons subject to a comprehensive prohibition *and* listed in a yet-to-be drafted annex to the Statute.[3] In short, the Rome Statute limits the International Criminal Court (ICC)'s jurisdiction over weapons prohibited under conventional and customary international humanitarian law.

Although Article 10 of the Rome Statute provides that such divergence shall not 'be interpreted as limiting or prejudicing in any way existing or developing rules of international law for purposes other than this statute', Article 21 nevertheless charges the ICC with applying 'the established principles of the international law of armed conflict' as a subsidiary means of interpreting the Statute's provisions. The result is an unresolved tension between the Statute's

---

[1] United Nations Diplomatic Conference of Plenipotentiaries on the Establishment of an International Criminal Court, *Rome Statute of the International Criminal Court (last amended January 2002)*, UN doc. A/CONF.183/9 (18 July 1998).

[2] ICJ, *Legality of the Threat or Use of Nuclear Weapons*, Advisory Opinion of 8 July 1996, para. 78 (hereafter, Nuclear Weapons Advisory Opinion).

[3] Rome Statute of the International Criminal Court, Art. 8(2)(b)(xx), Rome 17 July 1998, in force 1 July 2002, 2187 UNTS 90 (hereafter, Rome Statute).

purported codification of international humanitarian law and its divergent interpretation of specific international humanitarian law rules.[4]

Section A of this chapter provides a background on the role the debate over nuclear weapons played during the Rome Statute negotiations, and on the recent proposal to amend the Rome Statute to explicitly criminalise the threat or use of nuclear weapons. Section B analyses the two provisions of the Rome Statute that address the Statute's relationship to customary international law: Articles 10 and 21. While these provisions attempt to establish a dividing line between the Statute and custom, the distinction is not entirely clear, and is not consistently respected in practice. Section C assesses the impact of the Rome Statute's weapons provision on the status of nuclear weapons under international law. While the ICC does not have jurisdiction to adjudicate whether nuclear weapons are inherently indiscriminate or of a nature to cause superfluous injury or unnecessary suffering, other enforcement options remain, most promisingly, through adjudication in national courts or international ad hoc tribunals.

A.   Background: prohibited weapons under the Rome Statute

1.   *The Rome Statute negotiations: prohibited weapons*

Debate over explicitly criminalising use of nuclear weapons

Since the Rome Statute's inception, several non-nuclear weapon states and non-governmental organisation (NGO) activists have advocated for explicitly designating the threat or use of nuclear weapons in situations of armed conflict as a war crime subject to the ICC's jurisdiction.[5] Primarily, these efforts sought to ban the use of nuclear weapons within the category of prohibited means of warfare under international humanitarian law. A February 1997 Preparatory Committee (PrepCom) draft of the Rome Statute added nuclear weapons to the list of prohibited weapons in Article 8, along with, among others, the use of poison or asphyxiating gases.[6] Naturally, the nuclear weapon states parties

---

[4] See, e.g. M. McAuliffe deGuzman, 'Article 21: Applicable law' in O. Triffterer (ed.), *Commentary on the Rome Statute of the International Criminal Court: Observers' Notes: Article by Article* (Baden-Baden: Nomos Verlagsgesellschaft, 1999), p. 441 (opining on the interaction between Article 21 and the crimes listed in Article 8).

[5] See, e.g. UN, 'Rome conference, use of weapons of mass destruction should be included in criminal court's definition of war crimes, say several conference speakers', Press Release L/ROM/14, 18 June 1998; P. Kirsch and D. Robinson, 'Reaching agreement at the Rome conference' in A. Cassese *et al.* (eds.), *The Rome Statute of the International Criminal Court: A Commentary*, 3 vols. (Oxford University Press, 2002), Vol. I, pp. 79–80; M. Cottier, 'Article 8: War Crimes para. 2 (b) (xvii)–(xx)' in Triffterer, *Commentary on the Rome Statute*, pp. 240–1.

[6] *Ibid.*, p. 240.

to the negotiations protested any inclusion of nuclear weapons in the Rome Statute draft text.

The reference to prohibited weapons underwent several reformulations over the next year and a half. For example, during the December 1997 PrepCom, Switzerland recommended classifying as a war crime:

> employing weapons, projectiles and material and methods of warfare which are of a nature to cause superfluous injury or unnecessary suffering or which are inherently indiscriminate.[7]

By 6 July 1998 a range of options emerged in the draft text, reprinted here to illustrate the debate:

Option 1
Employing the following weapons, projectiles and material and methods of warfare which are of a nature to cause superfluous injury or unnecessary suffering

(i) Poison or poisoned weapons;

(ii) Asphyxiating, poisonous or other gases, and all analogous liquids, materials or devices;

(iii) Bullets which expand or flatten easily in the human body, such as bullets with a hard envelope which does not entirely cover the core or is pierced with incisions;

(iv) Bacteriological (biological) agents or toxins for hostile purposes or in armed conflict;

(v) Chemical weapons as defined in and prohibited by the 1993 Convention on the Prohibition of the Development, Production, Stockpiling and Use of Chemical Weapons and on Their Destruction;

(vi) Such other weapons or weapons systems as become the subject of a comprehensive prohibition, subject to a determination to that effect by the Assembly of States Parties, in accordance with the procedure laid down in article 111 of this Statute;

Option 2
Employing the following weapons, projectiles and material and methods of warfare which are of a nature to cause superfluous injury or unnecessary suffering or which are inherently indiscriminate:

(i) Poison or poisoned weapons;

(ii) Asphyxiating, poisonous or other gases, and all analogous liquids, materials or devices;

(iii) Bullets which expand or flatten easily in the human body, such as bullets with a hard envelope which does not entirely cover the core or is pierced with incisions;

(iv) Bacteriological (biological) agents or toxins for hostile purposes or in armed conflict;

---

[7] Preparatory Committee on the Establishment of an International Criminal Court, 1–12 December 1997, Working Group on Definitions and Elements of Crimes, Suggestion by Switzerland: Part D, UN doc. A/AC.249/1997/WG.1/DP.10, 9 December 1997.

(v)   Chemical weapons as defined in and prohibited by the 1993 Convention
         on the Prohibition of the Development, Production, Stockpiling and
         Use of Chemical Weapons and on Their Destruction;
(vi)   Nuclear weapons;
(vii) Anti-personnel mines;
(viii) Blinding laser weapons;
(ix)   Such other weapons or weapons systems as become the subject of a
         comprehensive prohibition, subject to a determination to that effect
         by the Assembly of States Parties, in accordance with the procedure
         laid down in article 111 of this Statute;

Option 3
Employing weapons, projectiles and material and methods of warfare
which are of a nature to cause superfluous injury or unnecessary suffering or which are inherently indiscriminate, in violation of international
humanitarian law.[8]

The International Committee of the Red Cross (ICRC) followed the negotiations closely, and provided feedback on specific language through written
statements tabled by the New Zealand delegation:

> ICRC expressed its preference of option 3 as this accurately reflects existing
> international law. However, if a list is chosen, subparagraph (vi) [of Option
> 1] becomes of extreme importance as it is essential that the use of other
> weapons prohibited by international law be added to the list. If option 1 is
> chosen, the chapeau must include the words 'or which are inherently indis-
> criminate' which reflects a fundamental rule of humanitarian law, recently
> reaffirmed by the International Court of Justice, and which led to the pro-
> hibition of some of the weapons in this list.[9]

In other words, the ICRC endorsed the list approach as a second-best alternative, even though the text of Option 1 limits the definition of weapons 'of a
nature to cause superfluous injury or unnecessary suffering' to those included
in the list.

States objecting to the more general principle approach found in Option 3
argued that the text did not define the crime with enough specificity to give
notice to potential defendants.[10] This concern animated several debates during the negotiations, and reflects the difficulty of converting rules of international humanitarian law expressed as general principles into specific rules
of criminal liability – including the prohibited conduct and requisite mental

---

[8] United Nations Diplomatic Conference of Plenipotentiaries on the Establishment of an
     International Criminal Court, Rome, 15 June–17 July 1998, *Official Records Volume III:
     Reports and Other Documents*, UN doc. A/CONF.183/C.1/L.53, 6 July 1998, p. 206.
[9] *Ibid.*, p. 225.
[10] H. von Hebel and D. Robinson, 'Crimes within the jurisdiction of the Court' in R. S. Lee
     (ed.), *The International Criminal Court: The Making of the Rome Statute*, 2nd edn (The
     Hague: Kluwer Law International, 2002), p. 114.

state. The Preparatory Committee accepted the concern that the general principle approach to prohibited weapons would prove too vague, which left the delegates to the Diplomatic Conference with the difficult task of determining exactly which weapons belonged on the list. The alternative to crafting a specific definition, leaving the details for interpretation by a judge in a future case, was hardly palatable to states concerned about ICC judges' accountability.

Canada had earlier proposed combining a list with a provision banning the use of 'such other weapons or weapons systems as become the subject of a comprehensive prohibition pursuant to customary or conventional international law',[11] undoubtedly with the recently concluded 1997 Anti-Personnel Mine Ban Convention (Ottawa Treaty) banning anti-personnel landmines in mind. This, too, was unpalatable to states concerned that the clause left the responsibility to identify specific weapons subject to a comprehensive prohibition to judicial interpretation, rather than the will of the states parties.[12] These states preferred to define explicitly the weapons whose use is prohibited, to avoid granting ICC judges the power to determine which weapons the provision prohibited and which weapons were allowed.

The issue of whether to include nuclear weapons in such a list generated so much controversy at the 1998 negotiations that certain non-nuclear weapon states succeeded in forcing an ultimatum upon the delegates to the Diplomatic Conference: if nuclear weapons were omitted from Article 8, so too would any explicit mention of chemical or biological weapons be omitted.[13] As a result, the status of a relatively uncontroversial provision, including biological and chemical weapons among the list of weapons whose use is prohibited, was held hostage to the nuclear weapons debate.

Article 8(2)(b)(xx) narrows the Court's jurisdiction over war crimes

On the morning of the last day of the Diplomatic Conference, the chair of the Committee of the Whole submitted a final proposal for the Rome Statute text, which excluded both nuclear and chemical weapons from the Statute.[14] With time running out, the delegates were left with the practical choice of either accepting this compromise solution or rejecting the proposal in its entirety.[15] Norway in particular expressed the concern that the nuclear issue might derail

---

[11] As quoted in von Hebel and Robinson, 'Crimes within the jurisdiction of the Court', p. 115, n. 105.

[12] *Ibid.*, p. 115.

[13] See, e.g. Cottier, 'Article 8: War crimes para. 2 (b) (xvii)–(xx)', p. 240–1; Kirsch and Robinson, 'Reaching agreement at the Rome conference', p. 80.

[14] W. Schabas, *An Introduction to the International Criminal Court* (Cambridge University Press, 2001), p. 17.

[15] C. Garraway, 'Article 8(2)(b)(xx) – Employing weapons, projectiles or materials or methods of warfare listed in the annex to the Statute' in R. S. Lee (ed.), *The International Criminal*

the Rome Statute negotiations completely.[16] Instead, the final text classified as war crimes in international armed conflict the use of 'poison or poisoned weapons' (Article 8(2)(b)(xvii)), 'asphyxiating, poisonous or other gases, and all analogous liquids, materials or devices' (Article 8(2)(b)(xviii)), and the use of expanding bullets (Article 8(2)(b)(xix)), while leaving the door open for the future inclusion of various types of weapons through a curious formulation in Article 8(2)(b)(xx).

Article 8(2)(b)(xx) classifies as a war crime:[17]

> Employing weapons, projectiles and material and methods of warfare which are of a nature to cause superfluous injury or unnecessary suffering or which are inherently indiscriminate in violation of the international law of armed conflict, *provided that* such weapons, projectiles and material and methods of warfare are the subject of a comprehensive prohibition *and* are included in an annex to this Statute, by an amendment in accordance with the relevant provisions set forth in articles 121 and 123 [emphasis added].

Compare this formulation to Article 35(2) of 1977 Additional Protocol I to the Geneva Conventions:[18]

> It is prohibited to employ weapons, projectiles and material and methods of warfare of a nature to cause superfluous injury or unnecessary suffering.

The delegates to the Diplomatic Conference restricted the scope of the Rome Statute with regard to the protections contained in Article 35(1) of 1977 Additional Protocol I by adding that weapons 'of a nature to cause superfluous injury or unnecessary suffering' are criminalised *only* if they are (1) 'the subject of a comprehensive prohibition' and (2) 'included in an annex' to the Rome Statute. This annex to the Rome Statute does not yet exist.

Article 8(2)(b)(xx) of the Rome Statute similarly adopts a more narrow version of the text of Article 51(4) of 1977 Additional Protocol I, which outlines the rule against indiscriminate attacks. Article 51(4) contains no qualifier based on whether the weapons used are subject to a comprehensive prohibition:

> Indiscriminate attacks are prohibited. Indiscriminate attacks are: (a) those which are not directed at a specific military objective; (b) those which employ a method or means of combat which cannot be directed at a specific military objective; or (c) those which employ a method or means of combat the effects of which cannot be limited as required by this Protocol; and

---

Court: *The Making of the Rome Statute*, 2nd edn (The Hague: Kluwer Law International, 2002), p. 182.

[16] Kirsch and Robinson, 'Reaching agreement at the Rome conference', p. 80.

[17] Article 8 defines war crimes subject to the Rome Statute's jurisdiction.

[18] Protocol Additional to the Geneva Conventions of 12 August 1949, and relating to the Protection of Victims of International Armed Conflicts (Protocol I), Geneva, 8 June 1977, in force 7 December 1978, 1125 UNTS 3 (hereafter, 1977 Additional Protocol I).

consequently, in each such case, are of a nature to strike military objectives and civilians or civilian objects without distinction.

At present, the use of nuclear weapons fails to meet the 'comprehensive prohibition' criterion contained in Article 8(2)(b)(xx), as well as the requirement of being placed in an annex. Other weapons of mass destruction, such as biological and chemical weapons, appear far more likely candidates for inclusion in the annex to which Article 8(2)(b)(xx) refers. For example, the 1997 Anti-Personnel Mine Ban Convention[19] may be cited as evidence of a comprehensive – although not universal[20] – prohibition of anti-personnel mines. For nuclear weapons, however, there is no clear comprehensive prohibition of either use or possession.[21] The 1968 Nuclear Non-Proliferation Treaty (NPT) explicitly permits nuclear weapon states (NWS) parties to the Treaty to retain nuclear arms, and includes the NWS' obligation to negotiate in good faith towards eventual disarmament (Article VI). Also, the various treaties establishing nuclear weapon-free zones, inter alia in Africa[22] and Latin America,[23] establish only regional support for a ban on nuclear weapons. For their part, nuclear-armed states have consistently maintained that international law permits the use of nuclear weapons under specific circumstances[24] and that their possession may in fact promote peace and security through a deterrent effect.[25]

[19] Convention on the Prohibition of the Use, Stockpiling, Production and Transfer of Anti-Personnel Mines and their Destruction, Oslo, 18 September 1997, in force 1 March 1999, 2056 UNTS 211, 36 ILM 1507 (hereafter, the Anti-Personnel Mine Ban Convention).

[20] There were 161 states parties to the Anti-Personnel Mine Ban Convention as of November 2013. 'States Parties to the Convention', *Convention on the Prohibition of the Use, Stockpiling, Production and Transfer of Anti-Personnel Mines and their Destruction*, available at: www.apminebanconvention.org/states-parties-to-the-convention/.

[21] See, e.g. Nuclear Weapons Advisory Opinion, p. 266, para. 105(2)(B) ('There is in neither customary nor conventional international law any comprehensive and universal prohibition of the threat or use of nuclear weapons as such').

[22] Treaty on the Nuclear-Weapon-Free Zone in Africa ('Treaty of Pelindaba'), Cairo, 11 April 1996, in force 15 July 1999, 35 ILM 698.

[23] Treaty for the Prohibition of Nuclear Weapons in Latin America and the Caribbean ('Treaty of Tlatelolco') Mexico City, 14 February 1967, in force 22 April 1968, 634 UNTS 326.

[24] See, generally Written Statement of the United Kingdom to the ICJ, Nuclear Weapons Advisory Opinion, 16 June 1995, p. 74 ('State practice regarding the possession of nuclear weapons necessarily implies that the use of nuclear weapons would be lawful in proper circumstances'); Written Statement of the United States to the ICJ, Nuclear Weapons Advisory Opinion, 20 June 1995, p. 48 ('[T]here is no general prohibition in conventional or customary international law on the use of nuclear weapons'); Written Statement of the Russian Federation to the ICJ, Nuclear Weapons Advisory Opinion, 19 June 1995, p. 18 ('The issue of legality of the use of nuclear weapons shall be dealt with on a case-by-case basis from a viewpoint of the correspondence of such use to criteria of self-defence and the above limitations').

[25] See, e.g. HM Government, 'Securing Britain in an Age of Uncertainty: The Strategic Defence and Security Review' (October 2010), p. 5, available at: www.direct.gov.uk/prod_consum_dg/groups/dg_digitalassets/@dg/@en/documents/digitalasset/dg_191634.pdf?CID=PDFandPLA=furlandCRE=sdsr; United States Department of Defense, *Sustaining*

Due to the current absence of any comprehensive prohibition of nuclear weapons, classifying their use as a war crime under the Rome Statute could occur through one of three separate avenues, all of which face formidable political obstacles to success. First, states could agree to a comprehensive ban on nuclear weapons and the Assembly of States Parties (ASP) could subsequently amend the Rome Statute to create an annex that refers to Article 8(2)(b)(xx) and includes nuclear weapons. Alternatively, the ASP could agree to amend the Rome Statute to remove the 'subject of a comprehensive prohibition' requirement from Article 8(2)(b)(xx) (though it would still need to be included in an annex). If the ICC thereafter determined that nuclear weapons are of a nature to cause superfluous injury or unnecessary suffering, or that they are inherently indiscriminate, the use of nuclear weapons would be effectively criminalised under the Rome Statute. Lastly, the ASP could agree to classify the use of nuclear weapons as an independent war crime under Article 8(2) – the tack Mexico chose. Given current political constellations and security interests, none of these options appear likely.

2. A return to the nuclear weapons debate: Mexico's proposal at the 2010 Review Conference

Attempt to evade the Article 8(2)(b)(xx) straitjacket

The ASP met in November 2009 to clarify the agenda and procedural issues in advance of the 2010 Review Conference of the Rome Statute. Consistent with the state's previous activism on nuclear disarmament,[26] Mexico pushed for explicitly criminalising the threat or use of nuclear weapons through the Rome Statute.[27] Rather than add nuclear weapons to the list of prohibited weapons in Article 8(2)(b)(xx), Mexico proposed to include the threat or use of nuclear weapons as a separate war crime under Article 8(2).[28] In so doing, Mexico attempted to sidestep the Article 8(2)(b)(xx) 'comprehensive prohibition' requirement. The proposal read simply:

US Global Leadership: Priorities for 21st Century Defense (January 2012), p. 5, available at: www.defense.gov/news/Defense_Strategic_Guidance.pdf.

[26] Mexico also opposed the omission of nuclear weapons from the Rome Statute during the 1998 negotiations. See 'Extract from Volume II of the Official Records of the United Nations Diplomatic Conference of Plenipotentiaries on the Establishment of an International Criminal Court (Summary Records of the Plenary Meetings and of the Meetings of the Committee of the Whole)' UN doc. A/CONF.183/C.1/SR.34, at 333, para. 111. See, also Written Statement of Mexico to the ICJ, Nuclear Weapons Advisory Opinion, 19 June 1995, p. 2, para. 2 (arguing 'the use or the threat of use of nuclear weapons is under no circumstance permitted under international law').

[27] Proposal of Amendment by Mexico, UN doc. C.N.725.2009.TREATIES-6, 29 October 2009, p. 1.

[28] *Ibid.*

Proposed amendment
   Add to article 8, paragraph 2, b), the following:
   ... Employing nuclear weapons or threatening to employ nuclear weapons.[29]

The representative for the Mexican delegation explained that Mexico already regards the use or threat of use of nuclear weapons as a violation of international law, due to the 'superfluous injury and unnecessary suffering' these weapons inflict.[30] Mexico's proposal did not garner enough support to be included in the 2010 Review Conference agenda, however.[31] According to the International Law Association Committee on the International Criminal Court: 'Mexico's proposal on nuclear weapons obviously constitutes a political statement, rather than a serious amendment that has any hope of success, even in an amended version.'[32] The official record of debate demonstrates that several states supported Mexico's advocacy, but the general consensus among the ASP was clear: 'much more work needed to be undertaken before conveying this issue to the Review Conference.'[33]

Barriers to a nuclear weapons amendment

Any amendment to the Rome Statute requires a two-thirds majority for passage,[34] but does not enter into force until one year after seven-eighths of all state parties to the Rome Statute have ratified the amendment. Moreover, amendments to Article 8 in particular are binding only for states that ratify the amendment:

> In respect of a State Party which has not accepted the amendment, the Court shall not exercise its jurisdiction regarding a crime covered by the amendment when committed by that State Party's nationals or on its territory.[35]

In practice, this means that even if an amendment to criminalise the (threat or) use of nuclear weapons were to gain the two-thirds majority required for passage and at least seven-eighths of all state parties ratified the amendment, the two nuclear-armed state parties to the Rome Statute, the United Kingdom

---

[29] *Ibid.* (original emphasis).

[30] *Ibid.*, p. 3. Mexico did not elaborate, however, on how the international humanitarian law rule against the use of weapons of a nature to cause superfluous injury or unnecessary suffering relates to the legality of threats of use.

[31] International Criminal Court Assembly of States Parties, Part II: Resolutions Adopted by the Assembly of States Parties at 34–35, ICC-ASP/8/20 (18–26 November 2009), available at: www.icc-cpi.int/iccdocs/asp_docs/ASP8/OR/OR-ASP8-Vol.I-ENG.Part.II.pdf.

[32] International Law Association, 'Fourth Report of the Hague Conference (2010) International Criminal Court, Prepared by Professor Göran Sluiter and Professor William Schabas, Co-Rapporteurs' (2010), p. 6.

[33] International Criminal Court Assembly of States Parties, 'Annexes', ICC-ASP/8/20, p. 54, para. 36.

[34] Rome Statute, Art. 121(3).   [35] *Ibid.*, Art. 121(5).

and France, could nevertheless block the amendment from applying to their nationals or choose to withdraw from the Statute entirely.[36] There is also a concern that an amendment to criminalise the use of nuclear weapons might deter states from becoming parties to the Rome Statute. Article 120 specifies that no reservations may be made to the Treaty. Thus, once an amendment to the Rome Statute enters into force, all states that subsequently accede to the Treaty would have no choice but to accept the amendment. For states wavering over accession to the Rome Statute, there is a risk that the proposed amendment could tip the balance in favour of remaining outside the ICC.

B.   The Rome Statute and international humanitarian law: overlap, but not full convergence

By limiting international criminal responsibility to the use of weapons that are of a nature to cause superfluous injury or unnecessary suffering or that are inherently indiscriminate only where they are subject to a comprehensive ban and included in an annex to the Statute, the current wording of Article 8(2)(b) (xx) of the Rome Statute is clearly narrower than customary law.[37]

More ominously, Cassese cautions that as a result of the Rome Statute's current formulation, 'those weapons may eventually be regarded as lawful'.[38] Is Cassese's fear justified? The chapeau to Article 8 indicates that the drafters intended to avoid this unhappy result[39] by clarifying that the Article concerned the Court's subject matter jurisdiction, rather than an attempt to codify customary law: '*For purposes of this Statute*, "war crimes" means …'.[40] Article 10 of the Rome Statute attempts to prevent the Statute from narrowing customary international law, although Article 21 designates the law of armed conflict as a subsidiary source of law to aid the ICC judges in their interpretation of the Statute. The following sections examine the interplay among these three provisions in the light of existing scholarship on the relation between treaty law and customary international law.

1.   Article 10

Article 10 attempts to prevent the Rome Statute from limiting customary international law. It appears that this Article most likely has no independent legal effect; that is, it merely restates existing principles of interpretation. Nevertheless, there remains at least some cause for concern that Article 8(2)

---

[36] *Ibid.*, Art. 127(1).
[37] See A. Cassese, *International Criminal Law* (Oxford University Press, 2003), p. 60.
[38] *Ibid.*
[39] Schabas, *An Introduction to the International Criminal Court*, p. 23.
[40] Rome Statute, Art. 8 (emphasis added).

(b)(xx) could indirectly lead to the erosion of the customary international humanitarian law norm on which it is quite loosely based, depending on subsequent state practice and *opinio juris*.

Intention and content

At the behest of the Egyptian delegation to the Rome Statute negotiations, the Assembly of States Parties adopted Article 10, designed to end debate over which provisions of the Statute had achieved the status of customary international law and which had not.[41] An early draft of the Article, labelled 'Article Y', was designed to allay fears that any divergence between the text of the Rome Statute and rules of existing international law – such as the divergence in Article 8(2)(b)(xx) with regard to prohibited weapons – might erode or at least impede the development of international law.[42] Article 10 reads:

> Nothing in this Part shall be interpreted as limiting or prejudicing in any way existing or developing rules of international law for purposes other than this Statute.[43]

This Article does not appear, however, to preclude use of the Rome Statute as evidence of customary international law under all circumstances. The words 'limiting' and 'prejudicing' indicate the drafters' at least implicit intent to allow the Rome Statute to serve as evidence of a progressive development in international law. For example, Article 7(1)(g) of the Rome Statute classifies rape as a crime against humanity and Article 8(2)(c)–(e) applies many of the Statute's provisions on war crimes to both international and non-international armed conflicts.[44] Both of these provisions reach, if not exceed, the outer boundaries of customary international humanitarian law.

In support of Article 10's function as a floor rather than a ceiling for the development of international law, legal scholars have pointed to the Rome Statute's progressive provisions without reference to Article 10. References to the Rome Statute's role in the 'crystallization of war crimes committed in non-international armed conflict'[45] represent but one example. Similarly, the 2005 ICRC study of customary international humanitarian law also cites extensively Articles 6 through 8 of the Rome Statute.[46] The International Criminal Tribunal for the former Yugoslavia (ICTY) Trial Chamber in *Prosecutor v. Furundzija*,

---

[41] Von Hebel and Robinson, 'Crimes within the jurisdiction of the Court', p. 88.

[42] See *ibid.*, p. 88; O. Triffterer, 'Article 10' in O. Triffterer (ed.), *Commentary on the Rome Statute of the International Criminal Court: Observers' Notes: Article by Article* (Baden-Baden: Nomos Verlagsgesellschaft, 1999), pp. 315–16.

[43] Rome Statute, Art. 10.   [44] *Ibid.*, Art. 8(2)(c)–(e).

[45] See, e.g. C. Kreβ, 'International criminal law', para. 35, in *Max Planck Encyclopedia of Public International Law* (March 2009).

[46] J.-M. Henckaerts and L. Doswald-Beck, *Customary International Humanitarian Law*, 3 vols. (Cambridge University Press, 2005), Vol. I, pp. 4–5, 13, 35, 81, 89, 92, 94, 98–9, and 103.

writing before the Statute entered into force, described the relationship between the Statute and customary law as follows:

> In many areas the Statute may be regarded as indicative of the legal views, i.e. *opinio juris* of a great number of States. Notwithstanding article 10 of the Statute, the purpose of which is to ensure that existing or developing law is not 'limited' or 'prejudiced' by the Statute's provisions, resort may be had *cum grano salis* to these provisions to help elucidate customary international law. Depending on the matter at issue, the Rome Statute may be taken to restate, reflect or clarify customary rules or crystallise them, whereas in some areas it creates new law or modifies existing law. At any event, the Rome Statute by and large may be taken as constituting an authoritative expression of the legal views of a great number of States.[47]

In *Furundzija*, the Trial Chamber referred to the Rome Statute to help determine, inter alia, modes of liability under customary international law.[48] These examples support the view that Article 10 serves not as an absolute bar to the Statute's use as evidence of *opinio juris*. Its role as evidence of progressive development appears to be relatively widespread.

Legal effect

There is no analogue to Article 10 in the Statutes for the ICTY or for the International Criminal Tribunal for Rwanda (ICTR). In the case of the ICTY, the UN Secretary-General's report to the UN Security Council on the establishment of the Tribunal made clear that it was intended to apply 'existing international humanitarian law'.[49] This caveat was not codified in the ICTY Statute, but there is no support for concluding that this omission reflects any disagreement with the quoted paragraph of the Secretary-General's report.

In contrast to the drafters of the ICTY and ICTR Statutes, the participants at the Diplomatic Conference in 1998 included explicit language attempting to clarify the Statute's effect on developing international law. In this regard, it is worth asking whether the legal effect of Article 10 of the Rome Statute matches their intended purpose. The effect of this Article depends first on whether the customary international law rules referred to within the Rome Statute are peremptory (*jus cogens*) norms. If they are not, the result depends on the legal effect of a conventional rule that overlaps a customary rule.

---

[47] International Criminal Tribunal for the former Yugoslavia (ICTY), *Prosecutor v. Furundzija*, Case No. IT-95.17/1-T, Judgment of 10 December 1998, para. 227.

[48] *Ibid.*, para. 231.

[49] Report of the Secretary-General pursuant to paragraph 2 of Security Council Resolution 808 (1993), UN doc. S/25704, New York, 3 May 1993, p. 6, para. 29 ('It should be pointed out that, in assigning to the International Tribunal the task of prosecuting persons responsible for serious violations of international humanitarian law, the Security Council would not be creating or purporting to "legislate" that law. Rather, the International Tribunal would have the task of applying existing international humanitarian law').

Peremptory *(jus cogens)* norms   If the customary international law rules in question are peremptory norms of international humanitarian law, then Article 10 serves merely as a reminder of the existing rules of treaty interpretation. According to Article 53 of the 1969 Vienna Convention on the Law of Treaties (VCLT):

> A treaty is void if, at the time of its conclusion, it conflicts with a peremptory norm of general international law. For the purposes of the present Convention, a peremptory norm of general international law is a norm accepted and recognized by the international community of States as a whole as a norm from which no derogation is permitted and which can be modified only by a subsequent norm of general international law having the same character.[50]

A treaty cannot alter states' obligations to abide by a peremptory norm of international law. Thus, if the prohibition on weapons that are of a nature to cause superfluous injury or unnecessary suffering, or that are inherently indiscriminate, is a peremptory norm, then the Rome Statute cannot affect its status or content. Continuing with the example of prohibited weapons, if Article 8(2)(b)(xx) refers to a peremptory norm of customary international law, then the provision can only be interpreted to narrow the ICC's jurisdiction to adjudicate weapons prohibited under customary international law – the Article cannot affect the underlying customary international law rule itself.

Overlap between customary rule and conventional rule: two views   On the other hand, if the above customary international law rule is *not* peremptory, then the result is less straightforward. There are at least two competing views about the legal effect of an overlap between customary and treaty rules. The ICJ stated in *Military and Paramilitary Activities in and Against Nicaragua*:

> Even if a treaty norm and a customary norm … were to have exactly the same content, this would not be a reason for the Court to take the view that the operation of the treaty process must necessarily deprive the customary norm of its separate applicability.[51]

That is, the ICJ takes the view that a customary norm – even if codified in treaty form – continues to exist independently. Under this view, the customary rules embodied in the Rome Statute would continue to apply regardless of Article 10. For example, the Rome Statute's narrow interpretation of prohibited weapons in Article 8(2)(b)(xx) would preclude the ICC from exercising jurisdiction over the use of weapons not included in the list, but this provision would *not*

---

[50] Vienna Convention on the Law of Treaties, Vienna, 23 May 1969, in force 27 January 1980, 1155 UNTS 331; 8 ILM 679 (hereafter, VCLT), Art. 53.

[51] International Court of Justice (ICJ), *Military and Paramilitary Activities in and against Nicaragua (Nicaragua v. United States of America)*, Judgment of 27 June 1986, para. 175.

affect the underlying customary international law prohibition against the use of weapons that are inherently indiscriminate or of a nature to cause superfluous injury or unnecessary suffering.[52]

A second view of the relationship between treaty rules and customary international law holds that codification 'subsume[s]' the customary rule: the treaty rule replaces the customary rule in its entirety.[53] According to this view, in the absence of Article 10, the Rome Statute's definition of war crimes, crimes against humanity and genocide could replace the customary rules upon which these definitions were based. Of course, the Rome Statute cannot alter the obligations of states parties to the Statute vis-à-vis non-parties;[54] the customary weapons prohibition would continue to apply to non-parties. Nonetheless, given that there are currently 121 states parties to the Rome Statute, there are relatively few non-state members for which these obligations would remain in force.[55]

This second approach to overlap between treaty rules and customary rules, rather than the ICJ view, seems to hold greatest sway among states. Foreign ministries typically assign greater importance to treaty rules,[56] consistent with the canon of interpretation whereby the *lex specialis* prevails over a more general rule.[57]

---

[52] See 1977 Additional Protocol I, Arts. 35(2) and 51(4) (prohibiting, respectively, weapons 'of a nature to cause superfluous injury or unnecessary suffering' and 'attacks … which employ a method or means of combat … of a nature to strike military objectives and civilians or civilian objects without distinction'). Both rules are considered part of customary international law. See e.g. Henckaerts and Doswald-Beck, *Customary International Humanitarian Law*, pp. 40 and 237.

[53] See, e.g. M. E. Villiger, *Customary International Law and Treaties: A Manual on the Theory and Practice of the Interrelation of Sources* (The Hague: Kluwer Law International, 1997), p. 151, para. 228 (describing the various theories on the effect of an overlapping treaty and customary rule). See also P. Reuter, *Introduction to the Law of Treaties*, transl. J. Mico and P. Haggenmacher (London: Kegan Paul International, 1995), p. 141, para. 217 (criticising the ICJ decision in the *Military and Paramilitary Activities in and against Nicaragua* Case on the grounds that the ICJ's reasoning would preclude the use of reservations for treaties that codify customary international law).

[54] VCLT, Art. 30. See, also C. J. Borgen, 'Treaty conflicts and normative fragmentation' in D. B. Hollis (ed.), *The Oxford Guide to Treaties* (Oxford University Press, 2012), pp. 464–5 (describing the *lex prior* and *pacta sunt servanda* canons of treaty interpretation, whereby the earlier instrument prevails over the later one, particularly when the states parties to the first instrument are not identical to the parties to the second instrument).

[55] As of writing, there were 122 states parties to the Rome Statute. *ICC – The State Parties to the Rome Statute*, available at: www.icc-cpi.int.

[56] A. Aust, 'Vienna Convention on the Law of Treaties (1969)' para. 19, in *Max Planck Encyclopedia of Public International Law* (June 2006). See also Reuter, *Introduction to the Law of Treaties*, pp. 139–40, para. 216 ('[M]ost governments hold that the written treaty prevails').

[57] But, see International Law Commission, 'Conclusions of the work of the Study Group on the Fragmentation of International Law: Difficulties arising from the diversification and expansion of international law', para. 10 (2006) in *International Law Commission, Report on the Work of its 58th Session* (1 May to 9 June and 3 July to 1 August 2006) UN doc. A/61/10,

In addition, the perceived primacy of treaties can perhaps be at least partially explained by the treaty's status as both source and evidence of law:

> The treaty is a primary source in the sense that the treaty is not only the evidence of the law but also the source of its validity. On the other hand, written evidences not in treaty form are mere evidences; for the source of the validity of the law in this case is custom.[58]

In short, treaties provide a straightforward declaration of states parties' agreement to be legally bound by the treaty's provisions, whereas corresponding rules of customary international law require an inquiry into both their content and validity. While a treaty's content and validity derives directly from its text, customary international law emerges through accumulated evidence of state practice and *opinio juris*, often peppered with variations in the precise formulation of the rule. Baxter offers an additional, practical reason for favouring treaties:

> [They] provide a clear and uniform statement of the rule to which a number of States subscribe. There is no problem of varying inconsistent State practice of varying antiquity and varying authority. The treaty speaks with one voice as of one time.[59]

Debates over interpretation aside, the treaty provides a clearer expression of the rule than rules of customary international law shaped by divergent practice.

For all of the above reasons, the theory that treaty rules replace overlapping customary rules holds a certain appeal for states. If states tend to subscribe to this 'replacement' theory, then advocates of the customary international humanitarian law prohibition on weapons that are inherently indiscriminate or of a nature to cause unnecessary suffering or superfluous injury understandably breathed a sigh of relief upon the adoption of Article 10 of the Rome Statute. While the ICJ's position asserting the independent existence of overlapping treaty and customary rules appears logically sounder than the replacement theory, the ICJ view poses a few practical difficulties. First, even if a treaty precisely codifies a customary law rule, the differing rules for interpreting treaty versus customary law may lead to different interpretations over time.

---

para. 251 (noting that in addition to a conflict with a general rule that is *jus cogens*, the general rule may also prevail over the special rule when 'such prevalence may be inferred from the form or the nature of the general law or intent of the parties', when 'the application of the special law might frustrate the purpose of the general law', when 'third party beneficiaries may be negatively affected by the special law', and when 'the balance of rights and obligations, established in the general law would be negatively affected by the special law').

[58] R. Y. Jennings, 'The progressive development of international law and its codification', *British Yearbook of International Law* 24 (1947), 301–29, at 303.

[59] R. R. Baxter, 'Multilateral treaties as evidence of customary international law', *British Yearbook of International Law* 41 (1965–66), 275–300, at 300.

As a result, the law applicable to parties to the treaty may differ from the law applicable to non-parties:

> If ... [a treaty] is in fact declaratory of existing customary law, third states not parties to the treaty will, of course, be bound by identical rules derived not from the treaty but from customary law. But in practice the position can never be quite as simple as that ... After being reduced to written form the rule is almost bound to take on a rather different colour. The change of source from custom to treaty may seem to be purely formal and adjectival, but it has inevitable repercussions on the substance.[60]

Moreover, there is a practical difficulty involved in assessing the development of a customary international law rule that overlaps with a treaty rule: how should one evaluate subsequent state practice? If a state party is bound by a treaty rule identical to a pre-existing customary law rule, then it becomes nearly impossible to distinguish which rule led the state to adopt certain behaviour:

> [T]he formulation of a customary rule extending beyond the parties to the treaty is not in the first place determined by the treaty as such but by the fact that non-parties have applied its rules or recognized their customary character, or at least put up with their application by others in circumstances where they would normally have been expected to object.[61]

This is the classic Baxter paradox:[62] 'only the practice of non-parties is unqualifiedly constitutive of customary law.'[63] For example, the state practice of non-parties to the Rome Statute in recognising that the widespread or systematic use of rape as a tool of war can qualify as a crime against humanity forms the only unequivocal evidence of a developing norm of customary international law. One may point to the large number of states parties to the Statute as evidence of an emerging consensus prohibiting such crimes as a matter of international law, but states parties' behaviour in complying with the Statute's provisions tends to demonstrate no more than their observance of the rule *pacta sunt servanda*. But, as Villiger notes, '[e]xceptions are conceivable', as when a state party explains its behaviour in terms of compliance with the customary rule, independent of its obligations under the relevant convention.[64]

On the one hand, this result appears to grant non-parties to the Treaty disproportionate influence in determining the development of the customary

---

[60] Jennings, 'The progressive development of international law and its codification', pp. 304–5.

[61] Reuter, *Introduction to the Law of Treaties*, p. 109, para. 166.

[62] R. R. Baxter, 'Treaties and Custom', *Recueil des Cours* 129 (1970 I), 27–105, at 64, cited in T. Meron, 'The continuing role of custom in the formation of international humanitarian law', *American Journal of International Law* 90 (1996), 238–49, at 247.

[63] Villiger, *Customary International Law and Treaties*, p. 155, para. 234.

[64] *Ibid.* p. 183, para. 283.

rule. Alternatively, it reduces the number of states required to demonstrate widespread practice. If the states not party to the Rome Statute nevertheless recognise rape as an overt act under the statutory definition of a crime against humanity, leading to a binding customary international law rule, then states parties to the Rome Statute that subsequently decide to withdraw from the ICC's jurisdiction would remain nonetheless bound by the customary international law rule developed while the state remained a party to the Statute. In practice then, consent to this provision could no longer be withdrawn.

Cause for concern?   In sum, Article 10 has no independent legal effect if the underlying customary norm with which the Treaty overlaps is a peremptory norm or if one adopts the ICJ position that customary international law rules continue to exist independent of their codification in treaty form. If, on the other hand, an overlapping treaty provision displaces the customary rule in its entirety, then Article 10 would appear to protect customary IHL rules from regressive Rome Statute provisions such as Article 8(2)(b)(xx). This is not the case, however. The primary threat to customary international humanitarian law that Article 8(2)(b)(xx) represents comes not from the direct application of the Rome Statute, but rather from the development of state practice and *opinio juris* after the Statute's passage:

> [T]he more States parties adhere to the convention, the less States will engage in practice upon the customary rule which will eventually – and gradually – cease to attract the required widespread practice. As a result, the original customary rule may either be reduced to a special customary rule, or it may pass out of use – for instance, if it is modified by a new general customary rule that develops on the basis of a conventional rule.[65]

Provided the underlying customary rule is *not* a peremptory norm, the danger is that states will come to view the prohibition on certain weapons as coextensive with the Rome Statute, and begin gradually to develop state practice and *opinio juris* in support of the use of these weapons. Article 10 could not halt this development.[66]

---

[65] See Cassese, *International Criminal Law*, p. 60 (expressing concern that Article 8(2)(b) (xx) of the Rome Statute may weaken the customary international humanitarian law prohibition on weapons that are indiscriminate or of a nature to cause superfluous injury or unnecessary suffering).

[66] VCLT, Art. 38 ('Nothing in articles 34 to 37 precludes a rule set forth in a treaty from becoming binding upon a third State as a customary rule of international law, recognized as such'). See also Villiger, *Customary International Law and Treaties*, p. 159, para. 241 (asserting 'the existence of a customary rule simply cannot, and will not, depend upon conventional clauses').

2. *Article 21: sources of law*

Intention and content

Article 21 of the Rome Statute outlines the International Criminal Court's hierarchy of legal sources. The Court looks first to the Statute itself, and its rules of procedure and evidence.[67] Second, the Court shall apply 'where appropriate, applicable treaties and the principles and rules of international law, including the *established principles of the international law of armed conflict*'.[68] If these sources of law prove insufficient, Article 21 instructs the Court to apply 'general principles of law derived by the court from national laws of legal systems of the world'.[69] In addition, Article 21 also specifies that the Court may look to its own decisions for subsequent interpretation.

It could be argued that the reference to 'applicable treaties and the principles and rules of international law' simply restates Article 31(3)(c) of the VCLT, which provides that when interpreting the meaning of a treaty's provisions, 'any relevant rules of international law applicable in the relations between the parties' shall be taken into account. Article 21 nevertheless establishes a clear hierarchy of sources, by instructing judges to refer to the 'relevant rules of international law' only to resolve any ambiguity or lacunae in the Statute and its rules of procedure and evidence.

For terms left undefined in the Statute, such as 'inherently indiscriminate' and 'superfluous injury or unnecessary suffering', the reference to 'applicable treaties' in Article 21 of the Rome Statute permits ICC judges to refer in future cases to international law outside of the Rome Statute for questions of interpretation. In fact, the participants in the 1998 Rome Statute negotiations discussed in particular defining torture with reference to the 1984 Convention against Torture and Other Cruel, Inhuman, or Degrading Treatment or Punishment.[70]

Legal effect

For Article 8(2)(b)(xx), the plain wording of the 'provided that' stipulation indicates that this provision remains inoperative unless and until an annex containing a list of prohibited weapons is appended to the Statute. According to Article 21, if this annex were created, then the Court could look to IHL as a subsidiary means of interpreting the terms 'inherently indiscriminate' and 'superfluous injury or unnecessary suffering'. As McAuliffe deGuzman opines:

> Article 21 refers, in particular, to 'the established principles of the international law of armed conflict'. The Statute is silent, however, on the

---

[67] Rome Statute, Art. 21(1)(a).   [68] *Ibid.*, Art. 21(1)(b) (emphasis added).

[69] *Ibid.*, Art. 21(1)(c).

[70] P. Saland, 'International criminal law principles' in R. S. Lee (ed.), *The International Criminal Court: The Making of the Rome Statute*, 2nd edn (The Hague: Kluwer Law International, 2002), p. 215.

distinction between these principles and those embodied in the laws of armed conflict reflected in article 8 of the Statute.[71]

McAuliffe deGuzman's critique hints at the dilemma the ICC may face in the future for provisions of Article 8 that diverge from the law of armed conflict. For example, a rule of customary international law could develop whereby the rule of distinction becomes inextricably linked to the customary prohibition on weapons that are inherently indiscriminate. If these rules become inter-linked, might such weapons be criminalised under Article 8(2)(b)(i) and (ii), which criminalises intentional acts against the civilian population or civilian objects? Depending on whether intent can be inferred from the use of an inherently indiscriminate weapon, the answer may be yes.

As Gardiner notes, recent judicial decisions demonstrate international courts' increasing willingness to allow for an 'evolutionary interpretation by reference to developments in the law outside the immediate confines of a particular treaty'.[72] Although this is not a general rule, courts may determine the meaning of a term left undefined in a treaty by looking to contemporary rules of international law, regardless of the term's meaning at the time of the treaty's adoption.[73] Gardiner notes that the key factor in determining the time period for the relevant international law is the extent to which 'changed circumstances affect interpretation of a treaty', based on whether the treaty appears to allow for an 'evolutive' interpretation.[74]

This is not to argue that such a development with regard to prohibited weapons is necessarily likely, but rather to illustrate the somewhat fluid and ambiguous relationship between customary international humanitarian law and overlapping treaty provisions. Although Article 10 attempts to bar the Rome Statute from affecting customary international law, Article 21 allows customary international law to shape the Rome Statute.

C.   Implications of Article 8(2)(b)(xx) for nuclear weapons

1.   No change to lex lata … yet

At this stage, it is safe to assert that Article 8(2)(b)(xx) of the Rome Statute has not limited the prohibition of weapons that are inherently indiscriminate or of a nature to cause superfluous injury or unnecessary suffering. In fact, other provisions of the Rome Statute would almost certainly apply to the use of such

---

[71] McAuliffe deGuzman, 'Article 21: applicable law', p. 441.

[72] R. Gardiner, *Treaty Interpretation* (Oxford University Press, 2008), p. 252.

[73] See *ibid.*, pp. 252–3 (describing the continuing relevance of the inter-temporal principal, whereby courts determine the meaning of a treaty based on the applicable international law at the time the treaty was adopted).

[74] *Ibid.*, p. 254. However, see Article 22(2) of the Rome Statute.

weapons, not least the rule of distinction. Chapter 8 describes these potential bases for criminal liability under the Rome Statute in more depth.

Nevertheless, as this chapter has attempted to demonstrate, the Rome Statute cannot preclude either a progressive or a regressive development of customary international law, regardless of Article 10. As Danilenko opines, in reference to the more progressive provisions of the Rome Statute:

> Whatever the status of these provisions included in the Rome Statute at this stage, one cannot exclude the possibility that in due time they may gradually pass into the body of generally binding law. It is well recognized that new rules embodied in a treaty may come to be regarded as general standards of behaviour even by States that are not parties to the treaty. The passage of treaty norms into the body of general law depends on the subsequent practice of States. If the subsequent practice supports innovations in the field of substantive criminal law, the Rome Statute will make an important contribution to the emergence of new customary law, even though Article 10 states that the relevant definitions of crimes cannot limit or prejudice in any way 'developing rules of international law for purposes other than this Statute'.[75]

This argument illustrates how pointing to specific provisions of the Rome Statute as evidence of a progressive development of customary international law represents a double-edged sword. Moreover, Article 21 opens up the possibility for customary international law to shape the Rome Statute, as a subsidiary means of interpretation. While neither of these observations need raise cause for alarm, they underscore the necessity of maintaining vigilance to prevent the dilution of customary international law.

2.   Alternative enforcement mechanisms for prohibited weapons

Despite the limits to the ICC's jurisdiction over crimes involving weapons prohibited under customary international humanitarian law, several mechanisms for enforcing this prohibition remain, although these vary considerably based on whether enforcement is binding and on the strength of the measures described.

First, states may prosecute or extradite individuals charged with violating the ban on weapons that are inherently indiscriminate or of a nature to cause superfluous injury or unnecessary suffering. States may initiate domestic enforcement through civilian courts or military tribunals, or through an international ad hoc tribunal, of which the ICTY and ICTR are just two of many

---

[75] G. Danilenko, 'ICC statute and third states' in A. Cassese *et al.* (eds.), *The Rome Statute of the International Criminal Court: A Commentary,* 3 vols. (Oxford University Press, 2002), Vol. II, p. 1895.

historical examples.[76] For example, the Norwegian General Civil Penal Code §16 grants civilian courts jurisdiction over war crimes, crimes against humanity and genocide.[77] In amending the General Civil Penal Code to include prohibited weapons not covered in the Rome Statute, the Norwegian Parliament's Judicial Committee explicitly stated its intention to widen the definition of war crimes under Norwegian law to comply with Norway's existing international humanitarian law obligations, regardless of whether the Rome Statute granted the ICC jurisdiction over the included crimes.[78]

Second, for weapons subject to a comprehensive ban, for example not including nuclear weapons, enforcement provisions also exist in certain conventions, although there is no systematic provision demanding that states parties institute individual criminal liability. In addition, these mechanisms generally do not impose binding enforcement obligations. The majority of convention enforcement provisions fall into some combination of: (1) a requirement to resolve disputes through negotiation, or (2) a procedure for requesting further investigation or assistance from a UN organ. For example, Article VI of the 1971 Biological and Toxin Weapons Convention (BTWC) permits any state party to lodge a complaint with the UN Security Council to the effect that another state party has not complied with its obligations under the Convention, and requires all states parties to submit to any eventual investigation the Security Council may undertake.[79] Article 14(4) of the Amended Protocol II to the 1980 Convention on Certain Conventional Weapons (CCW)[80] requires states parties to agree to resolve disputes over the implementation of the Treaty through negotiation 'bilaterally, through the Secretary-General of the United

[76] J. J. Paust, 'Crimes within the limited jurisdiction of the International Criminal Court' in J. Carey et al. (eds.), International Humanitarian Law: Origins, Challenges, Prospects (Leiden: Martinus Nijhoff Publishers, 2006), 'International Humanitarian Law: Prospects', p. 190.

[77] The General Civil Penal Code with subsequent amendments, the latest made by Act of 7 March 2008 No. 4, § 16.

[78] Justice Committee, Recommendation of the Justice Committee on Amendments to the Criminal Code 20 May 2005 No. 28, etc. (aggravating and mitigating circumstances, genocide, national independence, terrorism, peace, order and security, and public authorities), Innst. O. nr. 29 (2007–2008) (5 February 2008), § 5.2 ('The Committee agreed that the Norwegian penal provisions of genocide, crimes against humanity and war crimes should not only deal with the crimes included in the Rome Statute, but that these provisions also include the obligations of other conventions ratified by Norway and customary international law').

[79] Convention on the Prohibition of the Development, Production and Stockpiling of Bacteriological (Biological) and Toxin Weapons and on their Destruction, New York, 16 December 1971, in force 26 March 1975, 1015 UNTS 163), Art. VI.

[80] Convention on Prohibitions or Restrictions on the Use of Certain Conventional Weapons Which May be Deemed to be Excessively Injurious or to Have Indiscriminate Effects (and Protocols), Geneva, 10 October 1980, in force 2 December 1983, 1342 UNTS 137; as amended, Geneva, 21 December 2001, in force 18 May 2004.

Nations or through other appropriate international procedures'. Article XIV of the 1992 Chemical Weapons Convention (CWC) provides for disputes to be resolved through negotiation, or, dependent on the consent of both states, through adjudication in the ICJ.[81] Article 10 of the 2008 Convention on Cluster Munitions[82] provides for the same. Article 8 of the 1997 Anti-Personnel Mine Ban Convention permits parties to send another state party a 'request for clarification' through the UN Secretary-General regarding the receiving state party's compliance with the Convention.[83] Again, none of the above-mentioned treaty mechanisms apply to nuclear weapons.

Third, the Geneva Conventions and their Protocols include several enforcement mechanisms.[84] Geneva Convention, I Article 8; Geneva Convention II, Article 8; Geneva Convention III, Article 8; Geneva Convention IV, Article 9; and Additional Protocol I, Article 5 authorise the designation of Protecting Powers, charged with 'safeguard[ing] the interests of the Parties to the conflict'. Article 90 of Additional Protocol I allows twenty or more states parties to bring an International Fact-Finding Commission to investigate potential violations of international humanitarian law into existence. Article 89 of Additional Protocol I also calls on parties to cooperate with the UN in the case of serious violations of the Conventions. Lastly, the unique role of the ICRC is outlined in Geneva Convention I, Article 9; Geneva Convention II, Article 9; Geneva Convention III, Articles 9 and 126; Geneva Convention IV, Articles 10 and 143; and Additional Protocol I, Article 81.

Conclusion

The history of nuclear weapons under the Rome Statute dates back to the negotiations to create the statute, when a proposal to criminalise the use of nuclear weapons nearly derailed the entire negotiations. The resulting compromise provision gutted the proposed text embodying the customary international humanitarian law prohibition against indiscriminate weapons or weapons of a nature to cause superfluous injury or unnecessary suffering. Instead, Article 8(2)(b)(xx) explicitly criminalises the use of such weapons only insofar as they are listed in an annex to the Rome Statute that, at the date of writing, does not yet exist. State proponents of criminalising the use of nuclear weapons have

---

[81] Convention on the Prohibition of the Development, Production, Stockpiling and Use of Chemical Weapons and on their Destruction, Geneva, 3 September 1992, in force 29 April 1993, 32 ILM 800, Art. XIV.

[82] Convention on Cluster Munitions, Dublin, 30 May 2008, in force 1 August 2010, 48 ILM 354.

[83] Anti-Personnel Mine Ban Convention.

[84] Listed in K. Dörmann and L. Maresca, 'The International Committee of the Red Cross and its contribution to the development of international humanitarian law in specialized instruments', *Chicago Journal of International Law* 5(1) (2004–05), 217–32, at 225, n. 22.

not given up, however. In 2009 Mexico proposed an amendment to the Rome Statute to criminalise the '*threat* or use of nuclear weapons' (emphasis added), consistent with the formulation of the question the UN General Assembly put to the ICJ in the oft-debated Nuclear Weapons Advisory Opinion. Mexico's proposal gained only marginal support from the start, yet it illustrates the continuing debate over the status of nuclear weapons among states parties to the Rome Statute.

This chapter also examines the relationship between the provisions of the Rome Statute and overlapping provisions of customary international law, using the status of nuclear weapons as a catalyst for discussion. While there is a possibility that the Rome Statute's restrictive interpretation of the relevant provisions of Additional Protocol I to the Geneva Conventions could *indirectly* lead to a change in customary law, if state practice and *opinio juris* adopt the more restrictive interpretation for issues outside the Rome Statute's jurisdiction, this scenario appears highly unlikely.

Lastly, given that the Rome Statute does not grant the ICC jurisdiction over the violation of customary international humanitarian law regarding prohibited weapons, this chapter outlines the avenues that remain for enforcing these prohibitions. These enforcement mechanisms include domestic prosecution under national law, dispute resolution mechanisms developed under the various weapons conventions (often, negotiations or referral to the UN Security Council) and the specific IHL enforcement mechanisms enshrined in the Geneva Conventions and their Protocols, such as Protecting Powers and international fact-finding missions.

PART IV

International environmental law

10

Use of nuclear weapons and protection of the environment during international armed conflict

ERIK V. KOPPE

Introduction

Nuclear weapons are potentially the most destructive weapons ever invented. The almost unimaginable impact of the use of nuclear weapons, including on the environment, was recognised by the International Court of Justice (ICJ) in its 1996 Advisory Opinion on the legality of the threat or use of nuclear weapons[1] (hereafter, Nuclear Weapons Advisory Opinion). As the ICJ recognised, their characteristics render nuclear weapons:

> potentially catastrophic. The destructive power of nuclear weapons cannot be contained in either space or time. They have the potential to destroy all civilization and the entire ecosystem of the planet. The radiation release by a nuclear explosion would affect health, agriculture, natural resources and demography over a very wide area. Further, the use of nuclear weapons would be a serious danger to future generations. Ionizing radiation has the potential to damage the future environment, food and marine ecosystem, and to cause genetic defects and illness in future generations.[2]

In the case of a use of nuclear weapons, however, the Court's discussion of the relevant rules of public international law governing the protection of the environment is rather general. The Court stated in this regard:

> States must take environmental considerations into account when assessing what is necessary and proportionate in the pursuit of legitimate military objectives. Respect for the environment is one of the elements that go to assessing whether an action is in conformity with the principles of necessity and proportionality ...
>   The Court thus finds that while the existing international law relating to the protection and safeguarding of the environment does not specifically

---

[1] ICJ, *Legality of the Threat or Use of Nuclear Weapons*, Advisory Opinion, 8 July 1996, para. 35 (hereafter, Nuclear Weapons Advisory Opinion). For more information on the characteristics of nuclear weapons and the effects of nuclear explosions, see E. V. Koppe, *The Use of Nuclear Weapons and the Protection of the Environment during International Armed Conflict* (Oxford: Hart Publishing, 2008), pp. 47–105.

[2] Nuclear Weapons Advisory Opinion, para. 35.

prohibit the use of nuclear weapons, it indicates important environmental factors that are properly to be taken into account in the context of the
implementation of the principles and rules of the law applicable in armed
conflict.[3]

In view of the environmental consequences of the use of any nuclear weapon,
the general concern for the environment during armed conflict since 1972,[4]
and the development of specific rules of public international law in this area,
the ICJ's analysis might appear rather unambitious. Further, it is surprising that
the Court chose to discuss rules protecting the environment during armed conflict separately from its assessment of the legality of the use of nuclear weapons
under 'the law applicable in armed conflict, in particular humanitarian law'
(para. 36).

In view of recent developments relating to the possession and use of nuclear
weapons[5] and renewed interest in the law governing the protection of the environment in relation to armed conflict,[6] further clarification of the applicable
law is warranted. This chapter seeks to clarify the scope of the relevant rules
of the law of armed conflict and to assess, *in abstracto*, the legality of use of
nuclear weapons under these rules.[7] It first describes relevant rules of treaty law

---

[3] Nuclear Weapons Advisory Opinion, paras. 30, 33.

[4] Principle 26 of the Stockholm Declaration provides: 'Man *and his environment* must be
spared the effects of nuclear weapons and all other means of mass destruction' (emphasis
added) (UN doc. A/CONF.48/14/Rev.1). See also para. 5 of the 1982 World Charter for
Nature (A/Res/37/7), Principle 24 of the 1992 Rio Declaration (UN doc. A/CONF.151/26/
Rev.l (Vol. I), and A/Res/47/37 (protection of the environment during armed conflict) in
this context.

[5] See the International Conference on the Humanitarian Impact of Nuclear Weapons,
hosted by Norway in Oslo on 4–5 March 2013, available at: www.humimpact2013.no, and
Resolution 1 of the Council of Delegates of the International Red Cross and Red Crescent
Movement, Geneva, 26 November 2011, which focuses on the elimination of nuclear weapons. See also President Obama's announcement in Berlin on 19 June 2013 that he would seek
a further reduction of deployed nuclear weapons from the level established with Russia in the
New START treaty. See The White House, Office of the Press Secretary, 'Fact Sheet: Nuclear
Weapons Employment Strategy of the United States', 19 June 2013, available at: www.white-
house.gov/the-press-office/2013/06/19/fact-sheet-nuclear-weapons-employment-strategy-
united-states.

[6] In 2011 the International Law Commission (ILC) decided to include the protection of the
environment in relation to armed conflicts in its long-term programme of work. UN doc.
A/66/10, Report of the International Law Commission, Sixty-third session (26 April–3 June
and 4 July–12 August 2011), para. 365. See ILC, 'Protection of the environment in relation to
armed conflicts', last updated 5 June 2013, http://legal.un.org/ilc/guide/8_7.htm.

[7] Protection of the environment during armed conflict also follows from *jus ad bellum* and
jus pacis. The protection of the environment during armed conflict under *jus ad bellum*
follows from the establishment by the Security Council in 1991 of Iraq's responsibility for
all environmental damage resulting from its illegal use of force against Kuwait (Resolution

relating to the protection of the environment during international armed conflict (Section A). It then discusses protection of the environment during armed conflict under customary international law (Section B). The chapter ends with a brief conclusion.

A.   Protection of the environment under treaty law

The protection of the environment under the law of armed conflict is specifically regulated in four treaties:[8] the 1976 ENMOD Convention,[9] 1977 Additional Protocol I,[10] the 1980 Incendiary Weapons Protocol (Protocol III to the 1980 Convention on Certain Conventional Weapons)[11] and the 1998 Rome

---

687, para. 16). The protection of the environment during armed conflict under *jus pacis* follows from the continuing applicability of rules of international environmental law in the relationship between belligerents and non-belligerents and in the relationship between belligerents *inter se*. According to the ILC, treaties relating to the international protection of the environment are presumed to remain fully operational during armed conflict due to their subject matter. See Article 7 and Annex under (g) of the 2011 Draft Articles on the Effects of Armed Conflicts on Treaties (UN doc. A/66/10), which was commended by the UN General Assembly in its Resolution 66/98 of 9 December 2011. For a discussion of the protection of the environment during armed conflict under *jus ad bellum* and *jus pacis*, see Koppe, *The Use of Nuclear Weapons*, Chapters 4 and 5. On the relationship and overlap between *jus ad bellum* and *jus in bello*, see E. V. Koppe, 'Compensation for War Damages under Jus ad Bellum' in: A. de Guttry, H. H. G. Post and G. Venturini (eds.), *The 1998–2000 War between Eritrea and Ethiopia: An International Legal Perspective* (The Hague: T. M. C. Asser Press, 2009).

[8]   The law of neutrality, which is part of the law of armed conflict and which prescribes the inviolability of the territory of neutral states (see Article 1 of 1907 Hague Convention V Respecting the Rights and Duties of Neutral Powers and Persons in Case of War on Land), may have a significant impact on protection of the environment during armed conflict. However, the law of neutrality in case of environmental harm may have been effectively displaced by the continuing applicability of rules of international environmental law between belligerent states and non-belligerent states. For more discussion, including details of state practice regarding compensation paid by Allied Powers for damage caused in Switzerland by shockwaves from bombing attacks on a German border town during the Second World War, see Koppe, *The Use of Nuclear Weapons*, pp. 297–308 and 335–64.

[9]   Convention on the Prohibition of Military or any Other Hostile Use of Environmental Modification Techniques, New York, 10 December 1976, in force 5 October 1978, 1108 UNTS 151 (No. 17119).

[10]   Protocol Additional to the Geneva Conventions of 12 August 1949, and Relating to the Protection of Victims of International Armed Conflicts (Protocol I), Geneva, 8 June 1977, in force 7 December 1978, 1125 UNTS 3 (No. 17512).

[11]   Protocol on Prohibitions or Restrictions on the Use of Incendiary Weapons (Protocol III) to the Convention on Prohibitions or Restrictions on the Use of Certain Conventional Weapons which May Be Deemed to Be Excessively Injurious or to Have Indiscriminate Effects, Geneva, 10 October 1980, in force 2 December 1983, 1342 UNTS 137 (No. 22495).

Statute of the International Criminal Court (ICC Statute).[12] Of these four treaties, only 1977 Additional Protocol I is directly relevant to the present discussion. ENMOD is not specifically relevant because its Article I prohibits use of environmental modification techniques as such, irrespective of any use of nuclear weapons.[13] The 1980 Incendiary Weapons Protocol is not relevant since nuclear weapons do not fall within the definition of incendiary weapons under that Protocol.[14] Lastly, the ICC Statute leads to individual criminal responsibility rather than state responsibility and will therefore not be discussed in any detail.

1. *Articles 35(3) and 55, 1977 Additional Protocol I*

Additional Protocol I to the four 1949 Geneva Conventions was negotiated in Geneva between 1974 and 1977 and was intended to reaffirm and develop international humanitarian law (IHL). The Protocol merges the classic conduct of hostilities law of The Hague with the humanitarian law of Geneva, with a

---

[12] Rome Statute of the International Criminal Court, Rome, 17 July 1998, in force 1 July 2002, 2187 UNTS, 90 (No. 38544).

[13] Even if nuclear weapons were used to manipulate natural processes, for example to cause tsunamis or earthquakes as explained in the Convention's Understanding Relating to Article II, it would still be the use of the environmental modification technique, and not the use of nuclear weapons as such, that would constitute a violation of Art. I of ENMOD. Although reference to the use of herbicides in the Final Declaration following the Second Review Conference of the states parties to ENMOD in 1992 could be interpreted as broadening the scope of ENMOD ('The Conference confirms that the military or any other hostile use of herbicides as an environmental modification technique in the meaning of Article II is a method of warfare prohibited by Article I if such use of herbicides upsets the ecological balance of a region, thus causing widespread, long-lasting or severe effects as the means of destruction, damage or injury to any other Party'), the declaration cites the use of herbicides *as an environmental modification technique*, and thus does not serve as state practice to go beyond the text of the Convention. The ICJ did not discuss the legality of the use of nuclear weapons as such under ENMOD, despite views expressed by a number of states on this issue (Egypt and Iran argued that the use of nuclear weapons would violate ENMOD; the United States and the United Kingdom opposed this view). See further on the possible applicability of ENMOD to use of nuclear weapons: Koppe, *The Use of Nuclear Weapons*, pp. 130–4, 366.

[14] See the definition in Article 1(1), in which the Protocol defines an incendiary weapon as 'any weapon or munition which is primarily designed to set fire to objects or to cause burn injury to persons through the action of flame, heat, or combination thereof, produced by a chemical reaction of a substance delivered on the target'. Although nuclear weapons have significant incendiary effects (approximately 35 per cent of the explosive energy in the case of a fission weapon and 38 per cent in the case of fusion weapons), the primary effect of a nuclear explosion is a shock wave (approximately 50 per cent in the case of a fission weapon and 54 per cent for a fusion weapon). See Koppe, *The Use of Nuclear Weapons*, pp. 69, 73–4. Further, the heat of a nuclear explosion is not produced by a chemical reaction and the Protocol is annexed to the 1980 Convention on Certain *Conventional* Weapons, which would *ipso facto* render application to nuclear weapons problematic.

view to enhancing protection of the victims of armed conflict.[15] Among the Protocol's 102 Articles, two provisions specifically govern protection of the environment during international armed conflict: Article 35(3) and Article 55.[16] Article 35(3) provides that:

> It is prohibited to employ methods or means of warfare which are intended or may be expected, to cause widespread, long-term and severe damage to the natural environment.

Article 55 provides that:

1. Care shall be taken in warfare to protect the natural environment against widespread, long-term and severe damage. This protection includes a prohibition of the use of methods or means of warfare which are intended or may be expected to cause such damage to the natural environment and thereby to prejudice the health or survival of the population.
2. Attacks against the natural environment by way of reprisals are prohibited.

Both provisions aim to protect the natural environment during international armed conflict in the widest possible sense,[17] including the air and marine environment,[18] but do so in different ways. Whereas Article 35(3) lays down a basic rule on means and methods of warfare and is intended to protect the

---

[15] Nuclear Weapons Advisory Opinion, para. 75.

[16] For a discussion of the possible indirect protection of the environment provided by the customary and conventional rules relating to the protection of civilian objects, see Koppe, *The Use of Nuclear Weapons*, pp. 279–97. Although the environment may indeed qualify as a civilian object, it is submitted that, on the basis of a contextual interpretation of Art. 55, 1977 Additional Protocol I, and in light of the legislative history of Arts. 55 and 35(3), protection of the environment during armed conflict cannot be derived from Arts. 48, 51 and 52 of the Protocol. In relation to the prohibition of excessive collateral damage to the environment and in more detail, see E. V. Koppe, 'The principle of ambituity and the prohibition against excessive collateral damage to the environment during armed conflict', *Nordic Journal of International Law* 82 (2013), 53–87, at 68–75.

[17] C. Pilloud and J. Pictet, 'Article 55' in Y. Sandoz, C. Swinarski and B. Zimmerman (eds.), *Commentary on the Additional Protocols of 8 June 1977 to the Geneva Conventions of 12 August 1949* (Geneva: International Committee of the Red Cross (ICRC)/Martinus Nijhoff Publishers, 1987), para. 2126. See also Article II of ENMOD.

[18] The scope of Art. 35(3), 1977 Additional Protocol I does not appear to be limited to the consequences of land, air or naval warfare for the civilian population on land, as is the case for Art. 55 (see Art. 49(3) of the Protocol). Such would follow, among other things, from the text of the ICRC's Draft Protocol that would form the basis of the negotiations at the 1974–77 Diplomatic Conference. The ICRC envisaged the section on basic rules of the law of armed conflict as applying to 'military operations as a whole carried out within the general framework of land, air or sea warfare'. ICRC, *Draft Additional Protocols to the Geneva Conventions of August 12, 1949: Commentary* (Geneva: ICRC, 1973), p. 54, available at: www.loc.gov/rr/frd/Military_Law/pdf/RC-Draft-additional-protocols.pdf. See Koppe, *The Use of Nuclear Weapons*, pp. 154–67.

intrinsic value of the environment, arguably Article 55 aims to protect the environment as a civilian object (Article 55 is included in Chapter III of Part IV which deals with the protection of the civilian population, including civilian objects), in particular because of its importance for the health and survival of the civilian population. The former provision is therefore generally regarded as ecocentric while the latter is considered anthropocentric.[19]

Although states drafting 1977 Additional Protocol I were concerned for the environment in times of international armed conflict, particularly after witnessing the damage resulting from the war in Vietnam, they did not mean to prohibit ordinary battlefield damage. Indeed, during the Diplomatic Conference, the United Kingdom observed in relation to Article 55 that the provision struck the necessary balance, protecting the environment against severe damage 'while not making for instance, a tank commander whose tank flattened a clump of trees liable as a war criminal'.[20] Further, a conference report stated that:

> The time or duration required ... was considered by some to be measured in decades. References to twenty or thirty years were made by some representatives as being a minimum. Others referred to battlefield destruction in France in the First World War as being outside the scope of the prohibition.

The report also observed that:

> it is impossible to say with certainty what period of time might be involved. It appeared to be a widely shared assumption that battlefield damage incidental to conventional warfare would not normally be proscribed by this provision.[21]

For those reasons, it was agreed that only under exceptional circumstances would damage to the environment lead to a violation of the law of armed conflict. First, Articles 35(3) and 55 of 1977 Additional Protocol I only prohibit use of means and methods that are either intended or expected to cause damage to the environment. Accordingly, each provision prohibits not only deliberate or direct attacks on the environment, but also attacks where it is reasonably

---

[19] M. N. Schmitt, 'Green war: an assessment of the environmental law of international armed conflict', *Yale Journal of International Law* 22 (1997), 1–109, at 70–1. Since Art. 35(3) cannot be deduced from fundamental principles of the law of armed conflict (military necessity, distinction, proportionality and humanity), I have argued elsewhere that Art. 35(3) indicates the existence of a new fundamental principle of the law of armed conflict, namely the principle of ambituity. The word ambituity is derived from the Latin word *ambitus*, which means environment. The principle of ambituity would provide for an absolute limitation to the necessities of war. See Koppe, 'The principle of ambituity', 56–61.

[20] H. S. Levie, *Protection of War Victims: Protocol 1 to the 1949 Geneva Conventions*, 4 vols. (Dobbs Ferry: Oceana Publications, 1980), Vol. III, p. 272.

[21] Report of Committee III, Second Session (CDDH/215/Rev.1), in Levie, *Protection of War Victims*, Vol. II, pp. 276–7.

forseeable that they will lead to excessive collateral environmental damage.[22] This applies irrespective of the weapons used and requires those who deploy these means or methods of warfare to know or reasonably predict that the attack they will launch will have such detrimental effects. This is an important limiting factor since environmental harm is not always directly visible or demonstrable. Natural processes are difficult to analyse and military commanders may not know how certain activities will impact the environment over the long term.[23]

Second, it was agreed that the use of means and methods of warfare would only be prohibited if such means or methods of warfare would lead to 'widespread, long-term and severe' damage to the environment. Indeed, contrary to the drafters of the 1976 ENMOD Convention, the drafters of Articles 35(3) and 55 chose to include a cumulative damage threshold: widespread, long-term *and* severe.[24] Since these terms were not defined, they must be interpreted in accordance with the general rules of treaty interpretation as reflected in Articles 31 and 32 of the 1969 Vienna Convention on the Law of Treaties (VCLT).[25] Potentially, however, establishing the ordinary meaning of the terms widespread, long-term and severe[26] is a highly subjective exercise.[27] Although they indicate a high level of seriousness,[28] arguably they should be interpreted

---

[22] Schmitt, 'Green War', 72; M. Bothe, 'War and Environment' in R. Bernhardt (ed.), *Encyclopaedia of Public International Law. Volume Four: Quirin, Ex Parte to Zones of Peace* (Amsterdam: Elsevier, 2000), p. 1344; Y. Dinstein, *The Conduct of Hostilities under the Law of International Armed Conflict*, 2nd edn (Cambridge University Press, 2010), p. 204. See also J.-M. Henckaerts and L. Doswald-Beck (eds.), *Customary International Humanitarian Law*, 3 vols. (Cambridge University Press, 2005), Vol. II, p. 877. This interpretation is supported by declarations made by the UK and France upon ratification of 1977 Additional Protocol I, on 28 January 1998 and 11 April 2001, respectively. Both states stated that the risk of environmental damage as a result of the use of means and methods of warfare must be assessed 'objectively on the basis of information available at the time'. See www.icrc.org/ihl.

[23] W. D. Verwey, 'Protection of the environment in times of armed conflict: in search of a new legal perspective', *Leiden Journal of International Law* 8 (1995), 7–40, at 12.

[24] Article I of this Convention prohibits the use of environmental modification techniques for hostile purposes if they cause 'widespread, long-lasting or severe effects'.

[25] Vienna Convention on the Law of Treaties (VCLT), Vienna, 23 May 1969, in force 27 January 1980, 1155 UNTS 331 (No. 18232).

[26] See, e.g., M. Bothe, 'The protection of the environment in times of armed conflict: legal rules, uncertainty, deficiencies, and possible developments', *German Yearbook of International Law* 34 (1991) 54–62, at 56.

[27] See Justice Stewart's observation in relation to pornography and the first amendment. Rather than attempting to define pornography, he stated: 'I know it when I see it.' Justice Stewart, concurring, in US Supreme Court, *Jacobellis* v. *Ohio*, 378 US 184 (1964).

[28] After the 1990–91 Gulf War, it was doubted whether the damage resulting from the burning of oil wells and the oil spillage in the Persian Gulf would have met the damage threshold of Arts. 35(3) and 55 if the Protocol had been applicable. US Department of Defense, 'Report to Congress on the Conduct of the Persian Gulf War – Appendix on the Role of the law of War', *International Legal Materials* 31 (1992), 612–44, at 636–7. Similarly, the Committee

in accordance with current views on environmental damage and current standards of international environmental law.[29] After all, *tempora mutantur, nos et mutamur in illis*: times change and we change with them.

2. *Articles 35(3) and 55 and the use of nuclear weapons*

In view of the importance of Articles 35(3) and 55 of 1977 Additional Protocol I for protection of the environment during international armed conflict, it is important to establish the extent to which each provision would apply in the event of any new use of nuclear weapons. Apart from the fact that not all acknowledged and unacknowledged nuclear weapon states are parties to the Protocol (India, Israel, Pakistan and the United States are not, for instance), it has been widely argued that 1977 Additional Protocol I is not, as such, applicable to the use of nuclear weapons. This view was already reflected in the International Committee of the Red Cross (ICRC)'s general introductory note to its Draft Protocols, which were intended to be the basis for the negotiations in Geneva. In this introduction, the ICRC stated that it did not intend to 'broach' (i.e. discuss) problems relating to atomic, bacteriological and chemical warfare.[30]

This author does not find that argument particularly persuasive. Since the text of the Protocol is of general character and does not refer to any specific weapon or weapon category, it should therefore be presumed to apply to any type of weapon. Further, state practice, including by parties to the Protocol, is divided on whether the Protocol applies to the use of nuclear weapons. Some states are of the opinion that the Protocol, including Article 35(3), applies to all

---

established to review the NATO bombing campaign against the Federal Republic of Yugoslavia reported to the Public Prosecutor of the International Criminal Tribunal for the former Yugoslavia (ICTY) that damage resulting from the 1999 NATO bombing campaign did not meet the threshold of either provision. ICTY, 'Final Report to the Prosecutor by the Committee Established to Review the NATO Bombing Campaign against the Federal Republic of Yugoslavia', *International Legal Materials* 39 (2000), 1257–83, at 1262.

[29] Compare Art. 31(3)(c), VCLT, which provides that 'any relevant rules of international law applicable in the relations between the parties' must be taken into account, together with the context of a particular treaty.

[30] ICRC, *Draft Additional Protocols to the Geneva Conventions of August 12, 1949: Commentary*, p. 2. In 1956 the ICRC proposed amending the law of armed conflict to enhance protection of the civilian population in armed conflict. The draft included an implied prohibition on the use of nuclear weapons (Art. 14). It is believed that reference to use of nuclear weapons was the reason why the draft did not lead anywhere. ICRC Draft Rules for the Limitation of the Dangers Incurred by the Civilian Population in Time of War, 1956, in D. Schindler and J. Toman (eds.), *The Laws of Armed Conflicts; A Collection of Conventions, Resolutions and Other Documents* (Dordrecht: Martinus Nijhoff, 1988), pp. 251–7. C. Pilloud and J. Pictet, 'Part IV, Section I – General protection against the effects of hostilities' in Y. Sandoz, C. Swinarski and B. Zimmerman (eds.), *Commentary on the Additional Protocols of 8 June 1977 to the Geneva Conventions of 12 August 1949* (Geneva: International Committee of the Red Cross (ICRC)/Martinus Nijhoff Publishers, 1987), para. 1841.

weapon categories including nuclear weapons.[31] As discussed below, however, others hold firmly that the Protocol, or at least the new rules included therein, do not apply to use of nuclear weapons.[32] Although there was no 'need' for the Court 'to elaborate on the question of the applicability of Additional Protocol I of 1977 to nuclear weapons', the ICJ observed in its Nuclear Weapons Advisory Opinion:

> The fact that certain types of weapons were not specifically dealt with by the 1974–1977 Conference does not permit the drawing of any legal conclusions relating to the substantive issues which the use of such weapons would raise.[33]

A number of states made declarations upon signature and/or ratification of 1977 Additional Protocol I, including nuclear weapon states France and the UK.[34] France declared:

> Se référant au projet de protocole rédigé par le comité international de la croix rouge qui a constitué la base des travaux de la conférence diplomatique de 1974–1977, le gouvernement de la république française continue de considérer que les dispositions du protocole concernent exclusivement les armes classiques, et qu'elles ne sauraient ni réglementer ni interdire le recours à l'arme nucléaire, ni porter préjudice aux autres règles du droit

---

[31] India, for example, made an explicit statement to this effect upon the adoption of the Protocol by the Diplomatic Conference in 1977. CDDH/SR.39, Annex; VI, 113; Plenary Meeting of 25 May 1977, in Levie, *Protection of War Victims*, Vol. II, p. 279. Before the ICJ, within the framework of the Nuclear Weapons Advisory Opinion, Egypt, Malaysia, the Marshall Islands, Mexico, Nauru, Samoa and Solomon Islands stated, for various reasons, that the Protocol did apply to the use of nuclear weapons. See, e.g., oral statements (CR) of Egypt (CR 95/23, pp. 35–6), Solomon Islands (CR 95/23, p. 60), the Marshall Islands (CR 95/23, pp. 34–5) and Samoa (CR 95/31, p. 46), and written statements in relation to the request of the UN General Assembly of Mexico (para. 74), and of Nauru and Malaysia in relation to the request of the World Health Organization (respectively, pp. 51–2 and 18–19). Note, however, that the Marshall Islands, Malaysia and Nauru were not parties to the Protocol. Nauru acceded to the Protocol only in 2006.

[32] Before the ICJ, within the framework of the Nuclear Weapons Advisory Opinion, the UK, the United States, France, the Russian Federation and the Netherlands each stated that the new rules introduced in 1977 Additional Protocol I did not apply to the use of nuclear weapons. See, among other places, oral statements of the UK (CR 95/34, pp. 36–7), the United States (CR 95/34, pp. 73–5), France (CR 95/24, p. 23) and Russia (CR 95/29, pp. 44–5), and the written statement of the Netherlands in relation to the General Assembly request (para. 23). Note, however, that the UK and France were not party to 1977 Additional Protocol I when they made these statements before the Court, and that the United States is still not party to it.

[33] Nuclear Weapons Advisory Opinion, para. 84.

[34] Further declarations were made by Belgium, Canada, Germany, Italy, the Netherlands and Spain. Each state declared its understanding that 1977 Additional Protocol I only applied to conventional weapons. Ireland, however, expressed its uncertainty as to the applicability of the Protocol to the use of nuclear weapons. Reservations available at www.icrc.org/ihl.

international applicables a d'autres activités, nécessaires à l'exercice par la France de son droit naturel de légitime défense.[35]

The UK declared:

> It continues to be the understanding of the United Kingdom that the rules introduced by the Protocol apply exclusively to conventional weapons without prejudice to any other rules of international law applicable to other types of weapons. In particular, the rules so introduced do not have any effect on and do not regulate or prohibit the use of nuclear weapons.[36]

These declarations could be taken to amount to reservations according to Article 2(1)(d) VCLT. Apart from the view that both reservations are based on a misunderstanding of the scope of the Protocol, as was explained above, arguably both reservations are incompatible with the object and purpose of 1977 Additional Protocol I.[37] The object and purpose of a treaty must be established by discovering the 'essence' of a treaty, which can be derived from the title of a treaty, its preamble, a particular article, preparatory works or its general architecture.[38] The essence of the law of armed conflict, including 1977 Additional Protocol I, is the alleviation of the calamities of war in general,[39] and the protection of the victims of armed conflict in particular.[40] It is clearly contrary to

---

[35] 'Referring to the draft protocol prepared by the International Committee of the Red Cross, which was the basis of the work of the 1974–7 Diplomatic Conference, the Government of France continues to consider that the provisions of the Protocol concern exclusively conventional weapons, and that they can neither regulate nor prohibit the use of nuclear weapons, nor prejudice other rules of international law applicable to other actions necessary for France's exercise of its inherent right of self defence.' Unofficial translation.

[36] Available at: www.icrc.org/ihl.

[37] See Article 19(c) VCLT. Admittedly, however, no state has yet challenged the legality of the reservations as being incompatible with the Protocol.

[38] A. Pellet, 'Article 19: Formulation of reservations' in O. Corten and P. Klein (eds.), *The Vienna Convention on the Law of Treaties: A Commentary*, 2 vols. (Oxford University Press, 2011), vol. I, pp. 447–51.

[39] St Petersburg Declaration Renouncing the Use, in Time of War, of Explosive Projectiles Under 400 Grammes Weight, signed on 11 December 1868, in force 11 December 1868, reprinted in *American Journal of International Law* 1(2), Supplement: Official Documents, 1907, p. 95, preamble. According to the drafters of the St Petersburg Declaration, 'the only legitimate object which States should endeavour to accomplish during war is to weaken the military forces of the enemy' and that for that purpose it was 'sufficient to disable the greatest possible number of men'.

[40] The High Contracting Parties to 1977 Additional Protocol I believed it necessary 'to reaffirm and develop the provisions protecting the victims of armed conflicts and to supplement measures intended to reinforce their application'; and further reaffirmed 'that the provisions of the Geneva Conventions of 12 August 1949 and of this Protocol must be fully applied in all circumstances to all persons who are protected by those instruments, without any adverse distinction based on the nature or origin of the armed conflict or on the causes espoused by or attributed to the Parties to the conflict'. As such, this reflects the essence or global project of Additional Protocol I.

the aforementioned objects to exclude the use of the most destructive weapon ever invented from the scope of the (new) provisions of the Protocol, including its provisions on the protection of the (human) environment. As the Court recognised:

> These characteristics render the nuclear weapon potentially catastrophic. The destructive power of nuclear weapons cannot be contained in either space or time. They have the potential to destroy all civilization and the entire ecosystem of the planet. The radiation released by a nuclear explosion would affect health, agriculture, natural resources and demography over a very wide area. Further, the use of nuclear weapons would be a serious danger to future generations. Ionizing radiation has the potential to damage the future environment, food and marine ecosystem, and to cause genetic defects and illness in future generations.[41]

Assuming, however, that Articles 35(3) and 55 of the Protocol would indeed apply to a new use of nuclear weapons, it is likely that such use would breach both provisions. Although damage resulting from a nuclear explosion will depend on a number of factors, such as the type of explosion (sub-surface burst, surface burst or air burst), the type of nuclear weapon involved (fission/fusion weapon, enhanced radiation weapon), the environment where the explosion takes place and the weather at the time of, and after, the explosion, it is nonetheless likely that any nuclear explosion during an armed conflict would cause widespread, long-term and severe damage to the environment, and that such damage would be reasonably foreseeable.[42]

Both blast and heat will cause significant damage on the ground in case of an air burst, a surface burst or a shallow underground burst, and radioactive contamination resulting from the explosion could cover large areas and last for a significant period of time. Local fallout generally comes down within 24 hours after the explosion in a cigar-shaped pattern, downwind from 'Ground Zero', and is most damaging, since it contains between 40 per cent and 70 per cent of the total radioactivity, and may be of such intensity that certain areas will be severely affected and even remain unfit for human habitation for decades.[43]

[41] Nuclear Weapons Advisory Opinion, para. 35.

[42] Some authors assert that the drafters of Arts. 35(3) and 55 did indeed consider non-conventional means and methods of warfare, such as herbicides and chemical weapons, when they elaborated the two provisions. See, e.g., W. A. Solf, 'Article 55: Protection of the Natural Environment' in M. Bothe, K. J. Partsch, and W. A. Solf, *New Rules for Victims of Armed Conflicts: Commentary on the Two 1977 Protocols Additional to the Geneva Conventions of 1949* (The Hague: Martinus Nijhoff, 1982), p. 348; and F. Kalshoven, 'Reaffirmation and development of international humanitarian law applicable in armed conflicts: the Diplomatic Conference, Geneva, 1974–1977, Part II', *Netherlands Yearbook of International Law* 9 (1978), 107–38, at 130.

[43] In 1998, after sixteen tests over a time-span of twelve years at Bikini Atoll, the International Atomic Energy Agency (IAEA) considered the islands still generally unsafe for habitation forty years after the last test had taken place. The IAEA's conclusion was based on the

B.   Protection of the environment during armed conflict under customary international law

In addition to Articles 35(3) and 55, the environment is also protected under three rules of customary international law: Rules 43, 44 and 45 of the ICRC's 2005 Customary International Humanitarian Law Study (CIHL Study).[44] Rule 43 states:

> The general principles on the conduct of hostilities apply to the natural environment:
> A. No part of the natural environment may be attacked, unless it is a military objective.
> B. Destruction of any part of the natural environment is prohibited, unless required by imperative military necessity.
> C. Launching an attack against a military objective which may be expected to cause incidental damage to the environment which would be excessive in relation to the concrete and direct military advantage anticipated is prohibited.

Rule 44 states:

> Methods and means of warfare must be employed with due regard to the protection and preservation of the natural environment. In the conduct of military operations, all feasible precautions must be taken to avoid, and in any event to minimise, incidental damage to the environment. Lack of scientific certainty as to the effects on the environment of certain military operations does not absolve a party to the conflict from taking such precautions.

Rule 45 states:

> The use of methods or means or warfare that are intended, or may be expected, to cause widespread, long-term and severe damage to the natural environment is prohibited. Destruction of the natural environment may not be used as a weapon.

assumption that the local population would almost entirely consume locally produced food, and since substantial amounts of radioactive elements had entered the food chain around Bikini Atoll, this would lead to an annual dose that was considered too high by IAEA safety standards. P. Stegnar, 'Review at Bikini Atoll: assessing radiological conditions at Bikini Atoll and the prospects for resettlement', *IAEA Bulletin* 40(4) (1998), 15–18, at 15–17. Part of the Atoll has meanwhile been rehabilitated. See www.bikiniatoll.com and the Marshall Islands Program of the US Department of Energy at www.eh.doe.gov. Please note, however, that different species have different radio-sensitivities, and humans appear to be more sensitive to nuclear radiation than birds or trees: generally speaking, 'the higher the species on the evolutionary scale, the greater the sensitivity'. J. Rotblat, *Nuclear Radiation in Warfare* (London: Stockholm International Peace Research Institute (SIPRI)/Taylor & Francis, 1981), pp. 100–2. See also A. H. Westing, *Weapons of Mass Destruction and the Environment* (London: SIPRI/Taylor & Francis, 1977), pp. 21–2.

[44] Henckaerts and Doswald-Beck, *Customary International Humanitarian Law*, Vol. I, pp. 143–58.

Since it is unlikely that nuclear weapons would ever be used without (impera-tive) military necessity and highly unlikely that they would be used for the sole purpose of causing damage to the natural environment, this section only discusses the meaning and scope of Rules 43C and 44. The first sentence of Rule 45 generally reflects Articles 35(3) and 55, and indicates that, in the view of the ICRC, both provisions have developed into rules of customary international law, with the United States as a persistent objector to the first sentence of the customary rule in general, and France, the UK and the United States as per-sistent objectors to the application of the first sentence of the rule to the use of nuclear weapons.[45] As the scope of the prohibition to use methods and means of warfare expected to cause widespread, long-term and severe damage to the environment was discussed above, Rule 45 will not be further discussed here.

1.   Rule 43C: the prohibition on excessive collateral damage to the environment

The prohibition on launching an attack against a military objective that may be expected to cause incidental damage to the environment that would be exces-sive in relation to the concrete and direct military advantage anticipated (or, in short: the prohibition on excessive collateral damage to the environment) is a relatively new manifestation of the principle of proportionality. The prin-ciple of proportionality is a fundamental principle of the law of armed con-flict – despite not being referred to by the ICJ in the Nuclear Weapons Advisory Opinion – and a 'general principle on the conduct of hostilities' (chapeau Rule 43). The prohibition on excessive collateral damage to the environment appears to complement the Treaty and customary prohibitions on excessive collateral damage to civilians and civilian objects as laid down in Article 51(4) and (5)(b) of 1977 Additional Protocol I, and Rule 14 of the ICRC's CIHL Study. Rule 14 provides (under the heading 'Proportionality in Attack') that:

> Launching an attack which may be expected to cause incidental loss of
> civilian life, injury to civilians, damage to civilian objects, or a combination

---

[45] *Ibid.*, pp. 151–5. The ICRC's conclusion has not been generally accepted, however. In 1996 the ICJ rejected the claim that both provisions had customary equivalents (Nuclear Weapons Advisory Opinion, para. 31). In 2006 the drafters of the *Manual on the Law of Non-International Armed Conflict* concluded that Arts. 35(3) and 55 had not developed into rules of customary international law: M. N. Schmitt, C. H. B. Garraway and Y. Dinstein, *The Manual on the Law of Non-International Armed Conflict* (San Remo: International Institute of Humanitarian Law, 2006), p. 59. See similarly Y. Dinstein, *The Conduct of Hostilities under the Law of International Armed Conflict* (Cambridge University Press, 2004), p. 205; Schmitt, 'Green War', 76. Hulme is doubtful as to their customary status: K. Hulme, 'Natural Environment' in E. Wilmshurst and S. Breau (eds.), *Perspectives on the ICRC Study on Customary International Humanitarian Law* (Cambridge University Press, 2007), p. 232. For further references and discussion, see Koppe, *The Use of Nuclear Weapons*, pp. 220–4, 235–42.

thereof, which would be excessive in relation to the concrete and direct military advantage anticipated, is prohibited.

The customary prohibition on excessive collateral damage to the environment arguably emerged during the 1990s, triggered by damage to the environment caused by Iraq during the 1990–91 Gulf War.[46] Arguably the familiarity of states, and in particular their (military) legal advisers, with customary and conventional rules governing the protection of civilian objects under IHL, in combination with a growing concern for the environment, in particular after 1991, triggered the emergence of a specific customary prohibition on excessive collateral damage to the environment.

The existence of the customary prohibition is generally accepted in practice,[47] as is evident from a variety of sources, including treaties and other instruments, national practice, practice of international organisations and conferences, practice of international judicial and quasi-judicial bodies, and the practice of the International Red Cross and Red Crescent Movement.[48] In relation to Rule 43C, the ICRC refers, among other things, to the 1993 ICRC Guidelines for Military Manuals and Instructions on the Protection of the Environment in Times of Armed Conflict[49] and the 1994 San Remo Manual on International Law Applicable to Armed Conflicts at Sea,[50] both of which indicate general acceptance of the prohibition.[51]

Further, the ICRC refers to the (implicit) acceptance of the rule by the ICJ and the Committee Established to Review the NATO Bombing Campaign Against the Federal Republic of Yugoslavia. The Committee stated that 'military objectives should not be targeted if the attack is likely to cause collateral

---

[46] See also W. Heintschel von Heinegg and M. Donner, 'New developments in the protection of the natural environment in naval armed conflicts', *German Yearbook of International Law* 37 (1994), 281–314, at 294; J.-M. Henckaerts, 'Towards better protection for the environment in armed conflict: recent developments in international humanitarian law', *Review of European Community and International Environmental Law* 9 (2000), 13–19, at 18; L. Lijnzaad and G. J. Tanja, 'Protection of the environment in times of armed conflict: the Iraq-Kuwait War', *Netherlands International Law Review* 40 (1993), 169–99, at 184.

[47] Henckaerts and Doswald-Beck, *Customary International Humanitarian Law*, Vol. I, pp. 145–6. See also Koppe, *The Use of Nuclear Weapons*, pp. 261–8 for similar or additional evidence.

[48] Henckaerts and Doswald-Beck, *Customary International Humanitarian Law*, Vol. II: Practice, Part 1, pp. 844–59. Please note that the practice relied on by the ICRC relates to Rule 43 as a whole.

[49] ICRC Guidelines for Military Manuals and Instructions on the Protection of the Environment in Times of Armed Conflict (A/48/269, Report of the Secretary-General to the General Assembly on the Protection of the Environment in Times of Armed Conflict, of 29 July 1993, Annexing the ICRC Guidelines), Principle 4. See also the 1999 ICRC Model Manual, para. 702(e) and (f).

[50] San Remo Manual on International Law Applicable to Armed Conflicts at Sea, paras. 46(d) and 13(c).

[51] Henckaerts and Doswald-Beck, *Customary International Humanitarian Law*, Vol. I, p. 145.

environmental damage which would be excessive in relation to the direct military advantage which the attack is expected to produce'.[52] As noted above, in its Advisory Opinion the ICJ affirmed that: 'States must take environmental considerations into account when assessing what is necessary and proportionate in the pursuit of legitimate military objectives.'[53]

Additionally, the rule appears to be evidenced (without reference to the 'triple damage standard') by its reflection in military manuals, such as the US Commander's Handbook on the Law of Naval Operations,[54] as well as by a number of public statements by states within the framework of international organisations. Canada, for example, declared in 1992 to the Sixth Committee of the UN General Assembly:

> An important evolution was thus taking place which reflected the importance of the ecological point of view and which should be brought to bear on other questions, such as that of proportionality (the need to strike a balance between the protection of the environment and the needs of war) or that of the distinction between military and non-military objectives. Under the same principle, the environment as such should not be the object of direct attack, and this delegation would like to see that point reflected in the resolution to be adopted after discussion of the item.[55]

Finally, emergence of a customary international law prohibition on excessive collateral damage to the environment appears implicit in Article 8(2)(b)(iv) of the ICC Statute, which qualifies as a war crime:

> Intentionally launching an attack in the knowledge that such attack will cause incidental loss of life or injury to civilians or damage to civilian objects or widespread, long-term and severe damage to the environment which would be clearly excessive in relation to the concrete and direct overall military advantage anticipated.

Article 8(2)(b)(iv), which reflects Article 51(4) and (5)(b) of 1977 Additional Protocol I, is clearly inspired by Articles 35(3) and 55 of the Protocol. It appears to correlate the protection of civilian objects with protection of the environment as laid down in the Protocol.[56] Although Article 8(2)(b)(iv) provides for individual criminal responsibility for intentionally launching an attack which

---

[52] ICTY, 'Final Report to the Prosecutor by the Committee Established to Review the NATO Bombing Campaign against the Federal Republic of Yugoslavia', paras. 15 and 18.

[53] Nuclear Weapons Advisory Opinion, para. 30.

[54] NWP 1-14M, The Commander's Handbook on the Law of Naval Operations, para. 8.4.

[55] A/C.6/47/SR.8, Summary Record of the 8th meeting of the Sixth Committee of the General Assembly on 1 October 1992, para. 20. For further references, see Koppe, *The Use of Nuclear Weapons*, pp. 264–8.

[56] The distinction between civilian objects and the natural environment in Art. 8(2)(b)(iv) of the ICC Statute may be interpreted as an indication that the environment does not qualify as a civilian object but as an object *sui generis*.

causes excessive collateral damage to the environment, and which must also be widespread, long-term and severe, arguably the provision implies the existence of an independent and 'primary' rule of the law of armed conflict from which the war crime is derived. As such, this primary rule – as expressed in Rule 43C – partly underlies Article 8(2)(b)(iv).

For states parties to 1977 Additional Protocol I, this customary prohibition on excessive collateral damage to the environment complements Articles 35(3) and 55 of the Protocol.[57] In addition to an absolute prohibition to cause wide-spread, long-term and severe damage to the environment, states parties to the Protocol are also prohibited from causing excessive collateral damage to the environment during armed conflict. Since the two obligations are of different scope, it must be established which prevails, or rather which must be applied first. It is submitted that any military action that causes damage to the environment must first be assessed against this customary prohibition and only then, if no breach is established, against Articles 35(3) and 55 of the Protocol. The customary prohibition emerged later in time and provides relative protection to the environment (contrary to absolute protection of the environment under Articles 35(3) and 55). As such, it appears that the protection afforded by the law is significantly enhanced by the emergence of a customary prohibition on causing excessive collateral damage to the environment.

The relevance of the prohibition in the case of use of a nuclear weapon will depend on the circumstances of the case. As above, the damage resulting from nuclear explosions will generally be significant and foreseeably so. However, the extent to which any damage to the environment qualifies as 'excessive' will depend on the actual military advantage anticipated, as is apparent from the text of Rule 43C. If a military object qualifies as a highly valuable military target, then its destruction may justify considerable collateral damage. In contrast,

---

[57] The customary prohibition on excessive collateral damage to the environment must be distinguished from the prohibition on excessive collateral damage to civilian objects as provided under Art. 51(4) and (5)(b). Although it is arguable that the environment generally qualifies as a civilian object (see, for example, M. Bothe, C. Bruch, J. Diamond and D. Jensen, 'International law protecting the environment during armed conflict: gaps and opportunities', *International Review of the Red Cross* 92 (2010), 569–92, at 576), this author believes that the environment does not benefit from the same protection provided to civilian objects under conventional law, in particular Arts. 51 and 52. There is no indication that the drafters regarded the environment as a civilian object or that they considered the environment as being generally protected under Arts. 51 and 52 or their pre-existing customary equivalents. Arts. 35(3) and 55 qualify as stand-alone provisions, providing for specific protection of the environment, irrespective of their relationship with Arts. 51 and 52, and even though, in hindsight, Arts. 51 and 52 and their customary equivalents would have provided a more effective basis for protecting the environment during armed conflict. For more detail of the argument, see Koppe, 'The principle of ambituity', 68–75; and von Heinegg and Donner, 'New developments in the protection of the natural environment in naval armed conflicts', 289.

if a military object is not very valuable for military purposes and is not very important for the war effort, its destruction would not seem to justify considerable collateral damage. The prohibition on excessive collateral damage always entails a balancing of factors, and application of this test therefore depends on the circumstances of the case.

2.   Rule 44: the customary duty of care for the environment during armed conflict

A customary obligation to employ means and methods of warfare with due regard to the protection and preservation of the environment (Rule 44, first sentence)[58] appears to imply the existence of a general duty of care for the environment during armed conflict.[59] After all, 'due regard' is merely a standard to be applied, similar to the obligation to show 'due diligence', which must be applied to prevent transboundary environmental harm,[60] and which appears to be related to the general obligation on each state 'not to allow knowingly its territory to be used for acts contrary to the rights of other states'.[61] This obligation, also known under the maxim *sic utere tuo ut alienum non laedas*, is arguably based on a general duty of care similar to the one binding private individuals and legal persons, as recognised in the civil law of tort.[62]

According to the ICRC, Rule 44 follows from 'recognition of the need to provide particular protection to the environment as such'.[63] Rule 44 therefore qualifies as ecocentric, similar to Article 35(3) of 1977 Additional Protocol I. It reflects general concern for the environment during armed conflict dating back to 1972, as discussed above, and that is expressed most explicitly in UN General

---

[58] Henckaerts and Doswald-Beck, *Customary International Humanitarian Law*, Vol. I, Rule 44, pp. 147–51. The customary basis of Rule 44 has been criticised by Aldrich and to a lesser extent by Hulme. G. H. Aldrich, 'Customary international humanitarian law – an interpretation on behalf of the International Committee of the Red Cross', *British Yearbook of International Law* 76 (2005), 503–24, at 515; K. Hulme, 'Taking care to protect the environment against damage: a meaningless obligation?', *International Review of the Red Cross* 92 (2010), 675–91, at 686.

[59] See, Koppe, *The Use of Nuclear Weapons*, pp. 248–56.

[60] Nuclear Weapons Advisory Opinion, para. 29; ICJ, *Gabčíkovo-Nagymaros Project (Hungary/ Slovakia)*, Judgment, 25 September 1997 (*Gabčíkovo-Nagymaros* case), para. 53. ICJ, *Case Concerning Pulp Mills on the River Uruguay (Argentina v. Uruguay)*, Judgment, 20 April 2010 (*Pulp Mills* case), paras. 204–05.

[61] ICJ, *Corfu Channel Case*, Judgment, 9 April 1949, *ICJ Reports 1949* (*Corfu Channel* case), p. 22.

[62] See M. A. Fitzmaurice, 'The Corfu Channel Case and the development of international law' in N. Ando *et al.* (eds.), *Liber Amicorum Judge Shigeru Oda* (The Hague: Kluwer Law International, 2002), pp. 132, 137–9. Fitzmaurice relies, among other things, on the dissenting opinion of Judge Azevedo in this regard (Dissenting Opinion Judge Azevedo, pp. 84–5).

[63] Henckaerts and Doswald-Beck, *Customary International Humanitarian Law*, Vol. I, Rule 44, p. 147.

Assembly Resolution 47/37 of 25 November 1992[64] and the General Assembly's decision to declare 6 November the 'International Day for Preventing the Exploitation of the Environment in War and Armed Conflict'.[65]

The emergence of a duty of care for the environment during armed conflict was identified by the ICRC from a variety of sources, which include treaties and other international instruments and state practice, notably as set out in military manuals and in statements within international organisations and conferences.[66] For example, several military manuals provide that military operations must be carried out with due regard to the protection of the environment, such as the US Commander's Handbook on the Law of Naval Operations.[67]

Further, a number of states have affirmed (or at least implied) the existence of a duty of care for the environment during armed conflict. In 1991, for example, Canada issued a memorandum that implied the existence of such a duty of care;[68] and in 1995 and 1996 a number of states expressed concern for the environment during armed conflict and a need to show due regard before the ICJ within the framework of the Nuclear Weapons Advisory Opinion.[69] Although the Court did not acknowledge the existence of a duty of care for the

---

[64] The General Assembly 'expressed its deep concern about environmental damage and depletion of natural resources, including the destruction of hundreds of oil-well heads and the release and waste of crude oil into the sea, during recent conflicts' (Resolution 47/37, pre-ambular para. 3).

[65] Resolution 56/4 of 5 November 2001. The date of 6 November 2001 marked the tenth anniversary of the extinguishing of the last oil-well fire in Kuwait. W. J. Hybl, Representative of the United States, in Press Release GA/9946 of 5 November 2001, available at: www.unis. unvienna.org/.

[66] Henckaerts and Doswald-Beck, *Customary International Humanitarian Law*, Vol. II: Practice, Part 1, pp. 860–71. See also Koppe, *The Use of Nuclear Weapons*, pp. 248–56, for similar or additional evidence.

[67] NWP 1–14M, The Commander's Handbook on the Law of Naval Operations, Department of the Navy, Newport, RI, 2007, para. 8–4. See also the San Remo Manual on International Law Applicable to Armed Conflicts at Sea, in *International Review of the Red Cross* 309 (1995), paras. 44, 11, 46(c), and 13(c); and the ICRC Model Military Manual. A. P. V. Rogers and P. Malherbe, *Fight it Right: Model Manual on the Law of Armed Conflict for Armed Forces* (Geneva: ICRC, 1999), para. 702(c).

[68] The Memorandum stated that '[t]he customary laws of war, in reflecting the dictates of public conscience, now include a requirement to avoid unnecessary damage to the environment. This includes consideration of environmental effects in the planning of military operations.' Canadian Department of External Affairs, Legal Bureau, 'Memorandum; 12 July 1991; Armed Conflict and the Environment', in B. Mawhinney (ed.), 'Canadian practice in international law: at the Department of External Affairs in 1991–92', *Canadian Yearbook of International Law* 30 (1992), 347–64. See similarly Summary Record of the 18th meeting of the Sixth Committee of the General Assembly on 22 October 1991, UN doc. A/C.6/46/SR.18, para. 13; Summary Record of the 8th meeting of the Sixth Committee of the General Assembly on 1 October 1992, UN doc. A/C.6/47/SR.8, para. 20.

[69] Sri Lanka, for example, referred to the protection of the environment during armed conflict as an established principle of international law. Written Statement of the Government of Sri Lanka, 20 September 1994, in ICJ, *Legality of the Use by a State of Nuclear Weapons*

environment during armed conflict as such, it did observe that environmental factors and considerations must play an important role in the implementation of the law of armed conflict,[70] which suggests the existence of an obligation to show due regard for the environment during armed conflict. Finally, a duty of care for the environment is arguably evidenced by the first sentence of Article 55(1) of 1977 Additional Protocol I, which provides: 'Care shall be taken in warfare to protect the natural environment against widespread, long-term and severe damage.'[71]

A duty of care for the environment or an obligation to use methods and means of warfare with due regard for the environment during armed conflict entails that states must take 'all feasible precautions' in the conduct of military operations 'to avoid, and in any event to minimise, incidental damage to the environment'[72] (Rule 44, second sentence).[73] The second sentence of Rule 44 'operationalises' the more general obligation in the first sentence and appears to reflect the general principle of prevention, which qualifies as a principle of international environmental law.[74] The requirement to take all feasible

---

in Armed Conflict, 8 July 1996 (hereafter, WHO Advisory Opinion Request), p. 3. Iran, Sweden and New Zealand each expressed a concern for the environment during armed conflict. Written Statement of the Islamic Republic of Iran, Nuclear Weapons Advisory Opinion, p. 4; Written Statement of Sweden, WHO Advisory Opinion Request, p. 5; Written Statement of New Zealand, Nuclear Weapons Advisory Opinion, pp. 17–18. For further and other examples of national practice that also indicate a concern for the environment, see Henckaerts and Doswald-Beck, *Customary International Humanitarian Law*, Vol. II: Practice, Part 1, pp. 862–7.

[70] Nuclear Weapons Advisory Opinion, paras. 30, 32 and 33.

[71] According to Hulme, Rule 44 of the ICRC's CIHL Study requiring states to show due regard for the environment is not the same as the obligation to take care of the environment as laid down in Article 55 of 1977 Additional Protocol I. Hulme, 'Taking care to protect the environment against damage', pp. 679–80, 685–6, 691. Compare, however, Hulme's previous discussions of the relationship between Art. 55(1) and Rule 44. K. Hulme, *War Torn Environment: Interpreting the Legal Threshold* (Leiden: Martinus Nijhoff, 2004), p. 108; Hulme, 'Natural Environment', p. 218.

[72] Rule 44 does not refer to incidental damage to the environment that is excessive in relation to the concrete and direct military advantage anticipated, as Rule 43C does.

[73] The second sentence of Rule 44 is similar to Rule 15 (which reflects Art. 57(1) of 1977 Additional Protocol I), which states: 'In the conduct of military operations, constant care must be taken to spare the civilian population, civilians and civilian objects. All feasible precautions must be taken to avoid, and in any event to minimize, incidental loss of civilian life, injury to civilians and damage to civilian objects.' Rule 15 is further detailed in Rules 16–21.

[74] The principle of prevention was recognised by the ICJ in the 2010 *Pulp Mills* case (para. 101). See also Principle 2 of the 1992 Rio Declaration. Pursuant to the principle of prevention, states must at least carry out an environmental impact assessment prior to authorising a project that may have significant transboundary consequences and during the implementation of a project. *Pulp Mills* case, paras. 204–5. See also Principle 17 of the Rio Declaration. The principle of prevention is further reflected in the 2001 ILC Articles on Transboundary Pollution (UN doc. A/56/10, Draft Articles on Prevention of Transboundary Harm from

precautions 'objectifies' the behaviour of belligerents and requires that belligerents act reasonably or in conformity with what could be reasonably expected from that state under the specific circumstances. As such, an assessment must be made of all environmental risks.[75]

While the obligation to take all feasible precautions to avoid or minimise damage to the environment appears to require foreseeability of environmental damage, Rule 44 further states that '[l]ack of scientific certainty as to the effects on the environment of certain military operations does not absolve a party to the conflict from taking such precautions'. As such, the third sentence of Rule 44 goes further than the other rules of the law of armed conflict that protect the environment and that were discussed above. It reflects the precautionary principle,[76] which arguably qualifies as a principle of international environmental law,[77] and which is essential in view of the difficulty of analysing natural processes and assessing environmental damage.

Similar to the prohibition on excessive collateral damage to the environment, this customary duty of care for the environment complements Articles 35(3) and 55 of 1977 Additional Protocol I. For states parties to the Protocol, and for the same reasons as mentioned above in relation to the prohibition on excessive collateral damage to the environment, any military operation or use

---

Hazardous Activities, with commentaries, 2001). The Articles on Transboundary Pollution provide, in short, that the state of origin must take all appropriate measures to prevent significant transboundary harm or minimise the risk thereof. For that purpose, states must under certain circumstances carry out a proper environmental impact assessment.

[75] Compare Rule 18, which requires states to 'do everything feasible to assess whether the attack may be expected to cause' excessive collateral damage to the civilian population or civilian objects.

[76] See Henckaerts and Doswald-Beck, *Customary International Humanitarian Law*, Vol. I, Rule 44, p. 150.

[77] See Principle 15 of the Rio Declaration, which refers to a precautionary approach in case of scientific uncertainty. The formulation of Rule 44's second and third sentence indicates that the precautionary approach is part of the obligation to take all feasible precautions to avoid or at least minimise incidental environmental damage. A similar approach was taken by the Seabed Disputes Chamber of the International Tribunal for the Law of the Sea in its Advisory Opinion on Responsibilities and Obligations of States Sponsoring Persons and Entities with Respect to Activities in the Area of 1 February 2011. The Chamber held that 'it is appropriate to point out that the precautionary approach is also an integral part of the general obligation of due diligence of sponsoring States, which is applicable even outside the scope of the Regulations. The due diligence obligation of the sponsoring States requires them to take all appropriate measures to prevent damage that might result from the activities of contractors that they sponsor. This obligation applies in situations where scientific evidence concerning the scope and potential negative impact of the activity in question is insufficient but where there are plausible indications of potential risks. A sponsoring State would not meet its obligation of due diligence if it disregarded those risks. Such disregard would amount to a failure to comply with the precautionary approach' (para. 131). See also Separate Opinion of Judge Cançado Trindade, *Pulp Mills* case, paras. 52–3, 62–92.

of methods or means of warfare must first be assessed against the customary duty of care for the environment. Only if no breach can be established is it necessary to assess such operations against Articles 35(3) and 55.

Rule 44 or the duty of care for the environment is not weapon-specific and could arguably also extend to the use of nuclear weapons. Therefore, if applied to a hypothetical use of nuclear weapons, the relevance of a customary duty of care for the environment during armed conflict may be significant. In particular, the extent to which the nuclear weapon state has taken all feasible precautions to avoid, or in any event to minimise, collateral damage to the environment must be established. It is arguable that nuclear weapon states must assess the potential environmental harm of the use of nuclear weapons and if necessary call off an attack to avoid or at least minimise collateral environmental harm.[78] Such assessment would need to include a thorough investigation of the possibility of using alternative weapon systems. Nowadays, most nuclear weapon states possess highly sophisticated and powerful weapons that can hit targets over long distances with a high degree of accuracy, which means that use of nuclear weapons may not be necessary to destroy a military objective. Since there is no lack of scientific certainty as to the effects on the environment of the use of nuclear weapons, there is no need to discuss the obligation to take precautionary measures in conformity with Article 44C third sentence.

Conclusion

Nuclear weapons are the most destructive weapons ever invented. The consequences of a single nuclear explosion will likely be devastating, not only for man, but also for the environment. This chapter has sought to clarify the scope of the relevant rules of the law of armed conflict and to assess, *in abstracto*, the legality of use of nuclear weapons under these rules.

Articles 35(3) and 55 of 1977 Additional Protocol I both prohibit the use of methods and means of warfare that are intended or that may be expected to cause widespread, long-term and severe damage to the environment. This author has sought to argue that both rules must be taken into account by nuclear weapon states that have become party to 1977 Additional Protocol I, including France and the UK. In light of the effects of a nuclear explosion, in particular the effects of ionising or nuclear radiation, it is likely that the use of a nuclear weapon during armed conflict will cause widespread, long-term and

---

[78] Hulme, 'Taking care to protect the environment against damage', pp. 681–2. See also the illustrative list drawn up by Droege and Tsougas of measures that can be taken to show due regard for the environment: C. Droege and M.-L. Tsougas, 'The protection of the natural environment in armed conflict – existing rules and need for further legal protection', *Nordic Journal of International Law* 82 (2013), 21–52, at 33–5.

severe damage to the environment and will therefore be contrary to Articles 35(3) and 55, to the extent that these provisions are applicable.

This author has also argued that under customary international law, Rules 43C of the ICRC's CIHL Study (the prohibition on causing excessive collateral damage to the environment) and 44 (the general duty of care for the environment during armed conflict) must also be taken into account by all nuclear weapon states. Since both rules provide relative protection to the environment (contrary to the absolute protection of the environment under Articles 35(3) and 55) and since both rules emerged later in time, to the extent the rules are applicable any use of nuclear weapons must first be assessed against these customary rules. Only if no breach of these rules can be established, must the legality of that particular use be assessed – if applicable – against Articles 35(3) and 55.

Rule 43C, which prohibits excessive collateral damage to the environment, requires a balancing of values, namely expected environmental damage and the concrete and direct military advantage anticipated. The question of the extent to which the use of a nuclear weapon would be in conformity with this rule will therefore depend entirely on the circumstances of the case. Rule 44 prescribes that states must take all feasible precautions to avoid and in any event to minimise incidental damage to the environment. It is arguable that Rule 44 requires states to assess in advance the potential environmental harm of a particular method or means of warfare, including use of a nuclear weapon, and to assess to what extent the target can be neutralised by an alternative weapon system. Whether any use of a nuclear weapon is in conformity with this rule will therefore depend on the circumstances of each case, in particular efforts by the nuclear weapon state prior to its decision to employ nuclear weapons and the reasonableness of its decision.

This chapter shows that the rules of the law of armed conflict that protect the environment during armed conflict may provide additional parameters and significant impediments for a nuclear weapon state to employ nuclear weapons. These parameters have materialised over the last twenty to thirty years and reflect growing concern for environmental protection. Such protection is not only in the interest of all states, but also in the interest of mankind.[79] After all, 'the environment is not an abstraction but represents the living space, the quality of life and the very health of human beings, including generations unborn.'[80]

---

[79] *Gabčíkovo-Nagymaros* case, para. 53: 'The Court recalls that it has recently had occasion to stress … the great significance that it attaches to respect for the environment, not only for States but also for the whole of mankind.'
[80] Nuclear Weapons Advisory Opinion, para. 29.

11

Environmental approaches to nuclear weapons

MARTINA KUNZ AND JORGE E. VIÑUALES

Introduction

This chapter analyses the international regulation of nuclear weapons from an environmental law perspective. Since the International Court of Justice (ICJ) issued its Nuclear Weapons Advisory Opinion in 1996,[1] this question has been addressed mainly from two angles.

The most common approach to analysing the environmental regulation of nuclear weapons under international law has been through the lens of international humanitarian law (IHL). This line of scholarship has resulted in detailed assessments of the environmental coverage of some *jus in bello* instruments and rules. The IHL approach centres on Articles 35(3) and 55 of 1977 Additional Protocol I to the 1949 Geneva Conventions and customary international law, as well as the proscription of harm to the environment during hostilities arising from international criminal law.

Aside from these IHL rules, much has been written about whether international environmental law (IEL) remains applicable in times of armed conflict, with particular emphasis on the wording of certain multilateral environmental agreements (MEAs), as well as customary international law (pertaining to e.g. prevention and, arguably, precaution). Both this line of enquiry and the analysis of environment-related IHL rules focus on the broad question of environmental protection during armed conflict, and they seek to apply general conclusions derived from this context to the assessment of the legality of nuclear weapons.

However, these two approaches do not provide a complete picture of how international environmental law may capture a composite regulatory object such as nuclear weapons. Resort to nuclear weapons presupposes their production, testing, stockpiling, transportation and deployment before actual use in hostilities. International law governs parts of this more complex regulatory object in ways that have received less attention from commentators. It is important to assess potential breaches of international environmental law

---

[1] ICJ, *Legality of the Threat or Use of Nuclear Weapons*, Advisory Opinion, 8 July 1996, paras. 27–33 (hereafter, Nuclear Weapons Advisory Opinion).

through other activities involving nuclear weapons, albeit less dramatic than detonation in armed conflict, but nonetheless worthy of scholarly and advocacy consideration. In addition to looking at the production cycle, an environmental law perspective may also be useful in the aftermath of a disaster, to assess the burden of repairing damage, whether this is characterised as 'reparation' or, instead, by using euphemisms such as 'assistance', 'settlement', 'rehabilitation' or others.

In the limited context of this chapter, we cannot cover all these dimensions. Our purpose is more modest. We want to clarify what is known at this point and what requires further attention and research. Commentators have focused on two main angles, namely (1) the incorporation of environmental considerations into IHL rules, and (2) the applicability of environmental treaties during armed conflict. The first angle is discussed at length elsewhere in this volume.[2] We discuss the second in Section A of this chapter, providing an overview of the main issues and highlighting recent developments in international jurisprudence, which have so far been relatively neglected in the environmental literature. We propose a third angle in Section B of the chapter, on parts of international environmental law which may apply to nuclear weapons beyond a context of armed conflict, both through explicit restrictions on nuclear weapons in common areas and through indirect regulation, by recognising the by-products of the nuclear production cycle as pollutants covered by existing international environmental law.

A.   Applicability of environmental treaties to the use of nuclear weapons

When assessing to what extent international environmental treaties might apply to the resort to nuclear weapons, in addition to the usual criteria of applicability of a treaty (applicability *ratione personae, materiae, locis, temporis*), one needs to consider a number of challenges that have traditionally been raised by scholars and practitioners to the application of peacetime treaties in times of armed conflict.[3]

---

[2] See Chapter 10.

[3] For a succinct overview of the literature on this issue, see UNEP, *Protecting the Environment During Armed Conflict: An Inventory and Analysis of International Law* (Nairobi: UNEP, 2009), pp. 43–6 (hereafter, UNEP Report) and by largely the same authors but with more commentary, see M. Bothe, C. Bruch, J. Diamond and D. Jensen, 'International law protecting the environment during armed conflict: gaps and opportunities', *International Review of the Red Cross* 92 (2010), 569–92. Recent publications based on doctoral dissertations include S. Vöneky, 'A new shield for the environment: peacetime treaties as legal restraints of wartime damage', *Review of European, Comparative and International Environmental Law* 9 (2000), 20–32; S. Vöneky, 'Peacetime environmental law as a basis of state responsibility for environmental damage caused by war' in J. E. Austin and C. E. Bruch (eds.), *The Environmental Consequences of War: Legal, Economic and Scientific Perspectives* (Cambridge University

There are three types of effects that the outbreak of hostilities may directly or indirectly have on peacetime treaties, namely (1) affecting the continuance in force or in operation of such treaties for belligerent states (suspension, withdrawal, termination), (2) triggering a treaty-specific response (derogations, flexibilities, enhanced protection) and/or (3) giving rise to a norm conflict with respect to the law of armed conflicts. We will discuss each of these effects in turn, both with regard to particular environmental treaties and the default rules under the law of treaties. It is important to note at the outset that each and every one of these potential effects must at least be briefly considered before it is possible to ascertain whether a state has breached an environmental treaty in a given case. The above is the logical order in which to proceed. Indeed, if environmental treaties are suspended or terminated in armed conflict, whether automatically or not, it would be futile to even contemplate the second and third potential effect. Likewise, if a given treaty continues in operation but states are allowed under the treaty to derogate from its core provisions in situations of national emergency, no conflict of norms between such environmental treaty provisions and IHL rules can arise. Only if a relevant environmental treaty obligation survives all these preliminary tests may it be applicable to a case of nuclear weapons use.[4]

It is important to distinguish these potential effects of armed conflicts on treaties from the question of the material scope of the treaty. As a matter of

---

Press, 2000), pp. 190–225; S. A. J. Boelaert-Suominen, *International Environmental Law and Naval War: The Effect of Marine Safety and Pollution Conventions During International Armed Conflict* (Newport: Naval War College, 2000); E. Koppe, *The Use of Nuclear Weapons and the Protection of the Environment during International Armed Conflict* (Oxford: Hart, 2008); A. Loets, 'An old debate revisited: applicability of environmental treaties in times of international armed conflict pursuant to the International Law Commission's "Draft Articles on the Effects of Armed Conflict on Treaties"', *Review of European Community and International Environmental Law* 21 (2012), 127–36. Whilst there are a number of theories on the question of applicability of environmental treaties in times of armed conflict ('classification theory', 'intention theory', 'differentiation theory', 'sliding scale theory'), outlined in the abovementioned UNEP Report, in the following we will not engage in doctrinal discussions but simply present the legal issues that may arise with regard to the applicability of treaties to armed conflict situations under the general law of treaties and on the terms of the relevant environmental treaties themselves.

[4] An additional issue, beyond the scope of this chapter, is whether a breach of applicable environmental obligations would be excused by circumstances precluding wrongfulness under the customary law of state responsibility such as necessity or self-defence, but even excused conduct may imply a duty to compensate. See *Gabčíkovo-Nagymaros Project (Hungary/Slovakia)*, Judgment of 25 September 1997, ICJ Reports, p. 39, para. 48 ('the Court points out that Hungary expressly acknowledged that, in any event, such a state of necessity would not exempt it from its duty to compensate its partner'); ILC, *Draft Articles on Responsibility of States for Internationally Wrongful Acts, 2001* (United Nations, 2001), Art. 27(b) ('The invocation of a circumstance precluding wrongfulness in accordance with this chapter is without prejudice to ... the question of compensation for any material loss caused by the act in question').

course, if a treaty expressly excludes military conduct during armed conflicts from its scope *ratione materiae*, then the outbreak of hostilities does not have any effect on the (in)applicability of the treaty to such conduct, because it was not covered to begin with.[5] There is no evidence of an implicit carve-out of armed conflict situations in all peacetime treaties; thus, terms such as '*jus pacis*' or 'peacetime treaties' do not mean that such treaties are only applicable in times of peace, but that they are not specifically targeted at the regulation of armed conflict, hence they may be subject to the abovementioned effects.

Moreover, these effects are not specific to environmental treaties; they may occur in respect of any peacetime treaty, including human rights treaties, investment or trade agreements. International jurisprudence in the context of non-environmental peacetime treaties may therefore be relevant for the purposes of our enquiry.

1.   *Continued operation*

Termination of a treaty, its denunciation or the withdrawal of a party, as well as suspension of the operation of a treaty for some or all of its parties, may take place only in accordance with the provisions of the given treaty or under the default rules codified by the Vienna Convention on the Law of Treaties (VCLT).[6] However, the latter contains a general reservation in its Article 73 pursuant to which the Convention 'shall not prejudge any question that may arise in regard to a treaty from ... the outbreak of hostilities between States'. The International Law Commission (ILC) decided to address this point in 2004 and, in 2011, adopted a set of draft articles on the effects of armed conflicts on treaties.[7] The Draft Articles deal specifically with the first type of effect, continuance in operation and, *a fortiori*, continuance in force, hence we will briefly discuss the elements most relevant for the applicability of environmental treaties to the acts of belligerents.

---

[5] For instance, Art. 19(2) of the 1997 Terrorist Bombings Convention provides that 'the activities of armed forces during an armed conflict ... are not governed by this Convention'. No environmental treaty that we would know of contains such a carve-out, but some impose weaker obligations on armed forces at all times, which is different (see below). Also the exemption commonly found in civil liability conventions for damage caused in the course of hostilities does not mean that these treaties cease to apply in armed conflicts, but merely that private operators are not obliged to bear the costs caused by military conduct, while state responsibility for such conduct is unaffected.

[6] Vienna Convention on the Law of Treaties, Vienna, 23 May 1969, in force 27 January 1980, 1155 UNTS 331; 8 ILM 679 (hereafter, VCLT), Art. 42(2).

[7] ILC, *Draft Articles on the Effects of Armed Conflict on Treaties, 2011* (United Nations, 2011) (hereafter, ILC Draft Articles). The UN General Assembly took note of the Draft Articles in its Resolution 66/99 of 9 December 2011 and commended them to the attention of governments without prejudice to the question of their future adoption or other appropriate action, to be decided at a subsequent session.

The system proposed by the ILC is built in four stages. First and most import-antly, the Draft Articles state that armed conflict does not *ipso facto* terminate or suspend the operation of treaties between belligerents or with third states (Article 3). Second, not surprisingly, if a given treaty contains provisions regu-lating its operation in the event of an armed conflict, those provisions apply (Article 4). Third, when no such provisions exist, as is the case for the vast majority of environmental treaties,[8] the international rules on treaty inter-pretation apply in order to determine whether a given treaty is susceptible to be (unilaterally) suspended, terminated or denounced as a consequence of an armed conflict (Article 5). This determination must not only be based on the interpretation of relevant treaty provisions, but also take into account a var-iety of broader factors linked to the characteristics of the armed conflict and treaty considered, in particular the subject matter of the latter, with treaties on certain subjects – including those on environmental protection and water bodies – being presumed to continue in operation, in whole or in part, during armed conflict (Article 6, Article 7 and Annex). Fourth and finally, the con-tours of this ground for precluding the continued operation of certain treaties during hostilities, namely suspension, denunciation or termination of a treaty 'as a consequence of an armed conflict', are defined in the remainder of the Draft Articles, adapting the provisions of the VCLT to the context of armed conflict while referring to the rules of general international law for questions not treated in the Draft Articles.[9]

These contours specify, in short, that the right to suspend or withdraw from certain treaties in the event of an armed conflict, which is complementary to the customary grounds embodied in the VCLT,[10] may not benefit the aggres-sor state,[11] and is forfeited if the state expressly or by its conduct acquiesces in

---

[8] In R. Mitchell's database containing nearly 500 free-text searchable MEAs, the only treaty expressly regulating the issue of suspension of its operation during armed conflicts is the now obsolete 1954 OILPOL Convention, which provided in its Article XIX(1) that '[i]n case of war or other hostilities, a Contracting Government which considers that it is affected, whether as a belligerent or as a neutral, may suspend the operation of the whole or any part of the present Convention in respect of all or any of its territories' (data from Ronald B. Mitchell, 2002–2014, *International Environmental Agreements Database Project (Version 2013.2)*, available at: http://iea.uoregon.edu/).

[9] See Articles 8–18 of the ILC Draft Articles, and in particular commentary at Art. 8, which explains that the ILC intentionally omitted to treat matters of lawfulness of agreements on modification or suspension, such as the conditions for modification or suspension of a multilateral treaty by certain of the parties only, contained in Arts. 41 and 58 VCLT, 'prefer-ring to leave such matters to the operation of general rules of international law, including those reflected in the 1969 Vienna Convention' (para. 5). This is important for MEAs and the resort to nuclear weapons because of the number of parties and stakes involved. It may have been preferable to include such a reference to general international law in Art. 8(2) itself, similar to Art. 9(3), which refers to the 'applicable rules of international law'.

[10] ILC Draft Articles, Art. 18.   [11] *Ibid.*, Art. 15.

the treaty's continued operation.[12] It is crucial to note in this context that prior notification of the intention to suspend or withdraw from a treaty is a condition for its success, and may be met with objections, in which case states must pursue peaceful means of dispute resolution.[13] Under the ILC Draft Articles, treaties thus clearly continue in operation during armed conflict, except those that a state lawfully suspends with due prior notice, but environmental treaties are presumed not be susceptible to suspension due to their subject matter. In other words, according to the ILC the effect of the outbreak of an armed conflict on treaties is that an additional ground for suspension becomes available, but contrary to the VCLT grounds for suspension it depends on the subject matter of the treaty and a range of other factors.

As to whether the ILC Draft Articles reflect the current state of customary international law, their fundamental principle negating automatic suspension of treaties is consistent with the jurisprudence of the International Court of Justice. The Court has dealt with this question recently in two of its Advisory Opinions and one contentious case, and it has made no reference to the old doctrine of automatic suspension of the operation of peacetime treaties in the event of an armed conflict, focusing instead on the second and third types of effect, discussed below. With regard to human rights treaties, a subtle evolution of the ICJ's jurisprudence can be observed. While the 1996 Nuclear Weapons Advisory Opinion stated that 'the protection of the International Covenant of Civil and Political Rights does not cease in times of war, except by operation of Article 4 of the Covenant whereby certain provisions may be derogated from in a time of national emergency',[14] in the 2004 Wall Advisory Opinion the Court made an almost identical but significantly broader statement extending it to human rights conventions more generally.[15] This view on continued operation was again articulated and applied in a contentious case the following year.[16] Regarding explicit treatment of environmental treaties, the issue was only raised in the Nuclear Weapons Advisory Opinion, and as in the case of human rights treaties the Court rejected the challenge brought forth by certain nuclear weapon states to the continued operation of peacetime treaties during armed conflicts, but reassured these states at the level of norm conflicts between *jus pacis* on the one hand and *jus ad bellum* and *jus in bello* on the other hand that:

---

[12] *Ibid.*, Art. 12.   [13] *Ibid.*, Art. 9.

[14] Nuclear Weapons Advisory Opinion, para. 25.

[15] ICJ, *Legal Consequences of the Construction of a Wall in the Occupied Palestinian Territory,* Advisory Opinion, 9 July 2004 (hereafter, Wall Advisory Opinion), para. 106.

[16] ICJ, *Case concerning armed activities on the territory of the Congo (Democratic Republic of the Congo v. Uganda),* Judgment, 19 December 2005 (hereafter, *DRC* v. *Uganda* judgment), paras. 216, 219–20.

the Court is of the view that the issue is not whether the treaties relating to the protection of the environment are or are not applicable during an armed conflict, but rather whether the obligations stemming from these treaties were intended to be obligations of total restraint during military conflict.

The Court does not consider that the treaties in question could have intended to deprive a State of the exercise of its right of self-defence under international law because of its obligations to protect the environment.[17]

While the ICJ avoided referring to the classical theory of *ipso facto* suspension or termination of peacetime treaties during hostilities, such a doctrine featured in a recent award of the Eritrea–Ethiopia Claims Commission.[18] The Commission contended that in cases 'where the intention to maintain a treaty in operation during hostilities is not plainly apparent from the text or the surrounding circumstances', such as in the case at hand, the parties 'should be presumed to intend that such treaties be at least suspended during the hostilities'. The Commission referred to some old authorities to support this 'principle', but it did not take sufficiently into account the relevant ICJ jurisprudence or the work of the International Law Commission on the topic ongoing at the time. For this and other case-specific reasons[19] the award should not be seen as a challenge to the above-mentioned development.

It should be underscored that the issue of the current state of the law of treaties on this matter is highly relevant for our more specific question of the effect of armed conflicts on environmental treaties, as the latter, like most peacetime treaties, do not explicitly address their operation during hostilities. As a matter of fact, most major MEAs make no reference at all to armed conflicts. Examples include treaties as important as the Convention on the International

---

[17] Nuclear Weapons Advisory Opinion, para. 30. Some scholars have interpreted the first sentence of this excerpt as implying that the Court shied away from answering the question of continued operation of environmental treaties, but when compared to the structure of the section on human rights treaties where the Court also mentioned and rejected states' contention that they were not applicable, our interpretation seems more likely. Indeed, if environmental treaty obligations were inapplicable during hostilities, no conflict would arise between them and the law of armed conflict (i.e. no issue of total or partial restraint, no question of depriving a state of its right to self-defence, etc.).

[18] Eritrea–Ethiopia Claims Commission, Final Award – Pensions; Eritrea's Claims 15, 19 and 23 (December 19, 2005) pp. 6–8, available at: www.pca-cpa.org.

[19] It was a bilateral treaty that obliged Ethiopia to pay pensions to former Ethiopians living in Eritrea after it formally gained independence in 1993, but it was only an interim arrangement while the negotiations on a permanent solution continued (which were interrupted by the armed conflict) and in any event the treaty could be terminated by either of the parties upon twelve months' notice. Ethiopia argued that the treaty ended because of one of these two reasons, not *ipso facto* suspension under the law of treaties as the Commission itself acknowledged in para. 31.

Trade of Endangered Species,[20] the Convention on Migratory Species of Wild Animals,[21] the Montreal Protocol on Substances that Deplete the Ozone Layer,[22] the Basel Convention on Transboundary Movements of Hazardous Wastes,[23] the Convention on Biological Diversity,[24] the United Nations Framework Convention on Climate Change,[25] the Rotterdam Convention on Prior Informed Consent[26] or the Stockholm Convention on Persistent Organic Pollutants.[27] A number of environmental treaties do, however, contain provisions that expressly allow for derogations in exceptional circumstances such as armed conflicts, or that give leeway to states in the implementation of their substantive obligations by way of flexible formulations. Conversely, some treaties provide for unaltered or even enhanced environmental protection during armed conflicts. It is this treaty-specific response to such situations that we will discuss briefly in the following section.[28]

2. Treaty-specific response

Treaties expressly providing for unaltered or increased environmental protection

Some environmental treaties make it clear that they seek to prevent further deterioration of their environmental object of protection even in the event of an armed conflict.

By way of illustration, Article 11(4) of the World Heritage Convention (WHC) provides that the World Heritage Committee shall keep a 'List of World Heritage in Danger' in addition to the normal 'World Heritage List', including

---

[20] Convention on International Trade in Endangered Species of Wild Fauna and Flora, Washington, 3 March 1973, in force 1 July 1975, 993 UNTS 243 (hereafter, CITES).

[21] Convention on the Conservation of Migratory Species of Wild Animals, Bonn, 23 June 1979, in force 1 November 1983, 1651 UNTS 333, 19 ILM 15 (hereafter, CMS). See also Chapter 12 in this book.

[22] Montreal Protocol on Substances that Deplete the Ozone Layer, Montreal, 16 September 1987, in force 1 January 1989, 1522 UNTS 3 (hereafter, Montreal Protocol).

[23] Basel Convention on the Control of Transboundary Movements of Hazardous Wastes and their Disposal, Basel, 22 March 1989, in force 5 May 1992, 1673 UNTS 57 (hereafter, Basel Convention).

[24] Convention on Biological Diversity, Rio de Janeiro, 5 June 1992, in force 29 December 1993, 1760 UNTS 79 (hereafter, CBD).

[25] United Nations Framework Convention on Climate Change, Rio de Janeiro, 9 May 1992, in force 21 March 1994, 1771 UNTS 107 (hereafter, UNFCCC).

[26] Rotterdam Convention on the Prior Informed Consent Procedure for Certain Hazardous Chemicals and Pesticides in International Trade, Rotterdam, 10 September 1998, in force 24 February 2004, 2244 UNTS 337 (hereafter, PIC Convention).

[27] Stockholm Convention on Persistent Organic Pollutants, Stockholm, 22 May 2001, in force 17 May 2004, 2256 UNTS 119 (hereafter, POP Convention).

[28] See also UNEP Report, pp. 35–40.

'only such property forming part of the cultural and natural heritage as is threatened by serious and specific dangers, such as ... the outbreak or the threat of an armed conflict'. The Operational Guidelines further specify the criteria for the listing of a site on this list.[29] Here the occurrence of an armed conflict is a trigger for strengthening the protective regime of the affected World Heritage site that may go from a mere 'message of concern' sent by the Committee, to a system of international assistance to preserve the site as much as possible.[30] In this context it is also worth pointing to Article 6(3) of the same Convention in which states parties undertake 'not to take any deliberate measures which might damage directly or indirectly the cultural and natural heritage referred to in Articles 1 and 2 situated on the territory of other States Parties to this Convention'. Given the widespread and long-lasting impact of nuclear weapon detonation, it is highly likely that cultural and natural heritage in the sense of Articles 1 and 2 of the WHC would be damaged, be that in the immediate surroundings of the battleground or farther away, possibly even in a neighbouring country, and thus the state party using such weapons would prima facie be in breach of the Convention.

Other treaties arguably within this category are those that explicitly refer to nuclear weapons in their provisions. Examples include the treaties on Antarctica, outer space and the international seabed, discussed below. If a treaty prescribes the exclusively peaceful use of a common area and prohibits all military manoeuvres, particularly those involving nuclear weapons, it would go against its *raison d'être* to claim an exception or derogation for wartime situations.

Treaties allowing for reduced environmental protection under exceptional circumstances

A number of multilateral environmental agreements contain derogation clauses for exceptional circumstances threatening 'urgent national interest'[31] or 'the paramount interest of the State',[32] either contemplating the possibility

---

[29] UNESCO World Heritage Committee, 'Operational Guidelines for the Implementation of the World Heritage Convention', UN doc. WHC.13/01, July 2013, paras. 177–82, available at: http://whc.unesco.org/en/guidelines.

[30] *Ibid.*, paras. 183–9.

[31] Convention on Wetlands of International Importance especially as Waterfowl Habitat ('Ramsar Convention'), Ramsar, 2 February 1971, in force 21 December 1975, 996 UNTS 245, Art. 4(2).

[32] African Convention on the Conservation of Nature and Natural Resources, Algiers, 15 September 1968, in force 16 June 1969, 1001 UNTS 3, Art. XVII(1)(i). An important amendment to this Convention was adopted on 11 July 2003 deleting the exception for paramount interest of the state and replacing it with detailed environmental protection obligations for armed conflicts based on principles of international humanitarian law, but this amendment is not yet in force. See http://au.int/en/treaties.

of derogation from certain treaty obligations or specifying less stringent protection obligations in such cases.

For instance, Article 4(2) of the Ramsar Convention describes the protective regime that would apply under such exceptional circumstances:

> Where a Contracting Party in its urgent national interest, deletes or restricts the boundaries of a wetland included in the List, it should as far as possible compensate for any loss of wetland resources, and in particular it should create additional nature reserves for waterfowl and for the protection, either in the same area or elsewhere, of an adequate portion of the original habitat.

The rationale of this provision is considerably different from the one underlying Article 11(4) of the World Heritage Convention, discussed above. Whereas the latter seeks to preserve the endangered site as much as possible, Article 4(2) of Ramsar would – at least on its face – be confined to compensating the (admissible) loss in one place with enhanced protection in some other place. In other words, 'urgent national interest' would seem to override the protection of a listed wetland. In practice, however, the Secretariat keeps a list (the 'Montreux Record') similar to the List of World Heritage in Danger, and it has intervened in some cases to preserve existing sites as much as possible.[33] Moreover, this system could also apply when a listed wetland is threatened by nuclear-related activities short of detonation (see below).

Another relevant type of treaty consists of those establishing a system of civil liability of operators of hazardous installations such as oil tankers and civil nuclear facilities. These treaties are not primarily concerned with the international responsibility of the state detonating a nuclear weapon on or nearby such installations. Still, they are relevant for present purposes because they exempt economic operators from liability for damage arising from acts of armed conflict of any type, including the use of nuclear weapons,[34] and thus indirectly allow for reduced environmental protection in case of an armed

---

[33] By way of illustration, in the pending border dispute between Costa Rica and Nicaragua, where Costa Rica argued that Nicaragua was destroying a Ramsar-protected wetland as part of the construction works of a canal, the Ramsar Secretariat sent a mission to evaluate the impact of Nicaragua's actions on the relevant wetland. The ICJ encouraged this intervention by noting, in an order for provisional measures, that the Ramsar Secretariat was consulted by Costa Rica in connection with the protection of a wetland located in disputed territory. See ICJ, *Certain activities carried out by Nicaragua in the border area (Costa Rica v. Nicaragua)*, Request for the indication of provisional measures, Order of 8 March 2011, para. 86(2).

[34] See M. Fitzmaurice, 'International responsibility and liability' in D. Bodansky, J. Brunnée, and E. Hey (eds.), *The Oxford Handbook of International Environmental Law* (Oxford University Press, 2007), p. 1024ff; L. de La Fayette, 'International liability for damage to the environment' in M. Fitzmaurice, D. M. Ong and P. Merkouris (eds.), *Research Handbook on International Environmental Law* (Cheltenham: Edward Elgar, 2010), pp. 320–60.

conflict. However, some states have reserved their right to hold their operators liable under a strict liability regime even in the event of damage due to hostilities.[35]

3. Conflicts of norms

Even if continuance in force and in operation of relevant treaties is not threatened, and the most pertinent provisions are not subject to derogations, the application of environmental norms to a case of nuclear weapons use may still be impeded by the finding that other conflicting norms prevail over such norms in the given circumstances.

The International Law Commission has recently addressed the question of norm conflicts in the context of its work on fragmentation of international law,[36] providing a useful summary of the relevant practice and the different legal techniques for dealing with such conflicts.

Strictly speaking, true norm conflict arises only in the case of two mutually exclusive norms that would both independently be applicable to the case at hand and thus put the state in a situation of being unable to comply with both norms. As regards the relationship between IEL and IHL, this situation is unlikely to arise, because both bodies of norms aim at protection, not at destruction. A weaker type of norm conflict is relevant here,[37] between authorisations (or rights) and obligations, but there is an additional problem due to the fact that permissions to destroy are seldom made explicit in IHL treaties; they are arrived at by *a contrario* reasoning, which might not always be adequate, especially if such reasoning dates back to a time when international environmental law was still in an embryonic state.

There are three main conflict norms: *lex specialis*, *lex superior* and *lex posterior*,[38] each subject to limitations. The most relevant for our purposes are the principles of *lex specialis* for the relationship between IEL and IHL norms, and *lex superior* for the relationship between IEL obligations and the UN Charter, given Article 103 on the superiority of the Charter over other international obligations. There is also a distinction to be made with regard to the role to

---

[35] E.g. Germany and Austria's reservation to Article 9 of the Convention on Third Party Liability in the Field of Nuclear Energy, Paris, 29 July 1960, in force 1 April 1968, 956 UNTS 264 (reservation included in Annex I, para. 4).

[36] ILC, *Conclusions of the work of the Study Group on the Fragmentation of International Law: Difficulties arising from the Diversification and Expansion of International Law, 2006* (United Nations, 2006). See also the Report, finalised by the Study Group Chairman Martti Koskenniemi, 13 April 2006 (Doc. A/CN.4/L.682) on which the Conclusions are based.

[37] What Jenks called a 'divergence' as opposed to 'conflict', see W. Jenks, 'The conflict of law-making treaties', *British Yearbook of International Law* 30 (1953), 401–53, at 425–7.

[38] *Lex posterior* has found expression in Art. 30 VCLT, subject to the intention of the parties who may give precedence to the earlier treaty.

be played by these principles. They may either be seen to lead to the application of one of the conflicting norms at the exclusion of the other, or they may merely assist in the convergent interpretation of the norms in question. The ICJ clearly favours the latter approach, as evidenced in the excerpt of the Nuclear Weapons Advisory Opinion cited above, and in conformity with the Vienna Convention on the Law of Treaties.[39]

As for *lex specialis*, it is sometimes argued that IHL rules apply at the exclusion of other norms because they are specifically designed for the context of armed conflicts, or, in a milder version, that any other applicable norms would have to be interpreted in the light of IHL as the relevant *lex specialis*. The ICJ explicitly took this stance in its Nuclear Weapons Advisory Opinion with regard to the relationship between IHL and international human rights law (IHRL), reiterated it in the Wall Advisory Opinion, but notably abandoned any mention of *lex specialis* in the *DRC v. Uganda* case the following year and applied treaties of the two branches in parallel.[40] It remains to be seen whether the Court's jurisprudence will follow the same path in respect of the relationship between IEL and IHL, but chances are that it will, because IEL is as much *lex specialis* for the prevention and reparation of damage to the environment as IHL is specialised for situations of armed conflicts.

4. Summary

To summarise Section A on the applicability of environmental treaties to the use of nuclear weapons, we have argued that this question hinges mainly upon one's conception of the effects of armed conflicts on peacetime treaties. We have identified three such potential effects of the outbreak of an armed conflict: (1) a ground for suspension of peacetime treaties may become available, subject to procedural and substantive conditions (there is no automatic or implied suspension), (2) derogations or other flexibilities may become applicable, if and to the extent provided for by the treaty, and (3) a norm conflict with IHL rules may arise, if the norms are indeed incompatible (which is often doubtful) and if the conflict cannot be 'resolved' by convergent interpretation.

Having provided a brief overview of the steps in the analysis of the applicability of environmental treaties to the use of nuclear weapons in armed conflict, we will now consider all other activities involving nuclear weapons and the extent to which they are directly or indirectly regulated by international environmental law.

---

[39] The VCLT does not consecrate the principle of *lex specialis*, as *pacta sunt servanda* holds with respect to every treaty in its own right. Art. 31(3)(c) of the VCLT codifies the interpretation rule usually referred to as the principle of 'systemic integration'. See e.g. *Oil Platforms case (Islamic Republic of Iran v. United States of America)*, ICJ Reports 2003, 161, para. 41.

[40] See Chapter 17 of this volume for more details on this evolution of the Court's jurisprudence.

B.   Looking beyond the 'use' of nuclear weapons

1.   Explicit regulation of nuclear weapons in common areas

A number of activities involving nuclear weapons are expressly prohibited under international environmental law. It is worth recalling that, for the purpose of this chapter, IEL is broadly conceived as including the law of common areas (sea, space, Antarctica), even though protection of the environment may not always have been the negotiators' foremost concern.

The earliest multilateral environmental treaty explicitly governing nuclear weapons is the 1959 Antarctic Treaty, positing the principle of peaceful use of Antarctica and to this end stipulating that:

> [t]here shall be prohibited, inter alia, any measure of a military nature, such as the establishment of military bases and fortifications, the carrying out of military manoeuvres, as well as the testing of any type of weapon.[41]

The express reference to nuclear weapons can be found at its Article V, which provides that '[a]ny nuclear explosions in Antarctica and the disposal there of radioactive waste material shall be prohibited.'[42] Hence, under the Antarctic Treaty any activity involving nuclear weapons, such as their testing, stockpiling, emplacement, deployment, launching and detonation in or from Antarctica are prohibited.[43] The only exception to non-militarisation of Antarctica is the use of military personnel or equipment for 'scientific research or for any other peaceful purpose' (Article I(2)), an exception introduced into the treaty text by the US delegation due to their use of military vessels, aircraft and staff for the logistic support of their research stations.[44]

Only six years after the entry into force of the Antarctic Treaty, the 1967 Outer Space Treaty was adopted and promptly came into effect,[45] responding to concerns over a potential militarisation of outer space in the wake of the Cold

---

[41]   The Antarctic Treaty, Washington, 1 December 1959, in force 23 June 1961, 402 UNTS 71 (hereafter, Antarctic Treaty), Art. I(1).

[42]   *Ibid.*, Art. V(1), but subordinating the rule to any subsequent agreement on nuclear explosions and radioactive waste to which all of the parties with consultative status under the Treaty would be party (Art. V(2)).

[43]   Note that the enumeration in Art. I(1) (cited above) of what would be considered a 'measure of a military nature' is not exhaustive ('such as') and is preceded by 'inter alia' in order to further widen the scope. See the discussion of the treaty negotiations in J. Hanessian, 'The Antarctic Treaty 1959', *International and Comparative Law Quarterly* 9 (1960), 436–80, at 468.

[44]   *Ibid.*

[45]   Treaty on Principles Governing the Activities of States in the Exploration and Use of Outer Space, including the Moon and other Celestial Bodies, Washington/Moscow/London, 27 January 1967, in force 10 October 1967, 610 UNTS 205 (hereafter, Outer Space Treaty).

War powers' increasingly bold ventures into space in the 1960s.[46] The Outer Space Treaty mirrors the Antarctic Treaty in enshrining the principle of peaceful use of celestial bodies, but not of outer space as such. The only comprehensive prohibition of military use of space is that involving weapons of mass destruction. In particular, states parties undertake 'not to place in orbit around the earth any objects carrying nuclear weapons or any other kinds of weapons of mass destruction, install such weapons on celestial bodies, or station such weapons in outer space in any other manner'.[47] However, mere transit of earth-launched nuclear missiles through the orbit or outer space is not expressly prohibited.[48] The 1979 Moon Agreement,[49] while developing space law in other respects, does not expand the obligations with respect to nuclear weapons; it merely repeats the provisions of the 1967 Treaty. Moreover, while the earlier Treaty has been ratified by more than 100 states, the Moon Agreement lacks such widespread support.[50]

Yet another area beyond national jurisdiction where activities involving nuclear weapons have been explicitly restricted is the international seabed. Shortly after adopting the Outer Space Treaty, the international community concluded the 1971 Treaty on the Prohibition of the Emplacement of Nuclear Weapons and other Weapons of Mass Destruction on the Sea-bed and the Ocean Floor and in the Subsoil Thereof (Seabed Arms Control Treaty).[51] The title is explicit enough, as the basic obligation set out in Article I is 'not to emplant or emplace on the [international] seabed … nuclear weapons or any other types of weapons of mass destruction as well as structures, launching installations or any other facilities specifically designed for storing, testing or using such weapons'.[52] In case of doubt, states parties have the right to verify compliance by other states through on-site observations.[53]

As this brief overview of the most relevant multilateral environmental treaties regulating common areas shows, not only are nuclear explosions of any kind

---

[46] The first manned spaceflight took place in 1961 and the first man landed on the moon in 1969.

[47] Outer Space Treaty, Art. IV.

[48] On the political reasons for this, see E. Louka, *Nuclear Weapons, Justice and the Law* (Cheltenham: Edward Elgar, 2011), pp. 181–3.

[49] Agreement Governing the Activities of States on the Moon and other Celestial Bodies, New York, 5 December 1979, in force 11 July 1984, 1363 UNTS 3.

[50] The Outer Space Treaty has 102 states parties, while the Moon Agreement has only 15 states parties, and most importantly, none of the main space-faring nations. See www.unoosa. org/oosa/en/SpaceLaw/treatystatus/index.html.

[51] Treaty on the Prohibition of the Emplacement of Nuclear Weapons and other Weapons of Mass Destruction on the Sea-bed and the Ocean Floor and in the Subsoil Thereof, Washington/Moscow/London, 11 February 1971, in force 18 May 1972, 955 UNTS 115, 10 ILM 146 (hereafter, Seabed Arms Control Treaty).

[52] Seabed Arms Control Treaty, Art. I(1).

[53] Seabed Arms Control Treaty, Art. III.

prohibited in such areas,[54] but also a range of other activities, arguably covering the whole nuclear weapons 'life-cycle' – namely, production, assembly, storage, deployment, launching, dismantling and disposal of nuclear weapons, or any other act that would involve more than simple transit through the area in question. From an environmental perspective, given that any activity involving nuclear weapons may incidentally result in radiological contamination of the environment, it was wise to draft the relevant treaty provisions in broad terms, and to allow for reciprocal on-site inspection. Nevertheless, as most activities involving nuclear weapons tend to occur on state territory and not in common areas, it is important to assess the extent to which IEL may restrict such land-based activities.

2.   Indirect environmental regulation of nuclear weapons

Whereas nuclear weapons-related activities in common areas are explicitly restricted through multilateral treaties, the legal situation is less uniform for areas under national jurisdiction. However, it is worth recalling that 56 per cent of the world's land surface, which is inhabited by nearly 40 per cent of the world's population and governed by almost 60 per cent of the world's states (115 of 193 states), is part of a nuclear weapon-free-zone established by treaty.[55] Only nine states possess nuclear weapons, that is less than 5 per cent of all the states in the world, but these states represent 47 per cent of the world's population and 28 per cent of the earth's land area. These nine states are currently not covered by the Nuclear Non-Proliferation Treaty's (NPT's)[56] comprehensive prohibition on producing or otherwise acquiring nuclear weapons (Art. II). These states include the five permanent members of the UN Security Council, which are recognised nuclear weapon states (NWS) under the NPT, as well as India, Pakistan, Israel and the Democratic People's Republic of Korea, which are presently not parties to the NPT.[57]

Although these states are not bound by multilateral treaty obligations explicitly prohibiting nuclear weapons, that does not mean that IEL is irrelevant to these states' activities involving nuclear weapons. It is precisely when considering the whole range of nuclear weapons-related actions, beyond merely their use in armed conflict, that general IEL becomes most relevant. Nuclear weapons do not come out of the blue: they are designed, manufactured, assembled,

---

[54] The general expression of this rule is enshrined in Art. I(1) of the 1963 Treaty Banning Nuclear Weapon Tests in the Atmosphere, in Outer Space, and Under Water, discussed in Chapter 12.

[55] See Chapters 13 and 14.

[56] Treaty on the Non-Proliferation of Nuclear Weapons, Washington/Moscow/London, 1 July 1968, in force 5 March 1970, 729 UNTS 161 (hereafter, NPT). There are currently 190 parties to the NPT. See http://disarmament.un.org/treaties/t/npt.

[57] See Chapter 15.

transported, deployed, stockpiled, maintained, modernised and dismantled, to name just a few activities short of detonation that could generate nuclear pollution, but rarely attract the attention of international legal scholars. For the purpose of early prevention of a nuclear weapons catastrophe, focusing on the legal constraints on such preparatory activities is arguably more important than further stressing those on the *use* of these deadly weapons in armed conflict. Thus, it is worth assessing the ways in which IEL restricts nuclear weapon-related activities in times of peace before a situation of potential use arises.

All stages of the 'life-cycle' of nuclear weapons may cause pollution of the environment, and this not only through radioactive substances but also through hazardous chemicals used in the production and maintenance of these weapons.[58] Whereas in the early decades of nuclear weapon development after the Second World War modern IEL was still unborn, since the 1970s this field of international law has seen an impressive boom with a great number of multilateral treaties adopted in order to tackle global, regional and local transboundary environmental problems, and to a certain extent, even purely domestic environmental harm, such as harm to natural heritage sites or wetlands of international importance.[59]

With hundreds of multilateral environmental treaties currently in force,[60] it is impossible to discuss all potentially applicable agreements. Hence, in order to conceptualise the diversity and yet interrelatedness of environmental treaty systems, it is useful to distinguish treaties according to the environmental sphere they are designed to protect: atmosphere (air quality, ozone layer, climate change), hydrosphere (marine and fresh water), lithosphere (land and mineral resources) and biosphere (life in any of the other spheres). Radiological contamination stemming from nuclear weapon-related activities can occur in any of these four spheres and typically spreads to all of them through ecological cycles, air and water currents, and through migratory species. The state from whose territory the nuclear weapon pollution originates may thus be found in breach of a treaty that protects the affected spheres, or of corresponding norms of customary international law.

---

[58] For a detailed description of the environmental hazards arising from each stage of the production process, see A. Makhijani and S. Saleska, 'The production of nuclear weapons and environmental hazards' in A. Makhijani, H. Hu and C. Yih (eds.), *Nuclear Wastelands: A Global Guidebook to Nuclear Weapons Production and its Health and Environmental Effects* (Cambridge, MA: MIT Press, 1995), pp. 23–64.

[59] See P. H. Sand, 'The evolution of international environmental law' in D. Bodansky, J. Brunnée, and E. Hey (eds.), *The Oxford Handbook of International Environmental Law* (Oxford University Press, 2007), pp. 29–43.

[60] Ronald Mitchell's International Environmental Agreements Database Project currently includes 515 multilateral conventions and 219 related protocols since 1800, in addition to almost 1,500 bilateral environmental agreements. See R. B. Mitchell, 2002–2013, *International Environmental Agreements Database Project (Version 2013.1)*, available at: http://iea.uoregon.edu.

Specifically, the way in which international environmental law may be used by concerned states or non-state actors in order to curb the relevant activities of nuclear weapon states or demand clean-up is as follows. First and foremost, environmental pollution needs to be documented and, more challenging still, the causal link between a given activity involving nuclear weapons and the radiological contamination has to be proven or at least rendered highly likely. Second, depending on which of the four spheres is affected, potentially applicable treaties can be identified, taking into account the usual criteria of applicability (*ratione personae, loci, materiae, temporis*). Third, the avenues for redress provided by each of the applicable treaties for both state and non-state actors should be evaluated and compared as to their effectiveness and cost. This point merits further explanation.

International environmental law not having its own specialised judiciary,[61] unlike for instance international trade law or international criminal law, environmental claims are being brought before a wide range of 'borrowed fora', which are capable of hearing cases involving damage caused by nuclear weapons-related activities. In addition to traditional interstate dispute settlement by the ICJ, the International Tribunal for the Law of the Sea (ITLOS) or an arbitral tribunal, individuals can bring claims before regional human rights courts and thus indirectly pursue an environmental protection objective. The drawback of the human rights court approach is that individual compensation does not equal decontamination of the polluted area, and pure environmental damage is not addressed through this anthropocentric redress mechanism. The same considerations apply to foreign investors' environmental claims in international investment arbitration.[62] It is also worth pointing out that in borrowed fora, international environmental treaties usually do not confer jurisdiction and may not even be part of the applicable law. Rather, they are used to interpret the relevant treaty provisions forming the basis of the claim.

To the extent international adjudication focuses on reparation rather than prevention, and on damage to human health or property rather than to the environment per se, it may not be entirely adequate as a compliance control mechanism for MEAs. This difficulty is further compounded by the complexity of establishing causation in environmental litigation. It is hence not surprising that increasingly complex monitoring, assistance and 'non-compliance procedures' (NCPs) have been developed in order to verify and assist in treaty implementation before reaching a contentious stage where the state's responsibility

---

[61] The ICJ Chamber for Environmental Matters only existed from 1993 to 2006 and was never seized. On the patchwork of adjudicatory bodies dealing with environmental cases, see T. Stephens, *International Courts and Environmental Protection*, Cambridge Studies in International and Comparative Law (Cambridge University Press, 2009), pp. 21–55.

[62] On the adjudication of environment-related investment disputes, see J. E. Viñuales, *Foreign Investment and the Environment in International Law*, Cambridge Studies in International and Comparative Law (Cambridge University Press, 2012), pp. 83–132.

for an internationally wrongful act would be invoked.[63] Such NCPs can be triggered by a number of actors, depending on the treaty at hand, often including
the non-compliant state itself (e.g. if the state asks for assistance), other states
parties, treaty bodies and, less commonly, civil society actors such as non-
governmental organisations (NGOs).[64] In the event of pollution emanating from
a nuclear weapons production site or from a storage and maintenance facility,
for example in the form of radioactive gaseous emissions or contaminated cool-
ing water, the type of actor most likely to initiate a non-compliance procedure
is an NGO, or a treaty body if it is provided with the relevant data and competence. Environmental information-gathering is indeed a major issue in this
regard, as scientific measurement instruments are required in order to detect
and prove radioactivity in the surroundings of the relevant facilities, the location of which may not always be known. However, considerable technological
advances have been made by the International Atomic Energy Agency (IAEA)
in remote monitoring and environmental sampling in its compliance verification role under the NPT and comprehensive bilateral Safeguards Agreements.[65]
Furthermore, concerned citizens of states parties to the Aarhus Convention on
Access to Information, Public Participation in Decision-making and Access to
Justice in Environmental Matters[66] may also bring a complaint before the Aarhus
Compliance Committee if they consider, for instance, that they have not been
adequately informed about radiological contamination stemming from nuclear
weapons facilities, or not consulted in relevant decision-making.[67]

---

[63] See, e.g., M. Ehrmann, 'Procedures of compliance control in international environmental treaties', Colorado Journal of International Environmental Law and Policy 13 (2002),
p. 377–443; T. Treves, A. Tanzi and L. Pineschi (eds.), Non-Compliance Procedures and
Mechanisms and the Effectiveness of International Environmental Agreements (The Hague:
Asser Press, 2009); J. E. Viñuales, 'Managing abidance by standards for the protection of
the environment' in A. Cassese (ed.), Realizing Utopia: The Future of International Law
(Oxford University Press, 2012). For theoretical aspects see R. B. Mitchell, 'Compliance
theory: compliance, effectiveness, and behaviour change in international environmental
law', in D. Bodansky, J. Brunnée, and E. Hey (eds.), The Oxford Handbook of International
Environmental Law (Oxford University Press, 2007), pp. 893–921.

[64] Examples of the latter include the Aarhus Convention (discussed hereafter), the Alpine
Convention, and the Protocol on Water and Health to the UNECE Water Convention. See
F. R. Jacur, 'Triggering non-compliance procedures' in T. Treves, A. Tanzi and L. Pineschi
(eds.), Non-Compliance Procedures and Mechanisms and the Effectiveness of International
Environmental Agreements (The Hague: Asser Press, 2009), pp. 373–87.

[65] See, e.g., J. Scheffran, 'Verification and security in a nuclear-weapon-free world: elements
and framework of a nuclear weapons convention', Disarmament Forum 3 (2010), 51–64.

[66] Convention on Access to Information, Public Participation in Decision-Making and Access
to Justice in Environmental Matters, Aarhus, 25 June 1998, in force 30 October 2001, 2161
UNTS 447, 38 ILM 517 (1999).

[67] Ibid. See, e.g., S. Kravchenko, 'The Aarhus Convention and innovations in compliance with
multilateral environmental agreements', Colorado Journal of International Environmental
Law and Policy 18 (2007), 1–50.

As to the applicable law, this depends on where nuclear weapons pollution is found: (1) in the polluter state's territory itself, (2) in other states' territory, or (3) in areas beyond national jurisdiction. First, if evidence of contamination caused by nuclear weapons-related activities is found only in the territory of the polluter state itself, then global or regional treaties protecting sites, habitats, species, genetic resources or biodiversity as such are most relevant. Interstate dispute settlement is not likely to take place in this kind of situation because of a lack of legal interest, but non-compliance procedures may be effective, as well as human rights or investment law fora. Not only may substantive obligations to prevent and repair environmental harm be invoked, but also procedural rules of 'environmental democracy'.[68] As mentioned, the Aarhus Convention might be breached if access to information is refused or participation rights are not adequately fulfilled. However, under Article 4(4)(b) of the Convention, '[a] request for environmental information may be refused if the disclosure would adversely affect [i]nternational relations, national defence or public security'. The leeway granted by this exception is immediately restricted in paragraphs 6 (partial disclosure) and 7 (form of refusal and review of decision) of the same provision.

Second, if pollution originating in nuclear weapon-involving activities of one state can be found to have an impact on another state's territory, this constitutes a classical example of transboundary pollution to which the principle of 'no harm' and the prevention principle, as codified in Principle 21 of the Stockholm Declaration[69] and Principle 2 of the Rio Declaration,[70] would apply. Both principles are of a customary nature when the harm is significant.[71] Relevant procedural rules under the umbrella of the well-established duty to cooperate[72] include the conventional and customary duty to notify[73] and the

---

[68] M. Dellinger, 'Ten years of the Aarhus Convention: how procedural democracy is paving the way for substantive change in national and international environmental law', *Colorado Journal of International Environmental Law and Policy* 23 (2012), 309–66.

[69] Declaration of the United Nations Conference on the Human Environment ('Stockholm Declaration'), Stockholm, UN doc. A/Conf.48/14/Rev. 1(1973), 16 June 1972.

[70] Rio Declaration on Environment and Development, Rio de Janeiro, UN doc. A/CONF.151/26 (vol. I), 13 June 1992.

[71] Nuclear Weapons Advisory Opinion, para. 29; ICJ, *Gabčíkovo-Nagymaros Project*, para. 53; *Pulp Mills on the River Uruguay (Argentina v. Uruguay)*, Judgment of 20 April 2010, p.14, para. 101 (hereafter, *Pulp Mills* case). A treaty expression of this norm can be found, for example, in CBD, Art. 3.

[72] Declaration on Principles of International Law concerning Friendly Relations and Co-operation among States in accordance with the Charter of the United Nations, UN General Assembly Resolution 2625(XXV), UN doc. A/5217 at 121 (1970), adopted on 26 October 1970, Principle 4.

[73] CBD, Art. 14(1)(d); UN Convention on the Law of the Sea ('UNCLOS'), Montego Bay, 10 December 1982, in force 16 November 1994, 1833 UNTS 3, Art. 198 (hereafter, UNCLOS); Convention on Long-Range Transboundary Air Pollution ('LTRAP'), Geneva, 13 November

duty to conduct an environmental impact assessment (EIA).[74] This is the situation in which interstate arbitral or judicial dispute settlement is most likely, assuming the damage caused is worth the effort, but such arbitration or dispute settlement would probably be preceded by attempts at other mechanisms, such as mediation and conciliation, or any available non-compliance procedures.

Last but not least, if common areas are polluted through nuclear weapon-related activities, the prevention principle and the duty to conduct an EIA would still apply on a customary,[75] and to some extent conventional basis.[76] In particular, Part XII of the UN Convention on the Law of the Sea (UNCLOS) outlines a number of general obligations of states with respect to the prevention, reduction and control of all sources of pollution of the marine environment, including land-based, atmospheric, offshore and vessel-based pollution. For instance, Article 194(2) provides that 'States shall take all measures necessary to ensure that ... pollution arising from incidents or activities under their jurisdiction or control does not spread beyond the areas where they exercise sovereign rights in accordance with this Convention'.

UNCLOS Article 236 introduces an important carve-out, providing that '[t]he provisions of this Convention regarding the protection and preservation of the marine environment do not apply to any warship, naval auxiliary, other vessels or aircraft owned or operated by a State and used, for the time being, only on government non-commercial service'. However, this seemingly unambiguous exemption contains a caveat under which 'each State shall ensure, by

---

1979, in force 16 March 1983, 1302 UNTS 217, Art. 5; Convention on the Transboundary Effects of Industrial Accidents, Helsinki, 17 March 1992, in force 19 April 2002, 2105 UNTS 457, Arts. 10 and 17; Convention on Early Notification of a Nuclear Accident, Vienna, 26 September 1986, in force 27 October 1986, 1439 UNTS 275.

[74] *Pulp Mills* case, para. 204 ('it may now be considered a requirement under general international law to undertake an environmental impact assessment where there is a risk that the proposed industrial activity may have a significant adverse impact in a transboundary context'). The key treaty on this issue is the United Nations Economic Commission for Europe (UNECE) Convention on Environmental Impact Assessment in a Transboundary Context, Espoo, 25 February 1991, in force 10 September 1997, 1989 UNTS 310. For other treaties see the list of international instruments containing EIA commitments in Appendix 1 of N. Craik, *The International Law of Environmental Impact Assessment* (Cambridge University Press, 2010), pp. 283–93.

[75] International Tribunal for the Law of the Sea (ITLOS), *Responsibilities and Obligations of States Sponsoring Persons and Entities with Respect to Activities in the Area* (ITLOS Seabed Disputes Chamber), Advisory Opinion of 1 February 2011, 50 ILM 458 (2011), para. 145 ('the obligation to conduct an environmental impact assessment is a direct obligation under the Convention and a general obligation under customary international law') and para. 148 (transposing the customary duty to conduct an EIA in a transboundary context formulated by the ICJ in the *Pulp Mills* case to the context of areas beyond the limits of national jurisdiction).

[76] E.g. UNCLOS, Art. 206; Outer Space Treaty, Art. IX; Moon Agreement, Art. 7.

the adoption of appropriate measures not impairing operations or operational capabilities of such vessels or aircraft owned or operated by it, that such vessels or aircraft act in a manner consistent, so far as is reasonable and practicable, with this Convention'.

Similar provisions can be found in other treaties relating to the marine environment, whether they focus on a given area, such as the Barcelona Convention on the Mediterranean,[77] or on a source of pollution, such as the intentional waste dumping targeted by the 1972 London Convention and its Protocol of 1996.[78] The London Convention and its Protocol prohibit the dumping of materials above a certain level of radioactivity,[79] including nuclear weapons parts or waste thereof,[80] but exclude vessels and aircraft having immunity under international law from their scope, requiring only that such vessels and aircraft act in a manner consistent with the 'object and purpose' of the Convention.[81]

This apparent lacuna in the London Convention was the subject of extensive negotiations prior to the adoption of the 1996 Protocol. Most delegations supported a proposal inspired by the 1992 OSPAR Convention[82] and its Annex II on dumping, which states at Article 10(3) that '[n]othing in this Annex shall abridge the sovereign immunity to which certain vessels are entitled under international law'.[83] The wording that eventually prevailed, however, was a US

---

[77] See e.g. Convention for the Protection of the Marine Environment and the Coastal Region of the Mediterranean and its Protocols (1976/1995), Barcelona, 16 February 1976, in force 2 December 1978, as amended 10 June 1995, 1102 UNTS 27, Art. III(5).

[78] Convention on the Prevention of Marine Pollution by Dumping of Wastes and Other Matter, London, 29 December 1972, in force 30 August 1975, 1046 UNTS 120, 11 ILM 1294 (1972) (hereafter, London Convention); and 1996 Protocol thereto, London, 7 November 1996, in force 24 March 2006, 36 ILM 7 (1997) (hereafter, 1996 Protocol).

[79] The dumping of materials containing radioactive levels greater than *de minimis* concentrations as defined by the International Atomic Energy Agency is not permitted under the London Convention (see Annex I, paragraph 6) or the 1996 Protocol (see Annex I, paragraph 3).

[80] Indeed, military materials are not excluded from the scope of the prohibition, unlike the Joint Convention on the Safety of Spent Fuel Management and on the Safety of Radioactive Waste Management, Vienna, 5 September 1997, in force 18 June 2001, 2153 UNTS 303, which limits its applicability to spent fuel and radioactive waste from civilian applications (but contains an opt-in clause for nuclear weapon states to bring their military fuel and waste within the scope of the Convention, at Art. 3(3)).

[81] London Convention, Art. VII(4); 1996 Protocol, Art. 10(4).

[82] Convention for the Protection of the Marine Environment of the North-East Atlantic ('OSPAR Convention'), Paris, 22 September 1992, in force 25 March 1998, 2354 UNTS 67. The name 'OSPAR' reflects the treaty's origin as a revised combination of the 1972 Convention for the Prevention of Marine Pollution by Dumping from Ships and Aircraft ('Oslo Convention') and the 1974 Convention on Land-Based Sources of Marine Pollution ('Paris Convention').

[83] For further details see the account of the chair of the meeting that prepared the final negotiating text for the London Dumping Protocol: A. Sielen, 'The new international rules on

proposal to retain the original formulation but add an opt-in clause for states to bring their non-commercial governmental vessels under the coverage of the Convention.[84] States that elect to do so must enforce the Convention's provisions applicable to these vessels on their own; other states parties must continue to respect the vessels' sovereign immunity.[85]

Notwithstanding, the main problem with nuclear weapons pollution found 'only' in common areas, from whatever source, is not so much the stringent or diluted character of applicable norms, but rather the lack of effective monitoring and implementation mechanisms. There is the challenge of gaining access to reliable data, especially for diffuse land-based pollution sources. Moreover, the prospect of interstate adjudication for an obligation owed to the whole community of states to protect the marine environment beyond the limits of national jurisdiction remains to be tested.

Finally, in assessing indirect regulation of nuclear weapons, one cannot ignore the Achilles heel of the nuclear weapons industry: the special fissionable material used for weapon production called 'fissile material', mainly plutonium and highly enriched uranium. These materials possess an explosive character that normal fissionable materials used for energy generation do not. A progressive step would be to conclude a global, non-discriminatory, effectively verifiable fissile material treaty that not only bans future production but also requires states parties to eliminate their fissile material stocks both in civil and military applications (including thus not only nuclear weapons but also those power plants, research reactors and submarines that still run on highly enriched uranium). The eventual conclusion of such a treaty is not wholly unrealistic because it would attain two goals at the same time – eliminating the threat of nuclear terrorism and achieving nuclear disarmament. However, for the time being non-nuclear weapon states and civil society actors could exert pressure on nuclear weapon states by reminding them of their international environmental obligations through available compliance control and dispute settlement mechanisms.

Conclusion

We have argued in this chapter that there are at least three different ways to approach the issue of the protection of the environment from nuclear weapons. Two focus on the use of nuclear weapons during armed conflict: (1) examining environmental norms within international humanitarian law, and (2) asking whether and how multilateral environmental treaties continue to apply during hostilities. The third approach, in our view the one most in need of further

---

ocean dumping: promise and performance', *Georgetown International Environmental Law Review* 21 (2008), 295–336, at 333–4.
[84]   *Ibid.*; Art. 10(5) of the 1996 Protocol.   [85]   *Ibid.*

legal enquiry, takes a broader perspective and considers nuclear weapons as a complex regulatory object, which not only pollute the environment upon detonation, but already at the production and management stage. Thus, nuclear weapon states may be subject to environmental litigation or non-compliance procedures for breaching their international environmental obligations even absent nuclear detonation. Through such mechanisms, non-nuclear weapon states and civil society could signal their discontent with the current situation and add weight to the call for global nuclear disarmament.

12

The testing of nuclear weapons under international law

DON MACKAY

Introduction

This chapter analyses the status of nuclear testing under international law, including what types of nuclear weapons testing, if any, might violate international law; and whether nuclear weapons testing, in light of general treaty law, would be inconsistent with the object and purpose of the Comprehensive Nuclear-Test-Ban Treaty.

On 12 February 2013 the Democratic People's Republic of Korea (DPR Korea) announced that it had conducted its latest nuclear test, a contribution to the more than 2,000 tests conducted worldwide since the dawn of the nuclear weapons age in July 1945. DPR Korea's announcement drew international condemnation, including from members of the United Nations Security Council, which characterised it as 'a clear threat to international peace and security'.[1]

DPR Korea's test once more departed from a de facto moratorium observed by other states with nuclear weapons. Nearly two decades have passed since the five permanent members of the UN Security Council, all of which are nuclear weapon states, last conducted nuclear weapons tests; the former Soviet Union's last test took place in 1990, when it proposed a moratorium that was subsequently agreed to by the United Kingdom and the United States. The UK conducted its last test in 1991; the USA in 1992; and France and China in 1996. The opening for signature of the Comprehensive Nuclear-Test-Ban Treaty (CTBT)[2] on 24 September 1996 further underpinned the de facto moratorium among these states. The only three states that have tested since 1996 are all non-signatories to the CTBT. While India and Pakistan conducted two tests each in 1998, they soon announced unilateral moratoria on nuclear testing; thus, DPR Korea

---

[1] UN Security Council Press Release, 'Security Council and UN officials condemn DPR Korea's nuclear test', 12 February 2013. See also UN Security Council Resolution 2094, adopted on 7 March 2013 by unanimous vote. The Resolution condemned DPR Korea's most recent nuclear test and increased sanctions against the country.

[2] The Comprehensive Nuclear-Test-Ban Treaty, together with Annexes and Protocol, New York, 24 September 1996, not entered into force (hereafter, CTBT).

remains the only state that is continuing to test, with tests conducted in 2006, 2009 and 2013.[3]

The fact that the major nuclear weapon states have respected this de facto moratorium is consistent with increasing levels of concern about and condemnation of nuclear weapons testing by states that have elected not to acquire nuclear weapons. Many non-nuclear weapon states view each nuclear test as contributing to the improvement and renewal of weapon stockpiles, which reinforces their perception that nuclear weapon states are not genuinely committed to achieving nuclear disarmament, despite the promises they have made and the legal commitments they have entered into. Testing of nuclear weapons has also contributed to undermining the 1968 Treaty on the Non-Proliferation of Nuclear Weapons (NPT)[4] and the non-proliferation norm. While the five major nuclear weapon states are all parties to the NPT and have a disarmament obligation under Article VI of the Treaty, there is no consensus on what this obligation means in practice.[5]

While controversy remains over interpretation and compliance with the NPT's Article VI obligations, the broader international community has moved toward collectively viewing nuclear weapons testing as unacceptable. Accordingly, this chapter analyses the status of nuclear testing under international law, including what types of nuclear weapons testing, if any, might violate international law.

The chapter is divided into three sections. Using the South Pacific region as a focal point, Section A discusses and distinguishes between the health and environmental impacts of atmospheric and underground testing. Section B offers a brief overview of the current global and regional nuclear test ban treaties, with an emphasis on the CTBT, and then discusses the legal implications of these treaties with regard to testing. Section C addresses the international legal implications of nuclear weapons testing by analysing the 1974 nuclear test ban cases in the International Court of Justice (ICJ),[6] the ICJ's decision regarding New Zealand's 1995 application to reopen its 1974 *Nuclear Tests* case,[7] and

---

[3] See the website of the Preparatory Commission for the Comprehensive Nuclear-Test-Ban Treaty Organization (CTBTO) for a history of nuclear testing: www.ctbto.org/.

[4] Treaty on the Non-Proliferation of Nuclear Weapons, New York, 1 July 1968, in force 5 March 1970, 729 UNTS 161 (hereafter, NPT).

[5] For an extended discussion of NPT Article VI, see Chapter 16 in this book.

[6] ICJ, *Nuclear Tests* (*New Zealand* v. *France*), Judgment of 20 December 1974, ICJ Reports 1974 (hereafter, 1974 ICJ Judgment, New Zealand *Nuclear Tests* case); ICJ, *Nuclear Tests* (*Australia* v. *France*), Judgment of 20 December 1974. ICJ Reports 1974 (hereafter, 1974 *Nuclear Tests* case).

[7] Request for an Examination of the Situation in Accordance with Paragraph 63 of the Court's Judgment of 20 December 1974 in the *Nuclear Tests* (*New Zealand* v. *France*) Case, Order of 22 September 1995, ICJ Reports 1995, p. 288 (hereafter, 1995 ICJ Order Regarding New Zealand's Application to Reopen its *Nuclear Tests* case).

finally the implications, if any, of the ICJ's 1996 Nuclear Weapons Advisory Opinion for the testing of these weapons.[8]

The author concludes that it is not yet possible to reach the view that international law prohibits all forms of nuclear testing, although it is severely constrained. The ICJ has, so far at least, not definitively pronounced nuclear testing illegal, and the international treaty regime does not comprehensively render all testing illegal, although strides have certainly been made in the latter direction, including full test bans on certain types of testing, bans on testing in certain areas and greater acceptance of responsibility for the environmental repercussions of nuclear testing. Moreover, not all nuclear testing is yet in violation of customary international law. That said, there is cause for optimism that a customary norm against all nuclear testing is emerging.

A. Environmental and health impacts of atmospheric and underground testing

1. Environmental impacts

With both the passage of time as well as advances in science, the negative effects from testing have become more apparent. A 2000 UN report on the effects of atomic radiation noted that '[e]nvironmental contamination by radioactive residues resulting from nuclear weapons testing continues to be a global source of human radiation exposure'.[9] Thus apprehension over nuclear testing is justified (and in many cases further heightened) by increasing awareness of the environmental and health implications of testing, particularly – but not limited to – testing in the atmosphere.[10] This concern over nuclear weapons testing is also coupled with increasing anxiety about the safety of nuclear activities generally, and scepticism about assurances given at government and operator levels, as evidenced most recently by the tragedy at the Fukushima nuclear plant in Japan.[11]

This section looks in particular at the South Pacific, a region that three nuclear weapon states have used as a testing ground. The consequences of testing are still evident today, with radioactive contamination around many former

---

[8] ICJ, *Legality of the Threat or Use of Nuclear Weapons*, Advisory Opinion of 8 July 1996, ICJ Reports 1996, para. 78 (hereafter, Nuclear Weapons Advisory Opinion).

[9] 'Report of the United Nations Scientific Committee on the Effects of Atomic Radiation', UN doc. A/55/46, New York, 2000 (hereafter, UN Atomic Radiation Report).

[10] See, e.g. *ibid.*, pp. 5–6; S. Simon *et al.*, 'Fallout from nuclear weapons tests and cancer risks', *American Scientist* 94(1) (2006), 48–57; United States Department of Health and Human Services, *A Feasibility Study of the Health Consequences to the American Population from Nuclear Weapons Tests Conducted by the United States and Other Nations* (2005).

[11] See, e.g. P. Figueroa, 'Risk communication surrounding the Fukushima nuclear disaster: an anthropological approach', *Asia Europe Journal* 11(1) (2013), 53–64.

test sites. Nearly fifty years after testing some areas, particularly in the Marshall Islands, remain so contaminated that they are uninhabitable.[12] A brief discussion on atmospheric and underground testing, including the environmental and health impacts of both, follows.

2.   Atmospheric and underground nuclear weapons testing

As the name suggests, atmospheric testing occurs when nuclear explosions are detonated in the atmosphere.[13] Although only one quarter of all nuclear tests were conducted in the atmosphere, this type of nuclear testing is perhaps the best known and is also the most environmentally damaging.[14] The 2000 UN report on the effects of atomic radiation confirms this, concluding that the 'main man-made contribution to the exposure of the world's population has come from the testing of nuclear weapons in the atmosphere'.[15] Atmospheric testing is especially harmful because it leads to the 'unrestrained release … of substantial quantities of radioactive materials', which leads to fallout being deposited all over the world.[16] Further, atmospheric testing is also dangerous because it 'has some of the widest contamination patterns; exposure to harmful radiation need not occur as a result of living or working near the site'.[17] For instance, inhabitants of the Marshall Islands exposed to nuclear fallout from US atmospheric tests experienced radiation poisoning, birth defects, thyroid tumours and leukaemia.[18] Besides very high levels of radiation, other types of environmental damage include physical destruction of the land and vegetation, as well as abnormal and diminished vegetation growth.[19]

Owing to health and environmental concerns, atmospheric testing eventually ceased, with the last atmospheric tests conducted by France in 1974 and by China in 1980. In their applications to the ICJ in the *Nuclear Tests* cases in 1973–74, Australia and New Zealand explained that due to France's atmospheric testing in the South Pacific, radioactive fallout had occurred throughout the region, with New Zealand providing evidence that milk products consumed by New Zealanders during the height of testing were contaminated by

---

[12] Davor Pevec, 'The Marshall Islands Nuclear Claims Tribunal: the claims of the Enewetak people', *Denver Journal of International Law and Policy* 35 (2006), 221–39, at 223.

[13] See CTBTO website: www.ctbto.org/.

[14] While this chapter focuses on atmospheric and underground testing, it is also important to note that nuclear tests have been conducted underwater and at high altitudes (e.g. 40 to 540 kilometres above ground). These tests, however, make up a small percentage of nuclear testing. See CTBTO website.

[15] UN Atomic Radiation Report.   [16] *Ibid.*

[17] J. Barkas, 'Testing the bomb: disparate impacts on indigenous peoples in the American West, the Marshall Islands, and in Kazakhstan', *University of Baltimore Journal of Environmental Law* 13 (2005), 29–54, at 34.

[18] *Ibid.*, at 39–40.   [19] *Ibid.*, at 40–2.

the fallout.[20] In an apparent response to both countries' claims, France publicly declared that it would move its nuclear testing underground in 1974. This declaration of an end to atmospheric testing became the basis for the Court's finding that it did not need to take a decision on Australia's and New Zealand's complaints.[21] Nevertheless, France went on to carry out underground testing in the Pacific region between 1974 and 1992, subject to continuous protests from New Zealand and other South Pacific States, as discussed in section C(2) of this chapter. France's sinking of the Greenpeace protest ship *Rainbow Warrior* at Auckland harbour in 1985 was followed by further litigation between New Zealand and France.[22]

Although less dramatic than atmospheric testing, underground testing comprised almost three-quarters of all nuclear tests conducted in the world.[23] Underground testing is defined simply as nuclear explosions staged below ground level.[24] This type of testing is considered to be safer than atmospheric testing, because the 'tests had much lower yields than atmospheric tests, and it was usually possible to contain the debris'.[25] The only known examples of exposure to radiation beyond the testing site have occurred when radioactive gases 'leaked or were vented'.[26] When venting occurs, however, large amounts of radioactive fallout and debris can be created.[27]

B.   The treaty framework for nuclear weapons testing

1.   *Treaty overview – regional and global treaties in effect*

Pending the entry into force of the CTBT, there is no comprehensive treaty prohibition on nuclear weapons testing. Thus while a series of regional treaties ban all nuclear weapons testing in certain areas, and the 1963 Partial Nuclear Test Ban Treaty (PTBT)[28] bans testing in the atmosphere, in outer space and underwater, no international treaty unequivocally renders all nuclear testing illegal.[29]

---

[20] Request for the Indication of Interim Measures of Protection submitted by the Government of New Zealand, 1974 *Nuclear Tests* cases, 14 May 1973, p. 81.

[21] 1974 *Nuclear Tests* cases, paras. 57–64.

[22] For more on the *Rainbow Warrior* arbitration between New Zealand and France, see D. MacKay, 'Nuclear testing: New Zealand and France in the International Court of Justice', *Fordham International Law Journal* 19(5) (1995), 1857–87.

[23] *Ibid.*   [24] See CTBTO website: www.ctbto.org/.

[25] UN Atomic Radiation Report.   [26] *Ibid.*

[27] See CTBTO website: www.ctbto.org/.

[28] Treaty Banning Nuclear Tests in the Atmosphere, in Outer Space and Under Water ('Partial Nuclear Test Ban Treaty'), Moscow, 8 August 1963, in force 10 October 1963, 480 UNTS 43 (hereafter, PTBT).

[29] Several relevant global and regional treaties include: The Antarctic Treaty, Washington DC, 1 December 1959, in force 23 June 1961, 402 UNTS 71 – this treaty has fifty states parties, including the five NPT nuclear weapon states, DPR Korea, India and Pakistan. This

Regional treaties establish nuclear weapon-free zones,[30] which create a binding commitment by the states parties not to acquire or test nuclear weapons, thereby

treaty prohibits any nuclear explosion in Antarctica and the testing of any types of weapons there; Treaty for the Prohibition of Nuclear Weapons in Latin America and the Caribbean ('Treaty of Tlatelolco'), Mexico City, 14 February 1967, in force 22 April 1968, 634 UNTS 281 – this was the first nuclear weapon-free zone treaty, and it prohibited the testing of nuclear weapons by any of the parties, or their engaging in, encouraging, authorising, or in any way participating in such testing. It does permit nuclear explosions for peaceful purposes, but this is subject to a moratorium until it becomes technically feasible to determine whether a nuclear explosive device is for peaceful purposes or not. It has two protocols, covering dependant territories, and negative security assurances; Treaty on the Principles Governing the Activities of States in the Exploration and Use of Outer Space, including the Moon and Other Celestial Bodies, Washington DC, London and Moscow, 27 January 1967, in force 10 October 1967, 610 UNTS 205 – also known as the Outer Space Treaty, this treaty has 102 states parties and prohibits the orbit of nuclear weapons in outer space and all military activity, including the testing of any type of weapon, on the moon and other celestial bodies; Treaty on the Prohibition of the Emplacement of Nuclear Weapons and Other Weapons of Mass Destruction on the Sea-bed and the Ocean Floor and in the Subsoil Thereof, Washington DC, London and Moscow, 11 February 1971, in force 18 May 1972, 955 UNTS 115 – this treaty, also known as the Seabed Treaty, has ninety-four parties, including four of the five NPT nuclear weapon states and India. It prohibits any implantation or emplacement of nuclear weapons, or any facility designed for testing nuclear weapons, on the seabed, the ocean floor, or the subsoil thereof beyond a 12-mile limit. It does not therefore include a state's territorial waters. States parties are also obliged not to participate, assist, encourage, or induce any state to carry out such actions; Treaty on the Southeast Asia Nuclear Weapon-Free Zone ('Bangkok Treaty'), Bangkok, 15 December 1995, in force 27 March 1997, 35 ILM 635 – each state party to the Treaty of Bangkok undertakes not to test any nuclear weapons inside or outside the zone. A Protocol covering negative security assurances has not yet been signed; African Nuclear-Weapon-Free Zone Treaty ('Treaty of Pelindaba'), Cairo, 11 April 1996, in force 15 July 2009, 35 ILM 698 – this treaty obliges parties not to test any nuclear explosive device, to prohibit testing in their territory, and not to assist or encourage testing by any state anywhere. There are also three protocols, one covering negative security assurances, and a second obliging nuclear weapon states not to test in the zone. Protocol III addresses the special situation of France and Spain with respect to territories over which these states exercise '*de jure* or de facto' authority. See also H. Winge Laursen, 'An introduction to the issue of nuclear weapons in Africa', International Law and Policy Institute (ILPI) Nuclear Weapons Project Background Paper No. 1 (May 2012), available at: http://nwp.ilpi.org/wp-content/uploads/2012/08/BP01–12_Africa.pdf; Treaty on a Nuclear-Weapon-Free Zone in Central Asia ('Treaty of Semipalatinsk'), Kazakhstan, 8 September 2006, in force 21 March 2009 – this treaty contains an obligation 'in accordance with the CTBT' not to carry out any nuclear explosions, to prohibit and prevent any nuclear explosion at any place under its jurisdiction or control, and not to cause, encourage or participate in any way in such an explosion.

30   See, e.g. P. Beaumont and T. Rubinsky, 'An Introduction to the issue of nuclear weapons in Latin America and the Caribbean', ILPI Nuclear Weapons Project Background Paper No. 2 (December 2012), available at: http://nwp.ilpi.org/wp-content/uploads/2012/12/BP02–12_LatinAmerica.pdf; Winge Laursen, 'An introduction to the issue of nuclear weapons in Africa'; H. Winge Laursen, 'An introduction to the issue of nuclear weapons in Southeast

seeking to keep their respective regions free of nuclear weapons.[31] While non-nuclear weapon states that are also parties to regional treaties on nuclear weapon-free zones already have legal commitments of similar effect under Articles I and II of the NPT, these treaties go further by banning nuclear weapons entirely from the region – including nuclear weapons under the control of the recognised nuclear weapon states – and establish a verification regime to ensure compliance with this ban. These regional treaties are usually further buttressed by Protocols to which nuclear weapon states can become parties.

The focus of this chapter's case study, the South Pacific, has several regional treaties relevant to nuclear testing. The 1986 Noumea Convention for the Protection of the Natural Resources and Environment of the South Pacific Region,[32] which entered into force in 1990, formed the basis of one of New Zealand's main legal arguments in its 1995 application to reopen its *Nuclear Tests* case (see discussion below). The Treaty requires states parties to take appropriate measures to limit environmental damage caused by nuclear testing.[33] It also requires parties to undertake an environmental impact assessment before embarking on any major project that would affect the marine environment.[34]

Another treaty of lasting significance for the region is the South Pacific Nuclear Free Zone Treaty (Treaty of Rarotonga), which was signed in August 1985 and entered into force in December 1986.[35] Parties to this Treaty agree to prevent the testing of any nuclear explosive device in their territory, and not to assist or encourage nuclear weapons testing by any state. The Treaty also contains three protocols, including one that covers negative security assurances, and another that guarantees that nuclear weapon states will not test in the zone.[36] France and the UK have signed and ratified all three protocols, while the Soviet Union (now the Russian Federation) and China have signed and ratified the second and third protocols. The United States, however, remains the only nuclear weapons state that has signed but not ratified any of the three protocols.[37]

Besides regional treaties, there are global treaties in effect, the most important of which is the PTBT. This Treaty has 126 states parties, including three of the five NPT nuclear weapon states, as well as India, Israel and Pakistan. China

---

Asia', ILPI Nuclear Weapons Project Background Paper No. 3 (June 2013), available at: http://nwp.ilpi.org/wp-content/uploads/2013/06/BP03–13_ASEAN_WEB.pdf.

[31] For more information on nuclear weapon-free zones, see Chapters 13 and 14.

[32] Convention for the Protection of Natural Resources and Environment of the South Pacific Region, Noumea, 24 November 1986, in force 22 August 1990 (hereafter, Noumea Convention).

[33] *Ibid.*, Art. 12.   [34] *Ibid.*, Art. 16.

[35] South Pacific Nuclear Free Zone Treaty, Rarotonga, 6 August 1985, in force 11 December 1986, UNTS 1445 (hereafter, Treaty of Rarotonga).

[36] *Ibid.*, Protocols 1–3.   [37] *Ibid.*

and France, however, are not party to the Treaty, which prohibits nuclear weapons test explosions and other nuclear explosions anywhere under a state party's jurisdiction or control in the atmosphere, beyond its limits (including outer space), underwater (including in a state party's territorial waters or on the high seas) or in any other environment if such nuclear explosion would cause radioactive debris outside the territorial limits of the state.[38] States parties are also obliged to refrain from causing, encouraging or participating in such tests.[39]

In addition to the PTBT, it is important also to mention the NPT. Although the NPT does not specifically prohibit nuclear testing,[40] it has this effect implicitly, as it obliges non-nuclear weapon states parties not to manufacture, receive, control or otherwise acquire any nuclear weapons or other nuclear explosive devices.[41] However, an important caveat is that the five nuclear weapon states parties (those states that manufactured and exploded a nuclear weapon or other nuclear explosive device prior to 1967) are not subject to any such prohibition under the NPT.[42] Moreover India, Pakistan, Israel and DPR Korea are not parties to the Treaty.

While various treaties ban nuclear testing in specific regions as well as certain types of nuclear testing and testing by particular states, they fall short of creating a complete nuclear testing ban. This, however, is the goal of the CTBT.

2.   The Comprehensive Nuclear-Test-Ban Treaty: history and overview

The idea of a limit or ban on nuclear weapons testing has existed for many years. Non-nuclear weapon states pressed for the conclusion of a comprehensive test ban treaty in annual resolutions at the UN General Assembly, but the nuclear weapon states appeared more interested in further weapons development than in a prohibition on testing.[43] Over the years, however, the idea gradually gained traction, even among states that possessed nuclear weapons.

In 1993 the Conference on Disarmament (CD),[44] a Geneva-based forum for arms control,[45] decided after many years of futile discussions to:

> [N]egotiate a universal and multilaterally and effectively verifiable comprehensive nuclear test ban treaty, which would contribute effectively to the prevention of the proliferation of nuclear weapons in all its aspects, to the

---

[38] PTBT, Art. 1(1).   [39] *Ibid.*, Art. 1(2).

[40] *Ibid.*, Art. 1(2). See preamble. This does, however, recall the stated aspiration in the PTBT to continue negotiations that would end all nuclear test explosions for all time.

[41] NPT, Art. 2.   [42] *Ibid.*

[43] See CTBTO website: www.ctbto.org/.

[44] For more information on the Conference on Disarmament, see International Law and Policy Institute, 'The Conference on Disarmament', ILPI Nuclear Weapons Project Nutshell Paper No. 3 (2012), available at: nwp.ilpi.org/wp-content/uploads/2012/03/NP03-12_CD.pdf.

[45] See generally, CTBTO website: www.ctbto.org/.

process of nuclear disarmament and therefore to the enhancement of international peace and security.[46]

Three years of difficult negotiations followed. As a consensus-based forum, the CD has often been plagued by gridlock, and attempts to reach an agreement on the CTBT were no exception. In 1996, however, a treaty text was forwarded to the UN General Assembly, which on 10 September of that year adopted a resolution annexing the CTBT.[47] Although the United States has not yet ratified the CTBT, President Clinton was the first leader to sign the Treaty, symbolically using the same pen that President Kennedy had used in signing the Partial Test Ban Treaty thirty-three years earlier.[48]

The key provisions of the CTBT contain some of the same obligations as in nuclear weapon-free zone treaties, but with global application. Each state party undertakes not to carry out any nuclear weapon test explosion or other nuclear explosion, and to prohibit and prevent any such explosion at any place under its jurisdiction or control. Each state party also agrees to refrain from causing, encouraging or in any way participating in any nuclear weapon test explosion or any other nuclear explosion.

To ensure that the test ban was 'effectively verifiable' in terms of the CD's negotiating mandate (which was essential for many delegations), the CTBT established a comprehensive International Monitoring System (IMS).[49] This system comprises 337 monitoring stations and laboratory facilities worldwide. It operates provisionally, pending the entry into force of the CTBT.[50] The CTBT also created an on-site inspection system, although this will only become operational upon the Treaty's entry into force.

A major obstacle for the entry into force of the CTBT is the stipulation that gives special status to forty-four states listed by the International Atomic Energy Agency as those that possessed nuclear power reactors or nuclear research reactors at the time of their participation in the negotiations through the CD. The Treaty will not enter into force until all forty-four identified states (the so-called 'Annex 2 States', because they are named in Annex 2 to the Treaty) have

---

[46] Conference on Disarmament, 'Mandate for an ad hoc committee under agenda item 1, "Nuclear Test Ban"', CD doc. CD/1238, adopted 25 January 1994.

[47] UN General Assembly Resolution 50/245 ('The Comprehensive Test Ban Treaty'), UN doc. A/RES/50/245, adopted on 10 September 1996 by 158 votes in favour, and 3 against (Bhutan, India, Libya) with 5 abstentions (Cuba, Lebanon, Mauritius, Syria and Tanzania).

[48] R. Johnson, 'Embedding the CTBT in norms, law and practice', Report for the United Nations Association – UK (UNA–UK, 2013), p. 5.

[49] CTBT, Art. IV(16).

[50] It has been suggested that, in several aspects, the capabilities of the verification system have proven better than foreseen in 1996, due to advances in science and technology. See A. Aust et al., A New Look at the Comprehensive Nuclear-Test-Ban Treaty (CTBT) (Clingendael: Netherlands Institute of International Relations, 2008), p. 50.

ratified it.[51] So far, thirty-six have ratified the CTBT, leaving eight ratifications necessary before the Treaty can enter into force.[52] Of these remaining states, all but DPR Korea, India and Pakistan have taken the initial step of signing the Treaty.[53]

Although the Treaty is unlikely to enter into force in the near future, the CTBT has received strong international support, with 183 signatories (including all five NPT nuclear weapon states), of which 159 have ratified the Treaty, including the NPT nuclear weapon states of France, Russia and the UK.[54] It is also important to note that of the five Annex 2 states that have signed but not ratified the CTBT, two are already under an obligation not to test nuclear weapons, by virtue of their non-nuclear weapon status under the NPT.[55]

3.   *The obligation not to test nuclear weapons under current treaty law and the legal implications of ratifying or signing the CTBT prior to its entry into force*

As previously discussed, most non-nuclear weapon states are bound by a treaty obligation not to test nuclear weapons, both by virtue of their being party to the NPT, and by being party to other treaties, including those establishing the nuclear weapon-free zones. The five NPT nuclear weapon states and those states that are not party to the NPT are, however, in a different legal situation. Although some are still subject to a patchwork of obligations and agreements not to test nuclear weapons in certain places and under certain circumstances, these states are not subject to any specific overarching treaty prohibition on testing. The question nonetheless arises as to whether these states are under

---

[51] This entry into force provision was created to appease some of the nuclear weapon states parties to the NPT – notably China, Russia and the UK – that did not want to accept restrictions on their nuclear programmes unless all 'threshold' or aspirant nuclear-weapon programmes were likewise curbed. See R. Johnson, 'Is it time to consider provisional application of the CTBT?', *Disarmament Forum Two* 26 (2006), 29–31; David S. Jonas, former General Counsel in the United States National Nuclear Security Administration, characterises this inflexible entry into force provision as 'a terrible strategic error' by the negotiators. See D. S. Jonas, 'The Comprehensive Nuclear Test Ban Treaty: current legal status in the United States and the implications of a nuclear test explosion', *International Law and Politics* 39 (2007), 1007–46, at 1009.

[52] The remaining eight states that must ratify the CTBT before it will enter into force are China, DPR Korea, Egypt, India, Iran, Israel, Pakistan and the United States. See CTBTO website.

[53] As has been pointed out, it is ironic that India, which first urged the negotiation of such a treaty, and the United States, which played a leading role in its elaboration, are among those that have not become parties to the treaty. See Aust *et al.*, *A New Look at the Comprehensive Nuclear-Test-Ban Treaty*, p. 1.

[54] For a full list of the signatories and ratifications to the CTBT, see the CTBTO website.

[55] Egypt and Iran. See CTBTO website.

an obligation not to test nuclear weapons as a consequence of either having signed or ratified the CTBT where they have done so (even though it is not yet in force), or through the development of customary international law against testing.

Considering first the CTBT, although it is not yet in force, it has been argued that as a consequence of ratifying or even just signing it, states are obliged not to conduct any nuclear weapons test explosions. This view is founded on Article 18 of the 1969 Vienna Convention on the Law of Treaties (VCLT),[56] which is generally regarded as declaratory of customary international law, although not all nuclear weapon states are party to it.[57] Specifically, Article 18 of the VCLT requires treaty signatories and contracting states (states that have consented to be bound, although the relevant treaty is not yet in force) to refrain from acts that would defeat the object and purpose of the treaty in question. There are, however, two provisos. A contracting state is relieved of this obligation if entry into force of the treaty is unduly delayed – a point addressed later in this section – and a signatory state is relieved of its obligation should it subsequently make clear its intention not to become a party to the treaty.

There is debate, however, as to whether a nuclear test by a contracting state or signatory state would 'defeat' the object and purpose of the CTBT. One narrow view is that such states are obliged not to do anything that 'would affect [their] ability fully to comply with a treaty *once* it has entered into force'.[58] Under this view, a signatory or contracting state would not necessarily be required to abstain from all acts that would be prohibited once the treaty enters into force. In the context of the CTBT, nuclear testing would thus not defeat the Treaty's object and purpose, since a state could just stop testing once the CTBT enters into force.[59]

This author believes, however, that there are problems with this narrow view. First, the ban on testing in the CTBT needs to be seen in the context of a broader object and purpose, as evidenced by the CTBT's preamble. In light of this, the object and purpose of the CTBT includes impeding the development and

---

[56] Vienna Convention on the Law of Treaties, Vienna, 23 May 1969, in force 27 January 1980, 1155 UNTS 331; 8 ILM 679 (hereafter, VCLT).

[57] For example, France, India, Pakistan and the United States are not parties to the VCLT. See United States Congressional Research Service, Library of Congress, *Treaties and Other International Agreements: The Role of the United States Senate: A Study Prepared for the Committee on Foreign Relations, United States Senate* (US Government Printing Office, 2001), p. 43; See generally, Jonas, 'The Comprehensive Nuclear Test Ban Treaty', 1033; A. Anastassov, 'Can The Comprehensive Nuclear-Test-Ban Treaty be implemented before entry into force?', *Netherlands International Law Review* 55 (2001), 73–97, at 77.

[58] L. Tabassi, 'The Nuclear Test Ban: *lex lata* or *de lege ferenda*', *Journal of Conflict and Security Law* 14 (2009), 309–52, at 317 (quoting A. Aust, *Modern Treaty Law and Practice* (Cambridge University Press, 2000), pp. 94–5) (emphasis added).

[59] See Aust, *Modern Treaty Law and Practice*, pp. 94–5, as discussed by Tabassi, 'The Nuclear Test Ban: *lex lata* or *de lege ferenda*', 316.

improvement of nuclear weapons, contributing to the prevention of nuclear weapons proliferation and to the process of nuclear disarmament, and contributing to the protection of the environment. Second, the testing of a nuclear weapon will change the status quo at the time of signature, both vis-à-vis other signatories and also in terms of the broader object and purpose noted above.[60] Third, it can be argued that the testing of a nuclear weapon is an act that would defeat the object and purpose of the CTBT because it would likely precipitate testing by other states in response. As former UN Secretary-General Kofi Annan said:

> a resumption of nuclear testing by one state could well lead to a single cascade of States seeking to acquire nuclear weapons, but also, a variety of cascades, with other states conducting their own nuclear tests, additional States acquiring nuclear devices, and existing nuclear-weapon States racing to expand or improve their nuclear capabilities.[61]

It is hard to see how testing by one state that could lead to a cascade of testing by others,[62] either immediately or over time, could be characterised as anything other than an act that defeats the object and purpose of the CTBT.[63]

Another debate regarding the application of VCLT Article 18 to the CTBT concerns whether the passage of seventeen years since the CTBT's opening for signature constitutes undue delay in the Treaty's entry into force. If so, this would satisfy one of the provisos in Article 18 of the VCLT, and entitle contracting states to take action that would defeat the object and purpose of the Treaty. This author notes, however, that despite the passage of time this is not

---

[60] Tabassi, 'The Nuclear Test Ban', 318

[61] Statement by UN Secretary-General Kofi Annan, 'Welcoming the launch of Ministerial Statement supporting Nuclear Test Ban Treaty', UN doc. SG/SM/10648, New York, 20 September 2006.

[62] Several moratoria on testing declared by nuclear weapon states are specifically conditional on others also abiding by their declared moratoria, e.g. Russia and the United States. See J. Medalia, *Comprehensive Nuclear-Test-Ban Treaty: Background and Current Developments* (Washington DC: Congressional Research Service, 2013), p. 57.

[63] This is consistent with views expressed by senior US officials, for example John D. Holum, former Under Secretary of State for Arms Control and Director of the Arms Control and Disarmament Agency, who stated that, 'It will be widely understood that in the case of the test ban, any nuclear explosive test would defeat the Treaty's object and purpose and therefore is legally prohibited from the time a country signs'. See 'Statement from Arms Control Director on Nuclear Test Ban Treaty Negotiations', 28 June 1996; Anastassov, 'Can The Comprehensive Nuclear-Test-Ban Treaty be implemented before entry into force?', 88 (citing a letter from former Secretary of State Madeleine Albright to several other foreign ministers); Masahiko Asada, 'CTBT: legal questions arising from its non-entry-into-force', *Journal of Conflict and Security Law* 7 (2002), 85–122, at 97 (referring to an opinion by the US Department of State that a breach of a prohibition on testing would be a violation of the Article 18 VCLT obligation. Asada points out that the technological know-how obtained through a prohibited test cannot be erased once obtained, and so is irreversible).

the usual situation of undue delay where the Treaty has fallen into abeyance or disuse. First, the CTBT's membership continues to grow, inevitably more slowly than at the start, since nearly all states have now signed and ratified the Treaty. Second, an annual resolution of the UN General Assembly continues to support the CTBT, calling on states outside it to sign and ratify, and there is also a biennial meeting of ratifying states convened by the UN Secretary-General pursuant to Article XIV.[64] Finally, the work of the Preparatory Commission for the CTBT Organization continues apace, with the IMS well established, supported by states, and correctly identifying the few recent nuclear tests. As a testament to the strength of the organisation and the system, signatory states normally meet twice a year for Preparatory Commission meetings and schedule Working Group sessions to discuss financial and administrative issues and the verification system.[65]

Another reason why the delay in the CTBT's entry into force is not an *undue* delay pursuant to VCLT Article 18 is that it had to be entirely foreseeable at the time of the CTBT's adoption. States understood from the outset that requiring the forty-four 'Annex 2' states to ratify the CTBT before it could enter into force imposed a very high threshold. Indeed, such a threshold was unprecedented, and the expectation had to be that entry into force would take considerable time, but this was the price states were prepared to pay to ensure that all nuclear-capable states would be bound by the Treaty. Therefore, this author argues that the point has not yet been reached where there has been undue delay in the entry into force of the CTBT, such as would satisfy the proviso in Article 18 and entitle contracting states to take action that would defeat the object and purpose of the Treaty.[66]

Insofar as Article 18's application to signatory states (i.e. those states that have signed but not ratified the CTBT) is concerned, it has been pointed out that there is an inherent weakness in relying on it because of its reversibility in that a state may withdraw its signature and thus nullify the obligation.[67] There is a precedent for this in the United States' withdrawal of its signature from the Statute of the International Criminal Court in 2002.[68] In fact it is not even necessary to take the step of withdrawing signature, since a signatory state could find other ways to make clear its intention not to become a party.

---

[64] See, e.g. UN General Assembly Resolution 67/415, adopted on 11 December 2012 by 184 votes to 1 with 3 abstentions.
[65] See CTBTO website.
[66] The Vienna Convention itself did not enter into force for more than eleven years, having been opened for signature on 23 May 1969 and entering into force on 27 January 1980.
[67] Tabassi, 'The Nuclear Test Ban: *lex lata* or *de lege ferenda*', 320
[68] Press Statement, International Criminal Court: Letter to UN Secretary-General Kofi Annan from Under Secretary of State for Arms Control and International Security John R. Bolton, 6 May 2002, available at: http://2001–2009.state.gov/r/pa/prs/ps/2002/9968.htm.

That said, the consequences of the United States' withdrawal of its signature with respect to the Statute of the International Criminal Court, although unfortunate, was not fundamentally damaging to the Court, which was able to continue to operate effectively, and the United States even maintained a level of cooperation with it.[69] In contrast, the consequence of a nuclear weapon state withdrawing its signature from the CTBT, or making clear in other ways that it no longer intended to become party, would be potentially fatal to the Treaty, and the resumption of testing by one nuclear weapon state could be expected to trigger testing by others. A responsible nuclear weapon state could therefore be expected to think very carefully before triggering such a potentially adverse and unstable chain of events and facing the inevitable international outcry.

Since, in this context, Article 18 VCLT applies only to states that have signed or ratified the CTBT, questions remain over the legal obligations of the thirteen states that have not signed or ratified the CTBT.[70] Of this group, nine are parties to the NPT as non-nuclear weapon states, and are thus unable to possess, and by implication, test nuclear weapons anyway irrespective of the CTBT. Some states have also specifically undertaken not to test as a result of their status as parties to a nuclear weapons-free zone treaty.[71] The remaining states are DPR Korea,[72] India and Pakistan, and the recently independent state of South Sudan.[73] These, then, are the only states that are not currently bound by treaty obligations to refrain from nuclear weapons testing. The first three are also the only states that have conducted nuclear weapon tests since the opening of the CTBT for signature.[74]

C.   Nuclear testing and the International Court of Justice

In addition to the relevant treaties, the ICJ has also heard arguments on the legality of nuclear weapons testing and on the legality of the threat and use of nuclear weapons. This chapter's case study, the South Pacific, was at the forefront

---

[69] See, e.g. H. H. Koh, Legal Advisor, US Department of State, Speech at the Annual Meeting of the American Society of International Law, Washington DC, 25 March 2010, available at: www.state.gov/s/l/releases/remarks/139119.htm (stating 'The Obama Administration has been actively looking at ways that the US can, consistent with US law, assist the ICC in fulfilling its historic charge of providing justice to those who have endured crimes of epic savagery and scope').

[70] The thirteen states that have not signed or ratified the CTBT include Bhutan, Cuba, DPR Korea, Dominica, India, Mauritius, Pakistan, Saudi Arabia, Somalia, South Sudan, Syrian Arab Republic, Tonga and Tuvalu. See CTBTO website.

[71] For a full list of signatories and parties to the NPT, see UN Office for Disarmament Affairs, http://disarmament.un.org/treaties/t/npt.

[72] On the basis that DPR Korea's withdrawal from the NPT has been effective.

[73] Realistically South Sudan can be removed from the equation, since it has neither the disposition nor the resources to test nuclear weapons.

[74] See CTBTO website.

of both instances in which litigation regarding nuclear testing was brought to the Court, first with the 1974 *Nuclear Tests* case, and second, in 1995, with a request to reopen its *Nuclear Tests* case. In addition to these two instances, the Court also issued its Advisory Opinion on *The Legality of the Threat or Use of Nuclear Weapons* in 1996. This section analyses the *Nuclear Tests* cases and the Advisory Opinion, and concludes that while the ICJ failed to give a definitive ruling regarding the legality of nuclear testing and nuclear weapons use, some support can be drawn for the existence of a customary international law norm banning atmospheric testing, particularly flowing from an obligation on the part of all states not to damage the environment. The ICJ's foray into this issue also affirms that nuclear weapons testing in particular and nuclear use in general continue to be much-contested issues globally.

1.   *The 1974* Nuclear Tests *cases*

The Pacific bears the scars of many years of nuclear testing, which began shortly after the end of the Second World War, and occurred on and off until 1996.[75] The United States tested nuclear weapons in the Marshall Islands for nearly twenty years, and the UK tested for almost a decade, both in Australia, and also in what is now a part of Kiribati.[76] France's nuclear testing programme in the South Pacific, a particular subject of this chapter's case study, began with atmospheric tests at Mururoa Atoll in 1966, and elicited protests from nations in the region that continued throughout the testing period.[77]

While France was not the only state to test nuclear weapons in the South Pacific, there was particular sensitivity surrounding its nuclear testing programme, since it continued to test much later in the region than other countries, far away from its metropolitan territory. After many years of objections to its nuclear testing,[78] in May 1973 Australia and New Zealand took their complaints to the International Court of Justice, lodging parallel applications as well as requests for interim measures of protection.[79]

---

[75] This section has been expanded upon from this author's previous work. See MacKay, 'Nuclear testing: New Zealand and France in the International Court of Justice'.

[76] See CTBTO website.   [77] *Ibid.*

[78] Application Instituting Proceedings Submitted by the Government of New Zealand to the ICJ, *Nuclear Tests* (*New Zealand* v. *France*), 9 May 1973 (hereafter, 1973 New Zealand Application).

[79] 1973 New Zealand Application; Request for the Indication of Interim Measures of Protection Submitted by the Government of New Zealand to the ICJ, *Nuclear Tests* (*New Zealand* v. *France*), 14 May 1973 (hereafter, 1973 New Zealand Request for Interim Measures); Application Instituting Proceedings submitted by the Government of Australia to the ICJ, *Nuclear Tests* (*Australia* v. *France*), 9 May 1973 (hereafter, 1973 Australia Application); Request for the Indication of Interim Measures of Protection Submitted by the Government of Australia to the ICJ, *Nuclear Tests* (*Australia* v. *France*), 9 May 1973 (hereafter, 1973 Australia Request for Interim Measures).

New Zealand's application argued that bans on nuclear testing that gave rise to nuclear fallout had essentially crystallised into customary international law. New Zealand asserted that international attitudes had 'matured' toward nuclear testing that gave rise to nuclear fallout, thus 'reject[ing] the notion that any nation has the right to pursue its security in a manner that puts at risk the health and welfare of other people'.[80] As general evidence of this, New Zealand cited the development of scientific knowledge regarding the effects of testing; numerous treaties and resolutions that banned certain types of nuclear testing; UN General Assembly resolutions that called for bans and limits on nuclear testing; and environmental developments such as the Stockholm Conference.[81] New Zealand also cited more specific evidence of this crystallisation, including obligations stemming from the Partial Test Ban Treaty,[82] the 1972 Stockholm Declaration,[83] principles of territorial sovereignty, and principles of international law based on the *Trail Smelter* case,[84] to name a few.

New Zealand requested the Court to declare that the 'conduct by the French Government of nuclear tests in the South Pacific region that g[a]ve rise to radioactive fallout constitut[ed] a violation of New Zealand's rights under international law, and that these rights would be violated by any further such tests'.[85] Rights that New Zealand asserted included that 'no such nuclear tests that give rise to radioactive fallout be conducted'; to 'preservation from unjustified artificial radioactive contamination'; that 'no radioactive material enter the territory of New Zealand' or 'cause harm, including apprehension, anxiety and concern, to the people and Government of New Zealand'; and 'to freedom of the high seas … without interference or detriment resulting from nuclear testing'.[86]

In addition to the application it submitted to the ICJ, New Zealand also submitted a request for interim measures. New Zealand feared that additional French nuclear testing was imminent, and it requested that France halt any testing that created fallout while the case was pending.[87] The Court granted

---

[80] 1973 New Zealand Application, para. 24.

[81] *Ibid.*, para. 26; see also 1973 New Zealand Request for Interim Measures for a more in-depth discussion of possible environmental effects from nuclear testing.

[82] Although France was not party to the PTBT. For a full list of signatories to the PTBT, see United States Bureau of Arms Control, Verification and Compliance, Treaty Banning Nuclear Weapons Test in the Atmosphere, in Outer Space and Under Water, available at: www.state.gov/t/isn/4797.htm#signatory.

[83] Declaration of the United Nations Conference on the Human Environment, Stockholm, 16 June 1972, UN doc. A/Conf.48/14/Rev. 1, 11 ILM 1416 (hereafter, Stockholm Declaration).

[84] *Trail Smelter Case (U.S. v. Canada)*, 3 R.I.A.A. 1905, 16 April 1938 and 11 March 1941.

[85] 1973 New Zealand Application, para. 28.

[86] *Ibid.*; see generally, 1973 New Zealand Request for Interim Measures.

[87] 1973 New Zealand Request for Interim Measures, para. 51.

this request, stating that it would do so 'in order to preserve the right claimed by New Zealand in the present litigation'.[88] Although the ICJ thereby ordered France to cease nuclear testing that led to radioactive fallout, France continued testing and declined to participate in the proceedings, arguing that the Court had no jurisdiction. Specifically, France asserted that New Zealand's basis for jurisdiction, which stemmed from both the General Act for the Pacific Settlement of International Disputes as well as the Statute of the Court,[89] was insufficient as the General Act was no longer valid (being a vestige of the League of Nations, which no longer existed). Additionally, France argued that its reservation to the Court's compulsory jurisdiction, which excluded jurisdiction for any 'disputes concerning activities connected with national defence',[90] applied here, as nuclear weapons testing was connected to national defence.

Despite France's assertions, the Court concluded that it had prima facie jurisdiction, and listened to oral submissions from Australia and New Zealand. However, while the case was underway, French officials announced that France was prepared to move testing underground once the current atmospheric testing was complete. Determining that these public statements were legally binding for France,[91] the Court held that New Zealand's and Australia's claims no longer had any object once France stopped testing in the atmosphere, and thus dismissed the cases.[92]

It is this author's opinion, however, that the Court's reading of the New Zealand application was somewhat strained. Unlike Australia's application, New Zealand's was not cast just in terms of atmospheric testing. While the Court did acknowledge that New Zealand did not specify a type of testing with which it took issue, it still concluded that since the application referred mostly to atmospheric testing, it was 'to be interpreted as applying only to atmospheric tests'.[93] Once the Court concluded that New Zealand's application only applied to atmospheric tests, it went on to demonstrate how New Zealand's application would lose its merit once the French stopped atmospheric testing. After the Court thus 'matched' New Zealand's (and Australia's) application, it did not give either country the opportunity to clarify what was laid down in their

---

[88] ICJ, *Nuclear Tests (New Zealand v. France), Interim Protection, Order of 22 June 1973*, ICJ Reports 1973, para. 31 (hereafter, 1973 ICJ Interim Order, New Zealand).

[89] 1973 New Zealand Application, para. 11.

[90] 1973 ICJ Interim Order, New Zealand, para. 16.

[91] For France's specific statements, see 1974 ICJ Judgment, New Zealand *Nuclear Tests* case, para. 35–6. France's public statements included: 'France will be in a position to pass on to the stage of underground explosions as soon as the series of tests planned for this summer is complete', as well as 'France, at the point which has been reached in the execution of its programme of defence by nuclear means, will be in a position to move to the stage of underground firings as soon as the test series planned for this summer is completed'.

[92] 1974 ICJ Judgment, New Zealand *Nuclear Tests* case; *Nuclear Tests* case (*Australia v. France*), Judgment of 20 December 1974, available at: www.icj-cij.org/docket/files/58/6093.pdf.

[93] 1974 ICJ Judgment, New Zealand *Nuclear Tests* case, para. 29.

applications, nor the chance to discuss whether the Court's approach was correct. The Court's judgment was therefore politically pragmatic, as it found a way to avoid having to issue a ruling on the hard legal issues and sidestepped the awkward and controversial political implications that could arise from such a ruling against a member of the UN Security Council P5.

While the Court did not answer the question of the legality of nuclear testing generally, its judgment nevertheless impacted on atmospheric testing specifically, as it held that France was legally bound by its statements not to test in the atmosphere. Additionally, the Court left the possibility for both New Zealand and Australia to reopen their applications if France did not comply with its publicly stated commitments.[94] This was found in paragraph 63 in the Court's judgment, which stated, 'if the basis of this Judgement were to be affected, the Applicant could request an examination of the situation in accordance with the provisions of the Statue'.[95] New Zealand would later use this paragraph as the foundation for its request to the ICJ to reopen the case in 1995, which is discussed below.

2.   New Zealand's application to reopen its Nuclear Tests case

While France halted its atmospheric testing as it promised, it continued underground testing in the South Pacific and extended its testing programme to Fangataufa Atoll. Then in 1992 France, along with several other nuclear weapon states, announced a moratorium on nuclear testing.[96] This moratorium was, however, broken in June 1995, when President Jacques Chirac announced that France would conduct a final series of eight nuclear weapons tests in the South Pacific in September of that year.[97] This announcement came only a month after the NPT had been extended indefinitely, with the nuclear powers agreeing to exercise the 'utmost restraint' in nuclear testing pending the entry into force of a comprehensive nuclear test ban treaty. Non-nuclear weapon states already felt deeply betrayed by China's resumption of nuclear testing within a month of the NPT's extension, and France's announcement that it would conduct testing outraged countries in the South Pacific even more.[98]

---

[94] *Ibid.*, para. 63.   [95] *Ibid.*

[96] A. Riding, 'France suspends its testing of nuclear weapons', *New York Times*, 9 April 1992, available at: www.nytimes.com/1992/04/09/world/france-suspends-its-testing-of-nuclear-weapons.html.

[97] C. Bierre, 'Chirac restarts nuclear tests to protect the "higher interests" of France', *Executive Intelligence Review (EIR) News Service*, 22(30) (1995), 51–2.

[98] G. Spencer, 'South Pacific nations condemn French decision to restart nuclear tests', *Associated Press*, 14 June 1995, available at: www.apnewsarchive.com/1995/South-Pacific-Nations-Condemn-French-Decision-to-Restart-Nuclear-Tests/id-c3c4916a0a143b8b430cda6b1578e605.

Although delegates from the South Pacific flew to Paris to convey the region's deep concern over the planned testing, France remained determined to conduct the tests. New Zealand responded by announcing it would take France back to the ICJ and attempt to reopen its earlier *Nuclear Tests* case. Five other South Pacific states subsequently intervened.[99]

New Zealand faced considerable legal challenges to successfully reopening the case, especially since the jurisdictional basis to bring a new case no longer existed due to France's denunciation of the General Act and its complete withdrawal from the compulsory jurisdiction of the Court in January 1974. However, there was strong belief in New Zealand and the region that all possible means should be used to fight the resumption of French testing. Since it was not possible to bring new proceedings against France, New Zealand had to request the reopening of the 1974 *Nuclear Tests* case by linking its current complaint to the Court's 1974 judgment. New Zealand thus used Paragraph 63 from the 1974 judgment as the basis for its argument to reopen its previous application. It knew that linking the 1995 application to the 1974 judgment would be difficult, though, as New Zealand's current complaint was founded on France's decision to conduct underground testing, not atmospheric testing. Therefore, New Zealand had to demonstrate that its initial application in 1974 was not exclusively based on atmospheric testing.[100]

New Zealand's new application asserted that paragraph 63 was a reservation that allowed for new visitation of the case should France violate its obligations. In relying on paragraph 63, New Zealand's opening statement in its 1995 application directly connected France's current actions and the 1974 judgment, arguing that France's renewal of nuclear testing would 'affect the basis of the Judgment rendered by the court on 20 December 1974 in the *Nuclear Tests Cases*'.[101] Further, New Zealand also asserted that the ICJ had not formally terminated the case, as the 'operative part of the Judgment ... contains no words that could be construed as showing any intention on the part of the Court formally to terminate the Case'.[102]

In addition to establishing a link to the prior case, New Zealand needed to address the issue that the 1974 case focused on atmospheric testing, while the current controversy involved underground testing. New Zealand tackled this by arguing that its previous case was not solely based on atmospheric testing. For instance, New Zealand noted that the Court's provisional orders from 1974 did not specifically mention atmospheric testing, and that 'in the operative part

---

[99] See ICJ, Written Proceedings, available at: www.icj-cij.org/docket/index.php?p1=3&p2=3 &k=cd&case=97&code=nzfr&p3=1.

[100] Request for an Examination of the Situation, submitted by the Government of New Zealand to the International Court of Justice (ICJ), *Nuclear Tests* case (*New Zealand* v. *France*), 21 August, 1995 (hereafter, 1995 New Zealand Request to Reopen its *Nuclear Tests* case).

[101] *Ibid.*, para. 1.   [102] *Ibid.*, para. 7.

of the Orders, the term "nuclear tests" was not limited by the use of the word "atmospheric".[103] Additionally, New Zealand voiced its displeasure over the fact that the Court had taken the liberty of discerning its 'object as being the termination of atmospheric testing', especially since its 1973 application did not specifically mention the type of testing with which it took issue.[104] New Zealand thus argued that its prior application was not limited to just atmospheric testing, and instead emphasised its 'concern at the risk of any contamination of the environment outside of French territory by radioactive material arising from nuclear testing of any kind'.[105] New Zealand summed up this argument by focusing on the newly realised negative environmental impact from undergrounding testing, noting that:

> The crucial point to recall is that no one had any idea at that time that the underground testing … could, or would in due course, lead to some of the results that it was thought the termination of atmospheric testing would avoid, namely, pollution of the marine environment by radioactive material. If it had been so contemplated, the Court could hardly have taken the view that the French renunciation of atmospheric testing could by itself have brought the 'dispute' to an end – for evidently it would not have.[106]

By emphasising that the basis of its 1973 application applied to the negative environmental effects of *any* type of nuclear testing, New Zealand argued that the Court's 1974 judgment 'must be measured not by reference to atmospheric testing as such, but rather by reference to the true and stated objective of the Application which was to prohibit testing likely to produce contamination of the Pacific marine environment by artificial radioactive material'.[107] Thus, New Zealand concluded that the basis of the Court's 1974 judgment had indeed been altered, which allowed it to request the reopening of the previous case.[108] Finally, in terms of potential jurisdictional problems, New Zealand argued that since the 'Court remains seized of the original case … the jurisdiction of the Court is the same as it was in 1973, based upon the 1928 General Act, as well as France's acceptance of the Optional Clause as it stood at the time of the original Application'.[109]

Having thus asserted the grounds for reopening the 1974 case, New Zealand's argument consisted of two main points: first, that France had an obligation to conduct an environmental impact assessment (EIA) before conducting underground testing, and second, that any French nuclear underground testing was in itself illegal under customary international law. New Zealand's first argument, for an EIA, was based both on France's treaty obligations under the Noumea Convention, which in short, called for a basic environmental

---

[103] *Ibid.*, para. 17.   [104] *Ibid.*, para. 19.   [105] *Ibid.*
[106] *Ibid.*, para. 67.   [107] *Ibid.*, para. 67.
[108] *Ibid.*, para. 71.   [109] *Ibid.*

impact assessment, as well as on customary international law, as expressed through multiple treaties, which also requires environmental impact assessments. Some of these instruments, which were modelled on the 1978 UN Environment Programme (UNEP) Draft Principles of Conduct, included the 1985 Association of Southeast Asian Nations (ASEAN) Agreement,[110] the 1985 European Community Environment Assessment Directive,[111] the 1992 Convention on Biological Diversity,[112] the Rio Declaration[113] (which France had supported) and the Euratom Treaty.[114] In recalling these various treaties and declarations, New Zealand noted that this was 'yet another illustration of the international standards accepted by France as applicable in this sphere of activity'.[115]

New Zealand's second argument, that French nuclear testing that caused the introduction into the marine environment of radioactive material was illegal under customary international law, relied on relevant treaties and declarations as well as on the precautionary principle.[116] In terms of relevant treaties and declarations, New Zealand listed several from which it believed all states derived general obligations, including the Stockholm Declaration, the Rio Declaration, the Noumea Convention and the Convention on Biological Diversity. In addition to these basic obligations, New Zealand also stated that 'special rules have developed in relation to conduct which involves, or may involve, the introduction of radioactive material into the oceans ... calling for the most extensive, if not absolute, prohibition'.[117]

---

[110] ASEAN Agreement on the Conservation of Nature and Natural Resources (ACNNR), Kuala Lumpur, 9 July 1985.

[111] European Union Council Directive 85/337/EEC on the assessment of the effects of certain public and private projects on the environment, 27 June 1985, CELEX-EUR Official Journal L 175, 5 July 1985, pp. 40–8.

[112] Convention on Biological Diversity, 5 June 1992, in force 29 December 1993, 1760 UNTS 79; 31 ILM 818.

[113] UN Conference on Environment and Development, Rio Declaration on Environment and Development, UN doc. A/CONF.151/26 (vol. I), 31 ILM 874.

[114] Treaty establishing the European Atomic Energy Community ('Euratom Treaty'), Rome, 25 March 1957, in force 1 January 1958, 298 UNTS 259.

[115] 1995 New Zealand Request to Reopen the *Nuclear Tests* case, paras. 91–5.

[116] For a more complete explanation of the precautionary principle, see Jon M. Van Dyke, 'Liability and compensation for harm caused by nuclear activities', *Denver Journal of International Law and Policy* 35 (2006), 13–46, at 19. 'The essential components of the precautionary principle are: developments and initiatives affecting the environment should be thoroughly assessed before action is taken ... the burden is on the developer or initiator to establish that the new program is safe ... alternative technologies should be explored ... the absence of full scientific certainty should not limit precautionary measures to protect the environment ... whenever serious or irreversible damage is anticipated, the action should be postponed or cancelled.'

[117] 1995 New Zealand Request to Reopen the *Nuclear Tests* case, paras. 98–9.

Besides pointing to a general ban on nuclear testing that caused the introduction of radioactive material, New Zealand asserted that France would violate specific treaties to which it was party should it resume nuclear testing. It
pointed to France's announcement of a moratorium on underground testing in
1992, the fact that it supported the 1992 UN Conference on Environment and
Development, which called on states to not 'allow the storage or disposal of
high-level, intermediate-level, or low-level radioactive waste near the marine
environment',[118] that it was a party to the Noumea Convention and its environmental obligations, that it had signed the Convention on the Protection of
the Marine Environment of the North-East Atlantic, that it was bound by the
amendment to Annex I of the 1972 London Convention, and finally that France
held itself to high standards regarding the disposal of nuclear waste in its own
metropolitan territory.[119] Using France's treaty obligations as evidence, New
Zealand contended that '[t]hese international and national instruments reflect
the view that the introduction of radioactive material into the marine environment is considered undesirable and is generally prohibited'.[120]

In addition to pertinent treaties, New Zealand also argued that France's
non-submittal of an environmental impact assessment was contrary to international law pursuant to the precautionary principle. Specifically, New Zealand
reasoned that the precautionary principle, which recently emerged as a:

> very widely accepted and operative principle of international law ... has the
> effect that in situations that may possibly be significantly environmentally
> threatening, the burden is placed upon the party seeking to carry out the
> conduct that could give rise to the environmental damage to prove that con-
> duct will not lead to such a result.[121]

Thus, New Zealand concluded that France had an obligation to 'provide evidence that the tests will not result in the introduction of any radioactive material to that environment', which in the case at hand would be an environmental
impact assessment.[122]

In addition to its two main arguments, New Zealand also drew attention to
the disarmament context in which the tests were taking place. For instance, the
request pointed to the obligations on states arising out of the PTBT, and also
the recent NPT Review and Extension Conference. Although France was not
party to the PTBT, New Zealand asserted that customary international law no
longer countenanced nuclear testing that caused radioactive contamination of
the environment outside the territory of the testing state.[123]

New Zealand thus sought relief in two respects. First, it requested that the
Court hold that French nuclear testing would violate several of New Zealand's

---

[118] *Ibid.*, para. 100.   [119] *Ibid.*, paras. 100–3.
[120] *Ibid.*, para. 104.   [121] *Ibid.*, para. 105.
[122] *Ibid.*, para. 108.   [123] *Ibid.*, para. 109.

rights under international law, which had also been listed in its 1973 application (see above discussion).[124] Second, New Zealand also sought a declaration
from the Court that it was 'unlawful for France to conduct such nuclear tests
before it has undertaken an Environmental Impact Assessment according to
accepted international standards', which would thus oblige France to show that
testing would not give rise to radioactive contamination of the marine environment prior to conducting it.[125]

Finally, as in 1973, New Zealand also submitted a request for provisional
measures, asking the Court to ensure that 'France refrain from conducting any
further tests at Mururoa and Fangataufa atolls', and to 'undertake an environmental impact assessment of the proposed nuclear tests',[126] pending the final
decision of the Court.[127] Shortly thereafter, applications to intervene in support
of the New Zealand case were filed by Australia, Federated States of Micronesia,
the Marshall Islands, Solomon Islands and Western Samoa.

France responded, as in 1973, that the Court had no jurisdiction to entertain
New Zealand's requests. France asserted that the original case concerned only
atmospheric testing, and 'that New Zealand had at the time considered itself
reassured by the shift to underground testing because of the safety guarantees it
offered'.[128] Thus, France concluded that 'in the event of a fresh application, New
Zealand would have had to indicate a "present-day" jurisdictional link between
itself and France'.[129] Nevertheless, in a departure from its stance in 1974, France
participated in the proceedings, including a public hearing where the Court
considered the question of whether the New Zealand requests fell within the
provisions of paragraph 63 of the 1974 judgment.[130] Additionally, during this
time France conducted its first test, which was followed by unrest in French
Polynesia.[131]

After hearing oral submissions, the Court held that New Zealand's application should not proceed further, as the original case that New Zealand
sought to reopen could only be seen in the context of atmospheric rather than

---

[124] *Ibid.*, para. 113.   [125] *Ibid.*

[126] Further Request for the Indication of Provisional Measures, submitted by the Government
of New Zealand to the ICJ, *Nuclear Tests* case (*New Zealand* v. *France*), 21 August 1995
(hereafter, 1995 New Zealand Request for Provisional Measures), para. 5.

[127] *Ibid.*

[128] 1995 ICJ Judgment Regarding New Zealand's Application to Reopen its *Nuclear Tests* case,
para. 39.

[129] *Ibid.*, para. 40.

[130] See ICJ Oral Proceedings, available at: www.icj-cij.org/docket/index.php?p1=3&p2=3&k=
cd&case=97&code=nzfr&p3=2; 1995 ICJ Judgment Regarding New Zealand's Application
to Reopen its *Nuclear Tests* case.

[131] P. Shenon, 'France, despite wide protests, explodes a nuclear device', *New York Times*, 6
September 1995, available at: www.nytimes.com/1995/09/06/world/france-despite-wide-
protests-explodes-a-nuclear-device.html.

underground nuclear tests.[132] The Court declared that it could not resume the case because it was constrained by the literal terms of its 1974 judgment, which was limited to nuclear testing in the atmosphere. By relying on procedural formalities, therefore, the Court was able to once again excuse itself from issuing an opinion on the merits of the case with the awkwardness that would have engendered

Nevertheless while the 1995 case did not rule on the legality of nuclear weapons testing, New Zealand's application was able to highlight on a global stage prominent arguments against nuclear testing and arguments for the need for environmental assessments and protections. Additionally, although the application was dismissed, it made a powerful argument that global views and norms were indeed turning increasingly against nuclear testing. This case showcased increasing concern for the environment under international law, with the Court determining that its order was without prejudice 'to the obligations of States to respect and protect the natural environment, obligations to which both New Zealand and France have in the present instance reaffirmed their commitment'.[133] It illustrated that while there might as yet be no comprehensive prohibition or international legal standard regarding underground nuclear testing, there remains concerted opposition to nuclear testing, and that all states, regardless of their views on nuclear testing, are still bound by certain environmental obligations. All of this added to the political and moral pressure being placed on France and any other nuclear weapon states contemplating testing, and was a further nail in the coffin of nuclear testing.

3.   The Nuclear Weapons Advisory Opinion

Less than a year later, the Court drew on the above environmental statement in its Advisory Opinion of 8 July 1996, on the *Legality of the Threat or Use of Nuclear Weapons*. While the Court held that there was neither authorisation nor prohibition of the threat or use of nuclear weapons in customary international law,[134] and did not specifically address nuclear testing, it commented that 'states must take environmental considerations into account when assessing what is necessary and proportionate in the pursuit of legitimate military objectives'.[135] The Court also recognised:

> that the environment is under daily threat and that the use of nuclear weapons could constitute a catastrophe for the environment … [T]he environment is not an abstraction but represents the living space, the quality of life and the very health of human beings, including generations unborn. The

---

[132]   1995 ICJ Judgment Regarding New Zealand's Application to Reopen its *Nuclear Tests* case, paras. 57–64.
[133]   *Ibid.*, para. 64.   [134]   Nuclear Weapons Advisory Opinion, para. 105.
[135]   *Ibid.*, para. 30.

existence of the general obligation of States to ensure that activities within their jurisdiction and control respect the environment of other States or of areas beyond national control is now part of the corpus of international law relating to the environment.[136]

The Advisory Opinion therefore supported stronger protection for the environment from nuclear activity under international law, and further strengthened the environmental arguments against nuclear testing.

Conclusion

Although the CTBT has not yet entered into force, realisation of a comprehensive ban on testing is not limited to specific treaty obligations. Viewed through the lens of increased environmental awareness and obligations, the creation and maturation of numerous regional and testing-specific treaties, international jurisprudence and various international declarations reflecting increased concern about and sensitivity to the unintended consequences of nuclear activities,[137] there is room for optimism that a full ban on nuclear testing will come to fruition. Indeed there is also the separate question whether, given the history and background of nuclear testing, a customary rule of international law has already developed that now obliges states to refrain from nuclear weapons testing irrespective of the CTBT.

It is well established that rules in treaty law and customary law dealing with the same subject matter can exist side by side. The two requirements for customary law, as found in Article 38(b) of the Statute of the ICJ, are state practice and *opinio juris*, which means that states, when carrying out their practice, do so because they believe it is a legal obligation.[138] Thus, when addressing whether a ban on nuclear testing has crystallised into customary international law, one must determine if both state practice and *opinio juris* support this. This determination, however, is much easier to make with respect to atmospheric testing than for underground testing.

---

[136] *Ibid.*, para. 29. The ICJ did not further elaborate on the international law concerning nuclear testing in its Advisory Opinion.

[137] For public opinion regarding recent nuclear disasters, see M. Cooper and D. Sussman, 'Nuclear power loses support in new poll', *New York Times*, 22 March 2011, available at: www.nytimes.com/2011/03/23/us/23poll.html?_r=2&; J. Makinen and R. Vartabedian, 'Containing a calamity creates another nuclear nightmare', *Sydney Morning Herald*, 9 April 2011, available at: www.smh.com.au/environment/containing-a-calamity-creates-another-nuclear-nightmare-20110408–1d7qn.html; R. Black, 'Fukushima: as bad as Chernobyl?', *BBC News*, 12 April 2011, available at: www.bbc.co.uk/news/science-environment-13048916.

[138] For a more detailed discussion of state practice and *opinio juris*, see I. Brownlie, *Principles of Public International Law*, 7th edn (Oxford University Press, 2008); and R. Jennings and A. Watts, *Oppenheim's International Law*, 9th edn, 2 vols. (Oxford University Press, 1992), Vol. I, p. 30.

In terms of state practice and atmospheric testing, no state has conducted atmospheric testing since 1980, with France as the last NPT nuclear weapon state concluding this type of testing in 1974. It is of course true that norms of abstention, such as refraining from nuclear weapons testing, can be harder to identify and crystallise as part of customary international law than norms requiring positive action. For example, nuclear weapon states have long argued that the lack of use of nuclear weapons since 1945 is not evidence of a customary ban on their use, but instead that deterrence works. When states discontinued testing in the atmosphere, however, they continued to test underground, showing that the discontinuation of atmospheric testing was a specific and deliberate decision.[139]

There is also a long-standing obligation to prevent transboundary harm arising from hazardous activities, as articulated in the *Trail Smelter* case in 1938,[140] and more recently recognised by the ICJ in its 1996 Advisory Opinion as well as the *Nuclear Test* cases. It has also been reflected in various international declarations over the years. There has also been increasing awareness of and sensitivity to the unintended consequences of nuclear activities, exacerbated by the Chernobyl disaster and more recently the tragedy at Fukushima.

In all the circumstances, including consistent state practice over recent years, it seems reasonable to conclude that there is now a legal norm against the atmospheric testing of nuclear weapons.

Whether there is a legal norm against the underground testing of nuclear weapons is more problematic. Unlike atmospheric testing, recent state practice regarding underground testing is not uniform. Certainly, since the CTBT was opened for signature in 1996, none of the NPT nuclear weapon states has conducted underground nuclear weapons tests. The three states that have tested since 1996 – India, Pakistan and DPR Korea – faced international criticism and sanctions, and India and Pakistan have since declared moratoria. State practice does therefore seem to be coalescing.

Finding evidence of relevant *opinio juris*, though, remains a challenge. Specifically, there is little evidence that states refrain from nuclear testing out of a sense of general legal obligation, apart from any applicable treaty obligations. This is consistent with the *Nuclear Tests* cases, and the ICJ's Advisory Opinion, which avoided pronouncing on the matter. It is also noteworthy that condemnatory statements from the UN Security Council regarding the nuclear testing by India and Pakistan, and even DPR Korea, have been cast in terms of threats posed to international peace and security rather than breaches of international legal obligations not to test.[141] Similarly, the individual statements of

---

[139] Tabassi, 'The Nuclear Test Ban: *lex lata* or *de lege ferenda*', 333.

[140] *Trail Smelter* case (*United States* v. *Canada*), Award of 16 April 1938, republished in III UN Reports of International Arbitral Awards (United Nations, 2006), pp. 1905–37, available at: http://legal.un.org/riaa/cases/vol_III/1905–1982.pdf.

[141] See analysis by Asada, 'CTBT: legal questions arising from its non-entry-into-force', 92–4.

condemnation from the NPT nuclear weapon states did not allege breaches of international legal obligations not to test.[142] Obviously such statements will have been carefully crafted, and it is reasonable to conclude that the omission of any suggestion of a legal breach was intentional. By not suggesting that testing has breached customary international legal obligations, the NPT nuclear weapon states are keeping open their own legal options should they wish to test in the future, unlikely as that may be.

Even if there was a general rule of customary international law prohibiting underground testing, India and Pakistan, and possibly DPR Korea, would doubtless argue that they have been persistent objectors to the applicability of any such rule to them.[143] This is because they made it clear from both their actions and statements that they do not consider themselves bound to refrain from testing nuclear weapons, especially since they are in possession of nuclear weapons and are not signatories to the CTBT or the NPT.

While it is therefore probably premature to conclude that there is yet a customary international law prohibition on nuclear testing in all its forms, states' options to test underground are clearly closing. In the case of the NPT nuclear weapon states, their self-denial by virtue of their moratoria, coupled with their legal obligations as contracting states or signatories to the CTBT and the other treaty obligations they have undertaken, together with their robust denunciation of those three states that have tested, means that their options are reducing by the day. Unlike India and Pakistan, and possibly DPR Korea, they are unable to avail themselves of any persistent objector status against the formation of customary law. In this situation, it will be increasingly difficult for India, Pakistan and DPR Korea to be holdouts. The unacceptability of nuclear testing to the international community at large is clear and unequivocal, and the journey enshrined in the CTBT seems to be reaching its natural end.

---

[142] With the exception of possible NPT obligations in the case of DPR Korea.

[143] Tabassi argues that DPR Korea would not benefit from persistent objector status as it has left it too late. Tabassi, 'The Nuclear Test Ban: *lex lata* or *de lege ferenda*', 348.

PART V

International disarmament law

13

International law, nuclear weapon-free zones and the proposed zone free of weapons of mass destruction in the Middle East

MARCO ROSCINI

Introduction

Article VII of the 1968 Treaty on the Non-Proliferation of Nuclear Weapons (NPT) supports the establishment of nuclear weapon-free zones (NWFZs) as a regional component of the non-proliferation regime.[1] In 1975 the UN General Assembly defined an NWFZ as:

> any zone, recognized as such by the General Assembly of the United Nations, which any group of States in the free exercise of their sovereignty, has established by virtue of a treaty or convention whereby: (a) the statute of total absence of nuclear weapons to which the zone shall be subject, including the procedure for the delimitation of the zone, is defined; (b) an international system of verification and control is established to guarantee compliance with the obligations deriving from that statute.[2]

Thus, according to the General Assembly, an NWFZ has two essential components: the total absence of nuclear weapons within the zone and the presence of an international verification and control machinery.[3]

This chapter is based on developments as of June 2013 and all websites were also last visited during that month.

[1] 'Nothing in this Treaty affects the right of any group of States to conclude regional treaties in order to assure the total absence of nuclear weapons in their respective territories.' Treaty on the Non-Proliferation of Nuclear Weapons, New York, 1 July 1968, in force 5 March 1970, 729 UNTS 161, Art. VII (hereafter, NPT).

[2] UN General Assembly Resolution 3472(XXX)B, UN doc. A/RES/3472(XXX)B, adopted on 11 December 1975.

[3] In 1976 a group of experts appointed by the Conference of the Committee on Disarmament presented a comprehensive study setting out the principles that should be taken into account in order to establish an NWFZ. According to the study, (1) disarmament obligations may be assumed not only by large groups of states, but also by smaller groups and even by individual countries; (2) the agreement must ensure the absence of nuclear weapons in the region; (3) the initiative for the creation of the NWFZ should come from regional states and participation must be voluntary; (4) ideally, all regional states (and in particular those militarily significant) should participate in the initiative; (5) an effective system of verification of

Five treaties establishing NWFZs have been concluded so far: the 1967 Treaty of Tlatelolco for the Prohibition of Nuclear Weapons in Latin America and the Caribbean, the 1985 Treaty of Rarotonga on the South Pacific NWFZ, the 1995 Bangkok Treaty on the South-East Asia NWFZ, the 1996 Pelindaba Treaty on the African NWFZ and the 2006 Semipalatinsk Treaty on an NWFZ in Central Asia.[4] All five treaties have entered into force. Mongolia has also unilaterally declared itself a nuclear weapon-free state[5] and Antarctica is free of weapons of mass destruction (WMDs) as a consequence of the 1959 Washington Treaty that demilitarised the continent and devoted it to exclusively peaceful purposes.[6] Together, these zones cover the entire Southern hemisphere and one unstable region in the Northern hemisphere.

While proposals for an NWFZ in the Middle East were put forward as early as 1962, in 1974 Iran and Egypt formally submitted a draft resolution to the UN General Assembly calling for the establishment of such a zone.[7] In 1990 Egypt proposed to broaden the scope of the zone and turn it into a WMD-free zone so as to encompass not only Israel's nuclear programme, but also the chemical and bacteriological weapons possessed by other Middle Eastern states. Since the 1980s the UN General Assembly has annually adopted a resolution by consensus supporting the initiative.[8] The WMD-free zone was also mentioned, among

---

compliance must be set up by the agreement; (6) cooperation on all peaceful uses of nuclear energy should be promoted; and (7) the treaty should be of unlimited duration. UN Centre for Disarmament Department of Political and Security Council Affairs, 'Comprehensive Study of the Question of Nuclear-Weapon-Free Zones in All Its Aspects (Special Report of the Conference of the Committee on Disarmament', UN doc. A/10027/Add. 1, New York, 1976 (hereafter, 1976 Comprehensive Study), Annex 1, para. 90. These guidelines were updated (but not substantially modified) by the UN Disarmament Commission in April 1999 ('Establishment of nuclear-weapon-free zones on the basis of arrangements freely arrived at among the States of the region concerned', UN doc. A/54/42, Annex I (hereafter, Report of the Disarmament Commission), text in 24 *United Nations Disarmament Yearbook* (1999), pp. 248ff.). It is to be noted that the 1999 guidelines, like those of 1976, are meant to guide states in establishing NWFZs but cannot be regarded as binding or exhaustive, or be interpreted such as to prejudice the establishment of an NWFZ.

[4] The text of the treaties is available on the website of the Agency for the Prohibition of Nuclear Weapons in Latin America and the Caribbean (OPANAL): www.opanal.org/NWFZ/nwfz.htm.

[5] Law of Mongolia on its nuclear-weapon-free status, adopted on 3 February 2000, available at: www.opanal.org/NWFZ/Mongolia/mongolia_en.htm.

[6] The Antarctic Treaty ('Washington Treaty'), Washington DC, 1 December 1959, in force 23 June 1961, 402 UNTS 71; 19 ILM 860, Art. I.

[7] UN General Assembly Resolution 3263(XXIX), UN doc. A/RES/3263(XXIX), 9 December 1974. A similar resolution has been adopted every year since then. See P. M. Lewis, 'A Middle East free of nuclear weapons: possible, probable or pipe-dream?', *International Affairs* 89 (2013), 433–50, at 435–6.

[8] The first resolution to be adopted by the UN General Assembly on the issue was Resolution 3263 of 9 December 1974. Resolution 46/30 of 6 December 1991 is the first to extend the initiative to all WMDs. The most recent resolution is so far Resolution 67/28 of 11 December 2012. The Arab League has also supported the initiative and called for the drafting of a treaty.

others, in Security Council Resolution 687 (1991) on Iraq. Concrete negotiations were, however, stalled for a long time. They gained renewed momentum at the 1995 Review and Extension Conference of the NPT, when the so-called Middle East Resolution was adopted as part of the package deal for Arab states to support the indefinite extension of the NPT.[9] The Resolution, which was reaffirmed at the 2000 NPT Review Conference,[10] endorsed the peace process in the Middle East, called on the remaining states not party to the NPT to accede as soon as possible and accept full scope safeguards of the International Atomic Energy Agency (IAEA), and called on all Middle East states and NPT parties, in particular the nuclear weapon states, to make every effort to establish a WMD-free zone in the region. The subsequent 2010 NPT Review Conference called for a conference, to be held in 2012, with a view to the establishment of the zone.[11] In October 2011 the UN Secretary-General announced that Finland had been chosen to host the conference with Jaakko Laajava, Under-Secretary of State in Finland's Ministry of Foreign Affairs, acting as 'facilitator'. However, the conference was postponed and it is unclear if and when it will take place.[12] In any case, the conference's purpose was never to adopt a treaty, but merely to be a further step in the negotiation process that should eventually lead to the long-term goal of drafting and adopting a treaty.

Significant political obstacles have hampered negotiations to establish the WMD-free zone, including the ongoing Israeli–Palestinian conflict, the insurgency in Iraq and the concerns over Iran's nuclear programme.[13] The recent uprisings in several Middle Eastern and North African countries, and in particular the non-international armed conflict in Syria, have also further complicated the matter. The main obstacle is, however, Israel's 'nuclear ambiguity'. Even though never officially confirmed, it is believed that after the 1967 Six Day War Israel acquired between 80 and 200 nuclear warheads.[14] Israel considers this a deterrent against threats from some of its neighbours. Nevertheless, this

---

[9] 1995 NPT Review and Extension Conference, 'Resolution on the Middle East', NPT/CONF.1995/32/RES/1, available at: www.un.org/disarmament/WMD/Nuclear/1995-NPT/pdf/Resolution_MiddleEast.pdf.

[10] 2000 Review Conference of the Parties to the Treaty on the Non-Proliferation of Nuclear Weapons, Final Document, Vol. I, NPT/CONF.2000/28, pp. 16–18, available at: www.un.org/disarmament/WMD/Nuclear/pdf/finaldocs/2000%20-%20NY%20-%20NPT%20Review%20Conference%20-%20Final%20Document%20Parts%20I%20and%20II.pdf.

[11] 2010 Review Conference of the Parties to the Treaty on the Non-Proliferation of Nuclear Weapons, Final Document, Vol. I, NPT/CONF.2010/50, pp. 30–1, available at: www.un.org/ga/search/view_doc.asp?symbol=NPT/CONF.2010/50(VOL.I)&referer=http://www.un.org/en/conf/npt/2010/&Lang=E.

[12] See the conclusion to this chapter.

[13] M. Hamel-Green, 'Nuclear-weapon-free-zone initiatives: challenges and opportunities for regional cooperation on non-proliferation', Global Change, Peace and Security 21 (2009), 357–76, at 361.

[14] Ibid., p. 362.

deterrent did not prevent the 1973 Yom Kippur War, Saddam Hussein's launch of Scud missiles in the 1991 Gulf War or the firing of rockets into Israel by Hezbollah and Hamas. On the contrary, it might have encouraged the acquisition of chemical weapons by other Middle Eastern states and perhaps also Iran's nuclear programme.[15] Israel continues to maintain that it is prepared to start discussions on a WMD-free zone only when peace with every state in the region is achieved, while Arab states see a WMD-free zone as an instrument to achieving peace in the Middle East.[16] In support of Israel's position, the United States has repeatedly declared that it 'would not support a conference in which any regional state would be subject to pressure or isolation'.[17]

This chapter explores the legal issues arising from the proposed WMD-free zone in the Middle East in light of existing NWFZ treaties. It first looks at the conditions for entry into force and termination of the treaty and then analyses obligations arising from NWFZ treaties for both regional and external states. Issues related to the navigational rights of external states are examined in Section E, while Sections F and G highlight the weaknesses of the NWFZ treaties in relation to their verification and enforcement. The conclusion examines the possible consequences of the postponement of the 2012 conference.

A.   Entry into force and termination of the treaty

A range of instruments can be used by a regional grouping of states to establish a WMD-free zone. All NWFZs in existence have been established by treaty, with the exception of Mongolia, which unilaterally declared itself denuclearised in 1992. Unilateral declarations can give rise to international obligations if they are made publicly and with the intent to be bound;[18] however, they hardly seem to be the most suitable instrument for the disarmament of a whole region, especially one prone to conflict. In principle, a zone could also be denuclearised as a consequence of customary international law, should the relevant state practice and *opinio juris* exist. This is not, however, the case in the Middle East, where state practice and *opinio juris* suggest exactly the opposite.

---

[15] *Ibid.*, pp. 362–3.

[16] Lewis, 'A Middle East free of nuclear weapons', 436.

[17] US Department of State, Press Statement, 23 November 2012, available at: www.state.gov/r/pa/prs/ps/2012/11/200987.htm.

[18] According to the International Court of Justice (ICJ), '[i]t is well recognized that declarations made by way of unilateral acts, concerning legal or factual situations, may have the effect of creating legal obligations … When it is the intention of the State making the declaration that it should become bound according to its terms, that intention confers on the declaration the character of a legal undertaking, the State being thenceforth legally required to follow a course of conduct consistent with the declaration. An undertaking of this kind, if given publicly, and with an intent to be bound, even though not made within the context of international negotiations is binding.' ICJ, *Nuclear Tests* case (*Australia* v. *France, New Zealand* v. *France*), Judgment of 20 December 1974, paras. 43 and 46, respectively).

As recommended in the above-mentioned General Assembly Resolution 3472 (XXX) B, the conclusion of a treaty among regional states therefore remains the best option to establish a WMD-free zone in the Middle East, as well as elsewhere. The treaty could be open to the signature of the named states,[19] might more generally refer to the region[20] or might use geographical coordinates to determine the extension of the zone.[21] While the Middle East is not a clearly geographically or politically defined region, a 1991 UN study endorsed by the League of Arab States suggested that the WMD-free zone treaty should be open to all Arab League members in addition to Iran and Israel.[22] Among them, however, some states are considered 'core countries', that is 'a smaller group essential to the initiation of any serious action for the establishment of the zone and a somewhat larger group whose accession to the arrangement establishing the zone might be necessary to bring it into force'.[23] In the IAEA's view, for instance, the zone should at least include 'the area extending from the Libyan Arab Jamahiriya in the West, to the Islamic Republic of Iran in the East, and from Syria in the North to the People's Democratic Republic of Yemen in the South'.[24]

Securing the participation of all states in case of universal non-proliferation treaties and of all zonal states in case of regional ones is considered to be vital

---

[19] See Treaty on the Southeast Asia Nuclear Weapon-Free Zone ('Bangkok Treaty'), Bangkok, 15 December 1995, in force 27 March 1997, 35 ILM 635 (1996), Art. 1 (hereafter, Bangkok Treaty); and Treaty on a Nuclear-Weapon-Free Zone in Central Asia ('Treaty of Semipalatinsk'), Semipalatinsk, 8 September 2006, in force 21 March 2009, Art. 1 (hereafter, Semipalatinsk Treaty).

[20] Art. 1 of the Pelindaba Treaty defines the African NWFZ as 'the territory of the continent of Africa, islands States members of OAU [sic] and all islands considered by the Organization of African Unity in its resolutions to be part of Africa'. Treaty on the Nuclear-Weapon-Free Zone in Africa ('Pelindaba Treaty'), Pelindaba, 11 April 1996, in force 15 July 2009, 35 ILM 698 (1996) (hereafter, Pelindaba Treaty).

[21] See Treaty for the Prohibition of Nuclear Weapons in Latin America and the Caribbean ('Treaty of Tlatelolco'), Mexico City, 14 February 1967, in force 22 April 1968, 634 UNTS 281, Art. 4(2) (hereafter, Treaty of Tlatelolco); and South Pacific Nuclear Free Zone Treaty, Rarotonga, 6 August 1985, in force 11 December 1986, UNTS 1445, Annex 1 (hereafter, Treaty of Rarotonga).

[22] Department of Disarmament Affairs, Report of the Secretary-General, 'Effective and verifiable measures which would facilitate the establishment of a nuclear-weapon-free zone in the Middle East, UN doc. A/45/435 (New York: United Nations, 1991), para. 66, available at: www.un.org/disarmament/HomePage/ODAPublications/DisarmamentStudySeries/ PDF/SS-22.pdf. The zone would also include peripheral states such as Comoros, Djibouti, Somalia and Sudan, which are members of the Arab League, but not, strictly speaking, Middle Eastern countries. Because of its NATO membership, Turkey is not expected to be included in the zone. African countries are already included in the African NWFZ established by the Pelindaba Treaty.

[23] Department of Disarmament Affairs, 'Effective and verifiable measures', para. 65.

[24] Quoted in ibid., para. 64.

for the success of the initiative.[25] This is because the proliferation of WMDs, or their renunciation, involves national security concerns of particular sensitivity and importance to governments. It is therefore not surprising that non-proliferation treaties usually require a very high number of ratifications for their entry into force. In some cases, the requirement that ratifications include those of certain states sets the threshold even higher: Article XIV of the 1996 Comprehensive Test Ban Treaty (CTBT), for instance, provides that the Treaty will enter into force 180 days after the date of deposit of the instruments of ratification of the forty-four states listed in Annex 2, that is those possessing nuclear power or research reactors at the time of the opening for signature of the Treaty. Considering the highly conflictual character of the region and the climate of mutual distrust among regional states, the entry into force of the WMD-free zone treaty in the Middle East will probably have to require ratification by all regional states, or at least 'core' states, in particular those with WMD capabilities and with nuclear reactors.[26] As this might take a long time, a mechanism providing for temporary entry into force might be added. Article 29(2) of the Treaty of Tlatelolco, for instance, provides that, whereas the Treaty fully enters into force only when all regional states and external powers have ratified the Treaty and protocols and have concluded safeguards agreements with the IAEA, '[a]ll Signatory States shall have the imprescriptible right to waive, wholly or in part, the requirements laid down in the preceding paragraph ... For those States which exercise this right, this Treaty shall enter into force upon deposit of the declaration, or as soon as those requirements have been met which have not been expressly waived.' A similar mechanism could be used in the Middle East context as well.

With regard to termination, it is well known that non-proliferation agreements, including the NWFZ treaties, contain very generous withdrawal clauses. In the Rarotonga and Bangkok Treaties (Articles 13 and Article 22, respectively), the right of withdrawal is triggered by the breach by another party of a provision essential to the achievement of the objectives of the Treaty.[27] The Treaties of Tlatelolco (Article 31), Pelindaba (Article 20) and Semipalatinsk (Article 16) allow withdrawal if a party 'decides that extraordinary events, related to the subject-matter of

---

[25] N. Ronzitti, 'Aspetti giuridici del progetto di zona priva di armi di distruzione di massa in Medio Oriente' in N. Ronzitti (ed.), *Una zona priva di armi di distruzione di massa in Medio Oriente: problemi aperti* (Rome: Istituto Affari Internazionali, 2012), p. 21.

[26] The Treaty of Tlatelolco entered into force after the ratification of the Treaty by all regional states and the ratification of Protocols I and II by the relevant external states, as well as the conclusion of a safeguard agreement with the IAEA by the regional states (Art. 29(1)). The Treaty of Rarotonga entered into force after eight ratifications (Art. 15), the Bangkok Treaty after seven ratifications (Art. 16), the Pelindaba Treaty after twenty-eight ratifications (Art. 18(2)) and the Semipalatinsk Treaty after the ratifications of all five regional states (Art. 15).

[27] Art. 13 of the Rarotonga Treaty also mentions the violation 'of the spirit of the Treaty', which is difficult to interpret.

this Treaty, have jeopardized its supreme national interests'. The withdrawal takes effect twelve months (three months for the Treaty of Tlatelolco) after the date of receipt of the notification by the Depositary or one of the regional organs. It seems unlikely that the WMD-free zone treaty in the Middle East would not include a similar provision, which is standard in most non-proliferation agreements.[28]

The NWFZ treaties do not set up any mechanism to review a party's decision to withdraw, but usually require that notification of withdrawal include a statement indicating the 'extraordinary events' jeopardising the party's supreme national interests. Even though the other parties could challenge the existence of such extraordinary events, the lack of any definition and the vagueness of this concept hardly make it an effective deterrent against unjustified exercise of the right of withdrawal. However, a role might be played by the International Court of Justice (ICJ) (in the unlikely event that its jurisdiction is established over the case), since a dispute among states parties as to whether a certain situation amounts to an 'extraordinary event' would be a legal dispute concerning the interpretation of a treaty under Article 36(2)(a) of the Statute of the ICJ. On the other hand, it is debatable that an act of withdrawal by a state party exercised according to the terms of the treaty could lead to application of Chapter VII measures by the Security Council against that state, as has been suggested.[29] In Resolutions 1718 (2006) and 1874 (2009), for instance, the Council demanded that the Democratic People's Republic of North Korea (DPR Korea) reaccede to the NPT after withdrawing from it, and adopted sanctions against DPR Korea.[30] As has been observed, these Resolutions 'would seem to carry serious implications with regard to the consensual nature of all of the sources of international law, which is in turn intimately linked to the sovereign character of states in the international legal system'.[31]

Considering the character of the region, it would also be important that the WMD-free zone treaty in the Middle East clarifies the impact of armed conflict on its provisions.[32] Most treaties, including existing NWFZ treaties, are silent

---

[28] On the 'special' character of these withdrawal provisions, see D. H. Joyner and M. Roscini, 'Withdrawal from and termination of non-proliferation treaties' in D. H. Joyner and M. Roscini (eds.), *Non-Proliferation Law as a Special Regime* (Cambridge University Press, 2012), pp. 151–71.

[29] M. I. Shaker, *The Nuclear Non-Proliferation Treaty: Origin and Implementation, 1959–1979*, 3 vols. (London: Oceana Publications, 1980), Vol. II, p. 896; M. Willrich, *Non-Proliferation Treaty: Framework for Nuclear Arms Control* (Charlottesville: Michie, 1969), p. 301.

[30] The position of the UN Security Council has been reaffirmed more recently in its Resolutions 2087 (2013) and 2094 (2013). UN Security Council Resolution 2087, UN doc. S/RES/2087, adopted on 22 January 2013; and UN Security Council Resolution 2094, UN doc. S/RES/2094, adopted on 7 March 2013.

[31] D. H. Joyner, 'The Security Council as a legal hegemon', *Georgetown Journal of International Law* 43 (2011–2012), 225–57, at 251.

[32] It is worth recalling that Israel considers itself in a state of armed conflict with some of its neighbours.

on the issue of whether the outbreak of an armed conflict between the parties suspends or terminates the treaty. The International Law Commission (ILC)'s Draft Articles on the effects of armed conflicts on treaties, adopted in 2011, do not include non-proliferation treaties in the indicative list of categories of treaties that continue in operation, in whole or in part, during armed conflict (Draft Article 7 and Annex).[33] Draft Article 14 also specifies that a party is always entitled to suspend in whole or in part the operation of a treaty if that operation is incompatible with the exercise of its right of individual and collective self-defence. Self-defence could, at least in theory, be exercised through the threat and the use of nuclear weapons: it is well known that the controversial paragraph 97 of the ICJ's Advisory Opinion on the *Legality of the Threat or Use of Nuclear Weapons* does not rule out the right to use such weapons 'in an extreme circumstance of self-defence, in which [a state's] very survival would be at stake'.[34] Of course, any self-defence reaction must be necessary and proportionate and also comply with *jus in bello*. Although the use of chemical and biological weapons is clearly a violation of international humanitarian law and a war crime, both in international and non-international armed conflicts,[35] the situation is more uncertain with regard to the use of nuclear weapons: they are, for instance, not mentioned in the Statute of the International Criminal Court (ICC), and the ICJ held that they are only 'generally' contrary to the rules of international law applicable in armed conflict.[36] Under Draft Article 14, then, should the prohibitions to possess and use nuclear weapons arising from the WMD-free zone treaty hamper the exercise of the right of self-defence by a state party in 'extreme circumstances', the state could suspend them in order to react against an armed attack (although the use would still have to be consistent with international humanitarian law). It would therefore be important to include a specific provision in the treaty affirming that it continues its operation even in case of armed conflict.

---

[33] The text of the Draft Articles adopted by the ILC on second reading can be found in *Report of the International Law Commission, Sixty-third session (26 April–3 June and 4 July–12 August 2011)*, General Assembly Official Records, Sixty-sixth session, Supplement No. 10 (A/66/10), pp. 175–8.

[34] ICJ, *Legality of the Threat or Use of Nuclear Weapons*, Advisory Opinion of 8 July 1996, para. 97 (hereafter, Nuclear Weapons Advisory Opinion). According to the ICJ, the legality of the threat depends on the legality of the use in the same circumstances. *Ibid.*, para. 47. See also Chapter 2 of this book. On threats as a self-defence measure, see J. A. Green and F. Grimal, 'The threat of force as an action in self-defense in international law', *Vanderbilt Journal of Transnational Law* 44 (2011), 285–329.

[35] Ronzitti, 'Aspetti giuridici del progetto di zona priva di armi di distruzione di massa in Medio Oriente', p. 39. See Rules 73–76, in J.-M. Henckaerts and L. Doswald-Beck (eds.), *Customary International Humanitarian Law*, 3 vols. (Cambridge University Press, 2005), Vol. I, pp. 256–67.

[36] Nuclear Weapons Advisory Opinion, para. 105(2)(E).

B.   Core obligations

By ratifying an NWFZ treaty, states first of all commit themselves not to possess or accept on their territory 'nuclear weapons' or 'nuclear explosive devices'. The broader notion of 'nuclear explosive device' is used in the Pelindaba, Rarotonga and Semipalatinsk treaties and should be preferred to 'nuclear weapon',[37] as the latter might leave some ambiguity on whether nuclear explosive devices for peaceful purposes are admissible.[38] The obligation not to possess applies to all zonal states and extends to all forms of control by the states parties anywhere (within or outside the zone, e.g. in a military base situated in an allied country not included in the NWFZ), as well as to manufacture and acquisition. The devices must be 'explosive', that is capable of releasing a considerable amount of nuclear energy in a very short time and in an uncontrolled manner.[39] This excludes from the scope of the prohibitions conventional and experimental nuclear reactors, reprocessed nuclear material and depleted uranium munitions that do not cause an *uncontrolled* blast or heatwave.

The Bangkok, Pelindaba, Rarotonga and Semipalatinsk Treaties specify that the definition of 'nuclear weapon' or 'nuclear explosive device' 'does not include the means of transport or delivery of such a weapon or device if separable from and not an indivisible part of it'.[40] Missiles capable of delivering nuclear weapons are therefore not prohibited by those treaties.

As mentioned above, in the Middle East WMD-free zone the object of the prohibitions to possess and control would extend to biological, chemical and radiological weapons because of the strategic link that states in the region have made among the various WMDs, with biological and chemical weapons being the 'poor man's nukes'.[41] The definitions of biological and chemical weapons could be taken from Article I of the 1972 Convention on the Prohibition of the

---

[37] On its meaning, see M. Roscini, *Le zone denuclearizzate* (Turin: Giappichelli, 2003), pp. 37–42.

[38] The problem arose in relation to the Treaty of Tlatelolco. *Ibid.*, pp. 263–5.

[39] See para. III(e) of the note of the Government of the Federal Republic of Germany issued at the moment of the signature of the NPT: 'At the present stage of technology nuclear explosive devices are those designed to release in microseconds in an uncontrolled manner a large amount of nuclear energy accompanied by shock waves, i.e. devices that can be used as nuclear weapons.' Available at: http://collections.europarchive.org/tna/20080205132101/www.fco.gov.uk/Files/kfile/024a_NonProliferationNuclearWeapons,0.pdf.

[40] Art. 1, Rarotonga Treaty. See also Art. 1 of the Bangkok, Pelindaba and Semipalatinsk Treaties.

[41] Egypt, Israel and South Sudan are among the states that have not yet adhered to the Chemical Weapons Convention. Egypt has said that it will sign and ratify it only after Israel accedes to the NPT. C. Baumgart and H. Müller, 'A nuclear weapons-free zone in the Middle East: a pie in the sky?', *The Washington Quarterly* 28 (Winter 2004–2005), 45–58, at 49. Chemical weapons were used in the Iran–Iraq War in the 1980s and by Iraq against the Kurds and in the ongoing armed conflict in Syria. Algeria and Libya were (or are) also suspected of having a chemical weapons programme.

Development, Production and Stockpiling of Bacteriological (Biological) and Toxin Weapons and on their Destruction and Article II of the 1992 Convention on the Prohibition of the Development, Production, Stockpiling and Use of Chemical Weapons and on their Destruction, respectively. There might, however, be a problem with radiological weapons, as no existing treaty provides a ready-made definition.

The second fundamental provision contained in the NWFZ treaties is the prohibition of stationing nuclear weapons or nuclear explosive devices within the zone, which is defined in Article 1(c) of the Semipalatinsk Treaty as 'implantation, emplacement, stockpiling, storage, installation and deployment'.[42] This prohibition distinguishes the NWFZ treaties from the NPT. The latter does not prohibit the presence of nuclear weapons on the territory of non-nuclear weapon states, providing that they do not acquire control over them (for instance, about ninety nuclear warheads are thought to be stationed in the US Ghedi Torre and Aviano military bases in Italy). On the other hand, the Treaties of Bangkok, Pelindaba, Rarotonga, Semipalatinsk and Tlatelolco prohibit the presence of nuclear explosive devices within the zones, regardless of which state owns or controls them. In the Middle East context, this might cause problems with regard to the US military bases in Bahrain (where the 5th fleet of the US Navy is stationed), Qatar (which hosts the forward headquarters of US Central Command), Kuwait, Oman, Saudi Arabia and the United Arab Emirates (UAE). The United States also has a commitment to Israel's security that has been frequently reaffirmed.[43] Furthermore, the United Kingdom and France have concluded defence agreements with several Gulf States, and Bahrain, Egypt, Jordan, Israel and Kuwait have the status of major non-NATO allies.[44] It is not clear whether these security agreements and alliances imply a threat or use of nuclear weapons and whether nuclear weapons are stored in foreign bases in the region, as this is left intentionally ambiguous.[45] Be that as it may, the conclusion of a security agreement with a nuclear weapon state or the participation in a nuclear military alliance is not as such inconsistent with the obligations arising from an NWFZ treaty. The answer would depend on the circumstances of each case: if 'a treaty or alliance ... does not envisage nuclear

---

[42] The definition is identical to that contained in Art. 1(d) of the Bangkok Treaty. Art. 1(d) of the Pelindaba Treaty and Art. 1(d) of the Rarotonga Treaty also include in the definition of stationing the 'transport on land or inland waters'. While in the Bangkok Treaty transport by states parties is the object of a specific prohibition (even though it is not qualified as a form of stationing), no prohibition of transport is contained in the Semipalatinsk Treaty. The Treaty of Tlatelolco, without using the word 'stationing', prohibits 'the receipt, storage, installation, deployment and any form of possession of any nuclear weapons, directly or indirectly' (Art. 1).

[43] R. Mulas, 'Nuclear weapon free zones and the nuclear powers – lessons for a WMD/DVs free zone in the Middle East', Policy Brief for the Middle East Conference on a WMD/DVs Free Zone, No. 5 (December 2011), pp. 6–7.

[44] *Ibid.*   [45] *Ibid.*, p. 7.

retaliation in support of an ally, nor include the stationing of nuclear weapons on the territory of that ally', then it would be 'no bar to the creation of a nuclear-weapon-free zone' and in such a case 'a non-nuclear weapon State allied to a nuclear-weapon State can … also be a party to a nuclear-weapon-free zone treaty'.[46] In order to avoid assuming conflicting obligations, the denuclearised states ought to verify that the NWFZ treaty is not in contrast with other agreements to which they are a party.[47]

Another problem relates to the distinction between stationing and other means by which nuclear weapons could be present within the zone. As in all NWFZ treaties, any ship and aircraft, including those carrying nuclear weapons, may visit ports and land in airfields, pursuant to the 1982 UN Convention on the Law of the Sea and other treaties regulating international navigation.[48] As a result, it would be important to clarify when such visits become 'stationing': no limits of number or duration are specified in existing NWFZ treaties.

The prohibition of the use of nuclear weapons by the states parties only expressly appears in the Treaties of Bangkok, Semipalatinsk and Tlatelolco.[49] One could nonetheless argue that such a prohibition is unnecessary as it is implied in the prohibition of possession and control. To avoid ambiguity, however, it would be advisable that the Middle East WMD-free zone treaty expressly contains such an important prohibition.

C.   Other obligations

Apart from the two core prohibitions of possession/control and stationing, the NFWZ treaties also contain other supplementary obligations not necessarily present in all five existing treaties. The Bangkok, Pelindaba, Rarotonga and Semipalatinsk Treaties require states parties to conclude an agreement with the IAEA for the application of safeguards in accordance with the NPT and to refrain from providing source or special fissionable material or related equipment to any non-nuclear weapon state unless that state has concluded a comprehensive safeguards agreement with the IAEA.[50] The provision of such material or equipment to nuclear weapon states is not prohibited, however. The Semipalatinsk Treaty is the first – and so far only – NWFZ treaty to refer to the 1997 IAEA Additional Protocol (INFCIRC/540 (Corr.)), which provides

---

[46]   1976 Comprehensive Study, Annex I, para. 92.

[47]   Report of the Disarmament Commission, para. 32. This reference to compatibility with previous international and regional agreements was deemed necessary by the delegates from the United States, the UK, France and Poland. Disarmament Commission, Press Release DC/2641, 30 April 1999, p. 22.

[48]   See below, Section E.

[49]   Art. 1, Treaty of Tlatelolco; Art. 3, Bangkok Treaty; Art. 3, Semipalatinsk Treaty.

[50]   Annex 2 to the Rarotonga Treaty; Art. 9, Pelindaba Treaty; Art. 5, Bangkok Treaty; and Art. 8, Semipalatinsk Treaty.

for more intrusive and comprehensive verification measures.[51] Under the safe-guards system based on the previous INFCIRC/153, the possibility for the IAEA to detect clandestine nuclear activities is limited, as inspections focus on declared nuclear material and on strategic points in declared facilities. By con-trast, under the Additional Protocol, states parties grant the IAEA the author-ity to inspect undeclared facilities and to access all parts of a state's nuclear fuel cycle and any other location where nuclear material is or may be present. In the Middle East, the Additional Protocol is in force in Jordan, Kuwait, Libya and the UAE. Bahrain, Iran, Iraq, Morocco and Tunisia have signed, but not yet ratified the Protocol.

The Rarotonga, Bangkok, Pelindaba and Semipalatinsk Treaties obli-gate states parties not to conduct nuclear tests and require them to prevent such tests in their territories (the Semipalatinsk Treaty expressly refers to the CTBT).[52] They do so regardless of test yield, and whether tests are conducted in the atmosphere or underground. Article 18 of the Treaty of Tlatelolco allows nuclear explosions for peaceful purposes, but regional states and the nuclear powers have interpreted this provision as prohibiting all explosions.[53] The pro-hibition of nuclear testing is usually conceived of as a nuclear non-proliferation measure designed to prevent the development of new types of arms and the modernisation of existing arsenals. In the NWFZ treaties, however – where regional states (with few exceptions) never had nuclear ambitions – the main purpose of this prohibition is to delegitimise nuclear explosions by the nuclear powers.[54] For instance, the South Pacific NWFZ was established mainly in order to prevent France from conducting further nuclear tests in the region.[55]

The Pelindaba Treaty is the only NWFZ treaty that prohibits military nuclear research and that requires states parties to declare, dismantle and destroy or convert nuclear explosive devices and the facilities for their manufacture.[56] This provision was included with South Africa's nuclear facilities in mind and should also be included in a Middle East WMD-free zone to cover Israel's mili-tary nuclear activities and materials, as well as some Arab states' chemical facil-ities. The dismantling of WMD arsenals should precede the entry into force of

---

[51] Art. 8.

[52] Art. 6, Rarotonga Treaty; Art. 3, Bangkok Treaty; Art. 5, Pelindaba Treaty; and Art. 5, Semipalatinsk Treaty.

[53] Roscini, *Le zone denuclearizzate*, pp. 263–4.

[54] As acknowledged in the guidelines adopted by the Disarmament Commission in 1999, NWFZs are 'a useful complement to the international regime for the prohibition of any nuclear-weapon-test explosions or any other nuclear explosion'. Report of the Disarmament Commission, para. 37.

[55] As far as Central Asia is concerned, the Soviet Union conducted more than 450 atmospheric and underground nuclear tests in Semipalatinsk between 1949 and 1989. A. J. González, 'Radioactive residues of the Cold War period: a radiological legacy', *IAEA Bulletin* 40(4) (December 1998), 1–11, at 4.

[56] Arts. 3 and 6, respectively.

the WMD-free zone treaty and be conducted under the supervision of international inspectors.[57]

The Pelindaba Treaty is also the only treaty that prohibits taking, assisting with or encouraging any action aimed at an armed attack 'by conventional or other means' against nuclear installations situated within the zone.[58] This is an important provision that supplements existing *jus ad bellum* and *jus in bello* rules. Indeed, neither Article 51 of the UN Charter nor customary law appear to rule out attacks on nuclear installations in self-defence if this is both necessary and proportionate.[59] Under *jus in bello*, however, they can only be attacked if they are a 'military objective' as defined in Article 52(2) of 1977 Additional Protocol I to the four 1949 Geneva Conventions, and the attack is not 'expected to cause incidental loss of civilian life, injury to civilians, damage to civilian objects, or a combination thereof, which would be excessive in relation to the concrete and direct military advantage anticipated'.[60] Furthermore, for states parties to 1977 Additional Protocol I, nuclear electrical generating stations can only be attacked if the additional stricter conditions set out in Article 56 on installations containing dangerous forces are also met.[61] The inclusion

---

[57] N. Fahmy and P. Lewis, 'Possible elements of an NWFZ in the Middle East', *Disarmament Forum* (2011/2), p. 45, available at: http://nwp.ilpi.org/wp-content/uploads/2011/10/Possible-elements-of-an-NWFZ-in-the-Middle-East1.pdf.

[58] Art. 11.

[59] In its judgment in the *Oil Platforms* case, the ICJ pointed out that '[t]he United States must also show that its actions were necessary and proportional to the armed attack made on it, and that the platforms were a legitimate military target open to attack in the exercise of self-defence'. *Case concerning Oil Platforms (Iran v. United States)*, Merits, Judgment of 6 November 2003, para. 51. This seems at first sight to suggest that Art. 51 of the UN Charter extends to targeting issues and could be invoked to prohibit *all* attacks against nuclear installations in the light of the IAEA General Conference Resolution that declares 'that all armed attacks against nuclear installations devoted to peaceful purposes should be explicitly prohibited'. IAEA General Conference Resolution, GC(XXVII)/RES/407, adopted on 9 November 1983, para. 1. The significance of para. 51 of the *Oil Platforms* Judgment, however, should not be overstated. Arguably, what the Court meant here, perhaps not in the clearest way, is what it had already said in the Nuclear Weapons Advisory Opinion, para. 34, i.e. that any use of force in self-defence has to comply not only with *jus ad bellum* requirements (armed attack, necessary and proportional reaction), but also with the *jus in bello* (principle of distinction). There is nothing in para. 51 suggesting that the Court is reasoning only from the perspective of *jus ad bellum*.

[60] Protocol Additional to the Geneva Conventions of 12 August 1949, and relating to the Protection of Victims of International Armed Conflicts (Protocol I), Geneva, 8 June 1977, in force 7 December 1978, 1125 UNTS 3, Art. 51(5)(b) (hereafter, 1977 Additional Protocol I). According to Art. 52(2), 'military objectives are limited to those objects which by their nature, location, purpose or use make an effective contribution to military action and whose total or partial destruction, capture or neutralization, in the circumstances ruling at the time, offers a definite military advantage'.

[61] Under Additional Protocol I, Art. 56(1) and (2): '1. Works or installations containing dangerous forces, namely dams, dykes and nuclear electrical generating stations, shall not be

of a provision such as Article 11 of the Pelindaba Treaty in the Middle East WMD-free zone treaty would therefore outlaw all residual cases of attacks on nuclear installations that would otherwise escape the *jus ad bellum* and *jus in bello* provisions.[62] The IAEA General Conference has, for instance, stated that 'it would further the cause of peace to extend the prohibition of armed attack so as to protect all nuclear installations devoted to peaceful purposes'.[63] The prohibition of attacks on nuclear installations would also have another aspect of particular interest in the context of the Middle East if one recalls the recent case of the Stuxnet malware that damaged centrifuges at the Natanz uranium enrichment facility in Iran.[64] The question is whether a cyber attack would amount to an 'armed attack' in the sense of a provision such as Article 11 of the Pelindaba Treaty. The fact that the provision refers to attacks 'by conventional or other means' seems to allow a broad interpretation, at least with regard to cyber operations that produce consequences comparable to those of attacks conducted with kinetic weapons.[65]

A further aspect of NWFZ treaties, which distinguishes them from other non-proliferation treaties, is that they also contain provisions intended to protect the natural environment, such as the prohibition on dumping radioactive

made the object of attack, even where these objects are military objectives, if such attack may cause the release of dangerous forces and consequent severe losses among the civilian population. Other military objectives located at or in the vicinity of these works or installations shall not be made the object of attack if such attack may cause the release of dangerous forces from the works or installations and consequent severe losses among the civilian population ... 2. The special protection against attack provided by paragraph 1 shall cease: (a) for a dam or a dyke only if it is used for other than its normal function and in regular, significant and direct support of military operations and if such attack is the only feasible way to terminate such support; (b) for a nuclear electrical generating station only if it provides electric power in regular, significant and direct support of military operations and if such attack is the only feasible way to terminate such support; (c) for other military objectives located at or in the vicinity of these works or installations only if they are used in regular, significant and direct support of military operations and if such attack is the only feasible way to terminate such support.'

[62] In the Middle East WMD-free zone, the prohibition should also cover attacks against installations containing chemical or biological substances.

[63] IAEA General Conference Resolution, GC(XXVII)/RES/407, adopted on 9 November 1983.

[64] D. P. Fidler, 'Was Stuxnet an act of war?', *Privacy Interests* 9 (July/August 2011), 56–9.

[65] On cyber operations and *jus ad bellum*, see M. Roscini, 'World wide warfare: *jus ad bellum* and the use of cyber force', *Max Planck Yearbook of United Nations Law* 14 (2010), 85–130. On *jus in bello* aspects, see, e.g., M. N. Schmitt, 'Wired warfare: computer network attack and *jus in bello*' in M. N. Schmitt and B. T. O'Donnell (eds.), *Computer Network Attack and International Law* (Newport, CT: US Naval War College, 2002), pp. 187–218. See also *Tallinn Manual on the International Law Applicable to Cyber Warfare* (Cambridge University Press, 2013).

substances at sea,[66] the obligation not to allow other states to dispose of radio-active waste in a State party's territory[67] and the obligation to ratify the 1986 Vienna Convention on Early Notification of a Nuclear Accident.[68] Furthermore, according to Article 6 of the Semipalatinsk Treaty:

> Each Party undertakes to assist any efforts toward the environmental rehabilitation of territories contaminated as a result of past activities related to the development, production or storage of nuclear weapons or other nuclear explosive devices, in particular uranium tailings storage sites and nuclear test sites.[69]

The obligation is, however, one only of conduct, not of result (the environmental rehabilitation of contaminated territories), and is presumably triggered by the request for assistance of the state to which the contaminated territories belong.

Considering that terrorism has affected most, if not all, states in the Middle East and that the region has served as a hub for illicit nuclear trafficking, it would be important that the WMD-free zone treaty in the Middle East contains provisions on the prevention and repression of illicit nuclear activities by non-state actors. Indeed, in Resolution 1540 of 28 April 2004 the UN Security Council expressed its concern for 'the threat of illicit trafficking in nuclear, chemical, or biological weapons and their means of delivery, and related materials, which adds a new dimension to the issue of proliferation of such weapons and also poses a threat to international peace and security', and required all states to adopt 'effective laws which prohibit any non-state actor to manufacture, acquire, possess, develop, transport, transfer or use nuclear, chemical or biological weapons and their means of delivery'. It further required that states 'take and enforce effective measures to establish domestic controls to prevent the proliferation of nuclear, chemical, or biological weapons and their means of delivery, including by establishing appropriate controls over related materials'. Some measures against non-state actor activities are contained in existing NWFZs. Under Article 10 of the Pelindaba Treaty and Article 9 of the Semipalatinsk Treaty, for instance, each state party undertakes to maintain 'effective standards of physical protection of nuclear material, facilities and equipment to prevent its unauthorized use or handling or theft'. Measures adopted must be 'at least as effective' as those called for by the 1980 Convention

---

[66] Art. 7, Pelindaba Treaty; Art. 7, Rarotonga Treaty; Art. 3, Bangkok Treaty.
[67] Art. 3(2), Semipalatinsk Treaty.   [68] Art. 6, Bangkok Treaty.
[69] The provision was added in order to address the problem of the areas contaminated as a result of the nuclear-related activities carried out in Central Asia during the Soviet era, such as weapons storage and testing, uranium mining and plutonium production.

on the Physical Protection of Nuclear Material[70] and by the recommendations and guidelines developed by the IAEA in this field.[71]

Finally, it is also worth noting that the NWFZ treaties do not prohibit the production of fissile material: this prohibition is only contained in the 1992 Joint Declaration on the Denuclearization of the Korean Peninsula.[72]

D. Obligations of states outside the region

The typical structure of an NWFZ treaty regime includes protocols attached to the main treaty. One is addressed to states outside the region that are *de jure* or de facto internationally responsible for non-independent territories situated within the zone (if any).[73] By ratifying these protocols, such states commit themselves to respect at least some prohibitions of the NWFZ treaties with regard to the territory for which they are internationally responsible. These external states may continue possessing nuclear weapons even after ratification

---

[70] The Convention requires each state party 'to take appropriate steps within the framework of its national law and consistent with international law to ensure as far as practicable that, during international nuclear transport, nuclear material within its territory, or on board a ship or aircraft under its jurisdiction insofar as such ship or aircraft is engaged in the transport to or from that State, is protected at the levels described in Annex 1'. Convention on the Physical Protection of Nuclear Material, New York, 3 March 1980, in force 8 February 1987, 1456 UNTS 101, Art. 3 (hereafter, 1980 Physical Protection Convention). The purpose, which is instrumental to Arts. I, II, and III of the NPT, is to prevent fissile material that could be used to construct a nuclear device from being stolen. Of the potential parties to the Middle East WMD-free zone, only Egypt, Iran, Iraq, Somalia and Syria have not yet ratified the 1980 Physical Protection Convention.

[71] The recommendations, which were elaborated in 1972 by a panel of experts convened by the IAEA Director General, were revised in 1975, 1977, 1989, 1993, 1998 and 2010 (INFCIRC/225). See Fahmy and Lewis, 'Possible elements of an NWFZ in the Middle East', 46. Even though not per se legally binding, implementation of the IAEA recommendations is required by the agreements that the Agency concludes with states that it assists and by bilateral cooperation agreements in the field of nuclear energy.

[72] The text is available at: http://cns.miis.edu/inventory/pdfs/aptkoreanuc.pdf. The legal status of the document is unclear. In December 1993 UN General Assembly Resolution 48/75L, adopted by consensus, recommended 'the negotiation in the most appropriate international forum of a non-discriminatory, multilateral and internationally and effectively verifiable treaty banning the production of fissile material for nuclear weapons and other nuclear explosive devices'. UN General Assembly Resolution 48/75L, UN doc. A/RES/48/75L, adopted on 17 December 1997 by consensus. The 1995 NPT Review and Extension Conference's Decision 2 indicated '[t]he immediate commencement and early conclusion of negotiations on a nondiscriminatory and universally applicable convention banning the production of fissile material for nuclear weapons or other nuclear explosive devices' as an important measure towards full implementation of Art. VI of the NPT. Decision 2: Principles and Objectives for Nuclear Non-Proliferation and Disarmament, NPT/CONF.1995/32 (Part I), Annex, para. 4, available at: www.un.org/disarmament/WMD/Nuclear/1995-NPT/pdf/NPT_CONF199501.pdf.

[73] This Protocol is attached to the Pelindaba, Rarotonga and Tlatelolco Treaties.

of the protocol, but they cannot station or test them in their territories within the zone. This distinction has sometimes proven difficult to maintain in practice. For example, if a case involving Guantánamo Bay arose, it might not be easy to establish which state is responsible *de jure* or de facto for the territory.[74] Another controversial case is the inclusion of the Chagos Archipelago in the African NWFZ, over which both Mauritius and the United Kingdom claim sovereignty. This archipelago in the British Indian Ocean Territory hosts one of the most valuable US military bases in the region.[75] According to the map appended to the Pelindaba Treaty, the NWFZ covers the 'Chagos Archipelago – Diego García', albeit with a footnote (inserted at the British government's request) stating that the territory 'appears without prejudice to the question of sovereignty'. Upon signing the protocols, the United Kingdom noted that it did 'not accept the inclusion of [the Chagos Archipelago] within the African nuclear-weapon-free zone without their consent'.[76] The Russian statement referred to the UK claim and declared that it likewise did not consider itself bound by Article 1 of Protocol I with respect to the Chagos Archipelago.[77]

In the Middle East, the participation of Palestine in the WMD-free zone treaty might be problematic, and not only from a political perspective. According to the majority view, both the West Bank and the Gaza Strip are territories under belligerent occupation.[78] On 31 October 2011 UNESCO admitted Palestine as a Member State, and, on 29 November 2012, the UN General Assembly granted Palestine 'non-member observer state' status. Should Palestine therefore accede to the WMD-free zone treaty as a state, or should Israel as the Occupying Power assume the relevant, and more limited, obligations by ratifying a protocol addressed to states that are responsible for non-independent territories

---

[74] The question is whether the competence to denuclearise the territory rests on the United States, because of the lease of the territory from Cuba, or on Cuba itself, which has maintained sovereignty over the area. The former is probably correct, as the lease was specifically for the use of the territory for military purposes. Furthermore, since Cuba's sovereignty over Guantánamo Bay is reduced to a *nudum jus*, it would not be able to implement the denuclearisation obligations contained in the Treaty of Tlatelolco. See Roscini, *Le zone denuclearizzate*, pp. 123–5.

[75] P. H. Sand, 'Diego Garcia – a thorn in the side of Africa's nuclear-weapon-free zone', *Bulletin of the Atomic Scientists* (8 October 2009), available at: http://thebulletin.org/diego-garcia-thorn-side-africas-nuclear-weapon-free-zone.

[76] See UK: Signature of Protocol I to the Pelindaba Treaty, 11 April 1996, available at: disarmament.un.org/treaties/a/pelindaba_1/unitedkingdomofgreatbritainandnorthernireland/sig/cairo.

[77] See Russian Federation: Signature of Protocol I to the Pelindaba Treaty, 5 November 1996, available at: http://disarmament.un.org/treaties/a/pelindaba_1/russianfederation/sig/cairo. Problems have also arisen in the context of the Pelindaba Treaty with regard to the Canary Islands and Madeira, which Spain and Portugal refuse to see as 'African' dependencies. Roscini, *Le zone denuclearizzate*, p. 141.

[78] Ronzitti, 'Aspetti giuridici del progetto di zona priva di armi di distruzione di massa in Medio Oriente', p. 28.

within the zone? The latter solution would be politically unacceptable for the Palestinians, while the former would probably lead to the refusal of Israel (and perhaps also of the United Kingdom and the United States) to participate in the treaty. It should be recalled that the Palestinian Liberation Organization (PLO) enjoys some treaty-making power, at least for matters related to the right of self-determination of the people it represents.[79] A more practical option might be an ad hoc protocol signed by the PLO, with the caveat that the protocol does not affect the status of the territories.

Another protocol is addressed to the nuclear weapon states, which, by ratifying it, agree not to test any nuclear weapons within the zone.[80] These Protocols do not distinguish between atmospheric and underground nuclear tests and therefore complement the CTBT regime.

Finally, a protocol contains the negative security assurances provided by the NPT nuclear weapon states to the denuclearised states. These are, so far, the only legally binding nuclear assurances provided by the nuclear weapon states.[81] With the exception of China, however, the nuclear powers have issued declarations upon signature and/or ratification by which they have reserved the right to use or threaten the use of nuclear weapons in certain circumstances, in particular when a denuclearised state is in material breach of its denuclearisation obligations, or in case of an attack on the nuclear weapon state, its dependent territories, its armed forces or other troops, its allies or a state towards which it has a security commitment, carried out or sustained by a party to the NWFZ treaty in association or alliance with a nuclear weapon state.[82]

Furthermore, the negative security assurance protocols attached to only two of the treaties (Tlatelolco and Rarotonga) have been fully signed and almost fully ratified by the nuclear powers (the United States has yet to ratify the Rarotonga Protocol). China, France, the Russian Federation and the United Kingdom have ratified the Pelindaba Protocol I, but the United States has not. The Bangkok and the Semipalatinsk Protocols have not been signed or ratified by any nuclear power yet. Nevertheless, at the NPT Review Conference of May 2010 then-US Secretary of State Hillary Clinton announced that the US government would seek Senate advice and consent to ratify the Rarotonga

---

[79] For instance, the PLO signed the Oslo Accords in 1993 and 1995.

[80] This Protocol is not attached to the Tlatelolco and Semipalatinsk Treaties.

[81] At global level, the nuclear weapon states did not accept the inclusion of negative security assurances in the final text of the NPT for fear that their nuclear doctrines and alliances could be undermined, and so limited themselves subsequently to making unilateral statements in 1978 and 1995. In these statements, China was the only nuclear weapon state to offer unconditional assurances. In Resolution 984 (1995), the UN Security Council took note 'with appreciation' of the 1995 statements, which superseded those given in 1978. See Roscini, *Le zone denuclearizzate*, pp. 307–10.

[82] The statements can be read in the online treaty database of the UN Office for Disarmament Affairs, www.un.org/disarmament/HomePage/treaty/treaties.shtml. See also *SIPRI Yearbook*, 2010, pp. 495–7, 499, 500–1.

and Pelindaba Protocols.[83] As for the Bangkok and Semipalatinsk Protocols, Clinton declared that the US government is willing to continue consultations with zonal states in order ultimately to ratify these instruments.

The Protocol attached to the Bangkok Treaty has proved particularly controversial, as the obligation not to use or threaten the use of nuclear weapons applies anywhere 'within the Southeast Asia Nuclear Weapon-Free Zone'. This means that the nuclear weapon states would be prevented from using nuclear weapons against a state not party to the Treaty but whose territory is included in its geographical scope of application;[84] launching missiles with a nuclear warhead from ships, submarines or aircraft located within the zone (even to hit a target located outside it); and employing nuclear weapons against any vessel (even belonging to another nuclear weapon state) that is in the exclusive economic zone (EEZ) or on the continental shelf of the parties. This is one of the reasons why the nuclear powers, and the United States in particular, have so far refused to sign the Bangkok Protocol. This language should be avoided in the Middle East WMD-free zone treaty so as to secure the support of all nuclear weapon states.

Finally, as India and Pakistan are geographically very close to the Middle East and also de facto nuclear powers, they should also be invited to provide negative security assurances to zonal states.[85] Opening the relevant protocol to their signature, however, would entail recognising their nuclear status, to which NPT states parties are opposed. The problem could perhaps be solved by employing an open formulation that allows the accession of 'all powers possessing nuclear weapons', as in Protocol II of the Treaty of Tlatelolco, without taking position on the *de jure* or de facto character of such possession.[86]

Negative security assurances need not be granted with regard to chemical or biological weapons, as their use is already banned under the 1993 Chemical Weapons Convention and the 1925 Protocol for the Prohibition of the Use in War of Asphyxiating, Poisonous or Other Gases, and of Bacteriological Methods of Warfare (which do not distinguish between haves and have-nots), as well as from customary international law.[87]

---

[83] Hillary Rodham Clinton, US Secretary of State, 'Secretary Clinton's remarks at NPT Review Conference', New York, 3 May 2010, available at: www.voltairenet.org/article165279.html.

[84] This point is at present irrelevant, as all regional states have ratified the Bangkok Treaty. It cannot be excluded, however, that in the future they might withdraw from it.

[85] India has unilaterally declared that 'it fully respects the status of the NWFZ in South-East Asia', is 'ready to convert this commitment into a legal obligation' and 'remains responsive to the expressed need for such commitments from other nuclear-weapon-free zones also'. J. Prawitz, *Existing NWFZs: History and Principles*, Paper prepared for the Dag Hammarskjöld Foundation Seminar on Nuclear-Weapon-Free Zones: Crucial Steps Towards a Nuclear-Weapon-Free World, Uppsala, 1–4 September 2000, p. 33.

[86] Treaty of Tlatelolco, Art. 29.

[87] Ronzitti, 'Aspetti giuridici del progetto di zona priva di armi di distruzione di massa in Medio Oriente', p. 40.

E. The navigational rights of external states

One of the most controversial features of the NWFZ treaties is their delineation of maritime boundaries for the treaties' application. For instance, since
2002, when the Treaty of Tlatelolco first entered into force for the entire
Latin American and Caribbean region,[88] the zone of the Treaty's application
has included portions of international waters off the coast of Latin America,
defined by geographical coordinates.[89] The South Pacific NWFZ also encompasses ocean areas, but the main provisions of the Rarotonga Treaty only apply
to the waters under the sovereignty of the states parties and the airspace above
them (the only exceptions are the prohibition against parties dumping radioactive materials at sea and the prohibition against testing by the nuclear powers
of nuclear explosive devices).[90] The Bangkok Treaty explicitly includes within
the South-East Asia NWFZ the EEZ and the continental shelf of the parties.
Only the prohibition of dumping, however, seems to apply to those spaces, even
though the Treaty is ambiguous concerning the transit of nuclear ships.[91] The
Pelindaba Treaty, more cautiously, provides that the boundaries of the African
NWFZ correspond to the outer border of the territorial sea of the parties.[92]

The fact that marine areas are included in the NWFZs was of concern to
the nuclear powers as it could have affected the navigational rights of ships
carrying nuclear weapons of non-zonal states, and, ultimately, the nuclear
powers' deterrence policies.[93] This issue is particularly sensitive in the Middle
East. Indeed, several important straits would be partly or entirely encompassed
by the zone, for example the Straits of Bab al-Mandeb, Gubal, Hormuz and
Tiran, as well as the Suez Canal. The Bangkok Treaty contains a clause (Article
2(2)), which also appears in a shorter version in the Rarotonga and Pelindaba
Treaties, according to which nothing in the Treaty:

---

[88] As described above, Article 29 of the Treaty of Tlatelolco provides that the treaty does not
    enter into force until all Latin American and Caribbean states have deposited their instru-
    ments of ratification; however, states parties may voluntarily waive this requirement and
    assume their treaty obligations immediately, as many did. Cuba was the last state to ratify
    the treaty, in 2002. Organismo para la Proscripción de las Armas Nucleares en la América
    Latina y el Caribe (OPANAL), Status del tratado y sus protocolos adicionales, available at:
    www.opanal.org/opanal/Tlatelolco/P-Tlatelolco-i.htm.

[89] Before then, denuclearisation concerned only the whole of the territories of the states for
    which the Treaty is in force and which had issued the declaration of waiver provided for in
    Art. 29(2).

[90] Arts. 1 and 7, Rarotonga Treaty, and Art. 1 of Protocol 3.

[91] Art. 2(1).   [92] Arts. 1 and 2.

[93] The problem does not exist with regard to the transit of chemical and bacteriological weap-
    ons, which is prohibited as a consequence of the total bans on the possession of such weap-
    ons imposed by the Chemical Weapons and Biological Weapons Conventions. Ronzitti,
    'Aspetti giuridici del progetto di zona priva di armi di distruzione di massa in Medio
    Oriente' p. 34.

shall prejudice the rights or the exercise of these rights by any State under the provisions of the United Nations Convention on the Law of the Sea of 1982 (UNCLOS),[94] in particular with regard to freedom of the high seas, rights of innocent passage, archipelagic sea lanes passage or transit passage of ships and aircraft, and consistent with the Charter of the United Nations.[95]

Pursuant to this norm, if the law of the sea recognises the usual rights of navigation for vessels carrying nuclear weapons, denuclearised states could not prevent such vessels' passage.[96] In fact, both warships and vessels carrying nuclear materials enjoy the right of innocent transit and archipelagic sea-lanes passage pursuant to UNCLOS Articles 19, 22, 23, 38 and 53. Article 88 of UNCLOS, interpreted in connection with Article 301, only forbids those military activities at sea that involve the threat or use of force.[97] Furthermore, the coastal states only enjoy certain exploitation and exploration 'sovereign rights' over

[94]   United Nations Convention on the Law of the Sea, Montego Bay, 10 December 1982, in force 16 November 1994, 1833 UNTS 3 (hereafter, UNCLOS).

[95]   Art. 2(2) of the Rarotonga and Pelindaba Treaties provides that '[n]othing in this Treaty shall prejudice or in any way affect the rights, or the exercise of the rights, of any State under international law with regard to freedom of the seas'. The Tlatelolco Treaty does not contain safeguard clauses, and transit is not explicitly forbidden, but, according to the interpretation of the Comisión Preparatoria para la Denuclearización de América Latina (COPREDAL), it must be understood as being governed by the principles and rules of international law, that is it is for the territorial state, in the free exercise of its sovereignty, to grant or deny permission for such transit in each individual case, without prejudice to the normal rights of navigation. COPREDAL/S/30, 7 February 1967, quoted in A. García Robles, *El Tratado de Tlatelolco: Génesis, Alcance y Propósitos de la Proscripción de las Armas Nucleares en la América Latina* (El Colegio de Mexico, 1967), pp. 247–8.

[96]   Among regional states, Iran, Libya and the UAE have only signed UNCLOS, while Israel and Syria have not signed it. Arguably similar considerations might apply to overflight of aircraft of third states carrying nuclear weapons. M. Roscini, 'Something old, something new: the 2006 Semipalatinsk Treaty on a nuclear weapon-free zone in Central Asia', *Chinese Journal of International Law* 7 (2008), 593–624, at 609.

[97]   The Strait of Tiran between the Red Sea and the Gulf of Aqaba links the territorial sea with international waters and therefore the non-suspendable right of innocent passage applies to it (Art. 45(1)(b) of UNCLOS). Art. V of the 1979 Peace Treaty between Egypt and Israel reaffirms that '[t]he Parties consider the Strait of Tiran and the Gulf of Aqaba to be international waterways open to all nations for unimpeded and non-suspendable freedom of navigation and overflight. The parties will respect each other's right to navigation and overflight for access to either country through the Strait of Tiran and the Gulf of Aqaba.' See also Art. 14(3) of the 1994 Peace Treaty between Israel and Jordan. The transit passage regime should apply to the Strait of Hormuz, as it joins two parts of international waters or EEZs. Iran is not, however, party to the 1982 Convention on the Law of the Sea and has declared that it would apply the transit passage regime only to states that have ratified that convention, while for others the right of non-suspendable innocent passage as provided by the 1958 Geneva Convention applies (see N. Oral, 'Transit Passage Rights in the Strait of Hormuz and Iran's Threats to Block the Passage of Oil Tankers', *ASIL Insights*, Vol. 16, Issue 16, p. 3). The Strait of Bab al-Mandeb connects two EEZs (the Gulf of Aden and the Red Sea) and therefore the transit passage regime should apply to it. The Strait of Gubal

their EEZs and continental shelves, and freedom of navigation is preserved (UNCLOS Articles 56 and 77).[98]

The clause that preserves the navigational rights of ships of third states must be read together with another provision (contained in all treaties, with the sole exception of the Treaty of Tlatelolco), which recognises the right of each party to decide for itself 'whether to allow visits by foreign ships and aircraft to its ports and airfields, transit of its airspace by foreign aircraft, and navigation by foreign ships through its territorial sea or archipelagic waters and overflight of foreign aircraft above those waters in a manner not governed by the rights of innocent passage, archipelagic sea lanes passage or transit passage'.[99] This provision introduces a further exception to the general obligation upon states parties to an NWFZ treaty not to allow possession or control of any nuclear explosive device in their territory by anyone. Consequently, not only do the NWFZ treaties not prejudice the normal navigational rights of ships and aircraft under the law of the sea, including those carrying nuclear weapons, but they do not even require parties to prevent other forms of presence (provided they do not amount to stationing). This clause is unnecessary and represents a serious loophole in the denuclearisation regime and should therefore not be included in the Middle East WMD-free zone treaty.

One of the Middle Eastern states to be included in the WMD-free zone, Iran, borders the Caspian Sea. The Caspian is not actually a 'sea' but rather an international lake not governed by the law of the sea.[100] No agreement among the

is subject to the regime of international straits or, according to another school of thought, to the regime of passage that has been established for the Suez Canal. R. Lapidoth, 'Red Sea' in R. Wolfrum (ed.), *Max Planck Encyclopedia of Public International Law* (Oxford University Press, 2012), Vol. VIII, p. 695. The Suez Canal is an artificial waterway that is 'inland waters' of Egypt, but where the free passage of all ships, including warships, is provided by the 1888 Constantinople Convention. The Suez Canal is already included in the African NWFZ and, when signing Protocol III of the Pelindaba Treaty, France reaffirmed that 'the Treaty shall in no way impair the principle of free passage through the Canal, both in time of war and in peacetime'. France: Signature of Protocol III to the Pelindaba Treaty, 11 April 1996, available at: http://disarmament.un.org/treaties/a/pelindaba_3/france/sig/african+union.

[98] Iran, Oman, and the UAE have proclaimed EEZs. However, practice in relation to MOX (plutonium-uranium mixed oxide) shipments from Europe to Japan suggests the possible future emergence of a more restrictive regime according to which the coastal states may prohibit vessels carrying hazardous substances to enter their EEZ. See www.world-nuclear.org/info/inf39.html for the facts and my comments in M. Roscini, 'La zone dénucléarisée du sud-est asiatique: problèmes de droit de la mer', *Revue générale de droit international public* 105 (2001), 617–45, at 628–33.

[99] Bangkok Treaty, Art. 7. See also Rarotonga Treaty, Art. 5(2); Semipalatinsk Treaty, Art. 4; and Pelindaba Treaty, Art. 4(2).

[100] W. E. Butler, 'The Soviet Union and the continental shelf', *American Journal of International Law* 63 (1969), 103–7, at 106; R. R. Churchill and A. V. Lowe, *The Law of the Sea* (Manchester University Press, 1999), p. 60; M. Gramola, 'State succession and the delimitation of the Caspian Sea', *Italian Yearbook of International Law* 14 (2005), 237–72, at

littoral states has yet been reached on the delimitation of its waters. Its inclusion in the Middle East WMD-free zone might therefore raise many of the same thorny issues faced initially by the drafters of the Semipalatinsk Treaty.[101] The Semipalatinsk Treaty avoided wading into boundary disputes by adding a clause providing that '[n]othing in this Treaty shall prejudice or in any way affect the rights of any Central Asian states in any dispute concerning the ownership of or sovereignty over lands or waters that may or may not be included within this zone'. A similar provision should be included in the Middle East WMD-free zone treaty as well.

F.   Verification

UN General Assembly Resolution 3472 (XXX) B requires that NWFZs provide for an 'international system of verification and control'. In the NWFZ treaties, these tasks are usually performed by two parallel mechanisms, one entrusted to the IAEA and the other to regional bodies. The regional organs or organisations could be set up by the NWFZ treaty itself,[102] or could be already-existing regional organisations whose competencies are broadened.[103] These bodies typically receive the reports submitted by the states parties, carry out consultations, request clarifications and, in some cases, conduct inspections. However, only the Bangkok and Tlatelolco Treaties provide for 'challenge' inspections (i.e. at the request of a state party), while in the Rarotonga and Pelindaba Treaties the inspection machinery can only be triggered by the regional organs, and not requested by the parties themselves.[104] The weakest treaty from the regional verification point of view is the Semipalatinsk Treaty, as it neither envisages the establishment of an international organisation nor relies on existing ones, but simply provides for annual consultative meetings to review compliance, with decisions taken by consensus.[105]

The dual IAEA/regional verification system exists because the IAEA safeguards agreements, conceived in relation to Article III of the NPT, were not meant to monitor compliance with the broader obligations contained in an NWFZ treaty. Thus the two mechanisms do not overlap, but have different competences: the IAEA detects the diversion of fissile materials from peaceful

---

237–8; P. Tavernier, 'Le statut juridique de la mer Caspienne: mer ou lac?', *Actualité et droit international*, 20 October 1999, available at: www.ridi.org/adi/199910a1.htm.

[101] Roscini, 'Something old, something new', 606–7.

[102] The Tlatelolco Treaty established an international organisation (OPANAL), while the Pelindaba Treaty set up an African Commission on Nuclear Energy and the Bangkok Treaty the Commission for the South-East Asia NWFZ and an Executive Committee.

[103] The Rarotonga Treaty relies on the Pacific Islands Forum.

[104] Art. 16, Treaty of Tlatelolco; Annex to the Bangkok Treaty; Annex 4 of the Rarotonga Treaty; and Annex IV of the Pelindaba Treaty.

[105] Art. 10 and Annex.

to military uses, while the regional organs monitor compliance with the other denuclearisation obligations, in particular with the prohibition of stationing nuclear weapons within the zone.[106] In the verification context, the problem with a WMD-free zone in the Middle East is that there is no existing regional organisation that could step in for verification purposes: the Arab League does not include the main regional actors, that is Iran and Israel. Routine inspections might be entrusted to the IAEA, while a newly established organ or organisation might be given the right to conduct ad hoc or even special inspections.[107] This would, however, require careful consideration of the decision-making process in that organ or organisation. In the Middle East, the verification problem is further complicated by the fact that verification procedures need to be extended to chemical and biological weapons. Verification of chemical disarmament in the zone could be ensured through a reference in the treaty to the Organisation for the Prohibition of Chemical Weapons' verification activities, but at present there is no verification system applicable to biological weapons (although a protocol to the 1972 Bacteriological Weapons Convention has been proposed).[108]

G.   Enforcement

There are no specific regional mechanisms in the NWFZ treaties for enforcing the denuclearisation obligations in case of violations. The Bangkok, Pelindaba, Rarotonga and Tlatelolco Treaties only provide that the matter can or must be referred to the UN Security Council and/or General Assembly, the Organization of the American States (OAS), the African Union (AU), the Pacific Islands Forum or the IAEA.[109] The Semipalatinsk Treaty does not expressly envisage any role for the main UN organs in the enforcement process; however, this would not prevent the Security Council from handling a violation of the denuclearisation regime under Chapters VI or VII of the UN Charter. The IAEA Board of Governors might also report to the Security Council and to the General Assembly cases of non-compliance with the safeguards agreements, as well as suspend the IAEA's assistance to the wrongdoing state, call for the

---

[106] In the Middle East, Israel has always argued that verification should be regionally based, with national inspectors operating alone or in conjunction with the IAEA. Arab countries, on the other hand, would prefer to entrust verification to the IAEA.

[107] Fahmy and Lewis, 'Possible elements of an NWFZ in the Middle East', 48.

[108] Ronzitti, 'Aspetti giuridici del progetto di zona priva di armi di distruzione di massa in Medio Oriente', p. 43. It is worth recalling that Security Council Resolution 687 (1991) with regard to Iraq provides for verification measures that cover biological, chemical and nuclear weapons as well as ballistic missiles that are very intrusive, as they are not limited by time and place and do not require prior notification of inspection or right of refusal.

[109] Treaty of Tlatelolco, Art. 21; Rarotonga Treaty, Annex 4; Pelindaba Treaty, Annex IV(4); Bangkok Treaty, Art. 14(3).

return of materials and equipment, and/or suspend it from the exercise of the privileges and rights of membership.[110]

Apart from institutionalised reactions, states parties to a denuclearisation treaty that are injured by its violation could also individually resort to countermeasures under the law of state responsibility.[111]

Conclusion

The conference for a WMD-free zone in the Middle East, called for by the NPT 2010 Review Conference and supposed to take place in December 2012, has now been postponed *sine die*.[112] Although it was never intended to be a drafting conference, it would have been an important step in the negotiation and eventual adoption of a treaty establishing such a zone. As the conference has not been convened as of the date of writing, what are the possible scenarios?

The best-case scenario, supported by the co-sponsors of the Middle East Resolution and by the facilitator,[113] is that the conference takes place at the earliest opportunity before the 2015 NPT Review Conference. Certain regional states have, however, manifested their strong disappointment at the aborted 2012 conference. Indeed, the Middle Eastern states (with the exception of Israel) attach great importance to the WMD-free zone project, which was part of the great bargain for indefinitely extending the NPT in 1995. Arab League members have thus threatened to boycott the NPT Preparatory Committee meetings in preparation for the 2015 NPT Review Conference.[114] The worst-case scenario is that the possible abandonment of the WMD-free zone project will accelerate disaffection among Middle Eastern states towards the NPT, leading eventually to a chain of withdrawals from the Treaty. On the other hand, even though the language of Article X of the NPT is notoriously broad, it might nonetheless be difficult to categorise the postponement or even the demise of the WMD-free zone project as 'extraordinary events, related to the subject matter of this Treaty, [that] have jeopardized the supreme interests' of the Middle Eastern NPT Member States, allowing the withdrawal from the NPT. States parties could of course also resort to the general grounds for the termination of their participation in a treaty, contained in the 1969 Vienna Convention on the Law of Treaties

---

[110]   Statute of the International Atomic Energy Agency, New York, 23 October 1953, in force 29 July 1957, 276 UNTS 3, Article XII(C) of the IAEA Statute.

[111]   Roscini, *Le zone denuclearizzate*, pp. 370–81.

[112]   See Victoria Nuland, US State Department Spokesperson, 2012 Conference on a Middle East Zone Free of Weapons of Mass Destruction (MEWMDFZ), Press Statement, Washington DC, 23 November 2012, available at: www.state.gov/r/pa/prs/ps/2012/11/200987.htm.

[113]   Lewis, 'A Middle East free of nuclear weapons', 441–2.

[114]   E. M. Grossman, 'Arab League threatens nonproliferation event boycott', *Global Security Newswire*, 21 February 2013, available at: www.nti.org/gsn/article/arab-states-threaten-boycott-nonproliferation-conference.

(VCLT).[115] In response to the postponement of the WMD-free zone conference, Iran's ambassador to the IAEA, Soltanieh, claimed for instance that '[t]he US has taken the conference on banning nuclear weapons in the Middle East as hostage and this is a flagrant violation of the NPT'.[116] The reference to the United States' 'flagrant violation of the NPT' might presage Iran's possible invocation of the *inadimplenti non est adimplendum* clause contained in Article 60 of the VCLT. It is not clear, however, what the 'material breach' allegedly committed by the United States is in this case. It cannot be a 'repudiation of the Treaty not sanctioned' by the VCLT, as the United States has not denounced the Treaty. Therefore, the alleged breach could only be 'the violation of a provision essential to the accomplishment of the object or purpose' of the NPT (Article 60(3) of the VCLT). Be that as it may, in cases of treaties 'of such a character that a material breach of its provisions by one party radically changes the position of every party with respect to the further performance of its obligations under the treaty' (as the NPT arguably is), the other parties are only entitled to invoke the breach to suspend, and not to terminate, the operation of the Treaty in whole or in part with respect to themselves (Article 60(2)(c)).

In any case, despite postponement of the 2012 Conference, the news that the Middle East WMD-free zone project is dead is premature. The establishment of other NWFZs was also lengthy and problematic.[117] After all, it took thirty years for the first NWFZ – in Latin America and the Caribbean – to fully enter into force. Accordingly, the preparation of a carefully considered WMD-free zone draft treaty for negotiation remains essential for the ultimate success of the initiative: international lawyers have an important role to play in this regard and it is hoped that this chapter will contribute to the debate.

---

[115] It is true that the NPT was adopted before the VCLT and that the Convention does not apply to treaties concluded before its entry into force, but most rules contained therein are generally considered a codification of customary international law. Vienna Convention on the Law of Treaties, Vienna, 23 May 1969, in force 27 January 1980, 1155 UNTS 331; 8 ILM 679.

[116] 'Iran's IAEA envoy slams US blatant violation of NPT regulations', *Press TV*, 26 November 2012, available at: www.presstv.ir/detail/2012/11/26/274641/iran-raps-us-blatant-violation-of-npt.

[117] See Roscini, *Le zone denuclearizzate*, pp. 8–18.

14

Nuclear weapon-free zones: the political context

CECILIE HELLESTVEIT AND DANIEL MEKONNEN

Introduction

One of the most significant yet underexplored areas of international law governing nuclear weapons is the proliferation of nuclear weapon-free zone (NWFZ) treaties since the late 1950s. At present, over 100 countries world-wide are parties to an NWFZ treaty, representing over 50 per cent of the earth's surface. In the southern hemisphere the impact of NWFZs is even more sub-stantial: 99 per cent of all southern land areas are included within an NWFZ. Illustrative of how the NWFZ approach has engulfed the globe step by step, Michael Hamel-Green explains:

> The NWFZ approach can be likened to peeling an orange. First it was the denuclearization of the Antarctic – the area south of the 60° South lati-tude – achieved with the 1959 Antarctic Treaty. Next it was the whole of Latin America as a result of the 1967 Treaty of Tlatelolco. By the mid-1990s the whole southern hemisphere and large regions in the northern part were NWFZs, following the negotiation of treaties for the South Pacific, South-East Asia and Africa. More recently has been the establishment of new zones in Mongolia and Central Asia.[1]

Given such global growth, why have NWFZs garnered so little scholarly atten-tion? In part, their relative absence from the legal literature likely reflects a widespread yet inaccurate assumption that southern states are not key actors in the global nuclear weapons debate. The traditional nuclear weapons security paradigm, linked tightly to the now-defunct Cold War world order, assumes that non-proliferation and disarmament issues remain essentially the exclusive province of the nuclear weapon states (NWS) and their allies.

The present authors argue in favour of an alternative approach, however, viewing the spread of NWFZs as an innovative legal mechanism to bolster glo-bal nuclear non-proliferation and disarmament. Understanding the forces that have shaped this legal mechanism requires an in-depth examination of the pol-itical and historical context that permitted states to begin 'peeling the orange'.

---

[1] M. Hamel-Green, 'Peeling the orange: regional paths to a nuclear-weapon-free world', *Disarmament Forum* 2 (2011), 3–14.

In that vein, the purpose of this chapter is to highlight both how NWFZs arose and where the movement to create NWFZs may be headed in the future.

The first section of this chapter outlines the basic framework for NWFZs and their historical background. The second section reviews specific NWFZs, including those for uninhabited areas, those covering regional groupings of states and those that are unilateral (one-state) zones. The third section of this chapter briefly reviews aborted NWFZ projects, while the fourth section discusses several of the legal particularities of NWFZs. Lastly, the chapter concludes with an assessment of the impact of NWFZs and their potential role in future nuclear disarmament initiatives.

For an overview of the similarities and differences in the NWFZ treaties, see Figure 14.2 in the appendix to this chapter.

A.   Nuclear weapon-free zones

1.   Origins

The origins of the NWFZ concept are often traced to a proposal the USSR put before the UN Commission on Disarmament in 1956, designed to prohibit the installation of nuclear military formations in either East or West Germany and in the territories of neighbouring states.[2] Although this proposal was unsuccessful, it formed the inspiration for a Polish initiative known as the Rapacki Plan, put forward the following year.[3] The Rapacki Plan proposed a nuclear weapon-free zone for Central Europe. The proposal included an elaborate system of control, including aerial and ground control, and a supervisory body. It was suggested the plan be implemented in two stages: (1) a freezing of nuclear armaments in the zone, and (2) a reduction of conventional forces. The purpose was both to eliminate nuclear weapons and to reduce armed forces and conventional armaments so as to reduce tension and substantially limit the risks of conflict. The plan was never implemented, but is generally acclaimed as the major theoretical framework laying the groundwork for later NWFZ treaties.[4]

---

[2] Special Report of the Conference of the Committee on Disarmament, 'Comprehensive study of the question of nuclear-weapon-free zones in all its aspects', UN General Assembly, UN doc. A/10027/Add.1, 8 October 1975, p. 23, available at: www.un.org/disarmament/HomePage/ODAPublications/DisarmamentStudySeries/PDF/A-10027-Add1.pdf (hereafter, UN Comprehensive Study).

[3] P. Moorthy, *Nuclear Weapon Free Zone* (New Delhi: Concept Publishing Company, 2006), p. 6.

[4] For a detailed discussion on the Rapacki Plan, see U. Albrecht, 'The political background of the Rapacki Plan of 1957 and its current significance' in R. Steinke and M. Vale (eds.), *Germany Debates Defense: The NATO Alliance at the Crossroads* (New York: Sharpe, 1983), pp. 117–33; Z. Maruzsa, *Denuclearization in Central Europe? The Rapacki Plan during the Cold War* (May 2009), available at: www.coldwar.hu/html/en/publications/Online%20PublicationMar.pdf.

As early as 1959, the treaty establishing a nuclear-free zone in Antarctica was established, in anticipation of a possible nuclear arms race in uninhabited areas. During the 1960s China also proposed the creation of NWFZs, in Asia and the Pacific, intended to include the United States and the Soviet Union.[5] Following these and various other initiatives, in 1965 the UN General Assembly reaffirmed the right of groups of states to conclude regional treaties to assure the total absence of nuclear weapons in their respective territories.[6] This right was subsequently affirmed by the Nuclear Non-Proliferation Treaty (NPT), which stipulates that the Treaty does not affect 'the right of any group of States to conclude regional treaties in order to assure the total absence of nuclear weapons in their respective territories'.[7]

For non-nuclear weapon states (NNWS), NWFZs represented a third avenue that allowed them to take a stand on non-proliferation without joining either NATO or the Warsaw Pact. In 1974 UN General Assembly Resolution 3261 noted that obligations stemming from the creation of NWFZs may be assumed by groups of states, by entire continents, by regions of states or even by individual states.[8] The following year, UN General Assembly Resolution 3472(B) I, (1) defined an NWFZ as:

> any zone, recognized as such by the General Assembly of the United Nations, which any group of States, in the free exercises of their sovereignty, has established by virtue of a treaty or convention whereby:
>
> (a) The statute of total absence of nuclear weapons to which the zone shall be subject, including the procedure for the delimitation of the zone, is defined;
>
> (b) An international system of verification and control is established to guarantee compliance with the obligations deriving from that statute.[9]

The Resolution also stipulated that in every case of an NWFZ 'that has been recognized by the General Assembly, all nuclear weapon States shall undertake or reaffirm', in a legally binding instrument, to respect the 'statute of total absence' of nuclear weapons in the defined zone, to refrain from violations of the regime, and finally to 'refrain from using or threatening to use nuclear weapons against the States in the zone'.[10] Thus, the five NWS were effectively

---

[5] 'Statement of the Chinese government advocating the complete, thorough, total and resolute prohibition and destruction of nuclear weapons and proposing a conference of the government heads of all countries of the world', *Peking Review* 6(31) (2 August 1963), 7–8 (urging the creation of a 'nuclear weapon-free zone of the Asian and Pacific region, including the United States, the Soviet Union, China and Japan; a nuclear weapon-free zone of Africa; and a nuclear weapon-free zone of Latin America').

[6] UN General Assembly Resolution 2028, adopted on 19 November 1965.

[7] Treaty on the Non-Proliferation of Nuclear Weapons, New York, 1 July 1968, in force 5 March 1970, 729 UNTS 161, Art. VII (hereafter, NPT).

[8] UN General Assembly Resolution 3261 F (XXIX), adopted on 9 December 1974.

[9] UN General Assembly Resolution 3472B, adopted on 11 December 1975.

[10] *Ibid.*

given a veto power over the establishment of new NWFZs, at least for zones that would be recognised as such by the UN General Assembly.

2. *Political context*

While there were many efforts to create NWFZs during the Cold War, only two of the existing regional NWFZs were negotiated in this polarised climate. The Eastern and Western powers were sceptical, but consented to NWFZs on the premise that three conditions were met: (1) that all parties concerned gave their consent, (2) that the NWFZ would not alter the balance of power between East and West by giving a military advantage to either, and (3) that the NWFZ infrastructure contained effective control and monitoring mechanisms.[11] For example, the Treaty of Tlatelolco, drafted in the wake of the Cuban Missile Crisis, included negative security assurances from all of the permanent members of the Security Council. After the Cold War, negative security assurances by all – or even any – nuclear powers no longer appears to be a *sine qua non* for the establishment of an NWFZ. Two of the post-Cold War regional NWFZs (Bangkok and Semipalatinsk) have not yet received negative security assurances from the NWS, while the third (Pelindaba) has a protocol on negative security assurances that has been ratified by only three NWS. Negative security assurances thus appear less critical for the establishment of NWFZs than they were during the Cold War.

Another feature of NWFZs is their historic close association with the South and the Non-Aligned Movement (NAM). While there were proposals in the 1950s for the creation of NWFZs encapsulating European countries as well, the non-aligned countries launched their own proposals in the 1960s to make certain areas free of nuclear weapons, in particular the African continent and the Indian Ocean.[12] The desire to deny the NWS the use of the Southern hemisphere for nuclear military purposes was the main motivation behind the early proposals for the creation of NWFZs in various parts of the globe. The idea was to isolate non-aligned states from the rivalries between East and West.

These efforts eventually broadened to include conventional weapons and foreign military bases as well, as evidenced by proposals for a 'Zone of Peace' covering the Indian Ocean.[13] The NAM's attempt to broaden the zone agreement

---

[11] UN Comprehensive Study, pp. 25ff.

[12] See, e.g. Zone of Peace, Freedom and Neutrality Declaration, adopted by the Foreign Ministers at the Special ASEAN Foreign Ministers Meeting, Kuala Lumpur, 27 November 1971 (taking note of the Treaty of Tlatelolco and declaring that Indonesia, Malaysia, the Philippines, Singapore and Thailand 'are determined to exert initially necessary efforts to secure the recognition of, and respect for, South East Asia as a Zone of Peace, Freedom and Neutrality, free from any form or manner of interference by outside powers').

[13] S. Subedi, 'Problems and prospects for the Treaty on the Creation of Nuclear–Weapon-Free-Zone in Southeast Asia', *International Journal for Peace Studies* 4(1) (1999), available at: www.gmu.edu/programs/icar/ijps/vol4_1/subedi.htm.

to cover any type of unwanted military presence in the South may have had a certain detrimental affect on the appeal of NWFZs, especially for countries that might have agreed to refrain from having nuclear weapons but that nevertheless opposed a categorical prohibition on military forces from states outside the region.

Regional political dynamics also explain proposals to expand the types of weapons prohibited within a zone. In 1990 an Egyptian proposal for an NWFZ in the Middle East was broadened to also include chemical and biological weapons, converting the proposal into that of a Weapon of Mass Destruction-Free Zone (WMDFZ). This manoeuvre ensured Egyptian, Syrian and Iraqi chemical weapons would also be included in the subsequent negotiations, in an attempt to increase the likelihood of attracting Israeli interest in the proposal.[14] Accordingly, in April 1991 the UN Security Council officially adopted the objective of creating a WMDFZ in the Middle East.[15] Along the same lines, the negative security assurance the United States offered to the Treaty of Pelindaba in 1995 was contingent on no use of nuclear, biological or chemical weapons in Africa.[16]

Undoubtedly, the destructive potential of nuclear, biological and chemical weapons is significant, and disarmament efforts are inherently strenuous because the technology used in manufacture often has dual-use potential.[17] Nonetheless, introducing bans on other types of WMDs into NWFZ negotiations has had a tendency to complicate regional dynamics, since the number of states with arsenals of WMDs is substantially larger than the number of NWS. Promoting disarmament and non-proliferation of biological and chemical weapons – 'the poor man's nuclear weapon' – through NWFZs might generate greater support for NWFZs from the NWS, but this tactic also risks creating political gridlock by placing a broader range of interests on the negotiation table.

B.   Presentation of nuclear weapon-free zones

As mentioned above, NWFZs may be separated into three main categories: *geographical zones*, covering uninhabited territory or areas; *regional zones*, consisting of clusters of states or entire continents; and finally, *singular countries*.[18] For a map illustrating NWFZs' global reach, see the appendix to this chapter.

---

[14] UN General Assembly Resolution 45/435, adopted on 10 October 1990, p. 20.

[15] UN Security Council Resolution 687, adopted on 3 April 1991, para. 14.

[16] Press Briefing by Robert Bell, Senior Director for Defense Policy and Arms Control, National Security Council, 11 April 11 1996, available at: www.presidency.ucsb.edu/ws/index.php?pid=59365#axzz2hhVuheGM.

[17] See Convention on Cluster Munitions, Dublin, 30 May 2008, in force 1 August 2010, 48 ILM 354, Art. 1.

[18] The terminology used is from the UN Office for Disarmament Affairs (UNODA) website: www.un.org/disarmament/WMD/Nuclear/NWFZ.shtml.

1.   Geographical zones covering uninhabited areas

Antarctica: the Antarctic Treaty (1959)

The first global treaty on the prevention of proliferation of nuclear weapons was achieved in 1959 with the adoption of the Antarctic Treaty.[19] The Antarctic Treaty was the first multilateral agreement containing (by implication) provisions that ensured nuclear weapons would not be introduced into a specific territory. The zone extends to all territories south of 60° South latitude.[20] This is uninhabited territory with important environmental vulnerabilities.

Initiated by the United States, the Antarctic Treaty establishes a nuclear weapon-free and demilitarised zone by prohibiting the introduction of 'any measures of a military nature'; in other words, military bases, manoeuvres and the testing of weapons.[21] Twelve countries with interests in Antarctica agreed to ensure that the use of Antarctica be reserved exclusively for peaceful purposes.[22] The Treaty did not purport to solve conflicting territorial claims; rather, the aim was to allow scientific research in all corners of the continent regardless.[23] The Treaty does not prevent the use of military personnel and equipment for peaceful purposes. Introduction or testing of nuclear weapons in Antarctica would fall within the scope of the prohibition on testing any weapons contained in Article I.[24] Any type of explosion or disposal of radioactive waste is prohibited.[25]

The Antarctic Treaty does not prejudice the rights of any state under the international law of the high seas.[26] Lastly, provided all original contracting parties are also parties to later agreements on nuclear energy, such rules will apply to Antarctica as well.[27]

Outer space: the Outer Space Treaty (1967) and the Moon Treaty (1979)

Efforts to prevent the arms race from spreading to outer space materialised during the 1950s and early 1960s.[28] In 1961 the UN General Assembly suggested

---

[19] The Antarctic Treaty, Washington DC, 1 December 1959, in force 23 June 1961, 402 UNTS 71 (hereafter, the Antarctic Treaty).

[20] *Ibid.*, Art. VI.   [21] *Ibid.*, Art. I.

[22] The twelve countries with territorial claims in Antarctica parties to the Treaty are Argentina, Australia, Belgium, Chile, France, Japan, New Zealand, Norway, South Africa, the United Kingdom, the USSR (now Russia) and the United States.

[23] The Antarctic Treaty, Art. IV.

[24] UN Comprehensive Study, p. 12.

[25] The Antarctic Treaty, Art. V.

[26] See *ibid.*, Art. VI.   [27] *Ibid.*, Art. V(2).

[28] The USSR suggested a draft resolution to the UN General Assembly in 1958 banning the use of cosmic space for military purposes (Official Records of the General Assembly, Thirteenth Session, Annexes, Agenda Item 60, UN doc. A/C.1/L.291). In 1960 Western nations suggested a plan for prohibiting the placement of WMDs in outer space (Ten Nations Committee on Disarmament, Document TNCD/3, 1960), or vehicles carrying WMD (Ten Nations Committee on Disarmament, Document TNCD/5, 1960).

that the principles of international law apply to outer space and celestial bodies: they are 'free for exploration and use', but are 'not subject to national appropriation'.[29] In 1966 the United States and the USSR negotiated the Treaty on Principles Governing the Activities of States in the Exploration and Use of Outer Space, commonly known as the Outer Space Treaty.[30] Adopted on 27 January 1967, it now has 101 states parties.

Article IV of the Outer Space Treaty contains the operative provisions relating to nuclear weapons:

> States Parties to the Treaty undertake not to place in orbit around the earth any objects carrying nuclear weapons or any other kinds of weapons of mass destruction, install such weapons on celestial bodies, or station such weapons in outer space in any other manner.
>
> The moon and other celestial bodies shall be used by all States Parties to the Treaty exclusively for peaceful purposes. The establishment of military bases, installations and fortifications, the testing of any type of weapons and the conduct of military manoeuvres on celestial bodies shall be forbidden. The use of military personnel for scientific research or for any other peaceful purposes shall not be prohibited. The use of any equipment or facility necessary for peaceful exploration of the moon and other celestial bodies shall also not be prohibited.

This zone was reinforced by the subsequent Agreement Governing the Activities of States on the Moon and Other Celestial Bodies, also known as the Moon Treaty, adopted on 8 December 1979.[31] The Moon Treaty reaffirms that the moon can be used for peaceful purposes only. The Treaty prohibits states parties from 'plac[ing] in orbit around or other trajectory to or around the moon objects carrying nuclear weapons or any other kinds of weapons of mass destruction or plac[ing] or us[ing] such weapons on or in the moon'.[32] The utility of the Moon Treaty is limited, however, as it has been ratified by only fifteen states, none of which have self-launched space exploration programmes.[33] Resistance to the Treaty stems not from opposition to the provisions relating to peaceful use, but rather to the establishment in Article 11 of an

[29] UN General Assembly Resolution 1721 A (XVI), adopted on 20 December 1961; UN General Assembly Resolution 1962 (XVIII), adopted on 13 December 1963.

[30] Treaty on Principles Governing the Activities of States in the Exploration and Use of Outer Space, including the Moon and Other Celestial Bodies ('Outer Space Treaty'), London, Moscow and Washington DC, 27 January 1967, in force 10 October 1967, 610 UNTS 205 (hereafter, the Outer Space Treaty).

[31] Agreement Governing the Activities of States on the Moon and Other Celestial Bodies ('Moon Treaty'), New York, 18 December 1979, in force 11 July 1984, 18 ILM 1434 (1979) (hereafter, the Moon Treaty).

[32] *Ibid*, Art. 3(3).

[33] M. Listner, 'The Moon Treaty: it isn't dead yet', *The Space Review*, 19 March 2012, available at: www.thespacereview.com/article/2047/1.

'international regime' to oversee the disposition of any natural resources found on the moon.[34]

Seabed: the Seabed Treaty (1970)

Another treaty dealing with an uninhabited but environmentally vulnerable area is the Treaty on the Prohibition of the Emplacement of Nuclear Weapons and Other Weapons of Mass Destruction on the Sea-bed and the Ocean Floor and in the Subsoil Thereof, better known as the Seabed Treaty.[35] Motivated by the technological advances of oceanology during the 1960s and rising fear that the seabed would be a new arena for the arms race, the UN General Assembly examined the question of reserving the seabed and the ocean floor and subsoil for peaceful purposes in 1967 and 1968. The Nixon Administration expressed support for the idea, and a draft treaty submitted by the USSR was adopted in the UN General Assembly in 1970.[36]

The Seabed Treaty aims to eliminate the possibility of an underwater arms race and promote the peaceful exploration of water bodies. The Treaty stipulates that states parties shall refrain from implanting or placing any nuclear weapons or other WMD, launching installations or storing installations on the seabed, the ocean floor or its subsoil.[37] Any other facilities specifically designed for storing, testing or using such weapons are prohibited.[38]

2.   Regional zones

Latin America and the Caribbean: the Treaty of Tlatelolco (1967)

The first NWFZ treaty to cover a cluster of states was the Treaty of Tlatelolco,[39] initiated by Bolivia, Brazil, Chile, Ecuador and Mexico. The initiative to

---

[34] *Ibid*, Art. 11. See, M. Listner, 'Examining space law and policy, part V: the Moon Treaty of 1979', *theExaminer.com*, 26 October 2011, available at: www.examiner.com/article/examining-space-law-and-policy-part-5-the-moon-treaty-of-1979. See generally, M. Listner, 'The ownership and exploitation of outer space: a look at foundational law and future legal challenges to current claims', *Regent Journal of International Law* 75 (2003), 75–94.

[35] Treaty on the Prohibition of the Emplacement of Nuclear Weapons and Other Weapons of Mass Destruction on the Sea-bed and the Ocean Floor, and in the Subsoil Thereof ('Seabed Arms Control Treaty'), Washington DC, London and Moscow, 11 February 1971, in force 25 April 1969, 955 UNTS 115 (hereafter, the Seabed Treaty).

[36] UN General Assembly Resolution 2660(XXV), adopted on 7 December 1970.

[37] Seabed Treaty, Art. 1.   [38] *Ibid*.

[39] Treaty for the Prohibition of Nuclear Weapons in Latin America and the Caribbean ('Treaty of Tlatelolco'), Mexico City, 14 February 1967, in force 22 April 1968, 634 UNTS 281, Art. 4(2) (hereafter, Treaty of Tlatelolco). For more information about the issue of nuclear weapons in Latin America and the Caribbean, please see the webpages of the International Law and Policiy Institute's (ILPI) Nuclear Weapons Project: http://nwp.ilpi.org/?p=1851. The following countries have ratified the Treaty of Tlatelolco: Antigua and Barbuda, Argentina, Bahamas, Barbados, Belize, Bolivia, Brazil, Chile, Colombia, Costa Rica, Cuba, Dominica,

negotiate the Treaty was taken in the wake of the Cuban Missile Crisis. A major consideration was to block further proliferation or deployment by NWS of their existing nuclear weapons.[40] The Treaty of Tlatelolco therefore focused on undertakings by NWS not to use or threaten to use nuclear weapons against states in the zone: negative security assurances.

Inspired by the key features of the Rapacki Plan,[41] the Treaty provides for a complete ban on nuclear weapons, whether developed or acquired by signatories of the Treaty or introduced to the zone by nuclear weapon states.[42] The Treaty has a unique mechanism for entry into force. The text provides that it does not enter into force until all Latin American and Caribbean states ratify it, and until all of the NWS have ratified the additional protocol on negative security assurances. Realising, however, that this could take a very long time, a more flexible option was agreed: states parties, upon ratifying the Treaty, may opt to allow its provisions to enter into force for them immediately, and the Treaty then enters into force as soon as eleven states have chosen this option.[43]

Negotiated at the height of the Cold War, the Treaty of Tlatelolco is often cited as an example of a success story of how a treaty can be achieved even in the context of difficulties and setbacks affecting wider arms control and disarmament negotiations.

South Pacific: the Treaty of Rarotonga (1985)

The Treaty of Rarotonga, encompassing the South Pacific region,[44] opened for signature in 1985.[45] New Zealand and Australia first proposed the creation of an NWFZ in the South Hemisphere in 1962–63.[46] Support for the treaty grew

    Dominican Republic, Ecuador, El Salvador, Grenada, Guatemala, Guyana, Haiti, Honduras, Jamaica, Mexico, Nicaragua, Panama, Paraguay, Peru, Saint Kitts and Nevis, Saint Lucia, Saint Vincent and Grenadines, Suriname, Trinidad and Tobago, Uruguay and Venezuela. The Treaty's Protocol II on negative security assurances is ratified by China, France, the United Kingdom, the United States and the former Soviet Union (Russia).

[40] J. Goldblat, 'Nuclear-weapon-free zones: a history and assessment', *Non-proliferation Review* 4 (Summer 1997), 18–32, at 19; P. Beaumont and T. Rubinsky, 'An introduction to the issue of nuclear weapons in Latin America and the Caribbean', ILPI Nuclear Weapons Project Background Paper No. 2 (December 2012), available at: http://nwp.ilpi.org/wp-content/uploads/2012/12/BP02-12_LatinAmerica.pdf.

[41] Hamel-Green, 'Peeling the orange', 5.

[42] Treaty of Tlatelolco, Art. 1.   [43] *Ibid.*, Art. 29.

[44] South Pacific Nuclear Free Zone Treaty, Rarotonga, 6 August 1985, in force 11 December 1986, UNTS 1445 (hereafter, Treaty of Rarotonga).

[45] The following states are parties to the Treaty of Rarotonga: Australia, Cook Islands, Fiji, Kiribati, Nauru, New Zealand, Niue, Papua New Guinea, Samoa, Solomon Islands, Tonga, Tuvalu and Vanuatu.

[46] M. Hamel-Green, 'The Rarotonga South Pacific Nuclear-Free Zone Treaty' in R. Walker and W. Sutherland (eds.), *The Pacific: Peace, Security and the Nuclear Issue,* United Nations University Studies on Peace and Regional Security (London and New Jersey: Zed Books Ltd, 1998), p. 93

largely in response to the use of the South Pacific as a testing ground for nuclear weapons.[47]

In terms of content and scope, the Treaty of Rarotonga is similar to the Treaty of Tlatelolco, although the Treaty of Rarotonga also prohibits the dumping of radioactive waste.[48] Both Treaties prohibit testing nuclear weapons on the territory of the states parties to each Treaty.[49]

One unique feature of the Treaty of Rarotonga is that although the Treaty bans the permanent stationing of nuclear weapons within the zone, it explicitly allows each state party to 'decide for itself whether to allow' nuclear-armed forces from states outside the zone to travel through the state party's territorial waters or its airspace.[50] Australia sought this provision to allow US nuclear vessels to visit Australian ports.[51]

The Treaty of Rarotonga's Protocol II on negative security assurances and Protocol III on nuclear testing have both been ratified by China, France, the United Kingdom and the former Soviet Union, while the United States signed but did not ratify the protocols.

Southeast Asia: the Treaty of Bangkok (1995)

The Treaty of Bangkok is known in its full version as the Treaty on the South-East Asia Nuclear Weapon Free Zone.[52] It was adopted on 15 December 1995 and has ten states parties.[53]

The background for this Treaty dates to the 1971 Zone of Peace, Freedom and Neutrality in South-East Asia, an initiative of the Association of Southeast Asian Nations (ASEAN). Initially stalled due to the Cold War and the Thai-Philippine alliance with the USA, the 1992 Singapore Declaration relaunched the initiative with reference to 'changing circumstances'.[54] The altered conditions at the end of the Cold War allowed ASEAN to pursue the drafting of an NWFZ agreement, advanced by the founding members of ASEAN: Indonesia, Malaysia, the Philippines, Singapore and Thailand. The Treaty of Bangkok was

---

[47] For a detailed account of nuclear testing, with an emphasis on the South Pacific region in particular, see Chapter 12 in this book.

[48] Article 7.

[49] See Treaty of Rarotonga, Art. 6 and Treaty of Tlatelolco Art. 1.

[50] Treaty of Rarotonga, Art. 5.

[51] See Hamel-Green, 'The Rarotonga South Pacific Nuclear-Free Zone Treaty', p. 100.

[52] Treaty on the Southeast Asia Nuclear Weapon-Free Zone ('Bangkok Treaty'), Bangkok, 15 December 1995, in force 27 March 1997, 35 ILM 635 (1996) (hereafter, Bangkok Treaty). See, also H. Winge Laursen, 'An introduction to the issue of nuclear weapons in Southeast Asia', ILPI Nuclear Weapons Project Background Paper No. 3 (June 2013), available at: http://nwp.ilpi.org/wp-content/uploads/2013/06/BP03-13_ASEAN_WEB.pdf.

[53] Brunei Darussalam, Cambodia, Indonesia, Laos, Malaysia, Myanmar, Philippines, Singapore, Thailand and Vietnam.

[54] Singapore Declaration, 28 January 1992. See D. Weatherbee, *Historical Dictionary of United States – Southeast Asia Relations* (Lanham: Scarecrow Press, 2003), p. 329.

formally adopted in 1995, becoming the first NWFZ of the post-Cold War era and an early manifestation of the disarmament rush of the 1990s. It establishes an enhanced supervisory system comprising a commission and an executive committee, as well as procedures for fact-finding.[55]

In addition to emulating the same key denuclearisation features contained in the Treaty of Rarotonga and the Treaty of Tlatelolco, the Treaty of Bangkok went further by extending the Treaty's territorial zone of application to cover the exclusive economic zones (EEZ) of states parties to the Treaty.[56] The NWFZ thereby extends 200 nautical miles (370 km) off the coast of the member states. This is believed to have complicated the willingness of nuclear power states to provide negative security guarantees; no nuclear weapon state has yet signed the Treaty's Protocol on negative security assurances.[57]

Africa: the Treaty of Pelindaba (1996)

The African Nuclear-Weapon-Free Zone Treaty or the Treaty of Pelindaba was opened for signature on 11 April 1996 and entered into force in 2009.[58] The Treaty has thirty-six states parties.[59]

This Treaty covers, as its point of departure, the entire African continent, although not all states on the African continent are parties or even signatories.[60] The initiative for creating an African NWFZ dates back to the 1960s, when the Organization of African Unity (OAU, the predecessor to the African Union) committed to keeping the continent free of nuclear weapons by adopting the

---

[55] Treaty of Bangkok, Art. 8, 10, and 13.

[56] Treaty of Bangkok, Art. 2(1).

[57] Arms Control Association, www.armscontrol.org/factsheets/nwfz (stating 'Five nuclear weapons states and ASEAN members met in July 2012 to sign the treaty protocol. The treaty commission, however, postponed the signing of the protocol until November, requesting more time to review reservations that several of the NWS indicated that they would attach during ratification').

[58] Treaty on the Nuclear-Weapon-Free Zone in Africa ('Pelindaba Treaty'), Pelindaba, 11 April 1996, in force 15 July 2009, 35 ILM 698 (1996) (hereafter, Pelindaba Treaty). 'Pelindaba' was the name of a former nuclear weapons facility near Pretoria in South Africa. See, also H. Winge Laursen, 'An introduction to the issue of nuclear weapons in Africa', ILPI Nuclear Weapons Project Background Paper No. 1 (May 2012), available at: http://nwp.ilpi.org/wp-content/uploads/2012/08/BP01-12_Africa.pdf.

[59] Algeria, Benin, Botswana, Burkina Faso, Burundi, Cameroon, Chad, Comoros, Côte d'Ivoire, Equatorial Guinea, Ethiopia, Gabon, Gambia, Ghana, Guinea, Guinea-Bissau, Kenya, Lesotho, Libyan Arab Jamahiriya, Madagascar, Malawi, Mali, Mauritania, Mauritius, Mozambique, Namibia, Nigeria, Rwanda, Senegal, South Africa, Swaziland, Togo, Tunisia, United Republic of Tanzania, Zambia, Zimbabwe. UN Office for Disarmament Affairs, 'African Nuclear Weapon Free Zone Treaty (Pelindaba Treaty)', available at: http://disarma-ment.un.org/treaties/t/pelindaba.

[60] Contrast with, e.g., Article 2(1) of the Treaty of Bangkok: 'This Treaty and its Protocol shall apply to the territories, continental shelves, and EEZ of the States Parties within the Zone *in which this Treaty is in force*' (emphasis added).

Declaration on the Denuclearization of Africa.[61] The Declaration of Lusaka of 1970 likewise called for the establishment of an NWFZ on the African continent.[62] However, the first concrete step towards the adoption of a treaty took place only in 1996, after the Cold War. This was possible due to major changes in the global political order, leading to decreased US and Soviet strategic and military interest in Africa.

The Treaty requires each member state to 'prohibit in its territory the stationing of any nuclear explosive devices'. In terms of supervision, the Treaty authorises member states to inspect visits or transits by foreign nuclear-armed ships or aircrafts.[63] The Treaty of Pelindaba establishes a regional organisation, the African Commission on Nuclear Energy (AFCONE), to implement the Treaty.[64] In the event of complaints against a state party of breach of its obligations under the Treaty or its protocols, the AFCONE may request the International Atomic Energy Agency (IAEA) to conduct a 'special inspection'.[65]

Like the Treaty of Bangkok, the Treaty of Pelindaba is also seen as an early manifestation of the disarmament rush of the 1990s. The negative security assurances in the Treaty's supplementary protocols are in force, ratified by China, France and the United Kingdom. The question of the geographical scope of the zone, however, has been a point of contention. Although the United Kingdom has ratified the Treaty of Pelindaba's negative security assurance protocol, it objects to the extension of the treaty to the Chagos Archipelagos, and does not consider itself bound by the Treaty's restrictions in respect of Chagos.[66] For its part, the United States has signed but not ratified the protocols, due to the Treaty's stipulated scope extending to the US military base at Diego Garcia.[67] Like the United States, Russia has abstained from becoming a party to the Treaty's protocols.[68]

---

[61] Adopted by the Summit of the OAU at its first ordinary session, Cairo, 17–21 July 1964.

[62] Also known as the Lusaka Declaration on Peace, Independence, Development, Cooperation and Democratisation of International Relations, adopted 8–10 September 1970.

[63] Treaty of Pelindaba, Art. 4.

[64] *Ibid.*, Art. 12, and Annex III.   [65] *Ibid.*, Annex VI.

[66] For an overview of UK reservations upon signature and ratification to the Pelindaba Treaty, see O. Adenji, *The Treaty of Pelindaba on the African Nuclear Weapon Free Zone* (Geneva: United Nations Institute for Disarmament Research, 2002), pp. 149ff.

[67] The principal obstacle to US ratification was the impending threat of Libya's nuclear weapons programme, which has since been defused. A more persistent problem is the question about the Treaty's applicability to Chagos and Diego Garcia. P. Sand, 'African nuclear-weapon-free zone in force: what next for Diego Garcia?' *American Society for International Law Insight* 13(12) (28 August 2009), available at: www.asil.org/insights/volume/13/issue/12/african-nuclear-weapon-free-zone-force-what-next-diego-garcia.

[68] See Letter from the Russian Ambassador to the OAU Secretary General (Addis Ababa, 5 November 1996) (cited in J. Goldblat, *Arms Control: The New Guide to Negotiations and Agreements* (London/Thousand Oaks/New Delhi: Sage Publications, 2002), p. 211).

Central Asia: the Treaty of Semipalatinsk (2006)

The Treaty on a Nuclear-Weapon-Free Zone in Central Asia, also known as the Treaty of Semipalatinsk (or the Treaty of Semey), was adopted on 8 September 2006.[69] Five Central Asian countries have ratified the Treaty: Kazakhstan, Kyrgyzstan, Tajikistan, Turkmenistan and Uzbekistan.

In addition to adopting the same general prohibitions on nuclear weapons stipulated in other regional treaties, the Treaty of Semipalatinsk goes further by prohibiting the conduct of research on nuclear weapons,[70] and explicitly including the more intrusive IAEA additional protocol safeguards.[71] Its Protocol on negative security assurances has not been ratified by any of the NWS.[72] The Treaty also contains a provision obliging states parties to assist in environmental rehabilitation of contaminated areas.[73]

The former Soviet Union relied extensively on the Central Asian region for a range of nuclear weapon-related activities, including nuclear and missile testing, processing of nuclear fuels, stockpiling of strategic and tactical nuclear weapons, uranium mining and plutonium stockpiling. These countries once hosted over 700 tactical nuclear weapons, in addition to the over 1,400 former Soviet strategic nuclear weapons that Kazakhstan returned to Russia before joining the NPT in 1995.[74] The collapse of the Soviet Union made it possible to envisage a nuclear weapon-free zone in this area. The five Central Asian states took the initiative, and a treaty was concluded after nine years of negotiations. The zone was established independently of any negative assurances by the nuclear powers. The presence of Western military bases in the Central Asian region linked to the conflict in Afghanistan occasioned US, UK and French opposition to the Treaty of Semipalatinsk.

All state parties to the Treaty of Semipalatinsk, with the exception of Turkmenistan, are also parties to the Tashkent Treaty (1992), a security agreement with Russia under which aggression against one signatory will be perceived as aggression against all signatories. As this places Central Asia under the Russian nuclear umbrella, the United Kingdom, France and the United States consider the two agreements to be incompatible.

The Treaty of Semipalatinsk is yet another indication that the importance of support and acquiescence by nuclear powers to regional NWFZs – the *raison d'être* of regional NWFZs during the Cold War – has shifted. Although assurances from the nuclear powers are certainly important, they are not necessarily the main, much less the only, objective of regional NWFZs anymore.

---

[69] Treaty on a Nuclear-Weapon-Free Zone in Central Asia ('Treaty of Semipalatinsk'), Semipalatinsk, 8 September 2006, in force 21 March 2009 (hereafter, Semipalatinsk Treaty).
[70] Treaty of Semipalatinsk, Art. 1.   [71] *Ibid.*, Art. 8.
[72] *Ibid.*, Arts. 3 and 8.   [73] *Ibid.*, Art. 6.
[74] J. Dhanapala, Statement before the First Committee of the General Assembly, UN Doc. A/C.1/57/PV.2, 30 September 2002.

3.   Singular countries

A third type of NWFZ is based on a state's unilateral declaration. The status must be recognised by the UN General Assembly in order to be classified as an NWFZ.[75]

Mongolia was the first state to declare itself a single-state NWFZ, in 1992.[76] Mongolia's interest in creating an NWFZ derived from its history as a border country to two nuclear-armed states: the Soviet Union and China. By 1994 Mongolia had succeeded in obtaining commitments from its NWS neighbours to respect Mongolia's decision to remain free of nuclear weapons.[77] The UN General Assembly formally recognised Mongolia as an NWFZ in 1999.[78] Mongolia's domestic laws also confirm the country's NWFZ status and provide criminal penalties for violations.[79]

Austria is not formally classified as an NWFZ since it has not been recognised as such by the UN General Assembly, but Austria's domestic legislation effectively renders the state an NWFZ. A referendum held in 1978 showed strong popular discontent with a national nuclear power plant, leading to a prohibition on the establishment of nuclear power plants and any use of nuclear fissile materials in Austria, even for peaceful purposes.[80] A federal constitutional law adopted in 1999 underpins this self-declared denuclearised status.[81]

C.   Missing links

A number of proposals for NWFZs have been initiated in different parts of the world without coming to fruition. A brief overview of the most important missing links shows that initiatives for an NWFZ in Europe, the Middle East and South Asia have been repeatedly up for discussion. As attempts to create a WMD-free zone in the Middle East were the subject of Chapter 13, this section focuses on attempts to create an NWFZ in Europe and in South Asia.

There have been numerous attempts to create an NWFZ in Europe. As described earlier, in 1957 Poland put forward a proposal known as the Rapacki Plan, which involved creating a zone in Central Europe in which states would agree to not maintain, transfer or use nuclear weapons. The Rapacki Plan provided an elaborate system of control, including aerial and ground control,

---

[75] See UN General Assembly Resolution 3472 B, adopted on 11 December 1975.

[76] See generally J. Enkhsaikhan, 'Mongolia's status: the case for a unique approach', *Asian Affairs: An American Review* 27(4) (Winter 2001), 223–32, at 226.

[77] G. Verlini, 'Keeping nuclear weapons out', *IAEA Bulletin* 51–2 (April 2002), 44–7.

[78] UN General Assembly Resolution 53/77 ('Mongolia's international security and nuclear-weapon-free status), adopted on 12 January 1999.

[79] Verlini, 'Keeping nuclear weapons out', 45.

[80] See *Législations nucléaires des pays de l'OCDE, Réglementation générale et cadre institution- nel des activités nucléaires*, available at: www.nea.fr/html/law/legislation/fr/autriche.pdf.

[81] Bundesgesetzblatt Für Die Republik Österreich, 1999 (I), p. 1161.

and a supervisory body. It was never implemented, however, due to concerns over how the potential zone would affect the balance of power in Europe.[82] After the Cold War, certain proposals have surfaced in Eastern Europe. At the 1990 and 1995 NPT review conferences, Belarus and Ukraine proposed creating a European NWFZ.[83] These proposals have thus far failed to gain traction, however.

There have also been proposals for the creation of an NWFZ in Northern Europe. By 1957 Denmark and Norway had both refused to allow nuclear weapons to be stationed on their territory.[84] In 1963 Finland drew upon an earlier Swedish proposal to create a club of non-nuclear states. The Finnish proposal suggested the Nordic countries form their own NWFZ to confirm the Nordic countries' shared policy of barring the stationing of nuclear weapons on their territory.[85] Denmark and Norway, however, accepted NATO recommendations to keep the nuclear weapon option open in case a future military conflict rendered the stationing of nuclear weapons on Danish or Norwegian territory desirable.[86] The NWFZ initiative resurfaced in the 1970s, and was combined with negotiations on force and armaments reduction in Europe more generally. The Finns argued that arms control in Europe should not focus exclusively on the concerns of the great powers; an NWFZ would allow the legitimate security interests of smaller, neutral states to be taken into account.[87] The proposal failed, however, because it did not include Soviet nuclear arms on the Kola Peninsula.[88]

Soviet President Mikhail Gorbachev initiated a proposal for the denuclearisation of the Arctic and Northern Europe in 1987.[89] Denmark and Sweden

---

[82] For a detailed discussion on the Rapacki Plan, see generally Albrecht, 'The Political Background of the Rapacki Plan', pp. 117–33 and Maruzsa, *Denuclearization in Central Europe?*

[83] A. Sychou, 'Status of the Initiative to Create a Nuclear-Weapon-Free Space in Central and Eastern Europe' in UNIDIR, *Nuclear Weapon Free Zones in the 21st Century* (Geneva: UNIDIR, 1997), pp. 65–75.

[84] F. Griffiths (ed.), *Arctic Alternatives: Civility of Militarism in the Cirumpolar North* (Toronto: Dundurn, 1992), p. 270.

[85] L. Mampaey, 'Les zones exemptes d'armes nucléaires: état des lieux, bilan et nouveaux enjeux', Research Note, Groupe de Recherche et d'Information sur la Paix et la Sécurité (2010), p. 7.

[86] *Ibid.*

[87] *Ulkopoliittisia Lausuntoja ja Asiakirjoja 1973* (Helsinki: Publications of the Ministry for Foreign Affairs, 1974), p. 169. UN Comprehensive Study 1975, p. 36 n. 49. See also Mampaey, 'Les zones exemptes d'armes nucléaires', p. 7.

[88] J. Skogan, 'Militarization and confidence-building measures in the Arctic', in F. Griffiths (ed.), *Arctic Alternatives: Civility or Militarism in the Circumpolar North* (Toronto: Dundurn, 1992), p. 262.

[89] M. Gorbachev, 'Speech in Murmansk at the Ceremonial Meeting on the Occasion of the Presentation of the Order of Lenin and the Gold Star to the City of Murmansk', held in Murmansk, Russia (October 1987).

proposed denuclearisation of the Arctic again in 1988. Although the proposal was not adopted, Nordic states and civil society organisations have regularly promoted the idea of denuclearising the Arctic ever since.[90] With the exception of Sweden and Finland, however, all countries with jurisdiction in the Arctic belong to one of the nuclear umbrellas – a factor that complicates efforts to create an Arctic NWFZ.

There have been various attempts to establish an NWFZ in Southern Europe. A 1959 USSR proposal concerning the Balkans and the Adriatic was rejected by the United States for not addressing production and stockpiling.[91] Likewise, the United States rejected a USSR proposal made in 1963 concerning the Mediterranean Sea.[92] Numerous attempts during the Cold War to create an NWFZ were rejected out of fear that they were merely intended to alter the military balance of power in the designated area.

In 1972 the United States put forward a proposal to create an NWFZ in the Korean Peninsula. President Kim Il Sung of the Democratic People's Republic of Korea renewed the proposal in 1980, but the process stalled due to mistrust and disagreement over inspection issues.[93] In 1974 India conducted its first nuclear test. In response, Pakistan proposed to the UN General Assembly the creation of an NWFZ in South Asia.[94] Although calls to create an NWFZ in South Asia were repeated annually in the UN General Assembly,[95] the prospects for such a zone dimmed significantly after Pakistan conducted its first nuclear test in 1998.

D.   Legal particularities of nuclear weapon-free zones

1.   Definition of nuclear weapons

The treaties establishing NWFZs in uninhabited areas omit any definition of nuclear weapons, as does the NPT. Their prohibitions are also not restricted to nuclear weapons, but include other weapons of mass destruction as well.[96]

---

[90] M. Wallace and S. Staples, *Ridding the Arctic of Nuclear Weapons – A Task Long Overdue*, 2010, available at: www.arcticsecurity.org/docs/arctic-nuclear-report-web.pdf. See also 'Proceedings: Conference on an Arctic Nuclear-Weapon-Free-Zone' (Copenhagen: Danish Institute for International Studies, 2009).

[91] US Department of State, Historical Office, *Documents on Disarmament 1845–1959*, Vol. II (1960), pp. 1423–6 and 1434–6.

[92] *Ibid.*, pp. 242–3.

[93] Hamel-Green, 'Peeling the orange', 3–15.

[94] UN General Assembly Resolution 3265(XXIX) 1974, *Declaration and Establishment of a Nuclear-Free Zone in South Asia*, UN doc. A/RES/3265, adopted on 9 December 1974.

[95] See, e.g. UN General Assembly Resolution 42/29, adopted 30 November 1987 (listing previous UNGA Resolutions encouraging the creation of a South Asian NWFZ).

[96] See, e.g. Outer Space Treaty Art. IV, Seabed Treaty, Art. 1.

By contrast, all treaties establishing regional NWFZs define nuclear weapons or devices. The Treaty of Tlatelolco defines nuclear weapons as 'any device capable of releasing nuclear energy in an uncontrolled manner and which has a group of characteristics that are appropriate for use for warlike purposes'.[97] The Treaty of Bangkok adopts a less restrictive definition, extending it to 'any explosive device capable of releasing nuclear energy in an uncontrolled manner'.[98] The Treaty of Rarotonga broadened the definition to include 'a weapon or device capable of releasing nuclear energy, irrespective of the purpose for which it could be used', a definition repeated *verbatim* in the Treaty of Pelindaba.[99] The definition in the Treaty of Semipalatinsk adds 'irrespective of the military or civilian purpose for which the weapon or device could be used'.[100] The Treaties of Rarotonga, Pelindaba and Semipalatinsk all specify that the term includes weapons or devices in unassembled and partly assembled forms. All regional treaties explicitly exclude means of transport or delivery if separable from and not an indivisible part of the weapon.

2. *Prohibited activities*

The NWFZ treaties pertaining to uninhabited areas contain simple prohibitions adjusted to the risks of the area in question. While the Antarctic Treaty prohibits nuclear explosions, disposal of radioactive materials and testing of nuclear weapons,[101] the Seabed Treaty prohibits states parties from implanting or emplacing such weapons, from maintaining facilities designed for storage or use of them and from assisting other states in carrying out any of the prohibited activities.[102] Similarly, the Outer Space Treaty prohibits the placement of objects carrying nuclear weapons in orbit or on celestial bodies.

The regional NWFZ treaties have more elaborate prohibitions, albeit with a slightly different emphasis. The Treaty of Tlatelolco prohibits production, receipt, storage, testing or use of nuclear weapons.[103] The Treaty of Rarotonga stipulates the same prohibitions, and also bars states parties from seeking or receiving assistance to engage in any of the prohibited activities. That Treaty further develops the prohibitions of testing and adds a prohibition on dumping radioactive matter at sea.[104] The Treaty of Bangkok prohibits the development, possession, stationing, transport, testing and use of nuclear weapons.

---

[97] Treaty of Tlatelolco, Art. 5.
[98] Treaty of Bangkok, Art. 1(c).
[99] Treaty of Rarotonga, Art. 1(c); Treaty of Pelindaba, Art. 1(c).
[100] Treaty of Semipalatinsk, Art. 1(b).
[101] Antarctic Treaty, Art. I.1.
[102] Seabed Treaty, Art. I.1, 2.
[103] Treaty of Tlatelolco, Art. 1.
[104] Treaty of Rarotonga, Arts. 6–7.

Dumping and discharge of radioactive material is also prohibited.[105] The Treaty of Pelindaba adds a prohibition on research on the development of nuclear weapons,[106] as does the Treaty of Semipalatinsk.[107] The Treaty of Pelindaba also extends the general prohibition of production to require the physical destruction of facilities for nuclear weapons manufacture.[108]

3.   Territorial scope of application

Treaties establishing NWFZs are, as a point of departure, applicable in the territories of the states that are parties to the relevant treaties.[109] The treaties establishing NWFZs in uninhabited areas are to a large extent uncontroversial in scope. While the Antarctic Treaty refers to latitude as a reference for its scope of application, in Article VI, the Outer Space Treaty simply refers in its provisions to the moon, outer space, other celestial bodies and to objects placed in orbit around the earth. The Seabed Treaty defines its area of application as extending up to the 12-mile boundary of each state's territorial sea.[110] The 'landlocked' Treaty of Semipalatinsk applies to the territory of the five states parties.[111]

Controversies arise in particular for the maritime territorial scope of NWFZs. For example, the Treaty of Tlatelolco relies on longitude and latitude to define its outer territorial scope, and applies to the whole of the territory.[112] The inclusion of the Malvinas/Falkland Islands has provoked certain controversies. The Treaties of Rarotonga and Pelindaba define the territory covered by the zones as including land territory, territorial sea, archipelagic waters and the airspace above them as well as the seabed and subsoil beneath.[113] The Treaty of Pelindaba defines the nuclear weapon-free zone established by the Treaty as the entire African continent, but specifies that the Treaty obligations only apply on the territories of the states parties.[114] Thus the individual obligations in the respective treaties apply only to the individual states parties to the treaties.[115] The inclusion of archipelagic waters has raised issues about military bases in addition to questions of free passage. The Treaty of Bangkok extends its territorial application to the exclusive economic zone, reaching 200 nautical miles

---

[105]   Treaty of Bangkok, Art. 2.3.   [106]   Treaty of Pelindaba, Art. 3(a).

[107]   Treaty of Semipalatinsk, Art. 3.   [108]   Treaty of Pelindaba, Art. 6.

[109]   See also Chapter 13 on the proposed WMD-free zone in the Middle East.

[110]   Seabed Treaty, Art. 2.

[111]   Treaty of Semipalatinsk, Art. 1(a).

[112]   Treaty of Tlatelolco, Art. 4.

[113]   Treaty of Rarotonga Art. 1(b); Treaty of Pelindaba, Art. 1(b). Both treaties have appended maps.

[114]   Treaty of Pelindaba, Art. 2 (1): '*Except where otherwise specified*, this Treaty and its Protocols shall apply to the territory within the African nuclear-weapon-free zone' (emphasis added).

[115]   See e.g. Treaty of Pelindaba, Arts. 2–4.

into the ocean.[116] Despite an explicit exemption for transport,[117] this extensive scope has provoked the NWS.

4. Permanency

A key feature common to all treaties establishing NWFZs is that these treaties are perpetual. They remain in force indefinitely, although they provide mechanisms for individual member states to withdraw from the treaty. The perpetual duration of NWFZ treaties – arguably one of their core strengths – is widely attributed to the Rapacki Plan, which is the major inspiration for all NWFZ treaties.[118] The permissible reasons for withdrawal from an NWFZ vary. For example, the Treaty of Tlatelolco provides that a party may notify the Secretary-General of the state's intention to withdraw from the Treaty if 'there have arisen or may arise circumstances connected with the content of this Treaty or [its protocols] … which affect its supreme interests or the peace and security of one or more Contracting Parties'.[119] The Treaties of Pelindaba and Semipalatinsk contain similar formulations.[120] The Treaty of Rarotonga, by contrast, adopts a more restrictive framework, permitting withdrawal only 'in the event of a violation by any Party of a provision of this Treaty essential to the achievement of the objectives of the Treaty or of the spirit of the Treaty'.[121] The Treaty of Bangkok also allows withdrawal only in the event of another state party's violation.[122] Most treaties require twelve months' notice for withdrawal.[123] The Treaty of Tlatelolco and the Seabed Treaty require three months' notice, while the Antarctic Treaty requires two years.

5. Monitoring and enforcement

Perhaps the most important and innovative aspect of the treaties is that they provide comprehensive safeguards and enforcement mechanisms. Some NWFZ treaties establish their own regional monitoring bodies. For example, the Treaty of Tlatelolco establishes the Agency for the Prohibition of Nuclear Weapons in Latin America and the Caribbean (OPANAL).[124] Monitoring bodies with more extensive tasks were erected under the Treaty of Bangkok,[125] and the Treaty of Pelindaba established the African Commission on Nuclear

---

[116] Treaty of Bangkok, Art. 2.1.   [117] *Ibid.*, Art. 2.2(b).
[118] Hamel-Green, 'Peeling the orange' and Maruzsa, *Denuclearization in Central Europe?*
[119] Treaty of Tlatelolco, Art. 31(1).
[120] Treaty of Pelindaba, Art. 20; Treaty of Semipalatinsk, Art. 16.
[121] Treaty of Rarotonga, Art. 13.   [122] Treaty of Bangkok, Art. 22(2).
[123] See, e.g. Treaty of Pelindaba, Art. 20(2); Treaty of Semipalatinsk, Art. 16(b); Treaty of Rarotonga, Art. 13(2); Treaty of Bangkok, Art. 22(3).
[124] Treaty of Tlatelolco, Art. 7.   [125] Treaty of Bangkok, Arts. 7–9.

Energy.[126] The Treaty of Semipalatinsk adopts a different path, requiring that states in the region adopt the IAEA's Additional Protocol, which provides for expanded monitoring.[127] The establishment of independent monitoring mechanisms through NWFZ treaties is seen as a major factor in reducing zonal states' dependence on NWS negative security assurances.[128]

6.   Points of friction

Nuclear umbrellas have created several controversies. For example, the coexistence of the Russian nuclear umbrella, as negotiated in the Tashkent Treaty, and the NWFZ established under the Treaty of Semipalatinsk has raised questions about the status and implications of the two treaties, as four countries are parties to both.

Maritime extensions of the zones are particularly controversial. The United States has remained vitally interested in the transit of nuclear-armed ships and planes through NWFZ air and sea space, leading to a debate with New Zealand over the implications of the Treaty of Rarotonga shortly after that Treaty's adoption. Insisting that NWFZ treaties may not restrict rights of free passage and transit or freedom of the high seas, the United States continues to object to the extensive geographic scope of the Treaty of Bangkok in particular. No NWS has given negative security assurances to the Treaty of Bangkok, ascribed in part to ongoing EEZ boundary disputes in the region, and in part to limitations on the passage of nuclear-powered ships within the treaty zone.[129]

Despite the treaties' entry into force, doubts are sometimes raised about NWFZ enforcement. For example, in 2012 Argentina accused the United Kingdom of deploying nuclear-armed submarines off the coast of the Malvinas/Falkland Islands in violation of the Treaty of Tlatelolco – a charge the United Kingdom refused to confirm or deny.[130] Questions have also been raised about French respect for the Treaty of Rarotonga, given that state's extensive history of nuclear testing in the South Pacific Region.[131]

E.   Nuclear weapon-free zones after the Cold War

Although the concept of an NWFZ arose during the Cold War, two out of five regional NWFZs entered into force as late as 2009, underlining their

---

[126] Treaty of Pelindaba, Art. 12.   [127] Treaty of Semipalatinsk, Art. 8.
[128] Hamel-Green, 'Peeling the orange', 10.
[129] N. Klein, *Maritime Security and the Law of the Sea* (Oxford University Press, 2011), p. 52; D. Weatherbee, *Historical Dictionary of United States* (Lanham, MD/Toronto/Plymouth, UK: Scarecrow Press, 2008), p. 330.
[130] R. Carroll, 'Argentina accuses UK of deploying nuclear weapons near Falkland Islands', *Guardian*, 10 February 2012, available at: www.theguardian.com/uk/2012/feb/10/falkland-islands-argentina-uk-nuclear-weapons.
[131] See Chapter 12 for more information on French nuclear testing in the South Pacific.

contemporary relevance as instruments of denuclearisation. Geographically, NWFZs are thus far concentrated primarily in the Southern Hemisphere. The desire to secure the complete absence of nuclear weapons from a region is equally relevant – albeit more complicated – in the Northern Hemisphere, however, where vast areas are not covered by NWFZs.

NWFZs are perceived to have multiple purposes. Discussions at the UN also reveal that the objectives of NWFZs have been very much adjusted to the nuclear challenges of the twenty-first century. In 1999 UN guidelines identified some of the key objectives in establishing NWFZs as:

> strengthening the international non-proliferation regime; strengthening regional peace and security; strengthening the security of regional states; functioning as important regional confidence-building measures (CBMs); strengthening and complementing other non-proliferation instruments; and providing 'a means of expressing and promoting common values in the areas of nuclear disarmament, arms control and non-proliferation'.[132]

The environmental dimension evident in the Treaty of Semipalatinsk, for example, also deserves mention. In sum, an examination of the three main objectives of NWFZs – non-proliferation, disarmament and security enhancement – indicates that they remain highly relevant in a post-Cold War environment, in which the risks of proliferation are polymorphous threats and environmental considerations have enhanced importance, and where regional security organisations are increasingly assuming responsibility for measures affecting international peace and security.

1. Non-proliferation

In the post-Cold War era, NWFZs have assumed a more prominent role in preventing the spread of nuclear weapons to states no longer restricted by the interests of their NWS benefactor. The function of NWFZ agreements in protecting a zone or region from the strategic deployment of nuclear warheads by NWS now appears less critical compared with their effect in precluding regional competitors from obtaining nuclear weapons. Existing NWFZ agreements offer a model that may be adapted to the specific conditions of each region or geographical area and act as important tools for states wishing to create NWFZs in the future.

To be sure, all states currently belonging to NWFZs are also states parties to the NPT. Nevertheless, the additional monitoring mechanisms that NWFZs often establish and their function in forcing states to reaffirm the obligations to which they have already committed under the NPT imply that NWFZ

---

[132] See UN General Assembly, Report of the Disarmament Commission ('Establishment of nuclear-weapon-free zones on the basis of arrangements freely arrived at among the States of the region concerned'), UN Doc. A/54/42, Annex 1, adopted on 6 May 1999.

agreements and the NPT reinforce each other with respect to non-proliferation. By restricting the geographic area where such weapons may be lawfully stockpiled, tested or developed, such zones also contribute to reducing the military advantage of nuclear weapons.

The non-proliferation feature of NWFZ agreements has also gained increased momentum with the growing emphasis on the importance of protecting the environment, by limiting the geographic area at risk of radioactive contamination. The preamble to the Treaty of Rarotonga explicitly names keeping the region free of environmental pollution as one major objective.[133] The Treaty of Semipalatinsk also introduces the NWFZ as a tool to promote 'cooperation in the environmental rehabilitation of territories affected by radioactive contamination'.[134] The dangers stemming from testing, accidents and potential use of nuclear weapons are reduced for the globe as a whole by restricting the geographical areas in which nuclear weapons are located.

NWFZs are also perceived to provide security enhancement by 'spar[ing] nations concerned from the threat of nuclear attack or involvement in nuclear war', thereby contributing to strengthening international peace and security.[135] In the bi-polar world, NWFZs were seen as an instrument to encourage political détente, and it was repeatedly argued that NWFZs might provide a useful instrument in the quest for international security.[136] In the post-Cold War era, NWFZ agreements may also be viewed as instruments that can help build mutual trust in regions fraught with security-related tensions. NWFZs support and improve the verification regime. They may offer an additional layer of security to nuclear installations, reducing the risks of theft of fissile material or technology. An NWFZ may therefore increase the actual security of states by offering a more robust verification and monitoring regime, reducing risks of unintended or unwanted proliferation – in particular, that arising from non-state actors.

2.   Disarmament

The disarmament dimension of NWFZs has also been important since their origin. The aim was to make positive contributions towards 'general and complete disarmament' as set out in NPT Article VI.[137] As former UN Under-Secretary-General for Disarmament Affairs Jayantha Dhanapala noted, the establishment of an NWFZ has particular relevance in the global movement towards the elimination of nuclear weapons.[138] One path to achieving the goal

---

[133] See also Treaty of Rarotonga, Art 7.1.D.
[134] See Treaty of Semipalatinsk, Preamble and Art. 6.
[135] UN Comprehensive Study 1975, p. 38.   [136] *Ibid.*
[137] For a more detailed analysis of the legal interpretation of NPT, Art. VI, see Chapter 16.
[138] Dhanapala, Statement before the First Committee of the General Assembly.

of nuclear disarmament expressed in Article VI of the NPT would be the gradual elimination of nuclear weapons region by region through NWFZs.

The Mexican architect of the Tlatelolco Treaty, Alfonso Garcia Robles, argued that the zonal approach contributes to global denuclearisation by gradually shrinking the number of areas in which nuclear weapons are seen as a legitimate part of national or regional security.[139] Hamel-Green adds that NWFZs are not intended to 'supplant the need for negotiated, universally-applicable frameworks and instruments', but rather 'they … serve to gradually limit and delegitimize nuclear weapons at a regional level and to move towards a nuclear weapon-free world'.[140]

Questions linked to the total absence of nuclear weapons are, however, haunted by the same dilemmas and challenges as other weapons of mass destruction, namely the challenge of dual-use materials. Permitting the production of components for peaceful purposes makes the monitoring regime less stringent and more complex than that for weapons that do not have the same dual-use problem. On the other hand, NWFZs may promote regional cooperation in the peaceful uses of nuclear energy, and thereby help to address the dual-use problem.

Conclusion

The historical origins of NWFZ are intimately linked to the logics of the Cold War. A major impediment to the establishment of NWFZs during the Cold War was the perceived military advantage bestowed on one of the two global adversaries (a disadvantage for one was automatically regarded as an advantage for the other). This concern is no longer as salient with the end of bipolarity, although the relationship between nuclear umbrellas and NWFZs remains somewhat uneasy. The authors argue that contemporary challenges arising from new security threats, increased reliance on regional security arrangements and the growing prominence of environmental concerns indicate that, far from outgrowing its role, the NWFZ structure has become more relevant since the end of the Cold War.

NWFZs provide complementary machinery to other measures of disarmament, non-proliferation of nuclear weapons and the development of peaceful uses of nuclear energy. The potential of NWFZs in defusing the risk of regional nuclear arms races and decreasing the risk of nuclear weapons falling

---

[139] A. G. Robles, *The Latin American Nuclear-Weapon-Free Zone*, Occasional Paper 19, Stanley Foundation, Muscatine (May 1979). This paper was the basis for Robles' Nobel Lecture of 11 December 1982 when he received the Nobel Peace Prize jointly with Alva Myrdal for playing a central role in UN disarmament negotiations.

[140] Hamel-Green, 'Peeling the orange', 3.

into the hands of non-state actors are also increasingly important security considerations for the major nuclear powers.

The dynamics, strength and potential of different regions make the NWFZ a flexible instrument that can be adjusted to regional realities. Regional security arrangements require different optimal solutions for each region. Similar ideas have been expressed by Josef Goldblat, noting that the need for regional nuclear-free zones is justified by the dissimilar geographical circumstances, as well as different political, cultural, economic and strategic considerations of the states concerned, which do not all allow for a uniform pattern of denuclearised zones.[141]

Having seen how nuclear weapon-free zones cover substantial areas of the world and also cover a substantial number of states, NWFZs remain a key element in denuclearisation efforts. They are first and foremost aimed at non-proliferation and enhanced security in the areas they cover, but are also an important factor in the general disarmament discourse. Since the end of the Cold War, the rationale for the bipolar nuclear arms race has diminished, and hence the rationale for keeping the nuclear weapons debate strictly within the hands of the NWS should by implication have diminished. The zone countries may thus have a greater potential for influencing the debates on nuclear weapons, in various settings, than currently appears to be the case. In short, NWFZs remain highly relevant – and perhaps underexplored and underexploited – tools for nuclear non-proliferation and disarmament.

[141]   Goldblat, 'Nuclear-weapon-free zones', 18–31.

Appendix

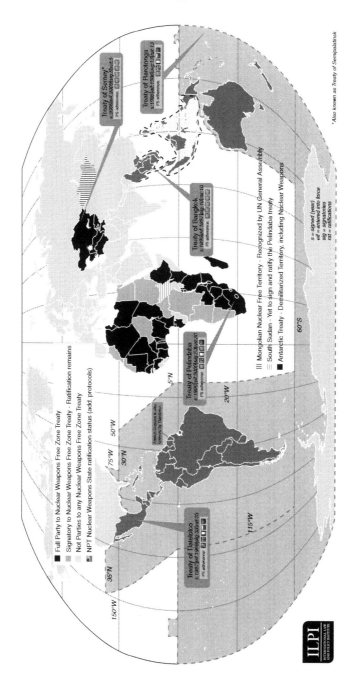

Figure 14.1

	Prohibition			Scope	Definition	Monitoring		Permanency	
	Use:	Stockpile:	Production:	Free Passage:	Definition:	Treaty body:	IAEA Safeguards:	Signatures:	Ratifications:
The Antarctic Treaty (1959)	Yes (Article V)			Yes (Article VI)	No	No	No	12	50
The Outer Space Treaty (1967)				Yes (Pream.)	No	No	No	89	101
The Seabed Treaty (1970)				Yes (Pream.)	No	Seabed Arms Control Treaty Review Conference (Article VIII)	No	84	94
The Treaty of Tlatelolco (1967)	Yes (Article 1A)	Yes (Article 1B)	Yes (Article 1A)		Yes (Article 5)	Agency for the Prohibition of Nuclear Energy in Latin America (Article 7)	Yes (Article 13)	33	33
The Treaty of Rarotonga (1985)		Yes (Article 3A)	Yes (Article 1A)	Yes (Article 2.2)	Yes (Article 1C)	Director of the South Pacific Bureau for Economic Cooperation and the Consultative Committee. (Article 9–10)	Yes (Annex 2)	13	13
The Treaty of Bangkok (1995)	Yes (Article 3.1.C)	Yes (Article 3.1.A)	Yes (Article 3.1.A)	Yes (Article 5.2)	Yes (Article 1C)	Commission for the Southeast Asia Nuclear Weapon-Free Zone (Article 8)	Yes (Article 5)	10	10
The Treaty of Pelindaba (1996)		Yes (Article 3, Article 4.1)	Yes (Article 3)	Yes (Article 2.2, Article 4.2)	Yes (Article 1C)	African Commission on Nuclear Energy (Article 12)	The IAEA can verify dismantling /destruction. (Article 6D)	52	31
The Treaty of Semipalatinsk (2006)	Yes (Article 3A)	Yes (Article 3A)	Yes (Article 3A)	Yes (Article 4)	Yes (Article 1C)	No.	Yes (Article 8)	5	5

Figure 14.2

Note: the authors gratefully acknowledge the assistance of Lars Jørgen Røed in the preparation of this figure.

| | | | | | Negative Security Assurances | | | |
Opened for signature:	Entered into force:	Delay (years):	Reservations:	Withdrawal:	P5 Protocol:	P5 Ratified:	Protocol prohibiting testing:	P5 Ratification:
1 December 1959	23 June 1961	2		Withdrawal is possible, effected two years after the receipt of notice. (Article XIIC)	No	n/a	No	n/a
27 January 1967	10 October 1967	1		Withdrawal is possible, effected if giving notice twelve months in advance. (Article XVI)	No	n/a	No	n/a
11 February 1971	18 May 1972	1		Withdrawal is possible, effected if giving notice three months in advance. (Article VIII)	No	n/a	No	n/a
14 February 1967	25 April 1969	2	No (Article 27)	Denunciation is possible, takes effect after three months. (Article 30)	No	n/a	No	n/a
6 August 1985	11 December 1986	1	No (Article 14)	Withdrawal is possible, effected if giving notice twelve months in advance. (Article 13)	Yes (Protocol I/Protocol II)	2/4	Yes (Protocol I/Protocol III)	2/4
15 December 1995	27 March 1997	2	No (Article 17)	Withdrawal is possible, effected if giving twelve months notice. (Article 22.2-3)	Yes (Protocol to the Treaty on Southeast Asia Nuclear Weapon-Free Zone)	0	No	n/a
11 April 1996	15 July 2009	13	No (Article 16)	Withdrawal is possible, effected if giving notice twelve months in advance. (Article 20)	Yes (Protocol I)	4	Yes (Protocol II)	4
8 September 2006	21 March 2009	3	No (Article 13)	Withdrawal is possible, effected if giving twelve months notice. (Article 16A-B)	Yes (Protocol to the Treaty on a Nuclear-Weapon-Free Zone in Central Asia)	0	No	n/a

Figure 14.2 (*cont.*)

15

The Nuclear Non-Proliferation Treaty

GRO NYSTUEN AND TORBJØRN GRAFF HUGO

I see the possibility in the 1970s of the President of the United States
having to face a world in which 15 or 20 or 25 nations may have these
weapons. I regard that as the greatest possible danger and hazard.

John F. Kennedy, 1963[1]

Introduction

The Nuclear Non-Proliferation Treaty (NPT)[2] was adopted in 1968, entered
into force two years later, and has since gained near universal adherence.[3]
The Treaty has generally been regarded as a 'grand bargain' in which the non-
nuclear weapon states (NNWS) forsake the nuclear option in exchange for a
legal obligation on the part of the nuclear weapon states (NWS) to refrain from
transferring the weapons to any other states, and to disarm and eventually
eliminate their arsenals. In 1995 the NPT states parties extended the Treaty's
initial lifetime of twenty-five years indefinitely, but the NPT has since come
under increasing pressure mainly due to a lack of implementation of the disarmament elements of the treaty.[4]

This chapter aims to give a brief overview of the historic background for the
NPT. The chapter begins by tracing the roots and rationale of the NPT, going

---

[1] Text of President Kennedy's News Conference on Foreign and Domestic Affairs, 22 March
1963 (quoted in E. B. Firmage, 'The treaty on the non-proliferation of nuclear weapons',
American Journal of International Law 63(4) (1969), 711–46).

[2] Treaty on the Non-Proliferation of Nuclear Weapons, New York, 1 July 1968, in force 5
March 1970, 729 UNTS 161 (hereafter, NPT).

[3] As of 2013, the NPT has 190 state parties. Israel, India, Pakistan and the Democratic People's
Republic of Korea are not parties. See UN Office for Disarmament Affairs, Treaty on the
Non-Proliferation of Nuclear Weapons, http://disarmament.un.org/treaties/t/npt.

[4] See Chapter 16 in this book for a discussion of the disarmament obligation in Article VI. It
should be noted, however, that as of writing (July 2014), the admissibility of a case regarding
the interpretation of Article VI of the NPT was ongoing in the ICJ, considering admissibility.
The case has been brought by the Marshall Islands against all nine nuclear weapons states.
The court may well consider the merits of the case when it comes to, at least, the United
Kingdom, because of its declaration on compulsory jurisdiction, while the situation with
respect to India and Pakistan is more complicated.

through some of the early discussions and negotiation process of key elements that were on the table, herein non-proliferation, peaceful use of nuclear energy, nuclear disarmament and security assurances.

The chapter then gives a summary of the Treaty's core content, while pointing to some of the inherently problematic questions regarding interpretation and implementation, before discussing some of the broader challenges to the regime, including its comparably weak normative status as well as its lack of clear obligations for the NWS to disarm and eliminate their arsenals.

A.   Background and summary of the NPT

At the beginning of the 1960s, a consensus began to develop in the international community on the need for serious action to be taken in order to prevent the humanitarian catastrophe that would result from a global nuclear war. In a speech to the UN General Assembly in September 1961, US President John F. Kennedy summed up the challenge succinctly: 'We must abolish these weapons before they abolish us.'[5] The sentiment was not new, but early post-Second World War plans aimed at ensuring that nuclear weapons did not become part of the geopolitical equation had failed,[6] and it gradually became evident that a new approach was needed. In a resolution presented to the General Assembly in 1958, the Republic of Ireland laid out two steps that were considered paramount in order to divert the world from its path towards nuclear annihilation: the prohibition of all forms of nuclear testing and the prohibition of the transfer of nuclear weapons to additional states.[7]

The issue of prohibiting testing was partially solved with the (Partial) Test Ban Treaty of 5 August 1963 (PTBT), which outlawed all nuclear explosions, whether peaceful or military, in the atmosphere, in outer space and underwater.[8] The Treaty was later given the prefix 'partial', both to underline the inherent limitations of the Treaty (it did not prevent states from undertaking testing underground) and also to distinguish it from its successor, the Comprehensive

---

[5] Address by President John F. Kennedy to the UN General Assembly, 25 September 1961, available at: www.state.gov/p/io/potusunga/207241.htm.

[6] The Baruch Plan was the first serious attempt to control nuclear energy and material. It was proposed by the US Representative to the UN Atomic Energy Commission (Baruch) in 1956, and involved the establishment of an International Atomic Development Agency that would seize control over all nuclear material internationally, and also maintain control over the whole fuel cycle. See e.g. Firmage, 'The treaty on the non-proliferation of nuclear weapons', 713.

[7] M. Shaker, *The Nuclear Non-Proliferation Treaty: Origin and Implementation 1959–1979*, 3 vols. (New York: Oceana Publications, 1980), Vol. I, pp. 3–9.

[8] Treaty Banning Nuclear Tests in the Atmosphere, in Outer Space and Under Water ('Partial Nuclear Test Ban Treaty'), Moscow, 8 August 1963, in force 10 October 1963, 480 UNTS 43.

Test Ban Treaty (CTBT),[9] which was adopted by the UN General Assembly on 10 September 1996 but has yet to enter into force. Despite its limitations, however, the PTBT had a significant impact and largely put an end to the race to build weapons of the 100-megaton category.[10] Moreover, the main reason for not including all forms of testing under the PTBT was the worry that this would be impossible to enforce. The scope of the Treaty was therefore limited to areas where testing could be detected from outside of the testing state's territory.[11] The PTBT was not ratified by all of the nuclear weapon states. For example, France continued atmospheric testing of nuclear weapons in the South Pacific region until the 1980s.[12]

Efforts to prevent the proliferation of nuclear weapons took several years to gain traction, but on 21 May 1968, after three years of negotiation in the Eighteen-Nation Disarmament Committee, the language of the Nuclear Non-Proliferation Treaty was finally adopted.[13] It established the two-tier system of nuclear weapon states and non-nuclear weapon states. The NWS were defined as those that had manufactured and exploded a nuclear weapon or other nuclear explosive device prior to 1 January 1967. This definition encompassed the (now) five veto-powers of the Security Council: China,[14] France, Russia (then the Soviet Union), the United Kingdom and the United States. In addition to the non-proliferation elements in Articles I and II, the Treaty guarantees all parties the 'inalienable right' to peaceful uses of nuclear technology in Article IV, and, in Article VI, also requires states parties to 'pursue negotiations in good faith' towards the reduction and eventual elimination of nuclear arsenals. The primary purpose of the Treaty, however, was to prevent further proliferation of the weapons. As Kaplan explains, the Treaty was intended 'to prevent an unstable arms race from multiplying in intensity as ever increasing numbers of nations attempt to acquire nuclear forces'.[15]

---

[9] UN General Assembly Resolution 50/245 ('The Comprehensive Test Ban Treaty'), UN doc. A/RES/50/245, adopted on 10 September 1996 by 158 votes in favour, and 3 against (Bhutan, India, Libya), with 5 abstentions (Cuba, Lebanon, Mauritius, Syria and Tanzania).

[10] Firmage, 'The treaty on the non-proliferation of nuclear weapons', 716; M. Willrich, 'The Treaty on Non-Proliferation of Nuclear Weapons: nuclear technology confronts world politics', *Yale Law Journal* 77(8) (1968), 1447–519, at 1459.

[11] E. Schwelb, 'The Nuclear Test Ban Treaty and international law', *American Journal of International Law* 58 (1964), 642–70.

[12] See Chapter 12 on nuclear testing.

[13] E. L. M. Burns, 'The Non-Proliferation Treaty: its negotiation and prospects', *International Organization* 23 (1969), 788–807.

[14] Taiwan, known as the Republic of China, was the permanent member of the Security Council at this time, although the People's Republic of China (PRC) carried out the test. See, e.g. CTBTO Preparatory Commission, 16 October 1964 – First Chinese Nuclear Test, available at: www.ctbto.org/specials/testing-times/16-october-1964-first-chinese-nuclear-test/. The PRC became a veto power in Taiwan's place in 1971.

[15] M. A. Kaplan, 'The Nuclear Non-Proliferation Treaty: its rationale, prospects and possible impact on international law', *Journal of Public Law* 18 (1969), 1–20, at 3.

Despite the inherently discriminatory framework of the NPT, calls for establishing a legal instrument to outlaw the proliferation of nuclear weapons did not come only from the nuclear 'haves'.[16] The need to outlaw the transfer of nuclear weapons was also recognised by NNWS, on the basis that the NNWS would refrain from acquiring nuclear weapons only if other NNWS were also denied that option.[17]

B. The negotiation process

The NPT negotiations took place in the Eighteen-Nation Disarmament Committee (ENDC), a forerunner to the current Conference on Disarmament (CD) in Geneva,[18] on the basis of a mandate from the UN Disarmament Commission.[19] The UN Disarmament Commission met for seven weeks between April and June 1965, with a view to adopting a mandate for negotiation of the NPT within the ENDC. Already during these discussions, the contours of what were to become the most contentious issues of negotiations began to show. The most pressing of these questions was how to fine-tune the language of the prophylactic paragraphs of the Treaty so as to satisfy both the Soviet Union and the United States, and also to provide the NNWS with sufficient confidence in the effectiveness of the non-proliferation obligations.[20]

A second challenge was the question of security guarantees, both negative and positive.[21] On the one hand, some NNWS wanted the NWS to guarantee that they would come to their aid if attacked (positive assurances). Others wanted the NWS to declare that they would not use nuclear weapons against any NNWS (negative assurances). India, for one, signalled early on that it would not sign a treaty that did not include adequate security guarantees.[22]

The question of security guarantees would also become part of a bigger debate on how to balance the different obligations of the Treaty. In exchange for forfeiting the option to develop nuclear weapons, the NNWS wanted something in return: access to peaceful nuclear energy and legally binding

---

[16] When the NPT was signed, five states had successfully tested a nuclear device: the United States (1945), the Soviet Union (1949), the United Kingdom (1954), France (1958) and China (1964).

[17] See e.g. Frank Aiken, Irish Minister for External Affairs, 31 October 1958 (quoted in Shaker, *The Nuclear Non-Proliferation Treaty*, Vol. I, p. 6).

[18] M. Sethi, 'Conference on disarmament: groping its way around', *Strategic Analysis* 28 (1999), 1275–88, at 1275–6.

[19] UN Disarmament Commission Resolution 130/225, adopted on 15 June 1965.

[20] Burns, 'The Non-Proliferation Treaty', 790.

[21] D. Bourantonis, 'The negotiation of the Non-Proliferation Treaty, 1965–1968: a note', *The International History Review* 19(2) (1997), 347–57.

[22] Firmage, 'The treaty on the non-proliferation of nuclear weapons', 719. In the end, India chose not to become a party to the NPT regime and has instead developed its own nuclear weapons. As of today, India is one of the four states that have nuclear weapons outside the NPT.

disarmament obligations for the NWS. The latter was considered particularly important, since the purpose of the Treaty was to bring the world closer to the full elimination of nuclear weapons. Many of the NNWS therefore considered the legal obligations on disarmament to be at the very heart of the Treaty,[23] and during the negotiations 'The three aspects of nuclear disarmament mentioned most often by the NNWS were an agreement ending the production of fissionable materials (in nuclear parlance, the "cut-off"), a comprehensive test ban agreement, and an agreement halting the production of delivery systems'.[24]

A fourth issue that drew some attention during the negotiations was verification and compliance measures. In order for the Treaty to be credible, it was considered essential to include verification provisions that would give states parties sufficient confidence and trust to ensure continued adherence to the regime. This would be particularly important if the Treaty were to allow access to the peaceful use of nuclear energy. The concept of safeguards was developed to describe the assurance that 'materials and equipment used in peaceful nuclear activities are not diverted to use in nuclear weapons programs'.[25] It was believed that without proper safeguard provisions, the Treaty would be ineffective.

A final point during the discussions of the mandate that was important for the non-aligned states was the status of regional treaties and frameworks under the NPT. Since the early 1960s momentum had built towards the establishment of nuclear weapon-free zones, in particular in Latin America and Africa. It was considered vital for the non-aligned states that these efforts be recognised and incorporated into the NPT. For the NWS, there was little reason to oppose this demand, as the regional prohibition regimes essentially consolidated the NPT compact and did little to complicate the NWS' continued possession of nuclear weapons.

The following sections describe the negotiations on each of these points in more detail.

1. Non-proliferation

As expected, much of the early disagreement between the two aligned blocs (East and West) concerned the interpretation of the concept of non-proliferation. From the US side, it was considered important that the Treaty did not challenge the nuclear sharing arrangements that were already in place in the North Atlantic Treaty Organization (NATO). Second, the Treaty should not preclude plans for a proposed Multilateral Force in NATO.[26] These positions

---

[23] See e.g. Burns, 'The Non-Proliferation Treaty', 793, 803; Shaker, *The Nuclear Non-Proliferation Treaty*, p. 782.

[24] Firmage, 'The treaty on the non-proliferation of nuclear weapons', 734.

[25] Willrich, 'The Treaty on Non-Proliferation of Nuclear Weapons', 1460.

[26] The idea of the multilateral force was to establish a nuclear-armed naval fleet that would be manned by nationals from several NATO states. The fleet would be under NATO command, and could therefore be a legal challenge under the NPT regime, even though the US would retain full control over the decision to use the nuclear missiles. For details,

were carefully carved into the first draft the United States presented on 17 August 1965, in which the prohibition on the transfer of nuclear weapons was limited to the transfer into 'national control of any non-nuclear state, either directly, or indirectly through a military alliance'.[27] This language would permit the transfer of control over the weapons – though not the decision to launch them – to an *international* entity.[28] As Shaker explains: 'the setting up of a new organization having independent power to use nuclear weapons would have been allowed, provided that no increase in the total number of states and "other organizations" having independent power to use nuclear weapons would have occurred.'[29]

For the Soviet Union, the language of the first US draft was unacceptable, not only because the prospect of a multilateral force in NATO was worrying, but more specifically because the reddest of all the Soviet red lines during the NPT negotiations was a legal sanction for placing nuclear weapons in West Germany.[30] Any language that could be interpreted in any way as a legal Trojan horse that could allow placement of nuclear weapons in West Germany was rejected outright.

In addition to the lack of clarity on multilateral nuclear sharing arrangements, the Soviet representative to the negotiations, Ambassador Tsarapkin, criticised the US draft for lacking a clear obligation on the part of the NWS not to allow NNWS 'the right to participate in the ownership, disposal and use of nuclear weapons', and, correspondingly, the draft did not stipulate any obligations on the part of the NNWS to refrain from the same.[31]

The Soviet Union presented its draft treaty on 24 September 1965, in which most of the alleged loopholes had been surgically closed. In effect, the Soviet proposal went so far as to prohibit all existing sharing arrangements in NATO, by stating that it would be illegal to transfer control, not merely of the weapons, but of the 'right to participate in the ownership, control or use of nuclear weapons', and also from transferring control over 'their emplacement and use, to units of the armed forces or military personnel of States not possessing nuclear weapons, even if such units or personnel are under the command of a military alliance'.[32] This proposal was politically unacceptable to the NATO states. By 1966 NATO had set up sharing arrangements such as the Nuclear Planning

---

see Burns, 'The Non-Proliferation Treaty', note on 791; H. A. Kissinger, *The Troubled Partnership* (New York: McGraw-Hill, 1965), p. 149; Shaker, *The Nuclear Non-Proliferation Treaty*, Vol. I, p. 140.

[27] UN Disarmament Commission, *Official Records of the Disarmament Commission (Supplement for January to December 1965)* (New York: United Nations, 1967), p. 41.

[28] Bourantonis, 'The negotiation of the Non-Proliferation Treaty', 349.

[29] Shaker, *The Nuclear Non-Proliferation Treaty*, Vol. I, pp. 215–16.

[30] Bourantonis, 'The negotiation of the Non-Proliferation Treaty', 349; Shaker, *The Nuclear Non-Proliferation Treaty*, Vol. I, p. 216.

[31] Shaker, *The Nuclear Non-Proliferation Treaty*, Vol. I, p. 218.

[32] USSR, Draft Treaty on Non-Proliferation of Nuclear Weapons, 4 ILM 1141 (1965).

Group, and the United States and its allies would not want to restrict their ability to use delivery systems owned by an NNWS ally in the case of war.[33]

The drafting tug-of-war between the superpowers over the basic provisions of the Treaty overshadowed all other issues during the first months of negotiations. Though there was a gradual convergence of views between the two, the real breakthrough did not come until US President Johnson realised that if he wanted the negotiation of the NPT to be successful, then 'the multilateral force (MLF) project would have to be abandoned'.[34] In a letter dated 23 June 1966, President Johnson instructed that the NPT be drafted in a simplified manner, based on Soviet suggestions on a treaty that would ban 'physical access' to nuclear weapons.[35] Similar concessions also had to be made by the Soviet Union, and a solution was not found until '[t]he Soviets finally agreed to wording permitting a continuation of NATO planning and participation based on the status quo. This would require no change in United States or West German participation in NATO but would preclude the creation of a Multilateral Force'.[36]

In August 1967 the United States and the Soviet Union each presented identical treaty drafts to the ENDC, and the language of Articles I and II remained largely unchanged in the text that was eventually adopted.

While the United States and the Soviet Union discussed the language of the non-proliferation provisions during this first year of the negotiations, some of the non-aligned states became increasingly frustrated. The superpowers 'visualized the treaty as an agreement between the United States and its allies on the one hand, and the Soviet Union and its allies on the other, ignoring the concerns of the states which were to forgo the option to acquire nuclear weapons'.[37]

To remedy this imbalance, the non-aligned states banded together to exert greater impact on the NPT's development.[38] In a resolution in the UN General Assembly in November 1965, the non-aligned states established a set of five principles that were to guide the ongoing negotiations:

(a) The treaty should be void of any loop-holes which might permit nuclear or non-nuclear Powers to proliferate, directly or indirectly, nuclear weapons in any form;

---

[33] For a tabular comparison of the two drafts, see UN Disarmament Commission, *Official Records of the Disarmament Commission (Supplement for 1966)* (New York: United Nations, 1967), p. 13.

[34] Burns, 'The Non-Proliferation Treaty', 971.

[35] G. T. Seaborg, *Stemming the Tide: Arms Control in the Johnson Years* (New York: The Free Press, 1987), p. 335 (quoted in G. Bunn, *Arms Control by Committee: Managing Negotiations with the Russians* (Stanford University Press, 1992), p. 74).

[36] Firmage, 'The treaty on the non-proliferation of nuclear weapons', 723.

[37] Bourantonis, 'The negotiation of the Non-Proliferation Treaty', 347–57.

[38] *Ibid.*, 350.

(b) The treaty should embody an acceptable balance of mutual responsibilities and obligations of the nuclear and non-nuclear Powers;

(c) The treaty should be a step towards the achievement of general and complete disarmament and, more particularly, nuclear disarmament;

(d) There should be acceptable and workable provisions to ensure the effectiveness of the treaty;

(e) Nothing in the treaty should adversely affect the right of any group of States to conclude regional treaties in order to ensure the total absence of nuclear weapons in their respective territories. [39]

In light of the perceived unwillingness to discuss issues beyond non-proliferation during the early rounds of the negotiations, the most important principle for the non-aligned states was the second one, regarding 'an acceptable balance of mutual responsibilities and obligations of nuclear and non-nuclear Powers'.[40] For the non-aligned states, the issues that would contribute to a better balance of rights and obligations in the Treaty included, inter alia, access to peaceful uses of nuclear energy; strong non-disarmament obligations for the NWS; and legally binding security assurances. As the negotiations proceeded, the non-aligned states gradually managed to exert greater influence over the Treaty text.

Peaceful use of nuclear energy

In 1968 more than forty NNWS possessed functioning nuclear reactors,[41] and for these states it was paramount that the NPT allow for the continued exploitation of peaceful uses of nuclear energy. In the typical jargon of the NPT, the right to peaceful use of nuclear energy is considered one of the three pillars of the Treaty (the other two being non-proliferation and disarmament). But since the technology required for the peaceful use of nuclear weapons is in essence the same as that used for military purposes, one of the fundamental challenges in the drafting of the Treaty was to find a way to resolve this dilemma.[42]

The proposed solution was to establish a neutral party that would regularly inspect all nuclear facilities in the NNWS, and the only real candidate for this role was the International Atomic Energy Agency (IAEA), formed in 1957 'to promote the peaceful use of nuclear energy and to seek to ensure that nuclear energy would not serve any military purpose'.[43] Perhaps surprisingly,

---

[39] UN General Assembly Resolution 2028 (XX), UN doc. A/RES/2028 (XX), adopted on 19 November 1965.

[40] *Ibid.*

[41] D. Fischer, *History of the International Atomic Energy Agency: The First Forty Years* (Vienna: International Atomic Energy Agency, 1997), p. 9; Firmage, 'The treaty on the non-proliferation of nuclear weapons', 711.

[42] Shaker, *The Nuclear Non-Proliferation Treaty*, Vol. I, p. 274.

[43] The IAEA was set up to 'accelerate and enlarge the contribution of atomic energy to peace, health and prosperity throughout the world'. Statute of the International Atomic Energy Agency, New York, 23 October 1956, in force 29 July 1957, 276 UNTS 3, Art. II.

the greatest barrier to negotiation of the safeguards provisions was not access to facilities in non-aligned states. Rather, it was the IAEA's role vis-à-vis the safeguard system already in place in Europe, through the European Atomic Energy Community. As Shaker notes, 'the Common Market countries were reluctant to allow the IAEA safeguards system to operate in their countries for fear it would result in abandonment of the Euratom system'.[44] At the same time, the Soviet Union and many of the non-aligned states in the ENDC made clear that they could not accept that the European NNWS would have a special status whereby they would end up inspecting themselves.[45] In the end, it fell to the United States to convince its allies of the need for a pragmatic solution.[46] The European states were ultimately persuaded to agree to a compromise that would allow them to negotiate safeguards agreements with the IAEA as a group, rather than as individual states.[47]

Peaceful nuclear explosions

Through his 'Atoms for Peace' speech to the General Assembly in 1953, President Eisenhower contributed to a spirit of optimism surrounding the peaceful uses of nuclear energy, including peaceful nuclear explosions.[48] While in retrospect one might wonder why the ENDC spent as much time as it did debating this issue, at the time there was in fact a genuine belief in the economic and developmental benefits of nuclear explosions.[49] As Firmage noted in 1969, 'from the use of nuclear explosives in the construction of a sea-level Atlantic-Pacific canal replacing the Panama Canal to the use of nuclear explosions to break copper ore bodies to permit direct recovery of copper, nations will continue to explore the peaceful uses of nuclear explosions'.[50]

The United States first raised the issue in negotiations in the middle of 1966, signalling that due to the indistinguishable nature of military and peaceful nuclear explosions, the latter could not be exempt from the general provisions

---

[44] Shaker, *The Nuclear Non-Proliferation Treaty*, Vol. I, p. 107.

[45] Burns, 'The Non-Proliferation Treaty', 799.

[46] Firmage, 'The treaty on the non-proliferation of nuclear weapons', 718. William C. Foster was Director of the United States Arms Control and Disarmament Agency.

[47] Burns, 'The Non-Proliferation Treaty', 801.

[48] UN General Assembly Official Records (VIII), 470th plenary, New York, 8 December 1953, available at: www.iaea.org/About/atomsforpeace_speech.html.

[49] See, e.g. Office of Scientific and Technical Information, US Department of Energy, *Plowshare Program*, undated, p. 1, available at: www.osti.gov/opennet/reports/plowshar.pdf (describing Operation Plowshare, a 'research and development activity to explore the technical and economic feasibility of using nuclear explosives for industrial applications'. Anticipated potential uses included 'large-scale excavation and quarrying' and 'underground engineering'). The Plowshare Program was eventually discontinued due to public opposition and a lack of commercial viability. *Ibid.*, p. 5.

[50] Firmage, 'The treaty on the non-proliferation of nuclear weapons', 732. Firmage was evidently very concerned about the issue of peaceful nuclear explosions, and states later in his article that 'Article V must work well or this source of pressure could lead to the eventual breakdown of the treaty'.

of Articles I and II. This raised concern among some of the NNWS, particularly India and Brazil, which considered protection of the potential developmental benefits of nuclear explosions to be vitally important.[51] In the end, the compromise solution was to allow NNWS access to the potential benefits of peaceful nuclear explosions through an 'appropriate international body with adequate representation of non-nuclear-weapon States'.[52]

Nuclear disarmament

In the UN General Assembly Resolution of November 1965, the role of the NPT as a 'step towards the achievement of general and complete disarmament and, more particularly, nuclear disarmament' was reiterated.[53] For many of the non-aligned states, this was interpreted to mean that concrete measures on nuclear disarmament should be included in the Treaty text. Such measures included, most notably, 'a comprehensive test ban and an agreement to cease the production of fissile material for weapons purposes', and later to end 'the production of offensive and defensive ballistic missiles'.[54]

The NWS strongly resisted the inclusion of such provisions in the Treaty, arguing that this would make the success of the NPT dependent on the negotiations of other treaties, which would weaken the NPT's prospects.[55] As Shaker notes, 'the American and Soviet treaty drafts of 1965, as far as arms control and disarmament were concerned, contained only preambular paragraphs', and this did not change until Mexico formally proposed specific text on a separate Treaty article in September 1967.[56] The Mexican proposal stated that the NWS would undertake to pursue negotiations 'in good faith, with all speed and perseverance', on measures including 'the prohibition of all nuclear weapon tests, the cessation of the manufacture of nuclear weapons, the liquidation of all their existing stockpiles', and on 'the elimination from national arsenals of nuclear weapons and the means of their delivery'.[57] The proposal was supported by Egypt, Canada and Sweden. Interestingly, however, Mexico noted when tabling the proposal that 'doubtless it would be an imperfect obligation, since it would not be accompanied by sanctions, but it would be more than a statement of intention', and moreover, that 'to stipulate that the non-proliferation treaty should include specific disarmament measures to be implemented by the nuclear Powers in the immediate future, would be tantamount to opposing the very existence of a non-proliferation treaty'.[58]

---

[51] *Ibid.*, 730.   [52] NPT, Art. V.

[53] See also Chapter 16 on the legal meaning and implications of Article VI.

[54] Burns, 'The Non-Proliferation Treaty', 802.   [55] *Ibid.*

[56] Shaker, *The Nuclear Non-Proliferation Treaty*, Vol. II, p. 556.

[57] Conference of the Eighteen-Nation Committee on Disarmament (United Nations), *Final Verbatim Record of the Conference of the Eighteen-Nation Committee on Disarmament [Meeting 331]* (Ann Arbor: University of Michigan Library, 2005), p. 10, available at: http://quod.lib.umich.edu/e/endc/4918260.0331.001?rgn=main;view=fulltext.

[58] *Ibid.*, pp. 9–10.

Eventually the text was watered down, and the references to specific measures removed, but the co-chairs accepted the inclusion of the Article as such, and the final version retained the basic structure of the Mexican proposal. The Article on nuclear disarmament constituted one of the key elements of the 'grand bargain', without which the NNWS would have been reluctant to agree to the regime.

2. Security assurances

With regard to security assurances, the basic premise was that the NNWS could not be expected to forfeit the nuclear weapons option if their current or future military adversaries would have free recourse to develop or otherwise acquire nuclear weapons. For a country like India, which had been in open war with China only three years prior to the commencement of the NPT negotiations, this was a genuine concern – not least since China successfully tested its first nuclear device in 1964. In addition, Brazil, the Federal Republic of Germany and Romania also raised this concern during the negotiations, demanding that legally binding security assurances be included in the Treaty.[59] Romania proposed a provision in the Treaty in which the NWS would guarantee not to launch or threaten to launch an attack with nuclear weapons on any NNWS.

Despite repeated attempts by NNWS to insert language on security assurances into the Treaty,[60] these efforts eventually failed. In the debates following the presentation of a new Treaty draft on 18 January 1968, the United States explained that 'the revised treaty draft does not deal with security assurances', but that the co-chairs – the United States and the Soviet Union – remained 'mindful of their pledge to provide the Committee with a recommendation for dealing with this complex and difficult problem'.[61] The co-chairs eventually decided to resolve the issue by preparing, together with the United Kingdom, a draft resolution on the matter that would be presented to the Security Council. The Resolution, adopted immediately after the final text of the Treaty was agreed, 'recognizes that aggression with nuclear weapons or the threat of such aggression against a NNWS would create a situation in which the Security Council, and above all its NWS permanent members, would have to act immediately in accordance with their obligations under the United Nations Charter'.[62] Algeria, Brazil, France, India and Pakistan abstained from voting.

---

[59] Firmage, 'The treaty on the non-proliferation of nuclear weapons', 740.
[60] See, e.g. *ibid.*, 740.
[61] Conference of the Eighteen-Nation Committee on Disarmament (United Nations), *Final Verbatim Record of the Conference of the Eighteen-Nation Committee on Disarmament [Meeting 357]* (Ann Arbor: University of Michigan Library, 2005), p. 15.
[62] UN Security Council Resolution 255 ('Question relating to measures to safeguard non-nuclear-weapon states parties to the Treaty on the Non-Proliferation of Nuclear Weapons'), UN doc. S/RES/255, adopted on 19 June 1968 by ten votes to nil with no abstentions.

For the non-aligned states, the Security Council Resolution was meagre compensation for the legally binding obligations they had demanded, since it added nothing to the legal protections already in place under the UN Charter.[63] As a result, the demand for legally binding security assurances has remained a subject for debate to this day.[64] While some of the NWS have issued unilateral declarations on the matter that go considerably further than the Security Council Resolution of 1968, these declarations do not have the same status as they would if included in the NPT.[65]

Duration

A final issue during the negotiations that merits mentioning was the Treaty's duration. At the time, the NPT was considered a temporary measure that would bring the world closer to general and complete disarmament. As a result, the drafters, in Article X(2), limited the Treaty's duration to twenty-five years, after which an indefinite extension of the Treaty would require the support of a two-thirds majority of states parties. In 1995 the Treaty was extended indefinitely at the NPT Review Conference,[66] under the understanding that the NWS would enhance disarmament measures in return.[67]

Adoption

After having agreed on the final text of the Treaty, the ENDC sent the Treaty text to the UN General Assembly (UNGA), a dual-step procedure that has also later been applied in the field of disarmament.[68] In the UNGA, the Treaty text was annexed to Resolution 2373 (XXII) of 12 June 1968, and adopted by

---

[63] Firmage, 'The treaty on the non-proliferation of nuclear weapons', 742.

[64] See Chapter 14 on nuclear weapon-free zones.

[65] See e.g. United States Department of Defense, *Nuclear Posture Review Report* (Washington DC: US Department of Defense, April 2010), p. viii, in which the United States pledges not to 'use or threaten to use nuclear weapons against non-nuclear weapons states that are party to the NPT and in compliance with their nuclear non-proliferation obligations'.

[66] Decision number 3 by the Review Conference reads as follows: 'Decides that, as a majority exists among States party to the Treaty for its indefinite extension, in accordance with article X, paragraph 2, the Treaty shall continue in force indefinitely.' NPT/CONF.1995/32 (Part I), Annex.

[67] The final documents contain numerous references to the need for full compliance with the disarmament obligation. Planned programmes of action include nuclear weapon states' 'systematic and progressive efforts to reduce nuclear weapons globally, with the ultimate goal of eliminating those weapons'. 1995 NPT Review and Extension Conference, Final Documents Part I, Decision 2, Article 4C. Decision 3 also emphasises that the ultimate goal is the complete elimination of nuclear weapons.

[68] Note, for example, the adoption of the Comprehensive Test Ban Treaty (CTBT) by the UN General Assembly. UN General Assembly Resolution 50/245 ('The Comprehensive Test Ban Treaty'), UN doc. A/RES/50/245, adopted on 10 September 1996 by 158 votes in favour, and 3 against (Bhutan, India, Libya), with 5 abstentions (Cuba, Lebanon, Mauritius, Syria and Tanzania).

a majority of 95:4, with 21 abstentions. The language of the Resolution is limited to 'commending' the Treaty, and expressing hopes of the 'widest possible adherence', which some states found to be a weak expression of support.[69]

Among the states abstaining from voting on the Treaty was Brazil, which criticised the draft for denying the NNWS full access to peaceful nuclear explosions, and for lacking both tangible disarmament commitments and security assurances.[70] India, which also abstained, criticised the Treaty for not providing for a cut-off in production of fissionable materials (the prevention of so-called 'vertical proliferation'), and the absence of any requirement that the NWS accept the safeguards provisions of Article III.[71]

C.   The three pillars of the NPT

With the historic narrative of the negotiations of the NPT as a backdrop, the following section provides a brief analysis of the three so-called pillars of the Treaty: non-proliferation, peaceful use of nuclear energy and disarmament. Given the substantial legal complexities and potential for interpretation as well as discussions on the implementation of the NPT, this chapter can only take a cursory look at some of the key features related to the three pillars.

1.   Articles I and II: non-proliferation

Articles I and II constitute the core of the NPT's non-proliferation obligations, and thus the prohibition on transfer of nuclear weapons. Article I obliges each of the NWS parties:

> not to transfer to any recipient whatsoever nuclear weapons or other nuclear explosive devices or control over such weapons or explosive devices directly, or indirectly; and not in any way to assist, encourage, or induce any non-nuclear weapon state to manufacture or otherwise acquire nuclear weapons or other nuclear explosive devices, or control over such weapons or explosive devices.

In Article II, the NNWS parties undertake not to:

> receive the transfer from any transferor whatsoever of nuclear weapons or other nuclear explosive devices or of control over such weapons or explosive devices directly, or indirectly; not to manufacture or otherwise acquire nuclear weapons or other nuclear explosive devices; and not to seek or receive any assistance in the manufacture of nuclear weapons or other nuclear explosive devices.

---

[69] Burns, 'The Non-Proliferation Treaty', 788.
[70] Firmage, 'The treaty on the non-proliferation of nuclear weapons', 719–20.
[71] *Ibid.*, 720.

Together, Articles I and II thus appear aimed at creating a watertight system for non-proliferation. As the discussion in the previous section revealed, however, many questions arise from these Articles – stemming both from the negotiation history and from legal ambiguity in the text as it stands. Although there are many interpretive debates over the text of Articles I and II,[72] this chapter discusses two of the most prominent: the definition of 'nuclear weapons' and the definition of 'manufacture'.

What is a 'nuclear weapon' under the NPT?

First, one important factor in the interpretation and implementation of Articles I and II is the absence of a definition of 'nuclear weapons'. According to Willrich, the omission made it easier for the United States to interpret nuclear weapons as only nuclear warheads, and not, for example, delivery systems. This made it possible for the United States to sell missiles to the United Kingdom, equipped with everything but the warheads.[73] The lack of a definition also helped to obscure the fact that in the negotiations, the Soviet Union more or less accepted the NATO sharing arrangements.[74]

The lack of a definition of nuclear weapons also made it easier to deal with the issue of military alliances. The NPT's prohibition against transfer of nuclear weapons to 'any recipient whatsoever' appears to constitute an outright prohibition on the transfer of nuclear weapons among the NWS themselves, including transfers to allies. But the question of how to deal with military alliances had been part of the discussion since the very beginning of the negotiation process. Already in August 1965 the United Kingdom had made clear to the members of the ENDC that: 'It is no part of [the Treaty's] purpose to place an embargo on all arrangements for sharing the control of nuclear weapons within NATO or any other alliance so far as they are not disseminatory.'[75] As Willrich also notes, the United States 'made clear throughout the negotiations its view that a non-proliferation treaty to which it would subscribe must not affect existing consultative and planning arrangements with its NATO allies'.[76] On the whole, the debate both in the ENDC and the UNGA shows that the issue of nuclear planning and sharing in NATO was a pivotal part of the discussion during much

---

[72] See e.g. D. Joyner, *International Law and the Proliferation of Weapons of Mass Destruction* (Oxford University Press, 2009).

[73] Willrich, 'The Treaty on Non-Proliferation of Nuclear Weapons', 1446.

[74] 'We may speculate why a definition was omitted from the Non-Proliferation Treaty. A definition similar to the Treaty of Tlatelolco would perhaps have highlighted the Soviet Union's concession to the status quo regarding the United States' arrangements within NATO.' Willrich, 'The Treaty on Non-Proliferation of Nuclear Weapons', 1463, n. 45.

[75] Conference of the Eighteen-Nation Committee on Disarmament (United Nations), *Final Verbatim Record of the Conference of the Eighteen-Nation Committee on Disarmament [Meeting 225]* (Ann Arbor: University of Michigan Library, 2005), available at: http://quod. lib.umich.edu/e/endc/4918260.0225.001/10?page=root;size=100;view=image.

[76] Willrich, 'The Treaty on Non-Proliferation of Nuclear Weapons', 1470.

of the negotiations, and that most non-nuclear weapon states must have been aware that the Treaty would not exclude all forms of nuclear sharing within security alliances.[77]

An important source of the US interpretation of these Articles is a note entitled 'Questions on the Draft Non-Proliferation Treaty Asked by US Allies Together with Answers Given by the United States'. The note was attached to a letter of 2 July 1968 to Secretary of State Dean Rusk, and as Shaker notes, it 'revealed important interpretations of the NPT by the US, especially with regard to alliance relationships and European unity'.[78] According to the US interpretation, the NPT would prohibit the transfer of control or ownership to a 'multilateral entity', but 'would not bar succession by a new federated European state to the nuclear status of one of its former components'. This was considered a very remote but realistic possibility at the time, and though this has never materialised, the reverse situation in fact arose with the end of the Cold War with the dissolution of the Soviet Union. Who would be in control of the nuclear weapons stationed in Ukraine? The issue was resolved as Russia effectively took control over all of Ukraine's nuclear weapons, but it nevertheless revealed that the NPT had no provisions to handle the potential dissolution of one of the NWS.[79]

What does 'manufacture' mean in the context of the NPT?

Another key discussion arising from Articles I and II is the definition of the term 'manufacture'. At what stage of the chain of events from the planning, researching, exploitation of uranium or other activities related to creating nuclear warheads will an activity be subsumed under the term 'manufacture'? The so-called 'Foster Criteria', named after then-director of the US Arms Control and Disarmament Agency William Foster, are often cited in connection with delimiting this term. As stated in his speech to the US Senate Foreign Relations Committee, the criteria include: 'Facts indicating that the *purpose*

---

[77] For the full verbatim records of all the meetings of the ENDC, see University of Michigan Digital Library, Eighteen Nation Committee on Disarmament, available at: http://quod.lib. umich.edu/e/endc/.

[78] Shaker, *The Nuclear Non-Proliferation Treaty*, Vol. I, p. 234.

[79] A second element in the US interpretation was that Articles I and II would *not* prohibit 'deployment of nuclear weapons within allied territory as these do not involve any transfer of nuclear weapons or control over them unless and until a decision were made to go to war, at which time the treaty would no longer be controlling'. 'Questions on the Draft Non-Proliferation Treaty Asked by US Allies Together With Answers Given by the United States' (quoted in US Senate, NPT Hearings, 90–2, pp. 262–3). The note thus suggests that in the case of war the Treaty would no longer be 'controlling', a suggestion that is obviously incorrect. The only means of avoiding the 'control' of the Treaty would be to withdraw from it in accordance with the provisions in Article X(1).

of a particular activity was the acquisition of a nuclear explosive device would tend to show non-compliance.'[80] It should be noted that the Foster Criteria do not represent a universally agreed – much less a legally binding – understanding of what the term 'manufacture' covers. For example, Joyner stresses that:

> The term 'manufacture' as used in Article II has been the subject of some controversy regarding its interpretation. Some current and former government officials and other observers, particularly in the US, hold that the prohibition on manufacturing a nuclear explosive device entails a scope which reaches far back along the knowledge acquisition and development line of a nuclear weapons program to the concept, capacity building, design, research and experimentation stages … However, this interpretation is incorrect by reference to the plain meaning of the terms of Article II, as confirmed by the negotiating history of the NPT.[81]

Joyner goes on to state, referring to the rules on treaty interpretation in the Vienna Convention on the Law of Treaties (VCLT), that the ordinary meaning of the term manufacture 'refers to the physical construction of a nuclear explosive device, or perhaps at its broadest reading, to the physical construction of the component parts of a nuclear explosive device'.[82] By implication, this understanding would mean that research and development activities that could be used to eventually manufacture nuclear devices might be allowed under the NPT.

Persbo argues against Joyner's understanding, claiming that this interpretation would in fact 'undermine the objectives of the treaty as stated in the preamble, namely that "the proliferation of nuclear weapons would seriously enhance the danger of nuclear war".'[83]

---

[80] Senate Committee on Foreign Relations, Remarks Submitted by William C. Foster, 89th Congress, 2nd session, 10 July 1968 (quoted in Joyner, *International Law and the Proliferation of Weapons of Mass Destruction*, p. 16 (emphasis added)). The statement goes on to give some examples: 'It may be useful to point out, for illustrative purposes, several activities which the United States would not consider per se to be violations of the prohibitions in Article II. Neither uranium enrichment nor the stockpiling of fissionable material in connection with a peaceful nuclear program would violate Article II so long as these activities were safeguarded under Article III. Also clearly permitted would be the development, under safeguards, of plutonium fueled power reactors, including research on the properties of metallic plutonium, nor would Article II interfere with the development or use of fast breeder reactors under safeguards' (quoted in E. Busch and D. Joyner (eds.), *Combating Weapons of Mass Destruction: The Future of International Nonproliferation Policy* (Athens, GA: University of Georgia Press, 2009), p. 295).

[81] D. Joyner, 'Iran's nuclear program and the legal mandate of the IAEA', *JURIST – Forum*, 9 November 2011, available at: http://jurist.org/forum/2011/11/dan-joyner-iaea-report.php.

[82] *Ibid.*

[83] A. Persbo, 'A reflection on the current state of nuclear non-proliferation and safeguards', Non-Proliferation Paper 8 (February 2012), 4–5.

Clearly, one major difficulty with applying the Foster Criteria to determine the meaning of 'manufacture' is that they presuppose that the activities' intent or purpose is known. Certain nuclear fuel activities carried out by Iran are, for example, likely to attract much more attention than similar activities carried out by other states, and thus the discussions pertaining to compliance with the prohibition on 'manufacture' inevitably become politicised.[84] Although space considerations preclude a full discussion of this topic here, the issue of non-compliance with, for example, inspection and verification regimes under the IAEA in implementing Article III is key in this discussion.

2.   Articles III–V: safeguards and peaceful use of nuclear technology

A second 'pillar' in the NPT 'grand bargain' is the right of all states parties to benefit from and take part in peaceful production and use of nuclear energy. This pillar is reflected in Articles III, IV and V of the Treaty.

Article III(1) of the NPT obliges each NNWS to:

> accept safeguards, as set forth in an agreement to be negotiated and concluded with the International Atomic Energy Agency in accordance with the Statute of the International Atomic Energy Agency and the Agency's safeguards system, for the exclusive purpose of verification of the fulfilment of its obligations assumed under this Treaty with a view to preventing diversion of nuclear energy from peaceful uses to nuclear weapons or other nuclear explosive devices … The safeguards required by this Article shall be applied on all source or special fissionable material in all peaceful nuclear activities within the territory of such State, under its jurisdiction, or carried out under its control anywhere.

This provision thus aims at ensuring that peaceful uses and production of nuclear energy will not be diverted to non-peaceful uses. The Article links safeguards to export controls by requiring the application of IAEA safeguards to nuclear exports to NNWS. It thus also constitutes an element of the overall non-proliferation regime, although it is not specifically crafted to ensure compliance with the prohibitions on transfer in Articles I and II.[85]

---

[84] For more on the discussions on the interpretation of 'manufacture', see also Joyner, *International Law and the Proliferation of Weapons of Mass Destruction*; A. Persbo, Vertic, Presentation to the International Law Association Roundtable 'Nuclear Weapons, Nuclear Energy and Non-Proliferation under International Law: Current Challenges and Evolving Norms'; J. M. Acton, 'The problem with nuclear mind reading', *Survival: Global Politics and Strategy* 51(1) (2012), 119–42, J. Acton and C. Newman, 'IAEA verification of military research and development, verification matters', VERTIC Research Report 5 (London: VERTIC, July 2006); L. Weiss, 'The Nuclear Nonproliferation Treaty: strengths and gaps' in H. Sokolski (ed.), *Fighting Proliferation, New Concerns for the Nineties* (Maxwell Air Force Base: Air University Press, 1996).

[85] For more detail on the IAEA safeguard system, see IAEA, www.iaea.org/safeguards/documents/safeg_system.pdf.

Article III contains several more detailed provisions on how the safeguards regimes are to be carried out. It ends by specifying that:

> Non-nuclear-weapon States Party to the Treaty shall conclude agreements with the International Atomic Energy Agency to meet the requirements of this Article either individually or together with other States in accordance with the Statute of the International Atomic Energy Agency ... Such agreements shall enter into force not later than eighteen months after the date of initiation of negotiations.

According to the IAEA, twelve non-nuclear weapon states parties to the NPT have not entered into safeguards agreements.[86] Among the states that have concluded agreements with the IAEA, but where there is disagreement as to the level of compliance, the ongoing discussions with Iran feature prominently.[87] There is no consensus on whether a potential violation of an IAEA agreement on verification would by implication also constitute a violation of the NPT.

Article IV states that all states parties shall have the right to 'develop research, production and use of nuclear energy for peaceful purposes', and, as described above, Article V ensures that all states parties shall have the right to benefit from 'any peaceful applications of nuclear explosions'.[88]

3. Article VI: disarmament

Article VI contains the disarmament pillar of the 'grand bargain', namely the obligation of all states parties to pursue the aim of nuclear disarmament, and thus (in due course) to spare the world from the potential hazards of existing nuclear weapons arsenals. Article VI obliges each of the parties to the Treaty to:

> pursue negotiations in good faith on effective measures relating to cessation of the nuclear arms race at an early date and to nuclear disarmament, and on a treaty on general and complete disarmament under strict and effective international control.

---

[86] IAEA, Factsheets and FAQs: NPT Comprehensive Safeguards Agreements, Overview of Status, available at: www.iaea.org/Publications/Factsheets/English/nptstatus_overview. html.

[87] In its 2013 report, the IAEA Board of Governors concluded that: 'While the Agency continues to verify the non-diversion of declared nuclear material at the nuclear facilities and LOFs declared by Iran under its Safeguards Agreement, as Iran is not providing the necessary cooperation, including by not implementing its Additional Protocol, the Agency is unable to provide credible assurance about the absence of undeclared nuclear material and activities in Iran, and therefore to conclude that all nuclear material in Iran is in peaceful activities.' IAEA Board of Governors, 'Implementation of the NPT Safeguards Agreement and relevant provisions of Security Council resolutions in the Islamic Republic of Iran', Report By the Director General, GOV/2013/40, 28 August 2013, 67.

[88] See Chapter 12 on nuclear testing.

As described earlier, this pillar was considered by the NNWS to be a core element of the bargain. In legal terms, however, the provision is rather unspecific compared to other disarmament regimes. To 'pursue negotiations in good faith' is a somewhat non-committal precursor to the actual substance of the Article (nuclear disarmament). Also, 'effective measures relating to' could be seen as a qualifier that potentially weakens the obligation to undertake 'cessation of the nuclear arms race at an early date', and 'nuclear disarmament'. The last part of the provision refers to the negotiation of a treaty on 'general and complete disarmament', but it is unclear if this was meant to be a treaty on nuclear disarmament or on disarmament of *all* weapons (conventional or not). The latter interpretation, introducing an obligation to eliminate all weapons, would arguably dilute and undermine the nuclear disarmament obligation by introducing a requirement widely perceived to be politically impossible.

Considering the 1965 UN Disarmament Commission Resolution in which nuclear disarmament was introduced as an essential element of the bargain,[89] it appears clear that the drafters' aim was to create a treaty on nuclear non-proliferation and disarmament and that this treaty would be a 'step towards the achievement of general and complete disarmament'.[90] There was thus no suggestion of a separate treaty on 'general and complete disarmament'.

Notwithstanding the fact that the disarmament obligations in Article VI appear unspecific, the International Court of Justice, in its Advisory Opinion on the *Legality of the Threat or Use of Nuclear Weapons*, unanimously stated that the text of Article VI meant that '[t]here exists an obligation to pursue in good faith and bring to a conclusion negotiations leading to nuclear disarmament in all its aspects under strict and effective international control'.[91]

Article VI has been subject to considerable debate over the years. While the NWS claim that advances with regard to disarmament have been made and many nuclear warheads have been dismantled, many NNWS express increased frustration over the fact that there are still over 17,000 nuclear warheads in the world.[92] It is not necessarily easy to determine to what extent 'good faith negotiations' to implement Article VI take place. These and other aspects of the content of Article VI are discussed in more detail in Chapter 16 of this book.

D.   The strengths and weaknesses of the NPT regime

The NPT has played, and continues to play, a crucial role in limiting nuclear arsenals in the world, and to limiting the number of states that have access

---

[89] UN Disarmament Commission Resolution 130/225, adopted on 15 June 1965.
[90] UN General Assembly Resolution 2028 (XX), adopted on 23 November 1965.
[91] International Court of Justice (ICJ), *Legality of the Threat or Use of Nuclear Weapons*, Advisory Opinion of 8 July 1996, para. 105(2)(F). See also Chapter 16 on Article VI.
[92] *SIPRI Yearbook 2013: Armaments, Disarmament and International Security*, 'Summary' (Stockholm International Peace Research Institute 2013), p. 12.

to these weapons. In the words of Russian disarmament diplomat and history professor Roland Timerbaev:

> the NPT, over the years, has been a reasonable success. If there had been no NPT, the total number of nuclear-weapon States (NWS) might have reached 30 or 40 by now.[93]

Seen in this perspective, the NPT has undoubtedly been a success. Although there are some cracks in the non-proliferation pillar walls, such as the fact that India, Pakistan and Israel never acceded to it, and that the Democratic People's Republic of Korea (DPR Korea) withdrew from the Treaty (asserting that it had the right to do so under NPT Article X),[94] the overall aim of preventing proliferation of nuclear weapons to NNWS has largely been achieved. This is perhaps the Treaty's most notable strength, and the foundation upon which all other issues discussed in the NPT framework is predicated. The norm of non-proliferation has today become firmly consolidated in the international community, something that has been illustrated, albeit in different ways, by cases where suspicions of nuclear weapons development have been raised, such as in the DPR Korea, Iraq, Libya and Iran.

At the same time, the plethora of issues drawn into the NPT review cycle discussions, with discussion topics ranging from a WMD-free zone in the Middle East, via the negotiation of a Fissile Material Cut-off Treaty (FMCT) and cuts in nuclear arsenals, to ratification of the CTBT, bears testimony to an underlying divergence in expectations among the states parties – a divergence that has been visible since before the NPT was negotiated. For some states the NPT is seen to have one and only one main function: namely, to prevent the spread of nuclear weapons. For others, perhaps for the majority of states, the NPT is still viewed as a grand bargain that is kept afloat by an intricate balancing of the Treaty's 'three pillars'. The problem with the notion of three equally important pillars of the NPT regime is that this political demand for 'balanced obligations', which can be traced back to UNGA Resolution 2028, is poorly reflected in the legal framework of the Treaty. The only prohibitions in the Treaty relate to proliferation. No amount of review conferences and outcome documents is likely to change this. The Treaty is essentially a non-proliferation treaty whose primary ambition was to 'freeze' the status quo with regard to possession of nuclear weapons.[95]

---

[93] International Atomic Energy Agency (IAEA), R. Timerbaev, 'What Next for the NPT?', available at: www.iaea.org/Publications/Magazines/Bulletin/Bull462/what_next.html.

[94] Each state party has the 'right to withdraw from the Treaty if it decides that extraordinary events, related to the subject matter of this Treaty, have jeopardized the supreme interests of its country. It shall give notice of such withdrawal to all other Parties to the Treaty and to the United Nations Security Council three months in advance. Such notice shall include a statement of the extraordinary events it regards as having jeopardized its supreme interests.' NPT, Art. X.

[95] Although many states wanted stricter obligations, particularly on the disarmament side. See, e.g. J. Ruzicka and N. J. Wheeler, 'The puzzle of trusting relationships in the Nuclear Non-Proliferation Treaty', *International Affairs* 86 (2010), 69–85, at 75.

1. *The NPT compared to other WMD regimes*

Since the NPT was a response to the specific political circumstances that existed at the time, it might seem unjustified to discuss the regime in light of how other weapons of mass destruction have been treated in international law. Still, if one disregards the political and 'mythological' aspects of nuclear weapons and simply regards them as weapons of mass destruction, the comparison with the other WMD regimes leaves the regime pertaining to nuclear weapons looking unambitious and inadequate.

The legal regimes applicable to comparable weapons (the other weapons of mass destruction: biological, bacteriological and chemical weapons) are, like the NPT, regimes of non-proliferation and disarmament (and they secure peaceful use).[96] This is also the case for regimes pertaining to anti-personnel mines and cluster munitions, though these will not be subject to further discussion here.[97]

The two other WMD conventions contain, as does the NPT, prohibitions against all forms of transfer. In its 'General obligations' provision, the Chemical Weapons Convention (CWC) specifies that it is prohibited to 'transfer, directly or indirectly, chemical weapons to anyone'.[98] An equivalent provision is found in the Biological Weapons Convention (BWC).[99] The NPT prohibition on transfer in Article I is equally clear: each nuclear weapon state party 'undertake[s] not to transfer to any recipient whatsoever nuclear weapons'.

The CWC also specifies that it is prohibited to 'develop, produce, otherwise acquire, stockpile or retain chemical weapons'.[100] The BWC contains the same provision.[101] The NPT contains its prohibition in Article II against both receiving and manufacturing or otherwise acquiring nuclear weapons. The NPT thus resembles the other two regimes in that it prohibits the 'manufacture' of nuclear weapons, and 'to seek or receive any assistance' to that end, but here the similarities between the regimes end. The difference between the regimes with

---

[96] Convention on the Prohibition of the Development, Production and Stockpiling of Bacteriological (Biological) and Toxin Weapons and on Their Destruction ('1972 Biological Weapons Convention'), London, Moscow, and Washington DC, 10 April 1972, in force 26 March 1975, 1015 UNTS 163 (hereafter, the 1972 Biological Weapons Convention); and Convention on the Prohibition of the Development, Production, Stockpiling and Use of Chemical Weapons and on their Destruction ('1992 Chemical Weapons Convention'), Geneva, 3 September 1992, in force 29 April 1993, 1974 UNTS 45 (hereafter, the 1992 Chemical Weapons Convention).

[97] Convention on the Prohibition of the Use, Stockpiling, Production and Transfer of Anti-Personnel Mines and their Destruction, Oslo, 18 September 1997, in force 1 March 1999, 2056 UNTS 211, 36 ILM 1507; and Convention on Cluster Munitions, Dublin, 30 May 2008, in force 1 August 2010, 48 ILM 354.

[98] 1992 Chemical Weapons Convention, Art. I(1)(a).

[99] 1972 Biological Weapons Convention, Art. 3.

[100] 1992 Chemical Weapons Convention, Art. I(1).

[101] 1972 Biological Weapons Convention, Art. I.

regard to the non-proliferation element is that the prohibition on transfer in the NPT only applies to the nuclear weapon states and the prohibition against receiving and manufacturing only applies to the non-nuclear weapon states. One might suggest that the prohibition on transfer by implication applies to all states, as one cannot reasonably transfer something one is not allowed to have in the first place. The prohibition on developing and manufacturing nuclear weapons, however, does not apply to the nuclear weapon states.

A non-proliferation regime that allows certain states to carry on manufacturing, producing and stockpiling weapons of mass destruction inevitably lacks moral legitimacy. Even the UN Charter, often subject to critique based on the inequality of its states parties, contains the same prohibition on the use of force, and the same exceptions, for all Member States, veto powers or not. There is no universal norm against production or proliferation of weapons of mass destruction to be extracted from a prohibition that does not apply equally to all. The issue of peaceful use is also present in the two other WMD regimes. Both the BWC and the CWC contain exceptions that allow peaceful use of substances that could be used to make biological or chemical weapons.[102]

The disarmament elements of the WMD regimes are also worth noting. Both the BWC and the CWC have extensive and detailed provisions on destruction of stockpiles, production facilities and so on within strict timelines and subject to verification measures.[103] As noted above, Article VI of the NPT, compared to the disarmament regimes in the two other WMD treaties, is unspecific. Being a treaty obligation, however vague, it remains the only legal commitment to nuclear disarmament that exists for the nuclear weapon states parties to the NPT, and may become the basis for future nuclear disarmament should the political climate change.

Comparing the NPT with the two other WMD regimes, however, the most striking difference is that the latter two contain prohibitions against use of the weapons in question.[104] The whole two-tier logic behind the NPT makes such a prohibition with regard to the use of nuclear weapons impossible. However, there is no escaping the fact that of the three kinds of WMD, nuclear weapons arguably have the most devastating impact from a humanitarian point of view. The NPT members recognised the particular humanitarian threat posed by nuclear weapons in the final document of the Review Conference in 2010, in which the states parties expressed their 'deep concern at the catastrophic

---

[102] See, e.g. 1992 Chemical Weapons Convention, Art. II(9).

[103] *Ibid.*, Arts. IV–V.

[104] See 1992 Chemical Weapons Convention, Art. I. The text of Article I of the Biological Weapons Convention does not explicitly prohibit use. The Convention's Review Conference has, however, specified that use of biological weapons 'is effectively a violation of Article I'. See, e.g. Final Document of the Fourth Review Conference, UN Doc. BWC/CONF/. IV/9 (25 November–6 December 1996). Moreover, the 1925 Geneva Gas Protocol already outlawed the use of bacteriological methods of warfare.

humanitarian consequences of any use of nuclear weapons'.[105] Both the BWC and the CWC, as successors to the Gas Protocol of 1925,[106] were negotiated and implemented based on the fact that these weapons could hardly be used consistent with the rules and obligations in international humanitarian law and the law of armed conflict.

The prohibitions against the use of chemical and biological weapons have gained near universal adherence and are seen as customary norms of undisputable legitimacy. This has become abundantly clear with the reactions against the use of chemical weapons in Syria in 2013, as the international community was holding the regime responsible for violations of a convention to which Syria was not even a party. It is unlikely that the establishment of such an undisputed customary law prohibition against use will develop within the NPT framework as long as the NWS parties continue to retain the right to actually use these weapons.

Conclusion

In the end, the NPT is a product of what was politically achievable at the time it was created. It is an instrument designed to alleviate one of the greatest fears of the 1960s: the possibility of 'a world in which 15 or 20 or 25 nations may have these weapons'.[107] It is thus a product of its historical context. Moreover, since nearly all states in the world eventually acceded to the regime, one could also claim that the 'balance of mutual responsibilities and obligations' was indeed 'acceptable'.[108] When a large number of states parties start to doubt the commitment of the NWS to fulfil their part of the bargain, this inevitably reduces confidence in and possibly adherence to the regime, which in turn threatens its viability.

To conclude, the NPT has largely succeeded in the task of preventing proliferation, while at the same time serving the role of promoting nuclear technology for peaceful uses. It has not in the same way, however, served as a key to nuclear disarmament. As a norm, reflecting the unacceptability of producing and retaining the option of using nuclear weapons, it remains unimpressive.

---

[105] 2010 Review Conference of the Parties to the Treaty on the Non-Proliferation of Nuclear Weapons, Final Document, NPT/CONF.2010/50 (Vol. I).

[106] Organisation for the Prohibition of Chemical Weapons, 'Basic Facts on Chemical Disarmament', available at: www.opcw.org/news-publications/publications/history-of-the-chemical-weapons-convention/.

[107] Text of President Kennedy's News Conference on Foreign and Domestic Affairs, 22 March 1963 (quoted in Firmage, 'The treaty on the non-proliferation of nuclear weapons', 711).

[108] See discussion on UN General Assembly Resolution 2028, above.

16

The legal meaning and implications of Article VI of the Non-Proliferation Treaty

DANIEL H. JOYNER

Introduction

This chapter interprets the legal meaning and implications of Article VI of the 1968 Nuclear Non-Proliferation Treaty (NPT),[1] which remains a constant source of debate between Nuclear Weapon States (NWS)[2] and Non-Nuclear Weapon States (NNWS)[3] Parties to the Treaty.[4] As the present author has considered previously,[5] NWS and NNWS have routinely talked past each other in their official diplomatic statements regarding Article VI. The text of Article VI indicates its origins as a product of compromise during the drafting of the NPT; yet, as explained in this chapter, Article VI contains legally binding disarmament obligations, which NWS officials have intentionally attempted to obfuscate. NWS and NNWS officials' interpretations of the Article VI obligations reflect profoundly different views of the measures needed to comply with this Article. This chapter expands on my previous analysis of Article VI in light of subsequently published NWS and NNWS statements, as well as providing a more detailed discussion of the interpretation of Article VI according to the principles of treaty interpretation outlined in the Vienna Convention on the Law of Treaties (VCLT).[6]

The chapter proceeds in five sections. Section A discusses the origins of the NPT, in order to explain the diplomatic compromise out of which Article VI arose. Section B reviews NWS and NNWS statements to Preparatory Committee (PrepCom) Meetings and Review Conferences (RevCon) since 2000, to illustrate the divergence in NWS and NNWS interpretations of Article VI. Section C discusses the interpretation of Article VI by the International Court of Justice

---

[1] Treaty on the Non-Proliferation of Nuclear Weapons, New York, 1 July 1968, in force 5 March 1970, 729 UNTS 161 (hereafter, NPT).

[2] As defined in Article IX(3) of the NPT, the five states parties are not prohibited from manufacturing or acquiring nuclear weapons according to the terms of the Treaty.

[3] All states parties to the NPT other than the five recognised nuclear-weapon states.

[4] See Chapter 15 for more information on the categories NWS and NNWS.

[5] D. Joyner, *Interpreting the Nuclear Non-Proliferation Treaty* (Oxford University Press, 2011), pp. 69–74.

[6] Vienna Convention on the Law of Treaties, Vienna, 23 May 1969, in force 27 January 1980, 1155 UNTS 331; 8 ILM 679 (hereafter, VCLT).

(ICJ) in its 1996 Nuclear Weapons Advisory Opinion,[7] as well as the legal status of this pronouncement. Section D engages in a systematic legal interpretation of Article VI, according to the framework outlined in Articles 31 and 32 of the VCLT. The chapter concludes with a few thoughts on how this analysis highlights both the promise and the limitations of Article VI.

A.   Drafting history of NPT Article VI

Although the drafting history of the NPT forms only a supplementary means of interpretation under the rules for treaty interpretation contained in the VCLT,[8] the historical record is nevertheless helpful in understanding the various interests at play during the negotiations. Unsurprisingly, the history reveals no common initial understanding of Article VI among the NWS and the NNWS. The give and take that led to the precise wording of this Article echoes the main divide prevalent today regarding its legal meaning and interpretation.

The origins of the NPT itself can be traced to post-Second World War concerns about the impact of recently developed nuclear technology on the future of international politics.[9] In a 1953 speech to the UN General Assembly, US President Dwight Eisenhower outlined as a part of his Atoms for Peace plan what was to become the basis for the NPT three-pillar framework: nuclear weapons non-proliferation, international sharing of the technology required to engage in peaceful uses of nuclear energy and nuclear disarmament.[10] Negotiations on a Treaty on the Non-Proliferation of Nuclear Weapons containing this three-pillar framework began only in 1965, however, with a UN General Assembly Resolution calling upon the UN Eighteen-Nation Disarmament Committee (ENDC) to 'take all steps necessary for the early conclusion of a treaty to prevent the proliferation of nuclear weapons'.[11] The General Assembly Resolution laid out a series of principles on which the NPT ought to be based. With respect to disarmament, the Resolution provided: 'The treaty should be a step towards the achievement of general and complete disarmament and, more particularly, nuclear disarmament.'[12]

---

[7] International Court of Justice (ICJ), *Legality of the Threat or Use of Nuclear Weapons*, Advisory Opinion of 8 July 1996 (hereafter, Nuclear Weapons Advisory Opinion).

[8] VCLT, Art. 32. See, also International Law Commission, *Yearbook of the International Law Commission: 1964: Documents of the Sixteenth Session Including the Report of the Commission to the General Assembly*, 2 vols. (New York: United Nations, 1964), Vol. II, p. 58, paras. 20–21 (stating '[S]ome caution is needed in the use of *travaux préparatoires* as a means of interpretation ... They are simply evidence to be weighed against any other relevant evidence of the intentions of the parties, and their cogency depends on the extent to which they furnish proof of the *common* understanding of the parties as to the meaning attached to the terms of the treaty' (emphasis added)).

[9] See Chapter 15 for a more comprehensive description of the negotiations.

[10] Joyner, *Interpreting the Nuclear Non-Proliferation Treaty*, pp. 9–11.

[11] UN General Assembly Resolution 2028, adopted on 19 November 1965.

[12] *Ibid.*

Of the five recognised NWS, China and France did not participate in the negotiations.[13] The United States and the Soviet Union entered the negotiations with copies of their own respective draft treaties in hand[14] – neither of which referred to disarmament.[15] The two countries ironed out their differences by August 1967, submitting identical draft treaties that included language on disarmament only in the preamble.[16] The NWS resisted any mention of disarmament in the text of the treaty itself, stating their fear that disagreements on nuclear disarmament might stall progress on non-proliferation.[17] Instead, they argued, disarmament should form the substance of a separate treaty, decoupled from the NPT.[18] The NNWS, however, viewed a disarmament obligation in Article VI as part of an implicit bargain between the NNWS and NWS: the former would give up any ambitions of acquiring nuclear weapons in exchange for the commitment of the latter to disarm in the future.[19]

The United States and the Soviet Union yielded to NNWS demands to include a disarmament obligation in Article VI.[20] The exact wording of the Article evolved over countless drafts. For example, Mexico originally proposed the phrase: 'to pursue negotiations in good faith'.[21] Shaker's monumental account of the NPT describes this choice of phrase as an alternative to a requirement to reach an agreement:

> Under the pressure of the non-aligned States as well as from some of their own allies, the two super-Powers merely accepted in the NPT to undertake to pursue negotiations in good faith, but not, as pointed out by one American negotiator, 'to achieve any disarmament agreement, since it is obviously impossible to predict the exact nature and results of such negotiations.'[22]

As Shaker explains: 'The obligation to pursue negotiations in good faith was lukewarmly admitted by a number of States, as the only solution acceptable to the two super-Powers.'[23] Sweden succeeded in adding the phrase 'at an early date' after the clause relating to the cessation of the nuclear arms race, in addition to adding 'nuclear' before 'disarmament' in the second clause.[24] In general, however, the NNWS lamented the absence of a timeline for implementation as well as the exclusion of NNWS proposals for more detailed lists of the required steps.[25]

The resulting treaty banned the proliferation of nuclear weapons to states other than the five recognised NWS;[26] confirmed the NNWS' right to exploit

---

[13] M. Shaker, *The Nuclear Non-Proliferation Treaty: Origin and Implementation 1959–1979*, 3 vols. (London; New York: Oceana Publications, 1980), Vol. II, p. 567.

[14] UN General Assembly Resolution 2028, UN doc. A/RES/20/2028, adopted on 29 November 1965, para. 2(c).

[15] Joyner, *Interpreting the Nuclear Non-Proliferation Treaty*, p. 17.

[16] Shaker, *The Nuclear Non-Proliferation Treaty*, pp. 565–6.

[17] *Ibid.*, p. 566.   [18] *Ibid.*   [19] *Ibid.*, p. 564.   [20] *Ibid.*, p. 566–7.

[21] *Ibid.*, p. 571, (emphasis added, internal citations omitted).   [22] *Ibid.*, p. 567.

[23] *Ibid.*, p. 572.   [24] *Ibid.*, p. 576.   [25] *Ibid.*, p. 575.   [26] NPT, Arts. I–III.

peaceful uses of nuclear energy;[27] and, in Article VI, established the parties'
disarmament obligations. NPT Article VI states, in its entirety:

> Each of the Parties to the Treaty undertakes to pursue negotiations in good
> faith on effective measures relating to cessation of the nuclear arms race at
> an early date and to nuclear disarmament, and on a treaty on general and
> complete disarmament under strict and effective international control.

The UN General Assembly adopted the draft on 12 June 1968, with France
abstaining.[28] France and China acceded to the NPT in 1992.[29]

B.   NWS and NNWS statements

As written about previously, the United States and the United Kingdom largely
appeared to share a common template when discussing their interpretation of
Article VI in statements at NPT PrepCom and RevCon Meetings from 2000
to 2008.[30] First, each state reiterated its commitment to its Article VI obligations, before pointing to reductions in their nuclear arsenals as proof positive
of compliance.[31] By not delving into the actual substance of the Article, these
statements failed to provide any detail on what precisely the text of Article VI
requires of NPT states parties. Rather, the US and British statements implied
that any action taken to reduce a state's nuclear arsenal, however small, fulfils
the requirements of Article VI. Moreover, the United States and the United
Kingdom disconnected their discussion of Article VI compliance from a hol-
istic assessment of their nuclear weapons arsenals, refusing to consider, for
example, whether Article VI applies to actions taken to maintain or upgrade
existing arsenals. Instead, NWS statements explicitly marginalised the importance of the NPT's disarmament pillar in comparison to the more pressing and
immediate concerns of non-proliferation.

---

[27] NPT, Arts. IV–V.

[28] Joyner, *Interpreting the Nuclear Non-Proliferation Treaty*, p. 20.

[29] Status of the Treaty, Treaty on the Non-Proliferation of Nuclear Weapons (NPT), available
at: http://disarmament.un.org/treaties/t/npt. In 1968 the Republic of China held China's
seat in the United Nations. The UN officially recognised the People's Republic of China as
the sole representative of China in 1971. UN General Assembly Resolution 2758 (XXVI),
adopted on 25 October 1971, para. 1.

[30] Joyner, *Interpreting the Nuclear Non-Proliferation Treaty*, p. 69.

[31] See, e.g., Statement on behalf of China, France, the Russian Federation, the United Kingdom
and the United States to the 2008 Non-Proliferation Treaty Preparatory Committee, delivered by Ambassador John Duncan, UK Ambassador for Multilateral Arms Control and
Disarmament, 9 May 2008. See also Statement by Ambassador Jean-Hugues Simon-Michel,
Permanent Representative of France to the Conference on Disarmament, Second Meeting
of the Preparatory Committee for the 2015 NPT Review Conference, General Debate,
Geneva 22 April 2012 (pointing to reductions in France's nuclear forces as evidence of the
state's compliance with its disarmament obligations).

The only possible exception to this NWS rhetorical template was China, which acceded to the NPT in 1992 and commented only sparingly on Article VI, suggesting that the Article requires nuclear disarmament at some future date.[32] For their part, Russia and France follow the same basic script as the United States and the United Kingdom, with the addition that both understand Article VI to refer to 'general and complete disarmament' as something broader than simply 'nuclear disarmament', thus posing obligations on NNWS as well.[33]

NWS statements during the early 2000s tended to neatly avoid identifying the precise content of the Article VI obligation, while simultaneously brushing aside allegations of their failure to comply with Article VI as a diversion from more critical concerns regarding nuclear proliferation.[34] For example, the United Kingdom's statement to the 2008 PrepCom invoked this line of reasoning, viewing the disarmament pillar as a distraction from the more urgent non-proliferation pillar:

> If one is truly committed to the goals of Article VI, if one is passionate about keeping nuclear weapons and fissile material for use in such weapons on a downward path – and I speak here as the representative of a country that has reduced its nuclear arsenal by 75% since the end of the Cold War – then you must be a non-proliferator.[35]

---

[32] Statement by HE Ambassador Li Baodong, Head of the Chinese Delegation at the 2010 Review Conference of the Parties to the Treaty on the Non-Proliferation of Nuclear Weapons, 4 May 2010, 3 ('All nuclear-weapon states should fulfil in good faith obligations under Article VI of the NPT, and publicly undertake not to seek permanent possession of nuclear weapons'). See, also Statement by HE Mr Cheng Jingye, Head of the Chinese Delegation to the Second Session of the Preparatory Committee for the 2010 Review Conference of the Parties to the Treaty on the Non-Proliferation of Nuclear Weapons, 28 April 2008 (stating that China has 'always stood for complete prohibition and thorough destruction of nuclear weapons and the conclusion of an international legal instrument in this regard').

[33] See Statement by Mikhail Ulyanov, Head of the Delegation of the Russian Federation, Director for the Department for Security Affairs and Disarmament, Ministry of Foreign Affairs of the Russian Federation, at the Second Session of the Preparatory Committee for the 2015 Review Conference of the Parties to the Treaty on the Non-Proliferation of Nuclear Weapons, 22 April 2013, p. 6; Statement by HE Mr Jean-Hughes Simon-Michel, Ambassador, Permanent Representative of France to the Conference on Disarmament, Head of the French Delegation, to the Second Session of the Preparatory Committee for the 2015 Nuclear Non-Proliferation Treaty Review Conference, 24 April 2013 (stating 'Nuclear disarmament is only meaningful if it does not lead to an arms race in other areas. This is why it needs to be carried out in the framework of general and complete disarmament, in accordance with Article VI of the NPT').

[34] See, e.g. Joyner, *Interpreting the Nuclear Non-Proliferation Treaty*, pp. 70–1.

[35] Statement by John Duncan, UK Ambassador for Multilateral Arms Control and Disarmament, UK General Statement to the 2008 Non-Proliferation Treaty Preparatory Committee, 28 April 2008.

In contrast, NNWS statements over the same period reveal a fundamentally different view of the nature of Article VI. The NNWS demonstrated no hesitancy in delving into the details of precisely how they understand Article VI to apply to concrete policies and actions; neither did the NNWS prove reticent in voicing their frustration at perceived NWS reluctance to comply with these obligations.[36]

During this period, the NNWS frequently bemoaned the lack of substantive discussion on Article VI – a provision the vast majority of NNWS interpreted to contain concrete disarmament obligations. The Indonesian statement to the 2008 PrepCom on behalf of the Non-Aligned Movement (NAM) criticised the NWS' continued efforts to 'develop and modernize their nuclear arsenals, imperilling regional and international peace and security, in particular in the Middle East'.[37] Indonesia's statement added that such actions 'illustrate a trend of vertical proliferation and non-compliance by NWS towards their commitments under Article VI of the NPT'.[38] Similarly, New Zealand's statement to the 2008 PrepCom on behalf of the New Agenda Coalition (Brazil, Egypt, Ireland, Mexico, New Zealand, South Africa and Sweden) noted that although it 'welcome[d]' proposals to reduce nuclear arsenals further, it did not condone plans to 'modernize other nuclear forces':

> The Coalition reiterates that States should not develop new nuclear weapons or nuclear weapons with new military capabilities or for new missions, nor replace nor modernize their nuclear weapon systems, as any such action would contradict the spirit of the disarmament and non-proliferation obligations of the treaty.[39]

These statements reflect an interpretation of Article VI as a substantive disarmament obligation. This is not just an obligation to pursue negotiations toward disarmament, but an obligation to achieve, at least in progressive fashion, the result of full nuclear disarmament. This interpretation views the obligation of good faith effort in Article VI as applying not just to negotiations

---

[36] See, e.g. Statement by Ambassador Hesham Badr, Assistant Minister of Foreign Affairs for International Organizations and Multilateral Affairs of Egypt, before the Second Session of the Preparatory Committee to the 2015 NPT Review Conference, General Debate, 23 April 2013, p. 3 (hereafter, Egyptian Statement to the 2015 NPT RevCon).

[37] Statement by Ambassador Gusti Agung Wesaka Puja of the Republic of Indonesia, on behalf of the Group of Non-Aligned States Parties to the Treaty on the Non-Proliferation of Nuclear Weapons, at the General Debate of the Second Session of the Preparatory Committee for the 2010 Review Conference of the States Parties to the Treaty on the Non-Proliferation of Nuclear Weapons, 28 April 2008.

[38] *Ibid.*

[39] Statement by Ambassador Don Mackay, Permanent Representative of New Zealand to the UN in Geneva, on Behalf of the New Agenda Coalition, to the Preparatory Committee for the 2010 Review Conference of the Parties to the Treaty on the Non-Proliferation of Nuclear Weapons, General Debate, 28 April 2008.

on disarmament, but also to state policies and state actions in the progressive direction of actual nuclear disarmament. This interpretation is essentially consistent with the interpretation of Article VI given by the International Court of Justice in its 1996 Advisory Opinion, discussed below.

In 2009 President Obama's Prague speech, which played an important role in the Norwegian Nobel Committee's decision to award him the 2009 Nobel Peace Prize,[40] announced a shift in US policy: '[T]oday, I state clearly and with conviction America's commitment to seek the peace and security of a world without nuclear weapons.'[41] At the same time, President Obama clarified that '[t]his goal will not be reached quickly – perhaps not in my lifetime.'[42] The 2010 US Nuclear Posture Review moderates this ambition even further, by stipulating a series of non-exhaustive conditions for full US nuclear disarmament.[43] Despite this substantial policy shift,[44] however, little seems to have changed in terms of the United States' understanding of the timeline for action or in terms of the concrete application of Article VI to specific nuclear policy actions.

The question of modernisation of nuclear arsenals, for example, remains a sticking point in NWS and NNWS discussions. At the 2013 PrepCom, the Indonesian representative, speaking on behalf of the NAM, reiterated the Movement's concerns, stating in no uncertain terms that the NAM perceived efforts to upgrade or modernise nuclear arsenals as a violation of Article VI:

> In order to comply with their obligations under Article VI of the Treaty, as well as with their commitments under the 13 practical steps and 2010 Action Plan on nuclear disarmament, the NWS must immediately cease their plans to further invest in modernizing, upgrading, refurbishing, or extending the lives of their nuclear weapons and related facilities.[45]

---

[40] Thorbjørn Jagland, Announcement of the 2009 Nobel Peace Prize, available at: www.nobelprize.org/mediaplayer/index.php?id=1173.

[41] Remarks by US President Barack Obama, Hradcany Square, Prague, Czech Republic, 5 April 2009.

[42] *Ibid.*

[43] US Department of Defense, Nuclear Posture Review Report (April 2010), p. xv (specifying '[t]he conditions that would ultimately permit the United States and others to give up their nuclear weapons without risking greater international instability and insecurity are very demanding. Among those conditions are success in halting the proliferation of nuclear weapons, much greater transparency into the programs and capabilities of key countries of concern, verification methods and technologies capable of detecting violations of disarmament obligations, enforcement measures strong and credible enough to deter such violations, and ultimately the resolution of regional disputes that can motivate rival states to acquire and maintain nuclear weapons. Clearly, such conditions do not exist today').

[44] See, e.g. Joyner, *Interpreting the Nuclear Non-Proliferation Treaty*, pp. 123–4.

[45] Statement by Ambassador Edi Yusup, Deputy Permanent Representative of Indonesia in Geneva, on behalf of the Group of Member States of the Non-Aligned Movement Parties to the Treaty on the Non-Proliferation of Nuclear Weapons, Cluster 1 Specific Issues: Nuclear disarmament and security assurance, to the Second Session of the Preparatory Committee

The Indonesian representative thus rejected the NWS' common refrain that Article VI has nothing to say regarding NWS' maintenance of their existing nuclear arsenals. In a statement that bears quoting at length, the Egyptian representative to the 2013 PrepCom outlines the sense of frustration evident among NNWS that reductions in NWS nuclear arsenals do not equal compliance with the requirements of Article VI negotiations to pursue negotiations in good faith toward a legally binding multilateral agreement on disarmament:

> Article VI of the Treaty clearly says that each party of the Treaty undertakes to pursue negotiations in good faith on effective measures relating to cessation of the arms race at an early date and to nuclear disarmament. Forty five years after the conclusion of this treaty such a multilateral negotiation did not start. In the meantime, we have agreed in the NPT review conference on the decision on the principles and objectives for nuclear non-proliferation and disarmament of 1995, the thirteen practical steps for the systemic and progressive efforts to implement Article VI of the Treaty of 2000, the twenty two actions on nuclear disarmament 2010, and yet not much had materialized in advancing the cause of nuclear disarmament. Instead, we are told that many efforts have been done to reduce nuclear arsenals through unilateral or bilateral initiatives and that the five nuclear weapon States have started a dialogue. Those are welcomed developments. But they are by no means a multilateral, legally binding and verifiable regime to achieve a nuclear disarmament.[46]

To summarise, government statements to the NPT PrepComs and RevCons since 2000 illustrate the divergence between how the NWS and NNWS interpret Article VI. The NWS avoid concrete discussion of precisely what the Article VI obligation entails, referring instead to nuclear arms reductions as evidence of their compliance, before urging the states parties to the NPT to focus on the more important problems of nuclear proliferation. In contrast, the NNWS statements reveal an unambiguous understanding of Article VI as an obligation to achieve the specific result of nuclear disarmament; and therefore to refrain from any action that would prolong the achievement of this result, including modernising existing arsenals.

C. ICJ interpretation of Article VI

The International Court of Justice has commented on the interpretation of NPT Article VI only once, in its 1996 Nuclear Weapons Advisory Opinion. The ICJ adopted an expansive interpretation of the legal obligation Article VI

---

for the 2015 Review Conference of the Parties to the Treaty on the Non-Proliferation of Nuclear Weapons, 25 April 2013, para. 6.
[46] Egyptian Statement to the 2015 NPT RevCon, p. 3.

imposes on states parties, but did not describe the legal reasoning that led to this conclusion in much detail:

> The legal import of that obligation goes beyond that of a mere obligation of conduct; the obligation involved here is an obligation to achieve a precise result – nuclear disarmament in all its aspects – by adopting a particular course of conduct, namely, the pursuit of negotiations on the matter in good faith.[47]

The Court's consideration of Article VI occurs at the very end of the Advisory Opinion, and is not directly connected to its conclusions regarding the question put to it. In his separate dissent, Judge Gilbert Guillaume stated as much, adding that although he 'fully approve[d] of this reference', and hoped it would advance nuclear disarmament, he 'would have preferred the Court' not include the above paragraph among the operative language of the Advisory Opinion, to avoid extending it beyond the scope of the General Assembly's request.[48]

The Court states in paragraph 98 of its Advisory Opinion that the interpretation of Article VI is relevant to the General Assembly's question regarding the use or threat of use of nuclear weapons when the question is 'seen in a broader context'. Whether relevant to the question or not, the Court's interpretation of Article VI almost certainly stretched its terms beyond their ordinary meaning. Compare the ICJ's analysis, printed above, to the text of Article VI, in full:

> Each of the Parties to the Treaty undertakes to pursue negotiations in good faith on effective measures relating to cessation of the nuclear arms race at an early date and to nuclear disarmament, and on a treaty on general and complete disarmament under strict and effective international control.

With respect, the ordinary meaning of Article VI suggests an obligation to 'undertake to pursue negotiations in good faith' to achieve a precise result; it does not impose an obligation to *achieve* this result. This is a small, but important difference. Moreover, it is worth repeating that the ICJ's sole discussion of NPT Article VI appears in an Advisory Opinion, in which the discussion does not relate directly to the General Assembly's question. As a result, the proper weight to be attached to the ICJ's interpretation of Article VI remains unclear.

---

[47] Nuclear Weapons Advisory Opinion, para. 99.

[48] Nuclear Weapons Advisory Opinion, Dissenting Opinion of Judge Gilbert Guillaume, para. 13. See also Nuclear Weapons Advisory Opinion, Dissenting Opinion of Judge Stephen M. Schwebel, p. 329 (concluding '[i]n any event, since paragraph 2 F is not responsive to the question put to the Court by the General Assembly, it is to be treated as dictum'); Nuclear Weapons Advisory Opinion, Dissenting Opinion of Judge Mohammed Shahabuddeen, p. 378 (stating '[t]he particular question as to the legal implications of Article VI of the Treaty on the Non-Proliferation of Nuclear Weapons ("NPT") is not before the Court; it does not form part of the General Assembly's question. It could well be the subject of a separate question as to the effect of that Article of the NPT, were the General Assembly minded to present one').

D.   Interpretation of Article VI

1.   *Vienna Convention on the Law of Treaties*

The starting point for treaty interpretation is Articles 31 and 32 of the 1969 Vienna Convention on the Law of Treaties. Beginning with an analysis of NPT Article VI according to VCLT Article 31(1), the ordinary meaning of NPT Article VI suggests the text can be divided into three separate obligations:

> Each of the Parties to the Treaty undertakes to pursue negotiations in good faith …
>
> (1) … on effective measures relating to cessation of the nuclear arms race at an early date;
> (2) … on effective measures relating to nuclear disarmament; and
> (3) … on a treaty on general and complete disarmament under strict and effective international control.

The undertaking, or obligation, in Article VI is thus an obligation to pursue negotiations in good faith toward these three delineated end results. Grammatically, the phrase 'on effective measures relating to …' appears to apply to both 'cessation of the nuclear arms race' and 'nuclear disarmament', while the subsequent comma suggests that the clause 'on a treaty on general and complete disarmament' should logically be read as 'undertakes to pursue negotiations in good faith … on a treaty on general and complete disarmament under strict and effective international control'. The phrase 'effective measures relating to' is logically unnecessary for the third clause, as its stated end result – 'a treaty on general and complete disarmament' – *is* the effective measure to be achieved.

The text alone does not indicate that there is a chronological ordering of these three obligations, apart from the reference to 'at an early date' for the cessation of the nuclear arms race. Thus, the absence of the phrase 'at an early date' suggests that the two remaining obligations, relating to nuclear disarmament and to a treaty on general and complete disarmament, are less urgent than the cessation of the nuclear arms race, but the ordinary meaning of the text provides no further clues on the precise timeline.

At any rate, the text does not imply, as has been suggested,[49] that negotiations on effective measures related to nuclear disarmament need only occur subsequent to and conditional upon negotiations of a treaty on general and complete disarmament. Arguments to the contrary focus on a single paragraph in the preamble, rather than the text of Article VI. The relevant preambular paragraph reads:

> The States concluding this Treaty, hereinafter referred to as the 'Parties to the Treaty' … Desiring to further the easing of international tension and

---

[49] C. A. Ford, 'Debating disarmament: interpreting Article VI of the Treaty on the Non-Proliferation of Nuclear Weapons', *Non-Proliferation Review* 14(3) (2007), 401–28, at 403.

the strengthening of trust between States in order to facilitate the cessation of the manufacture of nuclear weapons, the liquidation of all their existing stockpiles, and the elimination from national arsenals of nuclear weapons and the means of their delivery pursuant to a Treaty on general and complete disarmament under strict and effective international control …

Here, one commentator emphasises 'the elimination from national arsenals of nuclear weapons and the means of their delivery *pursuant to* a Treaty on general and complete disarmament' as a sign that the measures related to nuclear disarmament will occur through a treaty on general and complete disarmament.[50] As a matter of treaty interpretation, the preamble functions primarily as a source of the object and purpose of the treaty.[51] Although the preamble may comprise one element of the context of the treaty, as a means of deciphering the meaning of ambiguous terms, its value as an interpreted source should be examined critically.[52] Using the preamble to contradict the ordinary meaning of a treaty's terms, by imposing a conditionality requirement not found elsewhere, extends beyond the permissible uses of a preamble.

2. 'Each of the Parties to the Treaty undertakes to pursue negotiations in good faith'

The obligation to 'undertake … to pursue negotiations in good faith' applies to each of the three results. The first portion of the phrase – 'undertakes to pursue negotiations' – resembles Article 33 of the United Nations Charter, which requires all UN member states to 'seek a solution by negotiation' to 'any dispute likely to endanger the maintenance of international peace and security'.[53] Neither Article adopts a more direct formulation, for example by requiring parties simply 'to negotiate' or 'to reach an agreement'. Reading the phrase in its entirety, 'undertakes to pursue negotiations in good faith' makes clear that the obligation is not illusory, however. The ordinary meaning of the text does not imply an obligation to *achieve* the subject of the negotiations – the ICJ's statements to the contrary notwithstanding – but the addition of 'in good faith' in particular indicates that something more than 'going through the motions' is required for compliance.

The principle of good faith is an accepted general principle of international law that sheds light on the Article's correct interpretation.[54] As one commentator explains: 'the substance of the principle of good faith is the negation of

---

[50] *Ibid.*, at 404 (emphasis added).
[51] See R. Gardiner, *Treaty Interpretation* (Oxford University Press, 2008), pp. 186–7.
[52] *Ibid.*
[53] Charter of the United Nations, San Francisco, 26 June 1945, in force 24 October 1945, 1 UNTS XVI, Art. 33.
[54] I. Brownlie, *Principles of Public International Law*, 7th edn (Oxford University Press, 2008), p. 19.

unintended and literal interpretations of words that might result in one of the parties gaining an unfair or unjust advantage over another party.'[55] VCLT Article 31(1), excerpted above, also refers explicitly to the principle of good faith as an integral component of treaty interpretation, although the distinction between good faith in treaty interpretation and good faith in treaty implementation is sometimes unclear.[56]

The concept of good faith applies on two levels with respect to NPT Article VI: (1) good faith in interpreting the terms of the NPT in its entirety, and (2) interpreting the meaning of 'good faith' as it appears in the text of the Article. Although the remaining analysis in this section focuses primarily on task (2), it is worth bearing in mind that the VCLT Article 31(1) obligation to interpret a treaty's terms in good faith requires, at a minimum, that 'an interpretation of a term should be preferred which gives it some meaning and role rather than one which does not' and that an interpretation should be preferred that 'fulfils the aims of the treaty'.[57] As discussed above, the aims of the NPT comprise three pillars: non-proliferation, transfer of the benefits of peaceful nuclear energy and disarmament. Thus, where possible, the terms of the NPT should be interpreted to give each Article a meaning and role in fulfilling these three aims.

The ICJ has employed the principle of good faith specifically in negotiations in its jurisprudence in the 1969 *North Sea Continental Shelf* cases and the 1974 *Nuclear Test* cases, among others.[58] In the 1969 *North Sea Continental Shelf*

---

[55] A. D'Amato, 'Good faith' in R. Bernhardt, Max Planck Institute for Comparative Public Law and International Law (eds.), *Encyclopedia of Public International Law* (Amsterdam, London, New York, Tokyo: North-Holland, 1992), pp. 599–601.

[56] Gardiner, *Treaty Interpretation*, p. 148.   [57] *Ibid.*

[58] See generally, D. Koplow, 'Parsing good faith: has the United States violated Article VI of the Nuclear Non-Proliferation Treaty?, *Wisconsin Law Review* 301 (1993), 301–94; R. Singh and C. Chinkin, *Joint Opinion: UK Trident replacement a 'material breach' of the NPT*, 19 December 2005, para. 69 ('The Treaty obligation is thus not to disarm as such, but a positive obligation to pursue in good faith negotiations towards these ends, and to bring them to a conclusion. Good faith is the legal requirement for the process of carrying out of an existing obligation. In the *Nuclear Tests cases* the ICJ described the principle of good faith as *"one of the basic principles governing the creation and performance of legal obligations"* ... The obligation of good faith has been described as not being one *"which obviously requires actual damage. Instead its violation may be demonstrated by acts and failures to act which, taken together, render the fulfilment of specific treaty obligations remote or impossible."* In the context of an obligation to negotiate in good faith this would involve taking no action that would make a successful outcome impossible or unlikely') (quoting ICJ, *Nuclear Tests* case (*New Zealand v. France*), Judgment of 20 December 1974, ICJ Reports 1974; ICJ, *Nuclear Tests* (*Australia v. France*), Judgment of 20 December 1974, pp. 253; 457, para. 46); and G. Goodwin-Gill, 'State responsibility and the "good faith" obligation in international law' in M. Fitzmaurice and D. Sarooshi (eds.), *Issues of State Responsibility Before International Judicial Institutions* (Portland, OR: Hart Publishing, 2004), pp. 75, 84. See also International Association of Lawyers Against Nuclear Arms and the International Human Rights Clinic at Harvard Law School, *Good Faith Negotiations Leading to the Total Elimination of Nuclear Weapons: Request for an Advisory Opinion from the International Court of Justice* (Cambridge, MA:

cases, the ICJ discussed the principle of good faith in interpreting an agreement between Germany and the Netherlands that stipulated that the parties 'shall delimit the continental shelf of the North Sea as between their countries by agreement'.[59] The Court employed equitable principles to determine the substance of this obligation to agree:

> The parties are under an obligation to enter into negotiations with a view to arriving at an agreement, and not merely to go through a formal process of negotiation as a sort of prior condition for the automatic application of a certain method of delimitation in the absence of agreement; they are under an obligation so to conduct themselves that the negotiations are meaningful, which will not be the case when either of them insists upon its own position without contemplating any modification of it.[60]

The principle of good faith in negotiations is also discussed in the decisions of international arbitral tribunals. For example, in the 1957 *Lake Lanoux* arbitration, the arbitral panel stated, in dicta, that an 'obligation of negotiating an agreement' can be breached:

> [I]n the event, for example, of an unjustified breaking off of the discussions, abnormal delays, disregard of the agreed procedures, systematic refusals to take into consideration adverse proposals or interests, and, more generally, in cases of violation of the rules of good faith.[61]

In the context of NPT Article VI, the *Lake Lanoux* arbitral panel's definition of 'abnormal delays' appears applicable to the foot-dragging that has characterised disarmament efforts since the Treaty's entry into force. Although Article VI does not establish a timeline for achieving the three specific results, aside from the reference to 'the cessation of the nuclear arms race at an early date', at the time of writing this chapter, forty-five years have passed since the signing of the NPT.

In the 1982 *Kuwait* v. *Aminoil* arbitration, the tribunal elaborated on the substance of an 'obligation to negotiate':

> A scrutiny of the negotiations fails to reveal any conduct on either side that would constitute a shortcoming in respect of ... the general principles that ought to be observed in carrying out an obligation to negotiate, that is to say, good faith as properly to be understood; sustained upkeep of the negotiations over a period appropriate to the circumstances; awareness of

---

International Human Rights Clinic, Human Rights Program, Harvard Law School, 2009), pp. 29–32, available at: http://lcnp.org/disarmament/2009.05.ICJbooklet.pdf.

[59] ICJ, *North Sea Continental Shelf Cases* (*Federal Republic of Germany* v. *Denmark*; *Federal Republic of Germany* v. *Netherlands*), Judgment of 20 February 1969, p. 7, para. 2.

[60] *Ibid.*, at p. 47, para. 85.

[61] *Lake Lanoux Arbitration* (*France* v. *Spain*), Award of 16 November 1957, 24 ILR 101, p. 128.

the interests of the other party; and a persevering quest for an acceptable compromise.[62]

In the 1931 Advisory Opinion in *Railway Traffic between Lithuania and Poland*, the Permanent Court of International Justice (PCIJ) interpreted a Council of the League of Nations resolution: 'Recommend[ing] the two Governments … enter into direct negotiations as soon as possible in order to establish such relations between the two neighbouring States as will ensure "the good understanding between nations upon which peace depends".'[63] The PCIJ outlined the substance of the obligation to negotiate, distinguishing it from the obligation to 'reach an agreement':

> The Court is indeed justified in considering that the engagement incumbent on the two Governments in conformity with the Council's Resolution is not only to enter into negotiations, but also to pursue them as far as possible, with a view to concluding agreements … But an obligation to negotiate does not imply an obligation to reach an agreement.[64]

As these opinions make clear, the principle of good faith comprises an obligation to proactively, diligently, sincerely and consistently pursue negotiations.[65] Article VI delineates these three specific results, each discussed in turn.

3. Negotiations towards three separate results

Each of the Parties to the Treaty undertakes to pursue negotiations in good faith on effective measures relating to cessation of the nuclear arms race at an early date

With the break-up of the Soviet Union and the end of the Cold War, the nuclear arms race ended, at least quantitatively. Global nuclear stockpiles peaked during

---

[62] *Government of Kuwait v. American Independent Oil Company (Aminoil)*, Award of 24 March 1982, 66 ILR 519, p. 578.

[63] Permanent Court of International Justice (PCIJ), *Railway Traffic between Lithuania and Poland*, Advisory Opinion of 15 October 1931, PCIJ (ser. A/B) No. 42, para. 29 (citing Council of the League of Nations Resolution of 10 December, 1927).

[64] *Ibid.*, para. 31.

[65] See, e.g., ICJ, *Gabčíkovo-Nagymaros Dam Project (Hungary v. Slovakia)*, Judgment of 25 September 1997, para. 142, in which the Court held: 'What is required in the present case by the rule *pacta sunt servanda*, as reflected in Article 26 of the Vienna Convention of 1969 on the Law of Treaties, is that the Parties find an agreed solution within the cooperative context of the Treaty. Article 26 combines two elements, which are of equal importance. It provides that "Every treaty in force is binding upon the parties to it and must be performed by them in good faith." This latter element, in the Court's view, implies that, in this case, it is the purpose of the Treaty, and the intentions of the parties in concluding it, which should prevail over its literal application. The principle of good faith obliges the Parties to apply it in a reasonable way and in such a manner that its purpose can be realized.'

the Cold War despite nuclear proliferation since the fall of the Soviet Union.[66] Qualitatively, as the previous section on NWS and NNWS statements to the most recent PrepComs and RevCons indicate, the NWS continue to modernise and upgrade existing arsenals. This could be interpreted as a continuation of the nuclear arms race, but the present author is persuaded that these efforts are more appropriately viewed in terms of the nuclear disarmament obligation.

Each of the Parties to the Treaty undertakes to pursue negotiations in good faith on effective measures relating to … nuclear disarmament

As stated earlier, some NWS argue that this obligation applies only *pursuant* to a treaty on general and complete disarmament, based on the reading of a single paragraph in the preamble.[67] According to this view, the obligation to pursue negotiations related to nuclear disarmament does not exist independently. This chapter demonstrates why this view is incorrect as a matter of treaty interpretation methodology.

What, then, does this obligation imply? In the context of the entire Article, including the third clause, it is clear that the phrase 'nuclear disarmament' means something other than 'general and complete disarmament'. The nuclear disarmament clause also lacks any reference to a 'treaty … under strict and effective international control', suggesting that nuclear disarmament may proceed through means other than a treaty and need not be subject to international verification. Article VI thus grants relatively broader flexibility to determine how to meet this obligation – including, for example, through unilateral disarmament.

According to VCLT Article 31(3)(a), in interpreting the provisions of a treaty, recourse shall be made to 'any subsequent interpretive agreements reached between the parties regarding the interpretation of the treaty or the application of its provisions'. For the NPT, some commentators have dismissed out of hand any suggestion that the final documents of the review conferences meet the definition of subsequent agreements, because there is '[n]othing in them' that would so indicate.[68] This is a flawed reading of VCLT Article 31(3)(a). The term 'subsequent agreements' for Article 31(3)(a) purposes depends on 'whether the parties to a treaty have, subsequent to its conclusion, reached a firm agreement on what one of its provisions means. Thus it does not necessarily follow that such an agreement will be recorded in one of the forms commonly used for a treaty', although it does require that 'the official is sufficiently senior to have an

---

[66] See, e.g. Federation of American Scientists, Status of World Nuclear Forces, available at: www.fas.org/programs/ssp/nukes/nuclearweapons/nukestatus.html; United States Department of Defense, Fact Sheet: Increasing Transparency in the US Nuclear Weapons Stockpile (3 May 2010), available at: www.defense.gov/npr/docs/10-05-03_Fact_Sheet_ US_Nuclear_Transparency__FINAL_w_Date.pdf.

[67] Ford, 'Debating disarmament', 403.   [68] *Ibid.*, at 411–13.

authority to make an agreement binding the state'.[69] Accordingly, the relevant
question for determining whether NPT review conference final documents
constitute subsequent agreements under VCLT Article 31(3)(a) is whether the
substance of the document indicates 'an agreement as to the interpretation of
a provision'.[70]

In the 2000 Review Conference final document, adopted by consensus, Part
I addressed 'Review and operation of the Treaty', organised by Article. The section 'Article VI and eighth to twelfth preambular paragraphs' outlined thirteen
practical steps on which 'the Conference agrees ... for the systematic and progressive efforts to implement Article VI of the Treaty on the Non-Proliferation
of Nuclear Weapons'.[71] These thirteen practical steps include, among others,
achieving the Comprehensive Test Ban Treaty's entry into force,[72] the negotiation of a treaty 'banning the production of fissile material for nuclear weapons' through the Conference on Disarmament[73] and the implementation of
START II.[74] Given their adoption by consensus and as 'practical steps for the
systematic and progressive efforts to implement article VI', these practical steps
could arguably be considered a subsequent agreement clarifying the meaning
of 'effective measures ... relating to nuclear disarmament' under NPT Article
VI. According to this interpretation, the practical steps form a 'yardstick' for
measuring compliance with Article VI. Alternatively, the thirteen practical
steps could be considered a non-exhaustive list of effective measures from
which states could choose how best to comply with the Article VI obligation.

Practical step number six addresses the interpretation of Article VI directly, calling for 'An unequivocal undertaking by the nuclear-weapon States
to accomplish the total elimination of their nuclear arsenals leading to nuclear
disarmament, to which all States parties are committed under article VI'.[75] The
contrast between the reference to 'the nuclear weapon States' in the first clause
and the reference to 'all States parties' in the final clause demonstrates that the
obligation 'to which all States parties are committed under article VI' is 'nuclear
disarmament' alone. Practical step six thus adds to the text of Article VI in
that it requires states parties to *achieve* nuclear disarmament, rather than to
'pursue negotiations' to that end. The 2010 Review Conference final document

---

[69] Gardiner, *Treaty Interpretation*, p. 217.
[70] *Ibid.* (quoting International Law Commission, *Yearbook of the International Law
Commission: 1966: Documents of the Second Part of the Seventeenth Session and of the
Eighteenth Session Including the Reports of the Commission to the General Assembly*, 2 vols.
(New York: United Nations, 1966), Vol. II, p. 221, para. 14). See, also B. Carnahan, 'Treaty
review conferences', *American Journal of International Law* 81 (1987), 226–30, 229.
[71] 2000 Review Conference of the Parties to the Treaty on the Non-Proliferation of Nuclear
Weapons, Final Document, 3 vols. NPT/CONF.2000/28(Part I), Vol. I, Part I, pp. 14–15,
para. 15.
[72] *Ibid.*, at pp. 14–15, para. 15(1).   [73] *Ibid.*, at pp. 14–15, para. 15(3).
[74] *Ibid.*, at pp. 14–15, para. 15(7).   [75] *Ibid.*, at pp. 14–15, para. 15(6).

includes a nearly identical formulation with the alterations from the 2000 statement marked in italics:

> 79. *The Conference notes the reaffirmation by the nuclear-weapon States of their* unequivocal undertaking to accomplish, *in accordance with the principle of irreversibility*, the total elimination of their nuclear arsenals leading to nuclear disarmament, to which all States parties are committed under article VI of the Treaty.[76]

Grammatically, the sentence is ambiguous as to whether the NWS have reaffirmed only 'their unequivocal undertaking', or the second clause of the sentence as well: 'to which all States parties are committed under article VI of the Treaty'. Although the legal significance of this discrepancy remains unclear, the interpretation proffered in both the 2000 and the 2010 Review Conference final documents arguably clarifies the scope and meaning of Article VI by recognising a positive disarmament obligation.

Turning to the substance of the term 'nuclear disarmament', this refers to the complete elimination of a class of weapons, as opposed to 'nuclear arms control', which encompasses arms reductions more generally.[77] Thus, while both 'nuclear arms control' and 'nuclear disarmament' may appear identical in the short term, the distinguishing factor is the long-term aim. Therefore, the ordinary meaning of the term 'nuclear disarmament' indicates that negotiations on nuclear arms reductions undertaken absent a policy goal of nuclear disarmament do not meet the obligation set out in Article VI.[78]

Looking to the United States as a case study, the present author has written previously about US compliance with Article VI during the decade 1998–2008.[79] At that time, the Bush Administration's nuclear arms reductions fell squarely

---

[76] 2010 Review Conference of the Parties to the Treaty on the Non-Proliferation of Nuclear Weapons, Final Document, 3 vols. NPT/CONF.2010/50(Part I), Vol. I, Part I, at p. 12, para. 79 (emphasis added).

[77] See, e.g. G. Bunn and R. Timerbaev, 'Nuclear disarmament: how much have the five nuclear powers promised in the Non-Proliferation Treaty?' in J. Rhinelander and A. Scheinman (eds.), *At the Nuclear Crossroads* (Washington DC: Lanham, University Press of America, 1995), p. 13 ('"Disarmament" can sometimes mean reductions short of zero. However, the ordinary meaning of "nuclear disarmament" clearly *includes* zero even if it also includes reductions short of zero. Therefore, the obligation to negotiate measures "relating to … nuclear disarmament" seems to include, among other things, zero' (emphasis added)).

[78] On NWS policies related to nuclear arms control, see C. Chyba and K. Sasikumar, 'A world of risk: the current environment for US nuclear weapons policy' in G. Bunn and C. Chyba (eds.), *US Nuclear Weapons Policy: Confronting Today's Threats* (Washington DC: Brookings Institution Press, 2006), pp. 11–19; R. Speed and M. May, 'Assessing the United States' nuclear posture' in G. Bunn and C. Chyba (eds.), *US Nuclear Weapons Policy: Confronting Today's Threats* (Washington DC: Brookings Institution Press, 2006), pp. 248–86.

[79] Joyner, *Interpreting the Nuclear Non-Proliferation Treaty*, pp. 69–74, 95–108.

within the definition of arms control, which this author criticised as falling short of states parties' obligations set out in Article VI, as these reductions were taken absent any policy goal of disarmament. Does the Obama Administration's shift in policy amount to effective measures relating to nuclear disarmament? The present author is persuaded that, regardless of the stated end goal, the extensive delays and fuzzy timeline amount to a continued breach of the United States' Article VI obligations relating to nuclear disarmament. However, it should be noted that there is considerable disagreement among scholars on how the absence of a specific timeline within the text for meeting the obligations of Article VI should be interpreted. This allows the NWS to claim that they are demonstrating a will towards compliance, but with little basis other than a change of rhetoric. Furthermore, modernisation of existing arsenals does not appear consistent with the obligation to 'undertake to pursue negotiations ... relating to nuclear disarmament'. The 2010 US Nuclear Posture Review's argument that modernisation actually *contributes* to disarmament by allowing for a reduction in the quantity of nuclear weapons needed[80] is disingenuous at best.

> Each of the Parties to the Treaty undertakes to pursue negotiations in good faith ... on a treaty on general and complete disarmament under strict and effective international control

Understanding the meaning of 'general and complete disarmament' demands recourse to the 'historical line' that preceded the NPT's drafting.[81] In his chapter on this precise topic, Randy Rydell describes how the concept of general and complete disarmament encompasses nuclear disarmament, as well as a variety of additional arms control measures.[82] The term was first used in a 1927 League of Nations proposal to refer to the elimination of all military activities and armaments.[83] In 1959 the UN General Assembly used the phrase in Resolution 1378, which 'put "general and complete disarmament" on the General Assembly's agenda, where it has been ever since.'[84] Resolution 1378 provides: '*The General Assembly* ... 3. *Expresses the hope* that measures leading

---

[80] United States Department of Defense, Nuclear Posture Review Report (April 2010), p. xv ('As the United States reduces the numbers of nuclear weapons, the reliability of the remaining weapons in the stockpile – and the quality of the facilities needed to sustain it – become more important') and p. 37 ('To sustain a safe, secure, and effective stockpile today, with the ultimate goal of a world free of nuclear weapons in the future, we must prudently manage our nuclear stockpile and related Life Extension Programs (LEPs), while cultivating the nuclear infrastructure, expert workforce, and leadership required to sustain it').

[81] See Gardiner, *Treaty Interpretation*, p. 101 (describing 'tracing a historical line' among the permissible uses of preparatory works to a treaty, consistent with VCLT, Art. 32).

[82] See R. Rydell, 'Nuclear disarmament and general and complete disarmament' in D. Krieger (ed.), *The Challenge of Abolishing Nuclear Weapons* (New Brunswick: Transaction Publishers, 2009). See also Bunn and Timerbaev, 'Nuclear disarmament'.

[83] Rydell, 'Nuclear disarmament and general and complete disarmament', pp. 228–9.

[84] *Ibid.*, p. 231.

towards the goal of general and complete disarmament under effective international control will be worked out in detail and agreed upon in the shortest
possible time.'[85]

In 1961 the UN Permanent Representative for the Union of Soviet Socialist
Republics (USSR), Valerian Aleksandrovich Zorin, and the Representative for
the United States, Adlai Stevenson, submitted a joint letter to the UN General
Assembly, outlining the two states' agreed principles for disarmament.[86] The
two UN Representatives explain general and complete disarmament (GCD)
as follows:

> The programme for general and complete disarmament shall ensure that
> States will have at their disposal only such non-nuclear armaments, forces,
> facilities and establishments as are agreed to be necessary to maintain
> internal order and protect the personal security of citizens; and that States
> shall support and provide agreed manpower for a United Nations peace
> force.[87]

The intended measures included, inter alia, the 'disbanding of armed forces',
the 'elimination of all stockpiles of ... weapons of mass destruction' including means of delivery, the closure of all military academies and '[t]he dis-
continuance of military expenditures'.[88] The two states envisioned that GCD
would proceed 'in an agreed sequence, by stages', each subject to 'specified time
limits'.[89] The letter echoes the call for GCD under 'strict and effective international control', under the aegis of the United Nations.[90] The scope and level
of ambition evident in this proposed plan reflects a concept of GCD that would
undoubtedly attract far less enthusiasm among the Permanent Members of the
UN Security Council today, yet it is nevertheless helpful as a historical road-
map to the phrase's origin.

The preamble to the 1965 UN General Assembly Resolution calling for the
negotiation of the NPT referred to GCD as well:

> Convinced that the proliferation of nuclear weapons would endanger the
> security of all States and make more difficult the achievement of general and
> complete disarmament under effective international control.[91]

---

[85] UN General Assembly Resolution 1378, UN doc. A/RES/14/1378, adopted on 20 November
1959 (emphasis added).
[86] UN General Assembly, Letter dated 20 September 1961 from the Permanent Representatives
of the Union of Soviet Socialist Republics and of the United States to the United Nations,
addressed to the President of the General Assembly, transmitting a report of their
Governments containing a joint statement of agreed principles for disarmament negotiations, UN doc. A/4879, 20 September 1961.
[87] Ibid., at 2, para. 2.   [88] Ibid., at 2, para. 3.
[89] Ibid., at 2, para. 4.   [90] Ibid., at 2, para. 6.
[91] UN General Assembly Resolution 2028, UN doc. A/RES/20/2028, adopted on 29
November 1965.

As the historical context suggests, in the 1950s and 1960s states understood GCD to refer to a path towards not only disarmament of weapons of mass destruction, but also conventional disarmament that, with the benefit of hindsight, comes across as wildly optimistic. What then is the legal significance of this phrase in the third clause of NPT Article VI?

The 2000 NPT RevCon Final Document contains a single reference to GCD, which consists only of a restatement of the phrase itself;[92] the phrase is absent from the 2010 NPT RevCon Final Document. Returning to VCLT Articles 31 and 32, therefore, both the ordinary meaning of the term and the absence of subsequent agreements on its precise definition leave significant ambiguity as to what such a treaty on GCD would require. Beyond a relatively recent UN press release urging states to take measures towards disarmament involving conventional arms,[93] references to GCD in the context of NPT Article VI add little in the way of substance to the understanding of this obligation.

This leaves one with the somewhat unsatisfying conclusion that the GCD obligation under NPT Article VI, although concrete in referring to a treaty under 'strict and effective international control', has otherwise been neglected as a specific, binding obligation on states parties, such that the dividing line between compliance and non-compliance remains blurry. The ordinary meaning of the term GCD has evidently evolved from the notion of full military disarmament outlined, for example, in the joint letter the US and USSR Permanent Representatives submitted to the General Assembly in 1961, but it is unclear what the term's ordinary meaning is today.

Given that the reference to GCD appears within the context of a treaty relating to nuclear weapons, however, one could make a plausible argument that the ordinary meaning of the term refers to the general and complete disarmament of nuclear weapons.

Conclusion

While disagreement persists regarding the precise nature and scope of the obligation in Article VI, there are a few legal conclusions we can draw with certainty. First, Article VI is a binding legal obligation, not a goal. Moreover, the duty to pursue negotiations 'in good faith' – a legal term with content and a

---

[92] See, e.g. 2000 Review Conference of the Parties to the Treaty on the Non-Proliferation of Nuclear Weapons, Final Document, 3 vols. NPT/CONF.2000/28(Part I), Vol. I, Part I, pp. 14–15, para. 15(11) ('Reaffirmation that the ultimate objective of the efforts of States in the disarmament process is general and complete disarmament under effective international control').

[93] UN Department of Public Information, UN Secretary-General, 'World must Stay Fixed on Ultimate Objective of General and Complete Disarmament; Deterrence Only Invites Endless Arms Races, Says Secretary-General', UN doc. SG/SM/13608, DC/3295, 31 May 2011.

body of established jurisprudence – indicates that efforts to merely pay lip service to the idea of negotiation do not suffice. The 2010 NPT Review Conference Final Document reflects this understanding, as well as an evolving interpretation of the nuclear disarmament obligation to not only require state parties to pursue negotiations, but in effect also to move toward complete nuclear disarmament in good faith.

The interpretation of the general and complete disarmament obligation remains disputed. However, the most important legal conclusion about the GCD obligation in Article VI, in my opinion, is that it has no bearing upon what is the most important obligation in Article VI – the obligation of all NPT parties to move toward complete nuclear weapons disarmament in good faith.

So in summary, on the question of NWS compliance with the NPT Article VI obligation relating to nuclear disarmament, the evidence proffered by NWS themselves to establish their compliance with this obligation appears to be incomplete and erroneously offered. Furthermore, even proceeding to an analysis of the question of whether there has been in the practice of the NWS the pursuit of negotiations in good faith on effective measures relating to nuclear disarmament, the present author argues that when compared to the actual state practice of NWS, each and all of the NPT NWS are in non-compliance with the Article VI obligation relating to nuclear disarmament.

17

Armed non-state actors and 'nuclear terrorism'

STUART CASEY-MASLEN

A nuclear bomb can be built with a relatively small amount of nuclear material. A trained nuclear engineer with an amount of highly enriched uranium or plutonium about the size of a grapefruit or an orange, together with commercially available material, could fashion a nuclear device that would fit in a van like the one Ramzi Yousef parked in the garage of the World Trade Center in 1993. Such a bomb would level Lower Manhattan.

9/11 Commission Report[1]

Introduction

Nuclear terrorism – defined as intentional participation in a potential or actual act of terrorism using nuclear or radioactive materials or devices[2] – is arguably the ultimate fear of many national intelligence and security forces. In one such scenario a non-state actor[3] somehow obtains a nuclear weapon and detonates it in a city, killing tens of thousands or even hundreds of thousands of people, also engendering humanitarian, political, economic and environmental havoc.[4] In his fanciful 1991 novel *The Sum of All Fears*, the late Tom Clancy imagined the Popular Front for the Liberation of Palestine using fissile material from a 'lost' Israeli nuclear weapon to kill the United States Secretaries of State for Defense and Foreign Affairs along with thousands of spectators at the Super Bowl. The aim, however, was not only to massacre as many people as possible with the

---

[1] The National Commission on Terrorist Attacks Upon the United States, *The 9/11 Commission Report*, 2004, p. 380.

[2] See 2005 International Convention on the Suppression of Acts of Nuclear Terrorism, adopted by the United Nations General Assembly on 13 April 2005, Art. 2.

[3] There is no definition under international law of a non-state actor, although in its Resolution 1540, discussed below, the UN Security Council included in a footnote that 'for the purpose of th[e] resolution only', the following definition applied: 'individual or entity, not acting under the lawful authority of any State in conducting activities which come within the scope of this resolution'.

[4] See, e.g., M. Levi, *On Nuclear Terrorism* (Cambridge, MA: Harvard University Press, 15 May 2009).

bomb's detonation, it was also intentionally to provoke a nuclear response or even a nuclear war. Indeed, the title of Clancy's novel relates not to the fear – already significant – of a first detonation, but of an ensuing nuclear war.[5]

A.   Nuclear terrorism using a nuclear weapon

But is an attack by means of a nuclear weapon by an armed non-state actor within the realm of the possible? Admittedly, such actors have used other weapons of mass destruction over the last twenty years. On 20 March 1995 members of a religious cult used chemical weapons in attacks on the Tokyo subway that could have killed thousands.[6] According to the 9/11 Commission Report, alarmed by the chemical attack in Tokyo, then US President Bill Clinton 'made it the very highest priority for his own staff and for all agencies to prepare to detect and respond to terrorism that involved chemical, biological, or nuclear weapons'.[7] Allegedly – but highly controversially – chemical weapons have been used by rebel groups during the ongoing armed conflict in Syria.[8] A biological weapon attack has also occurred: soon after the 11 September 2001 attacks on the United States by al-Qaeda, letters laced with anthrax began appearing in US mail. Five US citizens were killed and seventeen others were rendered sick in

---

[5] Accordingly, one of the stated military rationales for retaining and eventually using nuclear weapons – to be able to respond to a threat or a detonation by a terrorist group – could even be seen as an additional incentive to such groups to acquire nuclear material. In this regard, Nick Ritchie refers to 'strongman rhetoric' by Professor Colin Gray, an expert on International Politics and Strategic Studies at the University of Reading, given in evidence to the United Kingdom's House of Commons Defence Committee in 2006: 'I certainly would not want terrorists and those who support them to say they can use weapons of mass destruction against Britain and we will do our best with conventional weapons to bring the roof down on their heads. I would like them to know they are messing with a nuclear power'. N. Ritchie, *A Nuclear Weapons-Free World: Britain, Trident, and the Challenges Ahead* (Basingstoke: Palgrave Macmillan, 2012), p. 89. See also J. Miller, *Stockpile: The Story behind 10,000 Strategic Nuclear Weapons* (Annapolis: Naval Institute Press, 2010), pp. 216–17; See, e.g., R. Ayson, 'After a terrorist nuclear attack: envisaging catalytic effects', *Studies in Conflict and Terrorism* 33(7) (2010), 571–93.

[6] In June 2012 Japanese police arrested the final fugitive they were seeking in connection with the sarin nerve gas attack in the Tokyo subway system of 20 March 1995 by members of the Aum Shinrikyo doomsday cult. The attacks killed thirteen people and injured 6,000, but could have killed thousands if the sarin had been dispersed differently. See, e.g., 'Archive: Nerve gas attack shocks Tokyo', BBC, 15 June 2012, available at: www.bbc.co.uk/news/world-asia-18455007; and 'Terror in Tokyo: the overview', *New York Times*, available at: www.nytimes.com/learning/general/onthisday/big/0320.html.

[7] The National Commission on Terrorist Attacks Upon the United States, *The 9/11 Commission Report*, 2004, p. 101.

[8] See, e.g., 'Russia will give UN "proof" of Syria rebel chemical use', BBC, 18 September 2013, available at: www.bbc.co.uk/news/world-middle-east-24140475.

what became the worst biological attacks in US history.[9] Although small-scale in terms of casualties in the grand scheme of things, the potential for harm is staggering. In March 2013 a senior United Kingdom counterterrorism official claimed that extremists had ever greater access to the information and technology required to create and spread germ agents or other biological weapons.[10]

In 1997 a group of Los Alamos weapons designers published an oft-cited article, 'Can Terrorists Build Nuclear Weapons?'[11] They discussed whether a terrorist group could build either a 'crude' nuclear weapon[12] or a more 'sophisticated' (and more powerful) device. A crude design (known euphemistically to weapons designers as a 'fizzle')[13] is one in which either of the methods successfully demonstrated in 1945 – the gun type and the implosion type – is applied. In the gun type, a subcritical piece of fissile material (the projectile) is fired rapidly into another subcritical piece (the target) such that the final assembly is supercritical without a change in the density of the material. In the implosion type, a near-critical piece of fissile material is compressed by a converging shock wave resulting from the detonation of a surrounding layer of high explosive and becomes supercritical because of its increase in density.[14] By 'sophisticated' nuclear device, they meant one 'with a diameter of about 1 or 2 feet and a weight of one hundred to a few hundred pounds, so that it is readily transportable (for example, in the trunk of a standard car)'.[15] While not minimising the risks of a more sophisticated nuclear weapon, they imply that the likelihood of a terrorist group being able to construct one is significantly less than one might fear:

> Merely on the basis of the fact that sophisticated devices are known to be feasible, it cannot be asserted that by stealing only a small amount of fissile material a terrorist would be able to produce a device with a reliable multikiloton yield in such a small size and weight as to be easy to transport and conceal. Such an assertion ignores at least a significant fraction of the

---

[9] US Federal Bureau of Investigations (FBI), 'Amerithrax or Anthrax Investigation', undated but accessed on 17 October 2010 at: www.fbi.gov/about-us/history/famous-cases/anthrax-amerithrax/amerithrax-investigation. The ensuing investigation by the FBI and its partners – code-named 'Amerithrax' – was one of the largest and most complex in the history of law enforcement.

[10] J. Kirkup, 'Biological attacks "getting easier for terrorists"', *Daily Telegraph*, 26 March 2013, available at: www.telegraph.co.uk/news/uknews/terrorism-in-the-uk/9955007/Biological-attacks-getting-easier-for-terrorists.html.

[11] C. Mark, T. Taylor, E. Eyster, W. Maraman, and J. Wechsler, 'Can Terrorists Build Nuclear Weapons?', Paper Prepared for the International Task Force on the Prevention of Nuclear Terrorism, Nuclear Control Institute, Washington DC, 1996, available at: www.nci.org/k-m/makeab.htm.

[12] *Ibid.*

[13] J. Bernstein, *Nuclear Weapons: What You Need to Know* (New York: Cambridge University Press, 2010), p. 258.

[14] Mark *et al.*, 'Can Terrorists Build Nuclear Weapons?'   [15] *Ibid.*

problems that weapons laboratories have had to face and resolve over the past forty years ...

For persons new to this business, as it may be supposed a terrorist group is, there is a great deal to learn before they could entertain any confidence that some small, sophisticated device they might build would perform as desired. To build the device would require a long course of study and a long course of hydrodynamic experimentation. To achieve the size and weight of a modern weapon while maintaining performance and confidence in performance would require one or more full-scale nuclear tests, although considerable progress in that direction could be made on the basis of non-nuclear experiments.[16]

They conclude that the production of sophisticated devices 'should not be considered to be a possible activity for a fly-by-night terrorist group', finding such a scenario conceivable only in the context of a 'nationally supported program able to provide the necessary resources and facilities and an established working place over the time required'. They do caution, though, that 'under the sponsorship of some malevolent regime, a team schooled and prepared in such a setting could be dispatched anywhere to acquire material and produce a device'. But the terrorist group 'would still have to obtain and set up the equipment needed for the reduction to metal and its subsequent handling and to spend the time necessary to go through those operations'.[17]

Others have argued that 'it is a relatively trivial challenge to make a gun-type weapon, like the Hiroshima bomb, from fresh weapons-grade HEU [highly enriched uranium] in metal form'.[18] According to the US Nuclear Control Institute, although the 9/11 attacks provided a 'wake-up call', a solid basis for concern existed long before:

It is ... clear that bin Laden was seeking nuclear explosive materials (plutonium or highly enriched uranium) and know-how for building atomic bombs, and other dangerous nuclear materials for use in 'dirty bombs' to spread radioactive contamination with conventional high explosives.[19]

In this regard, the 9/11 Commission Report cited testimony in February 2004 by George Tenet, the then Central Intelligence Agency (CIA) Director, who

[16] *Ibid.* [17] *Ibid.*

[18] L. Kirkham with A. J. Kuperman, 'Protecting US Nuclear Facilities from Terrorist Attack: Re-assessing the Current "Design Basis Threat" Approach', Working Paper 1, Nuclear Proliferation Prevention Project, University of Texas at Austin, 15 August 2013, p. 6. Weapons-grade HEU is generally defined as HEU enriched in the isotope of uranium-235 at 90 per cent or greater, although the HEU in the Hiroshima bomb had an average enrichment of only 80 per cent. US Government Auditing Office, *Nuclear Nonproliferation: US Agencies Have Limited Ability to Account for, Monitor, and Evaluate the Security of US Nuclear Material Overseas*, GAO-11-920 Washington DC, 2011, p. 2.

[19] Nuclear Control Institute, 'Nuclear Terrorism – How To Prevent It, Introduction', undated but accessed at: www.nci.org/nci-nt.htm#intro on 17 October 2013.

in the public portion of his worldwide threat assessment to the US Congress noted that Bin Laden considered the acquisition of weapons of mass destruction to be a 'religious obligation'.[20] He warned that al-Qaeda 'continues to pursue its strategic goal of obtaining a nuclear capability'. According to the 9/11 Commission Report, Khalid Sheikh Mohammed admitted that he considered targeting a nuclear power plant as part of his initial proposal for the planes operation and claimed that Mohammed Atta included a nuclear plant in his preliminary target list, but claimed that Bin Laden decided to drop that idea.[21] Tenet also asserted that 'more than two dozen other terrorist groups are pursuing CBRN [chemical, biological, radiological and nuclear] materials'.[22]

In late April 2011 the British newspaper, the *Daily Telegraph*, citing top-secret documents, referred to claims by Khalid Sheikh Mohammed during his interrogation at Guantánamo Bay whereby if Osama bin Laden were captured or killed by the USA, an al-Qaeda sleeper cell would detonate a 'weapon of mass destruction' in Europe, in a 'nuclear hell-storm'.[23] Further, according to the WikiLeaks files, a Libyan detainee, Abu Al-Libi, was said to have 'knowledge of al-Qaeda possibly possessing a nuclear bomb'. Sharif al-Masri, an Egyptian captured in 2004, allegedly claimed that Al-Libi had said the nuclear bomb's operatives 'would be Europeans of Arab or Asian descent'. The notes show that US interrogators spent large amounts of time trying to establish whether al-Qaeda had access to nuclear material.[24] Bin Laden was of course killed by a team of US Seals in Abbottabad, Pakistan, a week after the newspaper's exclusive.

B.   Other forms of nuclear terrorism

Although theft of a complete nuclear weapon has not been reported, there are confirmed cases of theft of weapons-usable material.[25] The International Atomic Energy Agency (IAEA) reported eighteen seizures of stolen HEU or plutonium in 1993–2007, but most of these cases involved very small quantities. Indeed, according to one analyst, 'if you add up all the reported attempts to sell highly enriched uranium or plutonium, even including those that have

---

[20] Testimony of George Tenet, 'The Worldwide Threat 2004: Challenges in a Changing Global Context', before the US Senate Select Committee on Intelligence, 24 February 2004; see also *9/11 Commission Report*, 2004, p. 380.

[21] *9/11 Commission Report*, 2004, Chapter 12, endnote 148.

[22] Testimony of George Tenet, 'The Worldwide Threat 2004: Challenges in a Changing Global Context'.

[23] H. Watt, 'Wikileaks: Al-Qaeda plotted chemical and nuclear attack on the West', *Daily Telegraph*, 26 April 2011, available at: www.telegraph.co.uk/news/worldnews/wikileaks/8472810/Wikileaks-Al-Qaeda-plotted-chemical-and-nuclear-attack-on-the-West.html.

[24] *Ibid.*

[25] Kirkham with Kuperman, 'Protecting US Nuclear Facilities from Terrorist Attack;', p. 5.

the scent of security-agency hype and those where the material was of uncertain quality, the total amount of material still falls short of what a bomb-maker would need to construct a single explosive.[26] (This does not, though, account for undetected cases of theft.)[27]

So if the likelihood of a terrorist group procuring or building a nuclear weapon is generally considered to be remote, the risk of one gaining access to sufficient fissile material to create a dirty bomb[28] and then detonating it is far higher. According to the IAEA, 'the radioactive materials needed to build a "dirty bomb" can be found in almost any country in the world, and more than 100 countries may have inadequate control and monitoring programs necessary to prevent or even detect the theft of these materials.'[29] The IAEA cite an incident when Chechen rebels placed a container of caesium-137 in a Moscow park in 1996 and then alerted reporters, but the device was not detonated.[30] Particular concerns also remain as to the risks of trafficking of nuclear materials. Security Council Resolution 1540 had called upon 'all States, in accordance with their national legal authorities and legislation and consistent with international law, to take cooperative action to prevent illicit trafficking in nuclear, chemical or biological weapons, their means of delivery, and related materials'.[31]

Another fear that continues to be expressed is a possible attack – suicide or other – on a nuclear power plant. According to the US Nuclear Control Institute:

> Trial testimony has revealed that Osama bin Laden's al Qaeda training camps offered instruction in urban warfare against enemies' installations

---

[26] B. Keller, 'Nuclear Nightmares', New York Times, 26 May 2002, available at: www.nytimes.com/2002/05/26/magazine/nuclear-nightmares.html?pagewanted=all&src=pm.

[27] Ibid., and see Kirkham with Kuperman, 'Protecting US Nuclear Facilities from Terrorist Attack', p. 5.

[28] As noted in the Introduction to this book, a dirty bomb is not a nuclear weapon but a conventional munition accompanied by radioactive material that is dispersed over a wide area upon detonation of the bomb. No nuclear fission or fusion occurs during this process.

[29] IAEA, 'Inadequate Control of the World's Radioactive Sources', undated, p. 1, available at: www.iaea.org/newscenter/features/radsources/rads_factsheet.pdf.

[30] Ibid., p. 2; and see Kirkham with Kuperman, 'Protecting US Nuclear Facilities from Terrorist Attack'.

[31] Resolution 1540 (2004), Operative Paragraph 10. Such 'related materials' were defined in a footnote in the Resolution (again, for the purpose of the Resolution only) as 'materials, equipment and technology covered by relevant multilateral treaties and arrangements, or included on national control lists, which could be used for the design, development, production or use of nuclear, chemical and biological weapons and their means of delivery'. Dan Joyner argues that under customary international law there exists an international crime of nuclear materials and commodities-smuggling. D. H. Joyner, 'Nuclear Materials and Commodities Smuggling, and International Criminal Law', NAPSNet Special Reports, 10 November 2011, available at: http://nautilus.org/napsnet/napsnet-special-reports/nuclear-materials-and-commodities-smuggling-and-international-criminal-law/.

including power plants. It is prudent to assume, especially after the highly coordinated, surprise attacks on the World Trade Center and the Pentagon, that bin Laden's soldiers have done their homework and are fully capable of attacking nuclear plants for maximum effect.[32]

In August 2013 a report by the Nuclear Proliferation Prevention Project (NPPP) at the University of Texas at Austin discussed 'radiological sabotage' of nuclear facilities by, inter alia, aircraft attacks, vehicle bombs, anti-tank weapons or the disabling of pumps.[33] The authors cited analysis by a member of the Union of Concerned Scientists of the consequences of an attack on the Indian Point nuclear power plant located 35 miles from New York City. It was claimed that an attack that resulted in a core meltdown and a large radiological release into the environment could cause 44,000 deaths in the short term and a further 500,000 deaths over the long term from radiation along with US$2 trillion in economic damage.[34]

The USA's Nuclear Regulatory Commission, the independent government agency charged with regulating the civilian use of nuclear materials, has required future power reactors to be designed to address attacks by commercial aircraft, but existing reactors are not obliged to make retrofits to do so.[35] The NPPP report concluded that although in 2001–10 the US nuclear industry spent a total of more than US$2 billion on security enhancements to the physical protection systems of nuclear power plants, 'it is difficult to know if those enhancements have been adequate'.[36]

C.   The international legal regimes governing nuclear terrorism

1.   UN Security Council Resolution 1540

The treaty regime prohibiting armed non-state actors' access to nuclear weapons and material is fragmented and often overlapping. As a result of US concern, on 28 April 2004 the United Nations Security Council, acting under Chapter VII of the 1945 UN Charter, adopted Resolution 1540 without a vote,[37] in which it affirmed that the proliferation of nuclear, chemical and biological

---

[32] Nuclear Control Institute, 'Nuclear Terrorism – How To Prevent It, Introduction'.

[33] Kirkham with Kuperman, 'Protecting US Nuclear Facilities from Terrorist Attack'.

[34] E. S. Lyman, 'Chernobyl on the Hudson? The Health and Economic Impacts of a Terrorist Attack at the Indian Point Nuclear Plant', Report Prepared for Riverkeeper, Inc., US, September 2004, pp. 5–6.

[35] M. Holt and A. Andrews, 'Nuclear Power Plant Security and Vulnerabilities', Report No. RL34331, Congressional Research Service, 23 August 2010, p. 5, available at: www.fas.org/sgp/crs/homesec/RL34331.pdf.

[36] Kirkham with Kuperman, 'Protecting US Nuclear Facilities from Terrorist Attack', p. 17.

[37] Resolution 1540 (2004), adopted by the Security Council at its 4956th meeting, on 28 April 2004.

weapons and their means of delivery[38] constitute a threat to international peace and security[39] and obliged all states to:

> refrain from providing any form of support to non-State actors that attempt to develop, acquire, manufacture, possess, transport, transfer or use nuclear, chemical or biological weapons and their means of delivery.[40]

The Resolution's adoption followed months of negotiations. The initiative had been outlined in September 2003 by US President George W. Bush in his speech to the UN General Assembly in which he called for a Security Council resolution that would 'call on all members of the UN to criminalize the proliferation of weapons of mass destruction, to enact strict export controls consistent with international standards, and to secure any and all sensitive materials within their own borders'.[41]

Thus, in the Resolution the Council also decided that:

> all States, in accordance with their national procedures, shall adopt and enforce appropriate effective laws which prohibit any non-State actor to manufacture, acquire, possess, develop, transport, transfer or use nuclear, chemical or biological weapons and their means of delivery, in particular for terrorist purposes, as well as attempts to engage in any of the foregoing activities, participate in them as an accomplice, assist or finance them.[42]

In total (depending on how they are counted) the Resolution creates more than 200 legally binding obligations for each state, covering specific proliferation-related activities that 'cut across the formerly distinct realms of proliferation of nuclear, chemical, and biological weapons and their means of delivery'.[43]

The Resolution makes it explicit that none of the obligations it sets out shall conflict with or alter the rights and obligations of states parties to, inter alia, the 1968 Treaty on the Non-Proliferation of Nuclear Weapons (NPT),[44] while recognising 'the urgent need for all States to take additional effective measures to prevent the proliferation of nuclear, chemical or biological weapons and their means of delivery'.[45] Under Article I of the NPT, each nuclear weapon state

---

[38] Means of delivery are defined 'for the purpose of this resolution only' as 'missiles, rockets and other unmanned systems capable of delivering nuclear, chemical, or biological weapons, that are specially designed for such use'.

[39] Resolution 1540 (2004), first preambular paragraph.

[40] Resolution 1540 (2004), Operative Paragraph 1.

[41] Cited in P. Crail, 'Report: Implementing UN Security Council Resolution 1540, A Risk-Based Approach', *Nonproliferation Review* 13(2) (July 2006), 355–99, at 356.

[42] Resolution 1540 (2004), Operative Paragraph 2.

[43] R. T. Cupitt, 'Nearly at the Brink: The Tasks and Capacity of the 1540 Committee', *Arms Control Today*, September 2012, available at: www.armscontrol.org/act/2012_09/Nearly-at-the-Brink-The-Tasks-and-Capacity-Of-the-1540-Committee.

[44] Resolution 1540 (2004), Operative Paragraph 5.

[45] Resolution 1540 (2004), twelfth preambular paragraph.

party undertakes 'not to transfer *to any recipient whatsoever* nuclear weapons or other nuclear explosive devices or control over such weapons or explosive devices directly, or indirectly', but the subsequent obligation is 'not in any way to assist, encourage, or induce any non-nuclear-weapon *State* to manufacture or otherwise acquire nuclear weapons or other nuclear explosive devices, or control over such weapons or explosive devices'.[46] Indeed, according to the US Department of State, the Resolution 'closes gaps in non-proliferation treaties and conventions to help prevent terrorists and criminal organizations from obtaining the world's most dangerous weapons'.[47]

A 1540 Committee, which functions as a subsidiary body of the Security Council, was established to promote effective implementation of the Resolution. Its mandate was extended first for two years by Council Resolution 1673 (2006) and then for a further three years by Resolution 1810 (2008). On 20 April 2011 the Security Council adopted Resolution 1977, which extends the mandate of the 1540 Committee for a period of ten years to 2021.[48] The Resolution provides for two comprehensive reviews, one after five years (i.e. in 2016) and a second before the end of the mandate 'prior to the renewal of its mandate'.[49] In its current Programme of Work (2013–14), which is renewed annually, the Committee, together with its four working groups, was planning to focus its attention on (a) monitoring and national implementation; (b) assistance; (c) cooperation with international organisations, including the Security Council Committees established pursuant to Resolutions 1267 (1999)[50] and 1373 (2001);[51] and

---

[46] Article I, NPT (emphasis added).

[47] US Department of State, 'UN Security Council Resolution 1540', undated but accessed on 17 October 2013 at: www.state.gov/t/isn/c18943.htm.

[48] Resolution 1977 (2011), adopted by the Security Council at its 6518th meeting on 20 April 2011, Operative Paragraph 2.

[49] Resolution 1977 (2011), Operative Paragraph 3.

[50] In the Resolution, the Security Council 'insist[ed] that the Afghan faction known as the Taliban, which also calls itself the Islamic Emirate of Afghanistan ... cease the provision of sanctuary and training for international terrorists and their organizations, take appropriate effective measures to ensure that the territory under its control is not used for terrorist installations and camps, or for the preparation or organization of terrorist acts against other States or their citizens, and cooperate with efforts to bring indicted terrorists to justice'. It further 'demand[ed] that the Taliban turn over Usama bin Laden without further delay to appropriate authorities in a country where he has been indicted, or to appropriate authorities in a country where he will be returned to such a country, or to appropriate authorities in a country where he will be arrested and effectively brought to justice'. Security Council Resolution 1267 (1999), Operative Paragraphs 1 and 2.

[51] Under Resolution 1373, the Council decided that all States should prevent and suppress the financing of terrorism, as well as criminalise the wilful provision or collection of funds for such acts. The funds, financial assets and economic resources of those who commit or attempt to commit terrorist acts or participate in or facilitate the commission of terrorist acts and of persons and entities acting on behalf of terrorists should also be frozen without delay. States should also ensure that terrorist acts are established as serious criminal

(d) transparency and media outreach.[52] For the UN Secretary-General, the Committee 'has a key role to play in ensuring that the world is a safe place and in allowing people in every country to pursue their lives free of fear of catastrophic attack by non-State actors'.[53]

Not everyone has been so positive about the Resolution or its implementation regime, however. As Crail noted in 2006:

> Even as a Security Council resolution, 1540 is not immune to the challenge of a lack of political will, a hindrance that many attribute to the current problematic state of nonproliferation norms in general. The threat of WMD terrorism and illicit trafficking is not a priority for many states, and there is some political opposition to the role of the Security Council in responding to this threat. Members of the Non-Aligned Movement (NAM) have expressed their concern about both the notion that the Security Council has now dictated domestic law for UN members, as well as the adoption of international obligations to nonproliferation outside the traditional negotiation process. Pakistan has been one of the resolution's more vocal critics in spite of voting in favor of its adoption. It not only expressed concerns during the negotiation process, but it has continued to express reservations since its adoption, including its belief that, 'the Security Council is not an appropriate body to deal with the issue of non-proliferation'.[54]

Nonetheless, as Masterson observes, the extension of the 1540 Committee's mandate for ten years from 2011 suggests that criticisms of the Resolution's sole focus on non-proliferation without adequate emphasis on disarmament and fear that the Resolution might be used to justify sanctions and other forms of coercion for states that did not adequately comply with the Resolution have been 'generally alleviated'.[55] Indeed, originally intended as a temporary

---

offences in domestic laws and regulations and that the seriousness of such acts is reflected in sentences served. Also under the Resolution, the Council established a Committee of the Council to monitor the Resolution's implementation and called on all states to report on actions they had taken to that end no later than ninety days thereafter.

[52] Programme of work of the Security Council Committee established pursuant to Resolution 1540 (2004) for the period from 1 June 2013 to 31 May 2014, para. 6, annexed to Letter dated 31 May 2013 from the Chair of the Security Council Committee established pursuant to Resolution 1540 (2004) addressed to the President of the Security Council, UN doc. S/2013/327.

[53] Remarks at Dinner hosted by the Permanent Representative of Saudi Arabia on the Occasion of the High-Level Event on Security Council Resolution 1540 (2004), New York, 10 December 2012, available at: www.un.org/zh/sc/1540/docs/Secretary_General_Statement_on_1540.pdf.

[54] Crail, 'Report: Implementing UN Security Council Resolution 1540', 359.

[55] K. E. Masterson, 'UN Security Council Resolution 1540 at a Glance', Arms Control Association, US, October 2012, available at: www.armscontrol.org/factsheets/1540. Reportedly, the ten-year period was a compromise between states favouring a traditional, short-term renewal and those who hoped to extend the Committee's mandate indefinitely.

committee to collect states' implementation reports and provide a summary report to the Security Council, 'the 1540 Committee has evolved into a more permanent body charged with collecting information on best practices, sharing information and outreach, and matching states' needs with offers of assistance.'[56]

2. The treaty regime

In addition to Security Council Resolution 1540 and other related Council resolutions, a series of treaties address the threat from nuclear terrorism.[57] There is considerable overlap between them, but perhaps the most comprehensive is the 2005 International Convention for the Suppression of Acts of Nuclear Terrorism (hereafter, the Nuclear Terrorism Convention). An Ad Hoc Committee commenced its work on the draft Convention in 1998, based on a text presented by the Russian Federation,[58] which culminated with the adoption of the Convention by the UN General Assembly on 13 April 2005, and its opening for signature on 14 September 2005. The Convention entered into force on 7 July 2007, in accordance with its Article 25(1), and as of October 2013 a total of eighty-eight states were party to it.

Delays in its adoption were, in part, due to the challenge of adopting a definition of nuclear terrorism. Given the obstacles in this regard in other negotiating fora (notably with respect to the draft Comprehensive Convention on

---

P. Crail, 'UN Bolsters WMD Nonproliferation Body', *Arms Control Today*, May 2011, available at: www.armscontrol.org.

[56] C. J. Harvey, 'Two Steps Forward, One Step Back: Slow, But Steady Progress Implementing UNSCR 1540', Nuclear Threat Initiative, 20 July 2011, available at: www.nti.org/analysis/articles/unscr-1540/.

[57] In particular the 1997 International Convention for the Suppression of Terrorist Bombings and the 1979 Convention on the Physical Protection of Nuclear Material, signed at Vienna and New York on 3 March 1980, and its 2005 amendment, which obliges States Parties to protect nuclear facilities and material in peaceful domestic use, storage, as well as transport. It also provides for expanded cooperation between and among states regarding rapid measures to locate and recover stolen or smuggled nuclear material, mitigate any radiological consequences of sabotage, and prevent and combat-related offences. The amendment has not yet entered into force. The amendments will take effect once they have been ratified by two-thirds of the states parties to the 1979 Convention. Fewer than half had done so as of October 2013.

[58] Russia introduced the Treaty in 1998 in response to the looming risks of nuclear materials falling into the hands of terrorist organisations as a result of the collapse of the Soviet Union. R. Dopplick, 'UN Adopts Nuclear Terrorism Treaty', International Law Blog Postings, Inside Justice, 19 April 2005, availablte at: www.insidejustice.com/intl/2005/06/19/un_adopts_treaty_on_nuclear_terrorism/. See also R. Perera, 'International Convention for the Suppression of Acts of Nuclear Terrorism', UN Audiovisual Library of International Law, undated but accessed on 15 October 2013 at: http://legal.un.org/avl/ha/icsant/icsant.html.

International Terrorism), the definition set out in Article 2 of the Convention is worth reproducing in full:

1. Any person commits an offence within the meaning of this Convention if that person unlawfully and intentionally:
    (a) Possesses radioactive material or makes or possesses a device:
        (i) With the intent to cause death or serious bodily injury; or
        (ii) With the intent to cause substantial damage to property or the environment;
    (b) Uses in any way radioactive material or a device, or uses or damages a nuclear facility in a manner which releases or risks the release of radioactive material:
        (i) With the intent to cause death or serious bodily injury; or
        (ii) With the intent to cause substantial damage to property or the environment; or
        (iii) With the intent to compel a natural or legal person, an international organization or a State to do or refrain from doing an act.
2. Any person also commits an offence if that person:
    (a) Threatens, under circumstances which indicate the credibility of the threat, to commit an offence as set forth in subparagraph 1(b) of the present article; or
    (b) Demands unlawfully and intentionally radioactive material, a device or a nuclear facility by threat, under circumstances which indicate the credibility of the threat, or by use of force.
3. Any person also commits an offence if that person attempts to commit an offence as set forth in paragraph 1 of the present article.
4. Any person also commits an offence if that person:
    (a) Participates as an accomplice in an offence as set forth in paragraph 1, 2 or 3 of the present article; or
    (b) Organizes or directs others to commit an offence as set forth in paragraph 1, 2 or 3 of the present article; or
    (c) In any other way contributes to the commission of one or more offences as set forth in paragraph 1, 2 or 3 of the present article by a group of persons acting with a common purpose; such contribution shall be intentional and either be made with the aim of furthering the general criminal activity or purpose of the group or be made in the knowledge of the intention of the group to commit the offence or offences concerned.

Thus 'unlawful and intentional' possession, use or threat of use of radioactive material or a device, or actual or threatened use or damage of a nuclear facility, as well as complicity in such acts, are all criminalised acts.

Another major negotiating challenge concerned the legality of the threat or use of nuclear weapons by states. Some states argued that since nuclear material and nuclear reactors are in the possession or control of states, the legality of the use or threat of use of nuclear weapons should be adequately addressed and, consequently, acts of state actors should be brought within the scope of the proposed convention. Others, however, asserted that the terrorism conventions were of a law enforcement nature, exclusively focused on the individual criminal responsibility of persons for specific acts of a terrorist nature, carefully excluding from their scope any question of state responsibility, which was regulated by other principles of international law. The position with regard to the Nuclear Terrorism Convention, they contended, could not be any different.[59]

The issue was finally resolved on the basis of a package comprising a preambular paragraph and an operative provision. Thus the preamble to the Convention notes 'that the activities of military forces of States are governed by rules of international law outside the framework of this Convention and that the exclusion of certain actions from the coverage of this Convention does not condone or make lawful otherwise unlawful acts, or preclude prosecutions under other laws'.[60] Within the text of the Convention itself, Article 4(4), following a proposal by Mexico, provided that:

> This Convention does not address, nor can it be interpreted as addressing, in any way, the issue of the legality of the use or threat of use of nuclear weapons by States.[61]

D. International humanitarian law and armed non-state actors

Today it is widely accepted that international humanitarian law (IHL) applies directly to armed non-state actors. This includes the protection provisions set out in Common Article 3 to the 1949 Geneva Conventions and customary and conventional rules governing the conduct of hostilities. In *Nicaragua* v. *United States of America*, for example, the International Court of Justice (ICJ) affirmed that Common Article 3 was applicable to the Contras, the non-state armed group fighting the government:

> The conflict between the contras' forces and those of the Government of Nicaragua is an armed conflict which is 'not of an international character'. The acts of the contras towards the Nicaraguan Government are therefore governed by the law applicable to conflicts of that character.[62]

---

[59] Perera, 'International Convention for the Suppression of Acts of Nuclear Terrorism'.

[60] Preambular paragraph 13. The provision was based on a similar provision in the 1997 Terrorist Bombings Convention, which excluded from its scope the activities of military forces of states.

[61] Similar issues relating to the scope of applicability of the Convention, addressing the question of responsibility of state actors in respect of acts of terrorism, and the exclusion of military forces of states from the scope of the Convention have resurfaced in the context of the ongoing negotiations on the draft Comprehensive Convention on International Terrorism. Perera, 'International Convention for the Suppression of Acts of Nuclear Terrorism'.

[62] ICJ, *Nicaragua* v. *United States of America*, 1986, para. 219.

The precise means by which international law binds non-state actors is, though, more debated. In 2004 the Appeals Chamber of the Special Court for Sierra Leone (SCSL) simply held, without offering any supporting evidence, that 'it is well settled that all parties to an armed conflict, whether states or non-state actors, are bound by international humanitarian law, even though only states may become parties to international treaties'.[63]

Several legal arguments have been advanced to explain why (or how) armed non-state actors are bound by certain international norms.[64] The first argument is based on the wording of Common Article 3, which states that it is directly binding on 'each Party to the conflict' – widely assumed to include non-state actors. A drawback of this approach is that it implies that where a treaty does not use such language, such as is the case with 1977 Additional Protocol II, it is not binding on a non-state actor that is party to the conflict.

According to another approach, customary international humanitarian law binds armed actors that are party to an armed conflict. Common Article 3 is also considered declaratory of customary international law and therefore applicable to each party to a conflict without formal ratification.[65]

A third approach, known as the doctrine of legislative jurisdiction, asserts that the rules of IHL bind any private individuals, including armed groups, through domestic law, via implementation of these rules into national legislation or direct applicability of self-executing norms.[66] This theory is, though, problematic, since what is at stake is not the fact that armed groups are subjects of domestic law but the direct regulation of the acts of such groups under international law.[67]

[63] SCSL, *Prosecutor* v. *Sam Hinga Norman*, Case No. SCSL-2004-14-AR72(E)), Decision on Preliminary Motion Based on Lack of Jurisdiction (Child Recruitment), Decision of 31 May 2004, para. 22.

[64] See, e.g., A. Bellal *et al.*, 'International law and armed non-state actors in Afghanistan', *International Review of the Red Cross* 93(881) (March 2011), 47–79.

[65] Thus, e.g., it has been asserted that 'there is now no doubt that this article [Common Article 3] is binding on states and insurgents alike, and that insurgents are subject to international humanitarian law … [a] convincing theory is that [insurgents] are bound as a matter of customary international law to observe the obligations declared by Common Article 3 which is aimed at the protection of humanity'. SCSL, *Prosecutor* v. *Morris Kallon and Brima Buzzy Kamara*, SCSL-2004–15-AR72(E) and SCSL-2004-16-AR72(E), Decision on Challenge to Jurisdiction: Lomé Accord Amnesty, Appeals Chamber, 13 March 2004, paras. 45–7.

[66] Yves Sandoz, Christophe Swinarski and Bruno Zimmermann (eds.), *Commentary on the Additional Protocols of 8 June 1977 to the Geneva Conventions of 12 August 1949* (Geneva: International Committee of the Red Cross (ICRC), Dordrecht: Martinus Nijhoff Publishers, 1987), p. 1345; Sandesh Sivakumaran, 'Binding armed opposition groups', *International and Comparative Law Quarterly* 55 (2006), 369–94, at 381.

[67] See, in this regard, Antonio Cassese, 'The status of rebels under the 1977 Geneva Protocol on Non-international Armed Conflicts', *International and Comparative Law Quarterly* 30(2) (1981), 416–39, at 429.

A fourth approach is based on the general principles governing the binding nature of treaties on third parties under the 1969 Vienna Convention on the Law of Treaties. This would entail enquiry into the intention of the contracting states to impose duties on third parties and that the parties consent to be bound. However, this approach can easily be challenged on the ground that the Convention only addresses treaties between states creating obligations for other (third) states.

Fifth, one can consider that, when armed groups exercise effective power over persons or territory of a state, they are bound by that state's obligations.[68] This claim is unpersuasive, though, as Common Article 3 – in contrast to 1977 Additional Protocol II – does not require territorial control for applicability and, as Moir points out, not every group seeks to replace the state.[69]

Conclusion

Although spread across treaties and UN Security Council resolutions, today the normative framework prohibiting armed non-state actors access to, and use of, nuclear material for terrorism is sufficiently detailed and far-reaching. In 2007 Christopher Joyner argued while the Nuclear Terrorism Convention 'emerges as a necessary component of the legal regime to counter terrorist activities, it is not sufficient. The Convention articulates new norms for international behaviour by individual persons, it establishes international legal rules to support those norms, and it imposes on states duties to execute those rules. Still, paper norms do not resolve real world threats.'[70] He rightly notes that it is effective government policy, political will and international cooperation that will determine whether the 'sum of all fears' is to be successfully avoided.

---

[68] According to the ICRC, 'The obligation resting on the Party to the conflict which represents established authority is not open to question … [I]f the responsible authority at their head exercises effective sovereignty, it is bound by the very fact that it claims to represent the country, or part of the country.' Jean S. Pictet (ed.), *The Geneva Conventions of 12 August 1949: Commentary, Fourth Geneva Convention Relative to the Protection of Civilian Persons in Time of War* (Geneva: ICRC, 1958), p. 37.

[69] Lindsay Moir, *The Law of Internal Armed Conflict* (Cambridge University Press, 2002), pp. 55–6.

[70] C. C. Joyner, 'Countering nuclear terrorism: a conventional response', *European Journal of International Law* 18(2) (2007), 225–51, at 251.

PART VI

International human rights law

18

Human rights law and nuclear weapons

LOUISE DOSWALD-BECK

Introduction

Although the possible use of nuclear weapons is primarily discussed in the light of international humanitarian law (IHL), and their possession under disarmament and arms control law, there is no doubt that international human rights law (HRL) is directly relevant also. The existence of international human rights enforcement mechanisms means that the adverse effects of these weapons are directly justiciable. Both the European and Inter-American human rights courts have heard cases relating to armed conflicts and the African court is likely to do so too. The quasi-judicial committees set up under the United Nations human rights treaties, which hear both state reports and individual petitions, are also significant. All human rights treaty texts require states to ensure that violations do not take place, including through positive preventive measures. In this light it is significant that most states have included international human rights standards in their constitutions and national legislation. Human rights treaty bodies are required, by virtue of their mandate, to apply the human rights listed within their respective treaties. They have not hesitated to do so for cases relating to hostilities during armed conflict. Human rights violations are also subject to the scrutiny of UN Charter bodies, such as the Human Rights Council, the General Assembly and the Security Council, as well as similar regional bodies. The result is that it is impossible to consider nuclear weapons without analysing their possible effects in the light of HRL.

This chapter will first outline the main factors pertinent to the application of HRL to armed conflict situations, including issues relating to jurisdiction. Afterwards, it will examine the most relevant human rights that would be affected by any use of nuclear weapons, most notably the right to life, but also rights relevant to the suffering they cause and their adverse effects on health.

A.   Applicability of human rights law to nuclear weapons

1.   Application of human rights at all times

It is now almost uncontroversial[1] that HRL continues to apply, alongside IHL, during any armed conflict situation. Not only the terms of the treaties themselves,[2] but also the multitude of UN resolutions attest to this fact. Although on occasion a few states still make statements to the effect that in armed conflict only IHL applies, these same states have not been consistent in their approach, including by supporting resolutions insisting that other countries respect human rights and IHL during armed conflict.[3] Furthermore, any argument that IHL needs to be the yardstick in cases brought before human rights treaty bodies is firmly rejected. Rather, the treaty bodies concerned stated that they could only refer to IHL as a means to help the interpretation of the human rights concerned.[4]

The most relevant issue, therefore, is the extent to which IHL should be used to interpret various human rights. In its Advisory Opinion on Nuclear Weapons, the International Court of Justice (ICJ) stated that in effect only IHL really counts:

> The Court observes that the protection of the International Covenant of [sic] Civil and Political Rights does not cease in times of war ... In principle, the right not arbitrarily to be deprived of one's life applies also in hostilities. The test of what is an arbitrary deprivation of life, however, then falls to be determined by the applicable *lex specialis*, namely, the law applicable in armed conflict which is designed to regulate the conduct of hostilities. Thus whether a particular loss of life, through the use of a certain weapon in warfare, is to be considered an arbitrary deprivation of life contrary to ... the

---

[1] For a discussion of this point see: L. Doswald-Beck, *Human Rights in Times of Conflict and Terrorism* (Cambridge University Press, 2011), pp. 6–9 (hereafter, *Human Rights in Times of Conflict and Terrorism*).

[2] War and states of emergency are directly referred to in human rights treaties and their protocols.

[3] The most notable states in this regard are the United States and Israel. However, more recently the USA has stated that the 1966 International Covenant on Civil and Political Rights continues to apply in armed conflict for matters within its scope of application: Fourth Periodic Report of the United States to the UN Committee on Human Rights Concerning the International Covenant on Civil and Political Rights, 30 December 2011, para. 506. For an overview of references to human rights law in armed conflict by UN bodies between 2000 and 2010, and how states have voted, see I. Siatitsa and M. Titberidze, 'Human rights in armed conflict: ten years of affirmative state practice within United Nations resolutions', *Journal of International Humanitarian Legal Studies* 2 (2012), 233–62.

[4] Inter-American Commission on Human Rights (hereafter, IAComHR), Inter-State Petition IP-02, *Ecuador v. Colombia*, Report No. 112/10, 21 October 2010 (hereafter, *Ecuador v. Colombia* report), paras. 114–15 and 119, in which the Commission rejected Colombia's claim that only IHL applies; European Court of Human Rights (hereafter, ECtHR), *Georgia v. Russia*, Admissibility Decision of 13 December 2011, paras. 69 and 72, in which the Court rejected Russia's argument that in an international armed conflict only IHL applies.

Covenant, can only be decided by reference to the law applicable in armed conflict and not deduced from the terms of the Covenant itself.[5]

Although this author is of the opinion that an honest evaluation of the effects of nuclear weapons under IHL would result in a finding that they cannot be used in a way that respects that law, the above-quoted statement by the ICJ is hardly satisfactory. Indeed the Court itself realised this when it made a further pronouncement on the relationship between IHL and HRL in its Advisory Opinion on the Palestinian Wall:

> As regards the relationship between international humanitarian law and human rights law, there are … three possible situations: some rights may be exclusively matters of international humanitarian law; others may be exclusively matters of human rights law; yet others may be matters of both these branches of international law. In order to answer the question put to it, the Court will have to take into consideration both these branches of international law, namely, human rights law and, as *lex specialis*, international humanitarian law.[6]

This statement was repeated, but significantly without the words 'as *lex specialis*' in the subsequent case between the Democratic Republic of the Congo (DRC) and Uganda.[7] The ICJ's statement on the relationship between the two branches of law is general, with no indication as to which is to be preferred in any situation. In that case, which concerned the actions of Uganda in territory it occupied in the DRC, the ICJ simply listed the IHL and human rights treaties that bound the two states and applied their provisions equally. It cannot even be said that when there was a precise reference to an issue in IHL the Court used that law rather than HRL. In considering the looting of mineral and diamond mines, the Court used the more recent African Charter on Human and Peoples' Rights (ACHPR),[8] rather than the provision in the 1907 Hague Regulations[9] that applies to the use of natural resources in occupied territories.[10]

---

[5] International Court of Justice (ICJ), *Legality of the Threat or Use of Nuclear Weapons*, Advisory Opinion of 8 July 1996 (hereafter, Nuclear Weapons Advisory Opinion), para. 25.

[6] ICJ, *Legal Consequences of the Construction of a Wall in the Occupied Palestinian Territory*, Advisory Opinion of 9 July 2004, para. 106 (hereafter, Palestinian Wall Advisory Opinion).

[7] ICJ, *Case Concerning Armed Activities on the Territory of the Congo (Democratic Republic of the Congo v. Uganda)*, Judgment of 19 December 2005, para. 216 (hereafter, *DRC v. Uganda* judgment).

[8] African Charter on Human and Peoples' Rights, Nairobi, 27 June 1981, in force 21 October 1986, OAU Doc. CAB/LEG/67/3 rev. 5; 1520 UNTS 217; 21 ILM 58 (1982) (hereafter, ACHPR).

[9] Convention (IV) respecting the Laws and Customs of War on Land and its annex: Regulations concerning the Laws and Customs of War on Land, The Hague, 18 October 1907, in force 26 January 1910, 187 CTS 227; 1 Bevans 631.

[10] *DRC v. Uganda* judgment, para. 245. The Court used Art. 21(2) of the ACHPR on the right to property of dispossessed people, rather than Art. 55 of the 1907 Hague Regulations,

Human rights treaty bodies have on occasion made reference to IHL as a means to help interpret human rights provisions, but in reality this has always been to reinforce the human rights protection and not to limit it.[11] In the case of *Democratic Republic of the Congo* v. *Burundi, Rwanda and Uganda*, which concerned violations of the ACHPR during the occupation of parts of Congo by the respondent states, the African Commission made reference to parts of the Geneva Convention IV[12] and its Additional Protocol I[13] to reinforce its finding of violations of the right to property, the right to cultural development, and the prohibition of inhuman and degrading treatment under the ACHPR.[14] The Inter-American Court of Human Rights (IACtHR), after stating that IHL could be used to help interpret human rights provisions,[15] did so in order to underline the severity of the human rights violations in the context of an armed conflict.[16] The European Court of Human Rights (ECtHR) made use of the Geneva Conventions to counteract an argument by Turkey that soldiers often go missing in armed conflict, and therefore a duty to investigate their whereabouts under Article 2 of the European Convention on Human Rights (ECHR)[17] would be unrealistic. The Court used IHL to maintain its earlier jurisprudence that the right to life includes the duty to investigate the fate of persons who are, or may well have been, killed by state forces.[18]

This is not the place for an extensive analysis of the various theories as to the precise relationship between IHL and HRL. It is sufficient to note that HRL applies at all times and would therefore be relevant to any use of nuclear weapons. The way in which certain specific human rights have been interpreted in the context of armed conflict will be addressed below.

which was not even mentioned. It needs to be noted, however, that this IHL provision refers to the Roman law concept of 'usufruct', which did not take into account the fact that mines, unlike fruit trees, can be exhausted.

[11] For a more detailed discussion of the use of IHL by human rights treaty bodies, see Doswald-Beck, *Human Rights in Times of Conflict and Terrorism*, pp. 109–17.

[12] Convention (IV) relative to the Protection of Civilian Persons in Time of War, Geneva, 12 August 1949, in force 21 October 1950, 75 UNTS 287.

[13] Protocol Additional to the Geneva Conventions of 12 August 1949, and relating to the Protection of Victims of International Armed Conflicts (Protocol I), Geneva, 8 June 1977, in force 7 December 1978, 1125 UNTS 3 (hereafter, Additional Protocol I).

[14] AComHPR, *Democratic Republic of Congo* v. *Burundi, Rwanda and Uganda*, Decision (Comm. No. 229/99), 25 May 2006, paras. 79, 84, and 87–8.

[15] IACtHR, *Bámaca Velásquez* v. *Guatemala*, Judgment (Series C No. 70), 25 November 2000, para. 203.

[16] E.g. IACtHR, *Ituango Massacres* v. *Colombia*, Judgment (Series C No. 148), 1 July 2006, paras. 179–83, which concerned the destruction and looting of property.

[17] Convention for the Protection of Human Rights and Fundamental Freedoms, Rome, 4 November 1950, in force 3 September 1953, 213 UNTS 221 (hereafter, ECHR).

[18] ECtHR, *Varnava and Others* v. *Turkey*, Judgment (App. Nos. 16064/90, 16065/90, 16066/90, 16068/90, 16069/90, 16070/90, 16071/90, 16072/90 and 16073/90), 18 September 2009, para. 185.

B.   Application in all places?

1.   Treaty obligations

It is important to consider this issue because a use of nuclear weapons is more likely than not to be aimed at another state, or on the high seas, rather than within a state's own territory. The International Covenant on Civil and Political Rights (ICCPR)[19] specifies that it applies to all persons in a state's 'territory and subject to its jurisdiction'.[20] This has been interpreted both by the treaty body (UN Human Rights Committee) and by the ICJ as meaning not only within a state's territory but also where it has jurisdiction outside the national territory.[21] The ECHR, the American Convention on Human Rights (ACHR)[22] and the Arab Charter on Human Rights (AChHR)[23] all specify that they apply to all individuals within a state's 'jurisdiction'. The treaty bodies concerned have interpreted the term 'jurisdiction' to cover, in addition to a state's own territory, persons or areas over which a state has 'effective control'.[24]

The International Covenant on Economic, Social and Cultural Rights (ICESCR)[25] and the ACHPR have no jurisdiction clause. The approach of their respective treaty bodies is addressed in section C below.[26]

---

[19] International Covenant on Civil and Political Rights, New York, 16 December 1966, in force 23 March 1976, 999 UNTS 171 (hereafter, ICCPR).

[20] *Ibid.*, Art. 2(1).

[21] UN Human Rights Committee (hereafter HRCte), *Lopez Burgos* v. *Uruguay,* Decision (Comm. No. 52/1979), UN Doc. Supp. No. 40 (A/36/40) at 176, 29 July 1981, paras. 12.1 and 12.3; ICJ, Palestinian Wall Advisory Opinion, para. 108.

[22] American Convention on Human Rights, San José, 21 November 1969, in force 18 July 1978, 1144 UNTS 123; 9 ILM 99 (1969) (hereafter, ACHR).

[23] Arab Charter on Human Rights, Tunis, 22 May 2004, in force 15 March 2008, reprinted in 12 Int'l Hum. Rts. Rep. 893 (2005) (hereafter, AChHR).

[24] HRCte, General Comment No. 31: 'The nature of the general legal obligation on States Parties to the Covenant', UN doc. CCPR/C/21/Rev.1/Add.13, 29 March 2004, para. 10; ECtHR, *Al-Skeini and others* v. *United Kingdom*, Judgment (App. No. 55721/07), 7 July 2011, paras. 130–40; IAComHR, *Ecuador* v. *Colombia* report, para. 91. For a more detailed overview of the various situations in which the treaty bodies analysed whether there was jurisdiction see Doswald-Beck, *Human Rights in Times of Conflict and Terrorism*, pp. 9–29.

[25] International Covenant on Economic, Social and Cultural Rights, New York, 16 December 1966, in force 3 January 1976, 993 UNTS 3; 6 ILM 368 (1967) (hereafter, ICESCR).

[26] In the context of rights relating to health in cases not involving control of the territory or persons affected. These treaties have also been applied to cases abroad where there was some control. The ICJ, in its Palestinian Wall Advisory Opinion, used the same test as to its application as for the ICCPR, namely, where a state has effective control, to apply it to occupied territory: para. 112. The African Commission on Human and Peoples' Rights (AComHPR) only considered the imputability of the violations of the Charter to states that had invaded another state: AComHPR, *Democratic Republic of Congo* v. *Burundi, Rwanda and Uganda*, Decision (Comm. No. 227/1999), 25 May 2006, paras. 63–4.

In terms of jurisdiction, the main issue is whether the detonation of a nuclear weapon in a place outside a state's national territory, or other than where it has physical control of people or of an area of land or sea, amounts to 'effective control'. Several cases are relevant to this point. The first is one in which the Inter-American Commission on Human Rights (IAComHR) applied the American Declaration on the Rights and Duties of Man (ADHR) to the attack, by Cuban military planes, of a civilian plane over international waters. Although the ADHR has no jurisdiction clause, the Commission found that this action by the Cuban military planes was within Cuba's 'jurisdiction' because the effect of firing on the planes 'placed the civilian pilots ... under their authority'.[27] The IAComHR took the same approach when interpreting the jurisdiction clause in the ACHR. In an inter-state petition, Ecuador complained of human rights violations by Colombian military when, inter alia, they bombed from the air alleged FARC (Revolutionary Armed Forces of Colombia) camps within the territory of Ecuador. The Commission specified that in order to establish jurisdiction, 'it is necessary to determine whether there is a causal nexus between the extraterritorial conduct of the State and the alleged violation of the rights and freedoms of an individual'. It stressed that it is not necessary to show a territorial presence and the ability to respect the whole range of human rights duties in the context concerned, but rather that 'the obligation does arise in the period of time that agents of a State interfere in the lives of persons who are on the territory of the other State, for those agents to respect their rights, in particular, their right to life and humane treatment'.[28]

This approach by the IAComHR is to be compared with that by the ECtHR in a case concerning the bombing, from the air, of a Serbian television and radio station. The applicants in the case argued that the air superiority of the attackers amounted to 'effective control' and therefore should be considered to amount to 'jurisdiction'. The Court did not accept this argument, but without really addressing how or why airspace should be considered differently from presence on the ground. It concentrated rather on indicating that the existence of a jurisdiction clause must mean that it is not enough to prove imputability of an act to the states complained of, and that extra-territorial control is to be seen as an exception.[29] It should be noted, however, that a subsequent case, which concerned the killing of persons in Iraq by a Turkish helicopter near the frontier, came to a different conclusion. Here the ECtHR stated that it was 'not required to determine the exact location' where the people were killed by the helicopter fire; the fact that they were the victims of the shooting meant that

---

[27] IAComHR, *Alejandre and others* v. *Cuba (Brothers to the Rescue case)*, Case No. 11.589, Report No. 86/99, 29 September 1999, para. 25.

[28] IAComHR, *Ecuador* v. *Colombia* report, paras. 99–100.

[29] ECtHR, *Bankovic and Others* v. *17 NATO States*, Admissibility Decision (Grand Chamber) (App. No. 52207/99), 12 December 2001, para. 75.

they were 'within the jurisdiction of Turkey at the material time'.[30] However, it should be noted that Turkey did not contest jurisdiction in this case. A pending case that may be relevant is one brought by Georgia against Russia in the context of the armed conflict between them, which included air strikes covering an incursion by land forces. One of the issues raised was the extent of 'effective control' at any given time resulting in 'jurisdiction'. Although the case has been declared admissible, the Court decided to leave its decision on this point until its judgment on the merits.[31]

Thus far, therefore, the only treaty body to have created a doubt about application to attacks from the air on people or territory not controlled by the attacker is the ECtHR, but, as we have seen, it has not been totally consistent. The Inter-American Commission on Human and Rights (IAComHR) applied the ADHR and the ACHR to such a situation, although we have yet to see if the Inter-American Court would follow suit, or whether the African Court would do so. This problem is particular to application clauses in treaties. In the Nuclear Weapons Advisory Opinion the ICJ did not allude to this problem at all, but seemed to assume that human rights law would in principle apply, the only issue being that of interpretation of the right to life.

2. Customary human rights law obligations

In the case of customary HRL, the usual rules of state responsibility would apply; therefore, it would only be necessary to prove that the damage caused by a nuclear weapon is imputable to a state. Although there has been no equivalent study for HRL to the one undertaken by the International Committee of the Red Cross (ICRC) for IHL, there can be no doubt that fundamental rules of HRL have attained customary status.[32] This would be particularly true for those rules from which no derogation is possible, but it is also true for those rights that are the subject of international resolutions that do not depend on the ratification of a specific human rights treaty. In other words resolutions that call on all states to respect certain rights, or which condemn states for violations of certain rights, without any reference to treaty obligations, are a good indication of customary law, especially if such resolutions are frequently repeated. The same can be said for fact-finding missions and reports by United Nations

---

[30] ECtHR, *Mansur Pad and Others* v. *Turkey*, Admissibility Decision (App. No. 60167/00), 28 June 2007, paras. 54–5.

[31] ECtHR, *Georgia* v. *Russia*, Admissibility Decision (App. No. 38263/08), 13 December 2011, paras. 66–7.

[32] The existence of customary human rights law is reflected in the Basic Principles and Guidelines on the Right to a Remedy and Reparation for Victims of Gross Violations of International Human Rights Law and Serious Violations of International Humanitarian Law, UN General Assembly Resolution 60/147, UN doc. A/RES/60/147, adopted on 16 December 2005, Annex, Principle I.1.(b).

bodies on violations of human rights without requiring a reference to treaty provisions binding specific states.[33] The prohibitions of arbitrary deprivation of life and of inhuman treatment clearly fall into this category.[34]

The enormous damage caused by nuclear weapons means that the loss of life and suffering could well amount to not only a violation of the customary right to life, but also to a crime against humanity and therefore a breach of a peremptory norm of international law.[35] No prior wrong can justify a breach of a peremptory norm.[36] The obligation to refrain from a breach of such a norm is also one that is *erga omnes*. In particular, given that the geographical extent of damage caused by a nuclear weapon is likely to affect more than one nation, as well as common areas such as the high seas and international air space, the obligations of the responsible state would not be limited to the state attacked.[37]

3. Human rights obligations of non-state actors

Concern that one or more nuclear weapons could fall into the hands of non-state actors is reflected in UN Security Council Resolution 1540, which requires states to 'adopt and enforce appropriate effective laws which prohibit any non-State actor' from acquiring or using in any way 'nuclear ... weapons and their means of delivery, in particular for terrorist purposes'.[38] Non-state actors and individuals will be criminally responsible, of course, for war crimes, genocide and crimes against humanity, and the use of a nuclear weapon could well amount to one or more of these crimes. The issue here, however, is whether,

---

[33] See, e.g., for a summary of this point A. Clapham, *Brierly's Law of Nations*, 7th edn (Oxford University Press, 2012), pp. 237–39.

[34] For the frequency and range of resolutions on these subjects, see Siatitsa and Titberidze, 'Human rights in armed conflict', Section 3.A. Human rights treaty bodies have specified that violations of these rights require a judicial remedy for the victims: HRCte, *Bautista* v. *Colombia*, Decision (Comm. No. 563/1993), 13 November 1995, para. 10; IACtHR, *Zembrano Velez* v. *Ecuador*, Judgment (Series C No. 166), 4 July 2007, paras. 112, 114–15, 120, and 129–30; AComHPR, *Sudan Human Rights Organisation and Centre on Housing Rights and Evictions* v. *Sudan*, Decision (Comm Nos. 279/03 and 296/05), 27 May 2009, paras. 180–1; ECtHR, *Esmukhambetov and others* v. *Russia*, Judgment (App. No. 23445/03), 29 March 2011, para. 159.

[35] Para. 5 of the Commentary on Article 26 of the International Law Commission Draft Articles on the Responsibility of States for Internationally Wrongful Acts, with commentaries, 2001, Text adopted by the International Law Commission at its fifty-third session, in 2001, and submitted to the General Assembly as a part of the Commission's report covering the work of that session (A/56/10) (hereafter, ILC Articles on State Responsibility).

[36] *Ibid.*, Art. 26 and para. 4 of its commentary.

[37] *Ibid.*, Art. 33 and paras. 1 and 3 of its commentary.

[38] UN Security Council Resolution 1540, UN doc. S/RES/1540, adopted on 28 April 2004, para. 2. This resolution confirms the existing obligation under Art. I of the 1968 Nuclear Non-Proliferation Treaty (NPT) that prohibits the transfer of these weapons to non-state actors.

outside individual criminal responsibility, non-state actors would be responsible for human rights violations as such.

Human rights treaties for the most part directly address governments and hold them responsible for the behaviour of non-state actors if they did not exercise sufficient 'due diligence' to prevent or punish such behaviour. However, this is not the full picture. UN bodies have been addressing the behaviour of non-governmental actors in armed conflict by reference to both IHL and HRL. These UN bodies include those composed of state representatives, namely the Human Rights Commission/Council, the General Assembly and the Security Council, as well as persons mandated by them to look into these issues, in particular special rapporteurs, working groups and truth commissions.[39] Examples of reports include those of the four Special Rapporteurs on the conflict between Lebanon and Israel,[40] the Darfur Commission of Inquiry[41] and those of the Office of the UN High Commissioner for Human Rights on the human rights violations of non-state actors in Nepal.[42] There are also significant UN resolutions directly requiring named non-state actors to respect human rights law, in addition to IHL. These include those relating to the Taliban and other 'factions' in Afghanistan,[43] Sudanese rebel groups,[44] Al Shabaab and affiliates in Somalia,[45] al-Qaeda and other extremist groups in Mali,[46] and various rebel groups in the DRC.[47] The

[39] For an extensive work on this subject, see A. Clapham, *Human Rights Obligations of Non-State Actors* (Oxford University Press, 2006).

[40] UN Human Rights Council, Report on Mission to Lebanon and Israel (7–14 September 2006), UN doc. A/HRC/2/7, 2 October 2006, which points out, in para. 19, that given the practice of the UN Security Council of calling on certain armed groups to respect human rights, such groups should be so bound when they exercise sufficient control over territory and population and have an identifiable political structure.

[41] Report of the International Commission of Inquiry on Darfur to the UN Secretary-General, pursuant to Security Council Resolution 1564 of 18 September 2004, 25 January 2005, para. 413.

[42] See e.g. A. Clapham, 'Human rights obligations of non-state actors in conflict situations', *International Review of the Red Cross* 88 (2006), 491–523, at 507.

[43] E.g. UN General Assembly Resolution 49/207, adopted on 23 December 1994; UN General Assembly Resolution 50/189, adopted on 22 December 1995; UN General Assembly Resolution 55/174A, adopted on 19 December 2000; UN General Assembly Resolution 56/176, UN doc. A/RES/176, adopted on 19 December 2001; UN General Assembly Resolution 57/234, adopted on 18 December 2002; UN Security Council Resolution 1214, adopted on 8 December 1988; UN Security Council Resolution 1193, adopted on 28 August 1998; and UN Security Council Resolution 1333, adopted on 19 December 2000.

[44] UN Security Council Resolution 1574, adopted on 19 November 2004, preambular para. 11.

[45] UN Security Council Resolution 2067, adopted on 18 September 2012, para. 18.

[46] UN Security Council Resolution 2071, adopted on 12 October 2012, preambular paras. 4 and 14, and operative para. 5; UN Human Rights Council Resolution 17/20, adopted on 17 July 2012, para. 2.

[47] UN Security Council Resolution 1376, adopted on 9 November 2001, para. 5; UN Security Council Resolution 1417, adopted on 14 June 2002, para. 4; UN Security Council Resolution

Security Council has called on specific non-state actors to prevent violations of HRL against children during conflict, including by preparing concrete action plans to this end.[48] This practice shows that there appears to be an understanding that non-governmental entities with de facto authority over persons and/or territory need to take measures to respect human rights.[49] This would equally apply to any threat or use of nuclear weapons.

C. The most relevant human rights

1. The right to life

The right to life in the context of the basic aim of human rights

Although the main opinion of the ICJ referred to IHL as a means to interpret the right to life, Judge Weeramantry, in his Dissenting Opinion, decided to address the issue of the right to life within the context of human rights. Instead of looking at the details of what constitutes a deprivation of life within the technical language of the treaties, he rather addressed the teleological underpinnings of the right. Thus he pointed out the following:

> when a weapon has the potential to kill between one million and one billion people, as the WHO has told the Court, human life becomes reduced to a level of worthlessness that totally belies human dignity as understood in any culture. Such a deliberate action by a State is, in any circumstances whatsoever, incompatible with a recognition by it of that respect for basic human dignity on which world peace depends, and respect for which is assumed on the part of all member States of the United Nations.
>
> This is not merely a provision of the Universal Declaration on Human Rights and other human rights instruments, but is fundamental Charter law

---

1906, adopted on 23 December 2009, para. 10; UN Security Council Resolution 2076, adopted on 20 November 2012, para. 3; UN Security Council Resolution 2098, adopted on 28 March 2013, para. 8.

[48] UN Security Council Resolution 1539, adopted on 22 April 2004; UN Security Council Resolution 1882, adopted on 4 August 2009. See also, e.g., UN Security Council Resolution 2096, adopted on 19 March 2012, para. 32.

[49] Territorial control is specifically mentioned as an important factor for human rights obligations in UN reports, e.g. 'Report of the International Commission of Inquiry to investigate all alleged violations of international human rights law in the Libyan Arab Jamahiriya', UN Human Rights Council, UN doc. A/HRC/17/44, 1 June 2011, para. 72; UN Assistance Mission in Afghanistan and Office of the High Commissioner for Human Rights, 'Afghanistan, Annual Report on Protection of Civilians in Armed Conflict 2012', Kabul, February 2013; 'Report of the independent international commission of inquiry on the Syrian Arab Republic', UN doc. A/HRC/21/50, 16 August 2012, para. 10. On the other hand, fundamental human rights obligations, such as the prohibition of torture or enforced disappearances, have been stated to apply to individuals and non-state actors even without territorial control: UN Human Rights Council, Report of the independent international commission of inquiry on the Syrian Arab Republic, UN doc. A/HRC/19/69, 22 February 2012, para. 106.

as enshrined in the very preamble to the United Nations Charter, for one of the ends to which the United Nations is dedicated is 'to reaffirm faith in fundamental human rights, in the *dignity and worth* of the human person' (emphasis added). No weapons ever invented in the long history of man's inhumanity to man has so negatived the dignity and worth of the human person as has the nuclear bomb.[50]

In much the same vein, the Human Rights Committee has questioned whether nuclear weapons can be compatible with the right to life and the achievement of peace and security. In General Comment 6 it stated that:

> States have the supreme duty to prevent wars, acts of genocide and other acts of mass violence causing arbitrary loss of life. Every effort they make to avert the danger of war, especially thermonuclear war, and to strengthen international peace and security would constitute the most important condition and guarantee for the safeguarding of the right to life.[51]

The Committee further elaborated on the issue in General Comment 14, in which it expressed concern about the toll of human life caused by conventional weapons in armed conflict and about the development and proliferation of weapons of mass destruction:

> [I]t is evident that the designing, testing, manufacture, possession and deployment of nuclear weapons are among the greatest threats to the right to life which confront mankind today.[52]

In the opinion of the Committee: 'The production, testing, possession, deployment and use of nuclear weapons should be prohibited and recognised as crimes against humanity.'[53]

It is evident from these statements that the UN Human Rights Committee is most likely to consider any use of nuclear weapons to be a serious violation of the right to life, whatever the context, and whatever arguments might be made using IHL as a yardstick. On the other hand, testing would not necessarily amount to a loss of life or damage to health if no radioactivity were released, so that testing such weapons, together with their manufacture and possession, would relate more to the positive obligations of states to protect life.[54] This issue was not expanded on further in these General Comments.

---

[50] Nuclear Weapons Advisory Opinion, Dissenting Opinion of Judge Weeramantry, section III. 10.(f).

[51] HRCte, General Comment 6, on Art. 6 ICCPR, 30 April 1982, para. 2.

[52] HRCte, General Comment 14 on Art. 6 ICCPR, 9 November 1984, para 4.

[53] HRCte, General Comment 14 at para. 6. Actions other than deployment are, in most cases, unlikely to fall within the technical definition of crimes against humanity – see Chapter 8 of this volume.

[54] The requirement for states to 'adopt positive measures' to protect the 'inherent right to life' is stated in HRCte, General Comment 6, on Art. 6 ICCPR, 30 April 1982, para. 5.

Interpretation by treaty bodies in the context of specific cases

Cases concerning the death of civilians during attacks   When the ICJ gave its Advisory Opinion in 1996, it did not have the benefit of precedent from international human rights courts dealing with concrete cases concerning loss of life as a result of aerial bombardments during active hostilities. The most significant subsequent cases include those from the ECtHR relating to internal conflicts in Turkey and Russia. Unlike the other treaties that specify that the right to life will be breached if a person is 'arbitrarily deprived' of it,[55] the ECHR spells out that the use of force must not be more than 'absolutely necessary' to achieve certain aims, in particular to defend persons against 'unlawful violence' or for the purpose of 'quelling a riot or insurrection.'[56] The cases were brought by the relatives of civilians who died during combat operations against rebel groups. In order to ensure that the use of force is no more than 'absolutely necessary', the Court examined whether the planning of the operation was such as to avoid or minimise deaths. In this regard, the language used by the Court to evaluate whether the force used was not more than 'absolutely necessary' is similar to that required by IHL in that the Court refers to 'feasible precautions' in order to prevent or at least minimise loss to civilian life. Thus, in a case concerning a ground operation in Turkey, the Court stated:

> The force used must be strictly proportionate to the achievement of the aims set out in … Article 2 … the Court must, in making its assessment, subject deprivations of life to the most careful scrutiny, particularly where deliberate lethal force is used …
>
> The responsibility of the State is not confined to circumstances where there is significant evidence that misdirected fire from agents of the State has killed a civilian. It may also be engaged where they fail to take all feasible precautions in the choice of means and methods of a security operation mounted against an opposing group with a view to avoiding and, in any event, minimising, incidental loss of civilian life.[57]

The same approach was used in cases relating to air operations by Russian forces in Chechnya. After establishing that the existence of rebel groups using military power meant that the use of force by the government met one of the aims required under Article 2 ECHR,[58] the Court examined whether the means used was limited to what was 'absolutely necessary':

> The Court regards it as evident that when the military considered the deployment of aviation equipped with heavy combat weapons within the boundaries of a populated area, they also should have considered the dangers that

---

[55] ICCPR, Art. 6(1); ACHR, Arts. 4(1) and 5(2); ACHPR, Art. 4.

[56] ECHR, Art. 2(2)(a) and (c).

[57] ECtHR, *Ergi* v. *Turkey*, Judgment (App. No. 23818/94), 28 July 1998, para. 79.

[58] The Court accepted that the government needed to resort to the use of military force in order to regain control of the area and to 'suppress the illegal armed insurgency': ECtHR, *Isayeva* v. *Russia*, Judgment (App. No. 57950/00), 24 February 2005, para. 180.

such methods invariably entail. There is however no evidence to conclude that such considerations played a significant part in the planning ... there is no evidence that at the planning stage of the operation any serious calculations were made about the evacuation of civilians, such as ensuring that they were informed of the attack beforehand, how long such an evacuation would take, what routes evacuees were supposed to take, what kind of precautions were in place to ensure safety, what steps were to be taken to assist the vulnerable and infirm etc. ...

The planes ... carried heavy free-falling high-explosion aviation bombs ... with a damage radius exceeding 1,000 metres [which were] used against targets both in the centre and on the edges of the village ...

Even when faced with a situation where, as the Government submit [*sic*], the population of the village had been held hostage by a large group of well-equipped and well-trained fighters, the primary aim of the operation should be to protect lives from unlawful violence. The massive use of indiscriminate weapons stands in flagrant contrast with this aim and cannot be considered compatible with the standard of care prerequisite to an operation of this kind involving the use of lethal force by State agents.[59]

The same conclusion was reached in another case decided on the same day concerning air operations, in which the Court found a violation on the basis that the operation was not 'planned and executed with the requisite care for the lives of the civilian population'.[60]

In a more recent case, but also concerning air operations against Chechen rebels, the Court recognised that the Russian authorities 'had no choice other than to carry out aerial strikes' in order to retake a town that was heavily defended by 'well-equipped extremists, armed with a range of large-yield weaponry'.[61] The operation resulted in six deaths, sixteen injured and thirteen houses destroyed. The Court referred to the need to limit action to what was absolutely necessary to achieve this aim, saying that it was:

not convinced, having regard to the materials at its disposal, that the necessary degree of care was exercised in preparing the operation ... in such a

---

[59] ECtHR, *Isayeva v. Russia*, Judgment (App. No. 57950/00), 24 February 2005, paras. 189–91.

[60] ECtHR, *Isayeva, Yusopova and Bazayeva v. Russia,* Judgment (App. No. 57947–49/00), 24 February 2005, para. 199. In the *Isayeva* case mentioned above, the Court added the surprising and unnecessary reference to the fact that Russia had not derogated from Article 2 and therefore the situation needed to be evaluated in accordance with normal law enforcement measures. This addition was both strange (as the exception to 'lawful acts of war' in Art. 15 ECHR almost certainly is limited to international conflicts, inter alia given that Article 2(2)(c) includes the use of force during an insurrection to be limited to what is absolutely necessary) and also superfluous to the reasoning needed. In any event, the case of *Isayeva, Yusopova and Bazayeva v. Russia*, decided on the same day, came to the same conclusion without this reference.

[61] ECtHR, *Khamzayev and others v. Russia*, Judgment (App. No. 1503/02), 3 May 2011, paras. 179–80 (hereafter, *Khamzayev* case).

way as to avoid or minimise, to the greatest extent possible, the risk of loss
of life, both for the persons at whom the measures were directed and for
civilians.[62]

The Court noted in particular that the weapons chosen for the operation
against rebel forces within a populated area were 'high-explosive fragmentation bombs of calibre 250–270kg', which it then characterised as 'an indiscriminate weapon'.[63] In finding a violation, it stated that using such bombs in
a residential area was 'manifestly disproportionate' to the aim of dislodging
the rebels.[64]

What is striking about these cases is the lack of any consideration of
whether civilian deaths and injuries were or were not 'excessive' in relation
to the military objective being pursued.[65] The only possible significance of
the number of civilian casualties was in evaluating whether all reasonable
efforts were made to avoid such casualties. Thus, in the case of *Ahmet Özkan
and Others* v. *Turkey*, a violation was not found because 'only' one civilian
injury occurred during a military operation. This fact was used as evidence
by the ECtHR to arrive at the conclusion that the use of force by the security forces was not more than 'absolutely necessary' for repelling an attack
against them, that is that the security forces must have taken the necessary
care.[66]

The approach of the Inter-American Court, when analysing attacks by an
army, has been to stress that lethal force must be 'absolutely necessary in relation to the force or threat to be repealed. When excessive force is used, any
resulting deprivation of life is arbitrary.'[67] In the case *Santa Domingo Massacre*
v. *Colombia*, which concerned the dropping of cluster munitions aimed at guerrillas in Colombia, the Court made reference to IHL in order to help the interpretation of the right to life.[68] The bomblets fell on a hamlet, causing deaths
and injuries to civilians only, rather than on the place near the hamlet where
the guerrillas were supposed to be hiding. The majority of the judgment concentrated on the vague instructions given to the pilot as to how far from the
hamlet the guerrillas were hiding, the fact that the pilot would not have been
able to see exactly where the bomblets would fall, and military evidence that air

---

[62] *Ibid.*, para. 180.   [63] *Ibid.*, para. 185.   [64] *Ibid.*, para. 189.

[65] I.e. the principle of proportionality in attack in IHL as reflected in Additional Protocol I,
Art. 51(5)(b).

[66] ECtHR, *Ahmet Özkan and Others* v. *Turkey*, Judgment (App. No. 21689/93), 6 April 2004,
paras. 305–06.

[67] IACtHR, *Zambrano Vélez et al.* v. *Ecuador*, Judgment (Series C No. 166), 4 July 2007,
para. 84.

[68] IACtHR, *Santa Domingo Massacre* v. *Colombia*, Judgment (Series C No. 259), 30 November
2012 (hereafter, *Santa Domingo* case), para. 211.

support for the army on the ground was not really necessary. These elements were taken together with the fact that cluster bombs are area weapons, which Colombian air force instructions stated were to be avoided in a populated area, as well as the fact that there was no evidence that any regard at all was given to the presence of civilians in the vicinity. The Court concluded that there had been a violation of the right to life because precautions had not been taken to avoid or minimise civilian casualties.[69]

Unlike the ECtHR, the IACtHR in this case mentioned the IHL rule that civilian casualties must not be 'excessive in relation to the concrete and direct military advantage anticipated'.[70] However, the Court held that this rule was irrelevant as no military advantage took place.[71] In this regard, the IACtHR did not actually apply the IHL rule, which speaks of the advantage that is *anticipated* (which was the case here, i.e. the army and air force hoped to neutralise the guerrilla presence there). IHL does not limit the rule to what is in fact achieved.

It is not surprising to this author that the IACtHR in practice avoided trying to apply the IHL proportionality rule when it was able to base its judgment on insufficient precautions in attack. Those wishing to justify the use of nuclear weapons under IHL stress that the scale of civilian casualties would not always be disproportionate to the military advantage anticipated.[72] Although the IACtHR made reference to this IHL rule, it seems highly unlikely that a human rights treaty body would ever try to evaluate whether civilian casualties are not 'excessive' once it has become clear that all efforts had not been taken in the choice of weapons to minimise collateral effects. Although this author is of the view that nuclear weapons are indiscriminate because of the unforeseeable range and effects of any nuclear explosion, thereby making any IHL proportionality assessment impossible in advance, it is significant that proportionality of collateral damage has not in practice been the basis of human rights judgments in cases relating to bombardments.

---

[69] IACtHR, *Santa Domingo* case, paras. 216–30.

[70] Additional Protocol I, Art. 51(5)(b). Rule 14 of the ICRC Study on Customary International Law specifies that this rule also applies in non-international armed conflicts. J.-M. Henckaerts and L. Doswald-Beck, *Customary International Humanitarian Law*, 3 vols. (Cambridge University Press, 2005), Vol. I, pp. 46–50.

[71] IACtHR, *Santa Domingo* case, para. 215.

[72] Three judges in the Nuclear Weapons Advisory Opinion stated that in extreme cases, the use of nuclear weapons would not be prohibited because the collateral damage would not be disproportionate to the military need (Opinion of Judge Higgins, paras. 20–1; Opinion of Judge Guillaume, para. 5; Opinion of Judge Schwebel, paras. 22–4, quoting with approval the submission to the Court by the UK government to this effect).

Cases concerning death of fighters as a result of attacks and/or a lack of subsequent care   It must be stressed that the human rights understanding of 'proportionality' is different from that of IHL.[73] In HRL, proportionality is applied to the use of force as a whole, and not just to the extent of incidental damage to civilians. Therefore, if the force used to defeat fighters is excessive, the degree of the use of force would not be 'absolutely necessary' and therefore would be a violation of the right to life. This is combined with the duty under human rights law to take positive measures to protect life to the degree possible, including legislation, training, planning, subsequent medical care and investigation.[74]

Several cases illustrate this point. In the case of *Neira Alegría et al.* v. *Peru*, which concerned the use of force to suppress an armed riot in a prison, the Court found that although the detainees were highly dangerous and armed, the amount of force used was disproportionate. One hundred and eleven inmates died and thirty-four were injured, with many of the dead crushed to death. No effort was made to find and rescue any who might have still been alive. On this basis, a violation of the right to life was found.[75] In the well-known case of *McCann and Others* v. *United Kingdom*, the ECtHR found a violation of the right to life when insufficient planning prevented the arrest rather than the killing of three terrorists.[76] As noted above, the Court stated in the *Khamzayev* case that care must be taken to 'avoid or minimise, to the greatest extent possible, the loss of life, *both for the persons at whom the measures [are] directed* and for civilians'.[77] The importance of subsequent medical care to prevent the loss of life,[78] as well as the obligation to investigate the whereabouts of soldiers missing in action,[79] attest to the positive obligation to protect life to the greatest degree possible.

In the context of nuclear weapons, the huge number of deaths is unlikely to fall into what is 'absolutely necessary'. The element that is most striking is the effect of radioactive fallout. This will have the effect of killing both soldiers and

---

[73] See, e.g., on this subject Noam Lubell, 'Challenges in applying human rights law to armed conflict', *International Review of the Red Cross* 87(860) (2005), 737–54, at 745–6.

[74] The level of force that is 'absolutely necessary' in ordinary law enforcement situations will inevitably be much less than that needed in a situation of armed hostilities. For more detail, see Doswald-Beck, *Human Rights in Times of Conflict and Terrorism*, Chapter 6.

[75] IACtHR, *Neira Alegría et al.* v. *Peru*, Judgment (Series C No. 20), 19 January 1995, paras. 74–76.

[76] ECtHR, *McCann and Others* v. *United Kingdom*, Judgment (App. No. 18984/91), 5 September 1995, para. 213. Also HRCte, *Guerrero* v. *Colombia*, Decision (Comm. No. 45/1979), 31 March 1982.

[77] *Khamzayev* case, para. 180 (emphasis added).

[78] ECtHR, *Ahmet Özkan and Others* v. *Turkey*, Judgment (App. No. 21689/93), 6 April 2004, paras. 307–8. Although this case concerned a civilian, the principle would be the same for any person, as subsequently stated in ECtHR, *Varnava and Others* v. *Turkey*, Judgment (App. Nos. 16064/90, 16065/90, 16066/90, 16068/90, 16069/90, 16070/90, 16071/90, 16072/90 and 16073/90), 18 September 2009, para. 185.

[79] *Varnava and Others* v. *Turkey*, Judgment (App. Nos. 16064/90, 16065/90, 16066/90, 16068/90, 16069/90, 16070/90, 16071/90, 16072/90 and 16073/90), 18 September 2009, para. 185.

civilians long after the attack is over, due to the effects of radiation poisoning. This is not consistent with avoiding or minimising loss of life. The presence of intense radiation will also severely limit the ability to search for, rescue and care for the wounded after a nuclear weapon detonation. This too will amount to a violation of the right to life.

It should also be noted that the right to life can be relevant even if a person has not actually died; it is enough that he or she has been exposed to life-threatening treatment.[80]

Possible effect of derogation? A few human rights treaties allow states to derogate from certain human rights during times of war or other emergency.[81] With the exception of the ECHR, the right to life is specifically non-derogable. Therefore, the elements to be considered are those outlined above.

Article 15 of the ECHR specifies that the right to life may not be derogated from 'except in respect of deaths resulting from lawful acts of war'.[82] So far this provision has not been used to derogate from the right to life. It is likely that that the term 'war' was intended to encompass only international armed conflicts, and not internal ones. Article 15(2) of the ECHR was negotiated shortly after the Second World War when war was clearly understood to refer to international conflict. This understanding is confirmed by Article 2 of the 1949 Geneva Conventions, which apply to 'all cases of declared war or of any other armed conflict which may arise between two or more of the High Contracting Parties'. Another indication is the fact that Article 2(2)(c) of the ECHR includes 'action taken for the purpose of quelling [an] insurrection' as one of the reasons for the use of force, but subjects such use to the chapeau of paragraph 2, that is 'the use of force which is no more than absolutely necessary'. 'Insurrection' is the term formerly used in international law to denote what we now refer to as 'non-international armed conflict'. Even in international armed conflicts it would not be possible to derogate in such a way that would violate IHL. That is specifically stated in Article 15(2) ECHR. It needs to be added that the right may only be derogated from 'to the degree required by the exigencies of the situation'.[83] All treaty bodies have in practice interpreted this phrase strictly. A derogation is therefore not an elimination of a right but rather a restriction. In this light, even with a derogation, the ECtHR may well still judge a case on the basis of whether all feasible precautions were taken to limit the loss of life, in keeping with precautions in attack required by Additional Protocol I, Article

---

[80] ECtHR, *Makaratzis* v. *Greece*, Judgment (App. No. 50385/99), 20 December 2004, para 49; AComHPR, *Kazeem Aminu* v. *Nigeria*, Decision (Comm. No. 205/97), 11 May 2000, para. 18.

[81] ICCPR, Art. 4; AChHR, Art. 4; ACHR, Art. 27; ECHR, Art. 15.

[82] ECHR, Art. 15(2).

[83] This wording in Art. 15(1) ECHR echoes the limit in the derogation provisions of the other treaties (but which do not allow any derogation from the right to life).

57(1) and 57(2)(a)(ii),[84] rather than go down the route of primarily evaluating whether the loss of civilian life was 'excessive' in relation to the military objective sought.

Effect on future generations   In a case brought before the ECtHR, the applicant, who suffered from leukaemia, argued that the United Kingdom had violated her right to life by exposing her father to radiation during atmospheric nuclear tests in the 1950s. The Court stated that if the UK government at the time had known of a real risk for future generations, they should have informed her parents of the risk. In the event, this link was not known at that time and therefore no violation was found.[85] Although it is still not clear whether the children of men exposed to radiation will suffer adverse effects, such a connection is now not in doubt as far as pregnant women are concerned. Indeed the ICJ stated in its Nuclear Weapons Advisory Opinion that 'the use of nuclear weapons would be a serious danger to future generations ... [i]onizing radiation has the potential ... to cause genetic defects and illness in future generations'.[86] The children of women so exposed could therefore invoke a violation of the right to life further to the effects of a nuclear explosion.

2.   Prohibition of inhuman treatment

In addition to the fact that nuclear weapons are a threat to life, their effects on survivors are also significant. So far, the injuries sustained by conventional weapons during hostilities have been analysed by human rights courts primarily under the right to life, given that life was thereby endangered.[87] However, nuclear weapons cause particularly extreme suffering. Their horrific effects are well known: people can be rendered blind from seeing the first flash, those not killed have horrific burns and/or the horribly painful effects of radiation poisoning, and there are other serious long-term health effects, including damage to the thyroid gland and later development of cancers. Radiation adversely affects the immune system so that the injured will not recover in the way they could have from weapons without this effect. In addition to causing more deaths than otherwise, this prolongs suffering.[88]

---

[84] Also see 'Rule 15' in Henckaerts and Doswald-Beck, *Customary International Humanitarian Law*.

[85] ECtHR, *L.C.B.* v. *United Kingdom*, Judgment (App. No. 14/1997/798/1001ww), 9 June 1998, paras. 38 and 41.

[86] Nuclear Weapons Advisory Opinion, para. 35.

[87] An exception is the IACtHR *Santa Domingo* case, which also found the bombardment of a hamlet to be a violation of Art. 5(1) ACHR ('Every person has the right to have his physical, mental, and moral integrity respected').

[88] For a summary of the effects of a nuclear explosion on people, see, e.g., 'Categories of Medical Effects', available at: www.remm.nlm.gov/nuclearexplosion.htm.

Inhuman treatment has been described as that which 'causes severe suffering, mental or physical, which, in the particular situation, is unjustifiable'[89] and which attains a 'minimum level of severity'.[90] The assessment will depend on the circumstances of the case, such as the duration of the treatment and the situation of the victim.[91] It is important to note that inhuman treatment is not limited to persons in detention. It has been applied to people who lost their homes and livelihoods through deliberate burning and destruction,[92] as well as to the relatives of forcibly disappeared persons.[93] The IACtHR has found the same for relatives of persons who have been massacred or subject to extrajudicial executions.[94] Although 'inhuman treatment' has not directly been applied by a human rights treaty body to the use of a particular kind of weapon during armed hostilities, the justifiability of any particular use of weapon in police operations has been relevant to whether the pain or suffering engendered amounted to inhuman treatment.[95] In particular, force that is not necessary as a result of the victim's own behaviour (for example, to restrain a violent demonstrator) will amount to inhuman treatment if severe enough. Resistance to interrogation has not been accepted as a justification for the use of force.[96]

---

[89] European Commission on Human Rights (EComHR), *Denmark, Sweden, Norway and the Netherlands* v. *Greece*, Report of the Commission, 5 November 1969, *Yearbook of the European Convention on Human Rights*, Vol. 12-II (1969), p. 186.

[90] ECtHR, *Ireland* v. *United Kingdom*, Judgment (App. No. 5310/71), 18 January 1978, para. 162; AComHPR, *Huri-Laws* v. *Nigeria*, Decision (Comm. No. 225/98), 6 November 2000, para. 41.

[91] HRCte, *Vuolanne* v. *Finland*, Com.265/1987, Views, 7 April 1989, para. 9.2. See also Report of the Special Rapporteur on the question of torture, Commission on Human Rights, UN doc. E/CN.4/2006/6, 23 December 2005, paras. 38–40.

[92] ECtHR, *Selçuk and Asker* v. *Turkey*, Judgment (12/1997/796/998–999), 24 April 1998, paras. 77–9; ECtHR, *Bilgin* v. *Turkey*, Judgment (App. No. 23819/94)), 16 November 2000, paras. 99–103; IACtHR, *Ituango Massacres* v. *Colombia*, Judgment (Series C No. 148), 1 July 2006, paras. 272–74; AComHPR, *Sudan Human Rights Organisation and Centre on Housing Rights and Evictions* v. *Sudan*, Decision (Comm. Nos. 279/03 and 296/05), 27 May 2009, paras. 157–9.

[93] E.g. AComHPR, *Amnesty International and Others* v. *Sudan*, Decision (Comm. Nos. 48/90, 50/91, 52/91, and 89/93), 15 November 1999, para. 54; HRCte, *Quinteros* v. *Uruguay*, Decision (Comm. No. 107/1981, 21 July 1983, para. 14; ECtHR, *Kurt* v. *Turkey*, Judgment (App. No. 24276/94), 25 May 1998, paras. 133–4; IACtHR, *Heliodoro Portugal* v. *Panama*, Judgment (Series C No. 186), 12 August 2008, para. 163.

[94] E.g. IACtHR, *Valle Jaramillo et al.* v. *Colombia*, Judgment (Series C No. 192), 27 November 2008, paras. 119–22, which concerned the family of a murdered human rights defender; IACtHR, *Villagran Morales et al.* v. *Guatemala (Street Children case)*, Judgment (Series C. No. 63), 19 November 1999, paras. 173–4, which concerned the families of street children who had been murdered and the bodies abandoned.

[95] ECtHR, *Balçik and others* v. *Turkey*, Judgment (App. No. 25/02), 29 November 2007, paras. 30–4; ECtHR, *Ali Günes* v. *Turkey*, Judgment (App. No. 9829/07), 10 April 2012, paras. 42–3.

[96] E.g. ECHR, *Tomasi* v. *France*, Judgment (App. No. 12850/87), 27 August 1992, paras. 113–15.

We may derive from this that the existence of armed hostilities will not automatically justify any type of injury, however extreme, but will depend on whether the use of a particular weapon is absolutely necessary. In this regard, a certain similarity can be seen with the prohibition of the use of weapons that cause superfluous injury or unnecessary suffering under IHL. However, although it is notoriously difficult for states to admit that specific weapons, not banned by treaty or already obsolete, have such an effect under IHL, this problem is less likely to occur under human rights law. The effects of nuclear weapons are so atrocious, and so much worse than conventional weapons, that it is difficult to imagine a human rights treaty body considering that their use was sufficiently justified to prevent a finding of inhuman treatment.

3.   The right to a healthy environment

Relevance

The ICJ summarised the effects of nuclear weapons on the environment in its Advisory Opinion. In particular it specified that:

> [t]hey have the potential to destroy ... the entire ecosystem of the planet.
> The radiation released by a nuclear explosion would affect health, agriculture, natural resources and demography over a very wide area ... Ionizing radiation has the potential to damage the future environment, food and marine ecosystem, and to cause genetic defects and illness in future generations.[97]

Direct reference to the right to a healthy environment in human rights treaties

Two of the regional human rights treaties refer to this right directly. The 1981 ACHPR states, in Article 24, that '[a]ll peoples shall have the right to a general satisfactory environment favourable to their development'. The 1988 Additional Protocol to the American Convention on Human Rights in the Area of Economic, Social and Cultural Rights (ACESCR) provides in Article 11 that '[e]veryone shall have the right to live in a healthy environment' and that 'States Parties shall promote the protection, preservation and improvement of the environment'.

This right is perfectly justiciable. Human rights bodies, in particular the UN Human Rights Committee, have specified that so-called economic, social and cultural rights create obligations on states in three major ways. The first is the duty to *respect* rights, namely to not take measures that deprive people of resources they already have. The second is to *protect* rights, namely to adopt measures to protect persons from deprivation of their resources by companies

---

[97] Nuclear Weapons Advisory Opinion, para. 35.

or individuals. The third is to *fulfil*, namely helping people, as appropriate, to gain access to their care and livelihood.[98] The African Commission on Human and Peoples' Rights (AComHPR), following this typology, found a violation of the right to a healthy environment in a case concerning major damage to the environment in Ogoniland caused by the Nigerian National Petroleum Company working with Shell Petroleum Development Corporation. The lack of care violated the state's obligation 'to take reasonable and other measures to prevent pollution and ecological degradation'.[99] Indeed, in this case the government both directly and indirectly caused the damage, thus violating the duties to 'respect' and to 'protect' the right to a healthy environment.

The detonation of a nuclear weapon by a state would certainly amount to a violation of the duty to 'respect' this right and, if it was done by a non-state group, any lack of due diligence would amount to a violation of the duty to 'protect'.[100]

4. *The right to the highest attainable standard of health*

This right is specified in several human rights treaties.[101] Although being at the receiving end of any weapon will undermine health, the element that is important here is the damage to the natural environment caused by radiation that will adversely affect health over a long period of time. The direct connection between damage to the environment and damage to health was made by the African Commission, which found, in the Ogoniland case, a violation of not only the right to a healthy environment but also a violation of the right to the highest attainable standard of health based on the same factual elements.[102] The UN Committee for Economic, Social and Cultural Rights (ICESCR Committee) has similarly specified, in its General Comment on this right, that it includes the right to a healthy environment.[103] In particular, it specified that

[98] Eg. ICESCR Committee, General Comment No. 12: 'The right to adequate food (art. 11)', UN doc. E/C.12/1999/5, 12 May 1999, para. 15; General Comment No. 14: 'The right to the highest attainable standard of health (article 12 of the International Covenant on Economic, Social and Cultural Rights)', UN doc. E/C.12/2000/4, 11 August 2000, paras. 34–7; and General Comment No. 15: 'The right to water (arts. 11 and 12 of the International Covenant on Economic, Social and Cultural Rights)', UN doc. E/C.12/2002/11, 20 January 2003, paras. 21–9 and 44.

[99] AComHPR, *The Social and Economic Rights Action Center and the Center for Economic and Social Rights* v. *Nigeria*, Decision (Comm. No. 155/96), 27 October 2001, paras. 50–4.

[100] The respect, protect and fulfil typology is also applied to civil and political rights.

[101] ICESCR, Art. 12; ACHPR, Art. 16; ACESCR, Art. 10; Revised European Social Charter, Art. 11.

[102] AComHPR, *The Social and Economic Rights Action Center and the Center for Economic and Social Rights* v. *Nigeria*, paras. 50–4.

[103] ICESCR Committee, General Comment No. 14: 'The right to the highest attainable standard of health (article 12 of the International Covenant on Economic, Social and Cultural Rights)', UN doc. E/C.12/2000/4, 11 August 2000, paras. 4, 11, and 34.

'States should refrain from using or testing nuclear ... weapons, if such testing results in the release of substances harmful to human health'.[104] It is evident that the actual use of a nuclear weapon would have this effect.

The disruption of health services will be much worse than in the case of conventional weapons. Not only is there likely to be more destruction, death and harm within health services as such, but also the particular effects of nuclear weapons means that medical aid will be much more difficult to provide. An ICRC report points out that the scale of destruction and injuries, as well as the need for decontamination, will quickly overwhelm available emergency response capacities. There is also the very real problem of the exposure of assistance providers to radiation that will prevent or limit the aid they could give.[105]

D. Application of these rights during armed conflict

This is not the place to analyse all aspects of the application of economic, social and cultural rights during armed conflict, but rather to touch briefly on two of the most relevant points, namely extra-territorial application of these rights and how they have been applied to actual armed attacks.

1. Extra-territorial application of these rights

As already noted above, the ICESCR and the ACHPR do not expressly limit their application to where states have jurisdiction. It is significant that the ICESCR Committee has presumed that extra-territorial actions, in the form of sanctions against another state, are to take into consideration the rights of persons affected by them: '[w]hen an external party takes upon itself even partial responsibility for the situation within a country ... it also unavoidably assumes a responsibility to do all within its power to protect the economic, social and cultural rights of the affected population'.[106] Similarly, the AComHPR had no problem in evaluating whether an embargo by some states against another state

---

[104] *Ibid.*, para. 34.

[105] ICRC, 'Humanitarian Assistance in Response to the Use of Nuclear Weapons', February 2013. As a result, the Council of Delegates (a meeting of all Red Cross and Red Crescent Societies) has adopted a resolution that '*emphasises* the incalculable human suffering that can be expected to result from any use of nuclear weapons, the lack of any adequate humanitarian response capacity and the absolute imperative to prevent such use': Resolution I, 'Working towards the elimination of nuclear weapons', Council of Delegates 2011, reproduced in *International Review of the Red Cross*, 94(885) (2012), 347–415, at 358 (original emphasis).

[106] ICESCR Committee, General Comment No. 8: 'The relationship between economic sanctions and respect for economic, social and cultural rights', UN doc. E/C.12/1997/8, 12 December 1997, para. 13.

violated the human rights of the persons affected. In other words, the extra-territorial nature of the actions was not an issue, and the African Commission analysed the case on the merits of the embargo's effects.[107]

2. The duty to respect these rights and armed attacks

The ICESCR contains no derogation clause, and its limitation clause limits restrictions to those that 'may be compatible with the nature of these rights and solely for the purpose of promoting the general welfare in a democratic society'.[108] The ACHPR also has no derogation clause, but its limitation clause allows restrictions for the purpose of 'collective security'. However, the African Commission has not interpreted this in a way that could justify seriously undermining any portion of society. In the case concerning the mass eviction of persons in Darfur, the Commission found a violation of the right to health because 'the destruction of homes, livestock and farms as well as the poisoning of water sources, such as wells exposed the victims to serious health risks'.[109] It did not accept an argument of security because the security of the Darfurian population had considerably worsened.[110]

Similarly, interpretations of the ICESCR in the context of armed attacks have specified that the obligation to 'respect' entails 'the obligation not to destroy minimal essential levels of economic, social and cultural achievements'.[111] The ICESCR Committee regularly comments on violations of these rights during armed conflict, specifying in the context of its report on Colombia that 'it is precisely in situations of crisis, that the Covenant requires the protection and promotion of all economic, social and cultural rights ... to the best of its ability under the prevailing adverse conditions'.[112]

---

[107] AComHPR, *Association pour la sauveguarde de la paix au Burundi* v. *Tanzania, Kenya, Uganda, Rwanda, Zaire and Zambia*, Decision (Comm. No. 157/96), 23 May 2003, para. 75.

[108] ICESCR, Art. 4.

[109] AComHPR, *Sudan Human Rights Organisation and Centre on Housing Rights and Evictions* v. *Sudan*, Decision (Comm. Nos. 279/03 and 296/05), 27 May 2009, paras 165–6.

[110] *Ibid.*

[111] W. Kälin and L. Gabriel, *Human Rights in Times of Occupation: the Case of Kuwait* (Bern: Stämpfli for Law Books in Europe, 1994), Part I, Section II para. 4 (b), p. 24. With regard to all the obligations under the ICESCR, the Rapporteur noted that armed conflict may reduce available resources so that the guarantees of the Covenant may only apply 'to a limited extent', but these must not fall below the minimum core without genuine justification: UN doc. E/CN.4/1992/26, 16 January 1992, para. 52. For an analysis of practice on this subject, see A. Müller, 'Limitations to and derogations from economic, social and cultural rights', *Human Rights Law Review* 9(4) (2009), 557–601, at 574–5 and 579–83.

[112] ICESCR Committee, Concluding Observations: Colombia, UN doc. E/C.12/COL/CO/5, 21 May 2010, para. 7.

Reports of fact-finding missions by the UN have addressed the need to not recklessly undermine the right to health. In particular, in his report on Iraqi-occupied Kuwait, the Rapporteur stated that:

> not only in peacetime but also in times of armed conflict, the deliberate causing of large-scale environmental damage which severely affects the health of a considerable portion of the population concerned, or creates risks for the health of future generations, amounts to a serious violation of the right to the enjoyment of the highest attainable standard of health as embodied in article 12 of the [ICESCR].[113]

Such an effect will also in practice violate IHL, which is sometimes mentioned in reports on violations of human rights further to attacks.[114] It may be concluded, therefore, that the short-, medium- and long-term effects on a population further to any use of a nuclear weapon will certainly undermine the right to a healthy environment and to the highest attainable standard of health.

3. Violation of the rights to property, home, and private and family life

In a number of cases treaty bodies that do not have jurisdiction over economic and social rights have found a violation of certain civil rights as a result of damage to health caused by pollution, or lack of housing as a result of armed activities. In a landmark case concerning pollution from a factory affecting a residential neighbourhood, the ECtHR found a violation of the right to respect for private and family life because the government took no measures to remedy the problem.[115] The loss of home due to military activity, and inability to return or be provided with suitable alternative housing, have also resulted in violations of the right to family life, home and property.[116] Although these

---

[113] Report on the situation of human rights in Kuwait under Iraqi occupation, prepared by Walter Kälin, Special Rapporteur of the Commission on Human Rights, in accordance with Commission resolution 1991/67, UN doc. E/CN.4/1992/26, 16 January 1992, para. 208.

[114] E.g. report on the effect of rocket attacks in Report of the United Nations Fact Finding Mission on the Gaza Conflict, UN doc. A/HRC/12/48, 15 September 2009, paras. 1598, 1691 and 1748.

[115] ECtHR, *López Ostra* v. *Spain*, Judgment (App. No. 16798/90), 9 December 1994, paras. 51 and 57–8. Subsequent cases have stressed the importance of information to people considering living in an area, e.g. ECtHR, *Guerra and Others* v. *Italy*, Judgment (App. No. 116/1996/735/932), 19 February 1998, paras. 58 and 60.

[116] E.g. ECtHR Judgments: *Akdivar and Others* v. *Turkey*, Judgment (App. No. 21893/93), 30 August 1996, para. 88; *Bilgin* v. *Turkey*, Judgment (App. No. 23819/94), 16 November 2000, para. 108; *Ahmet Özkan and Others* v. *Turkey*, Judgment (App. No. 21689/93), 6 April 2004, paras. 405–6; *Dogan and Others* v. *Turkey*, Judgment (App. Nos. 8803–8811/02, 8813/02 and 8815–8819/02), 29 June 2004, paras. 154–9. IACtHR, *Moiwana Village* v. *Suriname*, Judgment (Series C No. 145), 15 June 2005, para. 134; IACtHR, *Ituango Massacres* v.

rights contain limitation clauses, and could also be derogated from, the treaty bodies concerned evaluated whether the supposed social or military need for the situation outweighed the suffering of the individuals concerned. In each instance this was not the case because either the destructive action was grossly disproportionate to the need, and/or the government did not take the necessary measures to remedy the situation to the best degree possible.

The enormous destructive effect of a nuclear detonation, as well as the long-term radioactive effects, is likely to result in the finding of a violation of some or all of these rights.

Conclusion

Although, in this author's opinion, an honest evaluation under IHL would result in the conclusion that nuclear weapons cannot be used in a way that respects that body of law, there is no doubt that human rights law does provide additional value. The most obvious point is that, unlike IHL, there are systems in place that enable individuals to take cases to courts in order to obtain redress for the damage that would be caused. Not only is this the case for those states that have human rights protections under their national law, but the existence of international courts and other treaty bodies also renders this possible. The reporting procedures of the treaty regimes and within the context of the UN Human Rights Council are also relevant.

The above analysis summarises the most relevant human rights affected by nuclear weapons. In the context of the right to life, the most significant fact is that international human rights courts primarily analyse whether sufficient effort was made to avoid or limit loss of life in cases where potentially lethal force cannot be avoided. The possible IHL justification that such loss is not excessive compared with the military advantage expected is not in practice a factor taken into account by such courts. This is important given the elastic nature that the so-called 'proportionality in attack' rule seems to enjoy, and the fact that insufficient precautions in attack are not listed as 'indiscriminate attacks' as such under IHL. The adverse effects on health also amount to several human rights violations. The positive obligations required under human rights law to ensure the proper respect of such law means that human rights courts insist that the law be effective, and not theoretical. Any use of nuclear weapons will, therefore, result in concrete human rights violations that are justiciable.

Although IHL aims to preserve life to the maximum degree possible whilst not undermining military necessity, and is certainly valuable to that end, the

Colombia, Judgment (Series C No. 148), 1 July 2006, paras. 182, 194, and 197; AComHPR, *Sudan Human Rights Organisation and the Centre on Housing Rights and Evictions* v. *The Sudan*, Decision (Comm. Nos. 279/03 and 296/05), 27 May 2009, para. 216.

foundation of human rights law is more squarely based on trying to ensure the short- and long-term respect of all human beings. As Judge Weeramantry pointed out, from a teleological point of view the effect of nuclear weapons is so profound, so long-term and widespread, that they undermine the very notion of human dignity that human rights is based on. Any reliance on these weapons is a sad reminder that much still needs to be done to achieve genuine peace and security.

19

The right to a remedy and reparation for the use of nuclear weapons

STUART CASEY-MASLEN

Introduction

This chapter picks up where Chapter 18 ended: with an understanding that international human rights law is directly relevant to nuclear weapons, and that any use of nuclear weapons outside testing would be highly likely to violate a range of human rights.[1] Such being the case, I suggest how international human rights law could offer remedy and reparation[2] in light of probably massive loss of life and destruction of property resulting from a nuclear weapon strike.[3]

In so doing, I look first at the basis of responsibility under human rights law for nuclear weapon use before turning to address the right to a remedy and reparation in general. The third section of the chapter considers who would be the duty bearers, for such a duty potentially goes beyond a user state. I then assess who could be the holders of a right to a remedy for nuclear weapon use: could

---

[1] I do not address the issue of whether the threat of use of nuclear weapons would itself constitute a violation of human rights, also giving rise to the right to a remedy. Any such threat, were it credible and foreshadowing imminent use, would likely generate mass panic even if not followed by actual use of the weapon.

[2] The precise distinction between the two concepts in legal terms is unclear. See, e.g., Redress, *Implementing Victims' Rights: A Handbook on the Basic Principles and Guidelines on the Right to a Remedy and Reparation* (London: The Redress Trust, March 2006), p. 8. Sometimes reparation is seen as a form of remedy (or vice versa); at other times remedies and reparations are seen as distinct forms of redress. The 2005 Basic Principles and Guidelines on the Right to a Remedy and Reparation for Victims of Gross Violations of International Human Rights Law and Serious Violations of International Humanitarian Law contain both terms, and they are frequently dealt with as separate notions in the body of the text; they also, though, refer to the need for 'available adequate, effective, prompt and appropriate remedies, *including* reparation'. 2005 Basic Principles and Guidelines, UN General Assembly Resolution 60/147, adopted on 16 December 2005, para. 2(c) (emphasis added). See further Art. 63(1), American Convention on Human Rights, San José, 21 November 1969, in force 18 July 1978, 1144 UNTS 123; 9 ILM 99 (1969) (hereafter, ACHR).

[3] Of course, as Archbishop Desmond Tutu stated at the inaugural ceremony of the ICC Trust Fund for Victims in 2004, 'The law alone cannot repair the scars of war' (cited in E. Kristjansdottir, 'International mass claims processes and the ICC Trust Fund for Victims' in C. Ferstman, M. Goetz and A. Stephens (eds.), *Reparations for Victims of Genocide, War Crimes and Crimes against Humanity: Systems in Place and Systems in the Making* (Leiden/Boston: Martinus Nijhoff, 2009), p. 168.

it extend, for example, to military personnel as well as to civilians injured by an explosion or the effects of nuclear fallout? Fifthly, I look at the forms of remedy that could be available to claimants, and seek to gauge which might be the most appropriate in case of a nuclear weapon strike. I advance some conclusions as to the *lex lata* in this area, as well as my view as to where the law might usefully evolve regarding remedies and reparations for mass atrocities.

A. The basis of human rights responsibility for nuclear weapon use

As Louise Doswald-Beck describes in Chapter 18, nuclear weapon use can violate a range of human rights. First and foremost would clearly be the rights to life and to freedom from torture or other forms of cruel, inhuman or degrading treatment. Other rights would likely include those to food, to an adequate standard of living, to freedom of movement or residence,[4] and to family life. This section considers what the basis would be to hold accountable the user of a nuclear weapon for such violations of rights.

A state (and potentially an armed non-state actor) could be held responsible for an unlawful use of nuclear weapons in a number of ways and potentially under several branches of international law. Most probably, use of a nuclear weapon would fall within *jus in bello* relating to international armed conflict. Accordingly there could be state responsibility for violation of international humanitarian law (IHL), as well as, potentially, on the basis of individual criminal responsibility under international criminal law, either on the basis that a weapon whose use was generally prohibited had been used (if the nuclear weapon(s) in question were so adjudged) or through use of a nuclear weapon in violation of IHL rules governing the conduct of hostilities. However, any payment of reparations (which is rare enough in and of itself) would tend to be made to the government of the victims[5] rather than directly to the victims themselves.[6]

---

[4] See, e.g. ACHR, Art. 22; and Inter-American Court of Human Rights (IACtHR), *Case of the Santo Domingo Massacre* v. *Colombia*, Judgment (Case No. 12.416), 30 November 2012, paras. 248–82.

[5] The term victim is used in this chapter to describe those directly or indirectly harmed in the context of an alleged human rights violation. Under paragraph 8 of the 2005 Basic Principles and Guidelines on the Right to a Remedy and Reparation for Victims of Gross Violations of International Human Rights Law and Serious Violations of International Humanitarian Law (discussed below), victims are defined as 'persons who individually or collectively suffered harm, including physical or mental injury, emotional suffering, economic loss or substantial impairment of their fundamental rights, through acts or omissions that constitute gross violations of international human rights law, or serious violations of international humanitarian law. Where appropriate, and in accordance with domestic law, the term "victim" also includes the immediate family or dependants of the direct victim and persons who have suffered harm in intervening to assist victims in distress or to prevent victimization.'

[6] As Ferstman *et al.* remark, reparation is understood as a right of victims not only as an interstate prerogative or an act of compassion or charity. Ferstman *et al.*, 'Introduction' to

In such a case there could also be corresponding responsibility under international human rights law. One example would be on the basis that a violation *in bello* of IHL thereby violated a human right (e.g. the right to life) through the application of the interpretative principle of *lex specialis*. As the International Court of Justice (ICJ) (in)famously stated in its Nuclear Weapons Advisory Opinion:

> The test of what is an arbitrary deprivation of life … falls to be determined by the applicable *lex specialis*, namely, the law applicable in armed conflict which is designed to regulate the conduct of hostilities. Thus whether a particular loss of life, through the use of a certain weapon in warfare, is to be considered an arbitrary deprivation of life contrary to Article 6 of the Covenant, can only be decided by reference to the law applicable in armed conflict and not deduced from the terms of the Covenant itself.[7]

Taking this approach, any violation of IHL rules governing the conduct of hostilities could inexorably result in a corresponding human rights violation. Clearly, the Court did not appear to see any impediment to extraterritorial application of the Covenant with regard to nuclear weapons. Indeed, it may be considered improbable that any state user of nuclear weapons would escape liability for human rights violations on purely jurisdictional grounds.

But what if the use was somehow in accordance with IHL? Let us imagine that a state has detonated a low-yield nuclear weapon on an isolated military base belonging to another state, or against troops conveniently amassed in the desert, or against a submarine armed with nuclear weapons on the high seas. Let us further assume – and it is a far-fetched assumption in my view – that the weapon's use was held to not violate the rules of proportionality or precautions in attack and that neither the weapon nor the method of its use were deemed to be 'of a nature to cause superfluous injury or unnecessary suffering' – what then? Would human rights still intervene to offer a remedy? Although purely speculative, and hopefully it will remain so, surely this would test the *lex specialis* approach to its breaking point.[8]

If, however, the use of the nuclear weapon was not only an act *in bello*, but also *ad bellum*, there could also be distinct and separate liability under human

---

Reparations for Victims of Genocide, War Crimes and Crimes against Humanity, pp. 8–9. See similarly T. van Boven, 'Victims' rights to a remedy and reparation: the new United Nations Principles and Guidelines' in C. Ferstman, M. Goetz and A. Stephens (eds.), *Reparations for Victims of Genocide, War Crimes and Crimes against Humanity: Systems in Place and Systems in the Making* (Leiden/Boston: Martinus Nijhoff, 2009), pp. 26–7. See also the situation with respect to the Eritrea–Ethiopia Claims Commission.

[7] ICJ, Nuclear Weapons Advisory Opinion, 1996, para. 25.

[8] For example, the European Court of Human Rights (ECtHR) has recognised in a number of cases that the use of certain weapons violates human rights even where such use does not appear, per se, to have violated IHL. In particular, courts have recognised the responsibility of the state to protect people from entering areas that are contaminated with landmines,

rights law for a violation of *jus ad bellum*. Arguably this liability could exist even for military victims of a nuclear attack. How could this happen? The Eritrea–Ethiopia Claims Commission made the (admittedly) controversial determination[9] that Eritrea had violated Article 2(4) of the 1945 United Nations Charter, which prohibits the use of force against the territorial integrity or political independence of another state. They did so 'by resorting to armed force on May 12, 1998 and the immediately following days to attack and occupy the town of Badme, then under peaceful administration by the Claimant, as well as other territory'.[10]

In its final award, the Claims Commission considered *ad bellum* claims in detail. It asserted that the law of state responsibility 'must maintain a measure of proportion between the character of a delict and the compensation due'. While it concluded that Eritrea's violation of *jus ad bellum* in May 1998 was serious, with serious consequences, it determined that the violation 'was different in magnitude and character from the aggressive uses of force marking the onset of the Second World War, the invasion of South Korea in 1950, or Iraq's 1990 invasion and occupation of Kuwait'. The Commission stated its belief that 'determination of compensation must take such factors into account'.[11] Use of a nuclear weapon in violation of *jus ad bellum* would certainly be considered an aggravating factor in any award of reparation.

The Commission also felt that an award of compensation 'should be limited as necessary to ensure that the financial burden imposed on Eritrea would not be so excessive, given Eritrea's economic condition and its capacity to pay, as seriously to damage Eritrea's ability to meet its people's basic needs'.[12] It noted that claims of compensation 'of this magnitude' might raise significant

---

both through adequate mine risk education and through clearance operations. In *Alkin* v. *Turkey*, for example, the Court affirmed that injury resulting from landmines is a violation of Art. 2 of the 1950 European Convention on the Protection of Human Rights and Fundamental Freedoms (ECHR) because the nature of the weapon makes their use unlawful: '[T]he Court considers that the laying of such indiscriminate and inhumane weapons as anti-personnel landmines, which affect the lives of a disproportionate number of civilians and children, amounts to intentional use of lethal force.' ECtHR, *Alkin* v. *Turkey*, Judgment (App. No. 75588/01), 13 October 2009, para. 30. Convention for the Protection of Human Rights and Fundamental Freedoms, Rome, 4 November 1950, in force 3 September 1953, 213 UNTS 221.

[9] See, e.g., C. Gray, 'The Eritrea/Ethiopia Claims Commission oversteps its boundaries: a partial award?', *European Journal of International Law* 17(4) (2006), 699–721; G. Nystuen and K. Tronvoll, 'The Eritrean–Ethiopian peace agreement: exploring the limits of law', *Nordisk Tidsskrift for Menneskerettigheter* 28(1) (2008), 16–37.

[10] Eritrea–Ethiopia Claims Commission, 'Partial Award, Jus Ad Bellum, Ethiopia's Claims 1–8 between The Federal Democratic Republic of Ethiopia and The State of Eritrea', The Hague, 19 December 2005, Section IV, para. 1.

[11] *Ibid.*, para. 312.　　[12] *Ibid.*, para. 313.

questions at the intersection of the law of state responsibility and fundamental human rights norms.[13] It had already concluded that 'in the circumstances' it 'need not decide the question of possible capping of the award in light of the Parties' obligations under human rights law'.[14]

Thus, the Commission only considered respect for fundamental human rights insofar as massive financial claims against Eritrea would impact on its ability to meet its own human rights obligations towards its own citizens. At no stage did the Commission discuss directly any potential liability upon Eritrea for human rights violations against Ethiopians for Eritrea's violation of *jus ad bellum*. The award it made was for inter-state compensation (although it noted the 'responsibility' upon Ethiopia to provide relief to the individual victims):

> The claims here are inter-State claims, not claims on behalf of specific individuals. Any compensation goes to the claimant State, not to injured individuals (although the Commission remains confident that the Parties are mindful of their responsibility, within the scope of the resources available to them, to ensure that their nationals who are victims of the conflict receive relief).[15]

Finally, there could be a violation of human rights law outside the conduct of hostilities (e.g. where a state used a nuclear weapon against its own people but not within a non-international armed conflict). This act, occurring in a situation of law enforcement, could potentially be dealt with by a regional human rights court as well as through reparations from the International Criminal Court, where it constituted a crime against humanity or possibly even genocide.[16] Trickier to deal with in a human rights framework would be a case where an armed non-state actor commits an act of terrorism by detonating a nuclear weapon in a public place (but see below).[17]

---

[13] Eritrea–Ethiopia Claims Commission, 'Final Award, Ethiopia's Damages Claims between The Federal Democratic Republic of Ethiopia and The State of Eritrea', para. 313.

[14] *Ibid.*, para. 23. [15] *Ibid.*, para. 82.

[16] The 1998 Rome Statute of the International Criminal Court empowers the Court to 'establish principles relating to reparations to, or in respect of, victims, including restitution, compensation and rehabilitation'. Rome Statute of the International Criminal Court, Rome 17 July 1998, in force 1 July 2002, 2187 UNTS 90, Art. 75. This provision also empowers the Court to 'determine the scope and extent of any damage, loss and injury to, or in respect of, victims'. Though see Ferstman *et al.*, 'Introduction' to *Reparations for Victims of Genocide, War Crimes and Crimes against Humanity*, p. 11: 'Funding reparations for mass victimisation from the resources collected from individual convicted perpetrators will be necessarily a challenge.' They note, however, that the ICC's Trust Fund for Victims 'should remedy some of the resource gaps created by indigent defendants unable to pay the reparations awards ordered against them'. *Ibid.*, p. 12.

[17] For a discussion of the likelihood of such an event, see Chapter 16.

B. The right to a remedy

It is fundamental to the notion of human rights that every victim of a human rights violation has the right to an 'effective' remedy. Indeed, the right to a remedy and reparation forms part of the corpus of customary law[18] and is arguably also a general principle of law.[19] The 1948 Universal Declaration of Human Rights (UDHR) saw the exercise of the right to a remedy purely in terms of national fora.[20] Today, however, the scope of the right is also well developed in international[21] and regional[22] human rights treaties, and has been clearly articulated by the various oversight and implementation mechanisms established under them.

Dinah Shelton observes that a remedy has two core elements, one substantive and the other procedural. The procedural element is the means by which redress for an alleged human rights violation may be sought. As South African Supreme Court Justice Albie Sachs declared, 'Justice is also in the process, not only in the outcome'.[23] The substantive element covers the outcome of such a process; that is 'the relief afforded the successful claimant'.[24]

---

[18] In 2001, in its judgment in the *Cantoral Benevides* case, for example, the Inter-American Court of Human Rights held that Art. 63(1) of the ACHR (governing remedy and reparation) 'embodies a rule of customary law that is one of the basic principles of contemporary international law as regards the responsibility of States. When an unlawful act imputable to a State occurs, that State immediately becomes responsible in law for violation of an international norm, which carries with it the obligation to make reparation and to put an end to the consequences of the violation.' IACtHR, *Cantoral Benevides* case, Judgment, 3 December 2001, Ser. C, No. 88 (2001), para. 40. See also Dinah Shelton, *Remedies in International Human Rights Law*, 2nd edn (Oxford University Press, 2005), pp. 27–9, 217.

[19] See, e.g., IACtHR, *Velasquez Rodriguez v. Honduras*, Judgment (Reparations) (Series C, No. 7), 21 July 1989, para. 25.

[20] 'Everyone has the right to an effective remedy by the competent national tribunals for acts violating the fundamental rights granted him by the constitution or by law.' Art. 8, Universal Declaration of Human Rights (UDHR), Paris, 10 December 1948, UN doc. A/810 at 71 (1948).

[21] See, e.g., International Covenant on Civil and Political Rights, New York, 16 December 1966, in force 23 March 1976, 999 UNTS 171, Art. 2; International Convention on the Elimination of All Forms of Racial Discrimination, New York, 21 December 1965, in force 4 January 1969, 660 UNTS 195, Art. 6; and the Convention against Torture and Other Cruel, Inhuman or Degrading Treatment or Punishment, New York, 10 December 1984, in force 26 June 1987, 1465 UNTS 85, Art. 14.

[22] Thus, the ECHR (Arts. 13 and 41), the ACHR (Art. 25), the 1981 African Charter on Human and Peoples' Rights (Art. 7) and the 2004 Arab Charter on Human Rights (Art. 12) all codify the right to a remedy for victims of human rights violations. African Charter on Human and Peoples' Rights, Nairobi, 27 June 1981, in force 21 October 1986, OAU Doc. CAB/LEG/67/3 rev. 5; 1520 UNTS 217; 21 ILM 58 (1982); and Arab Charter on Human Rights, Tunis, 22 May 2004, in force 15 March 2008, reprinted in 12 *International Human Rights Report* (2005), 893.

[23] Cited in Y. Danieli, 'Massive trauma and the healing role of restorative justice' in C. Ferstman, M. Goetz and A. Stephens (eds.), *Reparations for Victims of Genocide, War Crimes and Crimes against Humanity: Systems in Place and Systems in the Making* (Leiden/Boston: Martinus Nijhoff, 2009), p. 66.

[24] Shelton, *Remedies in International Human Rights Law*, p. 7.

In its judgment in the *Armed Activities on the Territory of the Congo* case, the ICJ affirmed 'that a State which bears responsibility for an internationally wrongful act is under an obligation to make full reparation for the injury caused by that act', although it left it to the parties to determine in the first instance through negotiations what the meaning of such 'full reparation' might be.[25] The Inter-American Commission on Human Rights and the European Court of Human Rights have both awarded remedies for those whose rights have been violated by unlawful weapon use.[26]

In 2006 the UN General Assembly adopted Resolution 60/147 without a vote, in which it 'adopted' the annexed Basic Principles and Guidelines on the Right to a Remedy and Reparation for Victims of Gross Violations of International Human Rights Law and Serious Violations of International Humanitarian Law. Ostensibly a soft law instrument,[27] a preambular paragraph nonetheless notes that the Basic Principles and Guidelines 'do not entail new international or domestic legal obligations but identify mechanisms, modalities, procedures and methods for the implementation of existing legal obligations under international human rights law and international humanitarian law'. Paragraph 3 referred to:

> The obligation to respect, ensure respect for and implement international human rights law and international humanitarian law as provided for under the respective bodies of law, [which] includes, inter alia, the duty to:
>
> (a) Take appropriate legislative and administrative and other appropriate measures to prevent violations;
>
> (b) Investigate violations effectively, promptly, thoroughly and impartially and, where appropriate, take action against those allegedly responsible in accordance with domestic and international law;
>
> (c) Provide those who claim to be victims of a human rights or humanitarian law violation with equal and effective access to justice ... irrespective of who may ultimately be the bearer of responsibility for the violation; and
>
> (d) Provide effective remedies to victims, including reparation.

To the extent that the Basic Principles and Guidelines 'do not entail new international or domestic legal obligations', these steps may reflect existing obligations of states under international law.

---

[25] ICJ, *Case Concerning Armed Activities on the Territory of the Congo (Democratic Republic of the Congo v. Uganda)*, Judgment of 19 December 2005, paras. 259–60.

[26] See generally, e.g., M. Burke and L. Persi Vicentic, 'Remedies and reparations', Chapter 18 in S. Casey-Maslen (ed.), *Weapons under International Human Rights Law* (Cambridge University Press, 2014).

[27] It is described by one commentator as a 'Magna Carta for victims'. Danieli, 'Massive trauma and the healing role of restorative justice', p. 65.

C.   Duty bearers

1.   The state

Front and centre in any accountability for human rights violations engendered by the use of nuclear weapons would clearly be a nuclear weapon-using state. The general obligation upon a state to make reparation for its violation of international law is long-standing. In 1928 the Permanent Court of International Justice (PCIJ) stated in the *Factory at Chorzów* case that:

> It is a principle of international law that the breach of an engagement involves an obligation to make reparation in an adequate form. Reparation therefore is the indispensable complement of a failure to apply a convention and there is no necessity for this to be stated in the convention itself.[28]

At the merits stage of the same case, the Court set out in more detail the content of the obligation of reparation:

> The essential principle contained in the actual notion of an illegal act – a principle which seems to be established by international practice and in particular by the decisions of arbitral tribunals – is that reparation must, as far as possible, wipe out all the consequences of the illegal act and re-establish the situation which would, in all probability, have existed if that act had not been committed.[29]

In 2001 the International Law Commission (ILC) codified these principles in Article 31(1) of its Draft Articles on Responsibility of States for Internationally Wrongful Acts (hereafter, Articles on State Responsibility), which provide that the responsible state 'is under an obligation to make full reparation for the injury caused by the internationally wrongful act'. In its Commentary on the Articles on State Responsibility, the ILC noted that the notion of 'injury' is to be 'understood as including any damage caused by that act' and that, in particular, '"injury" includes any material or moral damage caused thereby'.[30]

Furthermore, under international human rights law it is generally accepted that the state has the primary duty to respect and ensure human rights to all persons under its jurisdiction. This duty to provide a remedy includes not only situations where the state has itself failed to respect human rights but also where it fails to meet its obligations of due diligence to protect those under its

---

[28] PCIJ, *Case Concerning the Factory at Chorzów (Germany v. Poland)*, Judgment (Jurisdiction), No. 8, 1927, PCIJ Ser. A, No. 9, p. 21.

[29] PCIJ, *Case Concerning the Factory at Chorzów (Germany v. Poland)*, Judgment (Merits), No. 13, 1928, PCIJ Ser. A, No. 17, p. 47.

[30] ILC, Draft Articles on the Responsibility of States for Internationally Wrongful Acts, with commentaries, 2001, Text adopted by the International Law Commission at its fifty-third session, in 2001, and submitted to the General Assembly as a part of the Commission's report covering the work of that session (A/56/10), p. 91.

jurisdiction against unlawful use of weapons (for example, by third parties, including not only other states but also armed non-state actors). Under the 2005 Basic Principles and Guidelines the scope of the duty reflects the duty both to respect and to protect:

> In accordance with its domestic laws and international legal obligations, a State shall provide reparation to victims for *acts or omissions* which can be attributed to the State and constitute gross violations of international human rights law or serious violations of international humanitarian law. In cases where a person, a legal person, or other entity is found liable for reparation to a victim, such party should provide reparation to the victim or compensate the State if the State has already provided reparation to the victim.[31]

Consonant with public international law, state responsibility for reparation is generally owed to another state,[32] but recent jurisprudence in the ICJ[33] has shown how one state can bring a case for compensation against another on behalf of an individual. In June 2012 the Court ordered the Democratic Republic of Congo to pay compensation to Guinea for injuries resulting from violations of the human rights of a national of Guinea.[34] The ICJ judgment reinforces the understanding that violations of internationally protected human rights, like other violations of international law, give rise to a legitimate claim for a remedy, including monetary compensation. Moreover, where the human rights obligations are *erga omnes*, which means that they are obligations owed to the international community as a whole, then potentially any state has a legal interest in ensuring redress for the violation of a right enshrined in a treaty to which it is party. The ICJ noted, famously, in the *Barcelona Traction* case that:

> Such obligations derive, for example, in contemporary international law, from the outlawing of acts of aggression, and of genocide, as also from the principles and rules concerning the basic rights of the human person, including protection from slavery and racial discrimination.[35]

---

[31] 2005 Basic Principles and Guidelines, para. 15 (emphasis added).

[32] See, e.g., K. Hausler, N. Urban and R. McCorquodale, *Protecting Education in Insecurity and Armed Conflict: An International Law Handbook* (London: British Institute of International and Comparative Law/Doha: Education Above All, 2012), p. 224.

[33] The 1945 Statute of the International Court of Justice (ICJ) allows States Parties to declare that they recognise the jurisdiction of the Court concerning the 'nature or extent of the reparation to be made for the breach of an international obligation'. Statute of the ICJ, San Francisco, 26 June 1945, in force 24 October 1945, 3 Bevans 1179, Art. 36(2)(d).

[34] ICJ, *Ahmadou Sadio Diallo (Republic of Guinea v. Democratic Republic of the Congo)*, Judgment (Compensation owed by the Democratic Republic of the Congo to the Republic of Guinea), 19 June 2012.

[35] ICJ, *Case concerning the Barcelona Traction, Light and Power Co. Ltd.* (New Application: 1962) (*Belgium v. Spain*) (Second Phase), 1970, paras. 33–4. See also UN Human Rights Committee, General Comment No. 31: 'The nature of the general legal obligation on States Parties to the Covenant', UN doc. CCPR/C/21/Rev.1/Add.13, 29 March 2004, para. 2; and

These 'principles and rules concerning the basic rights of the human person' would certainly include the right to life and the right to freedom from torture and other forms of cruel, inhuman and degrading treatment: rights that would be violated by unlawful use of a nuclear weapon.

2. Armed non-state actors

Further, despite the continuing centrality of human rights obligations upon states, there is a clear trend towards considering that armed non-state actors are directly responsible for violations of human rights.[36] For example, the February 2012 report of the International Commission of Inquiry on Syria noted that, 'at a minimum, human rights obligations constituting peremptory international law (*ius cogens*) bind States, individuals and non-State collective entities, including armed groups. Acts violating *ius cogens* – for instance, torture or enforced disappearances – can never be justified.'[37] In July 2012 the UN Human Rights Council – a body composed of States – adopted a resolution on Mali in which it condemned:

> the human rights violations and acts of violence committed in northern Mali, in particular by the rebels, terrorist groups and other organized transnational crime networks, including the violence perpetrated against women and children, the killings, hostage-takings, pillaging, theft and destruction of religious and cultural sites, as well as the recruitment of child soldiers, and calls for the perpetrators of these acts to be brought to justice.[38]

Within the United Nations, the work of its Assistance Mission in Afghanistan (UNAMA) is particularly relevant. For several years now, UNAMA has explicitly sought to hold the Taliban and other 'anti-government elements' to account for violations both of IHL and of human rights. As it explains in its annual report on the protection of civilians:

> While non-State actors in Afghanistan, including armed groups, cannot formally become parties to international human rights treaties, non-State actors which exercise de facto control over some areas, such as the Taliban,

---

C. J. Tams and A. Tzanakopoulos, 'Barcelona Traction at 40: the ICJ as an agent of legal development', *Leiden Journal of International Law* 23 (2010), 781–800.

[36] Of course, the oversight mechanisms constituted by the human rights treaty bodies are addressed to states not to non-state armed groups.

[37] UN Human Rights Council, 'Report of the independent international commission of inquiry on the Syrian Arab Republic', UN doc. A/HRC/19/69, 22 February 2012, para. 106. Those who still reject the application of human rights law to entities other than states tend to refer to such entities as 'abusing' rather than 'violating' human rights.

[38] UN Human Rights Council Resolution 20/17, 17 July 2012, para. 2.

are increasingly deemed to be bound by international human rights obliga-tions.[39, 40]

On 28 April 2004 the UN Security Council unanimously adopted Resolution 1540 (2004) under Chapter VII of the UN Charter, affirming that the prolifer-ation of nuclear, chemical and biological weapons and their means of delivery constitutes a threat to international peace and security. The Resolution obliges states, inter alia, to refrain from supporting by any means non-state actors from developing, acquiring, manufacturing, possessing, transporting, transferring or using nuclear, chemical or biological weapons and their delivery systems.[41] While the Resolution is directed at states, it nonetheless indirectly affirms the illegality of any possession, let alone use, by armed non-state actors of nuclear weapons.

There may also be corporate liability for the commission of, or complicity in, human rights violations.[42] This could include liability for technical or mater-ial assistance to a person, group or state that used a nuclear weapon in viola-tion of international law. For example, Ralph Steinhardt has argued that the 'civil liability of corporations for their torts (and, in civil law jurisdictions, their delicts) plainly qualifies as a general principle of law recognised by civilised nations'. He concludes that: 'It may be that company-wide compliance pro-grammes, adopted to minimise the risk of alien tort litigation, become a free-standing means for assuring that corporations do not replace governments as the dominant perpetrator of human rights abuse.'[43]

D. Rights holders

Were a ground of action founded under international human rights law, clearly civilian victims of any nuclear attack (or their dependents) would be the primary

---

[39] See UN Secretary-General, Report of the Secretary-General's Panel of Experts on Accountability in Sri Lanka, 31 March 2011, para. 188. Also see UN Human Rights Council, 'Report of the International Commission of Inquiry to investigate all Alleged Violations of International Human Rights Law in the Libyan Arab Jamahiriya', UN doc. A/HRC/17/44, 1 June 2011.

[40] UNAMA, *Afghanistan, Annual Report 2012, Protection of Civilians in Armed Conflict*, February 2013, p. iv.

[41] See further Chapter 16 of this book.

[42] See generally R. G. Steinhardt, 'Corporate Responsibility and the international law of human rights: the new lex mercatoria' in P. Alston (ed.), *Non-State Actors and Human Rights* (Oxford University Press, 2005), pp. 205–14 (outlining the work of various intergovern-mental organisations in the articulation or enforcement of human rights norms for busi-nesses, including the UN, the World Bank, the International Monetary Fund, the OECD, the International Labour Organization, the World Trade Organization, among others).

[43] See R. G. Steinhardt, 'Weapons and the human rights responsibilities of multinational corporations', Chapter 17 in S. Casey-Maslen (ed.), *Weapons under International Human Rights Law* (Cambridge University Press, 2014).

rights holders.[44] The net could be cast widely, though. For instance, with respect to the crimes committed in Cambodia by the Democratic Kampuchea regime between 17 April 1975 and 6 January 1979 that are under the jurisdiction of the Extraordinary Chambers in the Courts of Cambodia (ECCC), victims are considered to be 'any person or legal entity who has suffered from physical, psychological, or material harm as a direct consequence':[45]

> For example: if you were detained or tortured, if you suffered from forced starvation, if you were forced to leave your home and to work hard labour against your will; if your parents, grandparents, or other family members were killed, abducted, detained, or tortured; if you lost your house, your rice fields, your animals, or other property, you may be considered a Victim.[46]

Victims can file complaints before the ECCC and can also apply to become civil parties to criminal proceedings.[47] Under the ICC Rules of Procedure and Evidence, a victim may also be an organisation or institution or other form of legal person, that is a company.[48]

What of the military? In the Eritrea–Ethiopia Claims Commission, Ethiopia had initially sought damages under twenty-three claims with respect to violations of *jus ad bellum*,[49] although it subsequently withdrew five of these.[50] None of the claims, however, addressed combatant deaths or injuries on the battlefield, so the Commission was not called upon to adjudicate that issue. Furthermore, prior to adjudication, Ethiopia withdrew its claim relating to the costs of administering prisoner-of-war camps. Nonetheless, the Commission did observe that Ethiopia's *jus ad bellum* claims 'often alleged injury connected with military activities that the Commission earlier determined were not themselves unlawful'. Since these acts were not themselves unlawful, the Commission held that they 'should not give rise to compensation *on the same basis* as violations of the *jus in bello*'.[51] That they do not give rise to compensation on the same basis as violations of *jus in bello* is clearly not the same as holding that they do not give rise to any right to compensation at all.[52]

---

[44] These may include future generations who would be at far greater risk of contracting certain diseases, such as leukaemia. See Chapter 17 of the present work.

[45] Extraordinary Chambers in the Courts of Cambodia (ECCC), 'Victims Participation' [*sic*], undated but accessed 1 June 2013, available at: www.eccc.gov.kh/en/victims-support/participation.

[46] *Ibid.*   [47] *Ibid.*

[48] Van Boven, 'Victims' rights to a remedy and reparation', pp. 35–6.

[49] Eritrea–Ethiopia Claims Commission, 'Final Award, Ethiopia's Damages Claims between The Federal Democratic Republic of Ethiopia and The State of Eritrea', The Hague, 17 August 2009, pp. 61–2, para. 273.

[50] *Ibid.*, p. 63, para. 274.   [51] *Ibid.*, para. 311 (emphasis added).

[52] Thus, when considering the military, it may be relevant that under the Iraq Claims Commission (discussed below) while there was no general eligibility for compensation, prisoners of war who had suffered 'mistreatment in violation of international humanitarian

Furthermore, responsibility towards military personnel may not only be against those using weapons. Thus, as Burke and Persi Vicentic observe, 'recent cases in the UK point to instances in which military victims of weapons might also be considered human rights victims and thus eligible for comprehensive reparations'.[53] Significant challenges must be overcome – notably combat immunity and jurisdictional issues – but certainty of failure of claims can no longer be assured. Among other cases, the use of combat immunity as a blanket defence was questioned in June 2011 in the case of *Smith and others* v. *Ministry of Defence* in the UK's High Court of Justice, wherein it was claimed that the Ministry of Defence had failed to take reasonable steps to protect the lives of soldiers from foreseeable risk posed by improvised explosive devices (IEDs),[54] and that in such circumstances the death or injury of active duty soldiers while in a combat situation may constitute a violation of the right to life. Significantly, the Court decided that the claim could not be summarily dismissed on the basis of combat immunity, but that it must be allowed to go forward and be considered on its merits. In its judgment in the case on appeal in June 2013, the UK Supreme Court endorsed the possibility of a claim by the families of deceased soldiers. The UK Ministry of Defence had argued that combat immunity applied to troops in action and that it was not 'fair, just or reasonable' to impose a duty of care on the Ministry when soldiers were on the battlefield. The Supreme Court, however, ruled that immunity did not apply in this case, deciding (by majority) that the doctrine of combat immunity should be construed narrowly and should not be extended beyond its established scope to the planning of and preparation for active operations against the enemy.

E.   The nature and scope of remedies

A comprehensive remedy to a human rights violation should serve at least four inter-related purposes. First, it should, to the extent possible, lead to full restitution (*restitutio in integrum*), that is the re-establishment of the situation before the harm was caused.[55] The second purpose of a remedy is to condemn the act that led to the violation and make it clear that there is a norm against

---

law' could lodge claims. Arguably this could also apply where there were violations of international human rights law. The present author is indebted to Charles Garraway for this observation.

[53] Burke and Persi Vicentic, 'Remedies and reparations'.

[54] An IED is an explosive device placed or fabricated in an improvised manner and designed to destroy, incapacitate, harass or distract. It may incorporate military explosive items, but is often constructed from non-military components.

[55] Of course, in many cases of human rights violations caused by weapon use *restitutio in integrum* is not possible. In such cases, courts determine a substitute remedy, often money, which seeks to restore the claimant as close as possible to his/her previous condition or provide something equivalent in value. Shelton, *Remedies in International Human Rights Law*, p. 11.

such behaviour. Third, and clearly leading on from the second, is the desire to deter future violations by essentially establishing a high 'price' for such behaviour. Finally, remedies should render justice by making the truth about human rights violations known, acknowledging the suffering of the victims, reintegrating them, and encouraging a process of reconciliation and forgiveness. Such restorative justice is often seen to be most relevant in instances of large-scale rights abuses that affect entire communities or societies.[56] It could be highly appropriate with respect to any use of nuclear weapons.

According to the 2005 Basic Principles and Guidelines, the procedural aspect of remedying a rights violation requires victims to enjoy the following:

(a) Equal and effective access to justice;
(b) Adequate, effective, and prompt reparation or redress for harm suffered; and
(c) Access to relevant information concerning violations and reparation mechanisms.[57]

For a rights violation to be remedied effectively, financial reparation should be provided within a reasonable time. Victims who have been disabled as a result of the unlawful use of weapons are often dependent on compensation or rehabilitation awards to pay for medical care or physical rehabilitation. Family members of those who have died may also depend on the income of the victim to survive. Recognising the urgency of reparations for such victims, the UN Compensation Commission for Kuwait (described below) accorded priority to cases of individual victims of the Iraqi invasion, including victims of landmines and other explosive devices, over those of businesses and states.

On many occasions, victims of human rights violations caused by weapons have been awarded reparations through national courts and national victims' laws and through regional courts. Some victims have also received compensation through friendly or out-of-court settlements. In both court decisions and settlements, financial compensation is the most common form of remedy, although arguably this is often designed more to meet rehabilitation needs than to address non-pecuniary damages of pain and suffering. Other decisions have provided victims with measures of satisfaction and guarantees of non-repetition in addition to financial compensation.

The common elements in an effective remedy are generally said to be restitution, compensation, rehabilitation, measures of satisfaction and guarantees of non-repetition.[58] These elements are summarised below. In many instances

---

[56] *Ibid.*, pp. 15–16.   [57] 2005 Basic Principles and Guidelines, para. 11.
[58] See, e.g., van Boven, 'Victims' rights to a remedy and reparation', pp. 38–9. Though see van Boven's agreement with Dinah Shelton's assertion that cessation is not part of reparation but part of the general obligation to conform to the norms of international law. *Ibid.*, pp. 24–5 note 12, and p. 38.

involving human rights violations caused by weapons, remedies are limited to compensation. In case of gross violations of human rights, such as those resulting from a nuclear strike, such financial reparations may be awarded to individuals, collectively to groups, and/or in ways that benefit the society as a whole.

Restitution is defined as those measures needed to restore the victim to his/her original situation before the violation. One common measure of restitution is the return of property for persons who have been driven from their homes and displaced (as would be the case as a result of radioactive fallout following the detonation of a nuclear weapon).

Compensation is awarded for any economically assessable damage as appropriate and proportional to the gravity of the violation. Compensation awards to victims may provide for both pecuniary and non-pecuniary damages, as well as expenses for legal costs.

Rehabilitation is the process of restoring physical and mental health of a victim after an attack on his/her physical or mental integrity. It could also be considered a form of restitution. This is particularly relevant for those weapons' victims who have been disabled and/or traumatised, since this form of remedy provides for appropriate medical and psychological care as well as access to legal and social services. Courts have awarded rehabilitation for weapons victims through financial compensation, providing the means for victims to be reimbursed for expenses already paid as well as to pay for future care.

National policies on reparations for large-scale human rights violations can include provisions that enable victims to access medical care and rehabilitation services for free. The national victims' law in Colombia, for example, calls for the dedication of resources to develop the national system of medical, rehabilitative and psychological care to benefit the rehabilitation of all victims of the conflict, including victims of landmines and other indiscriminate weapons, as well as other members of the community.[59] Among the human rights conventions, the 1984 Convention Against Torture, the 2006 Convention on the Rights of Persons with Disabilities and the 1989 Convention on the Rights of the Child all explicitly provide for rehabilitation of the victims of human rights violations.

Measures of satisfaction include, among other things, the verification of the facts and full and public disclosure of the truth, the search for the whereabouts of the disappeared, public apologies, judicial and administrative sanctions against persons liable for the violations, and commemorations and tributes to the victims. When victims of illegal weapons use receive 'no-fault' compensation, this falls short of remedying the human rights violation since it does not fully recognise the violation as such and fails to provide measures of satisfaction for the victim.

---

[59] Colombia Law No. 1448, 10 June 2011, Arts. 136–137.

In regard to a case of cluster munition use in Colombia, the victims have received financial compensation in the national courts, but those who gave orders for the use of the cluster munitions have not yet been held accountable for their actions. In its report on the merits of the case, the Inter-American Court concluded the state had not conducted serious, effective investigations to identify and penalise all those who had orchestrated or been involved in the attack.[60] Similarly, in the case of *Balaj et al. against UNMIK* [the UN Mission in Kosovo], claimants received compensation for their economic loss resulting from the use of a weapon but continued to pursue their claim for other forms of reparations:

> According to the complainants, the formal apology and acceptance of responsibility by the SRSG [Special Representative of the Secretary-General] and the payment of compensation are an insufficient acknowledgement of and redress for the fundamental human rights violations alleged by the complainants.[61]

In its decision to reopen the case, a Human Rights Panel agreed, acknowledging the claimants' interest in an effective criminal investigation: 'While the payment of a financial compensation may be relevant to any recommendation that the Panel chooses to make in respect of a "just satisfaction", a recommendation in respect of a lawful, public investigation into their complaints remains of the utmost personal importance to them.'[62]

Guarantees of non-repetition are those measures taken by the state to contribute to the prevention of future violations. Regarding the illegal use of weapons, a potentially effective guarantee of non-repetition is a comprehensive ban on the use of the weapon that has caused the human rights violation.

1. Remedies for nuclear weapon use

It is clear that individualised remedies for human rights violations might well not be realistic in the case of a nuclear weapon strike given the potentially huge number of victims. As suggested above, however, a range of broader measures, some societal, could be taken to redress the massive and widespread violations engendered by a nuclear strike. A national or international fund could be established for the victims. Rehabilitation of the contaminated areas in addition to support for the survivors and for the families of the deceased victims would be priorities (as well as significant challenges). Of course, those responsible

---

[60] Organisation of American States (OAS), 'IACHR Takes Case Involving Colombia to Inter-American Court', Press release, 28 July 2011, www.oas.org/en/iachr/media_center/PReleases/2011/077.asp.

[61] *Balaj (on Behalf of Mon Balaj), Shaban Xheladini (on Behalf of Arben Xheladini), Zenel Zemeli and Mustafa Nerjovaj against UNMIK*, Case No. 04/07, 11 May 2012, para. 68.

[62] *Ibid.*, para. 88.

for any unlawful strike would need to be identified, found and brought to trial in accordance with international law. An international commission of inquiry could be useful in establishing the facts.

Practice from the UN Compensation Commission

Of relevance to this discussion is the work of the UN Compensation Commission (UNCC), created to address Iraq's financial liability for its 'unlawful invasion and occupation of Kuwait' in 1990. The UNCC was established in 1991 as a subsidiary organ of the UN Security Council.[63] Security Council Resolution 687 had already 'reaffirmed', inter alia, that Iraq, 'without prejudice to the debts and obligations of Iraq arising prior to 2 August 1990, which will be addressed through the normal mechanisms, is liable under international law for any direct loss, damage, including environmental damage and the depletion of natural resources'.[64]

The UNCC accepted claims from individuals, corporations and governments (as long as the claims were submitted by governments), as well as those submitted by international organisations for individuals who were not in a position to have their claims filed by a government. More than 2.6 million claims were submitted for a total of more than US$350 billion in compensation.[65] A total of some $52 billion was awarded.[66] The UNCC's Governing Council identified six categories of claims (A through F): four for claims of individuals, one for corporations and one for governments and international organisations. Category 'B' claims were those submitted by individuals who suffered serious personal injury or whose spouse, child or parent died as a result of Iraq's invasion and occupation of Kuwait. Compensation for successful claims in this category was set at US$2,500 for individuals and up to US$10,000 for families.[67]

---

[63] UN Security Council Resolution 692, adopted on 20 May 1991.

[64] UN Security Council Resolution 687, adopted on 3 April 1991, para. 16.

[65] UNCC, 'The United Nations Compensation Commission', undated but accessed on 5 January 2013 at: www.uncc.ch/start.htm. Thus, as Edda Kristjansdottir observes, such mass claims processes show that 'where there is political will and some source of funds to pay compensation or property to restitute, the challenge of processing hundreds of thousands or even millions, of claims in a relatively short amount of time is not insurmountably difficult' E. Kristjansdottir, 'International Mass Claims Processes and the ICC Trust Fund for Victims' in C. Ferstman, M. Goetz and A. Stephens (eds.), *Reparations for Victims of Genocide, War Crimes and Crimes against Humanity: Systems in Place and Systems in the Making* (Leiden/Boston: Martinus Nijhoff, 2009), p. 169. See further L. A. Taylor, 'The United Nations Compensation Commission' in C. Ferstman, M. Goetz and A. Stephens (eds.), *Reparations for Victims of Genocide, War Crimes and Crimes against Humanity: Systems in Place and Systems in the Making* (Leiden/Boston: Martinus Nijhoff, 2009), esp. p. 213.

[66] UNCC, 'Status of Payment of Claims', 25 July 2013, available at: www.uncc.ch/status.htm.

[67] UNCC, 'Category "B" claims', undated but accessed on 5 January 2013, available at: www.uncc.ch/claims/b_claims.htm. The Commission received approximately 6,000 Category B claims submitted by forty-seven governments and seven offices of three international organisations, seeking a total of approximately US$21 million in compensation. In

That these payments might constitute a form of reparation for violations of human rights through aggression, rather than purely damages for losses as a result of the 'unlawful invasion', was seemingly not considered at the time, but there is no reason why this should not be the case in the future. In his 1992 report to the UN Commission on Human Rights,[68] Walter Kälin, the then UN Special Rapporteur on the Situation of Human Rights in Kuwait under Iraqi Occupation, addressed 'the human rights violations committed in occupied Kuwait by the invading and occupying forces of Iraq', consonant with his mandate.[69] Acts for which the Special Rapporteur found Iraq responsible included summary and arbitrary executions, widespread and systematic torture, deportation of large numbers of civilians to Iraq, the use of third-country nationals as 'human shields', and the extensive destruction of crucial infrastructure in Kuwait, including health care and educational facilities.[70] Similarly, the UN General Assembly Resolution that was adopted based on his report referred to the 'grave violations of human rights and fundamental freedoms *during* the occupation of Kuwait'.[71] There was thus no corresponding discussion of the violations of human rights not covered by the mandate but nonetheless occasioned by the unlawful invasion of Kuwait, even though they would later be covered by the UNCC to some extent.

F.   Ongoing human rights obligations

Of course, one issue is responsibility for the use of nuclear weapons. Whether or not any responsibility is established under international law, however, a state

December 1995 the Commission concluded the Category B claims processing programme. Payment of US$13.45 million in compensation was made available from January 1994 to December 1996 for distribution to 3,945 successful claimants.

[68] 'Report on the situation of human rights in Kuwait under Iraqi Occupation, prepared by Walter Kälin, the Special Rapporteur of the Commission on Human Rights, in accordance with Commission resolution 1991/67', UN doc. E.CN.4/1992/26, 16 January 1992.

[69] In Resolution 1991/67 the Commission requested its Chairman, after consultation with the Bureau, to designate a special rapporteur 'with a mandate to examine the human rights violations committed in occupied Kuwait by the invading and occupying forces of Iraq'. UN Commission on Human Rights, 'Situation of human rights in Kuwait under Iraqi occupation', 6 March 1991, UN doc. E/CN.4/RES/1991/67, para. 9.

[70] 'Report on the situation of human rights in Kuwait under Iraqi Occupation, prepared by Walter Kälin, the Special Rapporteur of the Commission on Human Rights, in accordance with Commission resolution 1991/67', paras. 242–7; and see L. Gabriel, 'Victims of gross violations of human rights and fundamental freedoms arising from the illegal invasion and occupation of Kuwait by Iraq', Paper in Seminar on the Right to Restitution, Compensation, and Rehabilitation for Victims of Gross Violations of Human Rights and Fundamental Freedoms, Maastricht, The Netherlands, 1992, available at: www.uu.nl/faculty/leg/nl/organisatie/departementen/departementrechtsgeleerdheid/organisatie/onderdelen/studieeninformatiecentrummensenrechten/publicaties/simspecials/12/Documents/12-04.pdf.

[71] UN General Assembly Resolution 46/135, 17 December 1991, Fifth preambular paragraph (emphasis added).

has ongoing legal obligations to protect, respect, and fulfil human rights.[72] Any nuclear strike on a populated area, no matter how small, would have catastrophic humanitarian consequences in the short term but also very serious effects over the medium and long term. Beyond the right to life, fundamental rights to health, to an adequate standard of living, to food and to education (among many others) would be gravely affected. While a great deal of latitude would be left to a victim state, close scrutiny of that state's reaction to the disaster would still need to occur, including with respect to its own mobilisation of resources and expertise; its willingness not only to countenance, but also wherever possible to facilitate the massive external support that would certainly be offered; and to its treatment of the wounded and sick without discrimination based on any grounds other than purely medical (e.g. triage).[73] As case law before the European Court of Human Rights as cited above has shown, responsibility for the effects of a weapon does not end at the moment of use.

Conclusion

As Yael Danieli reiterates, impunity, 'by definition, is the opposite of justice'.[74] Yet according to Cherif Bassiouni, 'International Law is not victim oriented.'[75] This chapter has sought to demonstrate that international human rights law does indeed offer a coherent framework for addressing and redressing use of nuclear weapons, should it ever occur again. There is a customary right to a remedy for violations of human rights, and it is very hard to imagine any use of nuclear weapons – even one that somehow complies with IHL – that would not be held to violate at least certain fundamental human rights of a range of individuals. Moreover, the scope of human rights protection is already broad and case law is broadening it still further: going beyond violations of IHL; extending binding obligations to non-state actors, such as rebel groups or companies; and potentially affording protection to military personnel as well as to civilian victims.

Compared with other mass atrocities, a nuclear weapon strike would not face many of the same evidentiary hurdles that frequently combine to deny justice.[76] In discussing compensation for the victims of chemical warfare in Iraq and Iran, Liesbeth Zegveld notes that 'proving the scope of their damage

[72] And, I would argue, at least with regard to the duty to *respect* fundamental human rights, also a non-state actor.

[73] Thus, for example, the 2005 Basic Principles and Guidelines provide (in para. 25) that: 'The application and interpretation of these Basic Principles and Guidelines must be consistent with international human rights law and international humanitarian law and be without any discrimination of any kind or on any ground, without exception.'

[74] Danieli, 'Massive trauma and the healing role of restorative justice', p. 45.

[75] M. Cherif Bassiouni, 'International recognition of victims' rights', *Human Rights Law Review* 6 (2006), 203–80, at 279; see Kristjansdottir, 'International mass claims processes', p. 167.

[76] See, e.g., L. Oette, 'Bringing justice to victims? Responses of regional and international human rights courts and treaty bodies to mass violations' in C. Ferstman, M. Goetz and

was not such a heavy burden for the chemical war victims' since 'their injuries were not disputed. To a large extent, they were still clearly visible. The victims of mustard gas still had scars of the blisters that resulted from second degree burns. In some instances, victims displayed symptoms of respiratory problems. Some suffered from sight deterioration over the years, a few ending up blind.'[77] A similar situation would arise from nuclear weapon use.[78]

Furthermore, the principles and the guidance offered by international human rights law could and should be central to the response to the catastrophe of a nuclear attack. The five principles of restitution, compensation, rehabilitation, measures of satisfaction and a guarantee of non-repetition would be central to such a remedy. And, today, we understand far better the role of transitional justice measures[79] and administrative reparations programmes[80] in addressing widespread and gross violations of human rights.

So, far from being irrelevant, as one might instinctively think, international human rights law should be at the centre of any legal response to a nuclear weapon strike. It should guide remedies for all the victims, whoever is held responsible. It should also help to guide and ensure a prompt, just and effective response by the 'victim' state to the short- and long-term needs of the hundreds of thousands, perhaps even millions of people who would be affected. Let us hope, of course, that this discussion remains an academic one.

A. Stephens (eds.), *Reparations for Victims of Genocide, War Crimes and Crimes against Humanity: Systems in Place and Systems in the Making* (Leiden/Boston: Martinus Nijhoff, 2009), p. 227.

[77] L. Zegveld, 'Compensation for the victims of chemical warfare in Iraq and Iran' in C. Ferstman, M. Goetz and A. Stephens (eds.), *Reparations for Victims of Genocide, War Crimes and Crimes against Humanity: Systems in Place and Systems in the Making* (Leiden/Boston: Martinus Nijhoff, 2009),, p. 378. See also Oette, 'Bringing justice to victims?', pp. 228–9.

[78] Thus, in this author's view, the failure of plaintiffs to secure damages from the Government of Japan in the case of District Court of Tokyo, *Ryuichi Shimoda et al.* v. *The State* (1963) would not be repeated today.

[79] According to the UN Secretary-General, transitional justice 'comprises the full range of processes and mechanisms associated with a society's attempts to come to terms with a legacy of large-scale past abuses, in order to ensure accountability, serve justice and achieve reconciliation. These may include both judicial and non-judicial mechanisms, with differing levels of international involvement (or none at all) and individual prosecutions, reparations, truth-seeking, institutional reform, vetting and dismissals, or a combination thereof.' UN Security Council, 'The rule of law and transitional justice in conflict and post-conflict societies, Report of the Secretary-General', UN doc. S/2004/616, 23 August 2004, para. 8.

[80] C. Correa, J. Guillerot and L. Magarrell, 'Reparations and victim participation: a look at the truth commission experience' in C. Ferstman, M. Goetz and A. Stephens (eds.), *Reparations for Victims of Genocide, War Crimes and Crimes against Humanity: Systems in Place and Systems in the Making* (Leiden/Boston: Martinus Nijhoff, 2009), p. 387.

PART VII

The legality of nuclear weapons under international law

20

Conclusions on the status of nuclear weapons under international law

GRO NYSTUEN

A certain level of what might be labelled nuclear weapons complacency still manifests itself in post-Cold War discussions on global security policy. The nuclear weapons 'logic', which essentially holds that one must have nuclear weapons in order to ensure that they will never be used, has helped to sustain a perception that we are thereby safe from their use. The fact remains, however, that nuclear weapons are still being produced, maintained and stockpiled in most parts of the world. The issue of legal regulation of nuclear weapons therefore remains vital because the potential for large-scale destruction and suffering as a consequence of their use is so enormous.

The aim of this book has been to give a *lex lata* (the law as it exists) analysis of the law in the chosen areas, in an effort to uncover the extent to which nuclear weapons are restricted (or not) under the relevant legal regimes. In accordance with the methodology of international law, the primary legal sources relied upon have been first and foremost international agreements and customary international law. While not an independent and binding legal source in itself, the 1996 Advisory Opinion of the International Court of Justice (ICJ) includes specific interpretations of such primary sources. The conclusions to be drawn from those and other legal sources drawn upon in this book are subject to debate, including among its various authors. In many instances there is no single or unequivocal legal answer.

A number of different legal regimes that explicitly or implicitly apply to nuclear weapons have been discussed in this book, in particular with a view to identifying restrictions on use, obligations to disarm, limitations on proliferation and other legal effects that would diminish the risks linked to nuclear weapons.

Starting with the legal regime governing the justness of and recourse to military force between states (*jus ad bellum*), and the contiguous rules on proportionality and necessity, it is asserted that these apply equally to all uses of force irrespective of weapon type, and thus no particular restrictions are imposed on nuclear weapons as such. This assumption also applies to the debate on threats (*ad bellum*): threatening use of force by nuclear weapons is governed by the same legal framework as general threats of the use of force in general.

In its Advisory Opinion, the ICJ may have contributed to confusion with regard to the *ad bellum* rules governing the justification for the use of military force on the one hand and the *in bello* rules governing the actual conduct of hostilities (and thus the use of weaponry) on the other. It is asserted here that these regimes are, as a matter of law, distinct and that they apply independently of each other. International humanitarian law (IHL) rules must apply irrespective of the *justness* of the use of force; otherwise they cannot reasonably apply at all.

The rules of IHL, governing how to conduct hostilities when an armed conflict takes place (*jus in bello*), are applicable and highly relevant for the potential use of nuclear weapons in an armed conflict. This is true in particular for the rules on distinction, proportionality and precautions in attacks, as well as the prohibition on means of warfare of a nature to cause superfluous injury and unnecessary suffering. The critical question is whether it is possible to imagine any use of nuclear weapons that would not violate one or more of these rules. There is no doubt that IHL places heavy restrictions on any perceived use, and would, in most foreseeable scenarios, in fact prohibit such use. Nuclear weapons are not, however, explicitly and without exception barred from use.

A separate question raised by the ICJ in its Advisory Opinion was whether *threats* of use of nuclear weapons can constitute a violation any of the IHL rules. The assertion here is that IHL in general does not regulate threats, save in a few explicit cases. Finally, in discussing the potential use of nuclear weapons as a belligerent reprisal under IHL, it is assumed that it would be almost impossible to imagine circumstances where use of nuclear weapons against civilians could meet the requirements of a lawful reprisal.

Given that use of nuclear weapons could constitute violations of IHL rules, such acts would potentially also be subject to rules and proceedings under international criminal law (ICL). The book hence assumes that use of nuclear weapons could, under certain circumstances and according to varying liability modes, constitute genocide, crimes against humanity and/or war crimes. This is deemed to apply irrespective of the discrepancy between the 1998 Rome Statute of the International Criminal Court (ICC) and other international legal regimes, including customary law, when it comes to specific references to prohibited weapons. The assertion here is that the lack of explicit ICC jurisdiction with regard to nuclear weapon use in the ICC Statute does not preclude the categorisation of such use as an international crime under other legal regimes.

It is a given that when discussing nuclear weapons, environmental issues must also be a key focus area. A number of international rules regarding the environment may be relevant for nuclear weapons. In this book it is argued that the rules under IHL that explicitly and implicitly protect the environment constitute significant impediments on any use of nuclear weapons, and would in most conceivable scenarios outlaw it.

The book also attempts to highlight international environmental rules that apply to nuclear weapons – not only to their potential use in an attack, but also to testing and to the release of pollutants at various stages of the weapons production cycle. IHL provisions relating to the environment are certainly relevant in the event of any nuclear weapon use, and advances in scientific knowledge about the effects of nuclear radiation only strengthen their importance. Environmental treaties not designed specifically with nuclear weapons in mind nevertheless regulate nuclear by-products as pollutants. Beyond discussing these rules, however, this book also addresses to what extent international environmental treaties remain applicable in armed conflict, in light of the Vienna Convention on the Law of Treaties as well as the International Law Commission's recent draft articles on the subject.

Lastly, any discussion of the environmental impact of nuclear weapons would be incomplete without mention of the legacy of nuclear testing. This book reviews the particular history of nuclear testing in the South Pacific, including case law from the ICJ and the development of international law in response to the devastation wrought. It is asserted that although the international environmental law framework applicable to nuclear weapons is more extensive than commonly assumed, it nevertheless remains inadequate in relation to the threat posed.

Among the most significant treaty regimes applicable to nuclear weapons are those establishing nuclear weapon-free zones. Covering large geographical areas and a large number of states, it is argued in this book that such zones represent an often underestimated legal and political dynamic with regard to disarmament as well as non-proliferation. As a potential instrument of disarmament in a very volatile region, the Weapons of Mass Destruction-Free Zone in the Middle East would serve a vital purpose if ever it were adopted. It is argued that while this process appears currently deadlocked politically, its future prospects are not necessarily hopeless.

The Nuclear Non-Proliferation Treaty (NPT) is a key legal instrument to specifically deal with nuclear weapons as such. It is asserted here that although the NPT has served the very significant purpose of largely preventing nuclear proliferation in the non-nuclear weapon states since its inception in 1968, it has proved less efficient with regard to nuclear disarmament by the nuclear weapon states. The NPT is also seen in light of the legal regimes pertaining to the two other weapons of mass destruction, the treaties on biological and chemical weapons. Contrary to what is the case for the two other weapons of mass destruction, the NPT does not contain a rule prohibiting use of nuclear weapons. The NPT obligation upon the nuclear weapon states to work for general and complete disarmament is, it is asserted here, a binding legal obligation and not just a political aspiration, and hence the NPT nuclear weapon states could be seen as in non-compliance with their obligations. On the topic of armed non-state actors and nuclear materials, it is asserted that an extensive and far-reaching normative framework exists that would outlaw, and hopefully to a certain extent prevent, nuclear terrorism.

Finally, this book argues that the treaty regime of international human rights can be applicable to the use of nuclear weapons. It notes the applicability of human rights law in armed conflict, and argues that relevant human rights, such as the right to life and the right to health, could be violated by such use. The right to a remedy for violations of human rights is also a key point here; it is argued here that any response to a nuclear attack should include inter alia restitution and compensation to victims.

A strongly polarised debate over nuclear weapons and their legality has taken place over the past decades. If this argument is simplified, one might say that one side has asserted that use of nuclear weapons is permitted under international law, whereas the other side has held that use, and even possession, of nuclear weapons constitutes a violation of international law. This debate peaked with the proceedings around the 1996 ICJ Advisory Opinion on the legality of nuclear weapons. Since the ICJ did not resolve the issue, the frontlines remained where they were, but now with the added element of both sides taking the Advisory Opinion as evidence that they were right. This stalemate over the legal issues might have contributed to pacifying the public debate rather than provoking involvement in efforts to diminish the risk of nuclear weapons use.

This book has thus sought to offer a dispassionate assessment of the state of the law. It has been demonstrated that various international legal regimes place heavy restrictions on *use* of nuclear weapons. It has also been established that there is no unequivocal and explicit rule under international law against such use. With regard to possession, production and stockpiling of nuclear weapons, a number of regimes are important regulatory frameworks that to a large degree have prevented nuclear proliferation. Unlike corresponding legal regimes that have banned other weapons because it is assumed that their use cannot comply with IHL requirements, nuclear weapon use, production, transfer and possession is not explicitly prohibited. Disarmament obligations on the nuclear weapon states remain contested, and remain challenging to enforce.

In sum, this book asserts that a multiplicity of international legal regimes govern different aspects of nuclear weapons, and that use of nuclear weapons in most instances would be outlawed. But a clear-cut and comprehensive prohibition of nuclear weapons is still missing.

SUBJECT INDEX

AUTHOR INDEX

Printed in Great Britain
by Amazon